T3-BOH-871

Reading Renunciation

Reading Renunciation

ASCETICISM AND SCRIPTURE IN EARLY CHRISTIANITY

Elizabeth A. Clark

PRINCETON UNIVERSITY PRESS

PRINCETON, NEW JERSEY

Published by Princeton University Press,
41 William Street,
Princeton, New Jersey 08540
In the United Kingdom: Princeton
University Press, Chichester, West Sussex

Library of Congress Cataloging-in-
Publication Data

Clark, Elizabeth A. (Elizabeth Ann), 1938–
Reading renunciation : asceticism
and Scripture in early Christianity /
Elizabeth A. Clark.
p. cm.
Includes bibliographical references
and index.

ISBN 0-691-00511-7 (alk. paper).—
ISBN 0-691-00512-5 (pbk. : alk. paper)
1. Asceticism—History—Early church, ca.
30–600. 2. Bible—Criticism, interpretation,
etc.—History—Early church, ca. 30–600.
I. Title.
BV5023.C53 1999
248.4′7′09015—dc21 98-55313 CIP

This book has been composed in Galliard

The paper used in this publication meets the
minimum requirements of
ANSI/NISO Z39.48-1992 (R1997)
(*Permanence of Paper*)

http://pup.princeton.edu

Printed in the United States of America

10 9 8 7 6 5 4 3 2 1

10 9 8 7 6 5 4 3 2 1
(Pbk.)

For Dale

Criticism is not a passage from text to reader: its task is not to redouble the text's self-understanding, to collude with its object in a conspiracy of eloquence. Its task is to show the text as it cannot know itself, to manifest those conditions of its making (inscribed in its very letter) about which it is necessarily silent.

Terry Eagleton,
Criticism and Ideology

To do away with the split between producing and consuming is first of all to affirm that the work acquires meaning only through the strategies of interpretation that construct its significances.

Roger Chartier, "Intellectual History or Sociological History? The French Trajectories"

Contents

Acknowledgments

This book has been a long time in the making—so long, in fact, that I fear I no longer remember all those who should be thanked for their various forms of assistance.

The National Endowment for the Humanities and Duke University provided a year of fellowship support in 1996, and the Arts and Sciences Research Council of Duke University kept me well supplied with graduate research assistants during the summer months. I thank NEH and Duke for their continuing support.

In addition to astute comments on my manuscript supplied by the two readers for Princeton University Press, Bart Ehrman, Dale Martin, Halvor Moxnes, and Randall Styers heroically read the entire manuscript at an earlier stage; Kalman Bland and James Goehring offered expert advice on particular sections. In addition, the Introduction received extensive comments from Daniel Boyarin, Jonathan Dollimore, Gail Hamner, Patricia Cox Miller, Mark Vessey, and Annabel Wharton. Many colleagues contributed help and suggestions on various points: Dyan Elliott, Sidney Griffith, Carol Meyers, Paul Strohm, Joseph W. Trigg, Robin Darling Young, and L. Michael White, among others. I thank them, and apologize to those whose comments and critiques have been incorporated into the manuscript without proper acknowledgment. All the remaining defects of the manuscript I must, of course, accept as my own responsibility.

Portions of some chapters were given as lectures at Austin Presbyterian Theological Seminary (Thomas Currie Lectures), Oberlin College (Haskell Lectures), St. John's Seminary, New Zealand (Selwyn Lectures), Washington University (Weltin Lecture), University of North Carolina at Chapel Hill (Christine de Pisan Lecture), the University of Michigan, Cambridge University, Boston University, Drake University, Union Theological Seminary, Amherst College, Australian Catholic University, the University of Oslo, as well as at annual conferences of the American Academy of Religion and the North American Patristics Society, and the Oxford International Patristic Conference in 1995. I thank these institutions and groups, as well as the audiences whose questions, criticisms, and comments helped me to formulate this book.

I have also been assisted by many fine research assistants in the Graduate Program in Religion at Duke University during the years I have worked on this book. I would especially like to thank Catherine Chin, who prepared the bibliography, and John Lamoreaux, who compiled the index. Julian Sheffield helped me with material at Union Theological Seminary (New York). I am very grateful for their intelligent assistance.

I have had many excellent talking partners in Durham and Chapel Hill during the years in which this book was being researched and written. Their cheerful company and intelligent conversation have made the hours of labor less onerous. I would especially like to mention my friends Sarah Beckwith, Kalman Bland, Stanley Chojnacki, Miriam Cooke, Bart Ehrman, Valeria Finucci, Gail Hamner, Barbara Harris, Bruce Lawrence, Donald Lopez, Dale Martin, Tomoko Masuzawa, Randall Styers, Kenneth Surin, and Annabel Wharton, in addition to the cadre of excellent graduate students who add much to the reading groups and academic life of this area. Having Dyan Elliott and Paul Strohm as visitors at the National Humanities Center for parts of 1996–98 enriched these years. I also wish to thank William and Carmela Franklin for the use of their marvelous home at General Theological Seminary (New York) during several of the summers when I was writing this book.

Some material in *Reading Renunciation* has appeared in earlier and different form in various journals, books, and conference volumes. Sections of chapters 5 and 7 were included in "Contesting Abraham: The Ascetic Reader and the Politics of Intertextuality," in *The Social World of the First Christians: Essays in Honor of Wayne A. Meeks*, ed. L. Michael White and O. Larry Yarbrough (Minneapolis: Augsburg/Fortress, 1995), pp. 353–65. Some portions of chapter 9 appeared in "Constraining the Body, Expanding the Text: The Exegesis of Divorce in the Later Latin Fathers," in *The Limits of Ancient Christianity: Essays on Late Antique Thought in Honor of R. A. Markus*, ed. William Klingshirn and Mark Vessey (Ann Arbor: University of Michigan Press, forthcoming 1999). Most of chapter 6 saw its first light as "Reading Asceticism: Exegetical Strategies in the Early Christian Rhetoric of Renunciation," *Biblical Interpretation* 5 (1997): 82–105. Some of chapter 4 appeared as "Perilous Readings: Jerome, Asceticism, and Heresy," in *Proceedings of the Villanova Patristic, Medieval, and Renaissance Conference* 19/20 (Villanova: Augustinian Historical Institute, 1996), pp. 15–33, and in "Spiritual Reading: The Profit and Peril of Figurative Exegesis in Early Christian Asceticism," in *Prayer and Spirituality in the Early Church 1996*, ed. Peter Ackroyd and Pauline Allen (Melbourne: Australian Scholarly Publishing, 1998), pp. 154–67. I thank these editors and publishers for granting me permission to publish this material in fuller form.

Gay Trotter, Staff Assistant of Duke's Graduate Program in Religion, saw the manuscript through too many revisions; her skill, efficiency, and patience made the technical side of the process much easier for me.

Last, *Reading Renunciation* is dedicated to my colleague and neighbor Dale Martin, whose critical intelligence, theoretical sophistication, scholarly acumen, and capacity for (non-renunciatory) fun both at home and abroad have greatly enhanced the last eleven years of my life in Durham.

Durham, North Carolina
June 1998

Abbreviation List

The following abbreviations for series of primary sources are used throughout:

CCL *Corpus Christianorum*, Series Latina (Turnhout, 1953–)
CSCO *Corpus Scriptorum Christianorum Orientalium*, Scriptores Coptici (Louvain, 1906–)
CSEL *Corpus Scriptorum Ecclesiasticorum Latinorum* (Vienna, 1866–)
GCS *Die Griechischen Christlichen Schriftsteller der ersten drei Jahrhunderte* (Leipzig, 1899–)
JSOT/ASOR *Journal for the Study of the Old Testament/American Society of Oriental Research*
NHC *Nag Hammadi Codices* (Leiden, 1972–84)
PG *Patrologia Graeca* (Paris, 1857–66)
PL *Patrologia Latina* (Paris, 1844–65)
PLS *Patrologia Latina Supplementa* (Paris, 1958–)
PO *Patrologia Orientalia* (Paris, 1906–)
SC *Sources Chrétiennes* (Paris, 1943–)
SubsHag *Subsidia Hagiographica* (Brussels, 1886–)

Other abbreviations:

ep., *epp.* *epistula*, *epistulae* (= *Letter*, *Letters*)
ET English translation
Hist. eccles. *Historia ecclesiastica* (= *Church History*)
Hom. *Homilia*, *Homiliae* (= *Homily*, *Homilies*)
Or. *Oratio* (= *Oration*)
q.v. *quod vide* (= which see)
Serm. *Sermo*, *Sermones* (= *Sermon*, *Sermons*)
s.v. *sub verbo* (= see under the word)

Throughout, modern chapter and verse divisions are cited for the book of Psalms.

Reading

Renunciation

CHAPTER ONE

Introduction

Reading Renunciation explores the exegetical problem confronting early Christian ascetic writers who wished to ground their renunciatory program in the Bible. Their "problem" arose because the Bible only sporadically supported their agenda; many verses appeared rather to assume that marriage and reproduction were the norm for godly living. To read the Bible as wholeheartedly endorsing their ascetic program challenged the Fathers' interpretive ingenuity as well as their comprehensive knowledge of Scripture. How, given the Bible's sometime recalcitrance, could the lived experience of Christian renunciants find a Scriptural justification? How might they derive a consistently ascetic message from the Bible? What ways of reading could they devise, or adapt from their culture, that enabled them to interpret their Scriptures ascetically? Could they understand asceticism as the "good news" of the New Testament without disparaging the Genesis command—also seen as God's word—to "reproduce and multiply"? This book analyzes how Christian authors from the second to mid-fifth centuries made meaning of Biblical texts in their own highly asceticized religious environments—or environments the authors wished to render highly ascetic.

In our time, "higher criticism" treats Biblical texts in a "pre-scriptural" fashion, that is, not "as Scripture."[1] The sacred status of these books is now often retrieved by Christians through the confession that, unscrolling from Genesis to Revelation, they constitute a "grand narrative" of God's unfolding plan for human history. Reading the Bible constituted a somewhat different enterprise for ancient Christian ascetics, who likewise saw a "grand narrative" in the Bible, albeit one that registered the hierarchically differentiated evaluation of humans based on their ascetic commitment. For early Christian renunciants, Biblical stories were not the prime carriers

[1] The phrase is Wilfred Cantwell Smith's, "Scripture as Form and Concept: Their Emergence for the Western World," in *Rethinking Scripture: Essays from a Comparative Perspective*, ed. Miriam Levering (Albany: State University of New York Press, 1989), p. 45.

of an ascetic revelation. To produce ascetic meaning, ancient Christian writers instead repositioned Biblical verses, liberating them from what we might consider their historical setting and from "authorial intention." Hence the "Scripturality" of a passage did not necessarily lie in a narrational episode taken as a whole, but rather in individual words and verses that could be recontextualized to promote the superiority of abstinence. Ancient Jews and Christians alike believed that revelation attends discrete words and verses quite apart from their textual emplotment.[2]

So different are ancient and modern (i.e., historical-critical) exegetical modes that only occasionally will I contrast interpretations devised by early Christian ascetic writers with those of our contemporaries, who are often keen to locate the "original" settings of Biblical texts and the "intentions" of their authors. I am interested rather in the history of the *effects* that Biblical texts produced in late ancient Christian communities, that is, in an asceticized *Wirkungsgeschichte.*

I hope also in this book to contribute to a history of early Christian reading. Specifically, I wish to align myself with those theorists and commentators who scrutinize the social location of writings and the institutional structures that variously support or challenge them, that "organize the relations between language and human agency."[3] Rejecting a "hermetic" approach to literature that cordons off texts,[4] I will argue for the imbrication of ascetic readings of the Bible in the lives of Christian renunciants—or those whom patristic authors labored to fashion as renunciants. For these authors, Biblical passages indeed produced "effects" in those

[2] In this respect, ascetic interpreters of the Bible in the early Christian era differ from the Christian readers of early modernity and beyond described by Wesley A. Kort; they rather resemble postmodern readers who, according to Kort, "disregard the restraints imposed on bits of texts by their larger textual residences" (*"Take, Read": Scripture, Textuality, and Cultural Practice* [University Park: Pennsylvania State University Press, 1996], p. 72).

[3] John Mowitt, *Text: The Genealogy of an Antidisciplinary Object* (Durham, N.C.: Duke University Press, 1992), p. 99.

[4] See, for example, criticisms of some poststructuralist approaches by Robert Scholes, *Protocols of Reading* (New Haven, Conn./London: Yale University Press, 1989), esp. chap. 3; idem, *Textual Power: Literary Theory and the Teaching of English* (New Haven, Conn./London: Yale University Press, 1985), esp. chap. 5; Fredric Jameson, *The Prison-House of Language: A Critical Account of Structuralism and Russian Formalism* (Princeton, N.J.: Princeton University Press, 1972); idem, *The Political Unconscious: Narrative as a Socially Symbolic Act* (Ithaca, N.Y.: Cornell University Press, 1981), p. 283n. 2; Valentine Cunningham, "Renoving That Bible: The Absolute Text of (Post) Modernism," in *The Theory of Reading*, ed. Frank Gloversmith (Sussex: Harvester; Totowa, N.J.: Barnes and Noble, 1984), pp. 1–51; Edward W. Said, "The Text, the World, and the Critic," in *Textual Strategies: Perspectives in Post-Structuralist Criticism*, ed. Josué V. Harari (Ithaca, N.Y.: Cornell University Press, 1979), pp. 161–88 (later to serve as the centerpiece of Said's book, *The World, the Text, and the Critic* [London/Boston: Faber and Faber, 1983]).

willing to hear their (allegedly) ascetic message. Early Christian communities were increasingly stratified and hierarchalized by an axiology—a theory of value—of "difference" centered on ascetic renunciation. I hope here to demonstrate how the interpretation of Biblical texts intersected with the lives of these early Christians and their communities.

In addition, I offer *Reading Renunciation* as a contribution to current discussions in the Humanities about texts, authors, and interpretation. In the traditional paradigm, readers play little role in the creation of meaning, a task that is reserved to authors. In recent years, however, texts have come to be seen less as the unified work of an original author than as a "tissue of quotations" embodying both a communal linguistic system and the words and ideas of previous authors.[5] Moreover, readers are now accorded a more positive role in the production of meaning,[6] in which the interaction of readers and the written is signaled by the word "textuality."

In this book, I will retain a "precritical" use of the word "text"[7] to indicate a particular Biblical verse or work by an early Christian author, since I thus deem it unhelpful for my purposes to erase the difference between Scriptural text and patristic commentary. The early Church insisted on a clear demarcation between these types of texts, and drummed out as "heretics" writers such as Valentinus who effectively elided the distinction.[8] On the other hand, with literary theorists I stress the creativity of readers and commentators in producing new meaning for earlier writings. Thus I argue that early Christian writers indeed created a new, asceticized Scripture—but by interpretation, not (usually) by a literal erasure or replacement of the Biblical words.

Literary theorist Roland Barthes hints at such a model when he claims that in arenas in which "monologism" is "Law" (so he alleges, for example, in the realm of Scriptural texts), changes in reading could yield

[5] Roland Barthes, "The Death of the Author," in idem, *Image, Music, Text*, trans. Stephen Heath (New York: Hill and Wang, 1977; French original of this essay, 1968), p. 146; Jacques Derrida, "Living On: Border Lines," in *Deconstruction and Criticism*, ed. Harold Bloom et al. (New York: Seabury/Continuum, 1979), p. 84: "text" as a "fabric of traces."

[6] Robert Young, "Post-Structuralism: An Introduction," in *Untying the Text: A Post-Structuralist Reader*, ed. Robert Young (Boston/London/Henley: Routledge and Kegan Paul, 1981), p. 8; Mowitt, *Text*, p. 7; Roland Barthes, "From Work to Text," in idem, *Image* (French original of this essay, 1971), p. 163. In the world of English-language criticism, Stanley Fish probably deserves pride of place for his emphasis on the role of the reader; see especially *Is There a Text in This Class? The Authority of Interpretive Communities* (Cambridge, Mass./London: Harvard University Press, 1980).

[7] Mowitt, *Text*, p. 94: "precritical" in the sense of "pre-poststructuralist."

[8] David Dawson, *Allegorical Readers and Cultural Revision in Ancient Alexandria* (New Haven, Conn./London: Yale University Press, 1992), pp. 128–29.

plural and diffracted meanings.[9] Although I would dispute Barthes' characterization of Scripture as "monologic"—recall Augustine's claim that the sheer multiplicity of Scriptural readings is a sign of divine generosity[10]—I agree with Barthes' thesis that different reading strategies make possible a variety of expositions that sometimes can appropriately be deemed "a new text."[11] Since in the case of Scripture, "what has been said cannot be unsaid, *except by adding to it*,"[12] the explication of Biblical verses became the accepted mode of meaning-production for the Christian interpreter.

Here, Jacques Derrida's notion of supplementarity, a word that suggests both "addition to" and "replacement for" an original text or practice,[13] is useful for my purposes. Commentary as supplement rests on the paradox that commentary must invoke an "absent presence" while at the same time holding at bay what is always already absent—in this case, for Derrida, the notion of an "original text." Derrida's discussion of commentary illuminates his larger theme, that Western philosophy since Plato has privileged speech over writing as the original, "truer," mode of communication; writing, by contrast, has been disparaged as a mere afterthought that never captures speech's fullness of presence. Derrida's project is to argue that the supposed "fullness of presence" of speech secures its very status by its implied contrast with the "absent," namely, writing.

Likewise for commentary, according to Derrida: commentary claims to secure the identity of the text, while in fact it "leaps over" it.[14] Elaborating this concept, Gayatri Spivak writes that although literary critics (such as herself)

> customarily say that the text is autonomous and self-sufficient, there would be no justification for our activity if we did not feel that the text *needed* interpretation. The so-called secondary material is not a simple adjunct to the so-called primary text. The latter inserts itself within the interstices of the former,[15] filling holes that are always already there. Even as it adds itself to the text, criticism supplies a lack in the text and the gaps in the chain

[9] Barthes, "From Work to Text," p. 160. By "monologism," Barthes means the insistence upon a single "correct" reading of a text.

[10] Augustine, *De doctrina Christiana* 3.27.38 (CCL 32, 99–100).

[11] Here, we can recall the "new texts" of the Bible produced in our time by liberation, womanist, and feminist theologians.

[12] Roland Barthes, "The Rustle of Language," in idem, *The Rustle of Language*, trans. Richard Howard (New York: Hill and Wang, 1986), p. 76.

[13] Jacques Derrida, *Of Grammatology*, trans. Gayatri Chakravorty Spivak (Baltimore/London: Johns Hopkins University Press, 1976; French original, 1967), pp. 144–45.

[14] Ibid., p. 159.

[15] "Latter" apparently (somewhat confusingly) refers to the "so-called secondary material" and "the former," to the "so-called primary text."

> of criticism anterior to it. The text is not unique . . . ; the critic creates a substitute. The text belongs to language, not to the sovereign and generating author.[16]

Derrida elaborates his notion of supplementarity—indeed, appears to have adopted it—from Rousseau's frequent use of the concept. Rousseau's examples, analyzed by Derrida, illustrate well how "the supplement," while claiming to "add on" to an original, actually comes to displace it. The first example Derrida raises for consideration is Rousseau's analysis of childhood education. Rousseau champions "Nature," which blesses the child with original endowments, yet admits the necessity of education to supplement the deficiencies of Nature. Problematically, what is added on—education—comes to displace the "original." Derrida writes, "the supplement comes *naturally* to put itself in Nature's place," as the "image and representation of Nature."[17] What was intended as a mere augmentation of the goods bestowed by Nature has usurped pride of place.

Derrida derives a second major example from Rousseau—masturbation—to illustrate the principle of supplementarity, an illustration that resonates with the theme of this book. As supplement, masturbation evokes "the absent," namely, sexual relations with an other, even in its very concentration on self. In his writings, Rousseau confesses that he was from youth through adulthood habitually engaged in masturbation. His practice could be seen as an addition to sexual relations with a partner—but it becamc, in Rousseau's view, a "dangerous supplement" in that it cheated "Nature" and, indeed, came to displace "Nature" entirely.[18] Seducing the youthful Rousseau away from "Nature," masturbation came to seem more "natural" to him than "Nature" itself.[19]

Derrida asserts that writing and commentary function in a manner analogous to Rousseau's masturbatory habits: allegedly (in the view of Western phallogocentric philosophy) a mere "image" of an original, writing/commentary displaces that which they were supposed merely to reproduce.[20] The analogy of commentary to an "absent sexuality" in Derrida's discussion of Rousseau seems especially pertinent to the renunciatory practices of the early Christian ascetics I will be discussing in this book: just as "the absent sexual" is deeply implicated in "the presence" of their renunciation, so "commentary" and "original" are deeply imbri-

[16] Gayatri Chakravorty Spivak, "Translator's Preface," Derrida, *Of Grammatology*, p. lxxiv.

[17] Derrida, *Of Grammatology*, p. 149.

[18] Rousseau, by his own confession, ceased to have sexual relations with Thérèse Levasseur, but continued to masturbate (Derrida, *Of Grammatology*, p. 156). Rousseau began a relationship with Thérèse (a hotel servant) in 1745, had five children by her (whom he sent to a foundling hospital), and married her in 1768.

[19] Derrida, *Of Grammatology*, p. 151.

[20] Ibid.

cated. Just as commentary, in traditional evaluations, was seen as secondary in relation to the "real text," and masturbation was disparaged in comparison to "real sex," early Christian advocates of asceticism worked a new displacement: "real sex" itself was depreciated in favor of sexual renunciation.[21]

A further discussion similarly stimulating for my project is Foucault's analysis of commentary. His inaugural lecture at the Collège de France in 1970, published as "The Order of Discourse,"[22] provides his fullest statement on the subject of commentary. Exploring how procedures of control both internal and external to the text govern reading and interpretation, Foucault notes the paradoxical quality of commentary as a means of interpretive discipline. Although primacy is usually assigned to the "original source," it is nonetheless commentary's role to state what the text has "silently articulated."[23] Claiming merely to repeat the original text, commentary presents itself as a repetition of "sameness," when in fact it operates differently.[24] Foucault elaborates:

> By a paradox which it always displaces but never escapes, the commentary must say for the first time what had, nonetheless, already been said, and must tirelessly repeat what had, however, never been said. . . . it allows us to say something other than the text itself, but on condition that it is this text itself which is said, and in a sense completed.[25]

Foucault's notion of "commentary" embodies a feature less manifest in Derrida's discussion of "text" that is useful for this book. For Foucault, "commentary" is subsumed in the more general category of "discourse," by which term he signals language's habitation in a social world. In an early critique contrasting Derrida's and Foucault's understandings of "text," Edward Said argued that "Foucault moves the text out from a consideration of 'internal' textuality to its way of inhabiting and remaining in an extratextual reality . . . by making the text assume its affiliation with institutions, offices, agencies, classes, academies, corporations, groups, guilds, ideologically defined parties and professions."[26] In Said's view, Foucault's project (unlike Derrida's) shows "that writing is no private ex-

[21] I thank Randall Styers for helping me with this formulation.

[22] English translation (by Ian McLeod) in *Untying the Text: A Post-Structuralist Reader*, ed. Robert Young (Boston/London/Henley: Routledge and Kegan Paul, 1981), pp. 48–78. This essay is also available in another translation (by Rupert Swyer) appended to Foucault's *The Archaeology of Knowledge*, trans. A. M. Sheridan Smith (New York: Pantheon, 1972), pp. 215–37.

[23] Ibid., pp. 56–58.

[24] Ibid., p. 59.

[25] Ibid., p. 58.

[26] Edward W. Said, "The Problem of Textuality: Two Exemplary Positions," *Critical Inquiry* 4 (1978): 701. I thank Gail Hamner for pressing me to reflect on these differences between Derrida and Foucault.

ercise of a free scriptive will but rather the activation of an immensely complex tissue of forces for which a text is a place among other places (including the body) where the strategies of control in society are conducted."[27] Thus Foucault, in Said's estimation, enables us "to understand culture as a body of disciplines having the effective force of knowledge linked systematically, but by no means immediately, to power."[28] Foucault's decisive placement of texts in extratextual realms marked by power relations finds an illuminating illustration in the world of early Christian ascetic writings, whose authors strove to create a hierarchy based on degrees of ascetic renunciation.

In the chapters that follow, I will explore how patristic exegesis of the Bible provided a "supplement," a "commentary," in the senses here elaborated. Professing to remain faithful to the Biblical passage at hand, ascetically inclined church fathers nonetheless produced new meaning that made the entire Bible speak to the practical as well as theological concerns of Christian renunciants.

By preserving a distinction between the "text" of Scripture and the "commentary"/"new text" of patristic interpreters, I imply that exegetical work—usually unacknowledged—had to be performed on various Biblical passages to bring them into accord with the ascetic predispositions of these commentators. For ancient commentators, all Scripture was revealed truth relevant to present Christian experience, not merely historical narration, and was to be aligned with their endorsement of asceticism's superiority. For interpreters of our own day, these exegetes' treatment of some Biblical passages instead suggests, in Stanley Fish's phrase, a "misprereading":[29] ascetic interpreters read so as to edify *their* religious and social situations, independent of the presumed assumptions, interests, and historical situations of the Biblical authors. It is the space *between* those differing assumptions, the distance—marked not just chronologically, but also axiologically—that is here to be explored.

I do not suggest that our contemporaries, in contrast to early Christians who were innocent of Biblical criticism, know the real meaning of the Bible. They had their presuppositions; we have ours. They could not approach this text without interpretation; neither can we. Rather, I argue that Christians' understanding of their faith developed considerably between the time of the first century and that of patristic writers committed to sexual renunciation as the highest form of the Christian life—rendered

[27] Ibid., p. 705.

[28] Ibid., p. 709. Said nonetheless faults Foucault "for his curiously passive and sterile view . . . of how and why power is gained, used, and held onto." For Said, this failure "is the most dangerous consequence of his [Foucault's] disagreement with Marxism" (p. 710).

[29] Stanley Fish, "Is There a Text in This Class?", in idem, *Is There a Text in This Class?*, p. 311.

highest precisely because "not all could receive it" (Matt. 19:12). It was not simply that the literary expression of the faith had changed by the later period; its content also shifted as sexual and other forms of renunciation were exalted as the pinnacle of Christian achievement. The writers whose works I examine, however, would resist the allegation that they were interpreting Biblical texts in ways other than those of the time and place of their composition: that is the assessment of *our* contemporaries, educated to perceive difference, to pry apart assumptions and interpretations—and motivated by a modern anti-asceticism.

Here, it is helpful to consider briefly the function of interpretation. Fredric Jameson's essay, "Metacommentary," provides a stimulus for reflection:

> The starting point for any genuinely profitable discussion of interpretation . . . must not be the nature of interpretation, but the need for it in the first place. What initially needs explanation is . . . not how we go about interpreting a text properly, but rather why we should even have to do so. . . . [T]he great traditional systems of hermeneutic . . . sprang from cultural need and from the desperate attempt of the society in question to assimilate monuments of other times and places, whose original impulses were quite foreign to them and which require a kind of rewriting . . . to take their place in the new scheme of things.[30]

Once a Biblical text—for example, Genesis—was deemed sacred literature, it could not be rejected, only interpreted. If every verse of Scripture was deemed meaningful, authoritative, and therefore unalterable and incapable of rejection,[31] hermeneutical strategies had to be devised to provide satisfactory explanations of apparent Scriptural divergences.

Yet the church fathers were impelled not just (as Jameson puts it) by the cultural need to assimilate the "monuments of other times and places," such as those of ancient Greece, but also by the religious need to assimilate the earlier traditions they claimed to own—in this case, both the Old and the New Testaments—to the demands of their new ascetic agendas. The distinctive feature of their ascetic program was to intensify

[30] Fredric Jameson, "Metacommentary," in idem, *The Ideologies of Theory: Essays 1971–1986*, vol. 1, *Situations of Theory*, Theory and History of Literature 48 (Minneapolis: University of Minnesota Press, 1988), p. 5 (originally in *PMLA* 86, no. 1 [1971]: 9–18).

[31] Augustine, *Contra Faustum* 11.6; 22.96 (CSEL 25, 321, 702–3). The difficulties that might ensue if Christians were to acknowledge that any verses of Scripture were not "truth" is well illustrated by Augustine's shocked reaction to Jerome's suggestion that Peter and Paul may have staged a mock controversy in Gal. 2:11–14; see Augustine, *epp.* 28 and 40 to Jerome (CSEL 34.1, 103–13; 34.2, 69–81), and Jerome, *ep.* 75 to Augustine (CSEL 34.2, esp. 285–314).

the "hardness" of the Bible's "hard" sayings and to fortify the "softer" ones through intertextual and other readings, thus furnishing interpretations that could be used to best more carnally minded Christians. Hence they developed a "pre-emptive" interpretation of texts[32] through ingenious hermeneutical strategies.

This book does not deal with all aspects of early Christian asceticism. It treats a single theme, sexual renunciation. Elaborating this particular feature of asceticism reveals my investment as a twentieth-century feminist scholar in issues of sexuality and gender. For many church fathers, by contrast, sexual abstinence was merely one, indeed initial, aspect of ascetic renunciation, which also included fasting, sleep reduction, and financial divestment, in addition to such "spiritual" virtues as the overcoming of anger and pride. Other topics, such as the ways that the doctrine of Mary's perpetual virginity was figured in ascetic rhetoric, are similarly absent from my account.

Some scholars may wonder why I have not organized the book around particular patristic authors, with chapters devoted to Augustine, Jerome, John Chrysostom, and so forth. They may further puzzle why I have not differentiated the writings of bishops, monastic leaders, hagiographers, and laity, the works of the orthodox from those of the heterodox. My response is that I am not here concerned to offer an overview of any particular church father's exegesis or to distinguish more from less religiously "correct" readings, but to dissect the interpretive devices that were employed to create ascetic meaning—and these devices, I have discovered, run across the spectrum of early Christian writers. Among "heretical" as well as among "orthodox" readers of Scripture, some tended more to figurative interpretations, others to more "literal" ones: there was no distinctively "heretical" or "orthodox" mode of reading. Likewise, I have not differentiated among the various kinds of writings that constitute my sources: Biblical commentaries, homilies, letters, polemical treatises, and moral exhortations, especially those dedicated to the promotion of celibacy.[33] Again, my approach is deliberate, for I aim not to focus on specific genres, but to illustrate how across the whole gamut of Greek and Latin patristic literature, Biblical verses could be pressed to promote an ascetic form of Christianity.

[32] The word is borrowed from Lee Patterson's discussion of Augustine in *Negotiating the Past: The Historical Understanding of Medieval Literature* (Madison: University of Wisconsin Press, 1975), p. 151.

[33] See Frances M. Young, *Biblical Exegesis and the Formation of Christian Culture* (Cambridge: Cambridge University Press, 1997), p. 247: there is no evidence "that particular reading strategies were confined to particular genres, or that distinct genres produced distinctive methodologies." Young here emphasizes the "remarkable continuity in the modes of exegetical practice found in the various different sorts of

I organized the research for this book around early Christian authors' use of particular Biblical verses. This mode of research in itself signals that *Reading Renunciation* is not a discussion of early Christian teachings on celibacy and marriage in general, but a close examination of the use of particular Biblical verses in the construction of ascetic meaning. Thus some important works that deal explicitly with ascetic concerns (Gregory of Nyssa's treatise *On Virginity* stands as case in point) receive relatively little attention insofar as they do not argue first and foremost through an appeal to particular Scriptural verses. In contrast, authors such as Jerome, Origen, and John Chrysostom, who promoted their agendas through detailed elaborations of Biblical texts, are more frequently quoted. Because of its emphasis on texts, this book may seem more literary than social historians would prefer. Although the opening chapter presents a historical overview of early Christian asceticism, readers must turn to other sources for more extensive social, historical, and theological analyses of the ascetic movement within patristic Christianity.

Reading Renunciation is organized into three distinct sections. I begin with a survey of past and present scholarship concerning early Christian asceticism that is designed to orient the nonspecialist. This historiographic overview is followed by a first section, "Reading for Asceticism," which sketches current understandings of early Christian reading and readers, and considers the relation between patristic exegesis and "pagan" and early Jewish interpretation. In this section I argue that allegorical exegesis is not so prevalent a mode of interpretation for early Christian ascetics as many scholars (myself included) have assumed; all too often, allegory allowed a *relaxation* of ascetic rigor that exegetes devoted to stringent renunciation were loath to countenance. Rather, a variety of alternative exegetical and rhetorical strategies (detailed in chapter 5) were employed in the ascetic interpretation of the Bible. Among these, intertextual exegesis, in which the Bible is seen as "self-interpreting and entire unto itself,"[34] holds a particularly prominent place. Following this analysis of hermeneutical strategies, chapter 6 describes three models of reading renunciation that illustrate how the exegetical strategies of John Chrysostom, Jerome, and Origen are linked with their various teachings on marriage, sexuality, and asceticism. Here, ascetic interpretation and ascetic praxis meet.

A second section, "Rejection and Recuperation: The Old Dispensation and the New," offers three narratives that illuminate the difficulties some Old Testament texts posed for ascetically inclined exegetes. How might the latter read Biblical verses that enjoined the faithful to "reproduce and

contexts in which early Christians were engaged in interpreting the scriptures."

[34] I thank Mark Vessey for this helpful phrase (private correspondence of March 28, 1998).

multiply," exalted the patriarchs' marital arrangements, and permitted divorce with an astounding ease? These texts, however, as well as those pertaining to Hebrew ritual law and sacrifice, were deemed part of Holy Scripture and thus had to be reconciled, not discarded; sometimes, surprisingly, even these passages could be reappropriated for the ascetic program through ingenious readings. This section, then, is organized around potentially troubling issues, especially issues posed by Old Testament texts that demanded skillful handling by ascetically inclined Christian exegetes.

The third section, "Reading Paul," contains two lengthy chapters that focus on particular Pauline and post-Pauline texts. One surveys the patristic exegesis of I Corinthians 7 (probably the most ascetically charged chapter of the New Testament); the other traces the hermeneutical problems the Deutero-Pauline and Pastoral Epistles posed for ascetically minded exegetes who believed that Paul of I Corinthians 7 had written these books and that their "messages" should thus conform to those of I Corinthians 7. How the Fathers brought these later New Testament books into conformity with their own rigorous ascetic agenda sets one major problem for this section.

Patristics scholars, I think, have often engaged in a formalistic approach to early Christian exegesis that ignores the ways in which the moral, religious, and social values of interpreters drive their exegeses. Throughout *Reading Renunciation*, my concern is to show how the Fathers' axiology of abstinence informed their interpretation of Scriptural texts and incited the production of ascetic meaning.

CHAPTER TWO

Asceticism in Late Ancient Christianity

I: Introduction

It is significant that the Society of Biblical Literature Group on Ascetic Behavior in Greco-Roman Antiquity, despite prolonged meetings throughout the 1980s, never reached consensus on a definition of asceticism. After scholars in the Group rehearsed the dictionary definition of "ascetic" ("given to strict self-denial, esp. for the sake of spiritual or intellectual discipline")[1] and noted its derivation from the Greek word for the physical training that an athlete might undertake,[2] questions of function, motivation, and purpose intruded to disturb the short-lived agreement. Group members disagreed as to whether they should stress deprivation, pain, and the "shrinking of the self" as definitive components of asceticism—or, conversely, the liberation of true "human nature." Such disagreements signal scholars' differing intellectual and ideological investments, the evidence they privilege as well as their own social and religious placements.

Participants in the Group finally settled on a definition of "ascetic behavior" (thus retreating from the "thing-in-itself" to its observed practices), namely, "ascetic behavior represents a range of responses to social, political, and physical worlds often perceived as oppressive or unfriendly, or as stumbling blocks to the pursuit of heroic personal or communal goals, lifestyles, and commitments";[3] "abstention or avoidance" lay at its core.[4] Writing for the *Encyclopedia of Religion*, Group member Walter O. Kaelber posits that asceticism, "when used in a religious context, may be defined as a voluntary, sustained, and at least partially systematic program of self-discipline and self-denial in which immediate, sensual or profane

[1] *Webster's New Collegiate Dictionary*, s.v. "ascetic."

[2] *Askēsis:* Liddell-Scott, *Greek-English Lexicon*, s.v.

[3] Vincent L. Wimbush, "Introduction," in *Ascetic Behavior in Greco-Roman Antiquity: A Sourcebook*, ed. Vincent L. Wimbush (Minneapolis: Fortress, 1990), p. 2.

[4] Ibid., pp. 10–11.

gratifications are renounced in order to attain a higher spiritual state or a more thorough absorption in the sacred."[5]

Although these latter definitions edge in a social-scientific direction, other approaches abound. A psychoanalytical description holds that asceticism "recognizes and manages drive or impulse, commonly called desire, by harnessing and directing resistance,"[6] and defines the phenomenon as "any act of self-denial undertaken as a strategy of empowerment or gratification."[7] Performance theory proffers this: "Asceticism may be defined as performances within a dominant social environment intended to inaugurate a new subjectivity, different social relations, and an alternative symbolic universe."[8] Even economic theory is not excluded in the following definition that underscores asceticism's structure of investment and profit: "Early asceticism is capitalism without money."[9]

However divergent these definitions, they share an etic, not emic, perspective: they are views of asceticism by "outsiders," not "insiders."[10] Christian devotees themselves might rather highlight the renunciant's desire to commune with God, to imitate the life of Jesus, or to recapture the life of Paradise. Yet whether we opt for "outsider" or "insider" descriptions, it is dubious that the study of early Christian renunciation locates an "essence" of asceticism that holds cross-culturally. Since asceticism has meaning only in relation to other behaviors in a given culture, scholars can best study the varying "structures of compensation," what ascetics give up and what they get, in various particular historical situations.[11]

The question of whether or not early Christian asceticism functioned as a radical critique of the larger society has much occupied scholars. On the one hand, it would seem that the ascetic's rejection of worldly values

[5] Walter O. Kaelber, "Asceticism," in *The Encyclopedia of Religion*, ed. Mircea Eliade (New York: Macmillan; London: Collier Macmillan, 1987), I:441.

[6] Geoffrey Galt Harpham, *The Ascetic Imperative in Culture and Criticism* (Chicago/London: University of Chicago Press, 1987), p. 61.

[7] Ibid., p. xiii.

[8] Richard Valantasis, "Constructions of Power in Asceticism," *Journal of the American Academy of Religion* 63 (1995): 797.

[9] Harpham, *Ascetic Imperative*, p. 30. Harpham also cites the case of Augustine, who passes from being a "word-vendor" (as a public orator; *Confessiones* 4.2.2) to the more sophisticated "capitalist" economy of textuality: here, for a small investment, he aspires to receive a larger return (p. 112).

[10] For a discussion of the history of the emic/etic distinction, see Paul Jorion, "Emic and Etic: Two Anthropological Ways of Spilling Ink," *Cambridge Anthropology* 8 (1983): 41–68.

[11] Geoffrey Galt Harpham, "Asceticism and the Compensations of Art," in *Asceticism*, ed. Vincent L. Wimbush and Richard Valantasis (New York/Oxford: Oxford University Press, 1995), pp. 359–60; cf. William E. Deal, "Towards a Politics of Asceticism," in the same volume, pp. 424–29,

implies a condemnation of the social order. Yet historian Philip Rousseau nonetheless suggests that early Christian ascetic ideals were more closely linked to those of "the world" than we may imagine:

> the stable society they [ascetics] created for themselves, with its own routine, its own economic endeavours and patterns of authority, became an invitation to others, a call to "conversion," to a new sense of purpose and direction. The models they espoused appeared, even at the time, "alternative," if not anarchic. Yet they made their points within the context of a growing public debate—about authority and leadership, about the mechanisms of social formation, about the nature of the very tradition to which Christianity was entitled to appeal. Although their own social system could never have usurped or absorbed all others, and their permanence, therefore, could only be assured on eccentric terms, the very tolerance and admiration of other people prove that they had a central role to play in the definition of Christian society.[12]

In the arena of gender relations, for example, monastic organization came more to conform to the customs of "the world" than to challenge them. In Susanna Elm's words, "Asceticism began as a method for men and women to transcend, as virgins of God, the limitations of humanity in relation to the divine. It slowly changed into a way for men as men and women as women to symbolize the power of the Church to surpass human weakness."[13] Since gender continued as a differentiating factor in the monastery, as in the larger society, the power (in theory) of a radical critique of worldly mores was blunted.

Despite dilemmas of definition, scholars of early Christianity largely agree that ascetic renunciation was one of the important characteristics of the early Christian movement. Yet even before Christian writers appropriated the word *askēsis* to name their ideal,[14] pagan writers had provided a safe passage for the concept from the realm of the physical discipline that an athlete might undertake to the philosopher's goal of self-restraint,[15] a

---

arguing for contextualization, a "politics of asceticism."

[12] Philip Rousseau, "The Structure and Spirit of the Ascetic Life," unpublished typescript, pp. 2–3.; cf. his forthcoming essay, "Monasticism," in *The Cambridge Ancient History* XIV.

[13] Susanna Elm, *"Virgins of God": The Making of Asceticism in Late Antiquity* (Oxford: Clarendon, 1994), p. 384.

[14] For discussions of the development of ascetic/monastic terminology, see E. A. Judge, "The Earliest Use of Monachos for 'Monk' (P. Coll. Youtie 77) and the Origins of Monasticism," *Jahrbuch für Antike und Christentum* 20 (1977): 72–89; Antoine Guillaumont, "Perspectives actuelles sur les origines du monachisme," in idem, *Aux Origines du monachisme chrétien*, Spiritualité orientale 30 (Bégrolles-en-Mauges: Abbaye de Bellefontaine, 1979), pp. 218–20; and Françoise-E. Morard, "Monachos, moine: histoire du terme grec jusqu'au 4e siècle," *Freiburger Zeitschrift für Philosophie und Theologie* 19 (1972): 332–411.

[15] See James E. Goehring, "Asceticism,"

goal that might not demand any more rigor than the moderate "care of the self" so engagingly described by Michel Foucault.[16] Christians claimed, however, that renunciation was not to be undertaken simply for the general well-being of the person, that is, not merely to achieve an appropriate balance between bodily desires and mental equanimity, but for the sake of a closer relation to God. While early Christian writers such as Clement of Alexandria acknowledged that other groups had cultivated self-restraint (so his catalog of Indian gymnosophists, Olympic contenders, and "Gnostic" devotees attests), they insisted that all ascetic practitioners who were not "orthodox" Christians were wrongly motivated and that their exertions and deprivations were thus for naught.[17]

Early Christian ascetics assumed that humans were transformable: the human person could be improved by ascetic practice. The standard textbook approach to asceticism that dualistically pits soul against body is in urgent need of nuance, for early Christian ascetics usually claimed that soul and body were tightly connected, that the actions and movements of one had a direct effect upon the other. And this effect was not just in the direction of the soul reining in the body: rather, ascetic practitioners believed that attention to the body's discipline could improve "the self." Thus, despite the obvious ways in which asceticism can appear as a pessimistic movement in its alleged flight from "the world," there is a certain optimism at its heart. Men and women are not slaves to the habitual,[18] but can cultivate extraordinary forms of human existence.

Beyond such intellectual and ideological differences in approach to early Christian asceticism, however, scholars of the phenomenon must also grapple with a wealth of new sources (archeological, epigraphic, papyrological, as well as textual) that continue to offer new data and perspectives for consideration. Indeed, scholars' knowledge of early Christian asceticism has expanded considerably even in the past few decades. Let me first review briefly some of the traditional approaches to early Christian asceticism before noting the new information and theories that call them into question.

---

in *Encyclopedia of Early Christianity*, ed. Everett Ferguson, 2nd ed. (New York/London: Garland, 1997), pp. 127–30.

[16] Michel Foucault, *The Care of Self*, trans. Robert Hurley (New York: Pantheon, 1986; French original, 1984). See Pierre Hadot, *Philosophy as a Way of Life: Spiritual Exercises from Socrates to Foucault*, ed. A. I. Davidson, trans. M. Chase (Oxford: Blackwell, 1995; French 2nd ed., 1987), chap. 7, for a discussion and critique of Foucault's approach.

[17] Clement of Alexandria, *Stromata* 3.1.1; 3.1.4; 3.3.24; 3.6.48; 3.6.50; 3.7.60 (GCS 52 [15], 195, 197, 206–7, 218, 219, 223–24).

[18] Robert A. F. Thurman, "Tibetan Buddhist Perspectives on Asceticism," in *Asceticism*, ed. Wimbush and Valantasis, pp. 108–9.

II: Changing Approaches to the Study of Early Christian Asceticism

The study of early Christian asceticism in recent years has retreated from the two questions that dominated discussion in decades past, namely, "Where did Christian asceticism come from?" and "Why did ascetic practitioners do what they did?" For convenience, we may label these the "origins" question and the "motivations" question. Both, I think, have proved unproductive for future research.

There is no doubt that by the later fourth century, the ascetic movement within Christianity had won many adherents. Even if we downsize the numbers furnished by such writers as Rufinus of Aquileia and Palladius—numbers suggesting that in the 370s, at the Egyptian monastic center of Nitria alone, three thousand or more ascetics were in residence, and that by the 390s, around five thousand;[19] or Jerome's (not credible) figure that by the late fourth century, the combined population of the several Pachomian monasteries farther south in the Thebaid stood at around fifty thousand[20]—it is safe to assume that retreat from "the world" was by that time considerable. Indeed, the very proliferation of Pachomian communities within the first two generations of cenobitic monasticism in Egypt testifies to the ever-increasing population that required these expanded quarters.[21] By the mid- to late fourth century, ascetic renunciation had also achieved popularity in the West, with virgins and monks attested not just for the Italian peninsula,[22] but for Gaul[23] and Spain[24] as well. Syrian

[19] Rufinus, *Hist. eccles.* 2.3–4 (PL 21, 511); Palladius, *Historia Lausiaca* 7 (Butler, p. 25). For a classic discussion of monasticism at Nitria and Scetis, see Hugh E. Evelyn White, *The Monasteries of the Wâdi 'N Natrûn*, pt. II, *The History of the Monasteries of Nitria and of Scetis*, ed. Walter Hauser (New York: Metropolitan Museum of Art, 1932).

[20] Jerome, *praef.*, Pachomius, *Regula* 7 (PL 23, 68). Palladius reports 7000 at Tabennisi and 1300 at Phbow in his day (*Historia Lausiaca* 32 [Butler, pp. 93, 94]).

[21] Derwas J. Chitty, *The Desert a City: An Introduction to the Study of Egyptian and Palestinian Monasticism under the Christian Empire* (Crestwood, N.Y.: St. Vladimir's Seminary Press, 1966), chap. 2.

[22] Italy: Rome (Jerome, e.g., *epp.* 22, 23, 24, 45; Ambrose, *De virginibus* 3.1.1); Bologna (Ambrose, *De virginibus* 1.10.60; *Exhortatio virginitatis* 1.1); Milan (Augustine, *Confessiones* 8.6.15). Rita Lizzi links the birth of asceticism in Italy to the resistance to Arianism; see her essay, "Ascetismo e monachesimo nell' Italia tardoantica," *Codex Aquilarensis* 5 (1991): 61.

[23] Gaul: Sulpicius Severus, *Vita Martini* (organized asceticism around Tours from the 360s). Honoratus founded his monastery on the island of Lérins probably in the first decade of the fifth century; Cassian, his near Marseilles around 415. See Rousseau, "The Structure," typescript, pp. 18–20. Robert Markus emphasizes the tendency of the Gallic church to recruit its bishops from monasteries: *The End of Ancient Christianity* (Cambridge: Cambridge University Press, 1990), p. 181.

[24] Spain: for a summary of the early evidence, see Adalbert de Vogüé, *Histoire lit-*

asceticism was also in full flower, as will be detailed below. In the same period, Palestine became a popular site for both transitory pilgrims[25] and more permanent ascetic practitioners.[26] The Palestinian monastery at Calamôn may have been founded at the turn to the fourth century, and others soon followed;[27] by the early Byzantine period, more than sixty monasteries existed in the Judean desert.[28] In Asia Minor, forms of ascetic practice associated with Eustathius of Sebaste preceded the Cappadocian Fathers' endorsement of monasticism in the second half of the fourth century.[29] Where and how did this movement arise, earlier generations of scholars asked? Their answers testify both to the divergent evidence to which they appealed and to their own ideological and religious presuppositions.

Thus Protestants of an older generation, more comfortable with Martin Luther's blessings on marriage and family than with the rigorous renunciations of the desert fathers, tended to downplay the very early manifestations of asceticism within Christianity, and to cast the blame for these developments on the dualism supposedly attendant upon the "Hellenization" of Christianity.[30] In this view, asceticism must have sprung from a

téraire du mouvement monastique dans l'antiquité. Première partie: Le Monachisme latin de la mort d'Antoine à la fin du séjour à Rome (356–85) (Paris: Les Editions du Cerf, 1991), pp. 190–99, 206–10; Virginia Burrus, *The Making of a Heretic: Gender, Authority, and the Priscillianist Controversy*, The Transformation of the Classical Heritage 24 (Berkeley/Los Angeles/London: University of California Press, 1995), esp. pp. 28–29, 37–38, 40–42, 82–84, 111–14. For a discussion of the anti-ascetic *Acta* of the Council of Saragossa in 380, see Virginia Burrus, "Ascesis, Authority, and Text: The Acts of the Council of Saragossa," *Semeia* 58 (1992): 95–108.

25 Especially the pilgrimage of Egeria: see her *Peregrinatio* (*Itinerarium*) (PLS 1, 1047–92); cf. Jerome, *ep.* 108.8–13, on Paula's pilgrimage through Palestine. See also John Binns, *Ascetics and Ambassadors of Christ: The Monasteries of Palestine 314–631* (Oxford: Clarendon, 1994), pp. 91, 95.

26 Such as Jerome, Paula, Rufinus, Melania the Elder, and Melania the Younger.

27 Binns, *Ascetics*, p. 155; cf. p. 245.

28 Yizhar Hirschfeld, *The Judean Desert Monasteries in the Byzantine Period* (New Haven, Conn./London: Yale University Press, 1992), p. xv; also discussed in Binns, *Ascetics*, p. 81. For books and libraries in the Palestinian monasteries, see Binns, *Ascetics*, pp. 57ff., 61, 65, 69, 70, 141–42.

29 See especially Philip Rousseau, *Basil of Caesarea* (Berkeley/Los Angeles/Oxford: University of California Press, 1994), chap. 7; Jean Gribomont, "Eustathe de Sébaste," in idem, *Saint Basile: Evangile et église. Mélanges* (Bégrolles-en-Mauges: Abbaye de Bellefontaine, 1984), I:95–106; idem, "Le Monachisme au IVe siècle en Asie Mineure: De Gangres au Messalianisme," in idem, *Saint Basile*, I:26–41. Susanna Elm, *"Virgins,"* p. 199, posits that the issue of the communal life of male and female ascetics, and the public role of women, were the decisive issues separating "orthodox" and "heretical" asceticism.

30 Adolph von Harnack's famous thesis: see his *Outlines of the History of Dogma*, trans. E. K. Mitchell (Boston: Beacon, 1957; German original, 1889), pp. 81, 133, 194–95. Such argumentation parallels that of several early church fathers (e.g., Hippolytus) who "blame" the importation of Greek philosophy into Christianity for the development of "heresy." More attention is given to early ascetic currents in Gerd Theissen, *Sociology of Early Palestinian Christianity*, trans. John Bowden (Phila-

later, "Greek" contribution to Christianity, since "we all know" that ancient Jews were not ascetic. Here, the view that asceticism may have been indigenous to the early Christian movement was not seriously countenanced.

It is puzzling that Protestants, so given to the study of the Bible, overlooked the ascetic dimensions of the New Testament itself. Already in 1892, Johannes Weiss in *The Proclamation of Jesus on the Kingdom of God* had trenchantly scored the ascetic dimension of the Synoptic Gospels in his critique of nineteenth-century Biblical interpretation. In the eschatological context of early Christianity, Weiss noted, a negative ideal of renunciation was championed for those who would follow Jesus. Riches were not to be used, but renounced, a view unwelcome to German Liberalism's notions of social improvement. As for Protestantism's exaltation of secular vocation as a manifestation of religious devotion, Weiss argued that Jesus and the first disciples *abandoned* their secular vocations. Nor is family life an evangelical value: the Gospel injunction to hate one's family for the sake of following Jesus, Weiss claimed, had been consistently ignored or diluted by Protestant interpreters.[31] Likewise, the tendency to interpret such passages as Paul's advice on celibacy and marriage in I Corinthians 7 as an aberration spurred by particular and temporary historical circumstances has been noticeable in Protestant circles.[32]

Rather than assign ascetic currents to the earliest days of Christianity, interpreters of the older school often cited the infusion of a dualistic Greco-Roman philosophy into the "purity" of Christian teaching to account for asceticism's rise: Platonic dualism was the leading culprit. Thus a "foreign" group of philosophers could be blamed for infesting Christianity with alien ideas. This view needs considerable tempering. While there is no doubt that within the movements we now label Middle Platonism and Neo-Platonism, body stood lower on the ontological scale than did soul or spirit, it was not a later Greek philosophy that first introduced ascetic notions into an otherwise world-affirming primitive Christianity. And contrary to popular opinion, it was not only philosophers who counseled bodily restraint to a populace wallowing in licentiousness—again, a textbook picture of the Roman world into which Christianity came. Rather, ideals of temperance and bodily discipline in matters of sex, diet, and exercise were often expressed throughout a spectrum of authors and texts, especially by medical writers.[33] Among the upper levels of society,

delphia: Fortress, 1978; German original, 1977), chap. 2.

[31] Johannes Weiss, *The Proclamation of Jesus on the Kingdom of God*, ed. and trans. R. H. Hiers and D. L. Holland (Philadelphia: Fortress, 1971; German original, 1892), pp. 105–12.

[32] For more recent assessments of the ascetic dimensions of I Cor. 7, see below, pp. 263, 264, 299, 321.

[33] Recent commentators cite works of (e.g.) Galen, Rufus of Ephesus, Caelius Au-

from which strata these authors largely came, "moderation" was a common watchword. Ascetic practitioners within Christianity may have engaged in more extreme renunciations than their pagan counterparts, but both groups agreed that the self-regulation of the body is a desideratum for all "rational" people.

Likewise, the argument that earliest Christianity's derivation from Judaism precluded any originary ascetic impulses has come under increasing scrutiny. With the discovery of the Dead Sea Scrolls and subsequent excavations at Qumran, scholars were forced to register the ascetic way of life that marked this form of Judaism. Despite the presence of a few female skeletons in the cemetery at Qumran,[34] the Qumran community appears to have been composed of male celibates.[35] Moreover, scholars such as Daniel Boyarin in his book *Carnal Israel* have given new prominence to such early Jewish texts as "The Testament of the Twelve Patriarchs," a treatise that is equally ambivalent about sexual relations as the Hellenistic Jewish author Philo of Alexandria and as early Christian ascetic texts. Boyarin argues that early Judaism moved away from the more skittish attitudes toward sex characteristic of documents written close to the time of the New Testament's composition, toward a stronger affirmation of body and marriage by the time that the Babylonian Talmud was compiled several centuries later.[36] If these suggestive arguments can be substantiated,

relianus, Celsus, and Soranus. For a popular overview of philosophers' and physicians' advice on bodily regulation in the imperial period, see Foucault, *The Care of the Self*, pt. 4.

[34] Roland de Vaux, *Archaeology and the Dead Sea Scrolls* (London: Oxford University Press, 1973), p. 47.

[35] For a more recent qualification of the Qumran requirement of celibacy, see Joseph M. Baumgarten, "The Qumran-Essene Restraints on Marriage," in *Archaeology and History in the Dead Sea Scrolls* (*Journal for the Study of Pseudepigrapha*, ed. Lawrence H. Schiffman, Suppl. 2, JSOT/ASOR Monograph 2) (Sheffield: Sheffield Academic Press, 1990), pp. 13–25. The "maleness" of the Qumran community had much earlier been noted by the ancient literary sources pertaining to the Essenes.

[36] Daniel Boyarin, *Carnal Israel: Reading Sex in Talmudic Culture*, The New Historicism 25 (Berkeley/Los Angeles: University of California Press, 1993), chap. 2; cf. Daniel Boyarin, *A Radical Jew: Paul and the Politics of Identity* (Berkeley/Los Angeles/London: University of California Press, 1994), p. 159. Boyarin's argument is somewhat hindered by the widespread recognition that "The Testament of the Twelve Patriarchs" contains Christian interpolations. See also Adalbert G. Hamman, "Les Origines du mônachisme chrétien au cours de deux premiers siècles," in *Homo Spiritalis: Festgabe für Luc Verheijen*, ed. Cornelius Mayer and Karl Heinz Chelius (Würzburg: Augustinus-Verlag, 1987), pp. 322–23, on ascetic currents in early Judaism. Will Deming argues that "The Testament of the Twelve Patriarchs" is pro-marriage, although anti-*porneia*; see his *Paul on Marriage and Celibacy: The Hellenistic Background of I Corinthians 7* (Cambridge: Cambridge University Press, 1995), esp. pp. 17–18. Deming nonetheless concedes that "The Testament of Naphtali" 2.9–10 warns that marital sex and prayer may be incompatible (pp. 123–26).

it is questionable whether scholars of early Christianity should claim that ascetic currents must have been a product of later Hellenization, not indigenous to the early Jewish-Christian movement.[37] Given considerations such as these, scholars of early Christian asceticism now deem it misguided to try to locate some particular moment after the late second century when Christianity took an ascetic turn. Rather, they prefer to trace parallel ascetic developments within various religious and philosophical groups of later antiquity.

The "motivations question" has likewise been restyled. A half-century ago, there were several dominant hypotheses as to why early Christians adopted asceticism: the question itself presupposes that ascetic strains entered the religion only at a later point of its development. In two of these motivational explanations, Constantine's conversion to Christianity and the faster pace of Christianization thereafter are privileged moments. One explanation held that with the increased rapidity of conversion, more ardent devotees sought a way of life that would distinguish them from the ordinary (and ever-swelling) ranks of lukewarm Christians, *hoi polloi* in the hierarchy of renunciatory enthusiasts. To be sure, many Christian texts suggest that by virtue of their renunciations, ascetics transcend the ranks of the commonplace: "Learn from me a holy arrogance," Jerome advises the teen-aged Eustochium, who had vowed herself to perpetual virginity, "if you are better than they."[38] Yet it must be noted that ascetic renunciants do not themselves appeal to such an explanation. The creation of "difference," of "distinction," I would argue, was surely a *function* of early Christian asceticism, but it fails to provide a documentable *motivation* for renunciation.[39] The *topos* of ascetic superiority may offer better access to the psyches of the framers of such language than to those of their ascetic subjects. Likewise, the functions that our contemporaries sometimes assign to ascetic renunciation after the fact perhaps differ from the motivations expressed by early Christian ascetic practitioners and their biographers.

A second explanation of ascetic motivation that privileges Constantine suggests that with the cessation of the Roman persecutions, a new means

[37] Gilles Quispel credits Erik Peterson and his students as pioneering this opinion: see Quispel, "The Study of Encratism: A Historical Survey," in *La Tradizione dell' enkrateia: Motivazione ontologiche e protologiche*, ed. Ugo Bianchi (Roma: Edizioni dell' Ateneo, 1985), pp. 42–47, 49. Also see Steven D. Fraade, "Ascetical Aspects of Ancient Judaism," in *Jewish Spirituality*, ed. Arthur Green (New York: Crossroad, 1986), I:253–88; and Marcel Simon, "L'Ascéticisme dans lẹs sectes juives," in *La Tradizione*, ed. Bianchi, pp. 393–426.

[38] Jerome, *ep.* 22.16 (CSEL 54, 163).

[39] The creation of "distinction" by means of religious practices is a theme emphasized by Pierre Bourdieu (borrowing from Durkheim); see chap. 8 below for discussion. Giving purely theological-philosophical "motivations" is Carlo Tibiletti, "Motivazioni dell' ascetismo in alcuni autori cristiani," *Atti della Accademia delle Scienze di Torino* 106 (1972): 489–537.

was sought by Christians to display their religious commitment: since physical martyrdom was no longer an option after Constantine's conversion, asceticism, considered a form of spiritual martyrdom, might prove an adequate substitute. As expounded by scholars such as Edward Malone in *The Monk and the Martyr*,[40] from the fourth century onward, those Christians aiming for "perfection" through renunciation were seen as seeking a form of spiritual martyrdom. Again, we must ask to what extent this supposed motivation stands largely as a rhetorical *topos*: although writers of the fourth and fifth centuries often inform renunciants that a glory like that of the martyrs awaits them in heaven, the claim is not emphasized by ascetic practitioners of themselves.

Another motivational explanation that earlier enjoyed some currency privileged the development of clerical hierarchy. With the rapid development of church office, especially in the fourth century, Christian worship became increasingly formalized and subjected to priestly authority; on this view, the wish to escape liturgical formality and hierarchical control for a freer style of Christian life accounts for the origins of asceticism. (This explanation often cites the advice of the desert fathers to "flee women and bishops.")[41] Yet this explanation too has its problems. We know, for example, that even desert hermits congregated for worship led by ordained priests and bishops, and hence do not appear anticlerical in principle. Moreover, a wider-ranging freedom may not have attended the ascetic life: does not the ascetic's submission to the control of an elder or an abbot seem at least as rigorous as the married Christian's submission to a bishop? Here it is worth noting that all the above explanations privilege the fourth century as the moment of monastic origins. I would argue to the contrary that although monasticism undoubtedly flourished in this era, we cannot posit the fourth century as the founding moment of Christian asceticism.

Still another motivational explanation also privileges the period of late antiquity, but takes its cue from the repressiveness of late Roman imperial bureaucracy that increasingly foisted the burden for the collection of taxes and the upkeep of civic structures on the curial class of towns and cities. On this view, the retreat (*anachōrēsis*) of the ascetic is linked to the flight of midlevel officials from towns and cities to escape the burdens of civic life. Evidence such as the following is cited in support of such a view: a law of Valentinian I and Valens dated to 370 C.E. instructs the Count of the Orient to "rout out" those who have abandoned their public duties and retreated to "solitary and secret places," joining up with *monazontes*.

[40] Edward Malone, *The Monk and the Martyr: The Monk as the Successor of the Martyr*, Studies in Christian Antiquity 12 (Washington, D.C.: Catholic University Press, 1950).

[41] John Cassian, *Institutiones* 11.18 (SC 109, 444).

Although such men act "under the pretext of religion," they in truth are "devotees of idleness." Those who refuse to return to their municipal duties, the law threatens, will lose their right to family property.[42] Does not such evidence suggest that monastic flight to the desert was an appropriate response for the most burdened classes? Here, the crumbling of governmental structures is seen as contributing to the attractiveness of Christian asceticism.

As a general explanation, however, this approach also fails: not only was asceticism a much earlier phenomenon within Christianity, but recent archeological studies suggest that fourth-century Roman towns and cities had not so precipitously declined by midcentury as earlier scholars had imagined,[43] an assumption on which this explanation depends. Moreover, this explanation would require that the curial class be identified as a prime constituency among the early monks. This claim, however, would be difficult to sustain, since the sources indicate a wide variety of social backgrounds among the early desert fathers.[44] Writers such as Augustine worry that the lower classes might flock to monasteries as a way to improve their social status,[45] a point that might not have troubled him if a sizable number of monks were derived from the decuriate. Although several laws of the period attempt to prevent town councillors from abandoning their civic duties,[46] as noted above, there is little direct evidence that many of these "political escapees" embraced the ascetic life of Christian renunciants.[47]

One further possible motivational explanation regarding monasticism's popularity pertains to women, who are better documented in the sources pertaining to asceticism than in much other early Christian literature. Can

[42] *Codex Theodosianus* 12.1.63. Contrast this law with that of Theodosius I in 390: monks are to be driven from the cities to desert places; they are to be "solitary" (*Codex Theodosianus* 16.3.1). Church councils such as that held at Saragossa in 380 also strike at clerics who out of "presumptuous vanity" abandon their posts to become monks (canon 6).

[43] See Claude Lepelley, *Les Cités de l'Afrique romaine au Bas Empire* (Paris: Etudes Augustiniennes, 1979), I, esp. Introduction and chap. 1. Bryan Ward-Perkins, *From Classical Antiquity to the Middle Ages: Urban Public Building in Northern and Central Italy A.D. 300–850* (Oxford: Oxford University Press, 1984), documents the shift from private patronage to imperial and Christian sponsorship of building projects.

[44] On the wealthier end, Isidore (Palladius, *Historia Lausiaca* 1); Amoun (*Historia monachorum* 22.1); Arsenius (*Apophthegmata patrum* [Arsenius 42]); on the humble end, Paul the Simple (Palladius, *Historia Lausiaca* 22); John of Lycopolis (Palladius, *Historia Lausiaca* 35); Sisinnius (Palladius, *Historia Lausiaca* 49).

[45] Augustine, *De opere monachorum* 22.25 (CSEL 41, 570–71).

[46] E.g., *Codex Theodosianus* 12.1.59; 12.1.62–64; 12.1.76; 12.1.82; 12.1.86–87.

[47] The most notable "political escapee," Arsenius, of senatorial rank, earlier held the post of tutor to the sons of Theodosius I, but he was of far higher social status than the curial-class officials who are the subjects of the above legislation; see *Apophthegmata Patrum* (Alphabetical), Arsenius.

we not posit that asceticism proved particularly attractive to Christian women insofar as it offered an alternative lifestyle to marriage and childbearing—and hence a motivation to renounce? A variety of evidence indeed suggests many women's desire for sexual renunciation. For example, ascetic sentiment dominates in fictional works that highlight women, such as the Apocryphal Acts of the Apostles; the alleged founder of communal monasticism, Pachomius, had a monastery built for his sister and other women renunciants;[48] and late-fourth- and fifth-century eyewitness reports stress the large number of women who adopted ascetic living in the Egyptian desert.[49]

Here again the problem is one of assigning causation: although some women derived advantage from undertaking the ascetic life, as I have detailed in a number of my own writings, it is less clear that women were *motivated* to renounce for the sake of benefits such as increased opportunities for travel (pilgrimage), for study and reflection, for the cultivation of friendships with scholarly and spiritually minded men, for monastic leadership, and for the receipt of honor through the exercise of patronage. If we accept the church fathers' rhetoric, we would also believe that women ascetics gained greater freedom from the tyranny of husbands and in-laws, from anxieties over the health and welfare of children, from concerns for the directing of extensive households which were serviced by dozens, even hundreds, of slaves. Whether the women themselves interpreted their celibacy as freedom, as did their male biographers, we have no sure way to know.[50] Yet we may note that ascetic women did not, any more than did ascetic men, explicitly appeal to such explanations: when we occasionally hear the words placed upon their lips by their biographers, devotion to God and repentance for sins are the reasons given for their renunciations.

Thus all attempts to find a sure moment of origin for early Christian asceticism or to locate the motivations of early ascetics seem problematic. There is now strong agreement that ascetic impulses are present in the

[48] *Vita Pachomii* (Bo) 27 (CSCO 89 = Scriptores Coptici 7, 26–27); cf. Palladius, *Historia Lausiaca* 33 (Butler, pp. 96–97). The chapter in the first Greek *Vita* of Pachomius that deals with the building of the women's monastery (chap. 32) was not contained in good condition in the manuscript on which Halkin based his text in SubsHag 19 but is found in Ms. 1015 from the National Library in Athens.

[49] Palladius, *Historia Lausiaca* 33 (Butler, p. 96); (Anonymous), *Historia monachorum* 5 (PL 21, 409); Marcellinus and Faustinus, *De confessione verae fidei* 99, cf. 93 (CCL 69, 384, 382).

[50] See Elizabeth A. Clark, "Friendship Between the Sexes: Classical Theory and Christian Practice," in idem, *Jerome, Chrysostom, and Friends: Essays and Translations* (New York: Edwin Mellen, 1979), esp. pp. 48–56; idem, "Devil's Gateway and Bride of Christ: Women in the Early Christian World," in idem, *Ascetic Piety and Women's Faith: Essays on Late Ancient Christianity* (Lewiston/Queenston: Edwin Mellen, 1986), esp. pp. 42, 46–48.

earliest extant Christian writings (Paul's letters) and that the Synoptic Gospels are replete with verses that Christians developed in a highly ascetic direction, for example, verses on the damnation that awaited a man who looked lustfully at a woman (Matt. 5:28) and the praise for those who became "eunuchs for the Kingdom of Heaven" (Matt. 19:12). Modern Biblical criticism (not available, of course, to patristic authors), which established that the Pastoral Epistles were not written by Paul himself, enables a recognition of anti-ascetic as well as ascetic strands in the New Testament itself. The Apocryphal Acts of the Apostles are now seen as developing the pro-ascetic trajectory of New Testament teaching: to read the Apocryphal Acts over against the anti-ascetic Pastoral Epistles is one enlightening exercise for which recent scholarship has provided considerable assistance.[51]

Ascetic teaching is likewise present in the writings of second-century authors such as Justin Martyr and Athenagoras, who defend Christianity's respectability by appealing to the loftiness of its sexual ethics. These authors claim that Christianity stands against second marriage, that many Christians "in every nation" have lived from childhood to old age in sexual abstinence, and that Christians cannot be blamed for child exposure, since for them the *only* purpose of marriage is the raising of children.[52] By the turn to the third century, Tertullian emerges as a strong critic of second marriage, which he scorns as an unnecessary decline into sexual indulgence.[53] Tertullian, in Peter Brown's phrase, was the first real spokesman for educated Christians "of the belief that abstinence from sex was the most effective technique with which to achieve clarity of soul."[54]

The Apocryphal Acts, probably composed largely in the third century (although in all likelihood based on earlier oral traditions), present the message of apostolic Christianity as one of asceticism, pure and simple. Thus the anonymous author of the *Acts of Paul and Thecla* (a text that probably dates to the second century) can "rewrite" the Gospels' Beatitudes to stress the centrality of asceticism in Christian teaching:

> Blessed are the pure in heart, for they shall see God.
> Blessed are those who keep the flesh pure, for they shall become the temple of God.
> Blessed are those who remain continent, for to them shall God speak.

[51] Dennis R. MacDonald, *The Legend and the Apostle: The Battle for Paul in Story and Canon* (Philadelphia: Westminster, 1983), esp. chap. 3.

[52] Justin Martyr, *Apologia I*, 15, 29 (PG 6, 349); Athenagoras, *Legatio pro Christianis* 33 (PG 6, 965, 968).

[53] See Tertullian, *De monogamia* (CCL 2, 1229–53).

[54] Peter Brown, *The Body and Society: Men, Women, and Sexual Renunciation in Early Christianity* (New York: Columbia University Press, 1988), p. 78.

> Blessed are those who have wives as if they had them not, for they shall inherit God.
>
> Blessed are the bodies of virgins, for they shall be well-pleasing to God and shall not lose the reward of their purity.[55]

Thus diverse evidence suggests that Christianity in the first through the third centuries—not just in the fourth—contained many testimonies to asceticism's popularity. In fact, early Christian writers warn against overly ascetic interpretations of Christianity, interpretations that the Fathers labeled "heretical" and from which they sought to distance themselves.

Rather than stress either origins or motivations, contemporary scholars of asceticism are more apt to explore the rhetoric of ascetic argumentation, the shifts in ascetic practice within particular geographical areas, the material supports that undergirded the ascetic lifestyle, and the forms of power (secular and political, as well as spiritual) that the ascetic practitioner was able to wield.

III: The Geographic Specificity of Early Christian Asceticism

Given such evidence of asceticism's popularity even in the earliest Christian centuries, scholars now concentrate on exploring its development in geographically specific areas, especially in Egypt, Syria, and Palestine.

Antony, the alleged founder of Egyptian asceticism, retreated to the desert in about 270.[56] Although Antony is customarily called the first desert ascetic, his *Vita* itself calls this claim into question by its report that in a neighboring village dwelt an old man who had devoted himself to the solitary's life from youth up, and that there were already "men of zeal" practicing renunciation whom Antony copied.[57] Jerome also maintains that Antony, in his old age, sought out Paul the Hermit who had preceded him in solitary ascetic living (Paul being 113 years old when Antony jour-

[55] *Acta Pauli et Theclae* 5–6 (Lipsius/Bonnet I:238–40). For a discussion of the asceticism of the Apocryphal Acts, see Yves Tissot, "Encratisme et Actes Apocryphes," in *Les Actes Apocryphes des Apôtres: Christianisme et monde païen*, ed. François Bovon et al., Publications de la Faculté de Théologie de l'Université de Genève 4 (Geneva: Labor et Fides, 1981), pp. 109–19.

[56] Armand Veilleux, "The Origins of Egyptian Monasticism," in *The Continuing Quest for God: Monastic Spirituality in Tradition and Transition*, ed. William Skudlarek (Collegeville, Minn.: Liturgical, 1982), p. 47. For a brief overview that sets Egyptian monasticism in a larger social and economic setting, see Roger S. Bagnall, *Egypt in Late Antiquity* (Princeton, N.J.: Princeton University Press, 1993), pp. 293–303.

[57] Athanasius, *Vita Antonii* 3–4 (PG 26, 844–45).

neyed across the desert to find him)—although Jerome's tale probably constitutes not "history," but reputational demotion.[58] By the 320s and 330s, the first inhabitants of rigorous ascetic groups at Nitria, Scetis, and "the Cells" are in place.[59] Pachomius' organization of communal monasticism is usually dated to the 320s,[60] and Palladius reports that by the end of the century the Pachomian monasteries boasted about seven thousand inhabitants.[61] So rapidly did monasticism's popularity develop that, in Athanasius' famous phrase, "the desert was made a city by monks, whose citizenship was that of heaven."[62]

Of interest to contemporary scholars are hints that early Egyptian asceticism may have been in a more tenuous state of "orthodoxy" than its later commentators found tolerable. Take the case of Antony. Robert Gregg and Dennis Groh have argued persuasively in their book *Early Arianism: A View of Salvation* that Antony's biographer Athanasius "polished up" Antony's image so that he emerged as a resolutely orthodox (by mid-fourth-century standards) fighter of Arian heretics.[63] Moreover, Samuel Rubenson's study of the letters of Antony, in which he argues convincingly for their authenticity (heretofore usually denied), shows an Antony far more at home with Origen's theology, soon to become suspect, than does Athanasius' representation of him in the *Life*.[64]

But Antony is not the only unsettling flashpoint regarding the "orthodoxy" of early Egyptian monasticism. Despite the church fathers' attempts to paint many so-called Gnostics as licentious libertines, the bulk of the evidence from the Nag Hammadi finds at midcentury suggests that much of early Egyptian Christianity that is customarily labeled "Gnostic" was resolutely ascetic, a point early stressed by Henry Chadwick in his memorable essay, "The Domestication of Gnosis."[65] Indeed, for some of

[58] Jerome, *Vita Pauli* 1, 7 (PL 23, 17–18, 22): Jerome appears to attempt the ouster of Antony from pride-of-place.

[59] Veilleux, "Origins," pp. 47–48; Chitty, *Desert*, pp. 11–13, 29–30.

[60] Chitty, *Desert*, pp. 10–11.

[61] Palladius, *Historia Lausiaca* 32 (Butler, p. 93).

[62] Athanasius, *Vita Antonii* 14 (PG 26, 865).

[63] Robert C. Gregg and Dennis E. Groh, *Early Arianism: A View of Salvation* (Philadelphia: Fortress, 1981), chap. 4. For earlier important discussions of the literarily constructed nature of the *Life of Antony*, see Richard Reitzenstein, "Des Athanasius Werk über das Leben des Antonius," *Sitzungsberichte*, Heidelberger Akademie des Wissenschaften, Philosophisch-Historische Klasse 5 (1914): 3–68; Karl Holl, "Die Schriftstellerische Form des griechischen Heiligenlebens," *Neue Jahrbücher für das Klassische Altertum* 29 (1912): 406–27.

[64] Samuel Rubenson, *The Letters of St. Antony: Origenist Theology, Monastic Tradition and the Making of a Saint* (Lund: Lund University Press, 1990), esp. chap. 4.

[65] Henry Chadwick, "The Domestication of Gnosis," in *Rediscovery of Gnosticism*, ed. Bentley Layton (Leiden: Brill, 1980), 1:3–16. Also see Robert McL. Wilson, "Alimentary and Sexual Encratism in the Nag Hammadi Tractates," in *La Tradizione*, ed. Bianchi, p. 319. Michael A. Williams argues that the older division of "Gnostics" into "ascetics" and "libertines"

the anonymous authors of the Nag Hammadi documents, Catholic Christianity's deficient embrace of ascetic practice was a point to be faulted. Some writers deemed "Gnostic" argued that if Catholics had received a genuine "baptism of truth," they would know that all things of the world must be renounced, including "the dominion of sexual procreation."[66] To what extent, scholars ask, did Catholic renunciation resemble Gnostic asceticism?

But more than the similar ascetic content of Gnostic and Catholic texts is at issue here: there is also the question of the actual sharing of documents. Once it was posited that among the cartonnage filling for the bindings of the Nag Hammadi codices were letters and rescripts possibly coming from nearby Pachomian monasteries,[67] a scholarly furor erupted over the relationship between the allegedly "orthodox" monasticism and the supposedly "heretical" Nag Hammadi documents. Frederik Wisse has argued that the Nag Hammadi texts probably did not look so "heretical" to the Pachomian monks, whose constituency may have been partly composed of former "Gnostics" retreating from their earlier allegiance. Equally important, Wisse added, it is "highly improbable" that either anchoritic or cenobitic monasticism arose only with "orthodox" Christianity.[68] Scholars were left with the delicate question, to what extent was "orthodox" Christian asceticism in Egypt influenced by, or parallel to, "Gnostic" asceticism—in many of its forms, also Christian?[69]

Similarly, the question of possible Manichean influences on the development of Christian asceticism in Egypt has been raised. Manicheanism ap-

---

needs serious revision: see *Rethinking "Gnosticism": An Argument for Dismantling a Dubious Category* (Princeton, N.J.: Princeton University Press, 1996), p. 140.

66 *Testimonium Veritatis* (NHC 9.3) 69, 30 (Nag Hammadi Studies 15:186, 124); cf. Klaus Koschorke, *Die Polemik der Gnostiker gegen das kirchliche Christentum* (Leiden: Brill, 1978), esp. pp. 113, 116–17.

67 John W. B. Barns, "Greek and Coptic Papyri from the Covers of the Nag Hammadi Codices: A Preliminary Report," in *Essays on the Nag Hammadi Texts: In Honour of Pahor Labib*, ed. Martin Krause (Leiden: Brill, 1975), pp. 9–18; Frederik Wisse, "Gnosticism and Early Monasticism in Egypt," in *Gnosis: Festschrift für Hans Jonas*, ed. Barbara Aland (Göttingen: Vandenhoeck & Ruprecht, 1978), p. 433. For a critique of Barns' position that rejects the hypothesis that the cartonnage material is Pachomian, see Clemons Scholten, "Die Nag-Hammadi-Texte als Buchbesitz der Pachomianer," *Jahrbuch für Antike und Christentum* 31 (1988): 144–72.

68 Wisse, "Gnosticism and Early Monasticism," pp. 433, 436, 440; the scribal colophons and decorations also suggest that the copyists did not think that the works were heretical (p. 435). Wisse argues against Torgny Säve-Söderbergh ("Holy Scriptures or Apologetic Documentations?: The 'Sitz im Leben' of the Nag Hammadi Library," in *Les Textes de Nag Hammadi*, ed. Jacques-E. Ménard [Leiden: Brill, 1975], p. 7), who holds that the Nag Hammadi documents were present in orthodox libraries to assist the monks in refuting the Gnostic heretics.

69 See Williams, *Rethinking "Gnosticism"*; Williams and other scholars now

pears to have had its origin in a Jewish-Christian baptismal sect, the Elchasaites,[70] an assumption that renders similarities between Manichean practice and Christian practice more understandable than was imagined before the discovery of the Cologne Mani Codex that describes Mani's "founding" of a new religion.

The process by which Manicheanism spread westward has received considerable attention in the past few decades.[71] It is now hypothesized that Manicheanism entered Egypt in the mid-third century, perhaps introduced by communities of merchants who were followed by Manichean missionaries.[72] Already by about 300 C.E., two Egyptian documents warn against Manicheanism, one from a Christian bishop who feared that Catholics might adopt the highly ascetic interpretation of I Corinthians 7 that Manicheans in his area were teaching.[73] Another Manichean document speaks of the Manichean mission in mid-third-century Egypt and mentions "collective houses" in which the Manichean "elect" lived. Were these like cloisters, scholars ask?[74] We are here reminded that the third quarter

---

question whether the label "Gnostic" is either accurate or useful.

[70] Albert Henrichs, "The Cologne Mani Codex Reconsidered," *Harvard Studies in Classical Philology* 83 (1979): 357–59, 366–67; also Samuel N. C. Lieu, *Manichaeism in the Later Roman Empire and Medieval China: A Historical Survey* (Manchester: Manchester University Press, 1985), pp. 28–37; doubted by J. Kevin Coyle, "The Cologne Mani Codex and Mani's Christian Connections," *Eglise et Théologie* 10 (1979): 179–93.

[71] Lieu, *Manichaeism*, pp. 67–68, 75, 81, 92; idem, "Some Themes in Later Roman Anti-Manichean Polemics: I," *Bulletin of the John Rylands Library of Manchester* 68 (1986): 434–35; Han Drijvers, "Facts and Problems in Early Syriac-Speaking Christianity," *The Second Century* 2 (1982): 170; Michel Tardieu, "Les Manichéens en Egypte," *Bulletin de la Société français d'Egyptologie* 94 (1982): 8–10. On Mani's letter to Edessa, see Reinhold Merkelbach, "Manichaica (1–3)," *Zeitschrift für Papyrologie und Epigraphik* 56 (1984): 45–48. Also see G. A. M. Rouwhorst, "Das Manichaeische Bemafest und das Passafest der Syrischen Christen," *Vigiliae Christianae* 35 (1981): 397–411; Henrichs, "The Cologne Mani Codex," pp. 352–53.

[72] G. Stroumsa, "Monachisme et Marranisme chez les Manichéens d'Egypte," *Numen* 29 (1982): 186, probably on the basis of the notice in the *Acta Archelai* that Scythianos, a Saracen merchant, carried Manicheanism to Egypt, married an Egyptian, and settled there; his disciple wrote books. See the fragments discussed in Peter Brown, "The Diffusion of Manichaeism in the Roman Empire," *Journal of Roman Studies* 59 (1969): 92–103.

[73] Papyrus Rylands 469, ed. in Alfred Adam, *Texte zum Manichäismus*, 2nd ed. (Berlin: de Gruyter, 1969), p. 175. See Ludwig Koenen, "Manichäische Mission und Klöster in Ägypten," in *Das Römisch-Byzantinische Ägypten (Akten des internationalen Symposions 26.–30. September 1978, Trier)*, ed. Günter Grimm et al. (Mainz am Rhein: Verlag Philipp von Zabern, 1983), p. 94; Tardieu, "Les Manichéens," p. 10.

[74] Stroumsa, "Monachisme," p. 188; Koenen, "Manichäische Mission," p. 98, uses the word "cloister." The text is edited by F. C. Andreas and W. Henning in *Mitteliranische Manichaia aus Chinesisch-Turkestan* II (Berlin: Sitzungsberichte der preussischen Akademie der Wissenschaften, 1933), pp. 301–2. The question of its reliability regarding date and place is raised by Samuel N. C. Lieu, "Precept and Practice

of the third century was supposedly the very time of Antony's retreat to the desert—and well before the development of Pachomian communal monasticism. Catholic monastic sources from or reporting on Egypt describe Catholic monks' encounters with Manicheans, but always distance their heroes from Manichean teachings.[75] It thus appears likely that Manichean and Christian asceticism developed almost concurrently in Egypt. Since the significance of Manichean asceticism for early Catholic asceticism has only recently begun to be explored, there is always the danger of overinterpretation on the basis of a few fragmentary remains; nonetheless the evidence is intriguing.

Despite the importance of Egypt as an early venue of Christian asceticism, we should be cautious not to adopt the "diffusionist" view that Egypt was the center from which all early Christian asceticism emerged; in other areas, such as Palestine, Mesopotamia, and Syria, asceticism probably developed independently of Egypt.[76] The attempt to link all Christian asceticism to a founding moment with Antony in Egypt seems aligned with the misplaced search for origins: a " 'big bang' theory of monastic origins," in James Goehring's evocative phrase.[77]

Syria is a second area of the early Christian world that has received considerable recent study as a center for asceticism's development. So strongly was ascetic practice rooted in early Syriac Christianity that over four decades ago the prominent scholar of Syrian asceticism, Arthur Vööbus, argued that celibacy was a virtual requirement for baptism in the early Syrian church.[78] This claim has since been nuanced,[79] but even so, there is good evidence from early Syriac texts that renunciation was a prominent feature of Christianity in that area: so we would gather from the second-century *Gospel of Thomas* and the third-century *Acts of Judas Thomas*, which proclaim that ascetic engagement is a norm for all Christians.[80] Also distinctive to Syria are the views and writings of the ascetic leader Tatian, who

in Manichaean Monasticism," *Journal of Theological Studies*, n.s. 32 (1981): 155–56.

[75] Athanasius, *Vita Antonii* 68 (PG 26, 940–41) cf. Stroumsa, "Monachisme," p. 185; (Anonymous), *Historia Monachorum* 10.30–32 (Festugière, pp. 87–88); Philostorgius, *Hist. eccles.* 3.15 (GCS 21, 46–47).

[76] See Rousseau, "Structure," typescript, p. 5; also see Antoine Guillaumont, "Perspectives actuelles," pp. 217–18.

[77] James E. Goehring, "The Origins of Monasticism," in *Eusebius, Christianity, and Judaism*, ed. Harold W. Attridge and Gohei Hata (Detroit: Wayne State University Press, 1992), p. 235.

[78] Arthur Vööbus, *Celibacy, A Requirement for Admission to Baptism in the Early Syrian Church* (Stockholm: Estonian Theological Society in Exile, 1951), esp. chap. 2.

[79] As explained by Syriac scholar Sidney Griffith, the evidence on which Vööbus drew (e.g., Aphraat, *Hom.* 7) dates only to the fourth and fifth centuries (personal communication).

[80] The third-century *Acts of Judas Thomas* make celibacy a requirement for baptism: see Vööbus, *Celibacy*, pp. 26–29, citing Act 13. Cf. *Gospel of Thomas* 75 (it is solitaries who will enter the bridal chamber).

deemed marriage to be *porneia* (fornication), and whose harmony of the Gospels, the *Diatesseron*, provided an ascetic rendition of the Gospel texts (e.g., references to Joseph as Mary's husband are omitted, as is mention of wine as the beverage preferred in the Kingdom of Heaven).[81] Special praise was reserved in early Syriac Christianity for the *ihidaye*, the "single ones," who within the structures of the church committed themselves to celibacy and to "singleness of heart" in imitation of the "singly-begotten one," Jesus.[82] From the fifth century on, there are reports of more extreme forms of asceticism—wandering, homelessness, living in common with the animals, wearing iron chains around the body, standing for years on pillars—although scholars such as Sidney Griffith argue that this fiercer variety of ascetic practice should not be dated too early (its previous placement in the mid-fourth century relied on texts that should probably be assigned to a somewhat later period).[83] The view that Syria represents the "Wild West" of early Christian asceticism demands some nuance,[84] given the incorporation of ascetics within the larger communal life of the Syrian church.

The third area here noted, Palestine, developed its own distinctive forms of monasticism as well. Jerome assigns to Hilarion, allegedly a follower of Antony, the impetus to ascetic practice in Palestine;[85] the *Life of Chariton*, however, rather credits *its* hero as originator (although his *floruit* should probably be moved from the mid-third to the early fourth century).[86] Another ascetic center, located near Eleutheropolis and dating from the mid-fourth century, is associated with Epiphanius, later bishop

[81] For a discussion of such omissions and emendations, see Arthur Vööbus, *History of Asceticism in the Syrian Orient: A Contribution to the History of Culture in the Near East*, vol. I, *The Origin of Asceticism: Early Monasticism in Persia*, CSCO 184 = Subsidia 14 (Louvain: CSCO, 1958), pp. 39–43. For a discussion of Tatian and the Encratites, see Georges Blond, "L'Hérésie' encratite vers la fin du quatrième siècle," *Recherches de science religieuse* 31 (1944): 157–210.

[82] Sidney H. Griffith, "Singles in God's Service: Thoughts on the Ihidaye from the Works of Aphrahat and Ephraem the Syrian," *The Harp* 4 (1991): 145–59; Guillaumont, "Perspectives actuelles," pp. 218–20.

[83] Sidney H. Griffith, "Asceticism in the Church of Syria: The Hermeneutics of Early Syrian Monasticism," in *Asceticism*, ed. Wimbush and Valantasis, pp. 220–21. Also see Jean Gribomont, "Le Monachisme au sein de l'église en Syrie et en Cappadoce," *Studia Monastica* 7 (1965): 17, discussing the evidence from Ephrem on "wanderers" detaching themselves from the church community.

[84] The phrase is from Peter Brown, *Body*, p. 334; critiqued by Griffith, "Asceticism," p. 220.

[85] Jerome, *Vita Hilarionis* 3, 13 (PL 23, 31, 34). Chitty, *Desert*, pp. 13–14, puts the founding of this monastic community at around 330, but cautions that Jerome's representation is not historically reliable.

[86] *Vita Charitonis* 2: Chariton fled the persecution of Aurelian (270–275 C.E.). The *Vita* comes from perhaps the fifth or sixth century, and is incorporated into Symeon Metaphrastes' *Vita Sanctorum, Mensis September* (PG 115, 899–918; ET by Leah DiSegni in Wimbush, ed., *Ascetic Behavior*, pp. 396–420).

of Salamis in Cyprus.[87] Early monasteries in the Palestinian desert were organized as "lavras," an allusion to the rows of stalls in a market that were replicated in the rows of caves providing shelter for the solitaries; communal worship and food production, however, suggest that these monks were not, strictly speaking, hermits.[88] Within a few decades, numerous monasteries had sprung up in Bethlehem and Jerusalem near the holy sites associated with Jesus' life: the monastic establishments of Jerome and Paula in Bethlehem, and of Rufinus, Melania the Elder, and Melania the Younger in Jerusalem, ensured their fame.[89] Thus asceticism flourished in widely separated areas of the Greco-Roman world. Some of its manifestations appear to have developed independently, while the borrowing of ascetic theory and practice seems clear in other cases.

IV: Forms of Ascetic Living

Another topic of recent interest is the variety of models for ascetic living. The distinction between anchorites or hermits, who lived alone, and cenobites, who lived in community, stands as a traditional differentiation, although modern commentators question the degree to which anchoritic monasticism was truly solitary.[90] Urban asceticism was an equally important phenomenon, although it received less attention from ascetic writers of the period who tend to romanticize the virtues of hermits in the Egyptian desert and other allegedly isolated regions. Recently, Susanna Elm has argued that urban asceticism was normative for parts of Asia Minor and that Basil of Caesarea's praise of country retreat for monks and nuns constituted one feature of his program to break with earlier (allegedly "heretical") ascetic patterns of a more urban nature.[91] Likewise, David Brakke's study of asceticism in Alexandria demonstrates the centrality of both female and male urban ascetics in Athanasius' struggle to maintain control of the Alexandrian church.[92] Despite such episcopal contests for dominance and for the maintenance of

[87] Sozomen, *Hist. eccles.* 6.32.2–3 (PG 67, 1389, 1392).

[88] Rousseau, "Structure," typescript, p. 6; Binns, *Ascetics*, pp. 109–11; Chitty, *Desert*, pp. 13–16.

[89] For Jerusalem monasteries: Palladius, *Historia Lausiaca* 46; 54; 61; (Gerontius), *Vita Melaniae Iunioris* 40–49. For Jerome's and Paula's Bethlehem monasteries: Palladius, *Historia Lausiaca* 41; Jerome, *ep.* 108.14; 108.20. For sixth-century material, see the *Lives* of Palestinian monks by Cyril of Scythopolis (*Kyrillos von Skythopolis*, ed. Eduard Schwartz, TU 49.2); also the fine study by Bernard Flusin, *Miracle et histoire dans l'oeuvre de Cyrille de Scythopolis* (Paris: Etudes Augustinniennes, 1983).

[90] Goehring, "Origins," p. 235.

[91] Elm, *"Virgins,"* pp. ix, 210.

[92] Brakke, *Athanasius*, pp. 9, 57–79. It is of interest that the female virgins appear to have given Athanasius considerable difficulty, since the Hieracites (deemed heretical by Athanasius) as well as the Arians made strong bids for the virgins' support.

"orthodoxy," urban ascetics may have been more tightly linked to the bishop and his establishment, as evidence suggests for Asia Minor,[93] Alexandria,[94] Milan,[95] and Hippo.[96] Moreover, papyrological and other evidence from Egypt shows that ascetics also abounded in smaller towns and engaged in the commercial life of the communities around them, selling goods and renting property.[97]

In the early Syrian church, as I have suggested, ascetics appear to have functioned within the larger structures of the church. Here, "fleeing the bishop," we may infer, was not thought necessary for ascetic practice; renunciants could qualify as "wanderers" (a common name for early Syrian ascetics) while remaining within their local communities.[98] Simply adopting an ascetic lifestyle while residing at home was another popular option, especially for female ascetics, some of whom stayed in their parental households, or, as widows, in their own homes (or palaces, as the case may be).[99] Susanna Elm has documented how prevalent this form of "household asceticism" was in Asia Minor; in the case of figures such as Basil of Caesarea, Gregory of Nyssa, and their sister Macrina, entire families came to adopt the ascetic life.[100]

Male ascetics as well practiced this "house asceticism," as testimony from Augustine, Paulinus of Nola, and Sulpicius Severus, among others, suggests.[101] Ownership of property was thus not absolutely condemned if

[93] Elm, *"Virgins,"* p. 310; Rousseau, "Structure," typescript, pp. 10, 18.

[94] Brakke, *Athanasius*, p. 2.

[95] Paulinus of Milan, *Vita Ambrosii* 10.49 (PL 14, 47); Augustine, *Confessiones* 8.6.15 (CCL 27, 122).

[96] For Augustine's establishment at Hippo, see George Lawless, *Augustine of Hippo and His Monastic Rule* (Oxford: Clarendon, 1987), chap. 5; Peter Brown, *Augustine of Hippo: A Biography* (Berkeley/Los Angeles: University of California Press, 1969), 198–200; Rousseau, "Structure," typescript, pp. 26–27 (Rousseau contrasts Augustine's pattern [a bishop learning to become a monk] with that prevalent in Gaul [monks learning to become bishops] [p. 27]); Markus, *End*, p. 160.

[97] Elm, *"Virgins,"* p. 358; Roger Bagnall, *Egypt in Late Antiquity*, pp. 298, 300; James E. Goehring, "The World Engaged: The Social and Economic World of Egyptian Monasticism," in *Gnosticism and the Early Christian World*, ed. James E. Goehring et al. (Sonoma, Calif.: Polebridge, 1990), pp. 137–44.

[98] For "wandering" as an important category in early asceticism, see Hans von Campenhausen, *Die Asketische Heimatlosigkeit im Altkirchlichen und Frühmittelalterlichen Mönchtum* (Tübingen: J. C. B. Mohr [Paul Siebeck], 1930), esp. pp. 6–7.

[99] See, for example, evidence in Jerome, *epp.* 23.2 (CSEL 54, 212); 47.3 (CSEL 54, 346); 108.5–6 (CSEL 55, 310–11); 127.8 (CSEL 56, 151); *Comm. in ep. ad Eph.*, *praefatio* 2 (PL 26, 507); (Gerontius), *Vita Melaniae Iunioris* 7, 36, 41 (SC 90, 140, 194, 204); Palladius, *Historia Lausiaca* 61 (Butler, p. 157); Paulinus of Milan, *Vita S. Ambrosii* 4 (PL 14, 28).

[100] Elm, *"Virgins,"* pp. 34–49, 92, 100, 134, 374–75; also see Rousseau, *Basil*, chap. 3.

[101] Augustine, *De moribus ecclesiae Catholicae* I.33.70 (PL 32, 1339–40); Possidius, *Vita S. Aurelii Augustini* 3 (PL 32, 36): Augustine returned "propriam domum agrosque." On Paulinus' arrangements, see

the renunciant adopted the correct attitude toward it, namely, not allowing himself or herself to be mentally captivated by wealth.[102] Jerome, John Cassian, and Benedict all express reservations about monks residing together in cities under no set rules, with money at their disposal to distribute as they pleased;[103] for Benedict, such men are "without a shepherd and in their own sheepfolds."[104] Yet the very evidence that these writers provide suggests that the practice was widespread.

Last, we should note the popular ascetic arrangement of "spiritual marriage," or "syneisaktism," in which men and women committed to Christian celibacy shared living quarters.[105] Although theologians and ecclesiastics authors rail against the practice for a variety of reasons—for example, it runs counter to the Christian freedom that asceticism promises and appears suspect to Christianity's critics—syneisaktism proved a popular ascetic lifestyle and continued as a practice into the Middle Ages.[106] Thus early Christian asceticism offered a variety of living arrangements, although, to be sure, not every arrangement was available to each ascetic; no doubt opportunities varied by region, and differed for men and women.

Despite the representations of early Christian ascetics as solitary hermits in the desert or the wilderness, most ascetic practitioners depended on considerable community support. An ascetic phenomenon that underscores this point is that of the pillar saints, the stylites, who spent their renunciatory careers atop narrow pillars and who from their lofty perches became the focus of intense admiration. Take the case of perhaps the most famous of the stylites, Simeon. After undertaking forty-day fasts, chaining himself to rocks, and engaging in other extreme ascetic practices for some years, Simeon took to a pillar, and then to a higher one. The fifth-century author who tells his story, Theodoret of Cyrrhus,[107] reports that at first, Simeon had to be tied to a beam attached to his pillar so that he would not topple over, but God soon gave him the grace to stand continuously without support. For twenty-eight years, he stood aloft—but his life was far from isolated. In addition to requiring a community of devotees who

---

Paulinus, *ep.* 5.4 (CSEL 29, 27); *Carm.* 11.11 (CSEL 30, 39); *Carm.* 21.386–569 (CSEL 30, 171–76), for numerous references to his buildings and property. For Sulpicius Severus, see Paulinus, *ep.* 24.3 (CSEL 29, 204): "domus tuae hospes es, ut sis hospitium domus."

[102] These are Paulinus' consoling words to Sulpicius Severus, *ep.* 24.2 (CSEL 29, 203); see also Paulinus, *ep.* 16.9 (CSEL 29, 122–23).

[103] Jerome, *ep.* 22.34 (CSEL 54, 196–97); John Cassian, *Conlationes* 3.18.7 (CSEL 13, 513–16); *Benedicti regula* 1.6–9 (CSEL 75, 18).

[104] *Benedicti regula* 1.8 (CSEL 75, 18).

[105] The classic study is Hans Achelis, *Virgines Subintroductae: Ein Beitrag zum VII Kapitel des I. Korintherbriefs* (Leipzig: J. C. Hinrichs, 1902).

[106] See Elizabeth A. Clark, "John Chrysostom and the Subintroductae," *Church History* 46 (1977): 171–85, for a list of the evidence.

[107] Theodoret, *Vita Symeonis* 26 (SC 257, 158–214).

would supply his bodily needs, Simeon like other "holy men" of late antiquity became a "power broker" for his community and for those who came from afar to seek his assistance. As Peter Brown has argued in his brilliant article, "The Rise and Function of the Holy Man in Late Antiquity,"[108] such men used the power accorded them to issue blessings and curses, to mediate disputes, to predict future events, to smooth human relations within their communities in an era when legal and other governmental structures were proving inadequate. So with Simeon: atop a pillar in alleged isolation, he performed cures, rendered sterile women fertile, foretold droughts, famines, and plagues, issued verdicts in legal and personal disputes, and exhorted eager mobs twice a day during festivals . . . all this, as his foot rotted under him. Such a story jolts our sense of ascetic "solitude," for Simeon, like many other ascetic practitioners, is thoroughly embedded in a community.

Indeed, although hagiographic literature stresses the separation of the ascetic from "the world," other evidence, especially that derived from archeological finds, suggests that ascetics were often more connected to it than we at first might imagine. Pachomian remains, as explicated by James Goehring, provide a good case in point. Although literary sources assert that Pachomius built his first monasteries in deserted villages, twentieth-century archeologists question whether the sites, at least as they developed, were as deserted as the texts claim. There was, for example, a sizable Roman settlement around the Pachomian monastery at Pbouw. Remains of two basilicas have been uncovered, one of them with five aisles, 36 meters wide by 72 meters long, with rose granite columns furnishing its internal pillars. Likewise, coins dating from the mid- and late fourth century at this site contribute to the impression that Pachomian ascetics of this period did not retreat to uninhabited wilderness. Moreover, some of the monastic *Rules* given by Pachomius' successor, Horsiesius, indicate that the monks had associations with laypeople living in towns and cities: the *Rules* stipulate how much time the monks may spend outside the monastery's walls, and regulate their work in nearby villages. Pachomian monks shipped the products they made to sites as distant as Alexandria.[109]

[108] *Journal of Roman Studies* 61 (1971): 80–101. Brown subsequently offered some emendations to his position in "The Saint as Exemplar in Late Antiquity," in *Saints and Virtues*, ed. John Stratton Hawley, Comparative Studies in Religion and Society 2 (Berkeley/Los Angeles/London: University of California Press, 1987), pp. 8–9 (emphasizing the holy man's exemplarity and his embeddedness in community). See Brown's retrospective discussion, "The Rise and Function of the Holy Man in Late Antiquity, 1971–1997," *Journal of Early Christian Studies* 6 (1998): 353–76.

[109] Goehring, "The World Engaged," p. 141; idem, "New Frontiers in Pachomian Studies," in *The Roots of Egyptian Christianity*, ed. B. A. Pearson and J. E. Goehring

Such data indicate that many monks were linked to the outside world to a degree that the literary evidence does not always suggest.

And it was not just monks living in community, that is, cenobites, who enjoyed these wider relations: stories of desert fathers who lived a more hermit-like existence report that they conducted a trade for their reed mats and other wares, journeying to nearby villages to sell them and to buy necessary supplies.[110] Evidence from documentary papyri supports the archeological data. To scholars' surprise, there have even been uncovered petitions concerning the reclamation of a dead monk's property.[111] Probably we should allow for more fluid relations between the desert and the town in considering early Egyptian monasticism.[112] Likewise for Palestine: as Israeli archeologist Yizhar Hirschfeld has demonstrated by comparing archeological with literary materials pertaining to early Palestinian monasticism, the "proximity to population centers was vital for the monks, especially in the initial stages of their settlement in the desert."[113]

Women renunciants stand as another notable topic in recent studies of early asceticism, and for good reason. Excluded from the priesthood and the ecclesiastical offices reserved for men, women could participate on a somewhat more equal footing in the ascetic life. Women figure prominently in ascetic texts of the early Christian period, whether we turn to the tales of Thecla and Drusiana (among others) in the Apocryphal Acts; to the catalogs of information on early ascetics supplied by such writers as Palladius and the anonymous author of the *History of the Monks of Egypt*; to reports on monasteries founded and monastic Rules adopted; or to full-blown *Lives* of ascetic practitioners. Renunciation, somewhat ironically, provided an avenue for patronage and for monastic leadership that was open to such wealthy aristocrats as Melania the Elder and her granddaughter Melania the Younger, to Jerome's friend Paula, and to John

(Philadelphia: Fortress, 1986), pp. 253–56. See also Goehring's helpful overview of early Christian asceticism, with many of the same emphases I make here, "The Origins of Monasticism," in *Eusebius, Christianity, and Judaism*, ed. Harold W. Attridge and Gohei Hata (Detroit: Wayne State University Press, 1992), pp. 235–55. It is not known whether the Roman settlement at Pbouw was still occupied when Pachomius founded this monastery (I thank James Goehring for this information).

[110] E.g., *Vitae patrum* 5.27; 6.11 (PL 73, 880, 890).

[111] James E. Goehring, "Through a Glass Darkly: Diverse Images of the APOTAKTIKOI(AI) of Early Egyptian Monasticism," *Semeia* 58 (1992): 30–35.

[112] See James E. Goehring, "The Encroaching Desert: Literary Production and Ascetic Space in Early Egyptian Christianity," *Journal of Early Christian Studies* 1 (1993): esp. 281–90, and "Withdrawing from the Desert: Pachomius and the Development of Village Monasticism" *Harvard Theological Review* 89 (1996): 267–85.

[113] Yizhar Hirschfeld, "The Life of Chariton in Light of Archaeological Research," in *Ascetic Behavior*, ed. Wimbush, p. 447.

Chrysostom's friend and benefactor, Olympias. Several such women provided vast funds for the construction of monasteries and often assumed the leadership themselves.[114] Various texts report that Melania the Elder's community on the Mount of Olives in Jerusalem had fifty virgins; that Olympias' monastery for women in Constantinople housed 250 women; and that Paula's in Bethlehem was sufficiently large so that the women were divided into three companies.[115] Although their male biographers do not reveal much about the women's leadership of the monasteries (albeit a great deal more about their strenuous renunciations), we here glimpse women in roles other than the domestic. That such activity was enabled by Roman law, which in this era encouraged husbands and wives to retain their property separately,[116] is an important and often-neglected fact that needs frequent repetition: these women, because they had financial and legal control over their own estates, could use their fortunes for the upbuilding of ascetic life. Of course, there were thousands more not of this social class who also flocked to monasteries, but of them we hear little in the sources; those who were accorded high status in the "outside" world tended to be those also honored in the literary sources pertaining to women's monasticism.[117] Moreover, "orthodox" Christianity had no special purchase on women renunciants: evidence gathered by recent scholars shows that Arian, Priscillianist, and other kinds of "heretical" groups were also adept—sometimes highly adept—at providing opportunities for female ascetics.[118]

[114] For an insightful response to Jack Goody's thesis (one aspect of which argued that the Church had an economic interest in tightening the degrees of relationship legally permissible so that it would benefit from the de-concentration of money amidst a small number of aristocratic families), see Rita Lizzi, "Una socièta esortata all' ascetismo: misure legislative e motivazioni economiche nel IV–V secolo D.C.," *Studi storici* 30 (1989): 129–53 (Lizzi argues that there was considerable direct giving to the Church, as the cases of these women suggest, without appealing to endogamy, as does Goody).

[115] Palladius, *Historia Lausiaca* 46 (Butler, p. 135); (Anonymous), *Vita Olympiadis* 6 (SC 13bis, 420); Jerome, *ep.* 108.20 (CSEL 55, 335).

[116] On the separation of marital property in the imperial period, see Susan Treggiari, *Roman Marriage: Iusti Coniuges from the Time of Cicero to the Time of Ulpian* (Oxford: Clarendon, 1991), chap. 11; Antti Arjava, *Women and Law in Late Antiquity* (Oxford: Clarendon, 1996), pp. 133–54.

[117] For evidence regarding less aristocratic communities, see Alanna Emmett, "An Early Fourth Century Female Monastic Community in Egypt?", in *Maistor: Classical, Byzantine and Renaissance Studies for Robert Browning*, ed. Ann Moffatt, Byzantina Australiensia 5 (Canberra: Australian Association for Byzantine Studies, 1984), pp. 77–83.

[118] Elm, *"Virgins,"* chap. 4 and pp. 199, 233; Brakke, *Athanasius*, pp. 57–79, for fights between Arians and supporters of Athanasius at Alexandria for the virgins' favor; Burrus, *The Making of a Heretic*, pp. 33–34, 40–42, 131, and passim. Augustine complains that Catholic virgins are going over to the Donatists: *Tract. Ioan.* 13.13.1–2.

V: Ancient Critiques of Asceticism and the Church Fathers' Response

To be sure, there were many in this era, Christians as well as non-Christians, whose enthusiasm for the ascetic enterprise was considerably less ardent than that of the ascetic writers and practitioners here noted. Jerome reports that many Roman nobles considered monasticism "strange, ignominious, and debasing"; pagan writers compare monks to swine and to elephants.[119] Within the Christian camp, some writers (such as Jovinian) thought that the exaltation of asceticism degraded marriage and established a hierarchy among Christians that was unbecoming to the baptized, who should all be "one in Christ."[120] As Kate Cooper has argued, the traditional criteria for social ranking were thrown askew by the new evaluational hierarchy based on degrees of ascetic renunciation.[121] More threatening, excessive ascetic fervor might be labeled "Manichean"—and here, we enter the realm of heresy charges.[122]

Many ascetically inclined church fathers believed that "Paul" in I Timothy 4:1–3 had predicted the coming of "heretics" who would forbid marriage and the eating of meat. Since they themselves, however, eschewed marriage and followed a sparse vegetarian diet, it was crucial for them to distinguish their own behaviors from those of dreaded opponents whose observed practice might all too readily be confused with their own.[123] The Fathers' self-defense rested on three points: that they did not forbid marriage, as did the alleged heretics, but only sought to regulate it;[124] that

[119] Jerome, *ep.* 127.5; Eunapius, *Vitae Sophistarum* 472; Libanius, *Oratio* 30.8. See L. Gougaud, "Les Critiques formulées contre les premiers moines d'occident," *Revue Mabillon* 24 (1934): 145–63.

[120] Jovinian in Jerome, *Adversus Iovinianum* 1.3 (PL 23, 224); also see David G. Hunter, "Resistance to the Virginal Ideal in Late-Fourth-Century Rome: The Case of Jovinian," *Theological Studies* 48 (1987): 45–64. Augustine as well testifies that "some" think some Catholic forms of asceticism have "gone too far": *De moribus ecclesiae Catholicae* 31.66 (PL 32, 1337–38).

[121] Kate Cooper, *The Virgin and the Bride: Idealized Womanhood in Late Antiquity* (Cambridge/London: Harvard University Press, 1996), pp. 82–83, 87.

[122] As Jerome came to fear: see *Adversus Iovinianum* 1.3 (PL 23, 223); *ep.* 49(48).2 (CSEL 54, 352).

[123] The desire to differentiate lies close to the surface in Augustine's *De moribus Manichaeorum* and *De moribus ecclesiae Catholicae*. See also Jerome, *ep.* 18.*3–4 (PL 30, 191–92): Catholic monks will be accused of Manicheanism for their restrictive diets. For an exhaustive discussion of how encratite themes get appropriated by the mainstream Church, see Giulia Sfameni Gasparro, *Enkrateia e antropologia: le motivazioni protologiche della continenze e della verginità nel cristianesimo dei primi secoli e nello gnosticismo*, Studia Ephemeridis "Augustinianum" 20 (Roma: Institutum Patristicum "Augustinianum," 1984).

[124] Tertullian, *De monogamia* 15 (CCL 2, 1250–51). Tertullian faults the Marcionites for disallowing baptism to any person who was not a virgin, widow, or celibate (*Adversus Marcionem* 1.29; 4.11).

they abstained from marriage by free will, not by coercion or prohibition;[125] and that their own motivations for abstinence were holy, not derived from a hatred of the Creator and creation.[126] Rather, they argued, it was "heretics" of various stripes ("Gnostics," Montanists, Marcionites, Manicheans, as well as unspecified dissenters)[127] who were the intended targets of "Paul's" warning.

In addition to their refutation of such "heretical" groups, the Fathers also fault such individuals as Tatian (who allegedly claimed that marriage is fornication),[128] in addition to the Encratites (considered Tatian's successors),[129] Saturninus,[130] and Julius Cassianus.[131] Athanasius and Epiphanius attack the fourth-century Egyptian ascetic leader Hieracas for positing that although marriage was allowable in Old Testament times, Christ's advent signaled a New Dispensation that requires sexual abstinence.[132] Moreover, the Fathers were eager to dissociate their position on second marriage from that of the Montanists, who firmly prohibited it: thus many Fathers allege that they, like Paul, concede (but do not encourage) second marriage after the death of a spouse.[133] To teach that Adam and Eve engaged in sexual union only after the Fall in Eden might be considered a Manichean position[134]—but this is in fact the view that Jerome, Gregory of Nyssa, and John Chrysostom themselves often espouse.[135] Differentiation became all the more necessary when theories and behaviors were similar.

[125] So Theodore of Mopsuestia, *Ad I. Tim.* (4:3); John Chrysostom, *Hom. 12 I Tim.* (4:1–3); Tertullian, *De cultu feminarum* 2.9; Clement of Alexandria, *Stromata* 3.7.58; 3.9.66.

[126] So Clement of Alexandria, *Stromata* 3.1.4; 3.3.12; 3.5.40; Origen, *Comm. I Cor.* 7:7; 7:18–20; Tertullian, *De ieiunio* 15; Jerome, *Adversus Iovianianum* 2.16.

[127] So Clement of Alexandria, *Stromata* 3.6.51; 3.12.85; Tertullian, *De ieiunio* 2 ("psychics" say this of the "New Prophecy"); Jerome, *Adversus Iovinianum* 2.16; Augustine, *Contra Faustum* 14.11; 15.10; 20.16; 30.1; *Contra Felicem* 1.7; *Contra Secundinum* 22.1; *Contra Adimantum* 14.2; Pelagius, *Comm. I. Tim.* 4:2.

[128] So Irenaeus, *Adversus Haereses* 1.28.1; Epiphanius, *Panarion* 46.2; Jerome, *Comm. Gal.* 3 (6:8); Hippolytus, *Refutatio omnes haereses* 8.16; Clement of Alexandria, *Stromata* 3.12.81. For an informative discussion of Tatian and the Encratites, see Sfameni Gasparro, *Enkrateia*, pp. 23–55, 78.

[129] Epiphanius, *Panarion* 47.1 (GCS 31, 215). See Blond, "L' 'Hérésie' encratite," pp. 175–76.

[130] Irenaeus, *Adversus haereses* 1.24.2 (PG 7, 675).

[131] Clement of Alexandria, *Stromata* 3.14.95 (GCS 52[15], 239–40).

[132] Athanasius, *ep. 1 ad virgines* (CSCO 150 = Scriptores Coptici 19, 83–86; Brakke, ET, pp. 282–83); Epiphanius, *Panarion* 67.1 (GCS 37, 132–34). See Brakke, *Athanasius*, p. 55: Hieracas "placed marriage in ancient history and its practitioners in a state just this side of ruin."

[133] So Jerome, *ep.* 41.3; *Comm. Tit.* 1:6 (Tertullian's *De monogamia* is here deemed heretical); Augustine, *Contra Faustum* 32.17; *De bono viduitatis* 4.6–5.7 (Tertullian went astray in his views, forbidding what Paul allowed).

[134] So Didymus of Alexandria, *Contra Manichaeos* 8 (PG 39, 1096).

[135] Jerome, *Adversus Iovinianum* 1.4; 1.16; Gregory of Nyssa, *De virginitate* 12.4–13.1; John Chrysostom, *Hom. 20*

Thus it is not surprising that the Fathers were accused of the very same "heresies" that they themselves often denounce. Manicheanism was the favorite "heresy" to allege against ascetic opponents in the late fourth and early fifth centuries, including both Jerome and Augustine, not least because in that period, Manicheanism had been legally proscribed.[136] The allegations against Jerome were prompted in part by his unguarded contempt for marriage in *Adversus Iovinianum*. Here, Jerome claims that when Paul wrote in I Corinthians 7:1 that it was "good not to touch a woman," he meant that so to touch was "bad." Moreover, if Paul thought that sexual intercourse impeded prayer (I Cor. 7:5), how much more did it impede the reception of the Eucharist! For Jerome, "all sexual intercourse is unclean in view of the purity of the body of Christ."[137] When criticized for "Manichean" leanings, Jerome bristled, alleging that only heretics would deny the goodness of marriage.[138] He claims that he had spoken "in great moderation" on the issue, and protests that his restraints on the married were considerably more gentle than were Paul's.[139]

Augustine, for his part, after a long career debating and writing against Manicheans (a movement to which Augustine himself had adhered in his youth),[140] was in his later years accused of Manicheanism: so Pelagian opponents such as Julian of Eclanum construed Augustine's theory of the transmission of original sin through the sexual act.[141] Is it not Manichean, they asked, to assert that no child can be conceived without receiving the stain of an inherited sin, a sin that he or she did not personally commit? Does not such a belief suggest that evil is an inevitable constituent of the material world, a view to be identified as Manichean? Augustine judged that he had adequately defended himself by rehearsing his views developed two decades earlier on the "goods" of marriage (offspring, fidelity, the sacramental bond),[142] but the accusations against him, some of which were

Gen. 1; *De virginitate* 14, 17. For the metaphysical and historical presuppositions of such a view, see Ugo Bianchi, "La Tradition de l'enkrateia: Motivations ontologiques et protologiques," in *La Tradizione*, ed. Bianchi, pp. 308–10.

[136] *Codex Theodosianus* 16.5.3 (372); 16.5.7 (381); 16.5.9 (382); 16.5.11 (383); 16.5.18 (389); 16.5.35 (399); 16.5.38 (405); 16.5.40 (407); 16.5.41 (407); 16.5.43 (408)—and so on, up to 435 C.E. (16.5.65.2).

[137] Jerome, *Adversus Iovinianum* 1.7; 1.8; 1.20 (PL 23, 229–30, 231, 249).

[138] Jerome, *ep.* 49 (48).11 (CSEL 54, 366).

[139] Jerome, *ep.* 49 (48).11; 49 (48).3 (CSEL 54, 365, 349).

[140] Augustine, *Confessiones* 3.11.20; 4.1.1 (CCL 27, 38, 40); *Contra ep. fundamenti* 10 (CSEL 25, 206); *De moribus Manichaeorum* 19.68 (PL 32, 1374); *De moribus ecclesiae catholicae* 18.34 (PL 32, 1326).

[141] Julian of Eclanum in Augustine, *Opus imperfectum contra Iulianum* 1.27; 1.66; 2.27.2; 2.202; 3.10 (CSEL 851, 23, 64, 181, 314, 355).

[142] Augustine, *De bono coniugali* 32(24) (CSEL 41, 266–67). For Augustine's moderating position as a "defence of Christian mediocrity," see Markus, *End*, pp. 45–46.

leveled in circles connected to the imperial court,[143] suggest otherwise. Christian writers of ascetic inclination, despite their efforts to distance themselves from excessively ascetic "heretics," could find instead that their own positions were conflated with those of their enemies. Since the alleged heretics, such as Augustine's Manichean opponent Faustus, often claimed that *they* were the true Christians, that *they* (unlike the Catholics) had renounced in accordance with Jesus' commands in the Gospels,[144] Catholic Christians had to walk a fine line to uphold their own ascetic values yet distinguish themselves from their "heretical" opponents. As Jerome put it, Catholics must keep to the king's highway, not turning to the left (i.e., to the lust of the Jews and the Gentiles) or to the right (i.e., to the errors of the Manicheans); although aspiring to virginity, they should nonetheless not condemn marriage.[145]

Thus the church fathers strove to protect themselves from allegations that their views bordered on a heretical disparagement of the Creator and the created world in all its materiality, that they differed little from the "heretical" opponents they themselves claimed to deplore.[146] Yet in this task of self-justification and self-protection, they faced the disturbing problem that the Bible only sporadically justified their ascetic agenda; many verses seemed rather to assume as a norm, even champion, marriage and reproduction. How to "read" the Bible so that it delivered a message wholeheartedly supportive of ascetic renunciation of an "orthodox" variety, so that it furnished a foundational rationale for the ascetic program, was a task that challenged the wits, ingenuity, and Biblical acumen of ascetically enthusiastic patristic writers. The following chapters investigate the interpretive strategies that the Fathers employed to produce properly asceticized Scriptures that supported their programs of renunciation.

[143] Augustine, *Contra duas epistolas Pelagianorum* 1.3.1; 1.4.2 (CSEL 60, 424–25).

[144] See, for example, the impassioned speech by Faustus that Augustine reports in his *Contra Faustum* (5.1) (CSEL 25, 271–72):

"Do I believe the Gospel? You ask me if I believe it, though my obedience to its commands proves that I do. . . . I have left my father, mother, wife, and children, and all else that the Gospel requires—and you ask if I believe the Gospel? . . . I have parted with all gold and silver, and have stopped carrying money in my purse; I am content with my daily food; I am not anxious for tomorrow and am without care for how I shall be fed, or with what I shall be clothed—and you ask if I believe the Gospel?"

[145] Jerome, *ep.* 49 (48).8 (CSEL 54, 361).

[146] That some Gnostic texts had far more resonance with the Old Testament than has often been admitted by either the church fathers or contemporary scholars is shown by Birger A. Pearson, "Biblical Exegesis in Gnostic Literature" and "Jewish Elements in Gnosticism and the Development of Gnostic Self-Definition," in idem, *Gnosticism, Judaism, and Egyptian Christianity* (Minneapolis: Fortress, 1990), esp. pp. 38, 126–27, 130.

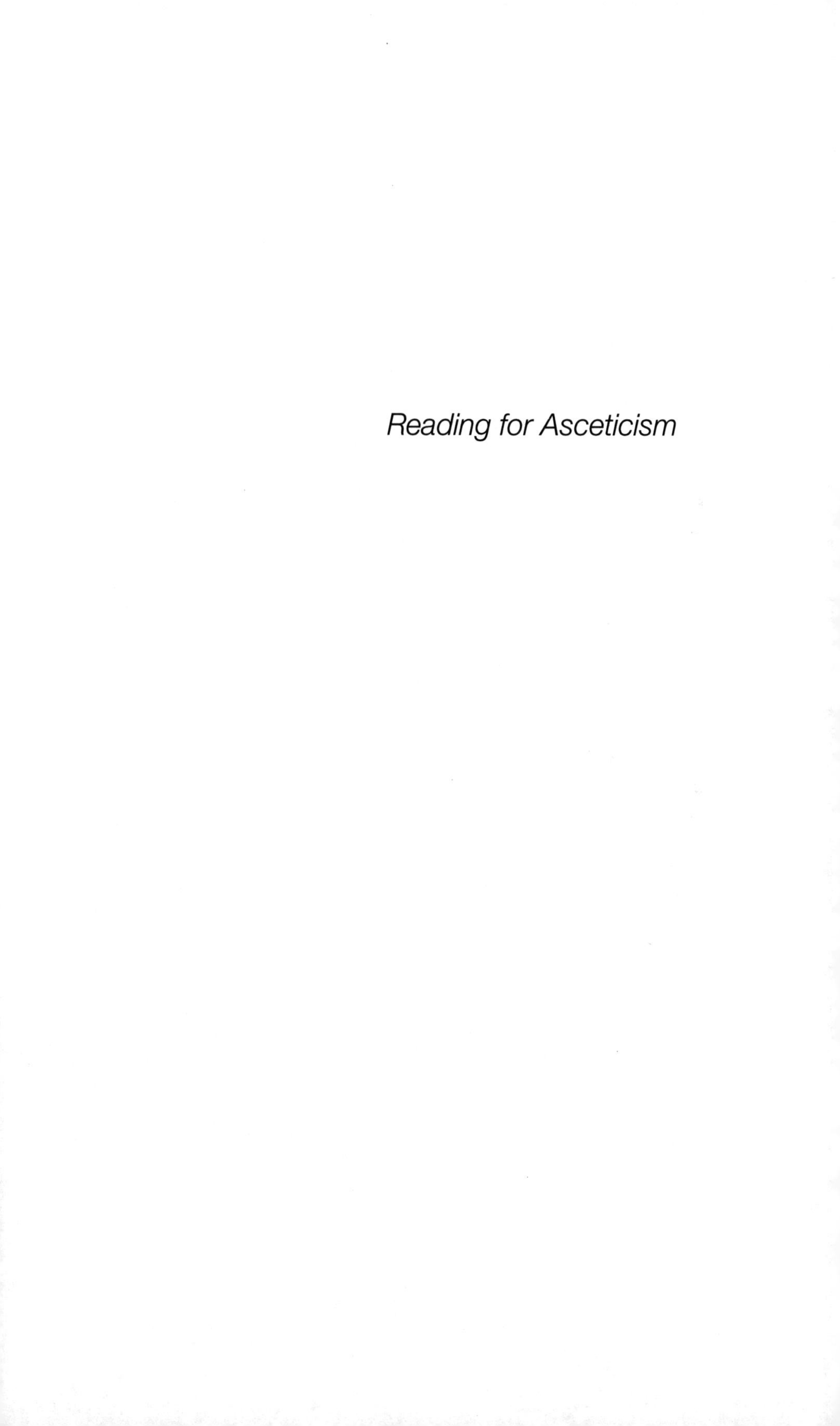

Reading for Asceticism

CHAPTER THREE

Reading in the Early Christian World

I: Christian Readers

A recent spate of scholarly works on the history of reading and writing has focused on the distinction between oral and literate cultures, and on the prevalence (or absence) of literacy at various historical periods. To place early Christians in this discussion has proved a vexing question. An important contribution to this exchange is classicist William V. Harris' *Ancient Literacy*, published in 1989. Arguing for a minimalist view of ancient literacy, Harris claims that not more than 10 percent of the adult population of the Roman Empire at the time of Christianity's origin was literate and that literacy declined from that already low percentage in later antiquity.[1] Despite Christianity's heavy reliance on the written word (Harris notes the "acute logorrhea" of church fathers such as Augustine and John Chrysostom),[2] Harris disclaims writing as the chief means of furthering the Christian missionary effort in the first three centuries of the new religion's existence.[3]

Harris' minimalist interpretation of literacy in the Greek and Roman worlds has not gone unchallenged. Indeed, earlier studies already had cast doubt on overly minimalist estimates by noting such details as that the Alexandrian Museum (i.e., Library) contained between one hundred thousand and two hundred thousand books;[4] that papyrus finds in Egypt prove the dissemination of both religious and secular texts in out-of-the-way places;[5] that the very process of Hellenization depended to a certain

[1] William V. Harris, *Ancient Literacy* (Cambridge/London: Harvard University Press, 1989), pp. 22, 282, 285.

[2] Ibid., pp. 305–6.

[3] Ibid., pp. 311–12, 316, 319, 322.

[4] Frederic G. Kenyon, *Books and Readers in Ancient Greece and Rome* (Oxford: Clarendon, 1932), pp. 26–27.

[5] Colin H. Roberts, *Manuscript, Society and Belief in Early Christian Egypt* (London: Oxford University Press, 1979), pp. 4, 70–71; P. E. Easterling, "Books and Readers in the Greek World: The Hellenistic and Imperial Periods," in *The Cambridge History of Classical Literature*, vol. I, *Greek Literature*, ed. P. E. Easterling and B. M. W.

extent on the availability of books;[6] that in Rome a book trade existed as early as the first century B.C.E., which developed considerably in the next few centuries;[7] that by the time of Constantine, there were twenty-eight public libraries in the city of Rome alone.[8] Although it could be argued that such data do not necessarily imply that there were more readers than Harris suggested, it does at the very least point to the presence of books, even in unlikely geographical areas, at the period of Christianity's early development.

Acknowledging the widespread illiteracy of late ancient peoples, works published since the appearance of Harris' book nonetheless nuance and even challenge his claims. Thus it has been posited that some who are labeled "illiterates" (or "slow writers") in ancient texts may have been able to read in a native language, if not in Greek.[9] Other scholars argue that Harris underestimated what has been called "sub-elite" literacy. On this view, many more people would have been able to make out business accounts or a simple text than could have read complicated poetry and prose, replete with allusions to the "high" works of Greek and Roman literature.[10] Many forms of employment, these scholars argue, would in fact

Knox (Cambridge: Cambridge University Press, 1985), p. 24.

[6] P. E. Easterling, "Books and Readers," p. 23; cf. Rosalind Thomas, *Literacy and Orality in Ancient Greece* (Cambridge: Cambridge University Press, 1992), p. 131.

[7] E. J. Kenney, "Books and Readers in the Roman World," in *The Cambridge History of Classical Literature*, vol. II, *Latin Literature*, ed. E. J. Kenney and W. V. Clausen (Cambridge: Cambridge University Press, 1982), pp. 19–22.

[8] Ibid., p. 24; evidence listed in Clarence Eugene Boyd, *Public Libraries and Literary Culture in Ancient Rome* (Chicago: University of Chicago Press, 1915), pp. 3–4. Just how "public" they were can be questioned; our evidence of their use comes from upper-class writers. Commentators note the real dangers of destruction of libraries by fire: Boyd, *Public Libraries*, pp. 8, 16–17, 47, 52; Kenney, "Books," p. 25.

[9] Thomas, *Literacy*, p. 154; Ann Ellis Hanson, "Ancient Illiteracy," in *Literacy in the Roman World*, ed. Mary Beard et al., Journal of Roman Archaeology Supplementary Series 3 (Ann Arbor: University of Michigan Press, 1991), p. 169. A classic essay on "slow writers" is Herbert C. Youtie, "Bradeōs graphōn: Between Literacy and Illiteracy," *Greek, Roman and Byzantine Studies* 12 (1971): 239–61.

[10] Keith Hopkins, "Conquest by Book," in *Literacy in the Roman World*, p. 158; cf. Jozsef Herman, "Spoken and Written Latin in the Last Centuries of the Roman Empire: A Contribution to the Linguistic History of the Western Provinces," in *Latin and the Romance Languages in the Early Middle Ages*, ed. Roger Wright (University Park: Pennsylvania State University Press, 1996), p. 32. Arguing that medievalists have underestimated the knowledge of simple written Latin used in the practical arena is M. T. Clanchy, *From Memory to Written Record: England, 1066–1307* (Cambridge, Mass.: Harvard University Press, 1979), p. 262. For the claim that the "ubiquitous presence of writing" on outdoor spaces in Rome between the third and first centuries B.C.E. testifies to a large literate population in the city, see Armando Petrucci, *Public Lettering: Script, Power, and Culture*, trans. Linda Lappin (Chicago/London: University of Chicago Press, 1993; Italian original edition, 1980), pp. 1–2.

have required at least minimal literacy.[11] Moreover, archeologists working in Britain had by the turn to the 1990s uncovered 997 documents (now called "the Vindolanda texts") that suggest the greater prevalence of literacy even at this distant outpost of the Roman Empire than had previously been imagined.[12]

Most striking is the realization that even if Harris were correct in his figure of a 10 percent (or less) adult literacy rate, this minimalist estimate still yields about two million readers in the Roman Empire.[13] And since books were often read aloud, people outside the literate classes might have been familiar with their contents. Moreover, for the people who themselves wrote books, a high literary culture served, in Keith Hopkins' phrase, as the "symbolic glue" that held together upper-class interests. "The whole experience of living in the Roman empire . . . ," he claims, "was overdetermined by the existence of texts."[14] Christianity, in contrast to "paganism," was highly dependent upon books for its teaching and ritual operations.[15]

The implications of these debates for my topic are weighty: if I wish to argue that the ascetic campaign in early Christianity was waged at least in part through texts, must I not assume both that at least a minority of Christians could read, and that there were books, the Bible and more, available to them? Here, Harry Gamble's study, *Books and Readers in the Early Church*, lends assistance. Gamble argues against an earlier position that emphasized the "oral" nature of early Christianity and claimed that the movement produced only "Kleinliteratur," literature of little cultural significance that matched the allegedly low social status of most early Christians. New Testament form criticism, which presupposed the oral nature of early Christian teaching, contributed to this judgment. In contrast, Gamble stresses the links between early Christian writing and the larger Greco-Roman literary tradition.[16] Indeed, revised notions of early Christianity's social constituency themselves suggest that the literary character of the movement needs reassessment, since as modern scholars extract more early Christians from the ranks of the destitute to which they

[11] Nicholas Horsfall, "Statistics or State of Mind?", in *Literacy in the Roman World*, pp. 63–65; cf. Hopkins, "Conquest," in *Literacy in the Roman World*, pp. 136–40.

[12] Alan K. Bowman, "Literacy in the Roman Empire: Mass and Mode," in *Literacy in the Roman World*, p. 120. Note also the 1800 manuscripts uncovered in a library at Herculaneum: see Harry Gamble, *Books and Readers in the Early Church: A History of Early Christian Texts* (New Haven, Conn./London: Yale University Press, 1995), p. 186.

[13] Hopkins, "Conquest," pp. 134–35.

[14] Ibid., pp. 143, 144.

[15] Ibid., pp. 148, 157; cf. Gamble, *Books*, p. 141. Mary Beard, on the other hand, argues for Roman religion's greater use of texts than is usually acknowledged: "Writing and Religion: Ancient Literacy and the Function of the Written Word in Roman Religion," *Literacy in the Roman World*, pp. 36–58.

[16] Gamble, *Books*, pp. 14–17.

had formerly been relegated, there is a strong chance that a higher percentage of them were literate,[17] education in antiquity being strongly tied to social class.

The relatively quick dissemination of such books as Irenaeus' *Against Heresies*, the *Shepherd of Hermas*, and Ignatius of Antioch's *Letters* all suggest a Christian reading public even in the earliest centuries, and with Christianity's increased prestige as an imperially sanctioned religion from the early fourth century onward, Christian books were produced to higher standards.[18] Such finds as the Nag Hammadi texts, the Dishna papers, and the Tura papyri in Egypt all testify to a surprising distribution of not just Christian texts ("heretical" as well as "orthodox"), but classical ones as well. Prolific writers such as Origen, Jerome, and Augustine had sizable personal libraries, and employed teams of stenographers and copyists to record their own extensive productions.[19] In addition, some ancient Christians owned the equivalent of "pocket books," miniature codices designed for private reading: of the approximately fifty-five such tiny codices known, the large majority contain Christian texts, with a heavy emphasis on apocryphal materials.[20]

Despite his compilation of detailed evidence, Gamble concedes that we have no reason to attribute higher levels of literacy to Christians in the Roman Empire than to their non-Christian neighbors. We thus confront a paradox: that although Christianity "placed a high value on texts," most Christians remained illiterate.[21] Moreover, Kim Haines-Eitzen argues,

[17] Ibid., p. 20.

[18] Ibid., pp. 82, 109, 111, 140–41, 78–79.

[19] Ibid., pp. 171–74, 120–21, 174–75; cf. Harald Hagendahl, "Die Bedeutung der Stenographie für die spätlateinische christliche Literatur," *Jahrbuch für Antike und Christentum* 14 (1971): 24–38. For Libanius' loathing of his era's increasing reliance on stenography, see Peter Wolf, *Vom Schulwesen der Spätantike: Studien zu Libanius* (Baden-Baden: Verlag für Kunst und Wissenschaft, 1952), pp. 54–55, with references. For Jerome's use of scribes, see Denys Gorce, *La Lectio divina des origines du cénobitisme à Saint Benoît et Cassiodore. T. I: Saint Jérôme et la lecture sacrée dans le milieu ascétique romain* (Wépion-sur-Meuse: Monastère du Mont-Vierge; Paris: Librairie Auguste Picard, 1925), p. 163. For a recently discovered reference to Jerome's stenographers, see Jerome in Augustine, *ep.* 27*.3 (CSEL 88, 133; Jerome here refers to two stenographers). Jerome claims that he could dictate one thousand lines a day: *Comm. in Eph.* 2, *praef.* Augustine allegedly dictated throughout the night: *ep.* 139.3; Possidius, *Vita Augustini* 24. Ambrose's biographer, Paulinus of Milan, reports that Ambrose wrote books in his own hand except when he was sick (*Vita Ambrosii* 38 [PL 14, 42]); the comment appears as an attempt to stress Ambrose's humility and simplicity, despite his privileged background.

[20] Gamble, *Books*, pp. 235–36; Roberts, *Manuscript*, pp. 11–12.

[21] Gamble, *Books*, pp. 10, 8. Frances M. Young has a somewhat more optimistic assessment of the early Christians, "[f]ew were literary, but many, in all probability, were literate" (*Biblical Exegesis and the Formation of Christian Culture* [Cambridge: Cambridge University Press, 1997], p. 14).

there is little evidence from the first or second century that Christian clergy endeavored to teach their illiterate congregations to read.[22] Earlier assessments of private Bible reading among ancient Christians, such as Adolf Harnack's, may overestimate the phenomenon: it appears that Harnack mistook prescription of Bible reading (by highly literate Christian authors) for description of actual practices, and failed to note that those preachers who exhorted to private Bible-reading, such as John Chrysostom, were addressing higher-class (i.e., more literate) congregations, unlike the norm for Christians-in-general.[23]

Even conceding widespread illiteracy among early Christians, we nonetheless know that inability to read did not exclude the uneducated from Christian culture; catechetical instruction prior to baptism, plus the frequent hearing of lengthy Scriptural passages, gave to the attentive a basic familiarity with Biblical texts and stories.[24] Moreover, recent discussions of literacy in contemporary largely "oral" societies[25] do not provide a sufficiently nuanced model for Christians of late antiquity, for oral and literate subcultures can function alongside each other in reasonably smooth harmony. As Rosalind Thomas expresses it in reference to earlier Greek cul-

[22] Kim Haines-Eitzen, "Hearing and Reading: Literacy and Power in the Early Christian Church," unpublished M.A. thesis, University of North Carolina-Chapel Hill, 1993, pp. 14, 30, 41–42, 92; she argues that ecclesiastical authorities neglected to teach illiterate Christians to read as part of a strategy to ensure their own authority. Alternatively, one might ask whether all laypeople had a vested interest in learning to read.

[23] Adolf Harnack, *Bible Reading in the Early Church*, trans. J. R. Wilkinson, Crown Theological Library 36 (London: Williams & Norgate; New York: G. P. Putnam, 1912), pp. 63–64, 68, 98, 105, 124; Harnack cites such authors as Origen, Augustine, and John Chrysostom. Harnack's emphasis on private Bible reading may relate to his strong Protestant bias: over against modern Catholic neglect of the Bible, the Protestant Reformers' "restoration" of the Bible to "the common people" is cited with approval (pp. 143, 148). Haines-Eitzen also faults Gamble for this overemphasis, "Hearing," p. 58n. 45.

[24] Gamble, *Books*, pp. 205–7. See also Victor Saxer, *Bible et hagiographie. Textes et thèmes biblique dans les Actes des martyrs authentiques des premiers siècles* (Berne: Peter Lang, 1986), p. 162, argues that there was a "biblical culture even among the most humble Christians."

[25] A sample of recent work in English on orality/literacy questions might include Walter J. Ong, *Orality and Literacy: The Technologizing of the Word* (London/New York: Routledge, 1982); Brian Street, *Literacy in Theory and Practice*, Cambridge Studies in Oral and Literate Culture 9 (Cambridge: Cambridge University Press, 1984); Jack Goody, *The Interface Between the Written and the Oral* (Cambridge: Cambridge University Press, 1987); Brian V. Street, "Orality and Literacy as Ideological Constructions: Some Problems in Cross-Cultural Studies," *Culture & History* 2 (1987): 7–30; Ruth Finnegan, *Literacy and Orality: Studies in the Technology of Communication* (Oxford/New York: Basil Blackwell, 1988); David R. Olson and Nancy Torrance, eds., *Literacy and Orality* (Cambridge: Cambridge University Press, 1991); Jonathan Boyarin, ed., *The Ethnography of Reading* (Berkeley/Los Angeles/Oxford: University of California Press, 1993).

ture, oral traditions are not "killed" when writing appears.[26] Moreover, the uses and functions of literacy in earlier societies need more careful elaboration. Medievalist Rosamond McKitterick reinforces this point:

> Literacy in any society, therefore, is not just a matter of who could read and write, but one of how skills function, the purposes they serve, and the adjustments—mental, emotional, intellectual, physical and technological—necessary to accommodate them. Above all, the functions and uses of literacy need to be established in relation to a particular society's needs.[27]

The "need" of an ascetic Christian culture for texts will become evident in the chapters that follow.

Yet a second point remains even more important: the authors who constitute our evidence for the study of "ascetic interpretation" in early Christianity themselves represent, for the most part, the dextrously literate classes. By the fourth century, it was largely "middling elites" who received the higher ecclesiastical offices of the Eastern Roman Empire.[28] In the West, although Augustine exemplifies "upward social mobility" in his rise to the episcopate,[29] he is manifestly outclassed by Ambrose of Milan, the first Western bishop who (probably) descended from the senatorial aristocracy of Rome.[30] These men had received the traditional grammatical and rhetorical education that ensured their place among the upper echelons of Roman society and that enabled them to enjoy the cultural benefits—

[26] Rosalind Thomas, *Literacy and Orality in Ancient Greece* (Cambridge: Cambridge University Press, 1992), p. 50.

[27] Rosamund McKitterick, "Women and Literacy in the Early Middle Ages," in idem, *Books, Scribes and Learning in the Frankish Kingdoms, 6th–9th Centuries* (Aldershot, U.K.: Variorum, 1994), p. 2.

[28] Richard Lim, *Public Disputation, Power, and Social Order in Late Antiquity*, The Transformation of the Classical Heritage 23 (Berkeley/Los Angeles/London: University of California Press, 1995), p. 139, citing A. H. M. Jones, *The Later Roman Empire 284–602* (Oxford: Basil Blackwell, 1964), II:925–29; cf. Aline Rousselle, "Aspects sociaux du recrutement ecclésiastique au IVe siècle," *Mélanges d'archéologie et d'histoire de l'Ecole Française de Rome* 89 (1977): 333–70.

[29] Augustine was the child of a minor Roman official who scrimped to educate his son (*Confessiones* 2.3.5 [CCL 27, 19]). Augustine later reports that as bishop of Hippo, he controlled property worth twenty times the value of his patrimony (*ep.* 126.7 [CSEL 44, 13]).

[30] For a discussion of Ambrose's lineage, now see Neil B. McLynn, *Ambrose of Milan: Church and Court in a Christian Capital*, The Transformation of the Classical Heritage 22 (Berkeley/Los Angeles/London: University of California Press, 1994), pp. 31–35 (who nonetheless cautions against inflating Ambrose's social background and status). Raymond Van Dam argues that in late antique Gaul, the "lateral mobility" into the episcopate for young men of good birth occasioned a fierce competition for episcopal slots: *Leadership and Community in Late Antique Gaul*, The Transformation of the Classical Heritage 8 (Berkeley/Los Angeles/London: University of California Press, 1985), pp. 153, 212.

social, intellectual, and ideological—of grammatical education.[31] As Peter Brown has recently argued, men like the Cappadocian Fathers and Ambrose had participated in the "system of grooming" provided by the ancient educational system that allowed pagan and Christian to share a common cultural ground.[32]

To be sure, the institutional power these Christian men came to wield shifted its location from imperial government to church office and monastic leadership; nonetheless, their power remained grounded in a literary culture that privileged written authority.[33] Despite the earlier assumptions that ancient Christianity constituted an oral culture (a view upheld in our time by as notable a critic as Paul Ricoeur),[34] the Fathers' grammatical education privileged writing over speech;[35] even the sometimes extemporaneous sermons of bishops such as John Chrysostom and Augustine were transposed into "literature."[36] Christian teaching probably did interrupt the classical notion that seriousness of content should be matched by impressiveness of style, since Christian authors argued that the most sublime subjects could be expressed in simple words.[37] Nonetheless, the writing process of Christian authors appears noticeably similar to that of their "pagan" counterparts. They too "edited" (i.e., "gave forth") their writings in public recitations and counted on their friends to circulate these works to a wider public.[38] Although some writing practices associated with

[31] Martin Irvine, *The Making of Textual Culture: 'Grammatica' and Literary Theory, 350–1100* (Cambridge: Cambridge University Press, 1994), p. 1.

[32] Peter Brown, *Power and Persuasion in Late Antiquity: Towards a Christian Empire* (Madison: University of Wisconsin Press, 1992), pp. 4, 34. Brown argues against overemphasizing the conflict between educated Christians and pagans in the fourth century (pp. 125, 128).

[33] Irvine, *The Making of Textual Culture*, pp. 20–21. For an informative overview of the fourth- and fifth-century Fathers' estimation of the benefits and perils of *grammatica* in the new Christian setting, see Robert A. Kaster, *Guardians of Language*, The Transformation of the Classical Heritage 11 (Berkeley/Los Angeles/London: University of California Press, 1988), pp. 70–95.

[34] Paul Ricoeur, "Epilogue: The 'Sacred' Text and the Community," in *The Critical Study of Sacred Texts*, ed. Wendy Doniger O'Flaherty (Berkeley, Calif.: Graduate Theological Union, 1979), pp. 275, 276.

[35] Irvine, *The Making of Textual Culture*, p. 4.

[36] It appears that stenographers took down the sermons as they were delivered; sometimes they were corrected later by the preachers. See Socrates, *Hist. eccles.* 6.4: Chrysostom used stenographers but went over the copy himself; cf. Eusebius, *Hist. eccles.* 6.23.1 on Origen's use of stenographers and calligraphers. Augustine preached extemporaneously but did not usually correct the stenographic account; see Roy Deferrari, "St. Augustine's Method of Composing and Delivering Sermons," *American Journal of Philology* 43 (1922): 211.

[37] Eric Auerbach, *Literary Language and Its Public in Late Latin Antiquity and in the Middle Ages*, trans. Ralph Mannheim, Bollingen Series 74 (New York: Pantheon/Random House, 1965; German original, 1958), pp. 37, 47, writing of Augustine's argument in *De doctrina Christiana*.

[38] Gamble, *Books*, pp. 83–85; Evaristo

Christians do seem distinctive (e.g., Christians made earlier and more extensive use of the codex than the roll/scroll),[39] the Fathers did not participate in a different literacy from that of their pagan contemporaries of similar class. Christian authors, like their pagan counterparts, sought patrons for their writing,[40] cultivated literary friendships with Christians of the highest aristocracy (including women),[41] solicited friends throughout the Mediterranean world to lend their books for copying, and shared the ones they themselves owned.[42] Of course, Christian authors now appeal to God for inspiration rather than to the Muses,[43] and profess (overmuch) their own lack of erudition, their inadequacy to the literary task,[44] but such are precisely the self-consciously rhetorical moves we might expect from learned men who had been schooled in and for "literature."

Contemporary scholars suggest that debates over "orthodoxy" and "heresy" were especially important in the early Christian production of texts, indeed, in the production of the text of the New Testament itself.[45]

Arns, *La Technique du livre d'après Saint Jérôme* (Paris: E. de Boccard, 1953), chap. 4, esp. p. 130. For practices of "publishing" among "pagan" writers, see James E. G. Zetzel, *Latin Textual Criticism in Antiquity* (Salem, N.H.: Ayer, 1984), pp. 233–35; Kenney, "Books and Readers," p. 19. On how literary texts were "edited" and circulated, see Raymond J. Starr, "The Circulation of Literary Texts in the Roman World," *Classical Quarterly* 37 (1987): 213–23—especially helpful in noting how "new" writers who did not stem from aristocratic circles themselves could gain entrée to them through literature (p. 223).

[39] Kenyon, *Books*, pp. 95–100; L. D. Reynolds and N. G. Wilson, *Scribes and Scholars: A Guide to the Transmission of Greek and Latin Literature*, 3rd ed. (Oxford: Clarendon, 1991; lst ed., 1968), pp. 34–35; Roberts, *Manuscript*, p. 20; Gamble, *Books*, pp. 62–63. Various arguments are given for the change: convenience, ability to have all the Gospels in one collection, ease of transport. Elizabeth Meyer (perhaps developing an argument from Roberts?) suggests that since the codex was the form used for law books, Christians' adaptation of this form suggests that they were seeking to invest their literature with the traditional authority of and reverence for legal documents (unpublished paper given at the American Historical Association, San Francisco, December 1994).

[40] Jerome provides a good example: see his prefaces to his translation of Proverbs, Ecclesiastes, and Song of Songs (PL 28, 1307); to his translations of Origen's *Hom. in Cant.* and *Hom. in Ezech.* (PG 13, 35–36, 665–66). For essays on literary patronage earlier in Rome, see Barbara K. Gold, ed., *Literary and Artistic Patronage in Ancient Rome* (Austin: University of Texas Press, 1982).

[41] E.g., Pelagius, Jerome, and Augustine all wrote to the Anician heiress Demetrias upon her decision for lifelong virginity: Pelagius, *Ad Demetriadem*; Jerome, *ep.* 130; Augustine, *ep.* 150 (addressed to Demetrias' mother and grandmother).

[42] E.g., Jerome, *epp.* 5.2; 10.3; 37.1; 49.4; 75.4; 85.3.

[43] E.g., Augustine, *Confessiones* 1.1; Faltonia Betitia Proba, *Cento* ll.9–22.

[44] E.g., (Gerontius), *Vita Melaniae Iunioris, prologus*; Gregory of Nyssa, *Vita Macrinae* 1.

[45] Bart D. Ehrman, *The Orthodox Corruption of Scripture: The Effect of Early Christological Controversies on the Text of the New Testament* (New York/Oxford: Oxford University Press, 1993); also see Kim Haines-Eitzen, "Hearing," chap. 3.

As Richard Lim has argued, where the interpretation of sacred texts was at stake, "the written word assumed greater importance."[46] In the first Christian centuries, debates (whether "real" or purely fictional) staged between Christians and Jews produced a "competitive exegesis" that issued in treatises such as Justin Martyr's *Dialogue with Trypho*.[47] Somewhat later, controversies between Christian groups regarding the nature of the Godhead, and with those beyond the pale, such as Manicheans, generated a flood of literature.[48] Augustine's debates with Donatists, and the records of church councils pertaining to the Donatist-Catholic controversy, furnish ample evidence of this point.[49] "Heresy," in fact, could be linked by patristic authors to "poor reading," a criticism that Augustine levels at his Manichean opponent Faustus.[50] Although the producers of ascetic literature only sometimes found themselves embroiled in debates over "heresy," controversies over asceticism itself, even within the "orthodox" camp, offered yet another arena for textual production by elite Christian writers.

Here, deceived by ascetic writers' rhetorical appeal to "simplicity," we may underestimate their dependence upon books, including the Bible. Granted that many of the Egyptian desert monks probably were illiterate (or at least were unable to read Greek),[51] and that the *Sayings of the Fathers* (*Apophthegmata Patrum*) originated in the oral relation between ascetic master and disciple.[52] Granted also that many sayings preserved in these collections suggest a hostility to "book-culture";[53] in some, highly educated monks decry their own secular learning, deemed worthless when compared to the "wisdom" of their unlettered colleagues.[54] Moreover, various of the *Sayings* express a monk's hesitation even to interpret Scripture: a brother might do best to remain silent.[55]

[46] Lim, *Public Disputation*, p. 22.

[47] Ibid., pp. 4–6.

[48] Ibid., chaps. 3 and 4.

[49] For a discussion of the Donatist debates, see Maureen A. Tilley, *The Bible in Christian North Africa: The Donatist World* (Minneapolis: Fortress, 1997).

[50] Augustine, *Contra Faustum* 6.9; 22.32; 22.49 (CSEL 25, 301, 625–27, 642).

[51] Douglas Burton-Christie, *The Word in the Desert: Scripture and the Quest for Holiness in Early Christian Monasticism* (New York/Oxford: Oxford University Press, 1993), pp. 59–60. Typical is the statement by the author of the *Historia monachorum* on Abba Or (2.5): he was illiterate, but God gave him grace to recite the Scriptures by heart. For a short survey of the development of Coptic in the third century, see Roger S. Bagnall, *Egypt in Late Antiquity* (Princeton, N.J.: Princeton University Press, 1993), pp. 238–40; for illiteracy in Egyptian villages, pp. 243–44.

[52] Graham Gould, *The Desert Fathers on Monastic Community* (Oxford: Clarendon, 1993), p. 24; Burton-Christie, *Word*, pp. 77, 79.

[53] *Verba seniorum* 5.6; 5.12 (PL 73, 889, 890).

[54] *Apophthegmata patrum* (Alphabetical) (Arsenius 5–6) (PG 65, 88–89); Evagrius Ponticus 7 (PG 65, 178); cf. Euprepius 7 (PG 65, 172), perhaps also to be attributed to Evagrius.

[55] Gould, *Desert Fathers*, pp. 78–80, citing *Apophthegmata patrum* (Poemen 8, Sisoes 17l, Antony 17). The desert fathers

Despite such concessions, counterevidence suggests that a reassessment of the *topos* of "unletteredness" may be in order. Was the monk who kept the stone in his mouth to learn silence[56] consciously parodying—and hence familiar with—the reported practice of the Greek orator Demosthenes, who aimed to speak more clearly and eloquently?[57] Although Pachomian monks allegedly repudiated Origen's writings and threw them in the river,[58] Samuel Rubenson's convincing argument for the authenticity of the letters of Antony, replete with Origenist sentiment, questions the "uncultivated" condition of these desert renunciants.[59] The probable association of the Pachomian monasteries at Pbouw and Šenesēt (Chenoboskion) with the Nag Hammadi "library," composed not just of Gnostic texts, but also of snippets of Plato's *Republic* and the *Sentences of Sextus*,[60] likewise casts doubt on the complete "unletteredness" of the Egyptian monks—a doubt strengthened by the quite probable association of the Dishna papers (containing parts of the *Iliad*, fragments of the *Odyssey*, and writings by Menander and Thucydides) with the Pachomians.[61] Finally, sketches of the desert monks, such as are found in the *Lausiac History*, sometimes mention that a particular monk is learned, or depicts him as writing;[62] although these reports may single out the literate

fear that their Scriptural interpretation might be wrongly motivated.

[56] *Apophthegmata patrum* (Alphabetical) (Agathon 15) (PG 65, 13).

[57] Plutarch, *Demosthenes* 11 (Loeb, *Lives* VII:26).

[58] *Vita Pachomii* (Gr.): *Vita Altera* 27; 68; *Vita Tertia* 56; 104; *Vita Quarta* 37 (SubsHag 19, 195, 240–41, 281, 307–8, 435). The repudiation of books is not mentioned in the Coptic versions of the *Vita Pachomii*; see James E. Goehring, "Monastic Diversity and Ideological Boundaries in Fourth-Century Christian Egypt," *Journal of Early Christian Studies* 5 (1997): 73–82, for a critical reading of the sources pertaining to monks and Origenism.

[59] Samuel Rubenson, *The Letters of Saint Antony: Origenist Theology, Monastic Tradition, and the Making of a Saint* (Lund: Lund University Press, 1990), esp. pp. 35–42, on the letters' authenticity; pp. 47, 59ff., 67–71, 86ff., for discussion of some Origenist themes. Critical of Rubenson's arguments for the influence of Origenist theology on early Egyptian monasticism is Graham Gould, "The Influence of Origen on Fourth-Century Monasticism: Some Further Remarks," in *Origeniana Sexta: Origène et la Bible/Origen and the Bible*, ed. Gilles Dorival, Alain Le Boulluec et al., Actes du Colloquium Origenianum Sextum Chantilly, 30 août–3 septembre 1993 (Leuven: University Press/Uitgeverij Peeters, 1995), pp. 591–98.

[60] See above, pp. 28–29. See also Clemons Scholten, "Die Nag-Hammadi-Texte als Buchbesitz der Pachomianer," *Jahrbuch für Antike und Christentum* 31 (1988): 144–72, for helpful examples of book possession.

[61] An inventory of the Dishna papers can be found in James M. Robinson, "The Pachomian Monastic Library at the Chester Beatty Library and the Bibliothèque Bodmer," *Occasional Papers* 15 (Claremont, Calif.: Institute for Antiquity and Christianity, 1990). My thanks to James Goehring for assistance with this material.

[62] Thus Sarapion is said to be "highly literate" (*eugrammatos*), and Evagrius Ponticus' writings are mentioned (Palladius, *Historia Lausiaca* 37, 38 [Butler, pp. 109, 120–21]).

few from their many illiterate colleagues, they nonetheless signal that the monks as a whole should not be portrayed as completely unlettered. Even in the *Sayings of the Fathers*, often thought to represent more accurately the "simple" monks than do literary productions such as the *Lausiac History*, there are references to scribes and the possession of books.[63] Likewise, even when a monk's selling his books to give to the poor is lauded, the very notice signals the presence and use of books by the more learned brothers.[64]

At the least, we may confidently claim that even if the alleged speakers of the *Sayings* were illiterate, those who compiled the documents that constitute our evidence were obviously not—nor were the authors of the highly elaborated and verbally ornate ascetic treatises on which this study is based. The latter were usually urban-based and urban-educated, in contrast to many of the unlettered desert monks from rural backgrounds. What then are we to make of the frequent appeals to "simplicity," to lack of literary cultivation, in the numerous texts pertaining to asceticism? I would suggest that once "simplicity" had been accepted as a prime Christian virtue, its cultivation was encouraged by and for all believers, even those who were far from "simple."[65] For sophisticated writers such as Augustine and John Chrysostom, the "simple" Christian virtues were to be pursued after the acquisition of *paideia*[66]—not in place of it. Several of the Fathers were rhetorically and literarily educated to such a high degree that they could not have discarded rhetoric even if they tried: such is Steven Oberhelman's recent judgment on Ambrose.[67] To claim oneself as humble, afflicted, and poor could also serve a theological purpose, namely, that through cultivating this self-understanding, Christians might imitate God's merciful condescension to humankind in the Incarnation.[68]

Here we face a paradox. The illiterate desert renunciants doubtless challenged the cultural norms shared by those initiated in youth to Greek and Latin literature, whatever their later religious commitments. In Peter

[63] *Apophthegmata patrum* (Alphabetical) (Abraham 3; Epiphanius 8) (PG 65, 132, 165).

[64] *Apophthegmata patrum* (Alphabetical) (Theodore of Pherme 1) (PG 65, 188). I thank James Goehring for pointing out the importance of such references. On the ideological uses of "simplicity," see James E. Goehring, "Monastic Diversity," pp. 77–81.

[65] Lim, *Public Disputation*, p. 30, cf. p. 214 ("the alliance between Christian virtue and holy simplicity against the empty sophistry of words").

[66] Brown, *Power*, p. 123.

[67] Steven M. Oberhelman, *Rhetoric and Homiletics in Fourth-Century Christian Literature: Prose Rhythm, Oratorical Style, and Preaching in the Works of Ambrose, Jerome, and Augustine*, American Philological Association American Classical Studies 26 (Atlanta: Scholars, 1991), p. 53.

[68] Brown, *Power*, pp. 155–57; cf. Averil Cameron, *Christianity and the Rhetoric of Empire: The Development of Christian Discourse* (Berkeley/Los Angeles/Oxford: University of California Press, 1991), pp. 68–69.

Brown's (customarily) pithy phrase, "[t]he monks could utter the *gros mots* that broke the spell of *paideia*."[69] Yet those who composed the literature of Christian asceticism were educated in the very grammar and rhetoric that the monks decry;[70] their simplicity was that of "the cultured, literate classes, not that of the poor and powerless."[71] Averil Cameron astutely notes this "convenience":

> this literature [on virginity] was typically a learned literature, whose practitioners had usually themselves received the best classical education available at the time. While encouraging virgins to avoid the classics, read Hebrew, and become learned in the Scriptures, they extolled uneducated "simplicity." Their praise of the unwashed and uncultured over and against the social advantages of civilization and learning, which they did not hesitate to display themselves in their own writing, is indicative of an area of deep ambiguity and uncertainty in contemporary Christian culture.[72]

Thus we may make sense of the literary rhetoric of debasement that undergirds the protests by writers that their talents are insufficient to their literary tasks.[73] Nor should we always take at face value the claim of hagiographers that their subjects were unlettered and uncouth,[74] subjects who are nonetheless represented as foiling Greek philosophers through the power of their God-given wisdom.[75] Although hagiography and stories of the desert fathers are often considered "low" Christian literature, not comparable to sophisticated theological treatises, it is nonetheless noteworthy that even these "artless" tales are constructed with literary skill and rhetorical power.

When we move from the desert to the city and from Egyptian peasants to urban renunciants, our evidence for ascetics' study of the Bible and later theological texts multiplies. Numerous references to the scholarly reading in which women ascetics engaged suggest that we are dealing with the higher social classes. The virgin is advised to be "a student of the Gospels"[76]: so Athanasius encourages his community of virgins at Alexandria.[77] In Ambrose's rendition of the Annunciation story, the Virgin Mary

[69] Brown, *Power*, p. 73; cf. pp. 39–40 on the shared bonds of *paideia*.

[70] Cameron, *Christianity*, p. 85.

[71] Irvine, *The Making of Textual Culture*, p. 191.

[72] Cameron, *Christianity*, p. 179. Oberhelman, *Rhetoric and Homiletics*, p. 121, similarly notes that Western ecclesiastical writers' "attacks on rhetorical devices, cries of 'content, not eloquence,' and demands for an unadorned style" were themselves "stated in the verbose and pedantic style of the period."

[73] See above, pp. 52, 55.

[74] Athanasius, *Vita Antonii* 1, 73 (PG 26, 841, 945). Cf. Rubenson, *The Letters of Saint Antony*, esp. pp. 91–109, for an argument against taking such assertions at face value.

[75] Athanasius, *Vita Antonii* 73–80 (PG 26, 945–956).

[76] Pseudo-Basil, *De virginitate* 2.41 (Amand de Mendietta/Moons, pp. 43–44).

[77] Athanasius, *De virginitate* (Lebon, p.

herself becomes a reader who provides a model for later virgins in her devotion to pious study.[78] In the *Life of Olympias*, the heroine is depicted as tossing off numerous citations from Paul's epistles;[79] whether or not she actually spoke this way is immaterial, since readers of her *Vita* need only think that she might have. Palladius, the author of the *Lausiac History*, ascribes an Origenist reading list to Melania the Elder that includes "three million lines of Origen and two and a half million lines of Gregory, Stephen, Pierius, Basil, and other worthy men," authors she allegedly read seven or eight times each.[80] Jerome encourages Eustochium to read, among the Latin ascetic authors, Tertullian on marriage, Cyprian on virginity, Damasus, and Ambrose's treatise on virginity composed for his sister.[81] Melania the Younger's biographer reports that she read through both Old and Testaments three or four times a year (which she also copied and distributed to "the saints");[82] that she was trained in Biblical interpretation;[83] that she wrote every day in notebooks ("without mistakes"); and that she read the Bible, collections of homilies, and the *Lives of the Fathers*, "as if she were eating dessert."[84] Of course, men of the educated classes also participated in this culture of ascetic learning. Sulpicius Severus, for example, praises Paulinus of Nola for making Sulpicius' *Life of Martin* of Tours available at Rome; it already was known in Africa and Egypt, according to its author.[85] Reading and writing were part of the life fabric of the ascetics whose interpretation of Scripture is the subject of my study.

Ascetics and their admirers composed a wide variety of documents describing and promoting their cause, from the sophisticated speculative theology of an Evagrius Ponticus to monastic rules, hagiographies large and small, letters and treatises directed not only to fellow ascetics, but also to lay Christians who are exhorted therein concerning proper conduct in

212; ET, Brakke, p. 305): the virgins claim that they have read Scripture "sufficiently"; cf. Athanasius, *ep. 1 ad virgines* (CSCO 150 = Scriptores Coptici 19, p. 79; ET, Brakke, p. 278).

[78] Ambrose, *Exp. Lucam* 2.15 (CCL 14, 38); *De virginibus* 2.2.10 (PL 16, 221).

[79] (Anonymous), *Vita Olympiadis* 17 (SC 13bis, 444, 446).

[80] Palladius, *Historia Lausiaca* 55 (Butler, p. 149); cf. 11 (Ammonius). Melania (the most likely reference) also is said by Jerome (*ep.* 133.3 [CSEL 56, 246]) to read Evagrius Ponticus; cf. Elizabeth A. Clark, *The Origenist Controversy: The Cultural Construction of an Early Christian Debate* (Princeton, N.J.: Princeton University Press, 1992), pp. 188–93.

[81] Jerome, *ep.* 22.22 (CSEL 54, 174–75). Little Paula, after her Greek and Latin instruction, should be taught to read not just the Bible, but Cyprian, Athanasius, and Hilary (Jerome, *ep.* 107.9; 107.12 [CSEL 55, 300, 302–3]).

[82] (Gerontius), *Vita Melania Iunioris* 26 (SC 90, 178).

[83] (Gerontius), *Vita Melania Iunioris* 21 (SC 90, 170, 172).

[84] (Gerontius), *Vita Melania Iunioris* 23 (SC 90, 174). Other references to women's ownership of books can be found in Palladius, *Historia Lausiaca* 60, 64.

[85] Sulpicius Severus, *Dialogus* 1.23 (CSEL 1, 175–76).

marriage and widowhood. Yet it was not just that ascetics produced texts: texts produced ascetics as well. There is a special relation between texts and ascetics' lives, in Douglas Burton-Christie's phrase, a "desert hermeneutic."[86] This "desert hermeneutic" constituted a seemingly circular process by which texts come to be expressed in lives—which then themselves become new "texts," new objects of interpretation.[87]

The desert fathers' "continuous rumination upon Scripture, their desire to embody the texts in their lives," writes Burton-Christie, was a primary source of the compelling spirituality that emerged from the desert.[88] Interpreting Scripture, he argues, became for the desert fathers "a means to transformation and holiness," with Biblical figures serving as exemplars for the monks' own sanctity.[89] The link that late antique philosophers often express between *paideia* and holiness is here reformulated as a "new *paideia* of the desert" based on Scripture.[90]

It was not, however, only desert renunciants who experienced this tight link between the ascetic text and the ascetic body. Urban ascetics participated in this book-culture as well. Indeed, most of the early Christian literature counseling renunciation was composed by ascetics living in towns and cities—and these ascetics were well-educated literary sophisticates, as the examples of Augustine, Ambrose, and John Chrysostom suggest. Even those ascetic writers who later took to monastic retreat (Jerome stands as case in point) were urban-educated. Burton-Christie's description of a "desert hermeneutic" here requires expansion to suit the circumstances of a wider circle of early Christian ascetic writers.

Urging the necessity of Christian books for those able to use them, Epiphanius claims that the mere physical act of seeing books provides a spur to righteousness and a deterrent to sin.[91] Could not literacy be understood as a necessary technique for those attempting to interpret God's will, especially since the divine author had not always provided clues as to

[86] Burton-Christie, *Word*, p. 4.

[87] Ibid., pp. viii, 20. Cf. Saxer, *Bible et hagiographie*, p. 261: in hagiography, the text fills up the place of the absent martyr. On the *Vitae* as productive of ascetic discipline, see Cameron, *Christianity*, p. 57. For an earlier statement of the close connection between sacred reading and ascetic bodies, see Gorce, *La Lectio divina*, I:359.

[88] Burton-Christie, *Word*, p. 297. Some might wish to add that "texts" could include much more than Scripture.

[89] Ibid., pp. 299 (cf. pp. 4–5 on the "quest for holiness"), 167–68. On the parallels between exegesis and asceticism, also see Verna E. F. Harrison, "Allegory and Asceticism in Gregory of Nyssa," *Semeia* 57 (1992): 114, 116.

[90] Burton-Christie, *Word*, pp. 54, 59. A similar view of the relation between the Biblical text and praxis was formulated by Frances Young, *Virtuoso Theology: The Bible and Interpretation* (Cleveland: Pilgrim, 1993; published originally as *The Art of Performance: Towards a Theology of Holy Scripture* [London: Darton, Longman and Todd, 1990]), pp. 147–48.

[91] *Apophthegmata Patrum* (Alphabetical), Epiphanius 8 (PG 65, 165).

the "correct" reading of a passage?[92] This moral transformation could even be expressed in the language of writing. Thus Basil of Ancyra posits that after we are "without the body," "every thought will show itself inscribed as by writing on the soul."[93] And for Origen, Mary's holy confession in Luke 1:38 ("I am a handmaid of the Lord") should be taken to mean "I am a tablet on which to be written"[94]: in Origen's rendition, Mary here-and-now becomes the *tabula rasa* that Basil of Ancyra imagines will be possible only in a bodiless state.[95]

The "desert hermeneutic" by which texts came to be expressed in lives—which themselves became new objects of interpretation— is well-illustrated in the case of full-blown hagiographies of ascetics, such as the *Life of Antony.*[96] Edith Wyschogrod sums up the process well:

> It is the life as narrated that exhorts the text's addressees to "make the movements" of the saint's existence after her/him. The success of the life's appeal is in part the result of sheer perlocutionary force: the indicative mood of the narrative's sentences carries imperative weight. Hagiography is historical to the extent necessary for saintly praxes to be experienced as imposing realizable demands on the lives of its addressees.[97]

And Wyschogrod adds, "Saints' lives are not only communicated *in* texts but *as* texts so that the character of textuality is pertinent to grasping saintly life and practice."[98]

Athanasius' *Life of Antony* is often singled out as the exemplary document for generations of Christians, itself formative for would-be ascetics. A dramatic example of such ascetic formation through this text is supplied by Augustine in the *Confessions*: he reports the case of two young government officials who immediately renounced careers and fiancées upon hearing the *Vita Antonii* read.[99] Likewise, the *Sayings of the Fathers* summed up in pithy pronouncements the virtues that would inform later generations of ascetic devotees. Hence Jerome enjoins Paulinus of Nola to adopt

[92] Jonathan G. Stratton, *The Problem of the Interaction of Literacy, Culture and the Social Structure, With Special Reference to the Late Roman and Early Medieval Periods.* Unpublished Ph.D. dissertation, University of Essex, 1978, p. 95.

[93] Basil of Ancyra, *De virginitate* 31 (Vaillant, pp. 24, 26).

[94] Origen, *In Lucam* frag. 17 (SC 87, 476).

[95] Basil of Ancyra, *De virginitate* 31 (Vaillant, pp. 24–25).

[96] For a fascinating discussion of how and why saints' *Lives* became a new way of teaching virtue, see Robert L. Wilken, "The Lives of the Saints and the Pursuit of Virtue," in idem, *Remembering the Christian Past* (Grand Rapids: Eerdmans, 1995), pp. 121–44.

[97] Edith Wyschogrod, *Saints and Postmodernism: Revisioning Moral Philosophy* (Chicago/London: University of Chicago Press, 1990), p. 28.

[98] Ibid., p. 30.

[99] Augustine, *Confessiones* 8.6.15 (CCL 27, 122–23).

the pattern of the earlier monks, to live like Paul (the first hermit, according to Jerome), Antony, Hilarion, and others.[100]

Thus a strong interrelation existed between the ascetic body and the ascetic text. Yet another text, lying behind the *Life of Antony* or the Pachomian *Rules*, was crucial for Catholic theoreticians and practitioners of asceticism to claim: the Bible. What would avail to copy the deeds of an Antony or a Melania, if they were not sanctioned, indeed encouraged, by Scripture? Although the monk's heart might be "a new book,"[101] at least one book—the Bible—was still essential to inspire and to transform lives.

Here arises the difficulty of "ascetic exegesis": how to bring the seemingly varied Biblical messages into a unified vision of Christianity that was ascetic to its core? How to interpret Biblical texts that seemed not just to tolerate, but to praise marriage and reproduction, abundant eating and drinking, the accumulation of possessions? How to claim that the New Testament's "good news" entailed a renunciatory commitment without implying that the Genesis commandment to "reproduce and multiply" was sadly misguided? Most pressing, how to advance an asceticizing Biblical interpretation that did not result in charges of "heresy"?

For despite the Fathers' occasional complaint that their "heretical" opponents were "poor readers,"[102] the latter seem all *too* artful in their Scriptural interpretations, appealing to "allegories, parables, and riddles."[103] Although Irenaeus, writing in the late second century, complains that his "Gnostic" opponents appeal to the "living voice" for their authority rather than to written documents,[104] patristic evidence more often suggests that "heretics" were highly adroit at mining the details of Scripture to press their own interpretations. And it was not just "heretics" who interpreted Scripture in ways that justified a laxer style of life;[105] so did "orthodox" Christians of a less rigorous stripe.[106] As John Chrysostom complained,

[100] Jerome, *ep.* 58.5 (CSEL 54, 534); cf. Jerome, *Vita Pauli* 1.1 (PL 23, 17–18): Paul, not Antony, was the first hermit.

[101] Brown, *Body*, p. 229.

[102] Augustine of Faustus the Manichean in *Contra Faustum* 22.32 (CSEL 25, 626–27). Cf. Augustine's complaint against Faustus as a "bad reader" in *Contra Faustum* 22.49 (CSEL 25, 642): was it only "in his own heart, as in a book of impious delusions," that he read about Jacob's four women fighting over their sexual rights to him?

[103] Tertullian, *Scorpiace* 11.4 (CCL 2, 1091). For Ambrose's preference for "literal" exegesis when combating Arian "figurative" deviations, see Luigi Franco Pizzolato, *La dottrina esegetica de sant' Ambrogio*, Studia Patristica Mediolanensia 9 (Milano: Università Cattolica del Sacro Cuore, 1978), p. 321.

[104] Irenaeus, *Adversus haereses* 3.2.1 (PG 7, 846). Irenaeus also complains that "Gnostics" read Biblical texts wrongly (e.g., *Adversus haereses* 3.7.1). Nonetheless, the Nag Hammadi texts themselves reveal a high literary culture.

[105] See Clement of Alexandria, *Stromata* 3.4.38.1 (GCS 52[15], 213), on heretics who interpret Mal. 3:15 as an exhortation to "libertine" living.

[106] (Anonymous), *De divitiis* 18.2; 18.10

reading does not suffice for a holy life unless knowledge is added to it; thus the Ethiopian eunuch of Acts 8, who could "read" but did not "understand," needed apostolic instruction.[107]

Had ascetically minded interpreters been willing to discard Hebrew Scripture, they would have eliminated a major source that accorded but poorly with the ascetic "turn" of fourth- and fifth-century exegetes. But this option was not open to Catholic Christians from the third century onward: the Church had fought (and won) the battle over the retention of the Old Testament in its struggle against Marcion. Once the decision was made to claim these Scriptures for Christianity, the difficulty of interpretation was pressed upon Christians who wished to read all of their sacred texts with ascetic eyes. Catholics could not argue, as did Faustus the Manichean, that parts of Scripture were spurious, or that the Paraclete would reveal which sections of the New Testament were authoritative:[108] *all* verses of the Bible were to be deemed holy and edifying. Catholics who suspected otherwise were not yet "good readers."[109]

II: The Sources of Early Christian Interpretation

To greater or lesser degrees, the church fathers were steeped in Greco-Roman rhetorical culture, yet this culture itself had changed significantly from earlier to later antiquity. As a centralized state displaced local centers, Roman law relied less on persuasive courtroom oratory and more on precedent and formulas, and the public, civic character of rhetorical culture shifted to a more literary (i.e., written) and personal mode.[110] George Kennedy describes this process as "letteraturizzazione," "the repeated slippage of rhetoric into literary composition."[111] Christianity was affected by this development as well: the

(PLS 1, 1408, 1411); (Anonymous), *De malis doctoribus* 10.3; 11.1 (PLS 1, 1433–34), cf. Burton-Christie, *Word*, pp. 163–64.

[107] John Chrysostom, *Contra Marcionistas et Manichaeos* ("Pater, si possibile est") 1 (PG 51, 31). In Irenaeus' view, Scripture could be clearly understood by all; the problem rather arises because "all" do not believe its contents (*Adversus haereses* 2.27.2 (PG 7, 803).

[108] Faustus in Augustine, *Contra Faustum* 18.3; 32.6 (CSEL 25, 499–500, 765–66).

[109] For the relations of heresy and literacy in the Middle Ages, see Brian Stock, *The Implications of Literacy: Written Language and Models of Interpretation in the Eleventh and Twelfth Centuries* (Princeton, N.J.: Princeton University Press, 1983), chap. 2.1; and *Heresy and Literacy, 1000–1530*, ed. Peter Biller and Anne Hudson (Cambridge: Cambridge University Press, 1994).

[110] George A. Kennedy, *Classical Rhetoric and Its Christian and Secular Tradition from Ancient to Modern Times* (Chapel Hill: University of North Carolina Press, 1980), pp. 111–12, 5.

[111] Ibid., p. 109. See Oberhelman, *Rheto-*

"simple, oral homily" was replaced by "the elaborate, epideictic sermon," a process particularly evident among such rhetorical virtuosi as Gregory Nazianzen and John Chrysostom.[112]

Schooled in both the elementary study of rhetoric (the *progymnasmata*) and in the more advanced rhetorical-literary curricula,[113] Christian bishops and monastic leaders increasingly exploited classical rhetoric for Christian purposes. They employed the conventions of rhetorical question, direct address, and invective to grip their audiences. Adept at the arts of comparison (*synkrisis*) and refutation (*anaskeuē*), they manipulated the schemes of antithesis, assonance, anaphora, and isocolon to promote their religious aims.[114] Their argumentation relied on *antiparastasis* (attributing views to an opponent which an author then refutes) and *biaion* (converting an opponent's stance to an author's own purposes).[115] "Style" became more massively important than most first-century Christians could have imagined.[116] Most important, if even humble Biblical texts could be construed as "literature," the canonical status of works such as the *Aeneid* could be discounted: such a displacement (Martin Irvine argues) is the final result of late ancient Christians' making of a "textual culture."[117]

But were Christian interpretive techniques appropriated only from Greco-Roman (i.e., "pagan") literary culture? Insofar as earliest Christianity constituted a sect of Judaism, did not Christians adopt interpretive techniques from early Jewish exegetes? Recent scholarship suggests that Greco-Roman and Jewish rhetorical culture shared certain modes of interpretation that became the common heritage of patristic Christianity. Since most church fathers knew little or no Hebrew, it is doubtful that their

---

ric and Homiletics, pp. 109–11, for a description of Augustine's sermonic style and the devices he uses; Augustine's style when writing/dictating, however, is more attentive to elaborate rhetorical and literary conventions (pp. 91–92).

[112] Kennedy, *Classical Rhetoric*, pp. 114, 145; see also Kennedy, *Greek Rhetoric Under Christian Emperors: A History of Rhetoric*, vol. 3 (Princeton, N.J.: Princeton University Press, 1983), p. 50.

[113] Outlined in Kennedy, *Greek Rhetoric*, pp. 60–65, 73.

[114] Kennedy, *Classical Rhetoric*, pp. 140, 134; *Greek Rhetoric*, p. 183. For analysis of Augustine's use of rhetorical/stylistic devices, see Christine Mohrmann, "Saint Augustin écrivain," *Recherches Augustiniennes* 1 (1958): 43–66.

[115] For examples of *biaion* and *antiparastasis*, see Kennedy, *Greek Rhetoric*, pp. 89–90. Also see David Weiss Halivni, *Midrash, Mishnah, and Gemara: The Jewish Predilection for Justified Law* (Cambridge, Mass./London: Harvard University Press, 1986), pp. 87–88, on Stammaitic interpreters (rabbis of the fifth and early sixth centuries) using such devices as pseudo-dialogue (e.g., offering false answers and then refuting them—seemingly a form of *antiparastasis*).

[116] Kennedy, *Classical Rhetoric*, p. 158. For the case of Athanasius, see G. Christopher Stead, "Rhetorical Method in Athanasius," *Vigiliae Christianae* 30 (1976): 121–37.

[117] Irvine, *The Making of Textual Culture*, pp. 178–79.

interpretive techniques could have been borrowed directly from the rabbis of their own era, although Origen may possibly have served as a conduit between the rabbis and Christian exegetes.[118] Some forms of exegesis, however, may have been adapted from pre-rabbinic Jewish sources by Christian interpreters.

The question of the relation between Jewish and Greco-Roman interpretive techniques has in recent decades been variously answered along a spectrum that either minimizes or maximizes the Hellenistic influence on Jewish thought. Thus Michael Fishbane, in his monumental volume, *Biblical Interpretation in Ancient Israel*, argues that the rabbis did not "have to look to the neighboring Alexandrian scribes," but "were themselves heir to an older, native tradition" of interpretation manifest in the Old Testament itself.[119] On this view, the rabbis were encouraged by Scripture itself to utilize such methods of interpretation as analogy, the resolution of apparent contradiction by appealing to a third text, and the closing of loopholes. Within Scripture itself, Fishbane argues, a saying could be decontextualized and relocated; contrasts could be drawn between "old" and "new" times that integrated the seemingly discrete events of history; shifts in the audience of a passage could create new meaning; the content of Biblical verses could be "spiritualized," as when military prowess is transformed into "spiritual fortitude."[120] These and other interpretive devices found within Scripture gave the later rabbis warrant to read in ways that brought new meaning to the sacred text. Indeed, Fishbane argues, these techniques of Jewish exegesis were developed long before there was such a thing as "Hellenistic culture." Thus for Fishbane,

[118] See David J. Halperin, *The Faces of the Chariot: Early Jewish Responses to Ezekiel's Vision*, Texte und Studien zum Antiken Judentum 16 (Tübingen: J. C. B. Mohr [Paul Siebeck], 1988), pp. 322–54; Reuven Kimelman, "Rabbi Yohanan and Origen on the Song of Songs: A Third-Century Jewish-Christian Disputation," *Harvard Theological Review* 73 (1980): 567–95; more generally, N. R. M. deLange, *Origen and the Jews: Studies in Jewish-Christian Relations in Third-Century Palestine* (Cambridge: Cambridge University Press, 1976). For Jewish and Christian interaction in Caesarea pertaining to the copying of Philo's works, see Dominique Barthélemy, "Est-ce Hoshaya Rabba qui censura le 'Commentaire Allégorique,'?" in idem, *Etudes d'histoire du texte de l'Ancien Testament*, Orbis Biblicus et Orientalis 21 (Fribourg: Editions Universitaires; Göttingen: Vandenhoeck & Ruprecht, 1978), pp. 140–73. Remaining skeptical of Origen's knowledge of contemporary rabbinic interpretation is Roger Brooks, "Straw Dogs and Scholarly Ecumenism: The Appropriate Jewish Background for the Study of Origen," in *Origen of Alexandria: His World and His Legacy*, ed. Charles Kannengiesser and William L. Petersen, Christianity and Judaism in Antiquity 1 (Notre Dame, Ind.: University of Notre Dame Press, 1988), pp. 63–95.

[119] Michael Fishbane, *Biblical Interpretation in Ancient Israel* (Oxford: Clarendon, 1985), p. 67.

[120] Ibid., pp. 412, 415, 417, 426.

the Jewish haggadah evolved from "native . . . cultural forms" and was not dependent on "the milieu of Greek or Roman rhetoric for its genesis."[121] Although Fishbane is careful to caution that trajectories between intra-Biblical exegesis and that of the rabbis and the Qumran community can only be suggested, not proved,[122] the import of his impressive study is to reduce Greco-Roman influence on the rabbis. On the other hand, Fishbane's book *could* be taken to imply that the ground was well prepared within Hebrew Scripture itself for the rabbis later to absorb Greco-Roman interpretive techniques.

David Daube, in contrast to Fishbane, argues not just that the rabbis were conversant with Hellenistic rhetorical conventions, but that "Rabbinic methods of interpretation derive from Hellenistic rhetoric."[123] In Daube's judgment, all seven of Hillel's norms of interpretation "betray the influence of the rhetorical teaching of his age."[124] Thus Hillel's first norm, *qal wahomer* ("from the light to the heavy") is known in Hellenistic circles as argumentation *a minori ad maius*, or more generally as *a fortiori* reasoning.[125] Daube also cites parallels from non-Jewish argumentation to Hillel's rule five, *kelal upherat* ("the general and the specific"), as he does for rule seven, *dabhar hallamedh me'inyano* (settling an ambiguity by adducing the context).[126] Likewise, the rabbinic use of *seres* (making logic of

[121] Ibid., p. 431.

[122] Ibid., p. 525.

[123] David Daube, "Rabbinic Methods of Interpretation and Hellenistic Rhetoric," *Hebrew Union College Annual* 22 (1949): 240. For a discussion of Daube's and Lieberman's positions, see Daniel Patte, *Early Jewish Hermeneutic in Palestine*, SBL Dissertation Series 22 (Missoula, Mont.: Scholars, 1975), pp. 113–15. Daube's position is substantially endorsed by William Horbury, "Jews and Christians on the Bible: Demarcation and Convergence [325–451]," in *Christliche Exegese zwischen Nicaea und Chalcedon*, ed. J. van Oort and U. Wickert (Kampen: Kok Pharos, 1992), p. 97; also by Philip S. Alexander, "Quid Athenis et Hierosolymis? Rabbinic Midrash and Hermeneutics in the Graeco-Roman World," in *A Tribute to Geza Vermes: Essays on Jewish and Christian Literature and History*, ed. Philip R. Davies and Richard T. White, Journal for the Study of the Old Testament, Supplement Series 100 (Sheffield: JSOT, 1990), esp. p. 103.

[124] Daube, "Rabbinic Methods," p. 251. For Hillel's seven norms of interpretation, see Hermann L. Strack, *Introduction to the Talmud and Midrash* (Philadelphia: Jewish Publication Society of America, 1931), p. 94; later expansions are on pp. 95–98.

[125] Daube, "Rabbinic Methods," p. 251. It is here worth noting that Christian exegetes pressing an ascetic line frequently use *a fortiori* argumentation as a "shaming device" to be deployed against the laxity of contemporary Christians ("if even . . . how much more"). For some notable instances of an appeal to pagans used to "shame" Christians, see Tertullian, *De monogamia* 17 and *De exhortatione castitatis* 13 (Dido); John Chrysostom, *Hom. 15 I Cor.* 1; for Israelites/Jews being used to shame Christians, John Chrysostom, *Hom. 13 Eph.*; *De virginitate* 30.1; for women being used to shame men, John Chrysostom, *Hom. 13 Eph.*; *Hom. 31 Rom.*; for low-class Christians shaming higher-class ones, John Chrysostom, *Hom. 35* and *36 Acta*.

[126] Daube, "Rabbinic Methods," pp.

a verse by separating and rearranging its parts) is, for Daube, simply a variation on the Greek rhetorical convention of *anastrophē* (inversion of the usual word order).[127]

Saul Lieberman nuances Daube's position: although the terminology of rabbinic interpretation may have been borrowed from Hellenistic rhetoric, the content remained "Jewish." Like Daube, Lieberman notes that Hillel's first norm of interpretation ("from the light to the heavy") is simply an *a minori ad maius* argument.[128] For Lieberman, however, the substance of Jewish exegesis was not "borrowed" from the Greeks. As he puts it, the "early Jewish interpreters of Scripture did not have to embark for Alexandria in order to learn there the rudimentary methods of linguistic research," even though their terminology may have been influenced by Greek rhetoric.[129]

In recent discussions informed by literary theory, several of Hillel's norms are given new life by their alignment with intertextual exegesis, to be discussed more extensively in chapter 5. Here, suffice it to note that the term "intertextuality" could be used to describe at least three of Hillel's norms of interpretation (three, four, and six): applying to several Biblical passages a rule which is found explicitly in only one of them ("building a family"); or the same technique, but based on two Biblical passages; or interpreting one passage by means of something similar in another passage.[130] These techniques all rest on the general principle that meaning is produced by reading texts in conjunction with other texts that are either explicitly or implicitly placed next to (or "inside") them, with power to constrain, expand, or explain.

Other techniques of rabbinical exegesis, particularly those employed in halakhic interpretation, also merit attention here. Midrashic exegesis frequently plays on a changed or double meaning of a word, rearranges the chronology or context of a passage, attends to the meaning (or alleged meaning) of names.[131] James Kugel's study, *In Potiphar's House*, supplies numerous examples of various Midrashic techniques: "transfer of affect," in which a motif that has been generated or elaborated to explain one text

---

252–53, 257.

[127] David Daube, "Alexandrian Methods of Interpretation and the Rabbis," in *Essays in Greco-Roman and Related Talmudic Literature*, ed. Henry A. Fischel (New York: Ktav, 1977), pp. 165–66. It is of interest that the word connotes "castration."

[128] Saul Lieberman, "Rabbinic Interpretation of Scripture," in idem, *Hellenism in Jewish Palestine: Studies in the Literary Transmission, Beliefs and Manners of Palestine in the I Century B.C.E.–IV Century C.E.*, Texts and Studies of the Jewish Theological Seminary of America 18 (New York: Jewish Theological Seminary of America, 5722/1962), p. 53.

[129] Ibid., pp. 53, 59.

[130] See Strack, *Introduction*, p. 94.

[131] See discussion in M. Gertner, "Mid-

comes to be understood as an explanation for another;[132] "back-referencing," in which a general maxim is particularized by being applied "backward" to an earlier historical figure;[133] "recycling" of answers from one problem to a new one.[134]

Such techniques also occur in early Christian ascetic exegesis, for Christianity as well as Judaism needed to find interpretive modes that brought the sacred texts of the past to bear upon present concerns—here, upon the issue of renunciation.[135] To be sure, it is doubtless true that rabbinic exegesis more frequently takes its point of departure from the peculiarity of a specific word[136] than does most Christian exegesis. In addition, there was more interest among rabbis than among Christians in such features of the text as the shape of letters and their numerical values[137]—again, interpretive techniques that made little sense for non-Hebrew readers and hence were not readily transferable to Greek and Latin texts. Moreover, it has been argued that in early Jewish exegesis, texts were correlated to other texts, not so much to "inner" or "hidden" meanings, as some commentators suppose for early Christian exegesis.[138] Despite such differences, many of the rhetorical strategies employed by the rabbis can be paralleled in

rashim in the New Testament," *Journal of Semitic Studies* 7 (1962): 270.

[132] James L. Kugel, *In Potiphar's House: The Interpretive Life of Biblical Texts* (San Francisco: HarperSanFrancisco, 1990), pp. 120, 255.

[133] Ibid., pp. 132, 173, 261.

[134] Ibid., pp. 251–52. Kugel's approach to Midrash is hotly disputed by Jacob Neusner, who accuses Kugel of dissolving the specificity of authorship, audience, time, and context of Midrash; the authorial intention behind the entire document needs to be kept in mind. See Neusner, *Midrash as Literature: The Primacy of Documentary Discourse* (Lanham, Md./New York/London: University Press of America, 1987), pp. ix, 15, 50.

[135] Such concern provides the very definition of Midrash for Addison G. Wright, "The Literary Genre Midrash," *Catholic Biblical Quarterly* 28 (1966): 456. Thus Jacob Lauterbach, writing many decades ago, notes the problems that occur within Judaism when the sacred text is set, and laws and customs have changed: "Midrash and Mishnah: A Study in the Early History of the Halakah," *Jewish Quarterly Review* 6 (1915–16): 53–54. David Stern also stresses the function of Midrash in "recuperating or salvaging the text—saving not only its meaning but its value, its felt importance in the life of the reader." Hence the interpreter is "literally a translator: one who carries the text across a divide, who negotiates the space between the text and its comprehension" (*Parables in Midrash: Narrative and Exegesis in Rabbinic Literature* [Cambridge/London: Harvard University Press, 1991], pp. 44–45).

[136] Wright, "The Literary Genre Midrash," pp. 247, 251. The "atomization" of texts in Midrash is discussed by David Stern, "Midrash and Indeterminacy," *Critical Inquiry* 15 (1988): 138, 150.

[137] Joseph Dan, "Midrash and the Dawn of Kabbalah," in *Midrash and Literature*, ed. Geoffrey H. Hartman and Sanford Budick (New Haven, Conn./London: Yale University Press, 1986), p. 128.

[138] Daniel Boyarin, *Intertextuality and the Reading of Midrash* (Bloomington/Indianapolis: Indiana University Press, 1990), pp. 20, 110, 116. Allegorical exegesis, it is here implicitly hinted, is aligned with Christianity.

Christian ascetic exegesis—and by church fathers with little or no knowledge of Hebrew, whose contact with the world of rabbinic Judaism was either nonexistent, limited, or decidedly hostile. That rabbis, church fathers, and "pagan" writers all exploited similar techniques suggests that the latter circulated widely (albeit in somewhat diverse forms) throughout the Greco-Roman world amidst that small intellectual elite whose lives were in part devoted to the explication of texts. The similarity of Jewish and Greco-Roman interpretive techniques and the complex interaction of their cultural milieus, I would posit, renders moot the question of the "origin" of Christian exegetical strategies.[139]

More important: the similarities of exegetical techniques between Jews and Christians provide a provocative anomaly when we reflect that the content of Christian exegesis promoted such different values (the rejection of marriage, sexual relation within marriage, and reproduction) than those held by the rabbis, whose allegedly "fleshly" (i.e., "literal") reading practices have been intriguingly explored by Daniel Boyarin in *Carnal Israel: Reading Sex in Talmudic Culture.*[140] Here, we are reminded of the "worldliness" of texts, that they "are always enmeshed in circumstance, time, place, and society,"[141] in the present case, in a Christian culture advocating a sexual and procreative renunciation that was largely foreign to Jewish contemporaries. As Boyarin argues in *Carnal Israel*, rabbinic Judaism advocated ascetic restraint in some areas of life, but not in those pertaining to marital sexuality and children.[142] In Boyarin's view, the rabbis' hearty embrace of marital sexuality developed in late antiquity from a more gingerly "ascetic" approach to women and sexual functioning in a slightly earlier period.[143]

Boyarin characterizes Augustine's "sexual exegesis" as follows: "Because the Jews reject reading 'in the spirit,' therefore they are condemned to remain 'Israel in the flesh.' Allegory is thus, in his [Augustine's] theory, a mode of relating to the body."[144] Boyarin here correlates a particular

[139] For a review of the parallels between Jewish and "pagan" Hellenistic interpretation, see Young, *Biblical Exegesis*, pp. 91–93; for those between Jewish and Christian interpretation, pp. 94, 208.

[140] Daniel Boyarin, *Carnal Israel: Reading Sex in Talmudic Culture*, The New Historicism 25 (Berkeley/Los Angeles/Oxford: University of California Press, 1993).

[141] Edward W. Said, "The Text, the World, and the Critic," in *Textual Strategies: Perspectives in Post-Structuralist Criticism*, ed. Josué V. Harari (Ithaca, N.Y.: Cornell University Press, 1979), p. 165.

[142] Boyarin, *Carnal Israel*, pp. 35, 71.

[143] Ibid., p. 63; cf. Jeremy Cohen, *"Be Fertile and Increase, Fill the Earth and Master It": The Ancient and Medieval Career of a Biblical Text* (Ithaca, N.Y./London: Cornell University Press, 1989), pp. 120–21; David Biale, *Eros and the Jews: From Biblical Israel to Contemporary America* (Berkeley/Los Angeles/London: University of California Press, 1997; original edition, New York: Basic, 1992), chap. 2.

[144] Boyarin, *Carnal Israel*, p. 8; cf. Daniel Boyarin, *A Radical Jew: Paul and the Politics of Identity* (Berkeley/Los Angeles/

mode of reading which tends to undercut physical "realities," namely, allegory, with a more "spiritualized," less "earthy" approach to the body—and these approaches he associates with patristic writers such as Augustine. According to the latter, the Jews, stubbornly "carnal" in their "literal" mode of exegesis, also remain "carnal" in their sexual concerns.[145] Without broaching the larger question of Jewish exegesis and Augustine's unflattering representation of it, I will in the next chapters question whether the Christian call to sexual renunciation was so tightly linked to an allegorical reading practice as Boyarin suggests.

There is no doubt, however, that Christian writers often faulted the "literalism" and "carnality" of Jewish Biblical interpretation. Yet more startling is the degree to which Christians *also* opted for "literal" readings on certain occasions, most notably those in which they could advance the ascetic program.[146] "Ascetic reading," I will argue, was not usually engaged via allegory: the Fathers devised many other ways to produce ascetic meaning. Yet recent scholars rarely hint that "monastic exegesis" sometimes appears puzzlingly similar to "rabbinic exegesis,"[147] a point to be detailed further in chapter 5. The freedom with which ascetically minded Christian exegetes borrowed the repertoire of interpretive strategies from their non-Christian neighbors is significant.

In the sections that follow, I have developed my own vocabulary to name the various rhetorical strategies and principles of interpretation by which the church fathers wrest ascetic meaning from Biblical passages. My explication begins with techniques that adhere most closely to the text and moves to other exegetical and rhetorical strategies that entail more ingenious textual displacements. There is a corresponding movement

London: University of California Press, 1994), p. 33.

145 The Christian accusation that the Jews read "carnally" often appears to mean that they did not give a Christological interpretation to texts.

146 Paul M. Blowers offers a good example of how Origen himself can "outliteralize" the rabbis. Blowers concludes that "there was no shared, highly articulated language about the method of rendering texts. Such debates thrived on rhetorical strategies and *ad hoc* arguments." Blowers thus notes that Origen alternatively rejects the rabbis' allegorical exegesis as well as their "literal" interpretation, and for the same reason: "to undermine the entire Jewish claim to the authoritative interpretation of the Bible" ("Origen, the Rabbis, and the Bible: Toward a Picture of Judaism and Christianity in Third-Century Caesarea," in *Origen of Alexandria: His World and His Legacy*, ed. Charles Kannengiesser and William L. Petersen, Christianity and Judaism in Antiquity 1 [Notre Dame, Ind.: University of Notre Dame Press, 1988], pp. 111, 113).

147 Jacques Biarne, "La Bible dans la vie monastique," in *Le Monde latin antique et la Bible*, ed. Jacques Fontaine and Charles Pietri, Bible de Tous les Temps 2 (Paris: Beauschesne, 1985), pp. 426–27. Biarne notes (with examples from John Cassian) the attention to words, association of ideas and words, and verbal similarities as examples of the rabbinic-monastic connection. We might add that such attention probably reflects Cassian's (hidden) debt to Origen.

from techniques that aim to retain the worthiness of the Israelite past to those that either openly denigrate it or at least consign its usefulness to the dustbin of ancient history. How these two trajectories cross and recross will become evident in the discussion to follow. Upon occasion, I will refer to rhetorical modes by their proper classical names (if indeed they have such), but in general I have chosen to devise a modern nomenclature to describe how the Fathers make ascetic meaning.

CHAPTER FOUR

The Profits and Perils of Figurative Exegesis

I: Revising Traditional Categories

The traditional categories through which early Christian exegesis is often described—"literal," "typological," "allegorical"—are less helpful for analyzing "ascetic exegesis" than some scholars might imagine. Contrary to my own expectation, I have discovered that typology and allegory, however much they may dominate other types of patristic interpretation, were underutilized interpretive tools in the church fathers' production of ascetic meaning from Biblical texts. Other interpretive strategies, to be detailed in chapter 5, particularly intertextual exegesis, proved on the whole far more useful. In some cases figurative interpretation of any sort seemed unnecessary to ascetically inclined exegetes because the unadorned—but carefully chosen—text seemed "normative," that is, already, as it stood, full of spiritual or moral meaning.[1] Indeed, in other circumstances figurative interpretation actually threatened to permit a dangerous relaxation of renunciatory rigor that ascetic enthusiasts were loath to grant. Here, the link between interpretive practice and forms of life becomes explicit.[2]

Just as problematic is the assignment of "literal" exegesis to Antioch and "allegorical" exegesis to Alexandria. Much so-called literal interpretation seems "figurative" to scholars of our own day. In actual exegetical practice,

[1] James Samuel Preus, *From Shadow to Promise: Old Testament Interpretation from Augustine to the Young Luther* (Cambridge, Mass.: Harvard University Press, 1969), p. 14, writing of Augustine's exegesis.

[2] Gerald Bruns employs this Wittgenstinian term in his discussion of Midrash: "The Hermeneutics of Midrash," in *The Book and the Text: The Bible and Literary Theory*, ed. Regina Schwartz (Cambridge/Oxford: Basil Blackwell, 1990), p. 200. Also note the comment of Ithamar Gruenwald: "interpretation is one of the ways in which spiritual adjustments and changes of behavior are introduced into a Scripture-oriented culture" ("Midrash and the 'Midrashic Condition': Preliminary Considerations," in *The Midrashic Imagination: Jewish Exegesis, Thought, and History*, ed. Michael Fishbane [Albany: State University of New York

such categories shade into and conjoin each other in ways that ignore their alleged boundaries.[3] Let me first comment on allegedly "literal" interpretation, and then turn to allegory and typology.

Scholars increasingly concede that the "plain sense" of a Biblical text, often identified as the "literal sense," is, in effect, simply what a given religious community understands it to be. Nothing "in itself," the so-called plain sense appears to be a function of communal use,[4] and cannot, in any case, be equated with the meaning that Jewish readers of the early Common Era derived from their Scriptures. Brevard Childs claims that what has often been assumed as the "literal" sense of a text (the *peshat*) is more aptly described as "that familiar and traditional teaching of Scripture which was recognized by the community as authoritative."[5]

In particular, the association of a "literal" or "Jewish" approach in early Christian exegesis with the so-called school of Antioch calls for reexamination. The traditional assessment of Antiochene exegesis (e.g., that of Diodore of Tarsus and Theodore of Mopsuestia) has been critiqued and revised by scholars such as Christoph Schäublin. Antiochene writers, Schäublin argues, were no more grounded in a "Jewish" exegesis than their Alexandrian counterparts: they had "as good as no understanding of Hebrew."[6] Like their Alexandrian rivals such as Origen, Antiochene

---

Press, 1993], p. 14).

[3] For a fine example of the blurring of categories in Jewish exegesis, see Elliot R. Wolfson, "Beautiful Maiden without Eyes: *Peshat* and *Sod* in Zohairic Hermeneutics," in *The Midrashic Imagination*, ed. Fishbane, pp. 155–203. Wolfson intriguingly points out how Biblical interpretation in the *Zohar* (often considered the epitome of "spiritualized" Jewish exegesis) "can be characterized as a form of hyperliteralism, for the very words of Scripture are transformed into vehicles for God's self-revelation" (p. 167). On the inadequacy of the traditional categories in general, see Frances M. Young, *Biblical Exegesis and the Formation of Christian Culture* (Cambridge: Cambridge University Press, 1997), p. 2.

[4] Hans Frei, "The 'Literal Reading' of Biblical Narrative in the Christian Tradition: Does It Stretch or Will It Break?", in *The Bible and the Narrative Tradition*, ed. Frank McConnell (New York/Oxford: Oxford University Press, 1986), p. 68; Kathryn E. Tanner, "Theology and the Plain Sense," in *Scriptural Authority and Narrative Interpretation*, ed. Garrett Green (Philadelphia: Fortress, 1987), pp. 64, 66, 63.

[5] Brevard S. Childs, "The Sensus Literalis of Scripture: An Ancient and Modern Problem," in *Beiträge zur alttestamentlichen Theologie: Festschrift für Walther Zimmerli zum 70. Geburtstag*, ed. Herbert Donner, Robert Hanhart, and Rudolf Smend (Göttingen: Vandenhoeck & Ruprecht, 1977), p. 81, discussing the article of Raphael Loewe, "The 'Plain' Meaning of Scripture in Early Jewish Exegesis," in *Papers of the Institute of Jewish Studies London I* (Jerusalem: Magnes, 1964), pp. 140–85, esp. 176–82. For an outline of five kinds of "literal" reading, see Young, *Biblical Exegesis*, pp. 188–89.

[6] Christoph Schäublin, *Untersuchungen zu Methode und Herkunft der Antiochenischen Exegese*, Theophaneia 23 (Köln/Bonn: Peter Hanstein Verlag, 1974), pp. 28–29. For an explanation of the alleged "Jewishness" of Theodore of Mopsuestia, see Frances M. Young, *Virtuoso Theology: The Bible and Interpretation* (Cleveland: Pilgrim, 1993), p. 100: Theodore rejected a

commentators were trained in the standard Greco-Roman methods of grammatical, rhetorical, and literary interpretation. Also like the Alexandrians, the Antiochenes believed that there was a "higher" sense of Scripture, *theōria*, that constituted its true meaning, its "treasure."[7] For Antiochenes as well as for Alexandrians, the divine inspiration of the text in the last analysis rendered purely philological considerations unimportant.[8] Nor can *theōria* be associated exclusively with Antiochene exegetes, Henri de Lubac argued a half-century ago, since Alexandrian interpreters such as Didymus the Blind and Cyril of Alexandria also employ the term frequently. Scholars should not imagine that *theōria* carries any distinctively Biblical or Christian meaning, de Lubac adds: the word is, in fact, borrowed from the Platonic tradition.[9] Alexandrians and Antiochenes, it appears, shared much in their interpretive practice.

Thus the sharp distinction often drawn between Alexandrian and Antiochene exegesis, Karlfried Froehlich concludes, should be deemed a "construct," by which he appears to mean a fictive assumption. Froehlich reminds readers both that Origen did not "deny the historical referent of most texts," and that "the Antiochene theologians admitted a higher sense of Scripture" (*theōria*) whose aim, like that of allegory, was to lead readers to a spiritual truth. (Froehlich notes, for example, Theodore of Mopsuestia's equation of Paul's use of *allēgorein* [Gal. 4:24] with his own *theōria* as an acceptable employment of figuration— unlike the wild ravings of

Christological interpretation of the Old Testament because it reduced the novelty of the Christian Dispensation; his "literal" reading of the Old Testament was thus deemed "Jewish." Although noting that the difference between Antiochene and Alexandrian exegesis should not be exaggerated, Robert M. Grant in an early work nonetheless stresses that the Antiochenes had a closer relation to "Jewish" exegesis than did the Alexandrians (*The Letter and the Spirit* [London: SPCK, 1957], p. 105). The misrepresentation of the "school of Antioch" (as both "Jewish" and "literal") is exemplified in Susan A. Handelman's *The Slayers of Moses: The Emergence of Rabbinic Interpretation in Modern Literary Theory* (Albany: State University of New York Press, 1988), p. 99.

[7] Schäublin, *Untersuchungen*, pp. 34, 172, 28–29, 41.

[8] Ibid., p. 173. Note also Maurice Wiles' warning that the Antiochenes are not to be treated as if they were modern critical historians: "Theodore of Mopsuestia as Representative of the Antiochene School," in *The Cambridge History of the Bible*, vol. I, ed. P. R. Ackroyd and C. F. Evans (Cambridge: Cambridge University Press, 1970), p. 491.

[9] Henri de Lubac, " 'Typologie' et 'allégorisme,' " *Recherches de science religieuse* 34 (1947): 204, 206–7. De Lubac thus seeks to undo the distinction between an Alexandrian "allegory" and an Antiochene "*theōria*" made by older scholars, e.g., A. Vaccari, "La *theōria* nella scuola esegetica di Antiochia," *Biblica* 1 (1920), esp. pp. 11–13. De Lubac's monumental history of early and medieval Christian exegesis is *Exégèse médiévale: Les quatre sens de l'Ecriture*, Théologie 41 (Paris: Aubier, 1959). Another early attempt to find some points of contact between the two "schools" is Jacques Guillet's "Les Exégèses d'Alexandrie et d'Antioche: Conflit ou malentendu?", *Recherches de Science Religieuse* 34 (1947): 257–302.

the Origenists.)[10] Almost all ancient Christian exegetes, of whatever school, aimed to uncover the spiritual or moral lesson of a text, which for them *was* its true meaning. They would, I think, have been puzzled by claims of twentieth-century scholars that only through the historical-critical approach to the Bible can "truth" be ascertained.

How the blurring of these traditional distinctions plays out in patristic interpretation is well illustrated in two recent articles on Alexandrian and Antiochene exegesis by John O'Keefe. O'Keefe argues that an "emerging consensus of scholars suggests that the difference between Alexandria and Antioch cannot be explained by an appeal either to method or to historical awareness."[11] Labeling Antiochene exegesis as "historical" and Alexandrian as "unhistorical" is incorrect, in O'Keefe's view, since "there was no historical-criticism in antiquity, and neither school was interested in history." Thus he concludes that "there are sound reasons to question any sharp distinctions drawn between the exegetical methods of the two schools." Explicating Cyril of Alexandria's *Commentary on Isaiah*, O'Keefe argues that this Alexandrian exegete's methodology was "essentially identical to that of his Antiochene counterparts."[12]

Likewise, the traditional distinction between "typology" and "allegory" held by an older generation of scholars, both Catholic and Protestant, is largely unprofitable for the discussion of ascetic exegesis. An overview of the twentieth-century debate about these terms provides a keen sense of the religious investments of various scholars who engaged in the discussion. For Protestant Biblical scholars writing at midcentury, typology, which linked earlier people and events, often of the Old Testament, to later Christian "fulfillments," was deemed an approved exegetical method insofar as it allegedly emphasized the centrality of history; those readers endorsing the Bible's message as "salvation history"—a major theme of

[10] Karlfried Froehlich, *Biblical Interpretation in the Early Church* (Philadelphia: Fortress, 1984), pp. 20–21. See Theodore of Mopsuestia's *Comm. Gal.* 4:22–31 (Swete I:72–87; ET in Froehlich, *Biblical Interpretation*, pp. 99–101; cf. his translation of selections from Diodore of Tarsus, which also emphasize the goal of attaining to *theōria* and identify it with Paul's *allēgorein* [pp. 85–88]). Cf. Robert M. Grant, *A Short History of the Interpretation of the Bible*, rev. ed. (New York: Macmillan, 1963), p. 93, on *theōria*. For a reconstrual of Antiochene and Alexandrian exegeses as "rhetorical" and "philosophical," see Frances Young, "The Rhetorical Schools and Their Influence on Patristic Exegesis," in *The Making of Orthodoxy: Essays in Honour of Henry Chadwick*, ed. Rowan Williams (Cambridge: Cambridge University Press, 1989), p. 188. For Young, Antiochenes were interested in "the narrative logic of the text" (p. 195); Origen, however, is "the first philosophical exegete" (p. 196); and now, see Young, *Biblical Exegesis*, chap. 8.

[11] John J. O'Keefe, "Impassible Suffering? Divine Passion and Fifth-Century Christology," *Theological Studies* 58 (1997): 42.

[12] John J. O'Keefe, "Christianizing Malachi: Fifth-Century Insights from Cyril of Alexandria," *Vigiliae Christianae* 50 (1996): 138, 140.

scholarship influenced by a Protestant "Neo-orthodoxy"—could embrace the notion of typology while simultaneously faulting allegory for its supposedly non- or antihistorical stance.[13] Thus Christian commentators such as G. W. H. Lampe, confessing the "real correspondences" of the two Testaments, appealed to typology in order to secure the unity they desired.[14] For Catholic patristic scholars as well of the same era, such as Jean Daniélou, typology (which he claimed had its roots in a Palestinian exegesis) was appropriated as an "authentic prolongation of the literal sense," whereas allegorical interpretation was deemed a foreign import rooted in a "pagan" philosophical approach that discounted history.[15] For Daniélou, Clement of Alexandria, Origen, Ambrose, and Gregory of Nyssa were the chief culprits among the Fathers employing this antihistorical form of analysis.[16]

Already in 1947, responding to Daniélou's first essays that sharply distinguished allegory from typology, Henri de Lubac argued that the terms were "neither scriptural nor truly traditional," and that early Christian authors themselves did not differentiate them in the way that Daniélou had suggested. According to de Lubac, Origen's allegory stems directly from Paul, and, in any event, is basically equivalent to what Daniélou labels "typology."[17] Rather than accepting at face value the Antiochenes' pejorative description of allegory as arbitrary and unhistorical, de Lubac urges modern commentators to develop a new vocabulary that avoids the pitfalls of the misleading distinction between typology and allegory.[18] It is my

[13] See James Barr, *Old and New in Interpretation: A Study of the Two Testaments* (London: SCM, 1966), pp. 103–4, for a discussion of von Rad, Eichrodt, and Noth. Cf. also A. C. Charity, *Events and Their Afterlife: The Dialectics of Christian Typology in the Bible and Dante* (Cambridge: Cambridge University Press, 1966), pp. 161–62. It is of interest that Rudolph Bultmann avoided associating typology with a diachronic notion of historical development; he recognized that linking *Urzeit* to *Endzeit* entails a "cyclic" notion of history (Rudolph Bultmann, "Ursprung und Sinn der Typologie als hermeneutischer Methode," *Theologische Literaturzeitung* 75 [1950]: 205, 208). Northrop Frye still understands typology as "diachronic" (*The Great Code: The Bible and Literature* [New York/London: Harcourt Brace Jovanovich, 1981], p. 83).

[14] G. W. H. Lampe, "The Reasonableness of Typology," in *Essays on Typology*, ed. G. W. H. Lampe and K. J. Woollcombe (London: SCM, 1957), pp. 18, 23, 29.

[15] Jean Daniélou, *Sacramentum Futuri: Etudes sur les origines de la typologie biblique*, Etudes de théologie historique (Paris: Beauschesne, 1950), pp. 15–16, 52, 45, 48, 252.

[16] Ibid., pp. 45, 94.

[17] De Lubac, " 'Typologie,' " pp. 180–81, 185, 197, 200, 221. For a discussion of Origen's contribution to the development of the medieval principle of "the fourfold sense" of Scripture, see de Lubac, *Exégèse médièvale*, I:198–207.

[18] De Lubac, " 'Typologie,' " pp. 204, 208, 209–11. Elsewhere, de Lubac champions the phrase "spiritual sense": " 'Sens spirituel'," *Recherches de science religieuse* 36 (1949): 542–76. For an early appraisal of the midcentury debate on allegory, see Walter Burghardt, "On Early Christian Exege-

hope that this book will make some small contribution to the development of such a vocabulary and to a revised understanding of one aspect of patristic exegesis.

A second challenge to Daniélou's position was proffered by R. P. C. Hanson in *Allegory and Event* (1959), a study of Origen's exegesis. Hanson argues that patristic allegory was *not* derived (as Daniélou had assumed) from an Alexandrian milieu, whether "pagan" or Philonic, but from Palestine. The Dead Sea Scrolls stand as a case in point. Moreover, Hanson claims, typology slips over into allegory more readily than Daniélou had admitted.[19] Despite these caveats, Hanson attacks Origen's allegorical approach for erasing the particularity of history and underestimating the doctrinal significance for exegesis of the Incarnation, the Word become flesh.[20] According to Hanson, Origen's "spiritual sense" is "governed by nothing but Origen's [own] arbitrary fancy. . . . "[21] Perhaps Origen so frequently resorts to allegory, Hanson speculates, "simply because he will not recognize an ordinary metaphor when he sees one."[22]

Yet the texts by which Hanson argued that Christian allegory had its roots in Palestine, not Alexandria—namely, the Dead Sea Scrolls[23]—enabled Biblical scholar James Barr to unravel Daniélou's claims even further. Barr noted that allegory (not merely typology) was also used by Jewish exegetes and was not always "antihistorical." Moreover, allegory is found in the New Testament itself: Sarah and Hagar as the "two Jerusalems" in Galatians 4:22–26, and the "muzzled ox" of I Corinthians 9:9, stand as examples.[24] Not only do the Dead Sea Scrolls contain a "Jewish" form of allegory (as Hanson had allowed); together with some intertestamental books such as Jubilees, they also demonstrate the diversity of Jewish exegesis.[25] *Heilsgeschichte*, Barr pointedly concludes, demands that we examine the *history* of Biblical interpretation, not just reaffirm formulas about "the acts of God."[26]

In the same years in which these debates raged, scholars of ancient allegory such as Jean Pépin were further deconstructing the categories of typology and allegory. For Pépin, much of what earlier scholars had cham-

sis," *Theological Studies* 11 (1950): 78–116.

[19] R. P. C. Hanson, *Allegory and Event: A Study of the Sources and Significance of Origen's Interpretation of Scripture* (Richmond: John Knox; London: SCM, 1959), pp. 128, 125; cf. Young, *Virtuoso Theology*, p. 81. Note also Rolf Gögler's argument that for Origen, "allegory" and "typology" cannot be sharply separated: *Zur Theologie des biblischen Wortes bei Origenes* (Dusseldorf: Patmos-Verlag, 1963), pp. 361, 359.

[20] Hanson, *Allegory*, pp. 197, 283, 363, 282.

[21] Ibid., p. 257.

[22] Ibid., p. 246.

[23] Ibid., p. 125.

[24] Barr, *Old and New in Interpretation*, pp. 105, 109–10.

[25] Ibid., pp. 128–29; Hanson, *Allegory*, p. 125.

[26] Barr, *Old and New in Interpretation*, p. 147.

pioned as typology was in actuality a variety of allegory. Thus, Pépin argues, Paul's use of "types" constitutes allegory, as do the Synoptic Gospels' parables and the Fourth Gospel's appeal to the "figures" (*paroimia*) in which Jesus spoke.[27] Paul himself had used the verb *allēgorein* in Galatians 4:24, Pépin notes, and in I Corinthians 10 had provided readers with an allegory of the Exodus.[28] Pépin's massive study elaborates a detailed scheme of how various Christian authors used and critiqued "pagan" and Biblical allegory.[29] Here again, the sharp distinction between typology and allegory was eroded.

Other scholars as well have commented on the difficulty of distinguishing between typology and allegory for the early Christian period. Literary theorist Erich Auerbach, for example, notes that *typos* was a word foreign to the ears of many Latin church fathers, who preferred the more all-encompassing *figura*, as had their pagan predecessors Varro, Lucretius, Cicero, and Quintilian.[30] Henri Crouzel, the eminent scholar of Origen's exegesis, argues that the differentiation between allegory and typology is in fact a creation of "the 'diachronic' historians," and notes that there is "no trace" of this distinction in the writings of Origen.[31] Andrew Louth remarks on the Latin Fathers' seeming reticence to speak of "allegory" or "typology"—in fact, the word *typologia*, he claims, dates only to around 1840. Thus, for Louth, Daniélou's sharp distinction between the two styles of exegesis is also to be faulted on purely linguistic grounds.[32] And from a different perspective, contemporary literary scholar Jon Whitman stresses that the alleged typological movement from "shadows" to "reality" deconstructs itself: "Once the process of relegating one Scripture to the shadows begins, it is difficult to stop the shadows from spreading."[33]

Yet if scholars increasingly reject the sharp distinction between allegory and typology, they have not abandoned the notion of figurative interpreta-

[27] Jean Pépin, *Mythe et allégorie. Les origines grecques et les contestations judéo-chrétiennes*, 2nd ed. (Paris: Etudes Augustiniennes, 1976; 1st ed., 1958), pp. 250n.13bis, 256–57.

[28] Ibid., pp. 247, 250.

[29] For Pépin's scheme, see pp. 260–61 of *Mythe*; subsequent chapters detail the options he sets forth on these pages.

[30] Erich Auerbach, *Scenes from the Drama of European Literature*, Theory and History of Literature 9 (Minneapolis: University of Minnesota Press, 1984; German original of "Figura," 1944), pp. 48, 14, 16–17, 20–25.

[31] Henri Crouzel, "La Distinction de la 'typologie' et de 'l'allégorie,' " *Bulletin de Littérature Ecclésiastique* 65 (1964): 171–72.

[32] Andrew Louth, *Discerning the Mystery: An Essay on the Nature of Theology* (Oxford: Clarendon, 1983), p. 118. Appreciative of Louth's attempt to reinstate the good name of allegory is Frances Young, "Allegory and the Ethics of Reading," in *The Open Text: New Directions for Biblical Studies?*, ed. Francis Watson (London: SCM, 1993), pp. 103–20.

[33] Jon Whitman, *Allegory: The Dynamics of an Ancient and Medieval Technique* (Cambridge: Harvard University Press, 1987), p. 68.

tion, more generally understood: there is no doubt that figurative reading was deemed essential by early Christian exegetes. Present scholarly interest has rather shifted to examine the *functions* of figurative reading. For the Greeks, Pépin argues, allegory "redeemed" a mythology replete with tales of divine misbehavior.[34] Although different philosophical schools might disagree on the meaning of the particular terms of the allegory (as Pépin shows in extensive detail), all assumed that it should portend *something*;[35] figurative reading was necessary to make sense of obscure or problematic texts and to serve as "the antidote of scandal."[36] For Philo too, albeit from a different religious perspective, allegory rescued the sacred texts from impiety[37] and enabled a universalizing of the Bible's messages that rendered them applicable to persons living in different times and places than ancient Israel.[38] Although some critics have faulted Philo for his alleged "erasure" of history, for his reading of the Bible as "symbolic,"[39] others, such as Joel Fineman, point to the beneficial cultural service that allegory plays in healing the gap between the reader's present and "a disappearing past, which, without interpretation, would be otherwise irretrievable and foreclosed."[40] Although early Christian writers impugn "pagan" authors' use of allegory, they themselves had even greater recourse to it, for Christians claimed that since *their* texts constituted a divine revelation, not a merely human construction,[41] all Scripture must be rendered edifying.

David Dawson's *Allegorical Readers and Cultural Revision in Ancient Alexandria*, published in 1992, explicitly highlights the role that allegory

[34] Pépin, *Mythe*, p. 45.

[35] Pépin, *Mythe*, pt. 1, outlines the approaches of the various philosophical schools in extensive detail.

[36] Gerald L. Bruns, "The Problem of Figuration in Antiquity," in *Hermeneutics: Questions and Prospects*, ed. Gary Shapiro and Alan Sica (Amherst: University of Massachusetts Press, 1984), pp. 147–48.

[37] Pépin, *Mythe*, p. 234.

[38] Auerbach, *Scenes*, p. 52. On Philo's "departicularization" of the text, see James L. Kugel, "Two Introductions to Midrash," *Prooftexts* 3 (1983): 140. For Daniel Boyarin, allegorical interpretation reveals "a profound yearning for univocity, a univocity which is only guaranteed by the positing of a spiritual meaning for language prior to its expression in embodied speech" (*A Radical Jew: Paul and the Politics of Identity* [Berkeley/Los Angeles/London: University of California Press, 1994], p. 16).

[39] So Daniélou, *Sacramentum*, p. 252. Cf. C. K. Barrett's view that Philo "depotentiated" the Old Testament: "The Bible in the New Testament Period," in *The Church's Use of the Bible, Past and Present*, ed. D. E. Nineham (London: SPCK, 1963), p. 4. Against such assessments, it should be stressed that Philo believed that the Mosaic laws were to be literally observed, even if spiritually "read."

[40] Joel Fineman, "The Structure of Allegorical Desire," in *Allegory and Representation*, ed. Stephen J. Greenblatt, Selected Papers from the English Institute, 1979–80, New Series 5 (Baltimore/London: Johns Hopkins University Press, 1981), p. 29. See also Morton W. Bloomfield, "Allegory as Interpretation," *New Literary History* 3 (1971–72): 302 (allegory "conquers time").

[41] Pépin, *Mythe*, pp. 274, 405–32; cf. pp. 455–59 on Origen.

played in the "culture wars" of late antiquity. "The very tensions between literal and nonliteral readings that characterized ancient allegory," Dawson writes, "stemmed from efforts by readers to secure for themselves and their communities social and cultural identity, authority, and power."[42] Dawson brilliantly elaborates his argument: allegorical readings can "domesticate" earlier texts now found culturally shocking; or, alternatively, critique the dominant culture "by giving cultural classics deviant meanings"; or, further, allow Scripture "to absorb and reinterpret culture," thus bringing culture into the Scriptural text.[43] Situating themselves and their communities with respect to the larger society via texts, allegorists exercise power through setting "one text over other texts and the worldviews they represent."[44] That figurative interpretation can be considered a social practice (not a "mental operation") has also been underscored by other commentators,[45] who note, as does Dawson, allegory's usefulness in situations of cultural disruption or polemic.[46] Allegory is thus not so much an abstract interpretive "method" as it is a kind of "spiritual" reading practice. In Gerald Bruns' words, the term "spirituality" should here be considered "a hermeneutical rather than a textual category."[47]

If such are the revised construals of so-called literal, typological, and allegorical interpretation by contemporary scholars, what were the functions of figurative exegesis (whether typological or allegorical) for early Christian readers and writers? How might interpretations that to us appear to "speak other" than their historical contexts suggest be used by early Christian readers to advance their own religious agendas? What were the profits—and the perils—of figurative readings?

II: The Profits of Figurative Reading

The Fathers employ "spiritual," that is, figurative, readings of Scripture for a variety of reasons. In some circumstances figurative interpretations were usefully deployed to counter the "literal" citation by "heretics," Jews and (to a lesser extent) "pagans" of various Biblical passages to fault Christianity's embrace of Hebrew

[42] David Dawson, *Allegorical Readers and Cultural Revision in Ancient Alexandria* (Berkeley/Los Angeles/Oxford: University of California Press, 1992), p. 2.

[43] Ibid., p. 10.

[44] Ibid., pp. 236, 5.

[45] Bruns, "Problem," p. 164. Cf. Bruns' "The Hermeneutics of Midrash," p. 200: "Midrash is not method but form of life."

[46] Fineman, "Structure," p. 28; Deborah L. Madsen, *Rereading Allegory: A Narrative Approach to Genre* (New York: St. Martin's, 1994), p. 135. On the use of typology in situations of contemporary crisis, see Michael Fishbane, *Biblical Interpretation in Ancient Israel* (Oxford: Clarendon, 1985), pp. 412–13.

[47] Bruns, "Problem," p. 148, cf. pp. 151, 164.

Scripture.[48] Against these opponents, the Fathers develop figurative readings that permit the retention of the Old Testament—indeed, claim it as a Christian book—yet give appropriately "spiritualized" interpretations to verses that otherwise might be taken as immoral, impious, meaningless, or "carnal" (i.e., "Jewish"). For the church fathers, the allegedly "literal" reading by "heretics" and Jews fails to acknowledge the moral or spiritual dimensions of *all* Scripture and does so with nefarious intent.

According to the Fathers, "literal" readings of the Old Testament were set forth by "heretics" to mock the Christian retention of the Old Testament. Thus Origen, in a work not extant but quoted by Jerome, rues the fact that "Gnostics" in their polemic against Catholics derive much mileage from a "fleshly" interpretation of Scripture.[49] In *On First Principles*, Origen provides examples of passages on which such "literal" readings might focus, namely, that God is "jealous," visiting the sins of the fathers unto children of the third and fourth generations (Exod. 20:5), and that "does evil befall a city, unless the Lord has done it?" (Amos 3:6). Armed with such verses, "heretics" abandon the God of the Old Testament and proclaim a perfect deity not related to the Creator.[50] Origen in his *Homilies on Genesis* also notes that the "Gnostic" Apelles mocked the story of Noah's ark by calculating that the dimensions of the ark given in Genesis 6 would have accommodated only four elephants, not all the clean animals who allegedly entered "seven by seven" or the unclean ones, "two by two" (Gen. 7:2).[51]

Yet another subject that Marcionites took delight to ridicule was circumcision. Interpreting the passages on "spiritual circumcision" in Romans 2:25–29, Origen reports some of the disturbing questions Marcion raised on the basis of a "literal" reading: Is not the omnipotent God able

[48] Although we might imagine that the problem was rather the opposite—"Gnostic" overallegorization, and indeed the Fathers complain of this (see Irenaeus, *Adversus haereses*, and Origen, *Comm. Ioan.* 10.13; 10.14; 10.16; 10.19)—the Fathers must defend their own Scriptures against overly literal readings. For a brief but instructive list of examples of "Gnostic" allegorization, see R. P. C. Hanson, "Biblical Exegesis in the Early Church," in *The Cambridge History of the Bible*, ed. Ackroyd and Evans, I:416–17. The pagan Celsus faults the Old Testament on such points as its alleged borrowing (in Celsus' view) of the Flood story from that of Deucalion. Origen responds that Celsus did not even notice the genuine problems in the story, for example, the measurement of the ark in relation to the number of animals it is said to contain (*Contra Celsum* 4.41–42). For a discussion of pagan criticism of Christianity, with useful attention to the pagan critique of the Bible, see Robert L. Wilken, *The Christians as the Pagans Saw Them* (New Haven, Conn./London: Yale University Press, 1984); chap. 6 on Porphyry is particularly helpful for this subject.

[49] Origen, *Stromata* 10, cited in Jerome, *Comm. Gal.* III (5:13) (PL 26, 435).

[50] Origen, *De principiis* 4.2.1 (GCS 22, 307).

[51] Apelles, cited in Origen, *Hom. 2 Gen.* 2 (GCS 29, 27–28).

to leave the sign of his eternal covenant anywhere except on the "obscene members"? Can this be a good God who wounds infants at their first glimpse of the new light? Is it not superfluous for God to make a bodily part that he then demands be cut off? Such are the impieties of a "literal" reading for Marcion, Origen complains, "whom it pleases to interpret nothing allegorically."[52]

A few centuries later, the Manichean opponents of Augustine could appear just as "literalizing" and for the same reason, namely, to encourage Catholics to abandon the Old Testament as a sacred book. One Manichean critique centered on the unworthy depiction of God in some passages. Commenting on Genesis 1:26 (humans' creation in the "image of God"), Manicheans scoffingly inquired if God had nostrils, teeth, a beard, internal organs? And if pious Christians rejected such anthropomorphisms, Manicheans countered that humans were not then in God's "image."[53] Over against such calumnies, Augustine announced in *On Genesis Against the Manichees* that he would go beyond a literal exposition of the text to a "figurative and enigmatic" interpretation.[54] Augustine here provides an instructive example of the utility of figurative readings in rebutting Manicheans' mockery of the Bible as "literally" interpreted.

Among the other allegorical interpretations he propounds in *On Genesis Against the Manichees*,[55] Augustine explains that "reproduce and multiply" (Gen. 1:28) refers to a spiritual, not a physical, union, since carnal fecundity came into the world only after the Fall. Augustine does not even take the birds and fish to reproduce physically; he interprets the reference in Genesis 1:22 to their fruitfulness to mean that the Jews "multiplied" greatly after their dispersion among the Gentiles.[56] In fact, Augustine claims that Genesis 1 does not pertain to bodily creation at all, which rather occurred only in Genesis 2, but to the creation of the "causal reasons." The woman's bringing forth is thus understood spiritually as the couple's production of good works. And Augustine reads Genesis 3 to mean that "manly reason" should not succumb to (feminine) *cupiditas*.[57] Moreover, he takes the Old Latin translation of Luke 20:34 ("the children of *this* world procreate and are procreated"—implying that there is some other world where they do not) as a reference to "fallen" humanity.[58] Here,

[52] Origen, *Comm. Rom.* 2.9 (12–13) (2:25–27) (Hammond Bammel, pp. 168–69).

[53] Augustine, *De Gen. contra Manichaeos* 1.17.27 (PL 34, 186).

[54] Augustine, *De Gen. contra Manichaeos* 2.2.3 (PL 34, 197).

[55] E.g., Augustine, *De Gen. contra Manichaeos* 2.10.13–14; 2.21.32 (PL 34, 203–4, 212–13).

[56] Augustine, *De Gen. contra Manichaeos* 1.19.30; 1.23.39 (PL 34, 187, 191–92).

[57] Augustine, *De Gen. contra Manichaeos* 2.7.9; 2.11.15; 2.14.20–21 (PL 34, 200–201, 204, 206–7).

[58] Augustine, *De Gen. contra Manichaeos* 1.19.30 (PL 34, 187): "Filii enim saeculi hujus generant et generantur."

Augustine devises figurative readings of Genesis and other passages in an attempt to rescue the alleged "carnality" of the Biblical text from Manichean detractors.

Manichean opponents especially chose to fault the behavior of the patriarchs as gleaned from a "literal" reading of Genesis; their criticism, and Augustine's response, occupies a significant portion of Book 22 of his *Against Faustus*.[59] Other of Augustine's anti-Manichean writings also show his determination to counter the Manichean critique of Scripture's "carnality" via spiritualizing interpretations. Thus the Manichean Adimantus taunts Augustine by setting the pro-reproductive passages of the Old Testament (such as Ps. 128:3–4, the blessing on one's wife as a "fertile vine") against the recommendation to "become a eunuch for the Kingdom of Heaven" in Matthew 19:12. Such disparities, according to Adimantus, should lead Christians to reject the Old Testament. Augustine counters that the book of Psalms should be read as a "figure"; this passage, he claims, refers to the growth of the Church, Christ's "wife."[60] Later in his career, when he was no longer battling Manicheans, Augustine rejects such overly spiritualized readings of "reproduce and multiply" (Gen. 1:28) that appeal, for example, to the "multiplication of virtue in the soul" on the basis of Psalm 128:3.[61] In his earlier polemics against Manicheans, however, Augustine deployed figurative exegesis to great advantage.

Augustine's opponent Faustus appears as sharpest Manichean critic of Catholics' retention of the Old Testament. Why should Christians revere the Old Testament, Faustus inquires, if they observe very few of its laws? The Jews, he alleges, could easily name the multifarious ways in which Christians fail to keep the Law.[62] Augustine concedes that it is probably "useless" to dispute with Faustus over "figurative" versus "literal" interpretation—after having written thousands of lines doing just that![63]

Moreover, we infer from Augustine's writings that clever Manicheans could quote "spiritualizing" passages from the New Testament—the Christians' *own* Scripture—to support their critique of Catholic exegesis and practice. Thus, Manichean critics asked, why retain the Old Testament when I Corinthians 13:9–10 counsels that "the imperfect passes away when the perfect has come"?[64] Or why accept New Testament passages pertaining to Jesus' earthly ancestry (e.g., Rom. 1:3) when Paul tells us

[59] Augustine, *Contra Faustum* 22.23–64 (CSEL 25, 618–60). See below, chap. 5, for further discussion.

[60] Augustine, *Contra Adimantum* 23 (CSEL 25, 182).

[61] Augustine, *De civitate dei* 14.21 (CCL 48, 443), an exegesis Augustine himself considered ca. 401, when he composed *De bono coniugali* (2.2).

[62] Faustus in Augustine, *Contra Faustum* 4.1; 6.1; 18.3 (CSEL 25, 268, 284, 492).

[63] Augustine, *Contra Faustum* 22.95 (CSEL 25, 701–2).

[64] Felix in Augustine, *Contra Felicem* 1.9 (CSEL 25, 811).

to "know Christ after the flesh no more" (II Cor. 5:16)?[65] Manichean exegetes could thus *both* "outliteralize" *and* "outspiritualize" Catholic readings, as the occasion prompted. The malleability of exegetical technique is here precisely registered.

Figurative exegesis likewise proved profitable in the church fathers' written polemics against Judaism. When combating Jewish opponents—whether real or hypothetical—Catholic writers faced grave exegetical dilemmas, since Jews (unlike "heretics") could with good reason claim that since the Hebrew Scriptures were "theirs," they enjoyed the privilege of determining their interpretation.[66] Of course, Jewish interpreters experienced their own exegetical problems, since many passages for which Christians gave "figurative" readings concerned the Temple and levitical rituals that had no practical import for Jews after the destruction of the Temple in 70 C.E.[67] Yet, arguing against Christian exegetes, Jews could note that Jesus had not fulfilled many Scriptural prophecies and hence lost his claim to messiahship; he had not, for example, "proclaimed release to the captives" (Isa. 61:1) or "cut off the chariot from Ephraim and the horse from Jerusalem" (Zech. 9:10).[68]

Against Jewish critics, second-century Christian writers developed interpretive strategies that gave figurative readings to various aspects of Old Testament teaching (especially those pertaining to ritual practice) and thereby "saved the text." Thus the author of the *Epistle of Barnabas* manipulates a variety of interpretive devices to rescue the Old Testament for Christian appropriation. For one, "Barnabas" (as we may call the anonymous author) claims that the Old Testament provides its own corrective interpretation: the prophets themselves railed against the Hebrews' rites and sacrifices, thus showing that they, like the later Christians, advocated their abolition. Moreover, since some Hebrew practices such as circumcision were not in any event unique to the Jews and hence not "sacred," they can now safely be abandoned. Last, the dietary laws were meant to symbolize moral virtues and vices: the prohibition against pork suggests that we should not associate with people who resemble swine; that against eating hare, that we should not be "corrupters of boys."[69]

[65] Faustus in Augustine, *Contra Faustum* 11.1 (CSEL 25, 313).

[66] For a discussion of a late Midrash that warns against Gentiles who translate the Torah and then claim, "We are Israel," see Marc Hirshman, *A Rivalry of Genius: Jewish and Christian Biblical Interpretation in Late Antiquity*, trans. Batya Stein (Albany: State University of New York Press, 1996), pp. 14–18.

[67] For a brief discussion of how *halakha* needed to be spiritualized after its literal fulfillment became impossible, see Joseph Heinemann, "Profile of a Midrash: The Art of Composition in Leviticus Rabba," *Journal of the American Academy of Religion* 39 (1971): 141.

[68] Origen, *De principiis* 4.2.1 (GCS 22, 306).

[69] *Ep. Barnabae* 2.4–3.5; 9.6; 10.3; 10.6 (Funk I:40, 42, 44, 66, 68).

Likewise, the mid-second-century author Justin Martyr argues in his *Dialogue with Trypho* that all features of the Jewish ritual law pointed ahead to Christianity. Thus the Passover lamb is a "type" of Christ; the offering of fine flours, a "type" of the Eucharistic bread; the bells on the high priest's robe, "types" of the Apostles. Why were such laws given to the Jews to be celebrated physically? Because of their wickedness, Justin answers; fleshly circumcision was ordained to separate the Jews from other nations and to ensure their suffering for sins that were to culminate in their murder of Jesus. Dietary laws, Sabbath observances, sacrifices—all these were instituted for the hardness of the Jews' hearts, as punishment for their wickedness.[70] Just as "Barnabas" claimed that the covenant was "ours, not theirs" (i.e., that it belonged to the Christians, not to the Jews),[71] so Justin argues against Trypho that the Scriptures are "ours, not yours."[72] God's gift of prophecy has been stripped from the Jews and bestowed on the Christians.[73]

It was not only second-century church fathers, however, who employed such figurative readings to counter "Jewish" interpretation. Two-and-a-half centuries later, Augustine still resorts to such exegesis when explaining Old Testament ceremonies and rituals: the festivals were an earthly "type" of heavenly ones, the Sabbath observances were "shadows of things to come" (Col. 2:17), and the sacrifices were "types" of the blood of Christ.[74] Thus could meaning be derived from such texts for Christian readers.

So too with Hebrew purity regulations. Since according to Titus 1:15, nothing is "unclean" in itself, should not Old Testament laws about the clean and unclean—corpses, lepers, emissions—be left aside?[75] Indeed, other Old Testament passages could be cited to counter verses pertaining to "impurity": had not God declared in Genesis 1:31 that everything he had created was "very good"?[76] A third topic that required figurative han-

[70] Justin, *Dialogus cum Tryphone Judaeo* 40–42; 16; 20–22 (PG 6, 561, 564–65, 509, 512, 517, 520–21, 524–25).

[71] *Ep. Barnabae* 4.6–7 (Funk I:46).

[72] Justin, *Dialogus cum Tryphone Judaeo* 29 (PG 6, 537). For Justin's "bracketing" of the covenant (there were righteous people both before and after), see Hirshman, *A Rivalry of Genius*, pp. 36–37. "Ownership" of Scripture also provides Tertullian with some rhetorical ammunition against "heretics": "Indeed, Marcion, by what right do you chop down my forest? Who gave you, Valentinus, the permission to divert [the streams] from my fountain? By what power, Apelles, do you remove my landmarks?" (*De praesciptione haereticorum* 37.3 [CCL 1, 217–18]).

[73] Justin, *Dialogus cum Tryphone Judaeo* 82 (PG 6, 669, 672). A famous example of Justin's appropriation of Hebrew Scripture concerns Isa. 7:14, which Justin insists (over against Jewish denials) refers to the virgin birth of Jesus (*Dialogus* 43; 66 [PG 6, 568–69, 628–29]).

[74] Augustine, *Contra Faustum* 18.5; 18.6 (CSEL 25, 493, 494–95).

[75] John Chrysostom, *Hom. 3 Tit.* 3–4 (2:1) (PG 62, 680–81).

[76] Augustine, *Contra Faustum* 31.4 (CSEL 25, 759).

dling concerned the wives and concubines of the patriarchs. If we were to take these passages as literally relevant for present-day Christians, Tertullian remarks, we would be required to admit that "types" remain.[77] Origen and Augustine, also knowing that "heretics" had an interpretive heyday with the sexual behavior of the patriarchs, suggested that the patriarchs' women must be understood in a more "spiritual" manner:[78] here, assistance was derived from Galatians 4:22–26 that set Hagar and Sarah as figures for the earthly and the heavenly Jerusalems.[79] Thus figurative interpretations that rescued Old Testament texts from an embarrassing "carnality" were useful to Christian exegetes in certain debates against Jewish or "heretical" approaches to Scripture.

Moreover, figurative readings of the Old Testament proved essential even when Jews or "heretics" were not the object of polemic: Christians of an "orthodox" stripe might also be edified by figurative interpretation. Indeed, all of Christian history could be inferred from the ancient narratives via figurative interpretation. Thus, according to Hippolytus, the story of Susanna and the Elders teaches that the Church is beset by evil plots from both Jews and Gentiles. Why was this tale of "salvation history" set forth in the figure of Susanna, Hippolytus asks? He answers with a citation from Paul: it is an example for us, "upon whom the end of the ages has come" (I Cor. 10:11).[80] Figurative interpretation thus shows Christians how the Old Testament predicts the New.[81] Even stories that recount wicked deeds—for example, those pertaining to Lot, his wife, and his daughters—can serve as warnings,[82] just as other stories provide positive examples for emulation.[83] Even if no clear "moral" or "literal" message can be derived from a passage, Origen and Augustine argue, Christians should believe that God has inserted perplexing verses into Scripture to spur them to "higher" spiritual interpretation—or at the very least, to exercise their minds.[84]

[77] Tertullian, *De exhortatione castitatis* 6.1 (CCL 2, 1023); cf. the spiritualizing interpretation of Ambrose, *De Iacob* 2.5.25: the two marriages of Jacob represent "grace" and the "law."

[78] Origen, *Stromata* 10, cited in Jerome, *Comm. Gal.* III (5:13) (PL 26, 434–35); Augustine, *De bono viduitatis* 7.10 (CSEL 41, 314).

[79] Discussed in such works as Augustine, *Contra Faustum* 22.51; *Tract. Ioan.* 11.7–15; *ep.* 185.9 and 11; Ambrose, *Exp. Luc.* 3.28–29; (Anonymous), *De castitate* 15.2; Origen, *Hom. 39 Luc.* 4, among others.

[80] Hippolytus, *Comm. Dan.* 1.15; 1.16 (SC 14, 98, 100).

[81] Augustine, *Contra Faustum* 4.2; 12.7–8 (CSEL 25, 269, 335–37).

[82] Augustine, *Contra Faustum* 22.41; 22.60; 22.62; cf. 22.83 (CSEL 25, 634–35, 655, 656, 658, 685–86).

[83] Augustine, *De peccatorum meritis* 2.10.12 (CSEL 60, 83–84) (of Daniel, Noah, and Job).

[84] Augustine, *De Gen. contra Manichaeos* 2.1.1 (PL 34, 195); *Contra Faustum* 6.7 (CSEL 25, 294–95); Origen, *De principiis* 4.2.2 (GCS 22, 310). In *De doctrina Christiana* 2.6.7 (CCL 32, 35), Augustine argues that God puts some obscure things in

"Ordinary" Christians as well might find various Scriptural passages puzzling. Augustine concedes that the Bible is crammed with details that seem pointless. Why, for example, would Genesis 2:21–22 emphasize that woman was taken from man's side while he slept? Why was it necessary for "Moses" to add that the ram who would substitute for Isaac as a sacrifice had its horns caught in a bush (Gen. 22:13)?[85] Yet since there are no meaningless or useless passages in Scripture, Augustine argues, even details that strike us as capricious must signify something.[86] Likewise, Origen fears that "simple" Christians, taking Biblical verses as they stand, confess about God what we would not wish to entertain even of "the most barbarous and unrighteous of men."[87] What are believers to make of such Biblical expressions as "the face of God" (Gen. 4:16), or of the "irrational" and "impossible" aspects of the Mosaic law? The best approach, Origen counsels, is to acknowledge that although all of Scripture has a spiritual meaning, not all has a "bodily" sense.[88]

"Literal" readings might also lead the simple-minded to adopt absurd practices in their attempt to emulate Biblical teaching. John Cassian, for example, reports that a pair of monks accepted too literally Jesus' injunction to "take up your cross" (Luke 9:23; 14:27; Matt. 10:38). Staggering under their wooden crosses, they became objects of ridicule for their monastic colleagues. Some parts of Scripture, Cassian comments, require allegorical interpretation. "Literal" interpretation, on the other hand, is "grass for the cattle," that is, for simple people without perfect understanding—yet Cassian hastens to modify his elitist presumption by citing Psalm 36:6, that the Lord saves both "man and beast."[89]

Moreover, when pagan critics such as Celsus accused Christian exegetes of resorting to allegory because they were ashamed of the plain meaning of Biblical stories,[90] Christians could counterclaim that "spiritual" interpretation was justified both because there already are allegories "in" the Bible[91] and because figurative reading properly illumines mysterious, but essential, dimensions of the faith. In addition, allegory enables a "present-

Scripture to "subdue our pride" and "forestall our mind's feeling of satiety."

85 Augustine, *Contra Faustum* 12.38 (CSEL 25, 364–65). Although Augustine does not here identify what the "type" means, the standard interpretation identified the Church as the "woman" coming from Christ's (= the Second Adam's) side.

86 Augustine, *Contra Faustum* 22.96 (CSEL 25, 702–3).

87 Origen, *De principiis* 4.2.1 (GCS 22, 308). Robert Grant claims that when Origen speaks of a "literal" exegesis, he means "the interpretation placed on Scripture by the simplest of simple believers," who understand "poetry as prose": see *A Short History*, p. 85.

88 Origen, *De principiis* 4.3.1; 4.3.2; 4.3.5 (GCS 22, 324, 325–27, 330–31).

89 John Cassian, *Conlationes* 8.3 (SC 54, 13).

90 Celsus in Origen, *Contra Celsum* 4.48 (GCS 3, 329).

91 Origen, *Contra Celsum* 4.49 (GCS 3, 321–22); cf. Augustine, *Contra Faustum* 22.95 (CSEL 25, 701–2).

ist" reading that allows any Biblical text to be brought within the religious experience of the Christian believer.

Sanctioning this "presentist" interpretation was I Corinthians 10:11, in which Paul notes various sinful deeds recorded in the Old Testament and comments, "Now these things happened to them as a warning, but they were written down for our instruction, upon whom the end of the ages has come." This verse was frequently cited by early Christian authors as a warrant for interpreting Old Testament texts as speaking to the experience of contemporary Christians. Thus the author of the pseudo-Titus epistle notes that the law prescribing penalties for a "betrothed virgin" guilty of sexual intercourse with another man (Deut. 22:23–24) was meant "for us, upon whom the end of the ages has come"—but the woman is now construed as "a virgin betrothed to Christ" who breaks her vow by engaging in sexual relation with a mere mortal.[92] Origen also appeals to I Corinthians 10:11 to argue that the "types and shadows" of the Old Testament were in fact meant to signal the coming of Christian truth; the Old Testament is not "ancient history," but is meant for us, here and now.[93] Thus when Moses comes "to us" and is united with "our Ethiopian" (i.e., the Gentile church that is able to interpret spiritually), the Law ceases to exist as figures and images and shows forth the Christian revelation.[94] Origen sounds this theme repeatedly in his homilies directed to Christian lay congregations, and this repetition is, I think, no accident:[95] it was the means by which Origen could make the texts of Hebrew history relevant to present Christian experience. Whether one takes a more or less sympathetic view to the "presentizing" tendency of allegorical interpretation—whether one aligns oneself with R. P. C. Hanson, who disdains this feature of allegory,[96] or with Andrew Louth, who notes the necessity of such interpretation for contemporary Christians[97]—it nonetheless provided Origen with a means of "listening across a historical gulf," in Louth's phrase.[98]

[92] Ps.-Titus, *Ep.* (de Bruyne, p. 50).

[93] Origen, *Comm. Ioan.* 1.6.8 (GCS 10, 11); *Hom. 2 Ex.* 1 (GCS 29, 155).

[94] Origen, *Hom. 7 Num.* 2 (12:8) (GCS 30, 39). I thank Joseph W. Trigg for his helpful comments on the meaning of "our Ethiopian" (in Origen's *Commentary on the Song of Songs* [2:1] the Ethiopian wife stands for the Gentile Church; the Gentile Church, since the coming of Christ, is able to understand Moses "spiritually," as the Jews cannot).

[95] In addition to the above, see Origen, *Hom. 10 Gen.* 2; *Hom. 38 Luc.* 3; *Hom. 4 Ezech.* 5; *Hom. 6 Ezech.* 4 for this theme.

[96] Hanson, *Allegory and Event*, pp. 280, 283. Also see Hanson, "Biblical Exegesis," in *The Cambridge History of the Bible*, ed. Ackroyd and Evans, I:436–37 (Origen's allegory is declared to be "disastrous").

[97] Louth, *Discerning the Mystery*, esp. p. 96. For an earlier appreciation of this point, see Henry Chadwick, "The Bible and the Greek Fathers," in *The Church's Use of the Bible*, ed. Nineham, p. 38.

[98] Louth, *Discerning the Mystery*, p. 107.

There were, then, several ways in which figurative interpretations profited early Christian readers: it served as a refutation of heretics' mockery of the Old Testament, sanctioned Christians' appropriation of those books from the Jews, made sense of passages that otherwise might be deemed incoherent, and allowed all of Scripture to be brought within the present experience of the Christian believer. Figurative interpretation was not to be renounced.

III: Figuration and Ascetic Exegesis of the Old Testament

Would figurative interpretation likewise serve the cause of asceticism? Many familiar interpretations of Biblical texts, as well as a multitude of more obscure ones, indicate that in some circumstances it might. Especially for the project of "desexualizing" the Old Testament, figurative exegesis proved highly beneficial. Here, Christian interpretation of Song of Songs stands as a prominent case in point. According to many early Christian commentators, the lovers in that book were Christ and the Church, or Christ and the individual soul—or both. Especially notable treatments of the theme can be found in Origen's *Homilies* and *Commentary on the Song of Songs*, Gregory of Nyssa's *Commentary* on that book, Ambrose's *On Virginity*, and a host of other writings.[99] Ascetically inclined writers, who understood the Song of Songs to depict Jesus' relation with virgins, sometimes produced rather prurient interpretations, such as Jerome's exposition to Eustochium (citing Song of Songs 3:1) that Jesus will visit her on her bed at night.[100] As Patricia Cox Miller notes, this is a peculiar form of "de-sexualization" that simultaneously eroticizes the relationship of Christ and the virgin.[101] Some verses of the Song of Songs proved particularly ripe for ascetic reconstruction. Thus the "garden enclosed, fountain sealed" (Song of Songs 4:12–13) could be taken to apply to virgins in general[102] and the Virgin Mary

[99] For a survey of themes and authors, see Elizabeth A. Clark, "The Uses of the Song of Songs: Origen and the Later Latin Fathers," in idem, *Ascetic Piety and Women's Faith: Essays on Late Ancient Christianity* (Lewiston/Queenston: Edwin Mellen, 1986), pp. 386–427. For an excellent discussion of Gregory of Nyssa's asceticizing *Commentary on the Song of Songs*, see Verna E. F. Harrison, "Allegory and Asceticism in Gregory of Nyssa," *Semeia* 57 (1992): 113–30.

[100] Jerome, *ep.* 22.17; 22.25 (CSEL 54, 166, 178–80).

[101] See Patricia Cox Miller, "The Blazing Body: Ascetic Desire in Jerome's Letter to Eustochium," *Journal of Early Christian Studies* 1 (1993): 21–45.

[102] Jerome, *epp.* 22.25; 49(48).21; *Adversus Iovinianum* 1.31; Ambrose, *ep.* 63.36; *Exp. Luc.* 4.13; 7.128; *De institutione virginis* 9.58–62; 17.111; Methodius, *Symposium* 7.1; Athanasius, *ep. 2 ad virgines* (3). The womb's representation as a stoppered

in particular.[103] "Putting off her garment" (Song of Songs 5:2–3) might be seen as an ascetic injunction to "put off vices"[104] or to "put off" the "garment of skins" acquired by the first sin (Gen. 3:21).[105] And the fate of the beloved who went out to seek her lover—being beaten by the watchmen (Song of Songs 5:6–7)—serves as a warning to the virgin to remain at home in her protected seclusion.[106] Thus verses from the Song of Songs that our contemporaries take as sexually charged could be read by the church fathers as portending "something else," namely, counsel for the celibate.

Of the early Fathers, Origen was especially adept at turning passages pertaining to marriage and reproduction into messages bearing less "carnal" import. Thus Abraham's marriage at age 137 to Keturah was not prompted by the revivification of his sexual desire at an advanced age, Origen argues; rather, the story constitutes an allegory of the lifelong acquisition of wisdom. Passages in Deuteronomy (7:14; 25:5–10) that appear to curse the unmarried or the sterile man cannot, in Origen's view, be read literally, or "all the virgins of the Church would appear to be placed under a curse."[107] That Samuel's father had two wives (I Sam. 1:2) stands not as a description of Israelite polygamy, but rather suggests that plural virtues, in this case, "grace" and "conversion," can exist simultaneously in the soul; Christians can in fact have many (not just two!) wives in this manner.[108] A higher principle of interpretation demands that we not read "increase and multiply" (Gen. 1:28) literally, Origen insists. In this case, the Genesis injunction is corrected by Luke 1:80, "growing and becoming strong in spirit."[109] Nonetheless, Origen expresses some unease about where this "spiritualizing" process might lead. While it is a simple matter for Christian exegetes to locate "types" when interpreting (for example) the meaning of the tabernacle, some rashly claim that *all* the "marriage and begetting" passages of the Old Testament are to be taken as "types," yet when others inquire, "types of what?," they are unable to answer. Some Scriptural passages, Origen suggests, may have to remain "mysteries."[110]

Ascetically inclined writers other than Origen also employed figurative readings to "desexualize" various Old Testament passages. Thus Athanas-

---

jar doubtless facilitated this interpretation.

[103] Jerome, *ep.* 49(48).21 (CSEL 54, 386); Ambrose, *De institutione virginis* 17.111 (PL 16, 347).

[104] Ambrose, *Exp. Luc.* 8.44 (CCL 14, 313).

[105] Gregory of Nyssa, *Comm. in Cant.* 11 (Jaeger VI:327).

[106] Jerome, *epp.* 22.25 (CSEL 54, 179–80), 107.7 (CSEL 55, 298).

[107] Origen, *Hom. 11 Gen.* 1 (GCS 29, 101).

[108] Origen, *Hom. 11 Gen.* 2 (GCS 29, 102–3).

[109] Origen, *Hom. 11 Luc.* 1 (SC 87, 188).

[110] Origen, *De principiis* 4.2.2 (GCS 22, 309–10).

ius informs the virgins to whom he writes that Isaiah 26:17–18 (a woman crying out in childbirth as a metaphor for pouring forth prayer to God) indicates the bringing forth of "true and immortal thoughts."[111] A man who leaves his parents to become "one flesh" with a wife (Gen. 2:24) serves as a lesson in Christology: Christ leaves his Father in heaven to come to the world (John 16:28) and leaves his mother (the synagogue) to join with his wife, the Church, becoming "two in one" (Eph. 5:31).[112] Deuteronomy 25:5–10 on levirate marriage does not now, on an allegorical reading, counsel recoupling, but urges every preacher of the Gospel to "raise up seed" for his dead brother, Christ.[113] And Old Testament verses that command washing after an emission of semen (Lev. 15:16–18) do not speak to a physical condition, but rather foretell Christian regeneration.[114]

Indeed, so eager are the Fathers to "asceticize" the Old Testament that they sometimes locate figures of ascetic renunciation in its pages, an exegetical strategy to be considered more fully in chapter 5. A few brief examples will here suffice. The sterility of various Old Testament women is seen as a "type" pointing ahead to virginity in general,[115] and Mary's virginal conception in particular.[116] The blessing on eunuchs in Isaiah 56:4–5 is taken to pertain not to fleshly begetting or lack thereof—merely "the shadow and letter of the law," according to Cyril of Alexandria—but to Jesus' injunction to "become eunuchs for the sake of the Kingdom of Heaven" (Matt. 19:12).[117] And in chapter 7, the stories of Abraham and Old Testament passages that praise reproduction will be examined as among those that stood ready for a spiritualizing exegesis. The Old Testament could thus be understood as modifying its own "pro-reproductive" message, as "desexualizing" its own teaching.

IV: Figuration and Ascetic Exegesis of the New Testament

Yet it was not only the Old Testament that needed to be "denaturalized." Certain New Testament passages as well benefited from a figurative reading. For example, the thirtyfold,

[111] Athanasius, *ep. 1 ad virgines* (CSCO 150 = Scriptores Coptici 19, 74; ET, Brakke, p. 275).

[112] Augustine, *De Gen. adversus Manichaeos* 2.24.37 (PL 34, 215–16).

[113] Augustine, *Contra Faustum* 32.10 (CSEL 25, 768–69).

[114] Clement of Alexandria, *Stromata* 3.12.82–83 (GCS 52 [15], 234): the author of the Law and of the Gospel, being one and the same, does not self-contradict. Hence marriage is still lawful for Christians, Clement concludes.

[115] Augustine, *Contra Secundinum* 22 (CSEL 25, 939–40).

[116] Ambrose, *De Isaac* 1.1 (CSEL 32.1, 641); John Chrysostom, *Peccata fratrum non evulganda* 6–7 (PG 51, 359–60).

[117] Cyril of Alexandria, *Comm. Is.* 5.3 (56:4–5) (PG 70, 1244–45).

sixtyfold, and hundredfold harvest of the Parable of the Sower becomes a stock example in Jerome's assessment of the rewards due respectively to the married, the widowed, and the virgins.[118] Likewise, the separation of the sheep from the goats in Matthew 25 could be held to signal the division of ascetics from nonascetics.[119] I John 3:9 ("He who is born of God does not sin, because his seed [RSV: 'nature'] abides in him") is taken to encourage the preservation of bodily chastity.[120] When the referent of Matthew 15:11 ("It is not what goes into the mouth that defiles a man but what comes out of the mouth, this defiles a man") was displaced from the mouth to another bodily organ, the verse could be deemed relevant to the monastic discussion of the polluting or nonpolluting effects of nocturnal emissions.[121] Biblical injunctions to "be like doves" acquire a peculiar force in Athanasius' *Second Letter to Virgins*: doves do not remove their clothes to bathe.[122] Almost any Biblical passage, it appears, could with the help of figurative interpretation become grist for the ascetic exegesis mill.

The most notable passage to receive a "dephysicalizing" treatment is Matthew 19's discussion of "eunuchs." Here we can safely claim that a "spiritual" interpretation of the passage had in fact *become* the "literal" understanding of the text by the fourth century: the exhortation was construed minimally as counseling sexual restraint, or ideally as exhorting to virginal commitment. Here, figuration proved beneficial for the ascetic cause. The church fathers' inventive interpretation of "eunuchs" is highly instructive and warrants further elaboration.[123]

Interpretations that suggest Jesus in Matthew 19:12 was recommending actual castration were denounced by the "mainstream" Church, as the evidence of the canons of various church councils that prohibit physical castration suggests.[124] "Becoming a eunuch for the Kingdom of Heaven" is rather read as an injunction to sexual chastity: so Tertullian,[125]

[118] E.g., Jerome, *epp.* 49(48).2 (CSEL 54, 353–54); 123.8 (CSEL 56, 82).

[119] Pseudo-Titus *Ep.* (de Bruyne, p. 60).

[120] *Testamentum Orsiesii* 20 (Boon, p. 121).

[121] Athanasius, *ep. ad Amunem* (PG 26, 1172). That the genitals constituted a "lower mouth" is a common assumption in ancient Greek texts.

[122] Athanasius, *ep. 2 ad virgines* (Lebon, p. 179; ET, Brakke, p. 297); cf. Matt. 10:16.

[123] For an informative brief survey of the treatments of Matt. 19:12 in patristic exegesis, see Walter Bauer, "Matt. 19, 12 und die alten Christen," in *Aufsätze und Kleine Schriften*, ed. Georg Strecker (Tübingen: J. C. B. Mohr, 1967; original, 1914), pp. 253–62.

[124] Nicaea, canon 1; *Canones apostolorum* 22–24; Second Synod of Arles, canon 7. See discussion of the evidence in the unpublished Ph.D. dissertation of Gary R. Brower, *Ambivalent Bodies: Making Christian Eunuchs*, Duke University, 1996. Note also the story in Justin Martyr (*Apologia* 1.29) of the Christian youth who sought permission to be castrated, but upon being denied it, led a life of chastity nonetheless.

[125] Tertullian, *De cultu feminarum* 2.9; *Ad uxorem* 1.6; *De monogamia* 3.7.

Cyprian,[126] Jerome,[127] Ambrose,[128] Pelagius,[129] the Pelagian author of the *De castitate*,[130] Sulpicius Severus,[131] and Augustine,[132] on the Latin side. Among the Greek writers, a figurative reading is favored by Clement of Alexandria,[133] Origen,[134] Athanasius,[135] Basil of Ancyra,[136] Gregory of Nazianzus,[137] John Chrysostom,[138] and Cyril of Alexandria.[139] These writers agree that Jesus recommends chastity—not castration.

Whether sexual abstinence—"becoming a eunuch for the Kingdom of Heaven"—was advised for *all* Christians, however, was a matter of debate. While most Christian authors, with Augustine at the forefront, argue that Jesus' comment, "not all can receive it," shows that dedication to celibacy is a matter of grace, not of free will,[140] others stress that *any* Christian who tried could fulfill the exhortation; here, verses such as "ask and it shall be given" (Matt. 7:7) are brought to bear on the text of Matthew 19.[141] Other writers such as Clement of Alexandria who were more sympathetic to marriage insist that "becoming eunuchs," in the sense of celibacy, means a rejection only of second, not of first, marriage.[142]

So far do some church fathers depart from an understanding of "physical eunuchs" that they even interpret the second category, "eunuchs made by men," in ways that "dephysicalize" them. Thus, according to Basil of

[126] Cyprian, *De habitu virginum* 4 (CSEL 3.1, 190).

[127] Jerome, *Adversus Iovinianum* 1.7; 1.12; 1.36; *epp.* 22.19; 49(48).15; 55.3; *In Math.* 3 (Matt. 19:12).

[128] Ambrose, *De officiis* 2.6.27; *De viduis* 13.75; *De virginitate* 28–30; *ep.* 16; *Exhortatione virginitatis* 3.18.

[129] Pelagius, *Ad Demetriadem* 9.3; 10.1; (Anonymous), *De virginitate* 2; (Anonymous), *ep.* 2 (= *Ad adolescentem*).6

[130] (Anonymous), *De castitate* 8.2; 13.2; 17 (PLS 1, 1477, 1492, 1503).

[131] (Anonymous), *ep. de virginitate* (= *Ad Claudiam*) 2 (CSEL 1, 226).

[132] Augustine, *Contra Faustum* 16.22; *Contra Adimantum* 3.4; 3.23; *De doctrina Christiana* 3.17.25; *De continentia* 1.1; *De bono viduitatis* 9.12; *De gestis Pelagianorum* 13.29; *De nuptiis et concupiscentia* 1.16.18; *De gratia et libero arbitrio* 4.7; *De coniugiis adulterinis* 2.12.12; *De sancta virginitate* 1(1); 23(23); 24(24); *Contra Iulianum* 5.9.39; 5.16.66; *Confessiones* 2.2; 8.1; *epp.* 188; 3*.3.

[133] Clement of Alexandria, *Stromata* 3.6.50 (GCS 52 [15], 219).

[134] Origen, *Comm. Matt.* 14.25; *Comm. I Cor.* 7:25; *Comm. Rom.* 2.9 (12–13).

[135] Athanasius, *ep. 1 ad virgines* (CSCO 150 = Scriptores Coptici 19, 85–86; ET, Brakke, p. 282).

[136] Basil of Ancyra, *De virginitate* 55; 57 (Vaillant, pp. 65, 67, 69).

[137] Gregory of Nazianzus, *Or.* 37.20 (PG 36, 305).

[138] John Chrysostom, *Hom. 62 Matt.* 3; *Hom. 78 Matt.* 1; *Hom. 23 II Cor.* 8; *Hom. 36 Ioan.* 2; *De virginitate* 13.3; 41.5; *Adversus eos qui apud se habent subintroductas virgines* 5.

[139] Cyril of Alexandria, *Comm. Is.* 5.3 (56:4–5) (PG 70, 1245); *Comm. I Cor.* 7:8 (PG 74, 872–73).

[140] Augustine, *De continentia* 1.1; *De gestis Pelagianorum* 13.29; *De nuptis* 1.16.18; *Contra Iulianum* 5.9.39; 5.16.66; *ep.* 188.

[141] So Origen, *Comm. Matt.* 14.25 (GCS 40, 346); cf. John Chrysostom, *De virginitate* 41.6 (SC 125, 242).

[142] Clement of Alexandria, *Stromata* 3.6.50 (GCS 52 [15], 219).

Ancyra, "eunuchs made by men" can refer to those who are devoted to virginity by education and watchfulness, such as is illustrated by the virgin guarded by her father in I Corinthians 7:37 (on Basil's interpretation of that vexing verse). Those who are physical eunuchs "by accident" thus do not count in the ranks of the "real" eunuchs to whom Jesus refers.[143] Basil of Ancyra knows of such—in fact, his discussion of castration shows him to be more medically knowledgeable than many other church fathers[144]—but physical eunuchs are not, he claims, what Jesus here intends. Likewise for Gregory of Nazianzus, even the "eunuchs made by men" are not those actually castrated, but "those whom reason has cleansed by cutting them off from the passions."[145] Here, a "spiritual reading" of Matthew 19:10–12 "dephysicalizes" the second category of eunuchs as well as the third, those who become eunuchs "for the sake of the Kingdom of Heaven." Figurative reading in these cases drove the interpretation of the passage in a direction acceptable to church teaching.

Figurative interpretation might in this instance ("becoming eunuchs") promote ascetic exhortation, but was such universally the case? Did a spiritualized reading always promote rigorous renunciation?

V: The Perils of Figurative Interpretation for Ascetic Exegesis

Allegory was not, however, consistently deployed to strengthen ascetic argumentation; on the contrary, it was sometimes used to foster a less rigorous renunciation. Patristic writers who freely revert to figurative exegesis in other circumstances often disclaim it in controversies with less ascetically rigorous opponents. Several examples alert us to the nonutility, indeed the dangers, of figurative interpretation for the promotion of ascetic renunciation. Such is especially the case with the interpretation of New Testament passages that themselves counsel renunciation: here, figurative exegesis could easily be understood as weakening the ascetic rigor which such verses appear to counsel.

Augustine's *On the Work of Monks*, for example, reveals the perils that allegorical exegesis might pose. In this case, allegory opened too broad a way for those who had supposedly committed themselves to the "narrow gate" (Matt. 7:13–14) of ascetic renunciation. In *De opere monachorum*, Augustine responds to a query of Bishop Aurelius of Carthage, who was

[143] Basil of Ancyra, *De virginitate* 57–58 (Vaillant, pp. 67, 69) (citing Is. 56:4–5).

[144] Basil of Ancyra, *De virginitate* 61 (Vaillant, pp. 75, 77, 79), a discussion of castration, pre-pubertal and post-pubertal, and its effects on sexual desire and ability. Basil notes that there are eunuchs of this sort in the Church (62).

[145] Gregory of Nazianzus, *Or.* 37.20 (PG 36, 305).

troubled by a dispute among some monks in his community.[146] One faction had disdained physical labor, citing Jesus' words in Matthew 6 on the carefree habits of the birds of the air and the lilies of the field, who did not sow, reap, or spin, and yet were provisioned by God (Matt. 6:26–33).[147] These verses, they insisted, were to be read "literally." But II Thessalonians 3:10 ("if any one will not work, neither let him eat"), they argued, was to be understood figuratively, "work" referring to "spiritual labors." Why, they asked, should monks be burdened with "the cares and labors of workers"? Appropriate "spiritual labors" might consist of reading prayers, psalms, and hymns with Christians weary from their worldly toils, of providing "spiritual refreshment" through consolation and exhortation.[148]

Eager to prove that the contested texts were in agreement and to discourage monastic indolence, Augustine argues that Paul engaged in physical labor, although he was not obliged to do so. Paul's occupation, tentmaking, was not to be allegorized, as the monks were proposing ("spiritual tentmaking"). Nothing prevents the monks from singing and praying *while* they undertake physical labor, Augustine notes[149]—a time-honored ascetic practice. Augustine especially wishes to prevent those of the lower social classes from imagining that the monastery would provide a life of ease denied them in their formerly humble circumstances.[150] Yet Augustine simultaneously insists that Paul as an ordained minister of God had the right not to perform physical labor, a right that neither the unordained Thessalonians nor the monks of Carthage could justifiably claim.[151]

Simple denunciation and chastisement are not, however, Augustine's only techniques. Rather, he provides the recalcitrant monks with what he considers to be a truly "literal" reading of the Matthew 6 passage that endeavors to beat them at their own game. Here, a manifestly "literal" interpretation proves to be *more* ascetically rigorous than the monks' spiritualized interpretation of "work." First, Augustine posits, to be "like birds" the monks will have to eat their grain raw: no full storehouses, no grinding and cooking of grain into bread. Monkish "birds" who try to abscond with grain to cook will be admonished, "Put that back! Birds don't behave like this!" The monks will rather be required to flit about the pastures, plucking what they can on the wing. But watch out—they are more apt to be arrested as thieves than shooed away as starlings if the

[146] Augustine, *De opere monachorum* 1.1–2 (CSEL 41, 531–32).

[147] Augustine, *De opere monachorum* 1.2 (CSEL 41, 532–33).

[148] Augustine, *De opere monachorum* 1.2 (CSEL 41, 532–34).

[149] Augustine, *De opere monachorum* 3.4; 19.22; 17.20 (CSEL 41, 535–36, 567, 564).

[150] Augustine, *De opere monachorum* 22.25; 25.32 (CSEL 41, 570–71, 577–79).

[151] Augustine, *De opere monachorum* 3.4; 14.15; 21.24 (CSEL 41, 536–37, 556, 569–70).

guards catch them! Should they not ask God to provide them with wings, so that they can make a speedy exit, Augustine muses? Moreover, won't flying out to the fields every day (chilly in the dead of winter!) interfere with their lives of monastic seclusion?[152] Augustine's witty exegetical posture here demonstrates both that he can "outliteralize" the recalcitrant monks and that his "literal" exegesis entails a more ascetically demanding interpretation of the monastic life than does their more figurative one.

A further issue among these monks also concerned Bishop Aurelius. The monks were wearing their hair long, appealing to the tradition of the Old Testament Nazirites (e.g., Num. 6:5). (As "birds of the air," Augustine sarcastically remarks, they seem to fear being "plucked.") The monks argue that far from neglecting Paul's words in I Corinthians 11:4 enjoining short hair for men, they take them seriously. To Paul's claim that long hair on men is "degrading," the monks reply, "We accept this degradation and disgrace because of our sins." Here was a case, an exasperated Augustine rejoined, where monastic pride had cloaked itself in false humility.[153]

The monks, however, were skillful exegetes—and allegorists. Paul indeed forbade "men" to wear long hair, they grant, but as monks who have "castrated themselves for the sake of the Kingdom of Heaven" (Matt. 19:12), they are no longer "men." Augustine hotly refutes the monks' interpretation: they are still "men," even if they engage in nothing of a sexual nature. Paul's words in Galatians 3:27–28 on "no male and female" mean that we should free ourselves from carnal lusts, not that sexual differentiation has been abolished. By parading their behavior as a form of holiness, the monks confuse other Christians about the correct interpretation of Scripture; they place stumbling blocks in the way of the weak, "for whom Christ died."[154] Allegory, Augustine here insists, is not to be used to justify a lax or eccentric monastic lifestyle.

A second topic that furnished a fertile arena for the development of figurative exegesis, and about which ascetically inclined authors likewise worried, was wealth. Especially problematic was the assertion attributed to Jesus in his story of the Rich Young Man that it is "easier for a camel to go through the eye of a needle than for a rich man to enter the Kingdom of God" (Mark 10:25 = Matt. 19:24 = Luke 18:25). Clement of Alexandria's treatise, *Who Is the Rich Man Who Will Be Saved?*, signals an early interpretive intervention. Clement's proposed solution provides another classic example of how a "spiritualized" reading might encourage a *weakening* of the ascetic rigor demanded by a more "literal" exegesis.

[152] Augustine, *De opere monachorum* 23.27; 23.2; 23.29 (CSEL 41, 573–76).

[153] Augustine, *De opere monachorum* 31.39 (CSEL 41, 590–91).

[154] Augustine, *De opere monachorum* 32.40; 33.41 (CSEL 41, 591–95).

Clement had learned that when wealthy Christians heard this saying, they had despaired of their salvation; thinking that all was lost, they had thrown themselves into the enjoyment of the present world.[155] Their despair is groundless, Clement assures them, for Jesus was in truth urging humans to renounce the passions of the soul that render them excited and anxious about material possessions. Moreover, poverty itself does not ensure righteousness; there are plenty of unrighteous poor, just as there are unregenerate pagans who give away their goods to secure more leisure for themselves, or to win "empty fame" through their benevolence.[156] Wealth should be considered among the *adiaphora*, the indifferent things; as something "external," it cannot hurt us if treated rightly.[157] Thus a person with material wealth can be simultaneously "rich in virtue" and "poor in spirit."[158] According to Clement, what amazed Jesus' disciples was not the injunction to renounce possessions—they already had—but their uneasy realization that they had not entirely "renounced the passions."[159] If in the midst of wealth we turn away from its power, we, like the camel, can pass through the needle's eye. Besides, Clement hints, the word "camel" may have a higher figurative meaning, as is expounded in a treatise entitled "Exposition of First Principles and of Theology." Although Clement does not tell his readers what this "higher interpretation" is (and the treatise has not been identified with any extant work)[160] we may hypothesize that it represented an early attempt to allegorize the "camel" into something that could slide through the eye of a needle.

The fate of this famous passage provides an interesting excursus on how the "ascetic stakes" could be *lowered* via allegorical interpretation. Origen, Jerome, and the anonymous Pelagian author of the treatise *On Riches* provide three fascinating readings. Origen in his *Commentary on Matthew*—perhaps surprising to some—does *not* shun a "literal" interpre-

[155] Clement of Alexandria, *Quis dives salvetur* 2.2 (GCS 17, 160). Markgraf's "Clemens von Alexandrien als asketischer Schriftsteller in seiner Stellung zu den natürlichen Lebensgütern," *Zeitschrift für Kirchengeschichte* 22 (1901): 487–515, remains useful in signaling the contradictions in Clement between world-affirmation and world-denial. The most extensive (and best) discussion of Clement's *Quis dives salvetur* is L. William Countryman's *The Rich Christian in the Church of the Early Empire: Contradictions and Accommodations*, Texts and Studies in Religion 7 (New York/Toronto: Edwin Mellen, 1980).

[156] Clement, *Quis dives salvetur* 3.1; 11.1–4 (GCS 17, 161, 166–67).

[157] Clement, *Quis dives salvetur* 15.3–4 (GCS 17, 169).

[158] Clement, *Quis dives salvetur* 19.1; 17.4 (GCS 17, 171, 170).

[159] Clement, *Quis dives salvetur* 20.4–5 (GCS 17, 173).

[160] Clement, *Quis dives salvetur* 26.8 (GCS 17, 177). Stählin hypothesizes that this was supposed to be a section of the *Stromata*, but the extant books do not contain it. See Otto Stählin's translation in the *Bibliothek der Kirchenväter*, 2nd ser., vol. 17 (Münich: J. Kösel and F. Pustet, 1936), p. 40.

tation as his "highest" reading, for a "literal" reading here encourages greater ascetic rigor. According to Origen, those who believe that Jesus' saying is too "hard" in view of human weakness and who use allegory to escape its force should be shamed by examples from pagan history such as Crates donating his wealth to the Thebans. Moreover, Origen continues, the book of Acts attests that the early Christian community shared its possessions; the fate of Ananias and Sapphira (namely, death: [Acts 5:1–11]) supports a "hard" interpretation of Jesus' saying.[161] Unlike Clement, who thought that the Rich Young Man had not yet renounced his passions and was being urged by Jesus to do so, Origen claims that he had. Otherwise, how could he have been so close to perfection? According to Origen, we ought not revert to "tropology" (by which he here appears to mean "figurative reading") to ease our moral difficulty. Origen acknowledges that there are spiritualizing interpretations of the passage: "riches" might signify "abstinence from sin." But he is drawn back to the "plainer" reading: "perfection" entails the actual renunciation of wealth, not just of vice.[162]

In other expositions, however, Origen proffered interpretations of "camels" that were to have a long history in Christian exegesis. One he appears to borrow from Philo:[163] in Hebrew law (Lev. 11:4) the camel is pronounced "unclean." Moreover, Origen adds, since this beast is "bowed," "deformed," it is doubly disqualified to pass through the eye of the needle, the narrow gate. Yet with God "all is possible": it is above human power to make the camel, or the rich man, ease through, but who of us, Origen asks, can understand the great mystery of God and God's power? Certainly we cannot without a revelation![164]

Origen's depictions of camels as unclean and as crooked (also noted in his *Contra Celsum*)[165] spurred the imaginations of later commentators. Moreover, a fragment of Origen's treatment of Matthew preserved in a catena encourages yet another possible exegesis: *kamelos* means not only an animal, but also a rope used on machines for lifting weights.[166] This interpretive option, here undeveloped by Origen, would give new hope to eager interpreters seeking to reduce the rigor of Jesus' injunction.

[161] Origen, *Comm. in Matt.* 15.15 (PG 13, 1296). Hanson (*Allegory*, p. 238) notes that Origen refrains from allegorizing the story of the Rich Young Man in his *Commentary on Matthew*, but does not discuss this point in relation to Origen's renunciatory goals.

[162] Origen, *Comm. in Matt.* 15.16; 15.17; 15.18 (PG 13, 1300, 1301, 1304).

[163] Philo, *De agricultura* 131–35: "chewing the cud" means meditating on what one has learned; "dividing the hoof" means separating good aspects of memory from evil.

[164] Origen, *Comm. in Matt.* 15.20 (PG 13, 1309, 1312).

[165] Origen, *Contra Celsum* 6.16 (GCS 3, 86–87).

[166] *Origenes Mattäuserklärung* (GCS 41, Katenenfragmente 390, 166).

Jerome's *Commentary on Matthew* (dated to 398)[167] borrows heavily from Origen, repeating such points as the story of Crates' renunciation of his property.[168] But Jerome introduces a new intertext (Is. 60:6) that would spur yet another interpretation among later exegetes. Isaiah 60 describes a joyous future in which the Gentiles will stream to Jerusalem; verse 6 depicts the camels of Midian and Ephah (i.e., non-Jewish locales) entering the city bearing gifts and tributes. Although this intertext would provide later exegetes a good opening to relate the "camel" of Matthew 19:24 to the issue of Jewish and Gentile salvation, Jerome does not here seize the opportunity. Rather, he stresses that camels *are* bowed, distorted by the depravity of their sin—yet they are nonetheless able to enter the gates of Jerusalem. Does not this verse encourage Christians to think that when rich men "lay down the heavy pack of their sins and all their crookedness of body, they will be able to enter through the narrow gate, the narrow way, which leads to life?"[169]

The anonymous Pelagian author of the treatise *De divitiis* (*On Riches*), writing probably in the early fifth century,[170] reaped the fruits of these earlier exegeses. In a scathing denunciation of rich Christians, the author mocks their allegorical interpretation of the "camel," which enables them to feel secure of their salvation. The author's allegorizing opponents (whether real or imagined) pose two interpretive ploys to rescue the text. The first cites the meaning of *kamelos* as a "rope," which we noted in the fragment of Origen. To these opponents, a "rope" going through the eye of a needle seemed far more likely than did a camel—that is, the degree of impossibility attending the rich man's salvation has here been reduced. The Anonymous' reply is scathing: a "rope" doesn't pass through a nee-

[167] J. N. D. Kelly, *Jerome: His Life, Writings and Controversies* (New York: Harper & Row, 1975), p. 222.

[168] Jerome, *In Math.* 3 (19:28) (CCL 77, 172).

[169] Jerome, *In Math.* 3 (19:24) (CCL 77, 171–72). Jerome comments on the "wide gate" as *saeculi voluptates* and on the narrow gate as *labores et ieiunia* earlier in his *Matthew Commentary* 1(7:13–14) (CCL 77, 43). The remains of Origen's *Homilies on Isaiah* do not run as far as chap. 60, so we cannot tell what he might have said about "camels" there. In Eusebius of Caesarea's *Commentary on Isaiah*, which may have been known to Jerome, the "Gentile" (= barbarian) aspects of the geographical locations from which the camels came are stressed (Eusebius, *Comm. in Is.* 2.50 [Isa. 60:6]; GCS Eusebius Werke 9, 372–74). By the time the sixth-century Latin interpreter who furnished a translation/commentary on Origen's *Matthew Commentary* (from book 12.9 onward = the *Vetus Interpretatio* accompanying Origen's *Matthew Commentary* in PG 13), Jews and "the people" are contrasted in the discussion of the camel of Matt. 19:24; the rich are "the Jews" and the *gentes* are "the poor" (PG 13, 1313–14).

[170] Since "riches" was an issue that Pelagians in Sicily were allegedly stirring up (see Hilary of Syracuse's letter to Augustine [*ep.* 156 in the epistles of Augustine, dated to about 414]), it is quite likely that the author of *De divitiis* may have been writing in the first dozen years of the fifth century.

dle's eye any more readily than does a "camel." The allegorists may industriously scout through *lanificia* (wool-working shops), but they will not find any "thread" called a "camel" that will pass through a needle's eye.[171]

Undaunted by this exegetical defeat, the allegorists try again, seemingly taking their cue from Jerome's treatment of Isaiah 60:6: here, they claim, "camel" is another word for "Gentiles," who are degraded through vice. Yet because the Gentiles have "bowed" (like camels?) to Christ, they have an easier way into the Kingdom of Heaven than do the Jews. Now cast as the Rich Man in the parable, the Jews have a more difficult entry into that Kingdom.[172] On the allegorists' reading, Jesus' saying has become a parable signaling the salvation of the Gentiles.

Again, the author of *De divitiis* scoffs at his interlocutors' interpretation. Although in other passages he borrows from Jerome's exegesis,[173] here he mocks it. Why, the author asks, are "Gentiles" represented by "camels"? There is no place in Scripture where Gentiles are so identified. Nor should the Rich Man be associated with "Jews." If the allegorists claim that the Gentiles are figured by camels because the latter are "bowed down" with sin (Jerome's interpretation), they should recall their Scriptures better: the Jews were "bowed down" with sin as well. Besides—a distinctively Pelagian touch—camels are "bowed" by nature, not by sinful deeds, whereas humans are not depraved by nature but through their own free choice (*arbitrio voluntatis*). The author acknowledges that Jesus sometimes compares humans to animals (recall Herod Antipas as the "fox" in Luke 13:32), yet Jesus used such analogies to indicate a similarity of character, not a likeness of bodily form.[174]

The anonymous author of *On Riches* attacks the very principles of his opponents' exegetical practice. On most points pertaining to ritual and morality, the opponents, like other Christians, read the Old Testament passages allegorically and the New Testament injunctions literally. Yet on the issue of riches, they reverse what is to be taken "according to the letter" and what "according to the spirit": here, they rush to affirm the permissibility of Abraham, David, and Solomon's possession of riches, whereas they approach the New Testament's more difficult injunctions

[171] (Anonymous), *De divitiis* 18.2 (PLS 1, 1408).

[172] (Anonymous), *De divitiis* 18.7 (PLS 1, 1410).

[173] Especially if we accept the hypothesis that the author of *De divitiis* was also the author of *De castitate*, which follows the arguments of Jerome's *Adversus Iovinianum*, but sharpens them. The *De divitiis* contains several "Hieronymean" forms of argumentation, such as linking the desire for the riches possessed by Old Testament heroes to circumcision, polygamy, and the practice of the ritual law ([Anonymous], *De divitiis* 9.4; cf. Jerome, *Adversus Iovinianum* 1.19).

[174] (Anonymous), *De divitiis* 18.7–8 (PLS 1, 1410).

regarding the renunciation of wealth allegorically. This practice, shameful to say, makes the New Testament the "figure" of the Old[175]—surely an objectionable reading of Scripture for Christians. Of course, the Anonymous concedes, Jesus can use metaphorical language when speaking of wealth. For example, in the Parable of the Sower and its interpretation given in Mark 4, riches are likened to "thorns" which choke the good seed of the Word.[176] Here, however, the meaning of the metaphor points in the same rigorous direction as the explicit command to renounce:[177] allegory has not been used to render our duties "lighter." Thus the topics of monks' work and of riches were allegorized by some exegetes in order to *lessen* the demands of a rigorous asceticism.

We find similar examples in the case of sexual renunciation. It is of interest that several of the passages here to be discussed pertain to the eschatological preaching attributed to Jesus in the Synoptic Gospels. These passages suggest that, given the coming cataclysmic end of the world, it might be better for his followers to abstain from marriage and childbearing. That the church fathers were not anticipating an imminent arrival of the eschaton is one matter, but that even writers who often promote a rigorous ascetic interpretation do not use press these verses for their own renunciatory agendas is surprising.

One interesting example is furnished by the Fathers' exegesis of the saying attributed to Jesus in Luke 21:23: "Woe to those with child and who give suck in those days!" Even writers who elsewhere press an ascetic agenda, such as Ambrose, do not always capitalize on this verse for their cause. The eschatological context of the verse drops out completely, and a new historical context—that of the later Fathers' worry over Manicheanism and related heretical movements—replaces it. Thus Ambrose fears that someone might infer from this passage that "conception is a crime." How to rescue the text from this implication? By allegory. Ambrose gives a spiritualizing interpretation: some people may indeed "produce vices," such as those married people at the time of Noah who (according to Luke 17:27) were punished for their alleged sins by the Flood. Others may "conceive" of good deeds, but fail to produce them. The truly blessed, however, are those who "become fathers" through the Gospel and are "mothers" who bear Christ, who bring forth justice and wisdom. According to Jesus himself, when they "do the will of God," they are counted as his "mother and brothers" (Matt. 12:48, 50).[178] Here, an alle-

[175] (Anonymous), *De divitiis* 18.10 (PLS 1, 1411).

[176] Cf. Mark 4:3–20 and parallels.

[177] (Anonymous), *De divitiis* 19.1 (PLS 1, 1412).

[178] Ambrose, *Exp. Luc.* 10.22–25 (CCL 14, 352–53).

gorical reading of "childbearing" *reduces* the ascetic import of the verses: married people who "bear good deeds" are *not* those upon whom Jesus pronounces "woe." In an alternative interpretation, Ambrose has Jesus pronounce the "woe" on those souls which bring forth something "stillborn," not faith.[179] Even more surprising, Jerome, the ascetic enthusiast, can read the Matthean version of the passage (Matt. 24:19) in a similar manner: Jesus pronounces "woe" on those whose souls have not been brought to perfect manhood.[180] No implied critique of actual marriage and childbearing is derived by Ambrose or Jerome from Jesus' pronouncement.

Another passage whose ascetic force was blunted via allegorical readings was Luke 12:51–53, the predicted eschatological divisions within the household. For Origen, the passage stands as an allegory of the faithful and the unfaithful, not as testimony to the dangers of familial ties.[181] Ambrose, for his part, focuses on one aspect of the text, Luke's mention that it is "five" family members who are divided against each other. Ambrose's allegorical interpretation weakens the saying's ascetic force: the "one" house stands for the one person in his unity; "two" portends body against soul; "three" denotes the three parts of the soul; and "five" signals the five senses.[182] On this interpretation, no warning is delivered that families will be torn apart by the stern proclamation of the Kingdom's imminence—or that domestic arrangements might be a hindrance to the following of Jesus.

Jerome's opponent Jovinian provides another instructive use of New Testament passages that detracts from an ascetic interpretation. Jovinian and Jerome waged a battle over the ascetic or nonascetic import of the parables, *themselves* figurative in nature. In this case, *both* writers employ figurative readings—but Jovinian aims to mute the rigorously ascetic direction of Jerome's allegorizing. Whereas Jerome interprets the Parable of the Sower to differentiate among virgins, widows, and married Christians, Jovinian focuses his interpretation on the types of soil: there is good soil and bad soil, so good Christians and wicked ones.[183] Likewise, I Corinthi-

[179] Ambrose, *De Cain et Abel* 2.1.1 (CSEL 32.1, 378).

[180] Jerome, *In Math.* 4 (CCL 77, 227). That both Ambrose and Jerome appeal to this interpretation suggests a common source in Origen; unfortunately, the fragments of Origen's *Matthew Commentary* do not run as far as Matt. 24 (the Latin commentary on Origen's *Matthew Commentary* [on 24:19] suggests that Origen may have given such an interpretation to the verse [GCS 38, 86–88]). Jerome reads the verse in a more ascetic, that is, "negative," direction in *Adversus Helvidium* 21 (a critique of marriage and childbearing).

[181] Origen, *Hom. Luc.* Greek frag. 81 (SC 87, 536–38).

[182] Ambrose, *Exp. Luc.* 7.138–40 (CCL 14, 261–62).

[183] Jerome, *Adversus Iovinianum* 2.19; 2.26 (PL 23, 327–28, 337).

ans 15 (which notes the varied brightness of the heavenly bodies) signals nothing to Jovinian about the relative degrees of sexual chastity, but merely the division between "spiritual" and "carnal" people.[184] For Jovinian, the Parable of the Laborers of the Vineyard (Matt. 20: 1–16) teaches that the workers all receive the same reward—not (as Jerome holds) that they are to be differentiated on the basis of their varying degrees of sexual renunciation.[185] And last, Jovinian does not interpret the "many mansions" of the Father's house (John 14:2) to portend a differentiation of rewards in heaven on the basis of ascetic renunciation, as does Jerome, but to predict the many churches that are spread throughout the world.[186] Here we have an interesting instance of a battle over *which* figurative interpretation should be preferred—a battle waged over already figurative Biblical verses.

A final example of how allegory was deployed in order to weaken the ascetic force of Biblical passages is found in the treatise *On Adulterous Marriages* that Augustine wrote to Pollentius, presumably a cleric,[187] on the issue of remarriage after divorce.[188] As is well known, Augustine strongly opposed divorce, claiming that a sacramental bond linked the couple even if they produced no children, and even if one of the parties proved unfaithful.[189] Augustine appeals to the story in John 8 of Jesus forgiving the woman accused of adultery to argue that Christian husbands should take back adulterous wives. Since the husband presumably has some sins to his own account, Augustine avers, he should not cast stones at his erring wife if she is repentant.[190] Thus far, we are prepared to think that Augustine holds a "hard" antidivorce position.

Yet in a few of his treatises written perhaps twenty-five years earlier than *On Adulterous Marriages*, Augustine had suggested an allegorized treatment of some divorce passages that might, to other eyes, open a way for a "laxer" interpretation—indeed, an interpretation that Pollentius presses. In these treatises, Augustine had struggled to reconcile two of the New Testament divorce texts. Jesus in Matthew 19:9 allegedly permits divorce only on the grounds of the wife's *porneia* ("sexual immorality"), yet Paul

[184] Jerome, *Adversus Iovinianum* 2.20; 2.23 (PL 23, 328, 333–34).

[185] Jerome, *Adversus Iovinianum* 2.20; 2.32 (PL 23, 328–29, 344).

[186] Jerome, *Adversus Iovinianum* 2.28 (PL 23, 338–39).

[187] For Pollentius' status and arguments concerning it, see Henri Crouzel, *L'Eglise primitive face au divorce*, Théologie Historique 13 (Paris: Beauchesne, 1971), p. 337n. 52.

[188] A fuller discussion of Augustine's exegesis of various Scriptural texts pertaining to divorce is found in chap. 9, below.

[189] Augustine, *De bono coniugali* 7 (6–7); 15(17) (CSEL 41, 195–97, 209–10).

[190] Augustine, *De coniugiis adulterinis* 2.6.5; 2.7.6 (CSEL 41, 387–88). In the latter passage, Augustine adds the revealing note that some were removing the John 8 story from Scripture on the grounds that women would think they could sin with impunity.

in I Corinthians 7:15, not mentioning *porneia*, allows for divorce if an "unbelieving" partner in a marriage does not wish to stay with the "believing" spouse. Since Augustine claimed that all parts of Scripture are in harmony with each other, he denied that Jesus and Paul could disagree on this important moral point. Thus he seeks a solution that rests on a figurative exegesis: the "unbelief" (or "paganism") that Paul mentions as the reason for divorce in I Corinthians 7 is really a code for "fornication"; *porneia*, conversely, is an "all-embracing category" that includes "every sinful corruption."[191] Thus, according to Augustine, the grounds for divorce given by Jesus and Paul are the same.

Such allegorizing, however helpful for reconciling seemingly disparate Scriptural texts, might open the way to less rigorous understandings of Christian morality, as we can see in Pollentius' reading of these same passages. Pollentius' line of argument, as recounted in *On Adulterous Marriages*, enabled remarriage after divorce from an adulterous spouse—an allowance, assumed by Roman law, that Augustine now unequivocally rejects. Pollentius based his argument for the right to remarriage on an allegorical reading of I Corinthians 7:39 (cf. Rom. 7:2–3): if Paul allowed the remarriage of widows after their husbands had died, why should not the adulterous spouse also be thought of as "dead"? Cannot "dead" mean "spiritually dead" as well as "physically dead"?[192] Adultery, on Pollentius' reading, occasions a "spiritual death" that enables an actual remarriage for the "innocent" spouse.[193]

Augustine does indeed hold that the "unbelief" of which Paul speaks in I Corinthians 7 is actually "fornication in the spirit."[194] But such allegorizing, however much it helps Augustine in theory to harmonize Jesus' and Paul's words,[195] permits the laxer practice that Pollentius now indulges and Augustine rejects. Yet if paganism is "spiritual fornication" for Augustine, why should he not grant that adultery is "spiritual death"? The most cogent reason appears to be Augustine's ascetic commitment. There should be no divorce, and if possible, no remarriage for "real" widows—and how much more no remarriage for "allegorical" widows whose husbands have become "spiritually dead" through adultery. Augustine is ada-

[191] Augustine, *De diversis quaestionibus octoginta tribus* 83 (CCL 44A, 248); *De serm. Domini in monte* 1.16.43–45 (CCL 35, 47–52). These treatises are dated variously between the late 380s and the mid-390s. It is noteworthy that Augustine did not join the debate over asceticism and "ascetic" interpretations of Scripture until 401 and the years thereafter.

[192] Augustine, *De coniugiis adulterinis* 1.1.1; 1.7.7; 1.13.14; 2.2.2 (CSEL 41, 347–48, 353–54, 361–62, 383–84).

[193] Augustine, *De coniugiis adulterinis* 2.4.3 (CSEL 41, 385–86).

[194] Augustine, *De coniugiis adulterinis* 1.18.20 (CSEL 41, 367–68).

[195] Augustine, *De coniugiis adulterinis* 1.3.3; 1.5.5; 1.7.7 (CSEL 41, 350, 351–52, 353–54).

mant: Paul here means only physical death, not "spiritual" death, not the "death of fornication," not the "death of the soul."[196] On this point, Augustine's stronger ascetic commitment drives the interpretation of a passage so as to dismiss an allegory to which he otherwise might himself resort to harmonize these troubling texts.

These examples demonstrate that allegory's utility—so clear in other areas of early Christian interpretation, such as Christology—was less patent in asceticizing exegesis. Moral rigor, it appears, could often be better promoted through other interpretations that countenanced no allegorical "widening" of the narrow gate. To these other reading strategies that supported a more rigorous asceticism I now turn.

[196] Augustine, *De coniugiis adulterinis* 2.12.12; 2.4.4–2.5.4 (CSEL 41, 395–96, 384–87).

CHAPTER FIVE

Exegetical and Rhetorical Strategies for Ascetic Reading

In this chapter, I survey the various ways in which the church fathers produce ascetic meaning from Scriptural texts, especially those of the Old Testament. As will become evident, the degree of exegetical work needed to render these texts as messages of sexual renunciation varied considerably: in some cases, passages stood ready-to-hand for appropriation, while in others, textual displacement, or even textual violence, was necessary to extract an ascetic meaning. I here identify eleven modes of reading, some closely related, that were frequently used by ascetically inclined church fathers. Although these modes of reading often have recourse to figurative interpretations, I wish here to signal the more particular hermeneutical strategies that the Fathers employed to produce ascetic meaning.

I: The Ascetic Old Testament

Despite the Fathers' frequent denigration of Old Testament laws and customs as "carnal," some characters, narratives, and sayings could be directly appropriated by the more ascetically inclined to advance their renunciatory cause. Passages that seemed "ascetically correct" as they stood will first be explored, verses that could be put to good use by ascetic exegetes who wished to stress Old Testament prefigurings of sexual renunciation. On this line of argument, a *continuity* is seen to run between the two Testaments. For example, stories of the initial barrenness of Old Testament women could be taken to signal the preaching of continence in the new order. Thus, according to John Chrysostom and to Ambrose, the sterility of Sarah, Rebecca, and Rachel was part of God's providential design to corroborate the Christian's faith in Mary's virginal conception.[1]

[1] John Chrysostom, *Hom. 49 Gen.* 2 (PG 54, 445–46); *Peccata fratrum non evulganda* 6–7 (PG 51, 359–60); Ambrose, *De Isaac* 1.1 (PL 14, 527).

Of the Old Testament passages that ascetically inclined commentators could readily appropriate, one set lauded the barren or eunuchs in a manner agreeable to Christian exegetes. Deutero-Isaiah, for example, offered two passages that received much comment from ascetic exegetes. Isaiah 54:1 (" 'Sing, O barren one, who did not bear. . . . For the children of the desolate one will be more than the children of her that is married,' says the Lord") was deemed highly serviceable. Since this verse was quoted by Paul in Galatians 4:27 to buttress his allegory of the two Jerusalems, its further elaboration proved easy. According to Augustine, Sarah, the barren woman ("Jerusalem above") bears more "children" than "the Jerusalem below" who is in bondage.[2] Ambrose cites the verse to virgins and widows to encourage them in their continence.[3] Jerome, for his part, claims that Isaiah 54:1 describes the situation of his patron Paula's barren (and now dead) daughter Paulina, who might well "sing," for although Paulina had died without producing children, her religious fervor had nonetheless enabled her to bear a "spiritual offspring," her husband Pammachius.[4] For the anonymous Greek author of the *Historia Monachorum*, Isaiah 54:1 predicted how the (spiritual) children of desert solitaries would prove more numerous than those of married women, a prediction already being fulfilled in the entrance of Gentiles (i.e., "pagans") to the Church.[5]

Even more argumentative power could be garnered by ascetically inclined exegetes from Isaiah 56:3–5: "let not the eunuch say, 'Behold, I am a dry tree.' For thus says the Lord: 'To the eunuchs who keep my sabbaths, who choose the things that please me and hold fast my covenant, I will give in my house and within my walls a monument and a name better than sons and daughters; I will give them an everlasting name which shall not be cut off.' " For ascetically minded Fathers, these verses declared the values of the new Christian Dispensation, no longer dominated by sin.[6] But the verses could be given a more specific connotation by linking them to Matthew 19:12 ("becoming a eunuch for the Kingdom of Heaven"):[7] then Isaiah could be understood to refer to "spiritual," not "physical,"

[2] Augustine, *Contra duas epistolas Pelagianorum* 3.4.13 (CSEL 60, 501).

[3] Ambrose, *Exhortatio virginitatis* 7.42 (PL 16, 364); *De viduis* 3.15 (PL 16, 252).

[4] Jerome, *ep.* 66.4 (CSEL 54, 651–52). In his *Comm. Is.* (15.1 [CCL 73A, 599–601]), Jerome emphasizes the allegorical use of these verses in Gal. 4, rather than pressing a decisively ascetic message.

[5] (Anonymous), *Historia Monachorum* 8.19 (SubsHag 53, 54).

[6] Jerome, *ep.* 22.21 (CSEL 54, 171–72); John Cassian, *Conlationes* 22.6 (SC 64, 123–24), also citing verses from Rom. 6 that Christians are no longer under the Law (i.e., of marriage).

[7] Augustine, *Contra Adimantum* 3.4; *De sancta virginitate* 24.24; (Anonymous), *ep. de virginitate* (= *Ad Claudiam*) 2; Basil of Ancyra, *De virginitate* 57; Cyril of Alexandria, *Comm. I Cor.* 7:8; *Comm. Is.* 5.3 (56:4–5).

eunuchs,[8] that is, those who voluntarily abstained from sexual relations, as was the usual Christian understanding of Matthew 19:12. Thus Cyril of Alexandria cites this verse in arguing that the "promise" (Rom. 9:6–8) pertained not, as the ancient Hebrews had imagined, to the "children of Abraham" who were to number like the stars in the sky (Gen. 15:5), but to those who have become "eunuchs for the sake of the Kingdom of Heaven." God does not reject those who are "dry vines" according to the flesh, for works of the flesh are not worthy of praise. The eunuchs who "observe the sabbath" (Isa. 56:4) are not the Jews, who worshiped in a "shadow" and a "type," Cyril claims, but those of the Church who have taken Jesus' teaching on eunuchs to heart.[9]

Some ascetic writers such as Ambrose stressed the "reward" that Isaiah here predicts eunuchs will receive (Isa. 56:3–5)—a signal of ascetic "distinction."[10] For the author of the pseudo-Clementine letters on virginity, the reward for "eunuchs" is manifestly "better" than that to be received by the chaste married of Hebrews 13:4.[11] The anonymous Pelagian who composed the treatise *On Chastity* cites Isaiah 56:3–5 to argue that the desire for heirs is foolish for those who are supposedly "disinherited" from the world: "eunuchs" gain a better inheritance.[12] The author of the letter *To Claudia*, pondering the reward here promised, alludes to an unnamed intertext (John 14:2) to support his claim that all the dwelling places of the divine mansions will be unlocked for virgins.[13] When the Old Testament, like the New, is understood to "spiritualize" the category of eunuchs (i.e., to take Isa. 56:3–5 as referring not to the castrated or impotent, but to those who voluntarily renounced sexual activity in the name of a loftier religious goal), a *continuity* between the two Testaments could be claimed, a continuity useful for anti-Manichean polemic.[14]

In addition, certain Old Testament characters—those for whom there is no mention of "wives"—could be retrieved from Hebrew "carnality" to stand as exemplars of Christian asceticism: their (allegedly) virginal

[8] E.g., Augustine, *De sancta virginitate* 24.24 (CSEL 41, 258–59); Basil of Ancyra, *De virginitate* 60 (Vaillant, pp. 73, 75). Jerome (*Comm. Is.* 15 [56:3–5]; CCL 73A, 631–34), contrasts the physical eunuchs with the spiritual ones (= virgins) who "castrate themselves for the sake of the Kingdom of Heaven" (Matt. 19:12), e.g., the disciple John.

[9] Cyril of Alexandria, *Comm. Is.* 5.3 (56:4–5) (PG 70, 1241–45). For other treatments of this verse, see Ps.-Basil, *De virginitate* 4.58 (Amand de Mendietta/Moons, p. 51); Julius Cassianus, *Peri enkrateias*, cited in Clement of Alexandria, *Stromata* 3.13.91 (GCS 52 [15], 238).

[10] Ambrose, *De institutione virginis* 6.45 (PL 16, 331–32).

[11] Ps.-Clement, *ep. 1 de virginitate* 4 (Funk, pp. 6–7).

[12] (Anonymous), *De castitate* 17 (PLS 1, 1500).

[13] (Anonymous), *ep. de virginitate* (= *Ad Claudiam*) 2 (CSEL 1, 226–27).

[14] So Augustine, *Contra Adimantum* 3 (CSEL 25, 121–22); *Contra Faustum* 14.13 (CSEL 25, 414–15).

status, in this reading, enables them to perform their heroic and miraculous deeds. Thus Elijah's bodily ascent to heaven at the moment he was to die (II Kings 2:11) is credited by several Fathers to his virginity;[15] for the same reason, Elisha was granted power to raise the widow's son (II Kings 4:18–37).[16] Why was Joshua allowed to enter the Promised Land when Moses was not (Deut. 34:5)?, Jerome asks—and answers, because Joshua had neither wife nor children, whereas Moses did.[17] That Jeremiah was commanded "not to take a wife in this place" (Jer. 16:2) was likewise understood to counsel a lifelong abstinence.[18] The story of Daniel furnishes still more examples: Daniel's three companions are taken to be eunuchs,[19] while Daniel himself is described either as a eunuch or a virgin.[20] Such "messages" could be brought into easy alignment with that of I Corinthians 7.[21]

Another set of verses that stood ready for the ascetic commentator to mine was Genesis 3:16–18, the "woes" placed upon woman for the first sin and the "thorns and thistles" that are predicted to attend earthly life "after the Fall." For ascetic exegetes, these verses do not constitute an etiology explaining various features of human life or the domestic customs of ancient Israel, but warn Christian women against marriage: pain in childbirth and domination by a husband are the "thorns" that virgins and widows are able to avoid. Many church fathers assure their readers that the curse on women in Genesis 3:16 will not be the lot of the celibate.[22]

[15] Ambrose, *De virginibus* 1.3.12; Jerome, *Comm. Zech.* 3 (10:8–10); *ep.* 22.21; (Anonymous), *Ev. Ps.-Matt.* 7; Athanasius, *ep. 1 ad virgines* (1, 7); cf. John Cassian, *Institutiones* 6.4.1; *Conlationes* 21.4.

[16] Jerome, *ep.* 22.21; *Comm. Zech.* 3 (10:8–10); *Adversus Iovinianum* 1.26; Athanasius, *ep. 1 ad virgines* (1, 7); John Cassian, *Institutiones* 6.4.1. According to the Anonymous version of the *Apophthegmata patrum* 232, it is the woman who, having had no sexual relation with men, is the enabling person.

[17] Jerome, *Adversus Iovinianum* 1.22 (PL 23, 251–52).

[18] Jerome, *Adversus Iovinianum* 1.33 (Jeremiah was a virgin); *ep.* 22.21; *Comm. Zech.* 3 (10:8–10); Ps.-Basil, *De virginitate* 4.59; Evagrius Ponticus, *Rerum monachalium rationes* 1–2. For Jeremiah's celibacy as "prefiguring" the New Testament recommendation, see Lucien Legrand, *La Virginité dans la Bible*, Lectio Divina 39 (Paris: Les Editions du Cerf, 1964), pp. 16–17, 22–25.

[19] Jerome, *Adversus Iovinianum* 1.25 (PL 23, 255).

[20] Origen, *Hom. 4 Ezech.* 5; 8 (SC 352, 174, 184); cf. Ezek. 14:14, 18; Ambrose, *De virginibus* 2.4.27 (PL 16, 225); cf. Augustine, *De peccatorum meritis* 2.10.12 (CSEL 60, 83): Daniel is a type of "continence." Ambrose's *De virginibus* appears to be based on Athanasius' *Letter to Virgins* (L. Th. Lefort, "Athanase, Ambroise et Chenoute: 'Sur la virginité,' " *Le Muséon* 48 [1935]: 55–73); for a modification, see Yves-Marie Duval, "La Problématique de la *Lettre au Vièrges* d'Athanase," *Le Muséon* 88 (1975): 405–33.

[21] Jerome, *ep.* 22.21 (CSEL 54, 172).

[22] Jerome, *ep.* 22.18–19; Ambrose, *De viduis* 13.81; Cyprian, *De habitu virginum* 22; *Ad Quirinum* 3.32; Methodius, *Symposium* 10.6; Ps.-Basil, *De virginitate* 3.46–47; Basil of Ancyra, *De virginitate*; Eusebius of Emesa, *Hom.* 6.5; 7.18; John Chrysostom, *Quod regulares feminae viris*

Although Eve's fate, and that of married woman after her, is symbolized by the "brambles," virgins will rather enjoy the "lilies" among which their Bridegroom (Christ) feeds, according to Song of Songs 2:16.[23] The escape from a husband's domination is often noted as a benefit of virginity that is here allegedly recommended,[24] as is avoiding the pain of childbirth.[25] No allegorization is needed to rescue such verses for the service of Christian asceticism. They were passages, in the Fathers' estimation, that already "spoke" Christian truth.

Yet still other passages were construed to mean that the Old Testament—like Christian ascetics—praised the renunciation of home, property, and children. Unlike the argument from the "difference in times," these readings were useful to signal the *continuity* between the two Testaments, both of which are here understood to counsel renunciation. Four Old Testament passages in particular are so read by ascetically inclined exegetes: Genesis 12:1 (Abraham's leaving homeland and kindred); Genesis 22:1–14 (Abraham's near-sacrifice of Isaac);[26] Deuteronomy 33:9 and Numbers 26:62 (the Levites' separation from relatives and property); and Psalm 45:10–11 ("Hear, O daughter, consider, and incline your ear; forget your people and your father's house; and the king will desire your beauty").

Abraham's abandoning of his homeland (Gen. 12:1) was a theme that, Jerome believed, offered counsel to Christian ascetics. Thus he encourages Eustochium to follow Abraham's example in departing his native land to dwell in "the land of the living" (cf. Ps. 27:13), associated by Jerome with the "land" of ascetic renunciation.[27] Likewise, he urges Paula after her daughter Blesilla's death to leave her country and kin, like Abraham.[28] According to Jerome, Abraham in forsaking his relatives was "the first to receive a promise of Christ."[29] Jerome also counsels a young Gallic monk, Rusticus, that if he wishes to be "perfect" (cf. Matt. 19:21), he should imitate the example of Abraham who deserted his country to obey

cohabitare non debeant 11; John Chrysostom(?), *De S. Thecla*.

[23] Jerome, *ep*. 130.8 (CSEL 56, 187); cf. *ep*. 22.3 (CSEL 54, 146).

[24] Cyprian, *De habitu virginum* 22 (CSEL 3.1, 203).

[25] E.g., John Chrysostom, *De virginitate* 65 (SC 125, 332); Ps.-Basil, *De virginitate* 3.46–47 (Amand de Mendietta/Moons, pp. 45, 47).

[26] Philo interprets Gen. 12:1–3 to mean that we, like Abraham, should leave the body, sense perception, and speech, that we should "depart" "from the pleasures and desires of the body" (*De migratione Abrahami* 1.2; 2.9). Likewise, Abraham's willingness to sacrifice Isaac indicates to Philo that the patriarch overcame the bond of kinship (*De Abrahamo* 32.170). Philo does not, however, make an explicit point regarding *sexual* renunciation. I thank Halvor Moxnes for encouraging me to pursue these Philonic parallels.

[27] Jerome, *ep*. 22.1 (CSEL 54, 172).

[28] Jerome, *ep*. 39.5 (CSEL 54, 304); she did, journeying to Palestine and settling there next to Jerome.

[29] Jerome, *ep*. 46.2 (CSEL 54, 330).

God's will.[30] Cassian, too, cites this verse to would-be monks: they should leave their former lives and possessions.[31]

Abraham's near-sacrifice of Isaac provided another useful narrative for ascetically inclined exegetes. Although Pelagius, Cassian, and Augustine all argue that if Abraham's deed had been undertaken on his own initiative, or if it were attempted today, it would be deemed either a temptation of the devil or a sign of madness,[32] the narrative could nonetheless be tamed to ascetic advantage. Aside from a Christological reading of the tale (Abraham's near-sacrifice of Isaac prepares us for God's act in offering *his* Son),[33] its susceptibility to ascetic interpretation made it a favorite for patristic writers who urged renunciation. Thus according to Ambrose, Abraham knew that "his son would be more acceptable to God when sacrificed than when whole"—and Christians, too, should be prepared for familial "sacrifice."[34] The (Pelagian?) author of the treatise *On Chastity* rebukes his Christian audience by means of this narrative: *they* worry about the world's continuation, while Abraham stood ready to sacrifice his son.[35] For Augustine, Abraham's near-sacrifice, understood as a renunciation of family ties, shows a devotion to the Kingdom of Heaven that Christians should emulate.[36] Appealing to this passage, Jerome urges Paula not to mourn excessively the death of her daughter Blesilla, since Abraham was willing to renounce *his* child.[37]

Others, such as Basil of Caesarea, however, could argue that Abraham's renunciation was not yet perfect, for although he had been ready to give his son, he had not yet given his riches.[38] And according to John Chrysostom, Hannah, the mother of Samuel, outstripped Abraham in virtue because she offered her child to God even *before* she was asked.[39] Despite such caveats, Abraham customarily served as an inspiring example of familial renunciation. His offering of Isaac was taken as encouragement for parents to offer *their* sons and daughters—in virginity.[40] And although few Christians would attempt to emulate Abraham by throwing their children onto

[30] Jerome, *ep.* 125.20 (CSEL 56, 142).

[31] John Cassian, *Conlationes* 3.6 (SC 42, 145).

[32] John Cassian, *Conlationes* 2.7 (SC 42, 118–19); (Anonymous), *De divina lege* 5.2 (PL 30, 110); Augustine, *Contra Faustum* 22.73 (CSEL 25, 670–71).

[33] John Chrysostom, *Hom. 25 Heb.* 2 (PG 63, 174).

[34] Ambrose, *De excessu fratris* 2.97 (CSEL 73, 302–3).

[35] (Anonymous), *De castitate* 13.5 (PLS 1, 1493).

[36] Augustine, *De bono coniugali* 20.24 (CSEL 41, 218).

[37] Jerome, *ep.* 39.6 (CSEL 54, 306).

[38] Basil of Caesarea, *Serm. de renunciatione saeculi* 1 (PG 31, 628).

[39] John Chrysostom, *Hom. 24 Eph.* 3 (PG 62, 173).

[40] Ps.-Basil, *De virginitate* 5.61–62 (Amand de Mendietta/Moons, p. 53); Eusebius of Emesa, *Hom. 7.* 25 (Buytaert I:192). For a similar offering of children to martyrdom, see Eusebius of Emesa, *Hom. 6.*29 (Buytaert I:171–72), recounting the story of Domnina and her daughters.

the fire, as did one monk eager to prove his ascetic commitment,[41] the story could be beneficially repeated to promote unfamilial values.

Two Old Testament passages pertaining to the Levites also were read to encourage ascetic interpretation, the verses declaring that the Levites had received no inheritance of land (Num. 26:62) and those that recount the blessing on Levi, who is said to renounce parents, brothers, and children (Deut. 33:9). Origen appears to have been the first church father to contrast the levitical order ("standing in" for Jesus) with the more "carnal" regulations of Moses, which do not enjoin renunciation: since Moses did not advocate the renunciation of possessions or relatives, his office is only a "shadow" of that of the Levites, who portend the more rigorous Christian ascetic divestment.[42]

Ambrose's reflection on the Levites in his *Exhortation to Virginity* is especially noteworthy. Pondering what Deuteronomy 33:8 ("I will give truth to Levi") might mean, Ambrose decides that the "truth" Levi was to receive portends "inviolate virginity," the condition into which we are born, not that to which we bind ourselves in cohabitation (*contubernium*). That the Levites received no land, moreover, suggests that they were not "earthly" but had their reward "above"—in contrast to most Jews, greedy for land and possessions, from which they reap only the "thorns and thistles" (Gen. 3:18) of anxieties. The lot of Christians, Ambrose advises, should be cast with Levi; their portion (i.e., their inheritance from Christ) is virginity and widowhood. Thus it is the continent, not the wife, who can say, "My portion is with the Lord" (Ps. 73:26). Moreover, Ambrose notes, it was only when the Levites disavowed their relatives that "truth" was given to them (Deut. 33:8–9), the "truth" of *integritas* (virginity, for Ambrose). The Levites' words to father and mother—"I know you not" (Deut. 33:9)—supply a worthy motto for Christian renunciants called to leave their parents (Matt. 4:21, 22).[43] In Ambrose's hands, the Levites signal a divestment that Christians are advised to emulate.

A final Old Testament example by which Christian ascetics encouraged young women[44] (and occasionally young men)[45] to "forsake their fathers' house" was Psalm 45:10–11. These verses constitute the opening salvo of Jerome's treatise to Eustochium concerning her virginal vow, and this

[41] *Apophthegmata Patrum* (Anonymous) (= *Verba Seniorum* 5) 14; 18 (PL 73, 952): the fire becomes "like dew."

[42] Origen, *Hom. 17 Jesu Nave* 2 (SC 71, 376); cf. Jerome, *Contra Ioannis Hierosolymitanis* 8 (PL 23, 378).

[43] Ambrose, *Exhortatio virginitatis* 6.35; 6.37; 6.39; 6.40–41; 7.44; 5.32 (PL 16, 361, 362, 363, 364, 360).

[44] Ambrose, *De institutione virginis* 1.2 (PL 16, 319); (Anonymous), *ep. de virginitate* (= *Ad Claudiam*) 14 (CSEL 1, 244); (Anonymous), *Ad virginem devotam* (PL 17, 579).

[45] John Cassian, *Conlationes* 3.6 (SC 42, 145). See the discussion below of gender-bending.

counsel of familial renunciation he links to Abraham's leaving his homeland.[46] Some years later, Jerome recited the same verses to Demetrias when she vowed herself to perpetual virginity: she is the queen of Psalm 45, forsaking her father's house.[47] Likewise, he encourages Furia to remain a widow through the recitation of these verses.[48] And according to the author of the *Vita Melaniae Iunioris*, these words (allegedly) convinced its heroine to renounce her property and worldly pursuits at the time of her father's death.[49]

There were, in addition, many individual verses, especially from the Wisdom literature, that could be swept into the service of ascetic exegesis. The dangers of "loose" or "foolish" women noted in Proverbs (6, 7, 9, 21, 25, 30) could stand as warnings against sexual involvement.[50] Wisdom of Solomon 4:1–2 (virtue is a better memorial than children) is read by ascetically inclined exegetes as an exhortation to virginity;[51] for Methodius, the verse suggests the moral "progress" that the Israelites had made since the era of the patriarchs.[52] Likewise, the warnings against sexual involvement that characterize the Wisdom of Ben Sirach are read straightforwardly by ascetically minded church fathers.[53] And that Job "made a covenant with his eyes not to look on a virgin's face" (Job 31:1) was a readily appropriable example for both married and more ascetically oriented Christians.[54] Such verses required little exegetical assistance in order to prove useful for ascetic exhortation.

Somewhat surprising, even the stories of the patriarchs contained details that could be isolated to argue that the latter were, if not precisely ascetics, nonetheless more chaste than some might have imagined from the narration of their sexual exploits in the book of Genesis. Here we may note that it is *not* allegorical exegesis that produces ascetic meaning, but a careful highlighting of particular details, more "literally" read, within the text. Here, atomization, close attention to one detail, might "rescue" a text that on the surface seemed to celebrate the patriarchal devotion to sexual relation and reproduction.

[46] Jerome, *ep.* 22.1 (CSEL 54, 143–44).

[47] Jerome, *ep.* 130.2 (CSEL 56, 177). Demetrias' father was conveniently dead by the time she made her ascetic commitment, a fact that perhaps made her renunciation of marriage more acceptable.

[48] Jerome, *ep.* 54.3 (CSEL 54, 468).

[49] (Gerontius), *Vita Melaniae Iunioris* 7 (SC 90, 140).

[50] Jerome, *Adversus Iovinianum* 1.7; *ep.* 22.14; Ps.-Clement, *ep. 2 de virginitate* 9; Athanasius, *ep. 1 ad virgines* (46–47).

[51] Ps.-Basil, *De virginitate* 2.43 (Amand de Mendietta/Moons, p. 45).

[52] Methodius, *Symposium* 1.3 (GCS 27, 12).

[53] Ps.-Clement, *ep. 2 de virginitate* 13; Athanasius, *ep. 2 ad virgines* (28); John Chrysostom, *Hom. 14 de statuis* 10; Augustine, *De nuptiis et concupiscentia* 1.29.32; *Contra Iulianum* 5.7.30.

[54] Athanasius, *ep. 2 ad virgines* (28); John Chrysostom, *Hom. 17 Matt.* 2; *Adversus eos qui apud se habent subintroductas virgines* 4 (anti-*subintroductae*); *Hom. 33 Matt.* 7 (love your wife instead).

Just as Abraham's departure from his homeland should incite ascetic Christians to "go forth" from the body's powerful desires, just as his near-sacrifice of Isaac should encourage Christians to set devotion to God before that to relatives,[55] so Abraham's willingness to put duty to God before any concern for Sarah's chastity (Gen. 12:10–20) illustrates, for ascetic readers like Ambrose, how "reason conquers devotion."[56] Startling to us, Ambrose can read the stories of the polygamous patriarchs as advocating "one marriage," a point he infers from reports that only the *first* wife of a patriarch shared his tomb—a detail that he probably garners from Origen's exegesis.[57] Even Jerome, usually eager to stress the "difference of times" between the two Testaments, singles out Isaac and his one wife, Rebecca, as standing against "the wantonness of second marriage."[58] Augustine, exegetically sanitizing the patriarchs' sex lives, argues that they engaged in sexual intercourse with their wives and concubines "without lust," obedient to God and eager to produce the genealogical line from which Christ would descend.[59]

Another feature of the patriarchal narratives that proved useful for ascetic argumentation was the late ages at which (some) of the patriarchs married. Thus for Gregory of Nyssa, Isaac did not wed until he was beyond the age of passion (according to Gen. 25:20, he was forty). After Isaac produced two sons, he closed his eyes and entered the realm of the unseen (Gen. 27:1: Gregory's interpretation of Isaac's fading eyesight).[60] John Chrysostom also notes Isaac's advanced age at marriage, which to him proves that Isaac married not for the sake of passion, but simply to obey God's providential order; after he begot his sons, Isaac had no more sexual union with his wife, Chrysostom assures his audience.[61] Abraham as well could be "rescued" in this manner for the ascetic cause: his marriage to Keturah took place (by Origen's calculation) when he was about 137, so Christians should not imagine that he was prompted to contract this mar-

[55] Ambrose, *De excessu fratris* 2.95; 2.97 (CSEL 73, 301, 303): we renounce relatives so God may preserve them, as he did Isaac.

[56] Ambrose, *De officiis ministrorum* 1.24.107–8 (PL 16, 60).

[57] Ambrose, *De viduis* 15.89 (PL 16, 276); cf. Origen, *Comm. I Cor.* 7:8–12 (Jenkins [1908], p. 504, of Abraham and Jacob).

[58] Jerome, *Adversus Iovinianum* 1.19 (PL 23, 248); they also prefigure Christ and the Church. No other wife or concubine is reported for Isaac, who serves for Ambrose (*De Isaac*) as an exemplar of the Word's future marriage with one woman, the Church.

[59] Augustine, *Contra Faustum* 22.50; 22.81; *De bono coniugali* 13.15; 22.27; *De bono viduitatis* 7.10; *Serm.* 51.25. Such works were composed before Augustine entered the debate with Pelagians; from that time on, he argued that since the sin of Adam and Eve, all humans (except for Mary) experienced concupiscence as a penalty for that sin.

[60] Gregory of Nyssa, *De virginitate* 7.3 (SC 119, 356, 358).

[61] John Chrysostom, *Hom. 24 Heb.* 2 (PG 63, 168).

riage out of "lust."[62] Thus even the patriarchs—most unlikely candidates—could be raised up as ascetic exemplars through close attention (aided by the Fathers' creative rhetoric) to particular details of the Genesis narratives. More examples of ascetic exhortation produced by "close reading" will be detailed below.

In these cases, Old Testament verses could be read with a minimum of exegetical labor to promote renunciation. Often some small detail of the narrative facilitated the claim that the Old Testament as well as the New encouraged ascetic divestment. How other, more recalcitrant, Old Testament passages could be interpreted so as to produce ascetic meaning is the subject of chapter 7 below.

II: Ascetic Translation

Translation from the Greek Bible, both the Septuagint and the New Testament, afforded another opportunity for Latin patristic writers to promote "ascetic" readings. If particular words could be ascetically nuanced in the process of translation, they could be read as manifestly advancing the program of renunciation. To be sure, even Greek-speakers might disagree on a word's ascetic weight: can, for example, *hagiasmos* ("holiness") be predicated of married people, who merely refrain from adultery,[63] or is it the special quality of virgins?[64] Translation from Greek to Latin, however, allowed ascetically inclined exegetes further scope. Thus Jerome translates *hagna* (Phil. 4:8: "whatever is holy") as *castitas*, which for Jerome usually applies only to the celibate.[65] Moreover, there could be opportunities for "ascetic" translation when the Greek word was unattested elsewhere and hence stood open to creative readings. Such is the case with the use of *agenealogētos* (RSV: "without genealogy") in Hebrews 7:3 to describe the priest Melchizedek as a "type" of Christ: Jerome conveniently translates the word as "unmarried" (*sine nuptiis*).[66]

Yet even words in customary Greek usage could also lend opportunities for Latin translators to express their own ascetic preferences. Take, for example, the Pastoral Epistles' recommendation of *sōphrosunē* (and related words) to matrons (I Tim. 2:15), bishops (I Tim. 3:2; Titus 1:8), and

[62] Origen, *Hom. 11 Gen.* 1 (GCS 29, 101). Augustine agrees: *De civitate Dei* 16.34 (CCL 48, 538–39).

[63] So John Chrysostom, *Hom. 30 Heb.* 1 (PG 63, 210); cf. *Hom. 33 Heb.* 3 (PG 63, 227–28).

[64] Origen, *Comm. I Cor.* 7:18–20, 28b (Jenkins [1908], pp. 507, 510). In *ep.* 130.11, Jerome translates *hagiasmos* as *castitas* but tells Demetrias that even this is not enough to win the virgin's crown.

[65] Jerome, *Adversus Iovinianum* 1.38 (PL 23, 277).

[66] Jerome, *Adversus Iovinianum* 1.23 (PL 23, 254).

presbyters (Titus 2:2). Some interpreters, to be sure, provide translations that do *not* press the text's meaning in an ascetic direction. Thus, for example, Pelagius, reading I Timothy 2:15 (that women should bring forth children, continuing in *sōphrosunē*), renders the Greek word as *sobrietas* ("sobriety" or "moderation"). Rather than wresting an ascetic meaning from the verse, however, Pelagius merely warns that *sola fides* ("faith alone") is not sufficient for salvation; Christians must aim by their *deeds* to be holy.[67] Likewise, Ambrosiaster (who translates *sōphrosunē* as *pudicitia*, "modesty" or "virtue") notes only that "Paul" here urges Christians to saving belief and reformed life. Commenting on I Timothy 3:2 (a bishop should be *sōphrona*), Ambrosiaster translates the word as *pudicum*, "modest," but nonetheless adds, in a more asceticizing vein, that those who refrain from marriage are considered more worthy of the clerical office.[68]

In the hands of ascetic enthusiasts such as Jerome, however, such verses of the Pastorals could be ascetically "improved" via translation. Thus Jerome translates the Pastorals' recommendation of *sōphrosunē* as *castitas*, "purity" or "chastity." Commenting on I Timothy 2:15, he claims that "Paul" here urges women to bear children who will remain virgins, thus compensating for their own "loss and decay" as matrons.[69] Jerome warns Christians not to accept the "faulty" translation of *sōphrosunē* as *sobrietas*,[70] although he himself can elsewhere translate the term *sōphrosunē* as *pudicitia*.[71]

Jerome likewise understands the recommendation that a bishop be *sōphrōn* (I Tim. 3:2; Titus 1:8) to mean *castus*, that is, according to Jerome, having "no sexual relation in the present." Moreover, the verses urge that bishops should teach *castitas* to any children they may have begotten *before* assuming episcopal office,[72] for no bishop, Jerome argues, may produce children *during* his episcopate.[73] In his comments on Titus 1:8 (that a bishop should be *castus*, "chaste" ("without sexual relation"), Jerome

[67] Pelagius, *Comm. I Tim.* 2:15 (PLS 1, 1349–50).

[68] Ambrosiaster, *Comm. I Tim.* 2:15; 3:2–4 (CSEL 81.3, 264, 265).

[69] Jerome, *Adversus Iovinianum* 1.27 (PL 23, 260). According to Jerome, the barren Paulina wished to "reproduce" so that she could bring forth virgins for Christ (*ep.* 66.3). Jerome's activities as a translator have been recently studied by Dennis Brown, *Vir Trilinguis: A Study in the Biblical Exegesis of Saint Jerome* (Kampen: Kok Pharos, 1992); Brown's interest is not, however, in Jerome's asceticizing translation.

[70] Jerome, *Adversus Iovinianum* 1.27 (PL 23, 260); for *sōphrosunē* as *sobrietas*, see n. 67 above on Pelagius. Ambrose recommends *sobrietas* to virgins, but instructs them that it does not mean "abstinence from wine" but from "corporalis lasciviae et saecularis iactantiae" (*Exhortatio virginitatis* 12.81 [PL 16, 375]).

[71] Jerome, *ep.* 107.6 (CSEL 55, 297).

[72] Jerome, *Adversus Iovinianum* 1.35 (PL 23, 270).

[73] Jerome, *Adversus Iovinianum* 1.34 (PL 23, 268).

elaborates other Biblical passages to argue his case. If even married laypeople must abstain from sexual relation for prayer (I Cor. 7:5), how much more should those who daily offer sacrifices on behalf of the sins of the people, that is, bishops? Likewise, Jerome cites I Samuel 21:1–6, the story of David's men being allowed the showbread if—and only if—they had abstained from women (and not just "other women," Jerome adds, but "wives"): such should be the case in regard to Christians' participation in the Eucharist, Jerome argues. Besides, since Paul in Galatians 5:23 includes "abstinence" (Jerome's translation of *enkrateia*) as among the gifts of the Spirit and recommends this to all Christians, "how much more" is "abstinence" incumbent upon bishops.[74] That *castitas* is the correct translation of *sōphrosunē* Jerome confirms by his reading of Romans 12:3: when Paul urges Christ's followers to think *eis to sōphronein* (RSV: "with sober judgment"), he means "with chastity," not merely "soberly."[75] Last, in discussing these passages from the Pastoral Epistles, Jerome translates the *presbytas* of Titus 2:2 simply as "old men" (*senes*), not as "priests." Although Jerome warns against their reveling in pleasure (thus setting a bad example for the younger men) and urges them to *sōphronas*, he does not, it seems, understand them to be clerical celibates.[76]

Likewise, in commenting on the virtue of *aphthoria* (RSV: "integrity") recommended to young men in Titus 2:7, Jerome posits that the correct translation is *incorruptio*, which he claims means "virginity." He compares this word to "Paul's" advocacy of *hagneia* in I Timothy 4:12, which he translates as *castitas*. Nonetheless, Jerome adds, since some understand *castitas* not to entail virginity, it was best for the Apostle to recommend both virtues. By preserving *castitas* in mind and *incorruptio* in body, Christians can fulfill the exhortation of I Corinthians 7:34 to be "holy in body and spirit."[77]

A second problem for Latin translators concerned the Greek Bible's use of the word *gunē*, which could mean either "woman" or "wife." Translating the word as *mulier* might pose difficulties for ascetic interpreters, for this general term designating adult females gave no way to distinguish the virginal from the nonvirginal among them. Especially when dealing with the Old Testament and with the Pastoral Epistles, in which there is no such category as "consecrated virgin," ascetic exegetes attempted to wrest the distinction from somewhat recalcitrant texts.

Thus some ascetically inclined Latin patristic authors simply supply their own contrast to "*mulier*": "*virgo*." According to Ambrose, for exam-

[74] Jerome, *Comm. Tit.* 1:8 (PL 26, 604).

[75] Jerome, *Adversus Iovinianum* 1.37 (PL 23, 274).

[76] Jerome, *Comm. Tit.* 2:2 (PL 26, 612–13).

[77] Jerome, *Comm. Tit.* 2:6–7 (PL 26, 618).

ple, when Song of Songs 1:8 calls the female protagonist "the first among women" (*mulieribus*, in Ambrose's rendition), this stands as no compliment: as merely a "woman," she denotes "the Synagogue," in contrast to the virginal Church, "without spot" (Eph. 5:27).[78] Likewise, in commenting on Mary Magdalene weeping at Jesus' tomb (John 20:11), Ambrose renders *gunē* as *mulier* since (he claims) she still hesitates in unbelief; if she had trusted in Jesus' resurrection, she would have been designated a *virgo*.[79] And if, according to Ambrose, *mulieres* are told in I Timothy 2:11 to "keep silent," "how much more" should a *virgo*:[80] an instructive example of *a fortiori* argumentation for ascetic purposes.

The translation of *gunē* posed special problems in two other cases as well: the Virgin Mary's designation as a *gunē* and the notice in I Corinthians 9:1–7 that an apostle (although not Paul) could travel about accompanied by a *gunē*. First, the case of Mary. Here the translation of *gunē* might depend on whether the interpreter believed that Joseph and Mary were truly "married." Although Augustine came to think so (the "sacramental bond" sealed their marriage despite their lifelong sexual abstinence),[81] in some of his earlier works he questioned the use of the word *gunē* for Mary. References to Mary as a *gunē* (Gal. 4:4; John 2:4) do not mean that she was a "wife" in a sexual sense, Augustine explains, but simply a member of the category "female." Augustine looks for assistance in the depiction of Eve as taken from Adam's side in Genesis 2: while Eve is still "untouched," he notes, she is called a *mulier*, a designation that might imply she was a "wife," not just a "woman." Hence Christians need not imagine that the designation of Mary as a *gunē/mulier* implies that she ever participated in sexual relations.[82]

Both the use of *mulier* as a word that merely marked out one sex and the appeal to Genesis 2:22–23 was also made by Pelagius,[83] whose discussion may rely on Origen's claim that *gunē* in Galatians 4:4 simply denotes Mary's sex, not her "corruption."[84] Origen (according to the Latin translation of his *Romans Commentary*) explains why Paul writes that Christ came *ex muliere* ("from" a woman) rather than *per mulierem* ("through"

[78] Ambrose, *Exhortatio virginitatis* 10.67 (PL 16, 372); cf. Origen's treatises on the Song of Songs for the casting of the synagogue/the Church as characters.

[79] Ambrose, *De virginitate* 4.17 (PL 16, 284).

[80] Ambrose, *Exhortatio virginitatis* 13.86 (PL 16, 377).

[81] Augustine, *De nuptiis et concupiscentia* 1.11.12–13 (CSEL 42, 224–25).

[82] Augustine, *Contra Faustum* 23.7 (CSEL 25, 712); *Tract. 10 Ioan.* 2 (CCL 36, 101); *Serm.* 51.11.18 (PL 38, 343). On the changing use of *mulier*, with reference to Augustine, see Christine Mohrmann, "Mulier. A propos de II Reg. 1, 26," *Vigiliae Christianae* 2 (1948): 117–19.

[83] Pelagius, *Comm. Gal.* 4:4 (PLS 1, 1280). The example of Eve as a *mulier* is found in the Latin tradition as early as Tertullian, *De virginibus velandis* 5.1–2 (CCL 2, 1214).

[84] Origen, *Hom. 8 Lev.* 2 (GCS 29, 395).

a woman) in Galatians 4:4 : namely, because no seed was involved in Jesus' conception.[85] This explanation also appeals to Cyril of Jerusalem: if Christ's birth had not been a virgin birth, Paul in Galatians 4:4 would have written that he was born "of man and woman," not merely "of woman."[86] According to Jerome, "through" a woman was a reading of the Galatians text that Marcion and other heretics espoused in order to deny that Jesus had real human flesh. Jerome's concern, however, is to rescue Mary's perpetual virginity from any insinuating implications of the word *mulier*: when she is called *mulier* in John 2:4 and described as a *coniuga* in Matthew 1:20, Christians are not to imagine that these designations detract from her virginal status; the words merely designate her sex.[87] Yet unlike Augustine in his later years, Jerome does not deem Joseph to be Mary's husband and hence the use of *mulier*, he thinks, is quite inexact. Those who imagine that the Virgin was married put the *mulier* before the *virgo*, Jerome complains.[88] Jerome's more ascetically aggressive reading stands against that of Tertullian, who believed that after Mary's virginal conception, her "womb was opened" and she became a "wife."[89] Tertullian argues that because at the time of her conception Mary was betrothed, it was appropriate for her to be called a *mulier*.[90] Ascetic readings have thus been strengthened in the passage of time between Tertullian and Jerome.

I Corinthians 9:5 also employs the word *gunē* in a manner that troubled patristic exegetes. Paul here asks if he and his companions do not have the right to be accompanied by (in alternative readings of the Greek text) an *adelphēn gunaika* or *gunaikas*, as "the rest of the apostles and the brothers of the Lord and Cephas"? Clement of Alexandria, a firm champion of Christian marriage against his "Gnostic" opponents, argues that since the apostles are here said to be married, marriage must be a blessed state for later Christians as well.[91] Tertullian, when in a generous mood toward marriage, interprets the *gunaikas* as "wives," but then retracts his seeming enthusiasm for marriage by noting that what is "merely permitted" cannot be said to be a "good." If the apostles had the *licentia* to take about wives, they also had the freedom to live by the Gospel more fully, that is, *not* to

[85] Origen, *Comm. Rom.* 3.7(10) (Hammond Bammel, pp. 255–56).

[86] Cyril of Jerusalem, *Or. Cat.* 12.31 (PG 33, 765).

[87] Jerome, *Comm. Gal.* 2 (4:4) (PL 26, 398). Jerome has the Matthew text describe Mary as an *uxor.*

[88] Jerome, *Comm. Gal.* 3 (5:18) (PL 26, 442), discussing 4:4.

[89] Tertullian, *De carne Christi* 23; cf. 20 (CCL 1, 914–15, 908–10).

[90] Tertullian, *De virginibus velandis* 6.1–2 (CCL 2, 1215). Tertullian struggles over the meaning of "women" in I Cor. 11:5–16 on the issue of veiling: *De virginibus velandis* 4.

[91] Clement of Alexandria, *Stromata* 3.6.53 (GCS 52 [15], 220). John Chrysostom's position on the marital issue is unclear: he reads a text of I Cor. 9:5 that has

"take about wives"—and so do other Christians.[92] In a rigorous mode, Tertullian proffers a more strongly ascetic reading of the verse: Paul does *not* here mean "wives," but "women" who ministered to the apostles, much like the women who are said in the Gospel to accompany Jesus (Luke 8:1–3; Matt. 27:55).[93]

Also rejecting the interpretation of *gunē* as "wife" in I Corinthians 9:5 are Augustine,[94] Jerome,[95] and Pelagius, the latter of whom proffers a "philological" reason for his decision: if Paul had meant "wives," the Latin text would use the word *duco* (the customary verb in Latin to denote "taking" a wife) rather than *circumduco*, which rather suggests the journeys through the provinces that men and women made together to promote the Christian mission.[96] Basil of Ancyra notes that although Paul had the freedom to take a wife, he did not use it; Paul would rather have "died" (I Cor. 9:15) than lose the glory of his virginity.[97] Jerome, reading I Corinthians 9:5 as "a sister, a wife" (raising the possibility that the words designated a sexless marriage), argues that Paul did not use this right because he did not wish to be judged by the consciences of unbelievers (I Cor. 10:29).[98] Thus the general understanding of more ascetically inclined patristic writers is that the *gunaikes* of I Corinthians 9:5 are women accompanying the apostles on their journeys, not "wives." Sexual renunciation here again is promoted through translation.

III: "Close Reading" of Problematic Texts

Although "close reading" practices were often criticized by more "spiritually minded" Christian exegetes as "literal," "carnal," and "Jewish,"[99] "close reading" techniques could *also*

---

adelphōn gunaika (*Hom. 21 I Cor.* 2 [PG 61, 172]).

[92] Tertullian, *Exhortatio castitatis* 8.3 (CCL 2, 1026–27).

[93] Tertullian, *De monogamia* 8.5–6 (CCL 2, 1240).

[94] Augustine, *De opere monachorum* 4.5 (CSEL 41, 539).

[95] Jerome, *Adversus Iovinianum* 1.26 (PL 23, 257).

[96] Pelagius, *Comm. I Cor.* 9:5 (PLS 1, 1207). For an informative discussion of changes in late Latin for expressions of a man's "taking a wife = marrying," see G. Q. A. Meershoek, *Le Latin biblique d'après Saint Jérôme: Aspects linguistiques de la rencontre entre la Bible et le monde classique*, Latinitas Christianorum Primeva 20 (Nijmegen/Utrecht: Dekker & Van de Vegt, 1966), pp. 56–61. Pelagius here favors the older expression (*uxores ducere*) rather than the newer (*nubere*).

[97] Basil of Ancyra, *De virginitate* 43 (Vaillant, p. 47).

[98] Jerome, *ep.* 123.14 (CSEL 56, 89).

[99] Daniel Boyarin, *Carnal Israel: Reading Sex in Talmudic Culture*, The New Historicism 25 (Berkeley/Los Angeles/Oxford: University of California Press, 1993), pp. 1–2, 8; see above p. 67–68. The theme of the Jews' "carnality" is a well-known patristic theme; Boyarin begins his discussion citing Augustine's words in *Tract. adversus Iudaeos* 7.9. "Close reading," in which con-

be employed to rescue Biblical verses that otherwise would be unusable for or even detrimental to the ascetic program. In contrast to some Old Testament passages, surveyed above, that could be read quite straightforwardly to prove that even the Old Testament advanced ascetic notions, "close reading" focused on less helpful passages to retrieve from them as well interpretations that fostered the ascetic cause. Some verses were thought to contain particular words or phrases that reduced their otherwise anti-ascetic tenor. Usually eschewing allegory, the close-reading exegete focuses on precise detail, on the "how" of the text's construction, to produce a more ascetic reading.[100]

Sometimes an interpreter need only scrutinize a passage's "chronology," the sequence of events, to locate an ascetic code. Thus Jerome, commenting on Ezekiel 24:18 ("So I spoke to the people in the morning, and at evening my wife died. And on the next morning I did as I was commanded"), finds the ascetic key in Ezekiel's receiving the gift of prophecy only *after* his wife died. "Note well," Jerome writes, "that when his wife was alive he was not free to admonish the people"—but upon his wife's demise, Ezekiel was at liberty to pursue his prophetic calling.[101] Just as Jeremiah's prophetic mission required that he not take a spouse "in this place" (Jer. 16:2), so Ezekiel had to await his wife's death: "neither he who wished to marry nor he who had married could prophesy freely in the married state," Jerome concludes.[102] Thus Ezekiel 24:18, "closely read," delivers the message that marriage and prophetic inspiration are incompatible.

A second example relying on a text's "chronology" concerns the patristic exegesis of Genesis 4:1: Adam "knew" his wife only *after* the first sin and the expulsion from Eden. Tertullian initiates this line of argument among Latin authors in an attempt to shame Christians into single marriage. In high rhetorical style, Tertullian exhorts:

> Return at least to the first Adam if you cannot return to the last! Once for all he tasted of the tree; once for all he felt sexual desire; once for all he covered his genitals; once for all he blushed in the presence of God; once for all he concealed his shame; once for all he was exiled from the paradise of chastity—once for all he then married.[103]

---

centrated attention is paid to the particular words and details of a text, is often associated with the New Criticism in literary studies.

[100] The "how" of a text's construction is a particular concern of many contemporary literary critics, especially those influenced by deconstruction; see, e.g., Robert Young, "Post-Structuralism: An Introduction," in *Untying the Text: A Post-Structuralist Reader*, ed. Robert Young (Boston/London/Henley: Routledge & Kegan Paul, 1981), p. 14, citing Shoshana Feldman.

[101] Jerome, *Adversus Iovinianum* 1.33 (PL 23, 267).

[102] Jerome, *ep.* 123.13 (CSEL 56, 86).

[103] Tertullian, *De monogamia* 17.5 (CCL 2, 1253).

The reading of Genesis 4:1 was further sharpened by Tertullian's successors, Ambrose and Jerome, to press a message not merely of single marriage, but of virginity. Urging his audience to virginal commitment, Ambrose advises that they return to the condition of Adam and Eve in Paradise. Since Scripture reports that it was "after Adam was ejected from Paradise that he knew his wife Eve," Christians are urged to "show forth what Adam was before the sin, what Eve was before she drank the poison of the slippery serpent."[104] Jerome's treatise to Eustochium continues this rhetorical line. Noting that the command to reproduce (Gen. 1:28) was fulfilled only after the expulsion of the first couple from Eden (Gen. 4:1–2), Jerome argues, "Let them marry and be given in marriage" on whom the curse of Genesis 3:18–19 falls; those unfortunates who have lost the "seamless" coat (John 19:23) must stitch "coats of skins" (Gen. 3:21) for themselves—in marriage. Eustochium is thus exhorted to preserve her "natural" condition, that which Adam and Eve had enjoyed before their sin, their expulsion from Eden—and their sexual relation.[105]

In the Greek patristic tradition, the argument that no sexual intercourse occurred before the expulsion from Eden was pressed to ascetic effect by both Gregory of Nyssa [106] and John Chrysostom. Again, "close reading" promoted—and reinforced—enthusiasm for renunciation. For Chrysostom, before the Fall and subsequent sexual union, Adam and Eve lived as angels in Paradise, without even the thought of sex. Those who now devote themselves to virginity replicate this angelic life that obtained before Genesis 4:1. According to Chrysostom, only after the sin and the expulsion did God provide the means for the human race to replenish itself; children become the consolation for death.[107] Thus the mere positioning of a verse—-Genesis 4:1—proved important for patristic commentators eager to wrest an ascetic message from the opening chapters of Genesis.

Another "close reading" that is partially anchored in the "chronology" of a text is Augustine's attempted rescue of Abraham, Sarah, and Hagar from the jibes of Manichean interpreters such as Faustus. Augustine argues that if Christians read Genesis 12–21 closely—as Faustus had not—they will comprehend the logic of the events there described, a logic that exonerates Abraham and Sarah. Augustine begins his lengthy defense by noting that although Sarah and Abraham both had a "natural desire" for children, Sarah knew that she was barren. Since she understood the point

[104] Ambrose, *Exhortatio virginitatis* 6.36 (PL 16, 361–62); cf. *De institutione virgines* 5.36 (PL 16, 329).

[105] Jerome, *ep.* 22.19 (CSEL 54, 169). Given such explications by Jerome of Gen. 1–4, it is hard to comprehend why John Oppel argues that, according to Jerome, Adam and Eve were "married" in the Garden of Eden ("Saint Jerome and the History of Sex," *Viator* 24 [1993]: 11).

[106] Gregory of Nyssa, *De virginitate* 12.4 (SC 119, 416–20).

[107] John Chrysostom, *Hom. 18 Gen.* 4 (PG 53, 153).

later explicated by Paul (I Cor. 7:4), that wives and husbands have power over each other's bodies, there was no arrogance in her suggestion that Abraham beget children with another woman. She hereby serves as proof that Abraham was not motivated by "animal passion," for no woman who loves her husband will send him into the arms of another if she knows that he is impelled by sexual desire!

Faustus had apparently argued that Abraham's union with Hagar showed that he mistrusted God's promise regarding the multiplication of his descendants (Gen. 12:2). Not so, Augustine retorts. Faustus has not read carefully, for Abraham had not yet in chapter 12 been told how this multitude of descendants would come about, whether from his own body (and, if so, by which woman) or by adoption; thus he first thinks of adopting his slave as a solution for his lack of progeny (Gen. 15:2–3). Only in Genesis 15:4 is Abraham informed that his heir will not be his slave, but a son from his own body. Yet even then, Augustine argues, God does not reveal whether the child will be born of Sarah or of another woman. If Faustus had read more closely, he would have seen that the sequence of events removes any suspicion of lascivious intent.[108] It is striking how frequently Augustine accuses Faustus not just of "impudence, ignorance, and malice," but also of not reading closely enough to follow the redeeming logic of a passage.[109]

Another type of "close reading" that yields an ascetic message rests on the separation of verses that, "artificially" united, had prompted a less ascetic interpretation. Origen's treatment of Matthew 19:3–9, Jesus' discussion of divorce with the Pharisees, offers a good example of this interpretive technique. Proscribing divorce, Jesus cites Genesis 2:24, that man and woman become "one flesh," and Genesis 1:27, that God in the beginning made them "male and female." Yet these passages are not linked in consecutive order in Genesis, Origen notes; in fact, they refer to two different aspects of creation. According to Origen, the "male and female" of Genesis 1 refers to that which was formed spiritually, not physically, "after the image of God" (Gen. 1:26). But the verses in Genesis 2 that pertain to leaving father and mother and becoming "one flesh" with a wife relate to physical beings, he who was "formed from the dust of the ground" and she who was taken from Adam's side. Origen argues that the spiritual creation of "male and female" of Genesis 1 is superior to the physical "man and woman" of Genesis 2.[110] When Jesus in Matthew 19:6 comments that man and woman are "two," he refers to those physically differentiated

[108] Augustine, *Contra Faustum* 22.31–32; cf. 23.6 (CSEL 25, 624–27, 711–12).

[109] Augustine, *Contra Faustum* 22.40; 22.32; 6.19; 23.6 (CSEL 25, 634, 625–27, 301, 711–12).

[110] For Origen on "male and female," see below, pp. 172–73.

beings. For them, he commends the "harmony" of marriage which is a "gift" from God—but, Origen interjects, readers should understand that celibacy is also a "gift" (I Cor. 7:7). Couples joined in marriage are further admonished that their unions should be like that of Christ's with the Church.[111] Thus according to Origen, sexual union was not part of God's original (and ideal) creation, but a consequence of the secondary and material formation of Adam and Eve. Here, Origen's dismemberment of Jesus' response to the Pharisees and the assigning of its Biblical citations to different "moments" of creation history enable a more ascetic message. "Close reading" locates details in seemingly recalcitrant texts that allow less ascetic interpretations to be checked by more ascetic ones. Other examples will be detailed in the chapters to follow.[112]

IV: Intertextual Exegesis

Intertextual exegesis, one of the most frequently employed modes of interpretation found in patristic literature, proved especially helpful to church fathers eager to press an ascetic message from the Bible. A popular concept in late-twentieth-century literary criticism, "intertextuality" also resonates with the practices of Midrashic interpretation, as noted above.[113] Given its frequent consideration in contemporary literary theory, some comments on how and why the term has attracted so much recent attention may here be in order.

Within poststructuralist literary theory, intertextuality was given special prominence by Julia Kristeva, who argues that "[e]very text builds itself as a mosaic of quotations, every text is absorption and transformation of another text."[114] As she acknowledges, Kristeva is much influenced by Bakhtin's "heteroglossia" and "dialogism," in which the varying "voices" speaking within a text interrupt any notion of its monological unity.[115] "Dialogism," Bakhtin posits, implies that writing

> cannot fail to be oriented toward the 'already uttered,' the 'already known.' . . . Only the mythical Adam, who approached a virginal and as yet verbally unqualified world with the first word, could really have escaped

[111] Origen, *Comm. Matt.* 14.16 (19:3–9) (GCS 40, 319–22).

[112] See especially in chap. 11 below the patristic discussion of the recommendation for the remarriage of young widows in I Tim. 5; as Jerome and John Chrysostom both note, a "close reading" of the text causes the anti-ascetic message to come unraveled.

[113] See discussion above, p. 65.

[114] Jeanine P. Plottel, "Introduction," in *Intertextuality: New Perspectives in Criticism*, ed. Jeanine P. Plottel and Hanna Charney (New York: Literary Forum 2, 1978), p. xiv, citing (in translation) Julia Kristeva's explanation of intertextuality in *Sēmeiōtikē* (Paris: Seuil, 1969), p. 146.

[115] Tzvetan Todorov, *Mikhail Bakhtin, The Dialogical Principle*, trans. Wlad Godzich, Theory and History of Literature 13 (Minneapolis: University of Minnesota Press, 1984; French original, 1981), p. 60.

> from start to finish this dialogic inter-orientation with the alien word. . . . Concrete historical human discourse does not have this privilege.[116]

Intertextuality thus stands *against* the notion of a book or poem's authorial "originality"[117] and *for* that of a text's productivity.[118] Texts are here seen as synchronous: whether as allusions or as explicit citations, intertexts stand on the same temporal plane as the passage-at-hand.[119]

Bakhtin's suggestion that literature of the Hellenistic era employs intertextual quotation[120] found a welcome audience in scholars of Biblical and post-Biblical literature. Michael Fishbane's *Biblical Interpretation in Ancient Israel* elaborates how the Hebrew Scriptures themselves employ intertextual readings,[121] while the essays in *Intertextuality in Biblical Writings* further detail the intertextual referencing found within the Jewish and Christian Scriptures.[122] Scholars of early Judaism, however, have most

[116] Mikhail M. Bakhtin, *The Dialogic Imagination: Four Essays*, ed. Michael Holquist, trans. Caryl Emerson and Michael Holquist (Austin: University of Texas Press, 1981), p. 279. For discussions of Bakhtin's notion of dialogism and its assimilation to "intertextuality," see also Julia Kristeva, "Word, Dialogue and Novel," in idem, *Desire in Language: A Semiotic Approach to Literature and Art* (New York: Columbia University Press, 1980, pp. 64–91; French original in *Sēmeiōtikē*, pp. 143–73); Todorov, *Mikhail Bakhtin*, chap. 5; Michael Holquist, "The Politics of Representation," in *Allegory and Representation*, ed. Stephen J. Greenblatt (Baltimore/London: Johns Hopkins University Press, 1981), pp. 163–83.

[117] Plottel, "Introduction," in *Intertextuality*, ed. Plottel and Charney, p. xv; cf. Geoffrey H. Hartman and Sanford Budick, *Midrash and Literature* (New Haven, Conn./London: Yale University Press, 1986), p. xii: intertextuality teaches that there are no "myths of private genius."

[118] Roland Barthes, "Theory of the Text," in *Untying the Text*, ed. Young, p. 39; Michael Riffaterre, *Text Production*, trans. Terese Lyons (New York: Columbia University Press, 1983; French original, 1979), p. 120; Tilottama Rajan, "Intertextuality and the Subject of Reading/Writing," in *Influence and Intertextuality in Literary History*, ed. Jay Clayton and Eric Rothstein (Madison: University of Wisconsin Press, 1991), p. 65 (intertextuality produces the ideology of the text).

[119] Ellen Van Wolde, "Trendy Intertextuality?", in *Intertextuality in Biblical Writings: Essays in Honour of Bas van Iersel*, ed. Sipke Draisma (Kampen: Kok, 1989), p. 46; Daniel Boyarin, *Intertextuality and the Reading of Midrash* (Bloomington/Indianapolis: Indiana University Press, 1990), p. 96. Thus, according to David Stern, "the most disparate and seemingly unrelated verses" (of the Bible) can be connected to create new meaning ("Midrash and Indeterminacy," *Critical Inquiry* 15 [1988]: 150).

[120] Bakhtin, *Dialogic Imagination*, pp. 68–70.

[121] Michael Fishbane, *Biblical Interpretation in Ancient Israel* (Oxford: Clarendon, 1985): see above, pp. 63–64, a Scriptural technique on which the rabbis built, according to Daniel Boyarin, "The Song of Songs: Lock or Key? Intertextuality, Allegory and Midrash," in *The Book and the Text: The Bible and Literary Theory*, ed. Regina M. Schwartz (Cambridge/Oxford: Basil Blackwell, 1990), p. 221.

[122] *Intertextuality in Biblical Writings*, ed. Draisma (see n. 119 above). A less self-consciously literary approach is taken by Frances Young, *Virtuoso Theology: The Bible and Interpretation* (Cleveland: Pilgrim, 1993; originally published as *The Art of Performance: Towards a Theology of Holy Scripture* [London: Darton, Longman and Todd, 1990]). Young uses the imagery of

fully capitalized on the concept. Thus in *Midrash and Literature*, editors Geoffrey Hartman and Sanford Budick claim that ancient Jewish Midrash constitutes a form of intertextual interpretation.[123] Commenting on literary scholars' recent interest in ancient Jewish modes of interpretation, David Stern warns against approaches that suggest there is "no closure" to the text, a position challenged by the rabbis' desire in Midrash "to recapture the fullness of divine presence." While conceding that the rabbinic understanding that texts hold multiple meanings and encourage interpretive playfulness resonates with late-twentieth-century literary theory, Stern argues that the rabbis' serious pursuit of "holiness" via interpretation sets an important limit to the parallels between early Jewish and poststructuralist reading.[124]

The most detailed investigation of intertextuality in early Jewish literature is Daniel Boyarin's *Intertextuality and the Reading of Midrash*. Boyarin summarizes the literary dimensions of intertextuality/dialogism: texts are understood to be "made up of a mosaic of conscious and unconscious citation of earlier discourse"; they may dialogically contest meaning within themselves. The ideological codes of a culture through which contemporaries assert what they think to be true, "natural," and possible spur new texts to be created from old. In the case of Midrash, meaning is produced for the present by the introduction of new material into the fissures and gaps of the ancient Biblical texts. Although this intertextual reading practice can be found in most cultures, Boyarin argues, the rabbis were uncommonly open in revealing the ideological codes that governed their interpretations.[125] Boyarin provides fascinating examples of how Midrashic intertextuality "works" as he reflects on its larger cultural function:

> Intertextuality is, in a sense, the way that history, understood as cultural and ideological change and conflict, records itself within textuality. As the text is the transformation of a signifying system and of a signifying practice, it

repetition of musical themes, the "quoting" or "alluding" to previous works of music, to explain what others now call "intertextuality" (p. 66). She also notes Origen's use of such exegesis (p. 152). Now see Young's *Biblical Exegesis and the Formation of Christian Culture* (Cambridge: Cambridge University Press, 1997), pp. 97–116 *passim*, on intertextual exegesis.

[123] Hartman and Budick, *Midrash and Literature*, p. xi; also see Susan A. Handelman, "Freud's Midrash: The Exile of Interpretation," in *Intertextuality*, ed. Plottel and Charney, pp. 99–112. For Midrash in relation to contemporary literary theory, see also Susan Handelman's *The Slayers of Moses: The Emergence of Rabbinic Interpretation in Modern Literary Theory* (Albany: State University of New York Press, 1982), and her "Jacques Derrida and the Heretic Hermeneutic," in *Displacement: Derrida and After*, ed. Mark Krupnick (Bloomington: Indiana University Press, 1983), pp. 98–129; and various essays in *The Book and the Text: The Bible and Literary Theory*, ed. Regina M. Schwartz (Cambridge/Oxford: Basil Blackwell, 1990).

[124] Stern, "Midrash," pp. 134–36, 141, 143, 149, 150, 161.

[125] Boyarin, *Intertextuality*, pp. 12, 92.

> embodies the more or less untransformed detritus of the previous system. These fragments of the previous system and the fissures they create on the surface of the text reveal conflictual dynamics which led to the present textual system.[126]

The church fathers, for their part, construct intertextual interpretations in several different ways. In its simplest form, a form that barely merits the label of "intertextuality," texts are placed next to each other to reinforce a point. Above, I noted how the juxtaposition of verses could lend an ascetic meaning to a particular Old Testament passage, such as Isaiah 56:3–5. Many more such juxtapositions of texts can be noted. Thus in the pseudo-Basilian treatise *On Virginity*, a catena of thirteen Biblical passages (plus a citation from the *Acts of Paul and Thecla*) are heaped up as ballast for parents hoping to press their children toward ascetic commitments.[127] The author of the pseudo-Titus epistle employs a similar device in arguing against a man's keeping a female servant. After appealing to the examples of Elijah, Elishah, and Jeremiah, who had male servants, the author inventively bolsters his point with a catena of verses: John 20:17 ("Touch me not . . . "), Mark 12:25 = Matthew 22:30 (no marriage in heaven), Psalm 4:8 ("sleep in peace . . . "), Proverbs 6:27 (if a man carries coals in his bosom, he will be burned), and other passages that allegedly encourage a virginal life.[128] Here, the piling up of diverse texts reinforces the ascetic message.

Aside from the mere accumulation of textual ballast, a prime function of intertextuality in ascetic exegesis, for which numerous examples will be found in the chapters that follow, is to press a mildly ascetic text in a more ascetic direction by the citation of other verses that are taken to counsel repudiation of "the world." Intertexts, whether overt or hidden, have the ability to reinforce or to constrain the text in ways that produce new textual meaning.[129] Here, two examples will suffice. In the first, Jerome writes to Exuperantius, a soldier, urging him to abandon his profession and become a monk. Since Exuperantius is not presently married, he should heed Paul's advice in I Corinthians 7:27, "Are you loosed from a wife? Seek not a wife." To drive home his ascetic exhortation, Jerome surrounds the Pauline counsel with other Biblical passages. First, Jerome cites a verse

[126] Ibid., p. 94.

[127] Ps.-Basil, *De virginitate* 58 (Amand de Mendietta/Moons, pp. 49, 51).

[128] Ps.-Titus *Ep.* (de Bruyne, pp. 54–56).

[129] On the constraining function of the intertext, see John Frow, "Intertextuality and Ontology," in *Intertextuality: Theories and Practices*, ed. Michael Worton and Judith Still (Manchester/New York: Manchester University Press, 1990), p. 45. Frow also provides a helpful note in distinguishing intertextual analysis from source criticism: "influence" is not the dominant category in the former analysis, but rather the integration of the intertext and the "work" that text and intertext perform on each other (p. 46).

from the Matthean "Messianic woes": Exuperantius should not come down from his "housetop" (of his ascetic resolve) to rescue the material goods inside (Matt. 24:17), for Jesus proclaimed unfit for the Kingdom any man who "puts his hand to the plough and looks back" (Luke 9:62). Jerome then appeals to Joseph, considered a model of chastity for his refusal of sexual relation with his master's wife (Gen. 39:6–23), and urges Exuperantius to leave his "garment in the hand of the Egyptian mistress" (thus simultaneously fleeing sex and abandoning his military garb) so that he may follow Christ "naked," the Christ who demands that his disciples renounce all (Luke 14:26–27). Next, the difficulty of the rich (like camels) passing through a needle's eye into the Kingdom (Matt. 19:24) is briefly remarked, as is the widow who gave her mite (Luke 21:1–4). Jerome rounds out this brief but Scripturally laden letter with a veiled allusion to the Parable of the Prodigal Son: having cast off all his goods, Exuperantius as a "new creature" will be rewarded by the father (God), who runs to meet him, gives him a robe, puts a ring on his finger, and kills for him the fatted calf[130]—in effect, a new (albeit dietarily inappropriate) provisioning for asceticism.

A second example of reinforcing a less renunciatory message by more ascetically stringent ones is furnished by Pelagius' cautionary comment on I Corinthians 7:33, that marriage entails "anxiety" about "worldly affairs." Pelagius strengthens Paul's warning by citing two other New Testament passages. Alluding to the Parable of the Sower, Pelagius argues that the seed sown among "thorns" (read: "of marriage") is choked so that the Word proves "unfruitful." In addition, Pelagius cites the example from the Parable of the Great Banquet of the man who declines the invitation to the banquet (i.e., the Kingdom) because he has taken a wife: marriage may inhibit a man's freedom for religious devotion. The cares that attend the state of marriage should thus warn Christians against it.[131] Paul's dissuasion from marriage has been reinforced by two ascetically construed intertexts.

Moreover, intertexts themselves can be made "more ascetic" by being brought into association with the main text. Such is the case in John Chrysostom's treatment of Colossians 3:5, "Put to death therefore what is earthly in you: immorality (*porneia*). . . . " Chrysostom comments that "Paul" places *porneia* first in the list of vices that need "putting to death," as he does "almost everywhere," and this because *porneia* is the passion with the strongest grip on humans. Chrysostom notes that Paul reinforces this view in I Thessalonians 4:3 by urging that men should "abstain from *porneia*." Chrysostom then adds a second intertext, I Timothy 5:22, the

[130] Jerome, *ep.* 145 (CSEL 56, 306–7).

[131] Pelagius, *Comm. I Cor.* 7:33 (PLS 1, 1204). Cf. Mark 4:1–9 and parallels; Luke 14:20.

recommendation that Christians not be hasty to "participate in another man's sin," but should rather keep themselves "pure" (*hagnos*).[132] Here, a general recommendation to "purity"—which in I Timothy 5:22 does not carry an overtly sexual connotation—is strengthened in an ascetic direction by its association with Paul's warning against *porneia*.[133] Thus an intertext is imbued with greater ascetic rigor than it otherwise might carry.

Some patristic champions of marriage, however, use intertextual exegesis not to urge a stringent renunciation, but merely to recommend restraint and decorum. Thus, for example, Clement of Alexandria's interpretation of "reproduce and multiply" (Gen. 1:28) is hedged about with Biblical verses that allegedly prohibit extramarital relation ("Do not scatter your seed everywhere," a counsel derived from the Parable of the Sower [Matt. 13]) and pederasty ("Do not eat hare and hyena" [Deut. 14:7], animals who in Clement's day were deemed "wanton" in their sexual practices). But within such moderating restrictions, according to Clement, reproduction is a good that signals humans' cooperation with God.[134]

Exegetes more intent on sexual renunciation, however, could press even recalcitrant texts in an ascetic direction through the skillful choice of intertexts. Gregory of Nyssa and Jerome furnish two useful examples. Pondering Genesis 1:27b ("male and female he made them")—a text usually cited to promote marriage—Gregory comments that sexual division was a departure from the "prototype," Christ, the "image" of God the Father, since in Christ there is "no male and female" (Gal. 3:28). Rather, Galatians 3:28 confirms Genesis 1:27a, the first half of the verse ("So God created man in his own [sexless] image . . . "). Although Gregory faults his "adversaries'" argument that sex and marriage occurred only after the first sin, he himself approximates their position by arguing that since there will be no marriage in the resurrection (Luke 20:35–36), singleness must have been the first condition of humanity as well,[135] since the end will resemble the origin. Christians of his era, Gregory suggests, would do well to emulate this condition of blessedness. The "male and female" of Genesis 1:27 has here been outflanked by the "no male and female" of Galatians 3:28 that constitutes the "image of God" (Gen. 1:27).

Jerome likewise can turn a resolutely nonascetic passage, this time from the Song of Songs, into an ascetic warning for virgins through the ingenious choice of intertexts. Jerome cites to Eustochium erotic verses from Song of Songs 5 that describe how the Song's heroine arises from her bed

[132] John Chrysostom, *Hom. 8 Col.* (3:5) (PG 62, 355).

[133] See Boyarin, *Intertextuality*, p. 112, for the notion that in intertextual commentary, "two signifiers . . . mutually read each other."

[134] Clement of Alexandria, *Paedagogus* 2.10.83 (GCS 12, 208).

[135] Gregory of Nyssa, *De opificio hominis* 16.7; 16.9; 17.1; 17.2 (PG 44, 181, 184, 188–89).

to admit her lover, but upon discovering that he had left, "sick with love" she combs the city to find him. Jerome admonishes Eustochium through the example of this young woman who wandered the streets to "seek him whom my soul loves" (Song of Songs 3:2). First, Eustochium's "lover" (Jesus) is not to be found in the streets, but rather in the "narrow way" (Matt. 7:14). Further, she should remember what befell the girl in the Song of Songs: the watchmen beat her and stripped her of her mantle (Song of Songs 5:7). Eustochium also should recall the story of Dinah (Gen. 34), who was raped when she went out "to visit the women of the land." Such is the fate of virgins who stray beyond their domestic seclusion. Since Jesus is a jealous lover, Eustochium should avoid contact with the lustful eyes of young men, or she may find herself barred from the bridal chamber (Matt. 25:10), left to feed the "goats" that are on Jesus' left side at the Last Judgment (Matt. 25:33, 41). Eustochium should rather secretly pray in her "closet" at home (Matt. 6:6); only then will Jesus come to her.[136] Ascetic seclusion is thus the moral Jerome here derives from the Song of Songs through intertextual argumentation. The chapters that follow detail many more examples of intertextual exegesis employed by the Fathers to press an ascetic message.

V: "Talking Back"

A common form of rabbinic exegesis involved verbal sparring, the quotation of Biblical passages against a debate partner: the polysemy of texts encouraged the proliferation of meaning through such verbal warfare.[137] Jesus himself, according to the Gospels, furnished an instructive example of such "talking back" in his encounter with the devil (Matt. 4:1–11 = Luke 4:1–12). When the devil tempts Jesus to turn stones into bread, Jesus replies with Deuteronomy 8:3 ("Man shall not live by bread alone . . . "). When the devil baits Jesus to fling himself from the Temple (since according to Ps. 91:11–12, God's angels will not let him fall), Jesus responds with "You shall not tempt the Lord your God" (Deut. 6:16). And when the devil offers Jesus the kingdoms of the world in return for worshiping him, Jesus retorts with Deuteronomy 6:13, "You shall worship the Lord your God and him only shall

[136] Jerome, *ep.* 22.25; 22.26 (CSEL 54, 180, 181).

[137] Handelman, "Freud's Midrash," in *Intertextuality*, ed. Plottel and Charney, p. 111: Midrash as "one long, elaborate talking cure." On disputation in the rabbinic study-houses and academies, see Ephraim E. Urbach, *The Sages: Their Concepts and Beliefs*, trans. Israel Abrahams, 2nd ed. (Cambridge/London: Harvard University Press, 1979; Hebrew original, 1969), pp. 620–30.

you serve." Jesus is here depicted as rhetorically defeating his satanic enemy by expert "back talk."[138]

In early Christian ascetic exegesis, "talking back" was deployed in numerous contexts: by "heretical" ascetics against more "carnal" Catholic Christians; conversely, by "anti-ascetics" who rebuke Catholic ascetics from the opposite flank; by exegetes who pit different Biblical passages by the *same* author against each other to press a more ascetic interpretation; and by ascetic practitioners in their battles against demons and demonically inspired thoughts. This exegesis is nothing if not polemical.

For astute readers of Scripture such as Faustus, the highly ascetic Manichean, numerous divergences in the Biblical text allowed a more ascetically stringent passage to "talk back" to, that is, to "correct," a less rigorous one. Thus Faustus cites the Evangelist Luke's less "carnal" naming of Jesus as "Son of God" (Luke 1:35) against Matthew's "Son of David" (Matt. 1:1). Likewise, the reference in Romans 1:3 to Christ as the "Son of David" is, according to Faustus, "corrected" by two verses: "even though we once regarded Christ from a human point of view, we regard him thus no longer" (II Cor. 5:16b) and "When I was a child, I spoke like a child, I thought like a child, I reasoned like a child; when I became a man, I gave up childish ways" (I Cor. 13:11). Although Faustus disputes the Pauline authorship of Romans 1:3 (Christ as the "Son of David"), he concedes that if Paul did in fact write this verse, he must have amended it later—and Faustus' Catholic opponents likewise can be "corrected" if they understand that the verses from Corinthians "answer back" Romans 1:3.[139]

On the other hand, anti-ascetics were also adept at deploying Scriptural passages to counter interpretations given by their more ascetically inclined colleagues. Particularly useful to the partisans of marriage and reproduction were verses from the Pastoral Epistles such as "to the pure all is pure" (Titus 1:5) and the prediction in I Timothy 4:1–4 of those latter-day deceivers of Christians who would wrongly forbid marriage and enjoin "abstinence from foods which God created to be received with thanksgiving by those who believe and know the truth." These verses, we are told, were favorites of the anti-ascetic Jovinian, who flung them at Jerome as the two authors sparred.[140] And according to Pelagius' scathing notice, the

[138] On Jesus' "performance" of "audacious midrash" ("he reads the scriptures in his own name by reading himself into them, making himself the secret of the Law"), see Gerald L. Bruns, *Inventions: Writing, Textuality, and Understanding in Literary History* (New Haven, Conn./London: Yale University Press, 1982), p. 37.

[139] Faustus in Augustine, *Contra Faustum* 3.1; 11.1 (CSEL 25, 262, 313–14).

[140] Jovinian in Jerome, *Adversus Iovinianum* 2.5 (PL 23, 304); cf. *ep.* 22.13 (CSEL 54, 160–61). The author of *De castitate* (16) reports that I Tim. 4:3 was Jovinian's

amatores luxuriae, the "lovers of [sexual] excess," in the Church quote Genesis 1:28 ("Reproduce!") in an attempt to counter Paul's counsel of sexual abstinence in I Corinthians 7.[141]

Moreover, passages of an ascetic cast can be cited by patristic exegetes to combat less ascetically directed ones by the same Biblical author. Here, the fact that the Fathers believed that Paul had written the Pastoral Epistles was of decisive importance, as was their belief that Solomon had composed both Proverbs and Ecclesiastes. In these situations, an author could be quoted against *himself* to produce a more ascetic meaning. Thus when Solomon is cited by Jovinian as an example of a married man who stood as a type of the Savior, Jerome counterargues that Jovinian should recall Solomon's seven hundred wives, three hundred concubines, and "others without number," women who led his heart away from the Lord (I Kings 11:3). Does Jovinian wish to endorse not just second and third marriages, but the more than one thousand sexual partners that Solomon had?[142] According to Jerome, the much-vaunted "wisdom of Solomon"—no doubt expressed in his alleged penning of such verses as "a time to embrace and a time to cease from embracing" (Eccles. 3:5b)—is brought to naught by the "foolishness" he displayed regarding women.[143] Yet Solomon also provided appropriate ascetic counsel in warning young men against "loose women" in the book of Proverbs, and it is *this* Solomonic counsel that Christians should accept, Jerome claims.[144] John Chrysostom, too, can pit Solomon against himself: although Solomon indulged himself in luxurious surroundings and beautiful bodies, in the end he confessed that "all is vanity."[145]

As for the New Testament, the author of the Pelagian(?) treatise *On Chastity* rudely (and rhetorically) inquires whether Paul "forgot" I Corinthians 7 when he wrote I Timothy 4:1–4, a passage that condemns those who preach abstinence from marriage; Paul's words on continence in I Corinthians, the author argues, appropriately "answer" the warning of I Timothy 4.[146] Likewise, John Chrysostom can quote Paul against "Paul," albeit less abrasively. He too cites I Corinthians 7 against I Timothy 4:1–4, claiming that although Paul (and Chrysostom himself) does not "forbid"

---

favorite passage. Tertullian in his Montanist phase wars against the "psychics" (i.e., Catholics) who cite I Tim. 4:1–2 to justify their dietary habits (*De ieiunio* 2.5 [CCL 2, 1258]).

[141] Pelagius, *Comm. I Cor.* 7:1–3 (PLS 1, 1198–99).

[142] Jovinian in Jerome, *Adversus Iovinianum* 1.5; 1.24 (PL 23, 227, 254–55).

[143] Jerome, *ep.* 125.1 (CSEL 56, 119).

[144] Jerome, *Adversus Iovinianum* 1.7; 1.28 (PL 23, 229, 260–61).

[145] John Chrysostom, *Adversus eos qui apud se habent subintroductas virgines* 12 (PG 47, 512–13).

[146] (Anonymous), *De castitate* 16 (PLS 1, 1498–99).

marriage, Paul also urged married people to live "as if not" (I Cor. 7:29).[147] The ascetic Paul here trumps the less rigorous Pastor.

Yet the Pastor could also be taken to trump *himself*, as is shown in the *Life of Olympias*. Olympias rejects the "law" of I Timothy 5:14 that young widows should remarry, favoring instead the Pastor's words in I Timothy 1:9, "For the law was not laid down for the righteous person, but for the unruly, the impure, and the insatiable." According to the author of Olympias' *Vita*, since she herself was not thus vice-ridden, she considered the "law" of remarriage inapplicable, and resisted the emperor Theodosius' entreaty that she marry one of his relatives.[148]

A last important use of "talking back" in ascetic exegesis pertains to monks' citation of Scriptural verses against demons or demonic "thoughts" (*logismoi*).[149] Here, Scripture is deployed in a prophylactic fashion, creating a protective exegetical barrier that shields the ascetic from demonic attack and fortifies his inner resolve. Athanasius' *Life of Antony* offers a good illustration. In Athanasius' rendition, not only did Scripture provide the motivation for Antony to renounce his property and adopt the ascetic life in the first place,[150] it also armed him with a battery of quotations with which to do battle against his demonic opponents. When the devil tempts him with sex, Anthony responds with "The Lord is my helper and I shall look upon my enemies" (Ps. 118:7).[151] When demons whip him, he recites Psalm 27:3, "Though an army should set itself in array against me, my heart shall not be afraid."[152] Jesus' temptation by the devil, according to Athanasius, set the pattern for Antony's "talking back" to the demons: Jesus had responded, "Be gone, Satan!"[153]

The demons who inhabit Evagrius Ponticus' *Antirrheticus* (*Talking Back*) appear the most clever of all. In addition to luring monks with sexual dreams[154] and transforming themselves into beautiful women to tempt the unwary,[155] the demons also recite Scriptural passages that affirm

[147] John Chrysostom, *Hom. 7 Matt.* 7 (PG 57, 80–81).

[148] (Anonymous), *Vita Olympiadis* 3 (SC 13bis, 410, 412).

[149] For an earlier assessment of this phenomenon, see Denys Gorce, *La Lectio divina des origines du cenobitisme à Saint Benoît et Cassiodore. T. I: Saint Jérôme et la lecture sacrée dans le milieu ascétique romain* (Wépion-sur-Meuse: Monastère du Mont-Vierge; Paris: Librairie Auguste Picard, 1925), p. 358.

[150] Athanasius, *Vita Antonii* 2 (PG 26, 841). Antony renounced his property after hearing passages from Acts 4 and Matt. 19:21, according to Athanasius.

[151] Athanasius, *Vita Antonii* 6 (PG 26, 849, 852).

[152] Athanasius, *Vita Antonii* 9 (PG 26, 856).

[153] Athanasius, *Vita Antonii* 37 (PG 26, 897), citing Matt 4:10.

[154] Evagrius Ponticus, *Antirrheticus* 2.15; 2.19; 2.34; 2.53; 2.60 (Frankenberg, pp. 486–87, 488–89, 492–93).

[155] Evagrius Ponticus, *Antirrheticus* 2.32 (Frankenberg, pp. 488–89); cf. *De diversis malignis cogitationibus* 26 long rec. (Muyldermans, p. 51).

the goodness of marriage and childbearing and that caution against excessive abstinence—-presumably, verses from Genesis and the Pastoral Epistles, here placed in the mouths of demons.[156] Evagrius supplies a catena of verses that the monk can chant to repel such demonic assaults. Some Scriptural verses are immediately appropriable, such as "everyone who looks at a woman lustfully has already committed adultery with her in his heart" (Matt. 5:28).[157] Others, such as Jeremiah 16:2 (the command that Jeremiah not take a wife "in this place"), acquire stronger ascetic force by being linked with I Corinthians 7:32–34 on the anxieties of marriage.[158]

According to Evagrius, some Scriptural passages could prove more useful to the ascetic as ammunition against demonic thoughts if they were decontextualized and reapplied to the monastic setting. Hence David's alleged expression of grief at Abner's murder ("God do so to me and more also, if I eat bread or drink water until the sun goes down" [II Sam. 3:35]) provides fortification for the monk whom gluttony tempts to eat at the *sixth* hour, that is, noon.[159] Judges 4:14 ("For this is the day in which the Lord has given Sisera into your hand"), when removed from its Biblical context that described the Israelites' "conquest" of Canaan, assists the monk who falls into despair that he can no longer bear the impure thoughts that sully his prayer.[160] For the monk whose unclean "thoughts" so tempt him that he does not keep vigil and pray, Jesus' words to his disciples in Gethsemane provide strength: "Watch and pray, that you may not enter into temptation" (Matt. 26:41).[161]

Thus Scripture itself provides the means of "talking back" to theological opponents, and a mental "stay" for the monk battling demonic temptation in his thoughts and dreams.

VI: Textual Implosion

Ascetically inclined exegetes, eager to wrest renunciatory injunctions from every possible Biblical passage, read many seemingly irrelevant verses as pertaining to sexuality and renunciation: texts that appear to modern scholars as inapposite are here understood as "imploding," collapsing into, these core issues. The most detailed

[156] Evagrius Ponticus, *Antirrheticus* 2.50 (Frankenberg, pp. 490–93).

[157] Evagrius Ponticus, *Antirrheticus* 2.56 (Frankenberg, pp. 492–93).

[158] Evagrius Ponticus, *Rerum monachalium rationis* 1 (PG 40, 1252–53).

[159] Evagrius Ponticus, *Antirrheticus* 1.7 (Frankenberg, pp. 474–75).

[160] Evagrius Ponticus, *Antirrheticus* 2.12 (Frankenberg, pp. 486–87). Evagrius borrows the Origenist theme that the "conquest" of Canaan signals the "conquest" of vice.

[161] Evagrius Ponticus, *Antirrheticus* 2.57 (Frankenberg, pp. 492–93).

example of this interpretive strategy can be found in the Fathers' commentary on I Corinthians 7:18–24, Paul's excursus on circumcision and slavery that is positioned in the midst of his larger discussion of marriage and celibacy. The discordant positioning of these verses enabled the ascetically minded to see "circumcision" and "slavery" as tropes pertaining to marriage and celibacy, and hence to read verses 18–24, as well as the rest of I Corinthians 7, as an exhortation to ascetic living. This interpretive strategy will be extensively elaborated in chapter 10.

Likewise, thoughts of food seemingly stimulated thoughts of sex. Thus Paul's words on not eating meat if it causes scandal to fellow Christians (I Cor. 8:13) could be cited to justify separating young female virgins from the male companions with whom they were "scandalously" living,[162] while similar verses pertaining to the problems at Corinth occasioned by meat-eating ("lawful but not helpful" [I Cor. 6:12]) could be quoted to discourage second marriage.[163] Another Pauline injunction on dietary restraint, "You cannot drink the cup of the Lord and the cup of demons" (I Cor. 10:21), could be coupled with "What fellowship has light with darkness? What accord has Christ with Belial?" (II Cor. 6:14b-15) to advise a woman who had divorced her dissolute first husband against second marriage: sensual pleasure is not concordant with Christian commitment, Jerome here argues.[164]

One developed example of "textual implosion" will here suffice to illustrate the principle. In Romans 2:29, Paul speaks of a "spiritual circumcision" that enables Gentile as well as Jewish Christians to be considered God's chosen people. But what does "spiritual circumcision" mean? Origen's discussion of this passage illustrates the way in which (seemingly) unrelated texts "implode" onto issues of sexual renunciation. Origen begins by linking "spiritual circumcision" to "cutting off the vices of the soul." Yet this interpretation, it appears, struck Origen as bland, since he seeks for another. That circumcision was performed on the eighth day gives Origen his interpretive key: the "eighth day" portends the "mystery of the future age," the age in which there will be "no marrying and giving in marriage" when we will be like "angels of God" (Matt. 22:30), "castrating" ourselves "for the sake of the Kingdom of Heaven" (Matt. 19:12). By adopting such behavior while still walking on this earth, we have our "conversation in heaven" (cf. Phil. 3:20).[165] Thus has the interpretation

[162] Cyprian, *ep.* 4(= 61).2 (CSEL 3.2, 473–74).

[163] Ambrose, *De viduis* 11.68 (PL 16, 267–68).

[164] Jerome, *ep.* 55.4 (CSEL 54, 494–95).

[165] Origen, *Comm. Rom.* 2.9 (12–13) (Hammond Bammel, p. 164). Origen goes on to consider whether "uncircumcision" might not refer to "those who use natural sexual intercourse in an immoderate and intemperate way," while "circumcision" could refer to those who use it "legitimately," that

of "spiritual circumcision" been "imploded" into the topic of sexual renunciation, and the "implosion," moreover, has received generous assistance from intertextual references.

VII: Changing Context

The passage of time from the days of the ancient Israelites to those of early Christianity necessitated a dehistoricization and relocation of Biblical texts to render them usable for the ascetic project. With the destruction of the Jerusalem Temple in 70 C.E., the ritual prescriptions of the Hebrew Scriptures were rendered at least partially moot; they had to be interpreted in some other way—and this for Jews as well as for Christians—if they were to retain their holy status. In addition, the larger saga of Israel's history—the Exodus, the defeat of Israel and Judah by their enemies, the Babylonian Captivity, the restoration to the land—supplied motifs that, when decontextualized, could be usefully deployed by ascetically minded exegetes. So too within the New Testament the provisions of the Household Codes, especially that of Ephesians 5, required interpretive assistance to be made meaningful for Christian ascetics. Through a decontextualized reading, the entire Bible could become a treasure trove for ascetic exegetes.

Chapter 8 details how the provisions of Israelite ritual law were reinterpreted as ascetic directives. Here it may be more briefly noted that various laws pertaining to purity and impurity were easily swept into the ascetic repertoire. If Exodus 19:22 suggests that an "unholy" man cannot be a priest, then the same could be said of Christian virgins.[166] Rules excluding the "impure" from the Israelite camp are taken by John Cassian as guidelines for the monastic community which must deal with the problem of the monks' nocturnal emissions.[167] The vows of the Nazirites and their segregation from other Israelites find their parallels in the vows of Christian virgins and their separation from other Christians, according to Methodius.[168] Ritual prescriptions could, it appears, quite easily be turned into ballast for the ascetic program.

So likewise with certain details of Israel's history, when read figuratively. The Israelites' Exodus from Egypt and their longing to return (Num. 11:5, 18) thus signals the ascetic's flight from the world and warns him not to yearn for "the fleshpots of Egypt." "Returning to Egypt" might be a special temptation for those monks who wish to visit their relatives,

---

is, only as much as is necessary to produce offspring (Hammond Bammel, p. 167).

[166] Gregory of Nyssa, *De virginitate* 23 (Jaeger VIII.1:342).

[167] John Cassian, *Conlationes* 22.5; 12.2 (SC 64, 121; SC 54, 122).

[168] Methodius, *Symposium* 5.1; 5.4 (GCS 27, 53, 56).

according to Basil of Caesarea,[169] while the fair "tents" of the embattled Israelites are transformed by Athanasius into monastic residences.[170] Injunctions regarding the treatment of female war captives (Deut. 21:10–13) deliver the ascetic message that "even" the ancient Israelites believed that sexual relations should be undertaken only for the procreation of children.[171] Jeremiah's weeping for the slain daughters of his people (Jer. 9:1) becomes an appropriate lament for "fallen" virgins[172]—as does the taunt for the "fallen" Babylon who "sits in the dust" (Isa. 47:1–3).[173] That Jeremiah was not taken as captive to Babylon (Jer. 40:1–4) signifies for Jerome the freedom and blessing accorded to virgins.[174] And the rapturous salute of Third Isaiah to the "people whom God has blessed" (by restoring their country) is read by the author of the pseudo-Clementine epistles on virginity as a fitting epithet for the abstinent.[175]

The New Testament as well contained passages that could be "improved" for the ascetic program through decontextualization. Especially was this the case with the Household Codes that assumed the patriarchal household as the model for Christian society, and of these, the version in Ephesians 5:21–6:9 proved particularly useful. "No one hates his own body" (Eph.5:29)—originally an injunction for husbands to love their wives—could be cited as a defense of Christian asceticism against those detractors who argued that rigorous ascetics must "hate their own flesh." Quoting this verse, Augustine retorts that ascetics attempt not to "rid" themselves of bodies, but rather to battle the passions that lead them astray.[176] That the Bride of Christ is to be "without spot or wrinkle" (Eph. 5:27) provided a key phrase that could be quoted variously to discourage second marriage[177] or to urge virgins to a life "without blemish."[178] Moreover, if Christ's "marriage" to the Church was the pattern for human marriage, as Ephesians 5 suggests, rigorously ascetic exegetes might argue that the best marriages should be sexless.[179]

[169] Basil, *Regulae fusius tractatae* 32.2 (PG 31, 996); cf. John Cassian, *Conlationes* 3.7 (SC 42, 148, 146).

[170] Athanasius, *Vita Antonii* 44 (PG 26, 908).

[171] Clement of Alexandria, *Stromata* 3.11.71 (GCS 52 [15], 228).

[172] Basil of Caesarea, *ep.* 46 (Loeb I:282, 284); John Chrysostom, *Ad Theodorum lapsum* 1.1 (PG 47, 277).

[173] Jerome, *ep.* 22.6 (CSEL 54, 150–51).

[174] Jerome, *Adversus Iovinianum* 1.33 (PL 23, 267).

[175] Ps.-Clement, *ep. 1 de virginitate* 9.4 (Funk, p. 16), citing Isa. 61:9.

[176] Augustine, *De doctrina Christiana* 1.24.24 (CCL 32, 19).

[177] Origen, *Hom. 17 Luc.* 10 (SC 87, 262).

[178] (Anonymous), *ep. de virginitate* (= *Ad Claudiam*) 11 (CSEL 1, 241); Gregory of Nyssa, *De virginitate* 1 (SC 119, 256).

[179] Jerome, *Comm. Eph.* 3 (5:22–24) (PL 26, 564–65). Origen hints at a similar meaning when he argues that the "solid food" of Eph. 5 stands against the concessive "milk" (i.e., sexual intercourse) that Paul grants to married couples in I Cor. 7:2 (*Hom. 7 Ezech.* 10 [SC 352, 270, 272]).

Some passages could acquire more specialized ascetic meanings by re-contextualization. Such is the case with Biblical verses that patristic exegetes deployed against the phenomenon of syneisaktism. Here, Job's confession that he had not "looked on a virgin's face" (Job 31:1) acquired pointed force as a warning against ascetic men and women living together, a situation in which "looking on a virgin's face" would be unavoidable.[180] Likewise, the injunction to be "without spot and wrinkle" (Eph. 5:27) militated against syneisaktic relationships, in which male and female ascetics shared a house: consecrated virgins must be especially "spotless," in Chrysostom's reckoning.[181]

As these examples show, dehistoricization and relocation of verses enabled ascetically inclined exegetes to expand their repertoire of appropriate passages with which to bolster the ascetic cause. Meaning was not to be mired in the trivia of ancient history—or even in a less rigorous Christianity.

VIII: Changing the Audience

Ascetic exegetes sometimes asked, who are the protagonists "in" the text, and to whom is the text directed? Answers to these questions could raise or lower the ascetic "weight" of any given Biblical passage. As chapter 10 details, it makes an interpretive difference whether an exegete assigns as the "speaker" of I Corinthians 7:1 ("it is good not to touch a woman") hypocritical pseudo-apostles, Corinthian Christians aiming at spiritual improvement, or Paul himself. Similar questions could likewise be put to other texts. Is it the disciples who reply to Jesus' injunction against divorce in Matthew 19, "If such is the case, it is not expedient to marry," or the hostile Pharisees?[182] Did Jesus intend his words on "becoming a eunuch for the sake of the Kingdom of Heaven" (Matt. 19:12) understood as a counsel of sexual abstinence, to dissuade widows and widowers from second marriage[183]—or to counsel the still-virginal from contemplating marriage at all?[184] Is the "yokefel-

The most frequent Biblical passage cited to encourage "sexless" marriage is I Cor. 7:29 ("as if not"): see, for example, Augustine, *De nuptiis et concupiscentia* 1.13.15; *De coniugiis adulterinis* 2.12.12; Jerome, *Comm. Eccles.* 3:5.

[180] John Chrysostom, *Adversus eos qui apud se habent subintroductas virgines* 4 (PG 47, 501); more generally of monks and virgins, see Athanasius, *ep. 2 ad virgines* (Lebon, p. 186; ET, Brakke, p. 301).

[181] John Chrysostom, *Quod regulares feminae viris cohabitare non debeant* 6 (PG 47, 526).

[182] Gregory of Nazianzus, *Or.* 37.9 (PG 36, 293).

[183] 182. So Clement of Alexandria, *Stromata* 3.6.50 (GCS 52 [15], 219); cf. Ambrose, *De officiis* 2.6.27 (PL 16, 118); *De viduis* 13.75 (PL 16, 270–71); Augustine, *ep.* 3*.3 (CSEL 88, 23).

[184] E.g., Cyprian, *De habitu virginum* 4; (Anonymous), *ep. de virginitate* (= *Ad Claudiam*) 2; (Anonymous), *De castitate* 8; Ps.-

low" whom Paul requests to help the Philippian women his wife?[185]—an interpretation that carried serious implications for Paul as an ascetic model. Does "Paul" in I Timothy 5:14 instruct "younger women" or "younger widows" to marry? (Their designation as *neōteras* leaves either interpretation as a possibility, but one with decided implications for the assessment of second marriage.)[186] Does I Corinthians 7:9 ("better to marry than to burn") give license to Catholic Christians ("psychics," i.e., people only of the "soul," not of the "spirit," in Tertullian's parlance of his Montanist days) to promise forgiveness for adulterers and fornicators?[187] When "Paul" forbade second marriage to priests (I Tim. 3:2; Titus 1:5), were his words meant *only* for the clergy—or are all Christians "priests," as Revelation 1:6 suggests?[188] Who were the wicked men of II Timothy 3:6–8 who enter women's houses and "capture" them with "counterfeit faith"? False monks?[189] Pelagians?[190] Were those told by Jesus to "depart into the fire" at the Last Judgment (Matt. 25:41) the "foolish virgins" who inhabit the first section of that chapter?[191]

Most important, who were the men of I Timothy 4:1–4 whom the Pastor predicted would come with false teachings that "sear the consciences" of Christians by forbidding marriage and enjoining food abstinence? Although anti-ascetic interpreters claimed that the verse predicted the advent of Catholic asceticism,[192] Catholic exegetes themselves responded either by denying the association or by arguing more forcefully that their own ascetic restraint was not "heretical"—and by volunteering the names of people and groups that the Pastor *did* predict: Marcion, Apelles, Tatian and the Encratites, Montanists, and Manicheans.[193] The passage, they argue, applies only to "heretical," not to Catholic, virgins.[194]

Those in the groups so branded, however, had their own interpretive ploys for the interpretation of "audience" in I Timothy 4:1–4. For Faustus

---

Clement, *ep. 1 de virginitate* 1; Eusebius of Emesa, *Hom.* 6.10; John Chrysostom, *Hom. 78 Matt.* 1.

[185] So Clement of Alexandria, *Stromata* 3.6.53 (GCS 52 [15], 220).

[186] By interpreting *neōteras* to mean simply "younger women," Clement of Alexandria avoids the connotation that second marriage (which he opposes) might be sanctioned by this Biblical passage (*Stromata* 3.12.89 [GCS 52 (15), 237]); see discussion below, p. 366.

[187] Tertullian, *De pudicitia* 1.15 (CCL 2, 1283).

[188] Tertullian, *De monogamia* 12.1–2 (CCL 2, 1247).

[189] Cf. Augustine, *ep.* 262.5 (CSEL 57, 624–25); Jerome, *ep.* 22.28 (CSEL 54, 185).

[190] Augustine, *epp.* 194.2; 199.22 (CSEL 57, 177, 263); Jerome, *ep.* 133.4 (CSEL 56, 247).

[191] John Chrysostom, *De virginitate* 4.1 (SC 125, 104).

[192] (Anonymous), *De castitate* 16.1 (PLS 1, 1498); cf. Jerome, *ep.* 22.13 (CSEL 54, 160–61).

[193] Augustine, *Contra Faustum* 30.1; *Contra Secundinum* 2; *Contra Adimantum* 14.1–2; Tertullian, *De ieiunio* 2; *De praescriptione haereticorum* 33; Jerome, *Adversus Iovinianum* 2.16; John Chrysostom, *Hom. 12 I Tim.* (4:1–3).

[194] John Chrysostom, *De virginitate* 5.2

the Manichean, the answer is simple: Paul could not have written I Timothy 4:1–4, given the ascetic tenor of his teaching elsewhere.[195] Tertullian, for his part, eagerly appropriates to himself as a "spiritual" Christian the abstinence from using "creatures of God" (I Tim. 4:4, a verse that predicts the coming of overly ascetic "heretics"), interpreting this verse via other ascetic injunctions from I Corinthians 7 and Matthew 19:12: abstinence is fitting to those "upon whom the end of the ages has come" (I Cor. 10:11).[196]

John Cassian's monastic treatises provide numerous examples of how Biblical verses, when removed from their original setting and applied to a solely monastic audience, bolstered the monks' ascetic commitment. Thus the *akatharsia* ("impurity") against which Colossians 3:5 warns is taken by Cassian to signal the dangers to monks of nocturnal emissions while asleep and of sexual thoughts while awake; this "impurity" will deprive the monk of "consecrated food" (i.e., the Eucharist) and will separate him from the "community of the camp" (Lev. 7:20; Num. 19:22; Deut. 23:10–11), that is, of the company of his monastic brothers.[197] The Lord's promise to Hosea that war will be abolished from the land and "I will make you lie down in security" (Hos. 2:18), when transposed from beleaguered Israel to the monastic dormitory, stands as a promise to the monk that he will no longer be plagued by the evils of the night.[198]

A shift in intended audience here allows Christians to advance their ascetic preferences, decry their opponents, and defend themselves against accusations of "heresy."

IX: Changing Sex: Gender-Bending

Numerous Biblical passages would lay ready-to-hand for ascetic exhortation and chastisement if they did not pertain to a person of the "wrong" sex. Not to be inconvenienced, patristic exegetes performed the appropriate "sex change" in the service of ascetic exegesis. Although some might view this exegetical practice as an illustration of Paul's claim that there is "no male and female" in Christ (Gal. 3:28), it appears that the Fathers were prompted more by the need to find fitting Biblical citations with which to exhort, upbraid, or shame fellow Christians.

(SC 125, 106, 108).

[195] Faustus in Augustine, *Contra Faustum* 30.1 (CSEL 25, 747–48).

[196] Tertullian, *De cultu feminarum* 2.9.6 (CCL 1, 363).

[197] John Cassian, *Conlationes* 12.2 (SC 54, 122).

[198] John Cassian, *Conlationes* 12.7 (SC 54, 132).

Passages that had originally referred to or addressed men could, with some assistance, be used to appeal to women. Such is the case with the men of I Corinthians 6:15 whom Paul rebukes for frequenting prostitutes, and with the Parable of the Prodigal Son. Basil of Caesarea, for example, writing of a female virgin who had "fallen," complains that she had "taken the members of Christ and made them members of a harlot." She, like the Prodigal Son, should return home, where the father (here, God) will welcome her, exclaiming, "This was my daughter who was dead and come to life."[199] Likewise, the author of the treatise *Ad virginem devotam* cites the words of the Prodigal Son, but renders them appropriate for a woman: the virgin he addresses should cry, "I am not worthy to be called your daughter."[200] Augustine, too, can readdress the question Paul asked the fornicating men of Corinth ("Do you not know that your bodies are members of Christ?") to wives in particular.[201]

Revelation 14:3–5 (the male virgins who were "undefiled by women") could also be reassigned to the female sex, "undefiled by men."[202] Cyprian explicitly addresses the issue of why women had been passed over in the Apocalypse's reference by appealing to the story of human creation in Genesis 2. He argues that since woman is a portion of man (Gen. 2:21–22), and since God always speaks to Adam—yet Adam and Eve are "two in one flesh" (Gen. 2:24)—then the "men" referred to in Revelation 14:4 denote women as well.[203]

The reverse sex-change operation could be performed as well. Thus John Cassian refers to male monastics as the princess of Psalm 45:10–11 who "leaves her father's house."[204] The author of the pseudo-Basilian treatise *On Virginity* places the words of the "loose woman" of Proverbs 5:3–4, who mixes bile with honey, on the lips of a man who, at the devil's instigation, seeks to lead virgins astray.[205] For Irenaeus, the "foolish virgins" of Matthew 25 with their untrimmed lamps signal "heretical" authors, presumably male, who obscure the meaning of the parables and thus will be shut out from the bridal chamber.[206] John Chrysostom feminizes his friend, the "fallen Theodore," as the "slain daughter" of Jere-

[199] Basil of Caesarea, *ep.* 46 (Loeb I:296, 308, 310).

[200] (Anonymous), *Ad virginem devotam* 2 (PL 17, 603).

[201] Augustine, *De bono viduitatis* 3.4 (CSEL 41, 308).

[202] (Anonymous), *ep. de virginitate* (= *Ad Claudiam*) 2 (CSEL 1, 226–27).

[203] Cyprian, *De habitu virginem* 4 (CSEL 3.1, 190).

[204] John Cassian, *Conlationes* 3.6 (SC 42, 145).

[205] Ps.-Basil, *De virginitate* 2.31–32 (Amand de Mendietta/Moons, p. 41).

[206] Irenaeus, *Adversus haereses* 2.27.2 (PG 7, 803). Conversely, in *Testamentum Orsiesii* 20 (Boon, p. 122), it is male monks who are depicted as the "wise virgins" of Matt. 25.

miah 9:1 for whom Chrysostom weeps; likewise, Theodore is the dissolute "Jerusalem" of Ezekiel 16 who pays her lovers rather than receiving a wage.[207] And Clement of Alexandria assures his readers that males—presbyters, deacons, and laymen—can all be "saved by childbearing" (I Tim. 2:15) if they keep their marriages "blameless."[208]

Song of Songs proved to be a popular source for "gender-bending" as well as for ascetic exegesis in general. "A garden enclosed, a fountain sealed" (Song of Songs 4:12)—so often cited to suggest the "sealed" virginity of religious women—can similarly be quoted to describe male ascetics.[209] Jerome, moreover, does not hesitate to depict his friend Pammachius as the female lover of the Song of Songs.[210]

And the Fathers did not merely cast their friends into these "feminized" portrayals; they also cast themselves. The Bohairic *Life of Pachomius* represents the monk Horsiesius, upon resuming the headship of his community, as reciting the words of Abigail upon hearing David's offer of marriage: "Behold, your handmaid is a slave to wash the feet of the slaves of my lord" (I Sam. 25:41).[211] Jerome depicts himself as the sinful woman of Luke 7:37–38, who washes Jesus' feet with his tears and dries them with his hair.[212] Judas Thomas, in the Acts named for him, sees himself as one of the "wise virgins" of Matthew 25, carrying his oil to meet the Bridegroom,[213] a role into which Jerome can also cast his male friend Rusticus.[214]

In a few instances, the customary understanding of *anthrōpos* as denoting both women and men as "human beings" was given an exclusively masculine edge—an ancient example of a practice all too familiar to modern women. Thus when Paul in Galatians 1:10 urges that Christians not strive to "please *anthrōpous*," Cyprian reads the verse as "pleasing *males*," a practice from which, he avers, female virgins should be dissuaded.[215] Likewise, John Chrysostom cites Paul's warning not to be "slaves [of] *anthrōpōn*" (I Cor. 7:23) to chastise male ascetics who live in syneisaktic relations with women: if Christian males are not to be "slaves of men," how much more should they not be "slaves of women!"[216] Through a linguistic "sex change," the patristic repertoire of verses promoting ascetic commitment could be expanded.

[207] John Chrysostom, *Ad Theodorum lapsum* 1.1; 1.13 (PG 47, 277, 296).

[208] Clement of Alexandria, *Stromata* 3.12.90 (GCS 52 [15], 237).

[209] *Testamentum Orsiesii* 20 (Boon, p. 121).

[210] Jerome, *ep.* 66.10 (CSEL 54, 660).

[211] *Vita Pachomii* 208 (Bo.) (CSCO 89 = Scriptores Coptici 7, 213).

[212] Jerome, *epp.* 11; 22.7 (CSEL 54, 41, 153).

[213] *Acta Thomae* 146 (Lipsius/Bonnet II.2:254–55).

[214] Jerome, *ep.* 125.20 (CSEL 56, 141).

[215] Cyprian, *De cultu virginis* 5 (CSEL 3.1, 190). *Anthrōpos* is linguistically masculine, although used for both sexes; similarly, the Latin *homo* refers to both men and women.

[216] John Chrysostom, *Adversus eos qui*

X: The Hierarchy of Voice

Ascetically inclined commentators found that their cause could also be promoted through careful attention to "voice" (and sometimes "tone") and to the authority of the speaker: considering who uttered a verse, how he or she said it, and with what authority, encouraged a flexibility of interpretation that could both explain (away) less helpful passages and accentuate those that encouraged ascetic commitment.

Three chapters that follow—"The Exegesis of Divorce," "I Corinthians 7 in Patristic Exegesis," and "From Paul to the Pastorals"—illustrate how the assignment of "voice" could lend authoritative weight to ascetic injunctions and "trump" less rigorous speakers. Thus, for example, in commenting on I Corinthians 7, the Fathers debated whether various verses represented the merely human and thus contestable opinions of Paul, or the indefeasible counsel of the Holy Spirit. Likewise, when the Paul of I Corinthians was set against the "Paul" of the Pastorals, the latter could be downgraded as offering mere "concessions" to the morally weak. Finally, Jesus' injunction against divorce was understood to overrule the freedom for (male-initiated) divorce granted by Moses. Somewhat harder to reconcile was Jesus' near-prohibition of divorce (Matt. 5:31–32; 19:9; Mark 10:11–12; Luke 16:18) with Paul's seemingly more tolerant advice in I Corinthians 7:10–16. Here, the more rigorous "voice," that of Jesus, was summoned to constrain Paul's presumed laxity. Among the numerous examples of "voice" to be detailed later, two can here suffice to illustrate the principle.

For Jerome, the seeming discrepancy between Jesus' and Paul's teaching on divorce could easily be resolved if readers took seriously the opening verse of I Corinthians 7 ("It is good not to touch a woman") as Paul's authoritative opinion on the issue of marriage: no man would be in a position to "put away a wife" (Matt. 19:7) if he had never acquired one.[217] Thus in Jerome's interpretation, Paul and Jesus share divine authority; there is no discrepancy between their teachings.

A second example, this time from Gregory Nazianzen, illustrates how the authority of Jesus' stringent teaching on divorce could be rendered even *more* authoritatively rigorous. Commenting on Matthew 19:9, Gregory argues that Jesus does not mean to fault only a woman's *porneia*, but a man's as well. Gregory frames a speech for Jesus, more expansive than the words assigned to him in Matthew, that corrects the presumption that only husbands may initiate divorce. An orator as consummate as Gregory

---

apud se habent subintroductas virgines 10 (PG 47, 509).

[217] Jerome, *Adversus Iovinianum* 1.7 (PL 23, 230).

himself, Jesus here solemnly pronounces, "I do not approve this custom." Gregory's ("feminist") Jesus explains how such a pernicious practice could have arisen: men who made the laws were hard on women but not on themselves. God, by contrast, deems that *porneia* is not permitted for *either* sex; both men and women should be punished for this infraction of God's will. Has not God enjoined that mothers as well as fathers be honored (Exod. 20:12)? Blessing and punishment should fall on the sexes equally.[218] Here, "Jesus" authoritatively rewrites his own words in Matthew to curtail the greater sexual freedom allowed to men.

In addition to authoritative voice, "tone" could also prove important for the production of ascetic meaning. A good example is furnished by Ambrose's treatment of Matthew 19:10, the disciples' reply to Jesus' injunction that a wife's *porneia* is the only grounds on which a husband could initiate a divorce. Here lay an interpretive dilemma. Should their reply—"If such is the case of a man with his wife, it is not expedient to marry"—be read as their shocked response to the "novelty" of Jesus' teaching? Should, in effect, the sentence be closed with an exclamation point? If so read, however, the disciples fail as suitably ardent proponents of the New (ascetic) Dispensation. A different "tone" is necessary if the disciples are to be rescued for the ascetic cause: the verse must be punctuated with a simple period. Hence Ambrose reads the verse flatly, so that the disciples here signal their ready agreement with Jesus that chaste "integrity" should be preferred to the burdens of marriage. Given Ambrose's assignment of "tone," the disciples are understood as already converted to the new virginal regime.[219] A similar treatment of this passage can be found in John Chrysostom's treatise *On Virginity.* According to Chrysostom, Jesus prudently waited to utter these words until his disciples were primed to receive his ascetic message, which Chrysostom firmly (unlike some modern commentators) links to the next verses, the exhortation to become "eunuchs for the Kingdom of Heaven" (Matt. 19:12).[220]

Augustine also offers a telling example of how the "tone" with which a reader invests a passage can promote ascetic interpretation. In his debate with Faustus the Manichean, Augustine seeks to rescue Paul from any unseemly appearance of anger in his outburst against the Galatian Judaizers, "I wish those who unsettle you would mutilate themselves!" (Gal. 5:12). Faustus has not read the passage in the right "tone," Augustine argues. Paul is actually pronouncing a *blessing* on those of whom he speaks, since he wishes them through their "mutilation" to become "eunuchs for the Kingdom of Heaven" (Matt. 19:12) whose sacrifice will be rewarded.

[218] Gregory of Nazianzus, *Or.* 37.6 (PG 36, 289).

[219] Ambrose, *De virginitate* 6.28–29 (PL 16, 286–87). Jerome also has the disciples agreeing with Jesus: "Our Lord thought well of their view" (*Adversus Iovinianum* 1.12 [PL 23, 238–39]).

[220] John Chrysostom, *De virginitate* 13.3

Far from uttering an angry curse, Augustine claims, Paul in true Christian spirit pronounces an "ingenious benediction" on those who heed Jesus' exhortation to ("spiritual") castration.[221] Here, a different assignment of "tone" both redeems Paul and promotes ascetic renunciation.

Ascetically inclined writers could also foster their cause by distinguishing, and reclassifying, "law" or "precept" from "counsel." According to Augustine, since Jesus' own utterances carry diverse levels of authority to suit different occasions,[222] he provides warrant for a reconsideration of what constitutes "law." In response to Faustus' critique that Catholics retain the Old Testament but do not keep its laws, Augustine argues that many of the commands given in the Old Testament should now be understood as "testimonies": such is the case with observing the Feast of Tabernacles or wearing garments of mixed wool and linen fabric. These practices, Augustine claims, echoing earlier Christian writers who explained the Old Testament ritual laws as "types," carry no authority for Christians, but merely point ahead to the fullness of Christian truth.[223] Such a reassignment of authority also applied to Old Testament stories and teachings on marriage and divorce, which otherwise for the Fathers pointedly signaled the "difference in times."

Yet it was not only Old Testament passages that required a reclassification of authoritative voice. Within the New Testament as well, the ascetic exegete could distinguish between "commands" or "precepts," on the one hand, and "counsels," on the other, while aligning both "commands" and "counsels" against "concessions." All major ascetic writers make much of these distinctions, which conveniently allow them to claim for the "counsel" of the celibate life a higher heavenly reward without overtly condemning the "concession" of marriage, thus averting accusations of "heresy."

Hence for Tertullian, Paul's "permission" for marriage does not make it a "good."[224] Paul "permitted" the remarriage of widows much as he "permitted" the circumcision of Timothy (Acts 16:3), in order to "become all things to all men" (I Cor. 9:22). But the Holy Spirit, carrying greater authority, may now recall that earlier indulgence, Tertullian argues.[225] Tertullian presses the text of I Corinthians 7 still further: when Paul claims the authority of the Holy Spirit (I Cor. 7:40) for his exhortation to continence, his words stand as an authoritative precept, not as a mere recommendation.[226]

(SC 125, 134, 136).

[221] Augustine, *Contra Faustum* 16.22 (CSEL 25, 465–66).

[222] Augustine, *Contra Faustum* 22.77 (CSEL 25, 676–77).

[223] Augustine, *Contra Faustum* 6.9 (CSEL 25, 301).

[224] Tertullian, *De monogamia* 3.3 (CCL 2, 1231); cf. *Ad uxorem* 1.3.2–3 (CCL 1, 375).

[225] Tertullian, *De monogamia* 14.1–3 (CCL 2, 1249); cf. *De exhortatione castitatis* 3.4 (CCL 2, 1018–22).

[226] Tertullian, *De exhortatione castitatis* 4 (CCL 2, 1020–22).

Different patristic writers variously nuanced their appeal to authority as it suited the occasion and their preferences. Thus for Ambrose, since exhortations to virginity and widowhood in Paul's writings are counsels, not commands, they receive a higher blessing because of their greater difficulty.[227] For the anti-ascetic Jovinian, however, Paul's caveat that he has "no commandment from the Lord" on virginity (I Cor. 7:25) proves that marriage should be lauded—while for his opponent Jerome, the verse implies exactly the opposite, namely, that virginity secures a higher blessing but one which Jesus declared "not all could receive" (Matt. 19:11).[228] According to Jerome, Paul concedes that he has "no commandment" so that all Christians may freely choose which mode of life they will adopt—and for which degree of reward they will strive.[229] For Pelagian authors, the "free choice" attending the counsel for virginity was especially important:[230] the counsel of "castrating oneself for the Kingdom of Heaven" brings a great blessing if it is an act of free will.[231] Yet, Pelagian authors warn, transgressing even one commandment imperils one's salvation (James 2:10);[232] hence a life of chastity cannot compensate for a Christian's failure to keep other commands.[233]

Concerning precepts and counsels, Augustine draws a subtle distinction even *within* one Scriptural verse. For Augustine, the first sentence of Paul's teaching in I Corinthians 7:27 ("if you are bound to a wife, do not seek to be loosed") constitutes a precept, an absolute command against divorce, whereas the second ("Are you loosed from a wife? Do not seek to be bound") stands as a counsel that gives Christians the opportunity for the higher choice of celibacy.[234] Thus while divorce is strictly prohibited, celibacy is encouraged but not required.

For Origen, Paul's repetition of "You shall not commit adultery" (Exod. 20:14) in Romans 13:9 stands as a command, but one on which Origen heaps scorn: forbidding adultery and fornication is like "milk for children" (I Cor. 3:2), a "milk" also attending Paul's concession for marriage in I Corinthians 7:2. Ephesians, which contains no warnings against adultery or fornication, provides "solid food" for the perfect who need no such commands.[235] For Origen, those who follow merely the precepts are

[227] Ambrose, *ep.* 63.35 (PL 16, 1250); *Ad viduis* 14.82 (PL 16, 273); cf. *Hexaemeron* 5.18.19.63 (CSEL 32.1, 187–88).

[228] Jerome, *Adversus Iovinianum* 1.12 (PL 23, 237–38).

[229] Jerome, *ep.* 22.20 (CSEL 54, 170–71).

[230] E.g., Pelagius, *Comm. I Cor.* 7:28 (PLS 1, 1203); (Anonymous), *De castitate* 9.1 (PLS 1, 1477–78).

[231] Pelagius, *Comm. I Cor.* 7:25 (PLS 1, 1202).

[232] (Anonymous), *De castitate* 10.8 (PLS 1, 1484).

[233] (Anonymous), *ep. de virginitate* (= *Ad Claudiam*) 4; cf. 13 (CSEL 1, 228–29, 243); Pelagius, *Ad Demetriadem* 4.4 (PL 30, 19–20); (Anonymous), *De malis doctoribus* 11.1 (PLS 1, 1434–35).

[234] Augustine, *De sancta virginitate* 15.15 (CSEL 41, 247–48).

[235] Origen, *Hom. 7 Ezech.* 10 (SC 352, 270, 272).

required to say, "We are useless servants," whereas those who commit themselves to virginity exceed the level of precept and can rightfully claim, "We are good and faithful servants" (cf. Luke 17:10; Matt. 20:23).[236]

Methodius, in an unusual interpretation of I Corinthians 7:1–2, assigns an even higher level of authority to Paul's teaching, "It is good not to touch a woman." Methodius argues that Paul in the opening verse of this chapter "commands" chastity and "not touching a woman," but then relaxes the "command" (*epitagē*) and gives "permission" for those unable to adopt this rigorous precept.[237] Here, the call for celibacy is transformed from counsel to precept—but one from which Paul quickly retreats after reconsidering the circumstances of his audience. Both the author of the *Apostolic Constitutions*[238] and John Chrysostom distinguish between the permission for marriage that Paul gives and his higher "wish" that all would freely choose virginity; Chrysostom adds that even if Paul issues "no command," he nonetheless himself provides an example that he urges Christians to emulate (I Cor. 7:7).[239] Last, Basil of Ancyra explicates why Paul says that he has "no command from the Lord" concerning virginity (I Cor. 7:25): since God had already pronounced "reproduce and multiply" (Gen. 1:28), Paul could issue no law requiring Christians to maintain lifelong virginity. This is why, Basil claims, we find no command for virginity among the Beatitudes. Positioned above the commandment, the virginal life is rather a matter of free choice.[240]

Thus do ascetically inclined patristic authors assign differing levels of authoritative tone to Scriptural passages in order to promote ascetic commitment—while seeking to avoid accusations that they have undone God's earlier commands or have invented more rigorous ones on their own authority.

XI: The "Difference in Times"

The patristic appeal to the "difference in times" (i.e., between that of the Old Testament and that of the New) was pressed in two different ways. Most obviously, it allowed for the contrast between the allegedly "carnal" mores of the Old Testament and the manifestly ascetic ones of the Christian era, thus creating not just "difference," but "distinction," for Christian renunciants. Yet in the

[236] Origen, *Comm. Rom.* 3.2.2–5 (3:12) (Hammond Bammel, pp. 213–14).

[237] Methodius, *Symposium* 3.12 (GCS 27, 40); cf. Origen, *Comm. Matt.* 14.23 (GCS 40, 339–40): these concessions are given for those who do not desire "the greater gifts" (I Cor. 12:31).

[238] *Constitutiones apostolorum* 4.14.1–2 (SC 329, 192). The author worries, however, that virgins may cast "reproach" on marriage.

[239] John Chrysostom, *De virginitate* 2.2 (SC 125, 100).

[240] Basil of Ancyra, *De virginitate* 55 (Vaillant, p. 65).

hands of exegetes eager to uphold the dignity of the Old Testament, the appeal to the "difference in times" could also serve as a means to excuse the behavior of Old Testament characters which otherwise would be deemed reprehensible: God had tolerated laxer sexual behavior in the world's infancy so that the Chosen People, the forerunners of the Savior, might be abundantly produced. Thus, according to John Chrysostom, Noah's drunkenness (Gen. 9:20–21) was perhaps excusable: he was considered "a righteous man, blameless in *his* generation" (Gen. 6:9)—although certainly not "blameless" by ascetic Christian standards.[241] Arguments from the "different times" proved useful in combating opponents, especially rigorously ascetic Manicheans, who rehearsed the foibles of the patriarchs as a ground for their rejection of the Old Testament. Thus, for example, when the Manichean Felix cites I Corinthians 13:9-10 (that the imperfect is to be put away when the perfect comes) as an injunction to set aside the Old Testament, Augustine counterargues that however reprobate its customs may seem to Christian eyes, the Old Covenant reveals God's plan of salvation.[242] Christians need not condemn "difference."

More often, the Fathers devised an "ascetic trajectory" that rose from the Old Testament to the New. Yet even here, the earliest moments of creation (Gen. 1–2) might be taken to signal the blessed regime of virginity and thus, in effect, to belong to the Christian Dispensation, not to Hebrew "carnality." But after the first sin and the expulsion from Eden came sexual relation—and concubinage, polygamy, incest, and divorce, to be corrected with the advent of the Christian Dispensation. This ascetic trajectory is especially favored by Gregory of Nyssa,[243] Jerome,[244] and John Chrysostom,[245] none of whom believed that sexual intercourse attended God's original plan for humanity. Others, conceding that marriage was established by God in the first chapters of Genesis, argued that God had nonetheless intended only *single* marriage: in Tertullian's famous formulation, the "one rib" (Gen. 2:22) signaled the "one wife" that Adam was to possess. Genesis 1–2 was also taken to teach that divorce was not to be countenanced. Thus Tertullian further argues that if Christians consider their Savior the "Alpha and Omega" (Rev. 1:8), they should believe that he restored the Edenic situation of "no divorce"—or better, of "the original integrity of the flesh."[246] According to John Chrysostom, the original "law of nature" given by God commanding a single marriage and forbid-

[241] John Chrysostom, *De virginitate* 83.1 (SC 125, 388).

[242] Felix in Augustine, *Contra Felicem* 1.9–10 (CSEL 25, 811–12).

[243] Gregory of Nyssa, *De virginitate* 12–13 (SC 119, 398–430).

[244] Jerome, *Adversus Iovinianum* 1.16; 1.18; 1.29 (PL 23, 246, 247–48, 262–63); *ep.* 22.19 (CSEL 54, 168–70).

[245] John Chrysostom, *De virginitate* 14.3; 14.5; 14.6 (SC 125, 140, 142, 144).

[246] Tertullian, *De monogamia* 4.2; 5.2–4 (CCL 2, 1233, 1234–35).

ding divorce preceded, and thus stood superior to, the Mosaic law that allowed for remarriage after divorce, as well as for bigamy.[247]

But where to mark the apex of this ascetic trajectory? Noting the (allegedly) lofty mores of primitive Christians against which the laxer behavior of a patristic author's contemporaries could be criticized proved a useful "shaming device," a favorite of John Chrysostom in castigating his congregation.[248] Yet praising Christian virginity encouraged the Fathers to believe that their *own* times, not those of the New Testament, enjoyed the most abundant outpouring of the Spirit, shown in the rapid spread of ascetic devotion.[249] On this latter trajectory, however, Montanists or Manicheans might claim that the New Testament revelation was not complete, but required later supplementation or correction, whether by the Holy Spirit[250] or by Mani. Thus the ascetic trajectory necessitated a delicate negotiation of its starting and ending moments.

In general, the church fathers approved the theme of God's progressive revelation to the human race. In simple form, they might claim that not all of Moses' commands were prompted by God (as shown by Jesus' critique of the Mosaic divorce laws in Matt. 19:4–8),[251] so that their amendment by Christians was in order. In the New Testament, Jesus' promise in the Gospel of John that the Paraclete would complete his revelation proved useful not just for Montanists,[252] but also for Catholic writers such as John Chrysostom, for whom the notion of progressive revelation could be used to explain why Jesus while on earth did not expound more explicitly the glories of virginity.[253]

A notable appeal to progressive revelation that both signals the "difference in times" and exalts the chaste standard of the Christian era can be found in Methodius' *Symposium*. Here, a female symposiast argues that the Old Testament originally allowed incestuous marriages, but overruled them in Leviticus 18:17–19. Next, the previous practice of polygamy was forbidden, then adultery. Later, marital continence was preached—but only now, in the Christian era, was virginity accorded its proper place.[254]

[247] John Chrysostom, *Hom. 13 Rom.* (7:25) (PG 60, 512).

[248] John Chrysostom, *Hom. 73 Matt.* 3–4 (PG 58, 677–78); *Hom. 3 Acta* (1:16) (PG 60, 34).

[249] E.g., Athanasius, *ep. 1 ad virgines* (CSCO 150 = Scriptores Coptici 19, 76; ET, Brakke, p. 276); cf. John Chrysostom, *Hom. 12 Rom.* (7:6) (PG 60, 498–99); *Hom. 13 Rom.* (7:14) (PG 60, 508).

[250] A special theme of Tertullian: *De monogamia* 14.3–4 (CCL 2, 1249); *De pudicitia* 1.20 (CCL 2, 1283).

[251] Origen, *Hom. 16 Num.* 4 (GCS 30, 142).

[252] Tertullian, *De monogamia* 14.3–4 (CCL 2, 1249).

[253] John Chrysostom, *De virginitate* 12.2 (SC 125, 128, 130), appealing to John 16:12 (Jesus will not reveal all now). According to Chrysostom, Jesus left to Paul to explicate a fuller teaching on virginity (*De virginitate* 12.3–4 [SC 125, 130]).

[254] Methodius, *Symposium* 1.2 (GCS 27, 9–10).

Here, a steady improvement of mores reaches its summit in the exhortations to sexual renunciation of Methodius' own day.

That "salvation history" had followed this increasingly ascetic trajectory was enabled by the Fathers' depictions of God as a patient parent, teacher, and physician, who accommodated his teachings or remedies to the abilities of his pupils and patients. John Chrysostom reasons that just as boys are not taught the most difficult concepts first, so God taught the Jewish "children" elementary lessons through their "schoolmaster," Moses.[255] Just as human parents, Chrysostom argues, expect better behavior of their children as they mature, so moral progress could be noted throughout "salvation history."[256] Methodius depicts the early Israelites as little calves whom God had allowed to frolic about before he enforced a stricter discipline upon them.[257] The ascetic message is clear: maturity demands more rigorous renunciation.

The analogy of God as a skillful physician also proved attractive to those expounding the ascetic trajectory. For Augustine, just as doctors prescribe divergent treatments for different days of an illness, so God varied his remedies with humans—but what God at first prescribed (e.g., marriage), he could later forbid.[258] For the anonymous author of the treatise *On Chastity*, the "good physician" image also befits Paul, who concedes marriage to those "patients" whom he deems too weak to bear the greater rigors of virginity. But why resort to "medicine" if you are not ill, the author pointedly inquires of his readers?[259]

Fortunately for the Fathers pressing this line of argument, a number of Scriptural verses lay ready to hand to reinforce the "difference in times." Notable was Ecclesiastes 3:5 ("a time to embrace and a time to refrain from embracing");[260] I Corinthians 10:11 ("these things are written down for our instruction, upon whom the end of the ages has come");[261] II Corinthians 5:17 ("old things have passed away, all has become new");[262] and Ephesians 4:13 (the achievement of "perfect manhood").[263] Moreover, Jesus' own teaching, such as his sharpening of the prohibition of

255 John Chrysostom, *Hom. 4 Col.* (1:25) (PG 62, 328–29).

256 John Chrysostom, *De virginitate* 84.1 (SC 125, 390).

257 Methodius, *Symposium* 1.2 (GCS 27, 10).

258 Augustine, *Contra Faustum* 32.14 (CSEL 25, 773–74).

259 (Anonymous), *De castitate* 9.2; 10.3 (PLS 1, 1478, 1480).

260 Jerome, *Adversus Iovinianum* 1.29; *epp.* 22.19; 107.13; *Comm. Eccles.* 3.5; Tertullian, *De monogamia* 3.8; Augustine, *De bono coniugali* 13.15; *De nuptiis et concupiscentia* 1.13.14–15; (Anonymous), *Admonitio Augiensis* (6).

261 Jerome, *Adversus Iovinianum* 2.4 (PL 23, 301); Ps.-Titus *ep.* (de Bruyne, p. 50); Origen, *Comm. Ioan.* 1.6.8 (GCS 10, 11).

262 Jerome, *Adversus Iovinianum* 1.37 (PL 23, 273); (Anonymous), *De castitate* 14.6 (PLS 1, 1495).

263 Origen, *Hom. 24 Num.* 3 (GCS 30, 231); cf. *Hom. 26 Num.* 1 (GCS 30, 243); John Chrysostom, *De virginitate* 16.1 (SC 125, 146).

adultery into the prohibition of lust (Matt. 5:27–28), indicates to several patristic authors the upward trajectory from the Old Dispensation to the New.[264]

That the provisions of the Old Law served as "types" and "shadows" of the New enabled a double message: that the stories of the Old Testament "foreshadowed" New Testament truth, but that the "spirit" had now, in Christian times, replaced the "letter."[265] Thus Origen and Augustine proclaim that although "types" had their place in the former era, they were no longer to be heeded by Christians.[266] No one should appeal to the patriarchs' wives and concubines as examples for the Christian present, Tertullian argues, for this would be to admit that "types" remain for Christians—which they do not.[267]

The items most frequently singled out by ascetically inclined Fathers to indicate the "difference in times" were not only procreation, polygamy, concubinage, and incest—but marriage as well. The practice of divorce also distinguished the Old Dispensation from the New, as chapter 9, "The Exegesis of Divorce," illustrates in detail.

Consistently, the ascetically minded Fathers sound the theme that "reproduce and multiply" (Gen. 1:28) is no longer in effect: the "time is wound up," according to Tertullian;[268] the "second decree" of continence has replaced the "first decree" of reproduction (so Cyprian);[269] the forest and harvest are ready to be cut down (so Jerome).[270] Even Augustine, who supports marriage for the sake of procreation, reminds readers that although in olden times it was necessary to have children, it is not so any longer—and cites Ecclesiastes 3:5 ("embrace and cease from embracing"), I Corinthians 7:29 ("have wives as if not"), and Matthew 19:12 ("eunuchs for the Kingdom of Heaven") to reinforce his point.[271] The anonymous author of the treatise *On Chastity* concedes that although it was "right" for Adam and Eve to procreate when the earth was barren, such is hardly the case at present, when the earth can scarcely sustain its population. For this author, the later commands of the New Testament annul the earlier ones of the Old; he cites II Corinthians 5:17 ("the old things are passed

[264] John Chrysostom, *De virginitate* 83.2; (Anonymous), *De castitate* 2; Cyril of Alexandria, *Comm. in Matt.* 5:27–28; Tertullian, *De pudicitia* 6.6; Augustine, *Contra Iulianum* 4.14.65.

[265] Gregory of Nazianzus, *Carm.* 2.3 (= *Exhortatio ad virgines*, 11.27–29 [PG 37, 635]).

[266] Origen, *Comm. Ioan.* 1.6.8 (GCS 10, 11); Augustine, *Contra Faustum* 31.4 (CSEL 25, 759).

[267] Tertullian, *De exhortatio castitatis* 6.1 (CCL 2, 1023).

[268] Tertullian, *De pudicitia* 16.19 (CCL 2, 1314); cf. *Adversus Marcionem* 1.29.4: the one who said Gen. 1:28 ("reproduce") can also say I Cor. 7:29 ("wives as if not") (CCL 1, 473).

[269] Cyprian, *De habitu virginem* 23 (CSEL 3.1, 203).

[270] Jerome, *Adversus Helvidium* 21 (PL 23, 215).

[271] Augustine, *De coniugiis adulterinis* 2.12.12 (CSEL 41, 395–96).

away, and all is made anew") to buttress his claim.[272] Basil of Caesarea's comment is perhaps the bluntest. Replying to an inquiry about the licitness of a man's marrying the sister of his deceased wife, Basil cites Leviticus 18 (on not uncovering the nakedness of one's relatives) and Pauline verses on "the shortness of time" (I Cor. 7:29–31), and concludes with a pointed rejoinder, "Don't read to me Genesis 1:28 or I'll laugh!" His correspondent has not appropriately distinguished "the times of the promulgation of the law," Basil complains.[273]

Likewise, the polygamy, concubinage, and incest reported in the Old Testament signaled the "difference in times" from the ascetic rigor appropriate to the New Dispensation. Various patristic authors took more or less generous approaches to the patriarchs' sexual behavior, a theme detailed more extensively in chapter 7. According to Tertullian, the patriarchs' numerous wives and concubines were "necessary" at the world's beginning, but now, in the Christian era, the reasons for the "necessity" had been "lopped off."[274] Augustine expands: the patriarchs engaged in polygamy for the sake of procreation, not out of "lust." This claim is reinforced (Augustine thinks) by the fact that it was the Israelite males who took several female sexual partners, not vice versa: a woman's fruitfulness is not enhanced by having more than one spouse, while a man's may be.[275] In any event, Christians should not judge this ancient custom as sinful for the patriarchs' time; Augustine reminds his readers that then there stood no legal prohibition against polygamy.[276]

In similar fashion, Augustine justifies the incest of the earliest Hebrews. The first progeny of Adam and Eve by necessity engaged in sister-brother marriages because there were no other people with whom they could mate. Yet since "nature" wishes for more people to be linked by ties of relation, the earlier practice of incest soon died out, even among impious idolaters.[277] In the case of Lot's drunken intercourse with his daughters, Augustine is careful to note that Scripture does not approve the deed; nonetheless, since these sexual acts were performed "without lust" and the daughters were motivated by their (mistaken) belief that the human race would die out if they failed to produce offspring, their behavior is in a sense justified.[278]

[272] (Anonymous), *De castitate* 14.4; 14.6 (PLS 1, 1495).

[273] Basil of Caesarea, *ep.* 160 (Loeb II:406, 408).

[274] Tertullian, *Ad uxorem* 1.2.2 (CCL 1, 374–75).

[275] Augustine, *De doctrina Christiana* 3.12.20; *De bono coniugali* 13.15; 15.17; *De bono viduitatis* 7.10; *Contra Faustum* 22.47–48; *Serm.* 51.15.25; 51.15.28.

[276] Augustine, *De doctrina Christiana* 3.14.22 (CCL 32, 91); *De civitate Dei* 16.38 (CCL 48, 544).

[277] Augustine, *De civitate Dei* 15.16 (CCL 48, 477–78).

[278] Augustine, *Contra Faustum* 22.45; 22.43 (CSEL 25, 637, 635–36).

Yet it was not just polygamy, concubinage, and incest that marked the "difference in times": so did marriage itself. For the more rigorously ascetic writers, the coming of virginity as a new way of life is *the* distinctive feature separating the Old Testament and the New.[279] Thus Jerome pits passages commanding childbearing (Gen. 1:28; Exod. 23:26) against the praise of I Corinthians 7 for virginity and sexual abstinence within marriage.[280] According to the author of *On Chastity*, once upon a time, under the Old Dispensation, God had sanctioned human marriage—along with circumcision and Sabbath observance—but this does not mean that God now desires these practices. If Christians acknowledge that "times differ" regarding circumcision and animal sacrifice, they should acknowledge that there is also a "difference of times" regarding the institution of marriage. Since there is a "time for everything" (Eccles. 3:1), behavior that was deemed lawful in the past no longer meets Christian standards.[281]

The Pelagian(?) author of the treatise *Admonitio Augiensis* also rhetorically sounds the theme of the "difference in times." In olden days, the author argues, married men without sons were thought to be under a curse; now, Christians are deemed blessed if they have wives "as if not" (I Cor. 7:29). Whereas Adam was told by God that it was "good not to be alone" (Gen. 2:18), now it is "well to remain as you are" (I Cor. 7:26). Once again, Ecclesiastes 3:5 is cited to reinforce the difference between those who are "two in one flesh" (Gen. 2:24) and those who are "two in one spirit" (I Cor. 6:16–17).[282]

Most sharply, the Pachomian monk Horsiesius reminds a correspondent that whereas Moses said, "Honor thy father and thy mother" (Exod. 20:12), the Son of God "corrects" this injunction with Luke 14:26: "If anyone comes to me and does not hate his own father and mother and wife and children and brothers and sisters, yes, and even his own life, he cannot be my disciple."[283] With such words, ascetically inclined church writers marked the sharp disjunction between the ascetic present and the Hebrew past. In the scheme of the "difference of times," unlike the practice of "close reading" or the locating of manifestly "ascetic" passages in the Old Testament, the discrepancies between Hebrew "carnality" and

[279] (Anonymous), *De castitate* 6.4 (PLS 1, 1497); Jerome, *Adversus Helvidium* 20 (PL 23, 213–14).

[280] Jerome, *Adversus Helvidium* 20 (PL 23, 213–14).

[281] (Anonymous), *De castitate* 15.3–4; 17 (PLS 1, 1497–98, 1499).

[282] (Anonymous), *Admonitio Augiensis* (PLS 1, 1702).

[283] Horsiesius, *ep.* 1.5 (CSCO 159 = Scriptores Coptici 23, 64). The Lucan passage is also cited with approval as encouragement to ascetic renunciation by Tertullian, *De idololatria* 12; Jerome, *ep.* 145; John Cassian, *Conlationes* 3.4; 21.9; Origen, *Hom. 17 Jesu Nave* 2; Basil of Ancyra, *De virginitate* 25; Evagrius Ponticus, *epp.* 55.3; 60.3; Basil of Caesarea, *Regulae fusius tractatae* 12.

Christian "spirituality" were most dramatically produced. Here, the difference between the Old and the New Dispensations could be scored to claim "distinction" for Christian ascetics. That an appeal to the "difference in times" flirted dangerously with a rejection of Old Testament teaching was understood by most church fathers, eager to escape accusations of "heresy." That their denigration of Old Testament mores might flame the fires of anti-Jewish sentiment appears less troubling to them than to us.

Through such diverse strategies of reading, early Christian authors were able to produce ascetic meaning from even the most unlikely Scriptural passages. In some cases, they located passages in the Old Testament that, with minimal interpretation, could be appropriated to further the ascetic cause; in other cases, a stronger ascetic meaning could be derived from a translation that pressured the text in a renunciatory direction. But if a text seemed "hopeless," Christian writers could at least appeal to the "difference in times" between the Old Dispensation and the New. The malleability of Scripture for the ascetic program is here strikingly manifest.

CHAPTER SIX

Three Models of Reading Renunciation

I: Introduction

The exegetical modes outlined above, I will argue, should not be understood as purely formal constructs: they were used by early Christian writers to counsel, exhort, and warn "real-life" audiences concerning issues of marriage, sexuality, and ascetic renunciation. Hence the Fathers' ways of interpreting Biblical texts correlate closely with their (somewhat) differing marital and ascetic axiologies. In this chapter I hope to show how the evaluations of marriage and asceticism by three patristic authors—John Chrysostom, Jerome, and Origen—relate to their respective modes of reading. Although other authors of the early Christian era might have served to illustrate my point, these three stand as particularly illuminating examples of how various interpretive strategies supported differing views of marriage and renunciation. Here, interpretive decisions—whether to emphasize or deemphasize the "difference in times," whether to employ intertextual rather than allegorical modes of exegesis—are seen to carry consequences for the bodies of Christians in the extratextual world. This discussion of exegesis and asceticism, then, serves as an introduction to the more specialized topical investigations of chapters 7 through 9, and to the exegesis of particular New Testament passages in chapters 10 and 11.

Each of these three distinct approaches to Biblical texts I will here explore offered different benefits and perils, each involved distinctive modes of exegesis. The first option—exemplified in some of John Chrysostom's writings—minimized the distance separating ancient Hebrew from contemporary ascetic ideals: the mores of the Israelites could be adroitly rescued and comfortably linked to the Christian Dispensation. This option firmly secured the Old Testament as the Church's book, so that (as Michael Fishbane has put it in a different context) there was "no past as such."[1] Forestalling allegations of a "heretical" rejection of the Old Testa-

[1] Michael Fishbane, *Biblical Interpretation in Ancient Israel* (Oxford: Clarendon, 1985), p. 413.

ment, this approach united the Hebrew past to the Christian present through a discursive privileging of the body in marriage. But where, then, might "difference" and "distinction" lie if Hebrew patriarchs and Christian ascetics were *not* to be hierarchically positioned in relation to each other? Where might lie the leverage by which contemporary commentators could claim the superiority of ascetics to nonascetics?

A contrasting interpretive option—represented here by Jerome—accentuated the divergence between the "carnality" of the Hebrew past and the ascetic superiority of the Christian present. This approach provided a ready avenue for ascetically inclined commentators to claim for contemporary renunciants not just difference, but "distinction." Moreover, the very act of "distinguishing" also conveniently served to highlight the religious superiority of the ascetic exegetes themselves, to establish *them* as authoritative interpreters of texts. Yet rejecting the celebration of marriage and procreation in the Hebrew Scriptures might prompt accusations of heresy: would not *too* strong an emphasis on "ascetic distinction" signal an abandonment of the Hebrew past and alienation from its God?

A third interpretive model—illustrated here through Origen's writings—circumvented the debate over the "difference in times" by abandoning any chronological trajectory between Hebrew past and Christian present: the text could be "saved" through a transhistorical reading of Scripture. Here, the interpreter was not forced to choose between "leaving the past as past" or transforming it into the Christian present. On this interpretive option, it was not so much physical bodies, whether in the service of marriage *or* of asceticism, that were differentiated, but the inner constitution of the human self, reason against sense, virtue against vice. But did not exegetes of this persuasion leave ascetic praxis to float free of any grounding in the Biblical text? Might Scripture itself not be rendered superfluous for the creation and maintenance of a Christian sexual ethic?

These three approaches to the Hebrew past—embracing it as the Christian present, distancing it as unedifying for contemporary ascetics, or bypassing it through a transhistorical reading—correlate, I will argue, with differing modes of exegesis. Both those interpreters who "unify" the times and those who "divide" them usually employ a quasi-literal and moralizing hermeneutic that relies heavily on intertextual exegesis, although their commentaries aim variously either to vindicate or to critique ancient Israelite (and some early Christian) mores. Those commentators who unify the Old Testament and the New, the Hebrew past and the Christian present, also link marriage and ascetic renunciation on a continuum of Christian practice. Yet if marriage is here "redeemed," "difference" has been displaced onto a hierarchy *within* marriage, a hierarchy that ranks husband over wife.

The proponents of the "difference in times," on the other hand, read both the Old Testament and the Christian present with more sharply asceticized eyes. Here, ancient Israelite sexual teaching and practice are deemed only selectively (and dubiously) recuperable for the Christian present. The Hebrew past is in a sense "foreclosed,"[2] worthy of only perfunctory efforts at redemption through interpretation. Although commentators of this persuasion faced allegations that they were flirting with heresy, if not embracing it, in their uncomplimentary treatment of the Old Testament, their exegeses created firm ground from which to proclaim a decisive "difference" between ascetics and nonascetics in the Christian present.

The third approach to the Hebrew past constructs no historical trajectory, either positive or negative, since Biblical narratives are seen to exist in the realm of timeless truth: on this transhistorical reading, the Old Testament proclaims the Christian message as fully as does the New—or the ascetic present. There is no worrisome gap between past and present because diachronic comparisons have been erased. Here, an allegorical style of exegesis will dominate. Biblical verses that refer to women, men, marriage, bodies, and sexual matters prompt reflection on the gendered nature of the human faculties ("sense" versus "reason," for example), or of the virtues and vices. Here, the materiality of the body is deflected onto an elaboration of hierarchically gendered virtue.

The church fathers typifying these three models in various ways create "difference," which, as Emile Durkheim taught us years ago, is built into the structure of religious language and practice.[3] More recently, "difference" and "distinction" have been analyzed by Pierre Bourdieu, who notes the "social magic" by which discontinuity and hierarchy is inevitably produced.[4] Ascetic exegesis, I will suggest, is precisely *about* the creation of hierarchy and distinction—although these are differently located by the three exegetes I will here discuss, John Chrysostom, Jerome, and Origen.

Although I will use these three authors as exemplars, others of course could be added. For example, Augustine, in his growing unease with allegorical interpretations of Genesis 1–3, in his tireless effort to rescue

[2] Joel Fineman, "The Structure of Allegorical Desire," in *Allegory and Representation*, ed. Stephen J. Greenblatt, Select Papers from the English Institute, 1979–80, New Series 5 (Baltimore/London: Johns Hopkins University Press, 1981), p. 29.

[3] Emile Durkheim, *The Elementary Forms of the Religious Life: A Study in Religious Sociology*, trans. J. W. Swain (London: George Allen & Unwin; New York: Macmillan, n.d.), pp. 145–47, 299–317. For a fuller discussion of the creation of "difference," see below, pp. 204–8.

[4] Pierre Bourdieu, *Language and Symbolic Power*, ed. J. B. Thompson; trans. G. Raymond and M. Adamson (Cambridge: Harvard University Press, 1991), p. 120; cf. *Distinction: A Social Critique of the Judgement of Taste*, trans. Richard Nice (Cambridge: Harvard University Press,

the Hebrew patriarchs from Manichean denigration, and in his warnings to proud contemporary ascetics lest they scorn the worthy Christian married, exhibits an exegetical pattern similar to Chrysostom's. Or again, the anonymous author of the allegedly Pelagian treatise *On Chastity* (*De castitate*) joins (and outdoes) Jerome in pressing an exegesis focused on the "difference in times," in which a sharp differentiation between an underasceticized Hebrew past is contrasted with a more richly renunciatory Christian present. And Origen, for his part, would find a worthy exegetical partner in Evagrius Ponticus, who also effects a transhistorical reading of the Bible that renders numerous passages of Hebrew Scripture, in allegorical guise, useful for Christian ascetics. And he, too, following Origen, will place "differentiation" and "distinction" not onto the realm of ascetics versus nonascetics (as does Jerome), nor onto a hierarchy within marriage (as does Chrysostom), but onto the genderized human faculties, virtues and vices.

II: John Chrysostom

John Chrysostom will serve as an example of the Fathers interested to "unite the times." Chrysostom denies that there is (or should be) a yawning gap that divides the mores of the Old Testament from those of the New and of the Christian present: Old Testament characters and teachings are raised up as exemplary for Christian audiences. Thus in his later (unlike some of his earlier) writings, Chrysostom regularly lauds Old Testament heroes and heroines who married and reproduced. They can—with some exegetical assistance—serve as models, even as "shaming devices," for the married men and women who constituted his congregations at Antioch and at Constantinople. Linking the Old Testament and the New, Chrysostom also joins marriage and ascetic renunciation on a continuum of Christian practice. Yet if marriage is thus redeemed for the Christian life, "difference" has been displaced onto a hierarchy *within* marriage, of husband over wife. Daniel Boyarin in his fascinating study, *Carnal Israel*, has uncovered a similar pattern for rabbinical interpreters, whose exaltation of marriage and procreation, he argues, is firmly grounded in a marital hierarchy that requires the subordination of women.[5]

Admittedly, for some Biblical characters Chrysostom offers only a weak excuse for their shocking behavior: Lot's drunken intercourse with his daughters stands as an example. (According to Chrysostom, the daugh-

---

1984; French original, 1979).

[5] Daniel Boyarin, *Carnal Israel: Reading Sex in Talmudic Culture*, The New Historicism 25 (Berkeley/Los Angeles/Oxford: University of California Press, 1993), pp. 133, 196.

ters, believing that they were the last humans on earth, deceived their father who, in his drunken state, was unaware of what they were doing.)[6] For other characters, Chrysostom locates some detail of the text that, when "closely read," renders their behavior praiseworthy: Noah, for example, begot three sons, but only when he was past five hundred years old, thus providing a model of sexual restraint to Christian husbands.[7] Still others are more straightforwardly recuperable: Joseph fleeing from Potiphar's wife appears as a paragon of continence for present-day Christians.[8] Chrysostom especially likes to utilize the narratives of ancient Israelites as shaming devices for his contemporaries: that of Sarah, who (unlike arrogant Christian wives of Chrysostom's own day) willingly served her husband and his three visitors at Mamre;[9] and of Job, who, deigning not to "look on a virgin's face" (Job 31:1), signals "perfect chastity."[10]

Chrysostom's favorite model is perhaps Abraham. Chrysostom offers scant comment on Abraham's near-sacrifice of Isaac,[11] but focuses instead on the narratives pertaining to Sarah and to Hagar, aiming to exonerate the trio from allegations of moral turpitude. Thus Chrysostom praises Sarah's "righteousness" in volunteering Hagar's reproductive services; represents Sarah and Abraham as exempt from passion in their marital union (they wish only to produce children before they die); and argues that Abraham's sexual relation with Hagar was not motivated by the desire for pleasure. And because Abraham tenderly pardons Sarah's anger, recalling "the weakness of her sex," he provides an excellent example to contemporary Christian husbands.[12]

Turning to Abraham's "loan" of Sarah to foreign kings, Chrysostom argues that since even the patriarch's death could not have rescued Sarah from dishonor, why should he have sacrificed his own safety to no avail?[13] Rather, Abraham manifests his virtue in not falling prey to jealousy when other men lust after his wife. Sarah's acquiescence in the scheme also provides a model for Christian marriage: like every good wife, she takes her husband's advice even at the risk to her own honor. Her ready agreement signals a marital accord that Chrysostom recommends to contemporary married Christians.[14] Chrysostom here enlists the "two in one flesh" verse

[6] John Chrysostom, *Hom. 44 Gen.* 4; 5 (PG 54, 410–12).

[7] John Chrysostom, *Hom. 24 Gen.* 1 (PG 53, 207); *Hom. 21 Gen.* 5 (PG 53, 182).

[8] John Chrysostom, *Hom. 84 Matt.* 4 (PG 58, 756–58); *Hom. 49 Acta* (PG 60, 342); *De S. Pelagia* 1.2 (PG 50, 581). In *Hom. 3 de poenitentia* 3 Joseph is praised but conceded not to be a virgin (PG 49, 296).

[9] John Chrysostom, *Hom. 41 Gen.* 5 (PG 53, 381).

[10] John Chrysostom, *Hom. de continentia* (PG 56, 293).

[11] John Chrysostom, *Hom. 62 Gen.* 3 (PG 54, 535).

[12] John Chrysostom, *Hom. 38 Gen.* 1; 2; 4; 5 (PG 53, 351, 352, 353, 356–57).

[13] John Chrysostom, *De SS. Bernice et Prosdoce* 2 (PG 50, 631).

[14] John Chrysostom, *Hom. 32 Gen.* 5; 6 (PG 53, 299, 300); cf. *Hom. 45 Gen.* 3 (PG

to praise the couple's marital harmony[15]—not noting its inappropriateness to a situation in which a husband delivers his wife for the sexual use of other men! The theme of Chrysostom's glowing vindication of Abraham is nonetheless clear: so great is the unity between the Testaments that characters of the Old Dispensation should be emulated by Christians, although Chrysostom thinks that no Christian of his day could match the virtue of this noble patriarch.[16]

Chrysostom's erasure of difference between the ancient Hebrews and contemporary Christians finds its counterpart in his close alignment of asceticism with marriage: even the married among his hearers can be encouraged to abandon their more sumptuous lifestyles for a daily practice of monklike simplicity. Although Chrysostom clearly holds virginity to be the superior way of life,[17] his critique of marriage rests on its anxious preoccupation with worldly things, not on its innate defilement.[18] In fact, for Chrysostom, the purpose of marriage is to *keep* the body pure, to *prevent* humans from falling into sinful defilement.[19] Like his rabbinical contemporaries, Chrysostom claims that marriage serves as a "protective asylum" for continence.[20] Unlike Jerome, who dwells on the sexual dimensions of marriage to negative effect, Chrysostom rather stresses the bond between the partners[21]—for if sex were the essence of marriage, what would separate the activity of a prostitute from that of an "honest woman"?[22]

Indeed, the very Biblical passages through which Jerome signals the defilement of married sexual relations receive a quite different treatment from Chrysostom. Take, for example, Paul's advice in I Corinthians 7:5, that a married couple not separate sexually except for brief periods of prayer. For Jerome, this verse indicates that the sexual act is stained. Since

54, 416–17).

[15] John Chrysostom, *Hom. 45 Gen.* 2 (PG 54, 416).

[16] John Chrysostom, *De virginitate* 82.3–4 (SC 125, 384, 386).

[17] E.g., John Chrysostom, *De virginitate* 1.1; 8.4; 15.2 (SC 125, 92, 118, 146); *Hom. 49 Gen.* 2 (PG 54, 416).

[18] John Chrysostom, *Hom. 24 Eph.* 5 (PG 62, 174); *Hom. 14 I Tim.* 2 (PG 62, 572–73); *Mulier alligata* 4 (PG 51, 223–24); *Hom. de statuis* 15.3 (PG 49, 158); *Hom. 3 Tit.* 4 (PG 62, 682); but cf. *Hom. 7 II Tim.* 4 (PG 62, 641).

[19] John Chrysostom, *Hom. 59 Matt.* 7 (PG 58, 583); *Hom. 62 Matt.* 2 (PG 58, 597); *Hom. 19 I Cor.* 6 (PG 61, 160). Unlike Augustine, Chrysostom does not believe that children are the primary aim of marriage, which is the restraint of unruly sexual desire: see his *Propter fornicationes* 3 (PG 51, 213); *Hom. 21 Gen.* 4 (PG 53, 180); *De virginitate* 19.1; 25 (SC 125, 156, 174).

[20] John Chrysostom, *De virginitate* 9.1; 25; 30.2 (SC 125, 120, 174, 190); *Propter fornicationes* 2 (PG 51, 209); *Quales ducendae* 5 (PG 51, 232).

[21] John Chrysostom, *De non iterando coniugio* 2 (PG 48, 612); Sarah and Abraham's relation is thus emphasized in *Hom. 45 Gen.* 2–3 (PG 54, 416–17); *Serm. 6 Gen.* 2 (PG 54, 606–7).

[22] John Chrysostom, *De non iterando coniugio* 2 (PG 48, 612); cf. Tertullian, *De exhortatione castitatis* 9.

as Christians we should "pray without ceasing" (I Thess. 5:17), Jerome suggests that spouses might choose *never* to engage in sexual relations if they wish to fulfill their religious duties.[23]

For Chrysostom, Paul's words mean quite the opposite. He castigates matrons who effect a unilateral withdrawal from marital intercourse: they are "putting all asunder" (a phrase that ominously resonates with Jesus' teaching on divorce) and will be held responsible for their husbands' sin should the latter stray. Indeed, Chrysostom ventures, a breach is made in the marital union if husbands merely become quarrelsome when deprived of their customary sexual outlet. But how then can Chrysostom interpret Paul's concession that the couple withdraw from sexual relation in order to pray? Chrysostom resolves his sexual/textual dilemma by claiming that Paul here means "prayer with unusual earnestness," not just "ordinary prayer," which, he asserts, *does* allow the sexually active couple to "pray without ceasing." And if in Paul's view, even a non-Christian (hence "unclean") husband cannot transfer his "impurity" to his believing spouse or to his children, how much more pure must be the sexual relation of a Christian couple?[24]

Lauding the "cleanness" of marriage[25] allows Chrysostom to conjoin marriage and celibacy in the Christian present: this he does by making marriage more "like" celibacy. Laymen, he testifies, should live as monks, excepting the one point that they are married.[26] The wife is the only thing that stands between a monk and a married Christian man—and wives can be had "as if not" (I Cor. 7:29). Chrysostom argues that married Christians must observe just as difficult precepts as do those in monastic life, although he concedes that it is easier to keep them in a monastery than in "the world."[27] Unlike Jerome, he does not constantly harp on the "difference," the "distinction," that sexual renunciation creates. The hierarchical marking of bodies lies not so much *between* married and celibate as *within* the married state, where the "concord" Chrysostom so avidly recommends is exegetically established and maintained precisely on the basis of status differences between husband and wife.

Chrysostom's argument that marriage is a "monarchy," not a "democracy," rests on his claim that spousal equality produces strife and defeats the harmony that should epitomize the marital relation.[28] Believing

[23] Jerome, *Adversus Iovinianum* 1.7 (PL 23, 230); cf. Jerome, *ep.* 49 (48).15 (CSEL 54, 376).

[24] John Chrysostom, *Hom. 19 I Cor.* 2 (PG 61, 154–55).

[25] Chrysostom thinks that desire is "natural": *Hom. 2 Eph.* 3 (PG 62, 20); pleasure can be "chaste": *Hom. 7 Matt.* 7 (PG 57, 81).

[26] John Chrysostom, *Hom. 7 Matt.* 7 (PG 57, 80–81).

[27] John Chrysostom, *Hom. 7 Heb.* 4 (PG 63, 68); *Adversus oppugnatores* 3.14 (PG 47, 372–74).

[28] John Chrysostom, *Hom. 34 I Cor.* 3 (PG 61, 289–90); *Hom. 19 I Cor.* 1 (PG

that the wife *must* take second place if a happy household is to be established, Chrysostom summons up various Scriptural verses that reinforce the correctness of this marital hierarchy through appeals to God, Custom, and Nature.[29]

Thus Chrysostom writes that the "first empire" which God erected, the "first servitude" that he established, was within conjugal society.[30] If husbands attend to public affairs and wives devote themselves to the household, peaceful domesticity will be ensured; in this arrangement, the wife is neither dispensable (as she would be if the husband played both the public and the domestic roles) nor is she allowed to become insufferably proud (since she is excluded from the arena of public affairs).[31] Chrysostom's model is not, however, based on what we might call an ideology of "separate-but-equal-spheres," but on marital hierarchy. Thus although Chrysostom sometimes speaks of the *reciprocal* servitude of husband and wife in marriage, his analysis more frequently appeals only to *female* submissiveness. He also suggests that any presumed equality of the woman occasioned by her wealth and social status fades before what he calls "the law of obedience": in marriage, her assets do not obviate the requirement that she obey her "head."[32]

Chrysostom's interpretation of the necessary hierarchy within marriage is hermeneutically accomplished not through allegory,[33] but through intertextual exegesis, which he uses to constrain the Biblical text in a conservative direction. Here, texts are seen as mosaics that incorporate previous texts, transforming their meaning. Daniel Boyarin, describing the work performed by intertextual exegesis in rabbinic interpretation, notes that texts embody "the more or less untransformed detritus" of a previous cultural system, a "detritus" that creates "fissures . . . on the surface of the text," thus revealing the "conflictual dynamics" between the old and

61, 153); *Hom. 26 I Cor.* 2 (PG 61, 215); *Quales ducendae* 4 (PG 51, 231); on "harmony in marriage," *Serm. 6 Gen.* 2 (PG 54, 606–7).

[29] E.g., John Chrysostom, *Hom. 10 Col.* 1 (PG 62, 366); *Hom. 20 Eph.* 1, 4 (PG 62, 136, 141); *Hom. 37 I Cor.* 1 (PG 61, 316); *Hom. 26 I Cor.* 2 (PG 61, 215); *Serm. 2 Gen.* 2 (PG 54, 589).

[30] John Chrysostom, *Serm. 4 Gen.* 1 (PG 54, 594).

[31] John Chrysostom, *Quales ducendae* 4 (PG 51, 251).

[32] E.g., John Chrysostom, *De virginitate* 41.1; 55 (SC 125, 236, 302).

[33] Chrysostom takes Matthew 19's call for "eunuchhood" allegorically, as an injunction to celibate living, but this merely demonstrates that what had once been considered "allegory" could by the fourth century be classified as a literal reading of the text: John Chrysostom, *Hom. 36 Ioan.* 2 (PG 59, 205–6). In *Hom. 62 Matt.* 3 (PG 58, 599), "becoming a eunuch" is described as "putting away wicked thoughts"; actually to amputate the bodily member is called "a work of the devil" and is associated with the denigration of creation characteristic of Manicheanism. For how "old" allegory becomes a "new" literal meaning, see David Dawson, *Allegorical Readers and Cultural Revision in Ancient Alexandria*

the new.[34] Through such intertextual exegesis, Scripture could be affirmed as self-interpreting, as if the interpreter had played no role in the production of meaning, as if no conceptual cracks existed between the texts, and as if no political consequences attended the choice of intertexts. *Which* dominant texts controlled the interpretation of others was, in fact, fiercely contested.

In the present case, intertextual exegesis proves useful to Chrysostom in his prescription of female submission within marriage. He rests his claim on an interpretation of Genesis 1–3, interlarded with other Scriptural references that serve to constrain a more "progressive" reading. For example, in his *Sermons on Genesis*, Chrysostom interprets the creation story with the help of I Corinthians 11 as an intertext. The Genesis 1 account of male and female as created in the "image of God" is here "corrected" through I Corinthians 11, in which only males enjoy the blessing of "God's image." Why is this so? Chrysostom asks. And he answers: because the "image of God" means authority, and only males possess this quality. Like God in the heavens, so the male on earth has no superior and rules over all creation, including woman. She, on the other hand, is not called in I Corinthians 11 "the image of God," but only "the glory of man," because she is under his authority.[35] Thus the force of the creation of both sexes "in God's image," according to Genesis 1, is mitigated to send a message of female submission.

Elsewhere, in his longer *Homilies on Genesis*, Chrysostom also employs I Corinthians 11 as the intertext for Genesis 1–3, but here it is Paul's designation of man as the "head" and woman as the "body" that provides the correct interpretation of these chapters. This "natural" hierarchy of head over body was upset by the first sin, when the "body" (Eve) did not obey her "head" (Adam) and Adam, allured by the "body," put himself in submission to Eve by his acquiescence in sin.[36] Read with the help of I Corinthians 11, Genesis 1–3 conveys the message that the allegedly "natural" sexual hierarchy given at creation was disturbed by the first sin—and hence needs reinstating. I Corinthians 12 also here lends assistance to Chrysostom's argument: Paul's metaphor of bodily organs which accept without protest their assigned status and function prompts Chrysostom to feature woman not just as the "body," but as the "foot" who is to obey her "head."[37] Yet even more intertexts are brought to bear upon Genesis

(Berkeley/Los Angeles/Oxford: University of California Press, 1992), p. 8.

[34] Daniel Boyarin, *Intertextuality and the Reading of Midrash* (Bloomington/Indianapolis: Indiana University Press, 1990), p. 94. See the discussion above of intertextuality, pp. 122–28.

[35] John Chrysostom, *Serm. 2 in Gen.* 2 (PG 54, 589); cf. *Hom. 7 de statuis* 2 (PG 49, 93).

[36] John Chrysostom, *Hom. 17 Gen.* 4 (PG 53, 139).

[37] John Chrysostom, *Hom. 17 Gen.* 9 (PG 53, 145).

1–3: passages from late New Testament books are introduced to reinforce the casting of the first couple as "teacher and disciple, ruler and subject."[38] Thus in this explication as well, the intertexts supplying the themes of female inferiority and submission govern the interpretation of Genesis 1–3—and Chrysostom's understanding of what contemporary marital relation should be. He struggles to put a favorable light on his message of female subordination: preferable for woman to be subjected to man than for her to fall into the abyss, just as it is better for a horse to be reined in by the bit than to rush uncontrollably toward the precipice.[39]

Throughout his writings, Chrysostom, unlike Jerome, employs intertextual exegesis not so much to promote asceticism, but to enforce gender hierarchy within marriage. Also unlike Jerome, who appeals to women's unhappy subordination as a reason why they should opt out of marriage, Chrysostom believes that it is precisely *happy* marriages that are marked by female submission. Thus, when writing of the blissful union the Creator wished man and woman to enjoy, he sees no discrepancy in citing that prototypical text on female subordination, "The man is the head of the woman" (Eph. 5:23).[40] Chrysostom's more tolerant view of marriage is bought entirely at the price of wifely subservience. Blurring the distinctions between Old Testament and New, between ascetics and married, Chrysostom reserves the sharpest sense of "difference" for the husband/wife relation.

III: Jerome

The proponents of the "difference in times," on the other hand—and here Jerome will stand as a test case—read both the Old Testament and the Christian present with more sharply asceticized eyes. Here, ancient Israelite sexual teaching and practice are deemed only selectively (and dubiously) recuperable for the Christian present. Although commentators of this persuasion faced allegations that they were flirting with (if not embracing) heresy in their uncomplimentary treatment of the Old Testament, their exegeses created firm ground from which to proclaim a decisive "difference" between ascetics and nonascetics in the Christian present. Making little attempt to explain away the disturbing features of Hebrew Scripture, Jerome (like Chrysostom) develops a Midrashic style of intertextual exegesis, invoking one text to constrain another—but (unlike Chrysostom) a style that serves to create a sharp division between ascetics and nonascetics in the present. Jerome also elab-

[38] John Chrysostom, *Hom. 12 Col.* 5 (PG 62, 388).

[39] John Chrysostom, *Hom. 17 Gen.* 8 (PG 53, 145).

[40] John Chrysostom, *Hom. 14 Gen.* 4 (PG 53, 115).

orates an exegetical technique I have above called "textual implosion": here, Scriptural discussions on such diverse (and seemingly asexual) topics as food, slavery, and circumcision all stand in for discourse on sex and the body. Thus Jerome's exegesis effectively enlarges the number of Biblical passages that can be claimed as pertinent to discussions of sexuality and ascetic renunciation.

Pressing the "difference in times" that separates the mores of the Old Testament from those of the New and of later Christianity provided Jerome with the Biblical grounding from which to claim the superiority of ascetics to nonascetics in the Christian present. By his appeal to the "difference in times," however, Jerome put himself at risk for charges of heresy from those who believed he had "gone too far"[41] when he penned such sentences as "in view of the purity of the body of Christ, all sexual intercourse is unclean."[42] Jerome thus struggled to distance himself and his interpretations from those of Encratites, Marcionites, Manicheans, and Novatianists.[43]

Wishing not to incriminate himself further, Jerome rarely mocks the sexual exploits of Old Testament characters openly, an exegetical move we might have *expected* him to make in his concern to "distinguish the times." He is no Faustus the Manichean:[44] only occasionally does he explode in disgust at (say) Abraham's three wives.[45] Jerome has more subtle means of denigration and distinction, but before he resorts to them, he locates Old Testament passages that might, with interpretive assistance, yield an *ascetic* message.

Jerome's asceticizing interpretation of the Old Testament, and of Genesis in particular, provides an interesting contrast to John Chrysostom's readings of the same material: whereas Chrysostom appealed to the Genesis patriarchs to provide models of domestic harmony for contemporary

[41] Jerome's *ep.* 48 (49) is his defense for writing the *Adversus Iovinianum*; see also Augustine, *De sancta virginitate* and *De bono coniugali*. For comment, David G. Hunter, "Resistance to the Virginal Ideal in Late Fourth-Century Rome: The Case of Jovinian," *Theological Studies* 48 (1987): 45–64.

[42] Jerome, *Adversus Iovinianum* 1.20 (PL 23, 249): "omnis coitus immunda sit."

[43] Jerome, *Adversus Iovinianum* 1.3; 2.16 (PL 23, 223, 323–24); *epp.* 22.13; 22.38; 49(48).8; 49(48).9; 49(48).11 (CSEL 54, 161, 204–5, 361–63, 364, 366); *Comm. Tit.* 1:6 (PL 26, 599); *Comm. Gal.* 3 (6:8) (PL 26, 460).

[44] See especially Faustus' attack on patriarchal virtue in Augustine's *Contra Faustum* 22.

[45] Jerome, *Adversus Iovinianum* 1.19 (PL 23, 248): if Christians want repeated marriages like Abraham, they will have to follow him in circumcision as well (cf. Tertullian, *De monogamia* 6). For a discussion of Jerome's borrowing of ascetic argumentation from Tertullian, see Fr. Schultzen, "Die Benutzung der Schriften Tertullians *de monogamia* und *de ieiunio* bei Hieronymus *adv. Iovinianum*," *Neue Jahrbücher für deutsche Theologie* 3, no. 1 (1894): 487–502.

married Christians, Jerome looks for features of the text that can be made to carry an ascetic message for contemporary Christian renunciants. Thus in the story of Noah's ark, the animals' entrance "two by two" is not taken as an occasion to praise coupling; rather, Jerome notes that it was only the *unclean* animals who so marched.[46] Unlike Jovinian, who included Solomon in his list of the praiseworthy married, Jerome centers on a different "Solomon," the author of Proverbs, who teaches the dangers that women pose to men.[47] Nor is Jerome interested in Abraham's marital arrangements, but rather in his willingness to sacrifice his son, thus demonstrating a proper ascetic concern to renounce family.[48] Childlessness—not childbearing—serves for Jerome as an Old Testament motif that points ahead to the Gospel Dispensation.[49] And as a last resort, Jerome, like Origen before him, can simply interpret Old Testament passages on reproduction "spiritually," not literally,[50] thus making them suitably edifying for Christian ascetics.

Likewise, Jerome's approach to the story of creation rescues these texts for ascetic interpretation. Developing a historical trajectory that had much appeal for ascetic writers, Jerome argues that human life had begun on a virginal "high" in the Garden of Eden, but had plunged to the abyss with the institution of marriage and sexual intercourse.[51] Most of the behavior of Old Testament characters *after* Genesis 2 can be relegated to this swamp of carnality, but with the advent of Christian celibacy, the virginal Paradise of Genesis 1 and 2 can be regained.[52] The positioning of Genesis 4:1 ("Adam knew his wife Eve") *after* the story of the sin in the Garden provides Jerome with some helpful leverage: only after their expulsion from Eden did Adam and Eve descend to the life of sex and marriage.[53] "Close reading" here assists an ascetic interpretation of the creation story. Likewise, Jerome sounds the theme of "Alpha and Omega": the end—the Christian present—should be like the virginal beginning of Genesis 1.[54] Christian virgins can, however, avoid the "thorns and thistles" that were

[46] Jerome, *Adversus Iovinianum* 1.16; 1.17; 2.15 (PL 23, 246, 247, 319–20).

[47] Jerome, *Adversus Iovinianum* 1.28 (PL 23, 260–61); cf. *ep.* 22.12 (CSEL 54, 159).

[48] Jerome, *ep.* 39.6 (CSEL 54, 306); *Adversus Iovinianum* 1.19 (PL 23, 248); and of Isaac to die, *ep.* 66.7 (CSEL 54, 656).

[49] Jerome, *ep.* 22.21 (CSEL 54, 171–73).

[50] Jerome, *Comm. Zach* 3 (10:8–10) (CCL 76A, 843–44); *Tract. Ps. 127/8:3* (CCL 78, 266) ("your wife shall be a fruitful vine").

[51] On theories of historical decline in the ancient world, see Randolph Starn, "Meaning-Levels in the Theme of Historical Decline," *History and Theory* 14 (1975): 1–31.

[52] Jerome, *Adversus Iovinianum* 1.16; 1.29; 2.15 (PL 23, 246, 262, 319); *ep.* 22.19 (CSEL 54, 168–69).

[53] Jerome, *Adversus Iovinianum* 1.16; 1.29; 2.15 (PL 23, 246, 262, 319); *ep.* 22.19 (CSEL 54, 169).

[54] Jerome, *Adversus Iovinianum* 1.18 (PL 23, 247–48).

God's punishment for the first sin—the thorns and thistles of marriage, with its concomitant subjection of the woman to a husband.[55]

With Genesis 3, however, humans embarked on a downward course that, according to Jerome, characterizes most of the rest of the Old Testament. From here on in, the "difference in times" will be sounded, the New Dispensation positioned not just as "different" from the Old, but as decidedly superior to and corrective of it. Jerome garners Biblical verses that support this interpretation: I Corinthians 10:11 (we "upon whom the end of the ages has come"); II Corinthians 5:17 ("the old has passed away, behold, the new has come"); Ecclesiastes 7:8 ("better is the end of a thing than its beginning"); and Ecclesiastes 3:5 ("a time to embrace, and a time to refrain from embracing").[56] Such passages lend ballast to Jerome's claim that the time of the Law differs from the time of the Gospel.[57] Thus he informs a correspondent that Genesis 1:28 ("reproduce and multiply") is *not for us*, upon whom "the end of the ages has come" (I Cor. 10:11).[58] I Corinthians 7's preference for virginity and celibacy can be pitted against not only Genesis 1:28, but also against the curse on the barren in Exodus 23:26.[59]

It was not only the Old Testament, however, that required interpretive work to render it palatable, even useful, for Jerome's ascetic program. Jovinian, we gather, had also used New Testament passages to argue his case for marriage, enlisting such married exemplars as Zachariah and Elizabeth, and the Apostle Peter (presumably once married, because he had a mother-in-law). Jerome's retort is sharp: these figures are still "under the Law"; the message of the Gospel did not begin until the crucifixion. As for apostles such as Peter, Jerome comments that having "lost their virginity in Judaism," they did not regain it under the Gospel. Jerome contrasts Peter unfavorably with the virginal John, the disciple whom Jesus loved best (John 13:23; 19:26; 21:20)—the only disciple, on Jerome's account, pure enough to be entrusted with the care of the Virgin Mary after Jesus' crucifixion.[60]

A second interpretive problem regarding the New Testament faced Jerome when he confronted the Pastoral Epistles, since he, like his contem-

[55] Jerome *ep.* 22.3 (CSEL 54, 146); cf. *ep.* 130.8 (CSEL 56, 187).

[56] Jerome, *Adversus Iovinianum* 2.4; 1.37 (PL 23, 301, 273); *Comm. Iob* 42:12 (PL 26, 848); *Comm. Eccles.* 3:5 (CCL 72, 275).

[57] Jerome, *Adversus Iovinianum* 1.24 (PL 23, 254); *Comm. Gal.* 1 (2:19) (PL 26, 369–70); *Adversus Helvidium* 20 (PL 23, 213); *epp.* 22.21 (CSEL 54, 171–73); 69.5 (CSEL 54, 686–87); 123.11–12 (CSEL 56, 84–85).

[58] Jerome, *ep.* 123.12 (CSEL 56, 85).

[59] Jerome, *Adversus Helvidium* 20 (PL 23, 213).

[60] Jerome, *Adversus Iovinianum* 1.26 (PL 23, 256, 258–59); *Adversus Ioannem Hierosolymitanem* 35 (PL 23, 405).

poraries, believed they had been written by Paul.[61] One strategy Jerome adopts is to read the Pastorals *themselves* as ascetic texts whenever possible. This interpretive move was assisted by his translations from Greek to Latin that pressed verses in an ascetic direction: hence, as we saw above, Jerome usually renders the Pastorals' recommendation of *sōphrosunē* as *castitas*[62] or as *incorruptio*.[63]

Another way in which Jerome reconciles I Corinthians 7 with the Pastorals is to emphasize that the Pastorals' advocacy of second marriage for widows is meant only for the moral dregs of Christians, who need this concession to restrain themselves from prostitution and harlotry.[64] As for the Pastorals' advice on widows, Jerome notes that even within I Timothy 5, a distinction is made between two types of widows: the "good" ones who married only once and are attested for their righteous deeds and prayers, and the "bad" ones who remarried.[65]

For Jerome, the more ascetic portions of the Bible are seen as correcting the less ascetic. Thus he usually emends any reference to Genesis 2:24 (man and woman becoming "one flesh") with I Corinthians 6:17 ("becoming one spirit").[66] Conversely, the remarriage that Paul appears to tolerate in I Corinthians 7:39 receives a sharper condemnation in Jerome's exegesis by being aligned with the adultery of Matthew 5:32.[67] Jerome justifies this differentiation with the argument that the New Testament contains two rules, one for the "perfect" and one for the weaker brothers and sisters.[68]

Best of all, according to Jerome, would be for Christians to read the concession for sexual relations offered to the married in I Corinthians 7 in light of Ephesians 5, which he understands to counsel a nonsexual

[61] E.g., Jerome, *ep.* 123.5 (CSEL 56, 77–78).

[62] Jerome, *Adversus Iovinianum* 1.27; 1.35; 1.37 (*pudicitia*) (PL 23, 260, 270, 274); cf. *Comm. Tit.* 1:8; 2:3 (PL 26, 603, 615). Commenting on Titus 2:3–5, Jerome also translates words derived from *sōphrosunē* as *pudicas* and *castitas*; this virtue, he writes, stands "in first place," and he discusses it before he mentions what *in fact* stands in first place in the Greek text: "to love their husbands and children" (see PL 26, 615–16). For a discussion of the "ideology of translation," see Charles Martindale, *Redeeming the Text: Latin Poetry and the Hermeneutics of Reception* (Cambridge: Cambridge University Press, 1993), pp. 86–89. For a discussion of how *sōphrosune* becomes aligned with "chastity" in early Christian literature, see Helen North, *Sophrosyne: Self-Knowledge and Self-Restraint in Greek Literature*, Cornell Studies in Classical Philology 35 (Ithaca, N.Y.: Cornell University Press, 1966), chap. 9 (Jerome: pp. 358–60).

[63] Jerome, *Comm. Tit.* 2:6 (PL 26, 618): Jerome makes clear that he means "incorruption of the body."

[64] Jerome, *ep.* 79.10 (CSEL 55, 100).

[65] Jerome, *ep.* 123.3 (CSEL 56, 74–75).

[66] Jerome, *epp.* 22.1 (CSEL 54, 145); 55.2 (CSEL 54, 488 [citing I Cor. 6: 13–18]); *In Math.* 3 (19: 5, 6) (CCL 77, 166).

[67] Jerome, *ep.* 55.4 (CSEL 54, 492–93).

[68] Jerome, *Adversus Iovinianum* 2.6 (PL 23, 307).

relationship, like Christ's with the Church.[69] We can assess the immaturity of the Corinthians' faith, Jerome claims, by recalling the dreadful immorality that they had tolerated in their midst (he alludes to the narrative in I Cor. 5 of the man living with his father's wife). Paul's "concession" for marital relations was thus granted to those of still-carnal status, those on whom Jesus pronounced, "Woe to those who are with child and give suck in those days" (Matt. 24:19 = Mark 13:17 = Luke 21:23). In contrast, Jerome argues, the bride and groom of Ephesians 5 enjoy a spiritual (i.e., nonsexual) relationship, as do Christ and the Church.[70] Jerome's allegorical resolution of the issue in his *Ephesians Commentary* advises that if husbands (coded as souls) nourish their wives (coded as bodies), then wives may be raised up as "men" (i.e., as souls), diversity of sex will cease, and "like the angels" (Matt. 22:30 = Mark 12:25), there will be "no male and female" (Gal. 3:28).[71]

Jerome's ingenious exegeses not only establish *him* as a preeminent interpreter of the Bible,[72] they also serve to accentuate the "difference" that marks the "distinction" of Christian ascetics to nonascetics in his own day. Jerome is famed for interpretations that through hierarchically organized lists signal degrees of ascetic renunciation and the heavenly rewards awaiting those in each tier. Of these, his most famous is doubtless the interpretation of the hundredfold, sixtyfold, and thirtyfold harvests in the Parable of the Sower as virginity, widowhood, and marriage, respectively.[73] Unlike Augustine,[74] Jerome does not worry that Christian ascetics will fall victim to pride, glorying in their superiority to the married; to the contrary, he instructs them, "learn from me a holy arrogance: you are better than they."[75]

For Jerome, the great leveler of persons, the great equalizer of humans, is sexual desire—for all of us, he writes, are "at its mercy."[76] But it is precisely this equalizing that Jerome *resists*, and hence he counsels Christians of stronger moral fiber to surmount desire's leveling tendency. By contrast, to create "difference" and "distinction" through an ascetically oriented exegesis is Jerome's task. Two of his strategies are here worthy of mention.

[69] Jerome, *Comm. Eph.* 3 (5:22–24) (PL 26, 564–65) (unlike those who at the time of the Flood [and perhaps in Corinth?] were engaged in "buying, selling, and marrying" [Matt. 24:38]); on Eph. 5:28 (PL 26, 567).

[70] Jerome, *Comm. Eph.* 3 (5:22–24) (PL 26, 564–65).

[71] Jerome, *Comm. Eph.* 3 (5:29) (PL 26, 567–68).

[72] Note Jerome's admission that after *he* left Rome, Marcella was the foremost exegete left in the city: *ep.* 127.7 (CSEL 56, 151).

[73] Jerome, *Adversus Iovinianum* 2.19 (PL 23, 327).

[74] Cf. Augustine, *De sancta virginitate* 1; 38.39; 44.45; 55.56.

[75] Jerome, *ep.* 22.16 (CSEL 54, 163).

[76] Jerome, *ep.* 54.9 (CSEL 54, 475–76); cf. *ep.* 79.10 (CSEL 55, 99–100).

Jerome's first exegetical technique for creating "distinction" sweeps texts that seemingly have nothing to do with sex into the purview of ascetic argumentation through "textual implosion," an interpretive strategy detailed in chapter 5. Three topics in particular provide grist for Jerome's ascetically interpretive mill: Pauline texts on circumcision and uncircumcision, on the Strong and the Weak, on meat-eaters contrasted with milk-drinkers or vegetable-eaters, and on free and slave. All of these are read as ciphers for ascetic renunciation and marriage.[77] For Jerome, following Origen's exegesis of I Corinthians 7:17–24, Paul's references to circumcision serve as a code for virginity and to uncircumcision as a code for marriage:[78] thus Moses, by circumcising his son, was "cutting off marriage."[79]

In addition, Jerome turns Paul's discussions of food into discourse about sex. Paul's meat-eaters are identified with the Strong—and the Strong now, in the Christian present, opt for a life of chastity. The "milk" of marriage, Jerome claims, is appropriate only for the Weak, for "children."[80] Likewise, Paul's words on slavery are read as pertaining to marriage, while freedom attends the life of virginity.[81] Interpreting seemingly irrelevant Biblical passages as messages pertaining to marriage, sexuality, and celibacy, Jerome enlarges his cache of appropriate texts through which he can advance the ascetic cause.

Jerome's second exegetical strategy is to supply an intertextual commentary, a technique by which he reins in recalcitrant passages through those more friendly to ascetic interpretation. Two illustrations must here suffice to suggest how Jerome via intertextual exegesis "raises the stakes" for asceticism.

Adversus Iovinianum 1.7 provides a first instructive example. According to Jerome—who here interprets I Corinthians 7—when Paul in that chapter advises his male audience that it is "better for a man not to touch a woman," the passage should be read in light of verses from Proverbs 6, 7, and 9 that warn young men against dangerous women who "touch," "preying upon" their lives, and causing them to lose their understanding. The view Jerome here argues—that if "touching" is not good, then it is necessarily bad—becomes a misogynistic message of the dangers

[77] For these examples, Jerome appears to lean quite heavily on Origen's *Commentary on I Corinthians*, for which only fragments preserved in catenas survive; see especially Claude Jenkins, "Documents: Origen on I Corinthians," *Journal of Theological Studies* 9 (1908), for fragments on these topics (pp. 506–9).

[78] Jerome, *epp.* 128.3 (CSEL 56, 158); 49 (48).6 (CSEL 54, 358), citing *Adversus Iovinianum* 1.11 (PL 23, 235).

[79] Jerome, *Adversus Iovinianum* 1.20 (PL 23, 249).

[80] Jerome, *Adversus Iovinianum* 1.37 (PL 23, 275).

[81] Jerome, *ep.* 49 (48).6 (CSEL 54, 358–59), citing *Adversus Iovinianum* 1.11 (PL 23, 235–36); *ep.* 145 (CSEL 56, 306).

that women pose to men.[82] Paul's advice regarding male restraint is thus lent a different coloration by the insertion of an explicit message about "female danger."

A second example: in *Epistle* 123 to a Gallic widow, Geruchia, Jerome adroitly revises the message of I Timothy 5 that young widows should remarry. This advice, not at all to Jerome's taste, is explained away with the help of two intertexts that constrain the text of I Timothy 5. First, Jerome reminds Geruchia (and other readers) that Noah's ark (a figure for the Church) contains unclean animals as well as clean ones (Gen. 7:2); she can still be called a Christian if she remarries, but only an "unclean" one. Next, he summons up the Parable of the Sower, accompanied by his famous interpretation in which the hundredfold, sixtyfold, and thirtyfold harvests (virginity, widowhood, and a single marriage) leave no apparent room for remarriage if a Christian wishes to be present in Christ's Kingdom. For Jerome, second marriage is better represented as the weeds which take root in no good ground, but grow among the thorns (cf. Matt. 13:7 = Mark 4:7 = Luke 8:7).[83] By interlarding his exegesis of I Timothy 5 with such passages, Jerome seeks to ensure that his readers comprehend the lowly status of second marriage. The carnal "detritus" (in Daniel Boyarin's phrase) of the Pastoral Epistles is here reconfigured for the new message of female asceticism: texts have not been discarded, but constrained.

Thus Jerome treats the problematic texts of the Hebrew and early Christian past so as to distance the Christian present—an ascetic present—from them. "Distinction" applies only to Christian renunciants. Through an intertextual exegesis, Jerome has claimed the Bible for the ascetic cause.

IV: Origen

A different model for dealing with Scripture's recalcitrance for ascetically minded Christians is provided by Origen, whose exegetical technique is to remove Biblical narratives from the realm of chronology and relocate them in a transhistorical sphere through allegorical exegesis. There is no worrisome gap between past and present because diachronic comparisons have been erased. Although, to be sure, Origen is interested in ascetic *practice*, his writings directly concentrate on issues of sexuality less than we might expect. Rather, Biblical verses that refer to women, men, marriage, bodies, and the sexual prompt Origen's reflection on the gendered nature of human faculties (sense versus reason, virtue versus vice): bodies and sexuality are themselves allego-

[82] Jerome, *Adversus Iovinianum* 1.7 (PL 23, 228–29).

[83] Jerome, *ep.* 123.8 (CSEL 56, 81–82).

rized through a genderizing of ethical discourse. In contrast to Jerome's exegesis, the number of texts that on a "literal" reading speak to issues of human sexuality has here seemingly been reduced. Whereas John Chrysostom dwells upon the body in relation to marriage, and Jerome, in relation to ascetic renunciation, Origen will deflect the materiality of the body onto an elaboration of hierarchically gendered virtue (and onto the materiality of language itself).

Textbook descriptions of Origen's hermeneutical procedure often take at face value his rendition of his own exegetical method in *On First Principles* 4.2.4. Here, Origen claims that Scripture has a threefold sense, corresponding to the flesh, the soul, and the spirit—and latter-day commentators have often read his words as portending a literal, a moral, or an allegorical interpretation. Yet Origen's own discussion, as well as the investigations of recent scholars, should lead us to question this division. Origen himself admits that some passages have no "bodily" meaning at all,[84] and recent commentators note that the two allegedly "higher" forms of interpretation are not always readily distinguishable.[85] My concern here, however, is not to delineate the nomenclature of Origen's exegetical categories, nor to relate his exegetical procedures to his wider theology of redemption,[86] but to examine the work that various interpretive modes perform for an ascetic or nonascetic reading of Biblical passages.

As noted earlier, David Dawson's book, *Allegorical Readers and Cultural Revision in Ancient Alexandria*, highlights the role that allegory played in the "culture wars" of late antiquity. Dawson writes: "The very tensions between literal and nonliteral readings that characterized ancient allegory stemmed from efforts by readers to secure for themselves and their communities social and cultural identity, authority, and power."[87] With Dawson, I wish to note the social location and ideological power of exegetical modes of early Christian interpretation. Origen's use of allegory is instructive in this regard.

As is well known, Origen believed that a "literal" or "historical" reading of the Bible, New Testament as well as Old, might prove problematic,

[84] Origen, *De principiis* 4.2.5; 4.3.4; 4.3.5 (GCS 22, 314–15, 328–31).

[85] Joseph Wilson Trigg, *Origen: The Bible and Philosophy in the Third-Century Church* (Atlanta: John Knox, 1983), p. 126; Henri Crouzel, *Origen: The Life and Thought of the First Great Theologian*, trans. A. S. Worrall (San Francisco: Harper & Row, 1989; French original, 1985), p. 79; Bertrand de Margerie, *Introduction à l'histoire de l'exégèse*, vol. I, *Les Pères grecs et orientaux* (Paris: Les Editions du Cerf, 1980), pp. 123–24 (following themes developed by Jean Daniélou); Karen Jo Torjesen, *Hermeneutical Procedure and Theological Method in Origen's Exegesis* (Berlin/New York: Walter DeGruyter, 1986), p. 41; Gerald Bostock, "Allegory and the Interpretation of the Bible in Origen," *Journal of Literature and Theology* 1 (1987): 45–46.

[86] Already well done by (e.g.) Henri Crouzel, *Origen*, and Karen Torjesen, *Hermeneutical Procedure*.

[87] Dawson, *Allegorical Readers*, p. 2.

unprofitable, and even nonsensical. A more spiritualized approach, however, allows Christians to proclaim that *both* Testaments are truly "New."[88] With allegorical exegesis providing the means to overcome the "difference in times," Origen need not struggle to exonerate—or decry—the behavior of the patriarchs or ancient Hebrew practices; he sees for himself where a literal exegesis might lead.[89] Through allegory, by contrast, the "time" of the Old Testament engages present-day Christians through an exegesis that erases chronological difference: Old Testament narratives are not relegated to the dustbin of ancient history, but apply to *us*, here and now, to *our* state of virtue and vice.[90] It is, as both Andrew Louth[91] and Karen Torjesen[92] have emphasized, the "present" of the contemporary Christian hearer that Origen addresses. Yet there are other approaches than allegory to Biblical texts that enable Origen to derive a message for Christian audiences of his day.

When Origen engages in moral exhortation, for example, he often reads a text in a quasi-literal way. Thus, for example, the story of Moses' instructing the Israelites to abstain from sexual relation before God's appearance on Sinai (Exod. 19:10–15) contains a message of restraint which Origen effortlessly links with Paul's preference for celibacy in I Corinthians 7: Moses and Paul both teach that holiness sometimes entails abstention.[93] Moreover, in this moralizing interpretation, Origen employs the same kinds of intertextual exegesis as does Jerome in *his* explications of such passages. Thus Origen reads the narrative of the Israelites' purification before Sinai through the intertexts of not just I Corinthians 7, but Matthew 22:12 (the man without a wedding garment); Ecclesiastes 9:8 ("let your garments be clean at all times"); and Acts 10:15 and 11:9 ("what God has cleansed, do not call common").[94]

It is of interest that when Origen comments on a passage such as I Corinthians 7, whose message pertaining to marriage and asceticism appears to agree with his own views, his use of allegory is remarkably restrained. Thus although Origen understands Paul's references to circumcision and uncircumcision, slavery and freedom, as tropes for marriage and

[88] Origen, *Hom. 9 Num.* 4 (GCS 30, 59); cf. *Comm. Ioan.* 1.6 (8) (GCS 10, 11): the Old Testament, however, becomes "the Gospel" only after Christ's Incarnation.

[89] Origen, *Hom. 3 Lev.* 3 (SC 286, 128).

[90] Origen, *Hom. 2 Exod.* 1 (SC 321, 70); *Hom. 38 Luc.* 3 (SC 87, 444). See Frances M. Young, *Biblical Exegesis and the Formation of Christian Culture* (Cambridge: Cambridge University Press, 1997), p. 3: without the use of analogy and allegory, the Biblical text would be only of "archaeological interest."

[91] Andrew Louth, *Discerning the Mystery: An Essay on the Nature of Theology* (Oxford: Clarendon, 1983), pp. 96, 107.

[92] Torjesen, *Hermeneutical Procedure*, esp. pp. 12, 14, 61, 130–38.

[93] Origen, *Hom. 11 Exod.* 7 (SC 321, 350): Origen cites I Cor. 7:1, 29–31, 34.

[94] Origen, *Hom. 11 Exod.* 7 (SC 321, 350).

celibacy, the moral message that he draws from the chapter closely follows Paul's: marriage is for the "weak" who are in danger of falling into fornication if they try not to "touch a woman"; married couples should refrain from sexual relations during periods of prayer; second marriage, after the death of a spouse, although not recommended, is allowed for those who "burn"; the anxieties of the married life are contrasted with the freedom attending virginity—and so forth.[95] The fact that Origen here so easily adopts a relatively "plain" reading of the text is in keeping with the recent scholarly emphasis on Origen's concern to enable a "presentist"[96] or "existential"[97] approach to the Bible, or on the role of the hearer in completing the redemptive work of the Logos in revelation.[98] Yet the fact the Origen can derive an edifyingly ascetic message from an "unadorned" reading of such passages, just as he can through allegorical readings of other Biblical texts, is still not the whole story.

Somewhat surprising for an ascetic practitioner, however, Origen routinely interprets passages that, on a "literal" reading, pertain to men, women, and sex, in ways that efface their directly sexual reference. This practice contrasts with Jerome's, in which almost all Biblical texts relating to sex (and many which we would think do not) are lifted up for discussions promoting asceticism. Borrowing interpretive props from Philo,[99] Origen thus habitually codes "male" and "female" as either spirit, mind, or reason as opposed to soul,[100] flesh, and body.[101] For example, Abraham's marriage at age 137 to Keturah (Gen. 25:1) does not prompt a discussion of patriarchal marriage, but is read through Wisdom of Solomon 8:9 ("take wisdom as my wife"): the narrative thus stands as an exhortation for Christians to pursue learning throughout ripe old age.[102] Likewise, the two wives of Samuel's father (I Sam. 1:2) do not occasion either a defense or a denunciation of Hebrew polygamy, but spark a discussion of the multiple virtues Christians are urged to pursue.[103] Most important,

[95] The fragments of this chapter of Origen's *Commentary on 1 Corinthians* can be found in the *Journal of Theological Studies* 9 (1908): 500–510.

[96] Louth, *Discerning the Mystery*, p. 96.

[97] Bostock, "Allegory," p. 46.

[98] Torjesen, *Hermeneutical Procedure*, esp. pp. 12–14, 33, 61, 130–38, 147.

[99] See Richard A. Baer Jr., *Philo's Use of the Categories Male and Female*, Arbeiten zur Literatur und Geschichte des Hellenistischen Judentums 3 (Leiden: Brill, 1970), chap. 2, esp. pp. 38–44; also R. P. C. Hanson, *Allegory and Event: A Study of the Sources and Significance of Origen's Interpretation of Scripture* (Richmond: John Knox; London: SCM, 1959), pp. 247–48.

[100] E.g., Origen, *Hom. 1 Gen.* 15 (SC 7bis, 66); *Hom. 10 Exod.* 3 (SC 321, 316); *Comm. Matt.* 12.4 (GCS 40, 73).

[101] E.g., Origen, *Hom. 4 Gen.* 4 (SC 7bis, 152); *Hom. 5 Gen.* 6 (SC 7bis, 180); *Hom. 2 Exod.* 1 (SC 321, 70); *Hom. 22 Num.* 1 (GCS 30, 204–5).

[102] Origen, *Hom. 11 Gen.* 1 (SC 7bis, 278).

[103] Origen, *Hom. 11 Gen.* 2 (SC 7bis, 282); *Hom. 1 I Sam.* 5 (SC 328, 111–13): "conversion" and "grace" are the two emphasized here.

the Old Testament's blessings on reproduction must not be taken literally, but spiritually, so that injunctions to fecundity portend spiritual and moral growth.[104] Only the "Sadducees" (i.e., the Jews) would take literally such texts as Psalm 128:3 ("your wife shall be like a fertile vine"), Origen scoffs.[105]

Most striking, this desexualization of Biblical texts is firmly linked to an allegorized gender hierarchy, in which "male" is a code for all that is lofty, intellectual, spiritual, and virtuous, and "female" the code for the opposite—although Origen points to virtuous Old Testament heroines such as Deborah and Judith, as well as to exemplary women of his own day who are virgins and martyrs.[106] Despite his praises for such women, Origen consistently depicts "the female" not just as fleshly and hence "lower" than reason,[107] but as standing for vice and moral weakness. Thus, according to Origen, the reason why women are not counted in the census described in the book of Numbers is because "the feminine" signals slackness, idleness, and sloth, not worthy of being "reckoned."[108] Conversely, Origen argues that there are numerous men who are "womanish," who whimper that they are too "weak" to keep the commandments.[109] Yet Origen offers hope to all—male as well as female—who are called "woman": they can, with effort, be transformed into the ranks of "men,"[110] of "combatants."[111] Gender destabilization, it appears, occurs more readily in the realm of allegory than in the realm of the flesh here-and-now.[112]

Origen's transhistorical exegesis, then, effects a certain leveling of the Old and New Testaments: while both can contain "the good news," both also teem with unedifying passages that require exegetical assistance if they

[104] Origen, *Hom. 11 Luc.* 1 (SC 87, 188); *Hom. 39 Luc.* 3 (SC 87, 452); *Hom. 1 Gen.* 15 (SC 7bis, 67).

[105] Origen, *Hom. 39 Luc.* 3 (SC 87, 452).

[106] E.g., Origen, *Hom. 9 Iud.* 1 (SC 389, 210–12).

[107] Origen, *Hom. 4 Gen.* 4 (SC 7bis, 152); *Hom. 11 Num.* 7 (GCS 30, 89).

[108] Origen, *Hom. 1 Num.* 1 (GCS 30, 3).

[109] Origen, *Hom. 9 Jesu Nave* 9 (SC 71, 266).

[110] Origen, *Hom. 26 Num.* 1 (GCS 30, 243), citing Eph. 4:13; *Hom. 9 Jesu Nave* 9 (SC 71, 264, 266).

[111] Origen, *Hom. 26 Num.* 1 (GCS 30, 243).

[112] In *Comm. Ioan.* 6.20 (12) (GCS 10, 128–29), Origen disputes Heracleon's interpretation of John 1:23 (that "voice" became "speech"); such a transformation is just as improbable as if we were to say "that a woman was turned into a man." Perhaps the most noted passage on "gender transformation" is Origen's allegorical reading of Eph. 5:28, the borrowing of which by Jerome stirred up trouble for him at the time of the Origenist debate. See Elizabeth A. Clark, *The Origenist Controversy: The Cultural Construction of an Early Christian Debate* (Princeton, N.J.: Princeton University Press, 1992), pp. 123–24; also idem, "The Place of Jerome's Commentary on Ephesians in the Origenist Controversy: The Apokatastasis and Ascetic Ideals," *Vigiliae Christianae* 41 (1987): 154–71 (esp. 156–57), and "New Perspectives on the Origenist Controversy: Human Embodiment and Ascetic Strategies," *Church History* 59 (1990): 145–62.

are to prove uplifting for contemporary Christians. Allegorical exegesis enables Origen to turn his hearers' and readers' attention from the realm of the physical to that of the "inner person." "Difference" attends minds, spirits, and souls; "distinction" is achieved—for men *and* for women, for celibate *and* for noncelibate—through the cultivation of "manly virtue" and the suppression of "feminine vice." This is a message for *all* Christians, whatever their sexual status.

John Chrysostom, Jerome, and Origen, then, employ the exegetical techniques outlined in chapter 5 to quite varying ends. Exegesis here proves itself an essential tool in the shaping of early Christian sexual values. In the chapters to follow, particular issues of exegesis in relation to asceticism will be more closely detailed.

Rejection and Recuperation: The Old Dispensation and the New

CHAPTER SEVEN

From Reproduction to Defamilialization

I: Introduction

This chapter explores how the church fathers might appropriate for their own purposes an apparently "underasceticized" Hebrew (and earlier Christian) past. How could "Israel of the flesh," with its concern for abundant reproduction, inspire those who yearned for "Jerusalem above," where marriage and family were counted as naught? If "sacred literature" could not be rejected, only interpreted, hermeneutical strategies had to be devised to accommodate Biblical texts to an ascetic agenda: through delicate mining, recalcitrant passages would yield up treasures for the ascetic program. Although words had changed their "social atmosphere"[1] from the time of the Hebrew patriarchs to that of fourth-century Christian ascetics, new texts might be made from old if the "otherness" of the past could be removed.[2] Ancient history could be recuperated for the requirements of a later era if the gap between past and present could be healed—through interpretation.[3] None of this, of course, was explicitly stated by patristic interpreters: it is in the interests of commentary to "erase its own tracks."[4] By doing so, commentary *itself* could become the "new text."[5]

The blow to "family values" that attended the advent of Christianity is evident in the New Testament itself, for the Synoptic Gospels represent

[1] Mikhail M. Bakhtin, *The Dialogic Imagination: Four Essays*, ed. Michael Holquist; trans. Caryl Emerson and Michael Holquist (Austin: University of Texas Press, 1981), p. 277.

[2] Martin Irvine, *The Making of Textual Culture: 'Grammatica' and Literary Theory, 450–1100* (Cambridge: Cambridge University Press, 1994), pp. 86, 253.

[3] Joel Fineman, "The Structure of Allegorical Desire," in *Allegory and Representation*, ed. Stephen J. Greenblatt, Select Papers from the English Institute, 1979–80, New Series 5 (Baltimore/London: Johns Hopkins University Press, 1981), p. 29.

[4] Irvine, *The Making of Textual Culture*, p. 271.

[5] Roland Barthes, "Theory of the Text," in *Untying the Text: A Post-Structuralist Reader*, ed. Robert Young (Boston/Lon-

Jesus as unmarried, and his teaching often appears to oppose the family. Thus Jesus claims that he has come to bring a "sword" that will divide families (Matt. 10:34–39). A follower of Jesus must "hate his own father and mother and wife and children and brothers and sisters" (Luke 14:26). Jesus rejects his own blood-relations, claiming instead that those who do the word of God are his family (Matt. 12:46–49 = Luke 8:19–21 = Mark 3:31–35). The woman who calls out to Jesus, "Blessed is the womb that bore you and the breasts that you sucked!" is corrected by his reply, "Blessed rather (*menoun*) are those who hear the word of God and keep it!" (Luke 11:27–28). Most important for later developments were the verses praising those who become "eunuchs for the sake of the Kingdom of Heaven" (Matt. 19:10–12),[6] and those claiming that "in the resurrection they neither marry nor are given in marriage, but are like the angels in heaven" (Matt. 22:30; cf. Mark 12:25; Luke 20:35). Early Christians understood the latter to mean that even now they might participate in this "angelic" state—to be theirs more fully in the afterlife—by adopting lives of celibacy.

Such sayings attributed to Jesus may well have been prompted by the expectation of an imminent arrival of God's Kingdom. The followers of Jesus believed that God would soon break into human history to destroy the present era and create a new one in which the poor, the hungry, and the despondent would receive the rewards so frequently denied them (Luke 6:20–26 = Matt. 5:3–12). In this eschatological context, Christians understood that Jesus had called them to lives in which traditional values, especially those pertaining to the family, were displaced by an ethic of radical allegiance to God alone. When the Kingdom would come "like a thief in the night" (Matt. 24:42; Luke 12:39), all must be ready to greet Christ the Bridegroom, not to linger with earthly husbands.[7]

Unlike many modern Christian interpreters, especially Protestants who reject an axiology grounded on ascetic superiority, the church fathers accepted these sayings as normative for their own lives while simultaneously discarding the early Christian expectation of an imminent eschaton.[8]

---

don/Henley: Routledge and Kegan Paul, 1981), p. 44.

[6] See chap. 4 above for a discussion of the Fathers' interpretation of this decisive verse.

[7] For a useful collection of recent essays detailing the treatment of "the family" in early Christianity, see Halvor Moxnes, ed., *Constructing Early Christian Families: Family as Social Reality and Metaphor* (London/New York: Routledge, 1997).

[8] Tertullian, writing at the turn to the third century, retains some eschatological enthusiasm (perhaps in part stimulated by his later Montanist leanings?); Augustine, while writing his mammoth *On the City of God*, which details the history of the world from before its creation to its final consummation, does not position the latter event anywhere near the present era (*De civitate Dei* 20–21).

Rather, other arguments—such as an appeal to "the woes of marriage," or to the hope for a higher reward in the afterlife—that did not rest on the expectation of an immediate "end" were pressed to stimulate enthusiasm for ascetic renunciation.

Although Scripture itself provided ample fuel for the ascetic fire, a few early Christian authors thought that it could be further improved by creative recomposition. Thus the anonymous author of the *Acts of Paul and Thecla*, writing probably in the second century, offers a new version of the Beatitudes (Matt. 5:3–12; Luke 6:20–23) that includes the following verses:

> Blessed are those who keep the flesh pure, for they shall become the temple of God.
> Blessed are the continent, for to them shall God speak. . . .
> Blessed are those who have wives as if they have them not, for they shall inherit God. . . .
> Blessed are the bodies of virgins, for they shall be well-pleasing to God and shall not lose the reward of their purity.[9]

Such manifest additions to and substitutions within Scripture were considered unacceptable by Catholic authorities, although they might adduce the example of Thecla to inspire virginal commitment.[10] Other, more subtle, modes of reading Scripture could vindicate the ascetic program equally well. Through interpretation, numerous Old Testament passages praising reproduction and family life could either be brought into alignment with the ascetic agenda, or explained so that they posed no serious deterrent to a thoroughly asceticized comprehension of Scripture. Although, as we have seen, some Old Testament passages—for example, Abraham's leaving his home and relations (Gen. 12), or the blessing on eunuchs (Isa. 56:4–5)—were deemed reinforcing of the ascetic agenda, what might be done with verses that appeared to celebrate procreation or to reinforce "family values"? How were ascetic interpreters to move from "reproduction" to "defamilialization"? This chapter examines ascetic writers' treatment of Old Testament passages that challenged their penchant to read all of Scripture with ascetic eyes, as well as their citation of New Testament verses to justify their renunciatory ideology.

[9] *Acta Pauli et Theclae* 5–6 (Lipsius/Bonnet I:238–40).

[10] For a history of the Thecla legend and cult, see Gilbert Dagron, *Vie et miracles de Sainte Thècle: Texte grec, traduction et commentaire*, SubsHag 62 (Bruxelles: Société des Bollandistes, 1978). For a lively discussion of the "culture wars" that were fought in the early Church over the story of Paul and Thecla, see Dennis R. MacDonald, *The Legend and the Apostle: The Battle for Paul in Story and Canon* (Philadelphia: Westminster, 1983).

II: Reproduction

Genesis 1:28 and 2:24

In the opening chapter of Scripture stood a verse whose interpretation taxed the exegetical ingenuity of ascetic interpreters: "Reproduce, multiply, and fill the earth" (Gen. 1:28). That this verse stood as God's first commandment to the human race exacerbated the difficulty of its interpretation for ascetic exegetes.

Genesis 1:28 could, of course, be read allegorically so that "increase" was understood to enjoin spiritual growth: in this instance, unlike some others, allegory *assists* the agenda of renunciation. This interpretive tradition, stemming from Origen, took the verse to counsel the increase of "good thoughts and inclinations."[11] Jerome, in his more openly Origenist phase, reads the verse through the intertext of Proverbs 4:8, which enjoins its readers to "embrace wisdom."[12] Augustine, too, when battling Manicheans who reject the Old Testament as authoritative Scripture, resorts to a spiritualized interpretation in an attempt to sidestep Manichean charges that Catholics wallowed in the "filth" of reproduction.[13] Even later, at the turn to the fifth century, Augustine still muses whether Genesis 1:28 should not be taken as an injunction to "multiply virtue"[14]—a view he soon came to discard in favor of a more physical reading of "reproduce."[15]

In addition to its usefulness in rebutting pagans who deemed ascetic Christians to be hostile to the social order,[16] Genesis 1:28 also stood ready as textual ammunition against "heretics" who allegedly denigrated creation and, with it, reproduction: Marcionites,[17] Encratites,[18] Manicheans,[19] and Origenists.[20] In Ambrose's view, God had proclaimed at the beginning of Genesis that the purpose of marriage was to "fill the earth" precisely in order to "destroy heresy."[21] Against Christian renunciants of an excessively ascetic stripe that bordered on "heresy," the verse could be

[11] Origen, *Hom.1 Gen.* 14–15 (GCS 29, 18–19); cf. *Hom. Luc.* 11.1 (GCS 35, 77–78).

[12] Jerome, *Comm. Eccles.* 3:5 (CCL 72, 275).

[13] Augustine, *De Gen. adversus Manichaeos* 1.19.30 (PL 34, 187).

[14] Augustine, *De bono coniugali* 2.2 (CSEL 41, 188–89).

[15] Augustine, *De civitate Dei* 14.21 (CCL 48, 443); *Contra Iulianum* 4.14.69 (PL 44, 772–73).

[16] Tertullian, *De anima* 27.4 (CCL 2, 823); Clement of Alexandria, *Paedagogus* 2.10.83; 2.10.95 (GCS 12, 208, 214).

[17] Tertullian, *Adversus Marcionem* 1.29.4 (CCL 1, 473); Ambrosiaster, *Quaestiones Veteris et Novi Testamenti* 127.2; 127.17 (CSEL 50, 399, 406).

[18] Jerome, *Comm. Gal.* 3 (6:8) (PL 26, 460).

[19] Augustine, *Contra Secundinum* 21 (CSEL 25, 938–39); Ambrosiaster, *Quaestiones Veteris et Novi Testamenti* 127.2; 127.18 (CSEL 50, 399, 406).

[20] Theophilus of Alexandria, *ep. fest.*(404) (= Jerome, *ep.* 100).12 (CSEL 55, 225).

[21] Ambrose, *Exp. Luc.* 1.30 (CCL 14, 21).

cited to argue that a "lawful use" of the genital organs was not contrary to God's will.[22]

Yet for ascetic enthusiasts, an interpretive problem remained, since their anti-ascetic opponents frequently cited Genesis 1:28 to promote a laxer version of Christian sexual ethics. According to Jerome, Genesis 1:28 was a favorite text of his opponent Jovinian;[23] Pelagius also testifies that the *amatores luxuriae*, the "lovers of (sexual) indulgence," championed the verse to oppose Paul's recommendation of celibacy in I Corinthians 7.[24] According to the anonymous Pelagian author of *De castitate*, it is "wanton Christians," preferring "lust" to Christ, who appeal to the dual creation of "male and female."[25]

In response, one strategy espoused by those of stronger ascetic mettle was simply to deny that the verse applied to Christians. These rigorists cite Genesis 1:28 to signal the "difference in times" between the old and the new ways of life: since the time is "wound up," Tertullian argues, Christians might rather live "as if not" (I Cor. 7:29) than to fulfill Genesis 1:28.[26] According to Pelagius, those who believed that such decrees of "ancient times" applied to Christians should also marry their daughters (as did Adam) or sisters (as did Cain)[27]—manifestly absurd propositions. Likewise for Jerome, Genesis 1:28 does not apply to the Christian era, which is the time for the "axe to be laid to the root" (Matt. 3:10)—the "root" of reproduction.[28] Then, at the world's beginning, was "the time to embrace," but now, in the Christian present, is the time to "cease from embracing" (Eccles. 3:5).[29] Still, since God had pronounced these words at creation, there could be no "law" that required virginity of Christians, who thus demonstrate their superiority by adopting that which is "above the command"—and "above nature." A choice lies before Christians:

[22] Athanasius, *ep. ad Amunem* (PG 26, 1173).

[23] Jerome, *Adversus Iovinianum* 1.5 (PL 23, 225).

[24] Pelagius, *Comm. I Cor.* 7:1–3 (PLS 1, 1198–99). The response of Basil of Caesarea to such a juxtaposition is, "Don't make me laugh" (*ep.* 160 [Loeb II:408]).

[25] (Anonymous), *De castitate* 11.1 (PLS 1, 1489). Conversely, pro-marriage church fathers such as Ambrosiaster cite Gen. 1:28 to show that the Church still shares in the blessing of the Old Dispensation: see Ambrosiaster, *Quaestiones Veteri et Novi Testamenti* 127.2–3; 127.7 (CSEL 50, 399–400, 401). A concern to harmonize the Testaments in the face of Manicheans' disjunction of them stands behind Augustine's somewhat astonishing statement that the New Testament does not contain any precepts not already contained in the Old: *Contra Adimantum* 3 (CSEL 25, 121).

[26] Tertullian, *De pudicitia* 16.19 (CCL 2, 1314); *De exhortatione castitatis* 6.1 (CCL 2, 1023).

[27] Pelagius, *Comm. I Cor.* 7:1–3 (PLS 1, 1199); cf. (Anonymous), *Admonitio Augiensis* (PLS 1, 1702), where Gen. 2:24 ("two in one flesh") is also cited to mark the "difference in times" between the two Dispensations.

[28] Jerome, *ep.* 123.12 (CSEL 56, 85–86); cf. *Adversus Helvidium* 20 (PL 23, 213).

[29] Jerome, *Comm. Eccles.* 3:5 (CCL 72, 275).

they can follow Adam, who through the "voluptuousness of marriage" became the seed for the married life, or imitate the Lord, who through the purity of virginity became the seed for the age to come.[30] Creating dichotomies between "the first decree" and "the second decree," and between "earth" and "heaven," was a standard strategy for *enlarging* the gap between "the times."[31]

Yet why, given the superiority of virginity, had God enjoined reproduction in the first place? Several Fathers explain that God had originally pronounced "reproduce and multiply" as a benevolent response to the earth's barrenness, to the need for a human population to fill the earth;[32] nonetheless, they add, since the earth is now more than full, there is no further need for human increase.[33] At best, Christians who reproduce can be praised for supplying virgins for the Church.[34]

Moreover, "reproduce and multiply" could be cited to explain, indeed to justify, aspects of Old Testament sexual ethics that might otherwise appear dubious: precisely *because* the Israelites heeded God's command in Genesis 1:28, they indulged in levirate marriage,[35] reproduced copiously with wives and concubines,[36] and engaged in polygamy and plural marriages.[37] Although such practices cannot be countenanced in the New Dispensation, they are rendered more understandable by the Hebrews' desire to fulfill what they understood as a divine command for reproduction.

A similar uncertainty attends the interpretation of Genesis 2:24, that a man will leave his father and mother and become "one flesh" with his wife. Between the views of interpreters such as Jovinian who appeal to Genesis 2:24 as a sanction for the continuing goodness of marriage,[38] and those of writers who scorn the text as demonstrating the "difference in times" between two Dispensations,[39] several interpretive options were possible. The verse could be taken as advocating single marriage but pro-

[30] Basil of Ancyra, *De virginitate* 55; 54 (Vaillant, pp. 62–65).

[31] Jerome, *ep.* 22.19 (CSEL 54, 168); Augustine, *De Gen. adversus Manichaeos* 1.19.30 (PL 34, 187); Basil of Ancyra, *De virginitate* 54 (Vaillant, pp. 62–63). See above, pp. 145–52, for a discussion of the motif, the "difference in times."

[32] (Anonymous), *De castitate* 14.4 (PLS 1, 1495); John Chrysostom, *De virginitate* 19.1 (SC 125, 156, 158); Pelagius, *Comm. I Cor.* 7:1–3 (PLS 1, 1199).

[33] (Anonymous), *De castitate* 14.4 (PLS 1, 1495); Jerome, *Adversus Iovinianum* 1.16 (PL 23, 246); *Adversus Helvidium* 21 (PL 23, 215).

[34] Jerome, *ep.* 66.3 (CSEL 54, 650).

[35] Tertullian, *De monogamia* 7.2–3 (CCL 2, 1237).

[36] John Cassian, *Conlationes* 17.19 (SC 54, 263).

[37] Clement of Alexandria, *Stromata* 3.12.82 (GCS 52[= 15], 233); cf. the Arabic fragment (#4) of Clement's remarks on Matt. 19:3–5 (Fleisch, pp. 68–69): it was a necessity of that situation, since God had pronounced Gen. 1:28.

[38] Jovinian in Jerome, *Adversus Iovinianum* 1.5 (PL 23, 225).

[39] (Anonymous), *Admonitio Augiensis* (PLS 1, 1702).

hibiting divorce,[40] warning against the Manichean denigration of reproduction,[41] condemning same-sex relations,[42] or furnishing a lesson in Christology (Christ left his Father in Heaven and his mother the Synagogue to embrace his wife, the Church, becoming "two in one flesh,"[43] or, alternatively, the "two in one flesh" symbolizing the human and the divine in Jesus).[44] Read more ascetically, Genesis 2:24 signified the union in which Adam and Eve would be bound in their sinful state only *after* they were expelled from Paradise,[45] or—far better—the union the virgin will enjoy when she leaves her father and mother to become "one flesh" with her Bridegroom, Jesus.[46] In such ways could the sexual and procreative injunctions of the creation stories be modified to serve the ascetic program through the creation of "difference" between ancient Israelites and contemporary Christians.

III: Patriarchal and Other Old Testament Narratives

As we have seen, Abraham's abandonment of home and homeland (Gen. 12) and his near-sacrifice of Isaac (Gen. 22) were, with limited exegetical assistance, taken to counsel ascetic renunciation. Likewise, various features of the patriarchs' marriages, such as their late age at marriage, were thought to contain ascetic overtones.

Such texts, however, could also be read in a less ascetic direction, as providing salutary models of domesticity for Christians who had opted for the "lower way" of marriage.[47] The virtues of the patriarchal women could be highly lauded by advocates of marriage, with Rebecca receiving pride of place;[48] likewise, Sarah's wifely hospitality to the visitors at the oak of Mamre and her "service" to them and to Abraham (Gen. 18) is frequently

[40] Tertullian, *De monogamia* 4.2 (CCL 2, 1233); *De exhortatione castitatis* 5.2 (CCL 2, 1022); Ambrose, *De viduis* 15.89 (PL 16, 276); *Exp. Luc.* 8.7 (CCL 14, 300).

[41] Augustine, *Contra Adimantum* 3.3 (CSEL 25, 118); *Contra Secundinum* 21 (CSEL 25, 939); *De nuptiis et concupiscentia* 2.3.9 (CSEL 42, 260–61).

[42] John Chrysostom, *Hom. 4 Rom.* 2 (1:26–27) (PG 60, 418).

[43] Augustine, *De Gen. adversus Manichaeos* 2.24.37 (CSEL 34, 215–16); cf. *Serm. Den.* 12.2 (PL 46, 853).

[44] Augustine, *Hom. 1 I Ioan.* 2 (PL 35, 1979).

[45] Jerome, *Adversus Iovinianum* 1.16 (PL 23, 246); John Chrysostom, *Hom. 15 Gen.* 4 (PG 53, 123).

[46] Basil of Ancyra, *De virginitate* 50 (Vaillant, pp. 56–57).

[47] John Chrysostom, *Hom. 32 Gen.* 3–6 (PG 53, 296–302); *Hom. 38 Gen.* 1–5 (PG 53, 350–58); *Hom. 20 Eph.* 5 (PG 62, 141); Ambrose, *De virginibus* 1.7.34 (PL 16, 209); *De excessu fratris* 2.95–99 (PL 16, 1400–1402).

[48] Origen, *Hom. 12 Num.* 1 (GCS 30, 96–97; Rebecca = patience); John Chrysostom, *Quales ducendae sint uxores* 7 (PG 51, 235–37).

recommended.[49] Moreover, according to the defender of marriage, Clement of Alexandria, Abraham's "half-lie" in calling Sarah his "sister" (Gen. 12:12–19; 20:2–12) describes precisely the relation in which a good wife should stand to her husband.[50] That Sarah addressed Abraham as her *kyrios/dominus* ("lord") (Gen. 18:12) supported other Biblical verses that counseled the subjection of wives.[51] For Origen, ever-attentive to the precise wording of Biblical verses, the representation of Sarah as standing "behind" Abraham in Genesis 18:9–10 suggests the proper place for wives.[52] Moreover, in Origen's view, God's instruction to Abraham that he should "hearken" to Sarah (Gen. 21:12) should be read allegorically: Sarah represents the "virtue" to which men should attend so that wisdom will become their "sister" (Prov. 7:4).[53] Such features of the Genesis narratives could be cited by those churchmen eager to justify, even to praise, aspects of marriage.

More ascetically inclined interpreters, however, feared that too positive a reading of the patriarchal narratives might suggest that marriage stood equal to celibacy in the Christian scheme of values.[54] This argument is precisely the one advanced by Jerome's opponent Jovinian, who implies that the blessedness pronounced by God on the patriarchs was linked to their marital status. Duly noting Abraham's three wives, Jovinian submits that through his faith, this patriarch "received the blessing in begetting his son." Likewise Sarah, even in old age, "exchanged the curse of sterility for the blessing of childbearing." And by citing numerous New Testament verses that appear to assume marriage and family life as normative, Jovinian claims that God's blessing on marriage did not cease with the dawn-

[49] John Chrysostom, *Hom. 21 Rom.* 3 (PG 60, 606); *Hom. 30 Rom.* 4 (PG 60, 666); *Hom. 14 I Tim.* 2 (PG 62, 573); *Hom. 41 Gen.* 5 (PG 53, 581).

[50] Clement of Alexandria, *Stromata* 6.12.100–101 (GCS 52[15], 482). The author of *De castitate* (4.12) appears to suggest that the text means that Abraham was having sexual intercourse with a "relative"—something that Paul surely would not have countenanced, since he lay down rigorous rules even for married couples.

[51] So Jerome, commenting on wifely subjection in Eph. 5:22–23: *Comm. Eph.* 3 (5:22–23) (PL 26, 564). Jerome probably borrows from Origen his "higher" interpretation that "wives" signify "bodies" and "husbands" signify "spirit"; bodies are to remain in subjection to the spirit/mind. Cf. Augustine's advice to Ecdicia (*ep.* 262.7 [CSEL 57, 626–27]) and the anonymous Pelagian(?) author's letter *To Celantia* (*Ad Celantiam* 27 [CSEL 29, 455]).

[52] Origen, *Hom. 4 Gen.* 4 (GCS 29, 54). Origen also allegorizes the passage: the flesh (= the woman) should yield to reason (= the man).

[53] Origen, *Hom. 6 Gen.* 1 (GCS 29, 66–67). Origen argues that since God had pronounced women to be subject to their husbands (Gen. 3:16), Christians cannot read Gen. 21:12 "literally."

[54] Thus it is of interest that many of the references in the above paragraphs come from John Chrysostom. In chap. 6, I have suggested that such a reading of these narratives well fit his purpose of praising marriage—but marriage that involved, in the present, the subjection of women.

ing of the Christian era—thus cleverly defusing the ascetics' argument that childbearing was appropriate only for the world's beginning.[55] The anonymous Pelagian (?) author of *De castitate* likewise reports that opponents of a rigorous asceticism appealed to Abraham and the patriarchs as a justification for their own pro-marriage sentiments.[56] In addition, John Chrysostom reveals that detractors of Christian virginity argued that Abraham's married state could not be considered sullying if the continent Peter, Paul, John the Baptist, and John the Evangelist all wished to ascend to his "bosom" (Matt. 8:11).[57]

Christian authors of a more ascetic cast here walked a narrow line: they must simultaneously refute the pro-marriage arguments advanced by Jovinian, yet eschew the Manichean denigration of the Old Testament. Thus Jerome, despite his passionate refutation of Jovinian, shies away from stressing the sinful behavior of the patriarchs,[58] even when he presses the argument from the "difference in times." He cites II Corinthians 5:17 to remind Christians that "the old has passed away," and Song of Songs 2:11, that "the winter [of the Old Law] is past."[59] Jerome concedes that the Hebrew ancestors fulfilled God's command under the Law, but vigorously argues that Christians are called to fulfill God's different command under the Gospel.[60] Despite such ameliorating concessions, Abraham's three wives are too much for Jerome to countenance: if Christians wish to follow Abraham in his marital habits, they should also follow him in his circumcision. Jerome baits his readers: don't half follow Abraham and half reject him! Although Abraham served God in marriage, we "upon whom the end of the ages has come" (I Cor. 10:11) should serve him in virginity.[61] Commenting on the patriarchs' multiple sexual relations, Jerome pithily remarks, "The intimate partnerships of Mesopotamia died in the city of the Gospel."[62]

[55] Jovinian in Jerome, *Adversus Iovinianum* 1.5; 1.36 (PL 23, 225–27, 271).

[56] (Anonymous), *De castitate* 4.12; 11.1; 15.1–2 (PLS 1, 1472, 1489, 1496). The author's scathing retort is that Christians should better follow Abraham in his willingness to sacrifice his son (13.5), and that, in any event, it was not because Abraham had a wife that he "pleased God" (15.3).

[57] John Chrysostom, *De virginitate* 82.1 (SC 125, 382).

[58] Jerome even praises Abraham in *epp.* 66.11 (CSEL 54, 661–62); 125.20 (CSEL 56, 142); 108.31 (CSEL 55, 349), and uses him and Sarah as exemplars of asceticism in *Adversus Helvidium* 20 (PL 23, 214).

[59] Jerome, *Adversus Iovinianum* 1.37; 1.30 (PL 23, 273, 263). Jerome also appeals to the "difference in times" argument when faulting the sexual behavior of David and Solomon; "we have a different command," he claims, appealing to I Cor. 7:29 (the time is short, "have wives as if not") (*Adversus Iovinianum* 1.24 [PL 23, 255]).

[60] Jerome, *Adversus Iovinianum* 1.24 (PL 23, 255).

[61] Jerome, *Adversus Iovinianum* 1.19; 2.4 (PL 23, 248, 301).

[62] Jerome, *Adversus Iovinianum* 1.19 (PL 23, 248).

An even sharper critique of the patriarchs, and of Abraham in particular, is leveled by the author of *De castitate*, for whom there can be no chastity within marriage until all sexual activity is renounced.[63] According to this author, it is "wanton" Christians (Jovinian and his disciples?) who have raised the issue of how the patriarchs "pleased God" when they had not only plural wives, but also many concubines. Was not Abraham ranked as first among the patriarchs, these "wanton Christians" ask?[64]

The anonymous author's retort is sharp. If we take the patriarchs as examples, Paul's teaching becomes "superfluous" and "empty." Almost no Old Testament injunctions apply to Christians, the author avers; for our rule of faith, we must look to the New Testament alone. Moreover, it was not because Abraham had a *wife* that he pleased God, but because he was obedient. Since Abraham proved that he scorned the fruit of marriage (i.e., his son Isaac) by his readiness to sacrifice him (Gen. 22), how much more would he have despised marriage itself, had he been given the opportunity to renounce it! How eagerly he would have heeded Paul's words on celibacy, had they been directed to him![65]

Yet Christian writers of this sharp an ascetic cast had reason to fear that they would be lumped with the Manicheans, who were, judging from Augustine's polemics against them, resolute critics of the Old Testament praise for fecundity in general and of patriarchal behavior in particular.[66] Thus Augustine's protracted literary debate with the Manichean Faustus centered on the correct reading of the patriarchal narratives. According to Faustus, who was of a strongly ascetic bent, the promises to the patriarchs regarding the children they would beget and the riches they would accrue are "useless for the soul's salvation." Trusting in the Old Testament implies a denial that the New Testament promises are sufficient; in Faustus' view, Catholics, like an adulterous wife, rush to "serve two husbands." The Old Testament curse on those who "fail to raise up seed for Israel" (Deut. 25:5–10), Faustus claims, is contradicted by the chastity that Jesus recommended in the Gospels and hence must be rejected. The New Testament rather enjoins us to leave wife, children, home, and riches: Faustus confesses that as a true follower of Christ, he has done just that.[67]

[63] (Anonymous), *De castitate* 2.9.1; 10.3; 10.4; 10.15; 13.9 (PLS 1, 1465–66, 1478, 1480, 1489, 1490).

[64] (Anonymous), *De castitate* 11.1; 15.1 (PLS 1, 1489, 1496).

[65] (Anonymous), *De castitate* 11.2; 12.3–4; 15.3 (PLS 1, 1489–90, 1490–91, 1497–98).

[66] See such passages as Secundinus, *ep.* cited in Augustine, *Contra Secundinum* (CSEL 25, 896–97). According to Augustine, *Contra Adimantum*, Manicheans argue that pro-reproduction passages of the Old Testament (such as Gen. 1:26; 2:18–24; Ps. 128:3–4) are in contradiction to New Testament teaching (*Contra Adimantum* 3; 5; 23).

[67] Faustus in Augustine, *Contra Faustum* 10.1; 15.1; 14.1; 5.1 (CSEL 25, 310, 415–17, 403, 271).

The patriarchal narratives in particular stand among the Old Testament passages that Christians should find offensive, in Faustus' view. Here, Abraham's "defiling himself with a concubine" and being spurred by "an irrational craving for children" are ammunition for Faustus' arsenal. Moreover, Abraham cannot even be praised for his trust in God (as Catholic writers often claimed): his taking a concubine proves that he distrusted God's promise to Sarah, lack of faith thus exacerbating sexual sin. In addition, according to Faustus, Abraham's "selling" of Sarah to both Abimelech and Pharaoh indicates that he was motivated by greed and avarice. Sarah too is guilty for her conniving with Abraham in his sexual defilement with Hagar.[68] As for Jacob, his allowing four women to "pass him around" suggests to Faustus that this patriarch "led the life of a goat."[69] Thus Faustus declines the invitation of Matthew 8:11 to sit at table with the patriarchs in the Kingdom of Heaven: on the basis of their behavior, he avers, they should rather be consigned to the "dungeons below."[70] Faustus not only reproaches the patriarchs' morality, he also questions the authority of the texts describing them: did your writers forge these stories, he mockingly asks his Catholic opponents? It is not Manichean critics who have blasphemed the prophets and the patriarchs, for the Biblical authors have done well enough at that without assistance![71] No ingenious reading of Genesis can "save" Abraham and the patriarchs for Faustus.

How were the Fathers to answer such attacks on morally dubious narratives that nonetheless were counted as divinely revealed Scripture? For those eager to uphold the goodness of marriage against the onslaughts of "heretics," some explanation for the inclusion of these texts in the Scriptural canon was necessary.

Thus in addition to arguing that a "close reading" of the story of Abraham would exonerate the patriarch in the face of Faustus' rude accusations, as noted above,[72] Augustine insists that the patriarchs' sexual unions were motivated only by their desire to produce children, not by "lust": this is his recurrent theme throughout book 22 of the *Contra Faustum*, in which he attempts to dispel his Manichean opponent's sneering insinuations concerning the patriarchs' sexual behavior.[73] Neither was Sarah motivated by lust, Augustine reasons, since no wife who loves her husband

[68] Faustus in Augustine, *Contra Faustum* 22.5; 22.30; 22.33; 22.31 (CSEL 25, 594, 624, 627, 625).

[69] Faustus in Augustine, *Contra Faustum* 22.49; 22.98 (CSEL 25, 642, 704).

[70] Faustus in Augustine, *Contra Faustum* 33.1 (CSEL 25, 784): "poenali inferorum custodia."

[71] Faustus in Augustine, *Contra Faustum* 22.5; 22.3 (CSEL 25, 595, 593).

[72] See above, pp. 120–21, for an example of Augustine's attempt to give a "close reading" that rescues the text.

[73] Thus for Abraham, Jacob, and others, see Augustine, *Contra Faustum* 22.30; 22.31; 22.47; 22.48; 22.50 (CSEL 25, 624–25, 639–41, 643–44).

would encourage him in an extramarital relation if he were motivated by "animal passion." Sarah, like Abraham, tolerated his union with Hagar because she wanted the Israelite race to be upbuilt.[74] Similarly, Augustine argues that the patriarchs' polygamous relations themselves had a beneficial procreative purpose, since men can produce more children if they engage in intercourse with several women, whereas having several male partners is of no advantage for female procreativity.[75] Moreover, Augustine posits, polygamy is more consonant with the "order of nature" than is polyandry, for it is part of that "order" for men to rule over women.[76] The patriarchs were merely displaying their obedience to Paul's words in I Corinthians 7:4 in these activities, remembering that their bodies were under the power of their wives—who, according to Augustine, were urging these multiple unions for the sake of procreation.[77] Had the patriarchs and their wives been able to reproduce otherwise than through sexual intercourse, Augustine posits, they surely would not have indulged in the latter.[78] Most important, their reproduction points ahead in a figurative manner to Christianity's advent: are Christians not said to be the descendants of Abraham (Rom. 4)?[79] Finally, the patriarchs' women, according to Augustine, far from being objects of calumny, symbolize the various races who will compose the Church, all subject to one man, Christ:[80] thus is polygamy given an edifying cast.

Other Fathers, however, could, through figurative readings, press New Testament verses pertaining to Abraham and Sarah in a more precisely ascetic direction: here, "spiritual interpretation" *does* serve the ascetic cause. Origen, in *Homily 39 on Luke*, counsels his readers not to understand the alleged blessings on childbearing in the Old Testament in a "physical" manner; it is "Sadducees," he alleges, who read Psalm 128:3 ("Your wife will be like a fruitful vine within your house; your children will be like olive shoots around your table") to refer to pregnancy and

[74] Augustine, *Contra Faustum* 22.31 (CSEL 25, 625).

[75] Augustine, *De bono viduitatis* 7.10 (CSEL 41, 314); *De doctrina Christiana* 3.12.20 (CCL 32, 90); *Serm.* 51.25 (PL 38, 347–48); *Contra Faustum* 22.47 (CSEL 25, 639).

[76] Augustine, *De nuptiis et concupiscentia* 1.9.10 (CSEL 42, 314).

[77] Augustine, *De civitate Dei* 16.25; 16.38 (CCL 48, 529, 544); *Contra Faustum* 22.31; 22.49 (CSEL 25, 625, 642–43).

[78] Augustine, *De bono viduitatis* 7.10 (CSEL 41, 314).

[79] Augustine, *De doctrina Christiana* 3.12.20 (CCL 32, 90); *De civitate Dei* 16.32 (CCL 48, 536–37); *Contra Faustum* 22.51 (CSEL 25, 645); cf. Origen, *Hom. 5 Lev.* 2.3 (GCS 29, 336–37): the numerous descendants promised to Abraham in Gen. 15 are Christians (cf. Rom. 4). Augustine can also "read" Sarah as an allegory of the Church: see *Contra Faustum* 22.51; 22.38 (CSEL 255, 645, 631–32); *Tract. in Ioan.* 11.7; 11.13 (CCL 36, 114, 118); *De correctione Donatistarum* (= *ep.* 185).2.11 (CSEL 57, 9–10).

[80] Augustine, *De bono coniugali* 18.21 (CSEL 41, 214–15).

childbearing. Rather, Christians should recall the interpretation of Hagar and Sarah in Galatians 4 and opt for a "spiritual childbearing."[81] Pelagians of an ascetic stripe also appeal to Galatians 4 to counter pro-marriage opponents who argue that Abraham's unions with women stand as models for Christians: these stories are "figurative," the author of *De castitate* claims.[82] Most dramatically, if "God is able from these stones to raise up children to Abraham" (Matt. 3:9), Jerome argues, there is no need for his virginal protégée Eustochium to consider reproducing: if God has already made "children of Abraham" from "the hard stones of the Gentiles," he can surely provide people for the Church as he sees fit.[83]

A different notion of figurative reading is provided by the ascetically rigorous author of *De castitate*. Much in Scripture, this anonymous writer argues, should be read as a "figure." Thus in the Old Testament, marriage is a "figure"—and "figures" are meant to pass away when the reality they portend becomes present. Genesis 2:24 (that a man leaves his parents, cleaves to his wife, and they become "one flesh"), for example, is merely a "figure" for the relation of Christ and the Church, as Paul indicates in Ephesians 5:31–32. Likewise, and again on Paul's authority, Abraham's wife and concubine should be taken as "figures" pointing to the future "reality"; they serve to contrast "Mount Sinai, the present Jerusalem" with the "Jerusalem above" of Galatians 4:25–26. But for present-day Christians, according to the author of *De castitate*, marriage does not figuratively foreshadow *any* truth to come—so what could be its function? Note that the author does not here claim, as latter-day Christians might, that Galatians 4 provides an allegorical interpretation of Old Testament "realities"; rather, the "real" is located entirely on the side of the New Testament. Yet Abraham, in the end, is better disposed of than "interpreted," for this anonymous author. Borrowing Jerome's argument, he scoffingly concludes that if Christians wish to imitate Abraham by marrying, they should also undergo circumcision and offer animal sacrifice.[84] Here, figurative interpretation is not sufficient to "save" father Abraham.

Yet a last way in which patristic writers could turn the patriarchal narratives to a more ascetic purpose can be seen in the reading of these texts by John Chrysostom.[85] Chrysostom centers on the oft-repeated theme of

[81] Origen, *Hom. 39 Luc.* 3–4 (SC 87, 452, 454). It is probably such Origenist speculation that raises the ire of Theodore of Mopsuestia, who uses Gal. 4 to discuss the proper and improper uses of figuration in Scriptural interpretation (*Ad Gal.* 4:4 [Swete I:73–78]).

[82] (Anonymous), *De castitate* 15.2 (PLS 1, 1496–97).

[83] Jerome, *ep.* 22.19 (CSEL 54, 168).

[84] (Anonymous), *De castitate* 15.2; 15.4 (PLS 1, 1496–97, 1498).

[85] For a discussion of this and similar motifs, see Elizabeth A. Clark, "The Virginal *Politeia* and Plato's *Republic*: John Chrysostom on Women and Sexual Relation," in idem, *Jerome, Chrysostom, and Friends: Essays and Translations* (New York/Toronto:

the *sterility* of the patriarchs' wives (Sarah and Rachel, in particular) to drive home his point that conception is not a "natural" act resulting simply from sexual intercourse, but is a gift that God may grant or withhold. According to Chrysostom, these sterile patriarchal women who nonetheless give birth confirm faith in the divine purpose before God revealed the mystery of a virgin birth. Through divine grace, these women became fecund so that, in time, others would not disbelieve that a virgin had borne a child. Especially is this line of argument helpful against the Jews, Chrysostom adds; when they mockingly ask, "How can a virgin bear?", Christians should reply, "How can a sterile and decrepit woman have brought forth?"[86] Since Sarah, Rebecca, and Rachel were all virtuous women, Chrysostom reasons, their barrenness was not the result of sin. Rather, God acted through them so that centuries later, there could be no reason to doubt that a virgin had conceived and borne a child.[87]

Nonetheless, although the sexual behavior of Abraham, Isaac, and Jacob is not condoned for Christians of the present—who are to engage in no polygamy,[88] no relations with servant girls[89]—the church fathers judge this trio more generously than they do other Old Testament characters. For example, take the Fathers' treatment of the story of Lot's drunken intercourse with his daughters (Gen. 19:30–38). Writers such as Origen and Augustine partially excuse the daughters: although mistaken in their belief that if they did not reproduce, the human race would come to an end, they nonetheless acted from an understandable motive.[90] Lot, however, is less easily exonerated, standing as a negative example of and warning against the dangers of drunkenness.[91] Augustine, so eager to defend Abra-

---

Edwin Mellen, 1979), pp. 8–9; similarly, Clark, "Sexual Politics in the Writings of John Chrysostom," *Anglican Theological Review* 59 (1977):11–12.

[86] John Chrysostom, *Hom. 49 Gen.* 2 (PG 54, 445–46). For a similar argument, see Ambrose, *De Isaac* 1.1 (CSEL 32.1, 641–42).

[87] John Chrysostom, *Peccata fratrum non evulganda* 6–7 (PG 51, 359–60).

[88] Augustine, *De doctrina Christiana* 3.12.20 (CCL 32, 90); cf. *De bono coniugali* 15.17–16.18 (CSEL 41, 209–11). It is of interest that the *Damascus Document* (4.19–5.2) of the Dead Sea Scrolls, opposing polygamy, also appeals to Gen. 1: God made one male and one female; likewise, Noah and his sons each had one wife.

[89] Augustine, *Contra Faustum* 22.25 (CSEL 25, 620).

[90] Origen, *Hom. 5 Gen.* 4 (GCS 29, 61): as "girls," they did not have perfect knowledge; nonetheless, their incest is "purer" than the chastity of many women of the present; cf. *Contra Celsum* 4.45 (GCS 2, 317–18); Augustine, *Contra Faustum* 22.43 (CSEL 25, 635–36).

[91] Augustine, *Contra Faustum* 22.44–45; 22.60 (CSEL 25, 636–37, 655); Origen, *Hom. 5 Gen.* 3 (GCS 29, 62); Ambrose, *De virginibus* 1.8.53 (PL 16, 214); Clement of Alexandria, *Paedagogus* 2.9.81 (GCS 12, 207). Lot's hospitality to his (angelic) visitors stands as his one good deed: Origen argues that this deed alone saved him during the destruction of Sodom ("We do not read of any other good deeds of Lot") (*Hom. 5 Gen.* 1); Paulinus of Nola argues that in putting the needs of his guests and God before his family, Lot exemplified

ham, Isaac, and Jacob against Faustus' allegations of sexual misbehavior, plainly admits in this case that Lot's evil deed must be judged a crime. Yet Augustine can derive a larger theological moral from stories such as this: since Scripture frequently condemns fornication and adultery, the reader should know when to condemn such deeds, even in passages where the Scriptural author does not explicitly mention God's displeasure.[92] Moreover (in an argument that Augustine will transpose to an ecclesiological register in his later battle against Donatists),[93] the holy character of Scripture is not affected by reporting the wicked deeds of some of its actors.[94]

Indeed, Augustine's reflections on the disreputable acts of Old Testament characters remain among the most trenchant of any of the church fathers. Eager to defend the Catholic retention of the Old Testament as "Scripture," Augustine adroitly finds ways to explain seemingly dubious behavior when such explanations appear important to his argument, but also willingly condemns the behavior of characters whose actions he deems indefensible. Nonetheless, even those ancients who had acted wickedly could be summoned to score a theological point: although as God, Christ willed to be born miraculously of a virgin, as man, he chose to be born of both wicked and good ancestors. This theological moral had a present-day corollary for Augustine: since Christ himself descended from sinful people, "the nations" should not be deterred from coming to God merely because they, too, had sinful forefathers. Although Faustus the Manichean tries to discredit the Incarnation by heaping reproach on Christ's ancestors, Augustine deems that this strategy fails, for Christ openly called both the good and the evil to his marriage (Matt. 22:10).[95]

This concessive principle Augustine applies in his discussion of several prominent Old Testament figures. Concerning Judah's (unknowing) sexual relation with his daughter-in-law Tamar (Gen. 38), Augustine argues that God brought a good work out of this evil deed.[96] Acknowledging that Judah is "not much praised" in Scripture, Augustine nonetheless stresses that Christ was born from his tribe (Matt. 1:2–3; 2:6; Luke 3:33).[97] Here, Augustine's reading contrasts with John Chrysostom's, for whom Judah's sexual act does not constitute "adultery" because (according to Chrysostom) the latter depends upon the will, and since Judah

---

properly Christian ascetic virtue (*ep.* 13.21).

[92] Augustine, *Contra Faustum* 22.42; 22.61; 22.62 (CSEL 25, 635, 657–58).

[93] E.g., Augustine, *De baptismo* 1.16.25; 2.6.8; *De correctione Donatistarum* (= *ep.* 185).9.9.38–40: the Church and its sacraments are not sullied by sinful priests or laypeople.

[94] Augustine, *Contra Faustum* 22.61 (CSEL 25, 656).

[95] Augustine, *Contra Faustum* 22.64 (CSEL 25, 659–60).

[96] Augustine, *Contra Faustum* 22.83 (CSEL 25, 685).

[97] Augustine, *Contra Faustum* 22.60; 22.64 (CSEL 25, 655–56, 659–60).

did not view Tamar as his daughter-in-law but as a prostitute, his deed cannot thus be condemned.[98]

Augustine also faults both David and Solomon for their sexual misdeeds. Here, he engages the text in a more "literal" manner than does Origen, who argues, in contrast, that those who refuse to read allegorically II Samuel 11–12 (the episodes pertaining to David, Bathsheba, and Uriah) accuse David of intemperance, cruelty, and inhumanity.[99] Augustine, however, draws a distinction between the two Israelite kings.[100] According to Augustine, David had many virtuous deeds to his account but nonetheless sinned grievously in committing adultery with Bathsheba and in murdering her husband. Nonetheless, since David deeply repented of these acts and accepted God's chastisement, he is not to be unduly faulted.[101]

Solomon, on the other hand, receives no exoneration from Augustine, especially since this king began his career as "good" and degenerated into "evil," succumbing to the love of foreign women who led him astray to idolatry and apostasy from God. Since Scripture says nothing about his repentance and restoration to divine favor (as it did in the case of David), readers should acknowledge that there is nothing "good" to be symbolized in Solomon's behavior; he serves only as an example of wrongdoing. In Augustine's view, Scripture's condemnation of Solomon is far more serious than the "impudent and trivial charges" that Faustus has leveled.[102] Although the Manicheans are to be faulted for their overly literal and hy-

[98] John Chrysostom, *De SS. Bernice et Prosdoce* 2 (PG 50, 632). Chrysostom in this passage also argues that neither would the Egyptian who took Sarah be considered guilty of adultery, had the deed occurred, since he, too, was unaware of her true status as Abraham's wife.

[99] Origen, *Philocalia* 1.29 (*Comm. Ps. 50 [51]*) (SC 302, 212). Origen also deals with this problematic text in his *Comm. Rom.* 2.10.14 (Hammond Bammel, pp. 189–92), pondering what David might mean when he said "Against thee [God] only have I sinned" (Ps. 51:4; cf. II Sam. 12:13).

[100] Augustine in *De doctrina Christiana* 3.21.31 (CCL 32, 96) also makes this distinction, as well as in the passages from the *Contra Faustum* listed below.

[101] Augustine, *Contra Faustum* 22.66–67; 22.98 (CSEL 25, 661–64, 704). John Chrysostom makes a similar point regarding David: despite David's egregious fall, he repented and was restored to God's good favor—so much so that the memory of him was able to shield his son Solomon from the full brunt of God's wrath (I Kings 11:12–13), despite Solomon's sexual misconduct and idolatry (*Ad Theodorum lapsum* 2.2 [PG 47, 311]). Elsewhere, Chrysostom agrees with the Manichean estimate of these deeds as constituting adultery and murder, but stresses that God still favored David because of his repentance (*Hom. 26 Matt.* 6 [PG 57, 340–41]).

[102] Augustine, *Contra Faustum* 22.81; 22.88 (CSEL 25, 683, 693). In John Chrysostom's judgment, the progression of Solomon's morality is reversed: after a period of indulgence, Solomon acquired "philosophy" and recognized that "all is vanity" (Eccles. 1:2; 2:1–11) (*Adversus eos qui apud se habent subintroductas virgines* 12 [PG 47, 512–13]).

percritical reading of these patriarchal tales, Augustine nonetheless claims that there are no useless passages in Scripture:[103] even the stories that discredit Old Testament characters such as Solomon serve to warn present-day Christians to keep to a more ascetically rigorous path.

IV: Further Praise for Reproduction

Numerous passages in the Old Testament that blessed childbearing and cursed the unmarried and the barren were ripe for interpretations that better suited the ascetic cause. To be sure, such verses were highly useful in polemics against "heretics" who allegedly downplayed the goodness of human procreative capacities. For example, Theophilus of Alexandria develops catenas of such verses for his attack on the Origenists. According to Theophilus, since Origenists think that there would have *been* no bodies if a primeval sin had not occurred, marriage and childbearing for them must necessarily be condemned. Thus Theophilus cites Hannah's prayer for a child (I Sam. 1:10–11), God's blessing on the multiplication of the Israelites (Deut. 1:10–11; Is. 60:22), and the joy of seeing one's children's children (Ps. 128:6) as appropriate verses, among others, with which to chide Origenists.[104]

Other interpreters, however, preferred to read such passages figuratively. In this approach, the text could be "saved," but its "literal" meaning erased as unseemly for Christians of the New Dispensation. Here, allegorical exegesis did prove useful for the ascetic agenda. Origen is, as we would expect, the prime originator of such interpretations for Greek-speaking Christianity; blessings on the multiplication of the Israelites and physical childbearing, and the curses on the barren, are to be read "spiritually." Origen appeals to such verses as Ephesians 1:3, "[God] who has blessed us in Christ with every spiritual blessing in the heavenly places," as counterweights to the earthier interpretations of the Old Testament texts.[105] The psalmist's hope that wives will be "fertile vines" bearing many offspring (Ps. 128:3) must be interpreted spiritually as well, according to Origen: the children brought forth signify the many virtues, as is rein-

[103] Augustine, *Contra Faustum* 22.95–96 (CSEL 25, 701–3).

[104] Theophilus of Alexandria, *ep. fest.* (401) (= Jerome, *ep.* 96).18 (CSEL 55, 177–79); *ep. fest.* (404) (= Jerome, *ep.* 100).12 (CSEL 55, 225–26). For a discussion of Theophilus' attack on Origenism (as he understood it), see Elizabeth A. Clark, *The Origenist Controversy: The Cultural Construction of an Early Christian Debate* (Princeton, N.J.: Princeton University Press, 1992), pp. 105–21.

[105] Origen, *Hom. 39 Luc.* 3 (SC 87, 452).

forced by I Timothy 2:15, that "women shall be saved by childbearing."[106] Gregory of Nyssa subscribes to Origen's line of interpretation: motherhood as a blessing (Ps. 113:9) must be understood spiritually to refer to virgins' "bringing forth."[107]

Why such verses must be interpreted allegorically, Origen makes clear in his comments on Deuteronomy 7:13–14, a blessing on reproduction: this text cannot pertain to physical seed, or it would imply that "all the virgins of the church were under a curse." Commenting on Abraham's marriage to Keturah at the age of approximately 137 (Gen. 25:1), Origen reasons that the passage should be understood in conjunction with Wisdom of Solomon 8:9, which enjoins men to "take wisdom as [their] wife." Since there is no end of wisdom and learning, we can embrace it until the end of our days. *This* must be the meaning of the curse on the unmarried: they have not "married wisdom" in a manner appropriate to God's people.[108] Here, figurative interpretation rescues the text from "carnality."

Spiritual interpretation is also recommended by Augustine in his anti-Manichean polemic. When Adimantus the Manichean claims that Psalm 128:3 (the wife as a fertile vine producing numerous children) stands against Jesus' recommendation in Matthew 19:12 to "become eunuchs for the sake of the Kingdom of Heaven," Augustine counters that the language of the Psalms should be taken as a "figure," in this case, as a "figure" of the Church's future increase.[109] Elsewhere, in a similar interpretation, Augustine claims that these many children of Psalm 128 are available to Christians "spiritually," even those with no physical offspring.[110] As for the injunction concerning levirate marriage in Deuteronomy 25:5–10, Augustine instructs his Manichean opponent Faustus that the passage enjoins preachers of the Gospel to raise up "seed" (i.e., multiply Christian adherents) for their dead brother, Christ.[111]

The explication of such themes can also acquire an anti-Jewish cast. According to the Fathers, to take these passages "literally" is "reading like a Jew." Thus according to Origen, it is "Sadducees," that is, Jews, who interpret Psalm 128:3 (the fertile wife with her "shoots" of children) as pertaining to physical women and offspring.[112] Jerome agrees: Jews who belonged to the Old Law did not appreciate the glories of virginity and

[106] Origen, *Hom. 20 Num.* 2 (GCS 30, 188–89).

[107] Gregory of Nyssa, *De virginitate* 13.3 (SC 119, 430).

[108] Origen, *Hom. 11 Gen.* 1 (GCS 29, 101–2).

[109] Augustine, *Contra Adimantum* 23 (CSEL 25, 182).

[110] Augustine, *Enarr. Ps.* 127 (128).11–12 (CCL 40, 1875–77).

[111] Augustine, *Contra Faustum* 32.10 (CSEL 25, 768–69).

[112] Origen, *Hom. 39 Luc.* 3 (SC 87, 452).

read this verse "literally."[113] For Cyril of Alexandria, various Old Testament verses that celebrate childbearing reveal the "carnal" interpretation of the Jews who, lacking "the spirit," yearn to become physical mothers. Christians should understand such passages spiritually: "mothers" are souls that love God, and the "children" they produce are the virtues.[114]

Others, including Augustine, also read these passages as illustrating the "difference in times," since the values of the "old times" are no longer appropriate for Christians. When Faustus the Manichean objects that "raising up seed for Israel" (Deut. 25:5–10) stands in opposition to the chastity that Christ taught, Augustine counters first with the claim that the Old Testament, like the New, teaches chastity (he cites Isa. 56:4–5, the blessing on eunuchs). Next, however, he concedes that in ancient times begetting children was considered a civic duty; now, in the Christian era, we seek spiritual increase.[115] According to John Chrysostom, verses expressing fear that one's line be eradicated (e.g., I Kings 14:12; Job 18:17) were characteristic of the Old Law, under which children were seen as a replacement for oneself since the time that death had entered the world.[116] For John Cassian, the Septuagint reading of Isaiah 31:9 ("blessed is he whose seed is in Zion"), demonstrates the attachment to reproduction that was characteristic of the Law, so different from the advice of the New Testament, such as contained in Luke 14:26 (hating one's relatives), Luke 23:29 (the day when the barren will be blessed), and I Corinthians 7:29 (wives "as if not").[117]

Most surprising, Augustine, best-known as a defender of Christian marriage over against the ascetic onslaughts of both Manicheans and Catholics such as Jerome, also fails upon occasion to render a positive assessment of the pro-natal sentiments of the Old Testament. Writing on the topic of prayer to Anicia Proba, widow of Sextus Claudius Petronius Probus and grandmother of the much-acclaimed virgin Demetrias, Augustine examines the prayer of Hannah in I Samuel 1, who petitions God to make her fertile. Augustine concludes that Hannah's prayer finds almost no point of resemblance to the Lord's Prayer of Matthew 6 except for the sentiment, "deliver us from evil." In Old Testament times, Augustine instructs Proba, women thought it was an "evil" to bear no children, for this was the sole purpose of marriage. How much better it is for women to imitate the widow Anna of Luke 2, who spent day and night in the Temple pray-

[113] Jerome, *ep.* 22.21 (CSEL 54, 171); *Adversus Iovinianum* 1.22 (PL 23, 252).

[114] Cyril of Alexandria, *In Is.* 1.3 (4:1) (PG 70, 125, 128)

[115] Augustine, *Contra Faustum* 14.1; 14.13 (CSEL 25, 403, 414–15).

[116] John Chrysostom, *Propter fornicationes* 3 (PG 51, 213).

[117] John Cassian, *Conlationes* 21.32 (SC 64, 106–7).

ing! Augustine concedes, however, that Proba is no longer susceptible to the sentiments of Hannah's prayer, having been firmly established in her widowhood for some years.[118] Here, Augustine's exposition stands in contrast to that of John Chrysostom, who claims that although it is God who gives fecundity, Hannah by her prayer brought a great blessing—her son Samuel—to herself.[119]

As many of the above examples suggest, the Fathers readily resort to figurative interpretation when confronted with seemingly intractable verses. In these cases, since little about the texts suggested an easy "rescue" by other exegetical means, allegory proved indispensable for the advancement of the ascetic agenda.

V: Defamilialization

Many verses in the Synoptic Gospels urge relaxation—or abandonment—of family ties in order to follow Jesus, often in the context of eschatological expectation. With the delay (or failure) of the *parousia* and the nonfulfillment of the eschaton, these verses were stripped from their context and read as timeless injunctions for ascetic living: the content was appropriated, if not the probable motivation. Yet even some of the more "pro-family" teachings ascribed to Jesus (e.g., his repetition of the Mosaic command to "honor your father and your mother" [Exod. 20:12; Matt. 15:4]) could be tempered and nuanced to fit the dominant asceticizing message.

According to ascetically inclined church fathers, Jesus proclaimed the message of relinquishing home and family from the beginning of his ministry. Was this not the import of James and John's abandoning their father to follow Jesus (Matt. 4:21–22 = Mark 1:19–20)? In the second century, these verses on the renunciations of James and John were cited to urge converts to forsake their "pagan" parents and professions for the new religious cause;[120] in the fourth, to encourage would-be ascetics to renounce their (now often-Christian) families.[121] Thus Jerome argues that the call to "perfection" (Matt. 19:21) entails a willingness to leave one's country and kin.[122] He commends to the grieving Paula the model of James and John leaving their father: now, after the death of her daughter Blesilla, she can more fully "reject" her family for a commitment to renunciation.[123] Jerome likewise instructs Eustochium that Christ makes possible the for-

[118] Augustine, *ep.* 130.15.29 (CSEL 44, 74–75).

[119] John Chrysostom, *De Anna* 1.4; 2.1 (PG 54, 637–38, 645).

[120] Tertullian, *De idololatria* 12.3 (CCL 2, 1112).

[121] Ambrose, *Exhortatio virginitatis* 5.32 (PL 16, 360).

[122] Jerome, *Adversus Vigilantium* 14 (PL 23, 366).

[123] Jerome, *ep.* 38.5 (CSEL 54, 292).

mation of a new household, one in which James and John forsake their father.[124] And the pseudo-Basilian author of *On Virginity* in yet another gender-bending exegesis,[125] cites Jesus' call of James and John to exhort his (probably) female audience to "leave their boats and their nets"—and their fathers—for the ascetic life.[126]

The message of Jesus' call of James and John was conveyed even more sharply in his rebuke to the man who begged for time to bury his father before he followed Jesus (Matt. 8:21–22 = Luke 9:59–60). Jesus' reply—"Leave the dead to bury their own dead"—was read as a counsel to abandon family by Jerome[127] (who nonetheless protests that he did not hereby intend to sever households),[128] by John Cassian,[129] and by Evagrius Ponticus, who cites the verse to warn monks against the dangers of visiting their relatives.[130] Jesus' prediction that members of one's own family would become one's "foes" (Matt. 10:35–36 = Luke 12:52–53) could likewise be quoted to remind ascetics of the need for familial renunciation.[131] For Augustine (attempting to rebut Faustus' claim that Catholics were not committed ascetics), this pericope, including the exhortation to "take up the cross," proves that the "Strong" among Catholic Christians are urged to adopt renunciatory practices.[132] According to the Pelagian(?) author of the treatise *On Chastity*, the passage encourages Christians to "offend" our parents, if necessary, rather than God.[133] In an intertextual exhortation, Basil of Ancyra links Jesus' words on the household "foes" to Abraham's renunciation of homeland (Gen. 12:1), and ingeniously reinforces these verses with Paul's passionate query in Romans 8:35, "who can separate us from the love of God?" ("No one, certainly not families," is the presumably correct answer.) The awesome cosmic powers that Paul here names devolve for the ascetic onto the "powers and principalities" of the family.[134]

Other Gospel passages concerning the family also proved useful to ascetic exegetes. For the author of *On Chastity*, if even Jesus could ask, "Who

[124] Jerome, *ep.* 22.21 (CSEL 54, 173).

[125] For a description of gender-bending exegesis, see above, pp. 138–40.

[126] Ps.-Basil, *De virginitate* 8.113 (Amand de Mendietta/Moons, p. 63).

[127] Jerome, *ep.* 38.5 (CSEL 54, 292–93).

[128] Jerome, *ep.* 54.2 (CSEL 54, 467): here, Jerome reports that he did *not* cite these words in an antifamilial manner (which in fact he had in *ep.* 38.5), arguing rather that "whoever believes in Christ is alive."

[129] John Cassian, *Conlationes* 21.7 (SC 64, 81): the passage shows that "the duties of human charity are outweighed by the virtue of divine love."

[130] Evagrius Ponticus, *Rerum monachalium rationes* 5 (PG 40, 1257).

[131] Basil of Caesarea, *Serm. de renuntiatione saeculi* 1 (PG 31, 628–29); John Chrysostom, *De virginitate* 78.5 (SC 125, 374); cf. Jerome, *ep.* 14.3 (CSEL 54, 48–49).

[132] Augustine, *Contra Faustum* 5.9; cf. 5.1 (Faustus' eloquent testimony that he has left *his* family) (CSEL 25, 282, 271).

[133] (Anonymous), *De castitate* 17 (PLS 1, 1501–2).

[134] Basil of Ancyra, *De virginitate* 25 (Vaillant, p. 17).

are my mother and my brothers?" (Matt. 12:48 = Mark 3:33; cf. Luke 8:20–21), did not his rhetorical question suggest that the family is "foe"?[135] And Jesus' words on the divisions in households were allegedly cited by ascetics such as the Pachomian monk Theodore when he refused to return home from his monastic retreat despite his mother's woeful entreaties (and her solicitation of ecclesiastical authorities).[136] Since Jesus counsels that any part of the body that causes a person to sin should be "cut off" (Matt. 18:8–9 = Mark 9:43–46), why not "cut off" the relatives who injure our souls?[137]

Especially important was Luke's version of the pericope on the cost of discipleship (Luke 14:25–27), which strengthens Matthew's rendition (Matt. 10:37–38) in two ways: first, Christians should not merely love Jesus "more" than their relatives, they should "hate" the latter for Christ's sake; and second, according to the Lucan version (unlike the Matthean) a "wife" is included among the relatives that a man may "hate." Jerome correlates these Lucan verses with I Corinthians 7:29 ("If you are loosed from a wife, seek not a wife").[138] In addition, John Cassian reports a discussion between the would-be monk Theonas and his wife in which these verses figure prominently. Theonas reminds his wife, who resists their proposed separation, that she was intended to be a "helpmate" (Gen. 2:20–23), not to deprive him of his salvation, and he cites to her Jesus' words on "hating" a wife for the sake of following Christ.[139] Origen contrasts the verses with the provisions of the Mosaic law, which was unaware that both family and riches should be renounced.[140] While Christians of a more ascetic bent deem that the verses on "hating" the family outweigh the command to "Honor your father and mother" (Exod. 20:12),[141] those of a less ascetic stripe, conversely, quote the Mosaic command to "rein in" the sharpness of Luke 14:25–27: Jesus would not overturn a command of the Decalogue, argue Clement of Alexandria and Cyril of Jerusalem.[142]

Moreover, several patristic writers cite Luke's version, in preference to Matthew's or Mark's, of another pericope that names a "wife" among the things a man might be called to leave (Luke 18:29b). For the author of the pseudo-Basilian treatise *On Virginity*, the verse advises that it is the

[135] (Anonymous), *De castitate* 17 (PLS 1, 1502); Jerome, *ep.* 14.3 (CSEL 54, 48–49).

[136] *Vita prima graeca Pachomii* 37 (SubsHag 19, 22–23).

[137] Origen, *Comm. Matt.* 13.25 (GCS 40, 247).

[138] Jerome, *ep.* 145 (CSEL 56, 306–7).

[139] John Cassian, *Conlationes* 21.9 (SC 64, 84–85). Cf. Basil of Caesarea, *Regulae fusius tractatae* 12 (PG 31, 949): these are good verses to cite if a wife resists a husband's desire to enter a monastery.

[140] Origen, *Hom. 17 Jesu Nave* 2 (SC 71, 376).

[141] Horsiesius, *ep.* 1.5 (CSCO 159 = Scriptores Coptici 23, 64).

[142] Clement of Alexandria, *Stromata* 3.15.97 (GCS 52 [15], 24); Cyril of Alexandria, *Comm. Luc.* 14:26 (PG 72, 793).

married—not just virgins—who are called to rigorous renunciation, here, of a spouse.[143] Thus Jerome cites Luke 18:27–30 to argue that Jesus instructed Peter and other married disciples to dissociate from their wives. (In Jerome's view, although Peter while a disciple still had a mother-in-law [Mark 1:30], he no longer had a wife.)[144] And although Jerome notes the different magnitudes of "reward" the Gospels promise to followers of Jesus for leaving their families (Matt. 19:29 = Mark 10:29–30; cf. Luke 18:29–30), he does not remark that Matthew omits naming a "wife" among the relatives who should be "left"[145]: for Jerome, Luke's more rigorous rendition of the pericope appears preferable.

Another Synoptic passage seen to buttress the ascetic cause was the story of the woman married successively to seven brothers, whose situation posed the dilemma, "whose wife will she be in the resurrection?" (Matt. 22:23–33 = Mark 12:18–27 = Luke 20:27–40).[146] According to Mark's version, Jesus replies, "For when they rise from the dead, they neither marry nor are given in marriage, but are like the angels in heaven." In the second century, Jesus' response could be cited simply to argue the surety of resurrection from the dead against "heretics" who denied it, or to instruct Catholics about its form[147] (or in the late fourth century, to correct Origenist opinion concerning the resurrection body).[148] Ascetic interpreters, however, took a different line: if singleness is the condition of the angels, it is also recommended for us.[149] Not only are virgins counted "worthy" of that angelic state in the afterlife; even here and now, by adopting the "angelic" life they escape labor pains and the domination of a husband.[150] Gregory of Nyssa claims that if in our final condition humans are not to be married, we should here and now renounce marriage and continue as virgins.[151] Novatian adds a further touch: we will be not just "equal" but superior to the angels, for angels, unlike humans, have no flesh against which they must struggle.[152]

[143] Ps.-Basil, *De virginitate* 9.117 (Amand de Mendietta/Moons, pp. 63–64); the author hastily continues (9.118) that he is not encouraging the breaking up of marriages, but the "choking out of incontinence."

[144] Jerome, *Adversus Iovinianum* 1.26 (PL 23, 256): do not believe the Pseudo-Clementines(?) that give Peter a wife during the time he was an apostle (PL 23, 257).

[145] Jerome, *Adversus Iovinianum* 2.19 (PL 23, 327).

[146] Usually taken by modern Biblical scholars as a "trick" question; the Sadducees did not believe in resurrection.

[147] Thus Tertullian, *De resurrectione mortuorum* 36.3 (CCL 2, 968–69).

[148] Jerome, *Adversus Ioannem Hierosolymitanum* 23; 28; 31 (PL 23, 391, 397, 400): Luke 20:35–36 proves that sex is to be preserved; people *could* marry in the resurrection, but they won't.

[149] Athanasius, *De virginitate* 16 (Lebon, p. 217; ET, Brakke, p. 308).

[150] Cyprian, *De habitu virginum* 22 (CSEL 3.1, 202–3).

[151] Gregory of Nyssa, *De opificio hominis* 17.2 (PG 44, 188).

[152] Novatian, *De bono pudicitiae* 7

The Lucan version of this pericope ("the sons of this age marry and are given in marriage; but those who are accounted worthy to attain to that age and to the resurrection from the dead neither marry nor are given in marriage, for they cannot die anymore, because they are equal to angels and are sons of God, being sons of the resurrection") provides an even stronger impetus to renunciation here and now.[153] Thus more ardent ascetics such as Marcion cite Luke's version to argue that "this world," ruled by the Creator, should be renounced in favor of "that world," governed by the good God; the elect who belong to "that world" should not marry even in this life.[154] That the wording of Luke 20:34 was exploited by heterodox Christians is also implied by Clement of Alexandria's protest that some of his ("Gnostic") opponents are contrasting the "children of this age" with those of some other age in their discussion of the elect and the doomed.[155]

In addition to citing the above-mentioned Gospel passages that seemed manifestly to promote the ascetic cause, patristic exegetes could also "asceticize" various other Gospel passages by proffering motivations for various deeds or sayings, or supplying contexts that were not given (and probably unimagined) by the authors or redactors of the Scriptural texts. This technique, we may note, need not resort to allegory but provides a "supplement" that in effect reconstrues the text in accordance with the needs of later, ascetically inclined Christians.[156]

Thus, for example, while Matthew 5:28 (that any man who has looked lustfully at a woman "has already committed adultery with her in his heart") was readily appropriable for the ascetic program, further nuance could ensure that the verse was rendered applicable to celibates as well as to the married: thus patristic authors assume that *any* sexual desire, not just "adulterous" desires, is here signaled.[157]

(CSEL 3.3, 202–3); the theme is also stressed by John Chrysostom, *De virginitate* 10.3 (SC 125, 124).

[153] The Old Latin reading of the Lucan version, which refers to "begetting and are begotten" rather than "marry and giving in marriage," provided Augustine with Scriptural support for his theory of original sin: even regenerated parents beget children "of this world" (Luke 20:34), not regenerated children. See Augustine, *De peccatorum meritis* 2.9.11 (CSEL 60, 82–83); *Contra Iulianum* 6.13.40 (PL 44, 843–44); *De nuptiis et concupiscentia* 1.18.20 (CSEL 42, 232).

[154] Tertullian, *Adversus Marcionem* 4.38.5–7 (CCL 1, 648–49).

[155] Clement of Alexandria, *Stromata* 3.12.87 (GCS 52 [15], 236).

[156] Irvine, *The Making of Textual Culture*, pp. 39, 244, 246–47. On changing the contexts and audiences of a Biblical passage as a device of ascetic exegesis, see above, pp. 134–38.

[157] I have found nearly three dozen citations of this verse in the writers here consulted. The verse could be taken as an anti-adultery warning to the married (Lactantius, *De divinae institutionis* 6.23); as an attempt to steer men from lascivious thoughts (John Chrysostom, *Hom. 7 Matt.* 7); as a warning to virgins not to "lust" or

Other passages also could be "improved" with minor supplementation. Who are the "two masters" (Matt. 6:24 = Luke 16:13) that a follower of Jesus cannot serve? Not always "mammon" in contrast to "God," as in the Biblical text, but "the flesh,"[158] secular life[159]—or even the *subintroducta* with whom a monk may live (she constitutes a particularly hard "master," in John Chrysostom's opinion).[160] Why are some virgins of the parable (Matt. 25:1–13) called "wise" and others "foolish"? Although the "foolish" are often faulted by patristic exegetes for their failure to perform good deeds, especially almsgiving,[161] the parable could be given a more "sexual" turn: the "wise" ones were dedicated virgins who conducted themselves appropriately to their ascetic commitment,[162] while the "foolish" ones did not truly "marry Christ,"[163] failed to retain purity of spirit along with their purity of body,[164] engaged in syneisaktic relationships with male ascetics,[165] and "fell";[166] in Cassian's gender-bending interpretation, the "foolish virgins" were those monks who did not struggle to triumph over nocturnal emissions.[167] Likewise, since the Lord's Prayer does not specify the sins for which we need to ask divine forgiveness (Matt. 6:12 = Luke 11:4), Augustine could provide his own sexualizing interpretation: married Christians must beg forgiveness for the lust that prompts them to sexual intercourse unmotivated by the desire to produce children.[168] Such passages could be "asceticized" with only limited exegetical supplement.

---

they will lose their virginity (Jerome, *ep.* 22.5); and as a recommendation against marriage in the first place (Tertullian, *Exhortatio castitatis* 9: those who marry presumably "lust" after their chosen partners). For a discussion of this passage as a counsel of virginity in Coptic Christian writings, see Tito Orlandi, "Giustificazioni dell' encratismo nel testi monastici copti del IV–V secolo," in *La tradizioni dell' enkrateia: motivazioni ontologiche e protologiche. Atti del Colloquio Internazionale, Milano, 20–23 aprile 1982*, ed. Ugo Bianchi (Roma: Edizione dell' Ateneo, 1985), p. 355.

158 Jerome, *ep.* 49(48).20 (CSEL 54, 385), citing Gal. 5:17 (the "flesh lusts against the spirit"); Evagrius Ponticus, *ep.* 53.1 (Frankenberg, pp. 600–601).

159 Athanasius, *ep. 2 ad virgines* (Lebon, p. 184; ET, Brakke, p. 299); Pseudo-Titus *Ep.* (de Bruyne, p. 49).

160 John Chrysostom, *Adversus eos qui apud se habent subintroductas virgines* 6 (PG 47, 503).

161 A special theme of John Chrysostom; see his *Hom. 6 II Tim.* (2:26); *Hom. Philip.*, prologus; *Hom. 77 Matt.* 5–6; *Hom. 47 Matt.* 5; *Hom. 50 Matt.* 5.

162 Ambrose, *De institutione virginis* 17.110; *Exhortatio virginitatis* 10.62; Jerome, *ep.* 7.6; Pelagius, *Ad Demetriadem* 10; Ps.-Basil, *De virginitate* 7.78–80; Athanasius, *ep. 1 ad virgines* (21, 31).

163 Origen, *Comm. I Cor.* 7:28b (Jenkins [1908], p. 510).

164 Origen, *Hom. 1 Lev.* 5.2 (GCS 29, 288).

165 Pseudo-Titus *Ep.* (de Bruyne, p. 57).

166 Jerome, *ep.* 22.5 (CSEL 54, 150).

167 John Cassian, *Conlationes* 22.6 (SC 64, 121, 125). It is of interest that Augustine in *Serm.* 93.1–2 provides an "anti-ascetic" interpretation of this parable: since there are manifestly more than ten Catholic virgins, the parable must refer to *all* Christians.

168 For example, Augustine, *Contra Iulianum* 4.2.6; 5.9.39; *Opus Imperfectum* 1.67;

The Gospel of John also contains passages that ascetically inclined exegetes could "fill in" to enhance the call to renunciation. John 14:2 ("my father's house has many mansions") could be taken to signal not just a heavenly reward for ascetics, but a hierarchy among the "many mansions": virgins would receive the best apartments.[169] In addition, the Gospel of John's elusiveness regarding "the disciple whom Jesus loved" (John 13:23; 19:26; 20:2; 21:7) allowed early Christian exegetes not merely to identify the disciple with John himself, but to supply the reason—unexplained in the text—why he was so "loved." Why was he the disciple deemed worthy to be entrusted with the care of Mary after Jesus' crucifixion (John 19:26–27)? Why did he reach Jesus' tomb before Peter and "believe" (John 20:3–4, 8)? Why was he the first to recognize the risen Jesus on the shores of the Sea of Tiberius (John 21:1–7)? For ascetically inclined church fathers such as Jerome and John Cassian, commentary could supplement what the text had regrettably omitted: the disciple was "loved" for his commitment to virginity.[170] It was the disciple John's virginity that made him a suitable protector of Mary after Jesus' death[171]—and it likewise supplied the reason why he outstripped Peter in running to Jesus' tomb, and why he recognized Jesus first.[172]

The above examples suggest that when ascetically minded Fathers found Biblical verses that seemed to bolster the ascetic agenda, they arrogated them with relatively little exegetical manipulation. Other passages, also useful, needed more supplementary explanation to "produce" an ascetic directive. In these cases, however, figurative interpretation was held to a minimum: these Biblical texts were seen as themselves speaking an ascetic message. In contrast, the more recalcitrantly "pro-reproductive" passages of the Old Testament required a figurative reading so as to deliver a renunciatory moral—or, if they could not be so construed, relegated to the time

---

1.90; 1.98; 1.101; 1.104–6; 2.71; 2.212; 2.227; 3.116; 4.82; 6.15; 6.30; *Serm.* 261.10.10; 278.9.9.

169 Jerome, *Adversus Iovinianum* 2.28; *epp.* 3.5; 77.12; (Anonymous), *ep. de virginitate* (= *Ad Claudiam*) 2; *De divina lege* 7.2; Athanasius, *ep. 1 ad virgines* (20); Augustine, *De sancta virginitate* 26.26.

170 Jerome, *Adversus Iovinianum* 1.26 (PL 23, 258); John Cassian, *Conlationes* 16.14 (SC 54, 234). According to the *Apocryphal Acts of John* (11.3), John was a virgin. In *Comm. Is.* 15 (56:4–5) (CCL 73A, 634), Jerome calls John a *eunuchus* and claims that it was because of John's virginity that Jesus loved him best. For an interesting discussion of the topic of John's virginity in early Christian writings, see Eric Junod, "La Virginité de l'apôtre Jean: Recherche sur les origines scriptuaires et patristique de cette tradition," in *Lectures anciennes de la Bible*, Cahiers de Biblia Patristica 1 (Strasbourg: Centre d'Analyse et de Documentation Patristiques, 1987), pp. 113–36.

171 Jerome, *Adversus Iovinianum* 1.26 (PL 23, 259); Ambrose, *Exp. Luc.* 2.4 (CCL 14, 32).

172 Jerome, *Adversus Iovinianum* 1.26 (PL 23, 258, 259); and Jerome adds, why John was entrusted to be a Gospel-writer and Peter was not. According to Jerome,

of the Old Law, no longer fitting for Christians. Procreating Israelites could be exegetically displaced by renunciatory Christians. In the words of the author of a pseudo-Clementine *Epistle on Virginity*, Christian virgins—not, it is implied, Israel—are "a people whom the Lord has blessed (Isa. 61:9).[173] "Distinction" now lies with the renunciants, not with those who reproduce.

---

the blood of Peter's martyrdom washed away the stain he incurred by marrying.

[173] Ps.-Clement, *ep. 1 de virginitate* 9.4 (Funk, p. 16).

CHAPTER EIGHT

From Ritual to *Askēsis*

I: Ritual and Difference

In some quarters, the study of ritual has shifted emphasis in recent decades. Scholars have gradually abandoned the functionalist view that ritual serves to create social unity,[1] stressing instead its marking of social difference. In part, this shift signals a dissatisfaction with functionalism's inherently conservative emphasis on "societal balance," on the preservation of the *status quo*.[2] Informed by a more sharply critical analysis, theoreticians now note the gaps, the distinctions, the discrepancies of a society that ritual, far from healing, instead underscores and maintains. Differentiation is here seen as an activity that can be examined through a focus on ritual.[3]

Prominent among the terms now found in the discussion of ritual is, not surprisingly, "hierarchy." As early as Durkheim, hierarchy was understood as the primary feature characterizing systems of religious classification. According to Durkheim, such classificatory hierarchies were derived from existing social hierarchies that were projected onto "our conceptions

[1] Jonathan Z. Smith describes the "Protestantizing" thrust of much early study of ritual: "The study of ritual was born as an exercise in the 'hermeneutic of suspicion,' an explanatory endeavor designed to explain away." That is, many early studies of ritual held the "Protestant" view of the "emptiness of ritual," of ritual as a nonrational activity that (in practice) should be done away with, or (in theory) explained in some other terms. See Jonathan Z. Smith, *To Take Place: Toward Theory in Ritual* (Chicago/London: University of Chicago Press, 1987), p. 102. Cf. Mary Douglas, *Purity and Danger: An Analysis of Concepts of Pollution and Taboo* (New York/Washington, D.C.: Praeger, 1966), pp. 61–62.

[2] See, for one illuminating example, the critiques of Jeremy Boissevain, *Friends of Friends: Networks, Manipulators and Coalitions* (New York: St. Martin's; London: Macmillan, 1974), pp. 4–19. Michael Taussig, *Shamanism, Colonialism, and the Wild Man: A Study in Terror and Healing* (Chicago/London: University of Chicago Press, 1987), pp. 440–46, provides a fascinating example of the *disorder* that ritual highlights.

[3] Catherine Bell, *Ritual Theory, Ritual Practice* (New York/Oxford: Oxford University Press, 1992), p. 119. It is interesting to note that as early as Plato (*Sophist* 226d), *katharmos* can be defined as an aspect of "the science of division"; see discussion in Robert Parker, *Miasma: Pollution and Purification in Early Greek Religion* (Oxford: Clarendon, 1983).

of the world."[4] For a latter-day Durkheimian such as Pierre Bourdieu, however, Durkheim's one-directional axis from "the social order" to "conceptualization" demands nuance. More fully acknowledging the power of language in the creation of the social order, Bourdieu posits that although social groups produce concepts, these concepts *also* produce groups—"the very groups which produce the principles and against which they are produced."[5] Conceptualization and group formation are here dialectically understood. Furthermore, Bourdieu argues, society in effect "works" through the production of discontinuity and hierarchy, at the level both of the group and of conceptualization.[6]

In ritual studies, scholars such as Louis Dumont (a specialist in Hinduism) and Catherine Bell (an expert in ancient Chinese religion) have stressed the links between ritual and hierarchy. Although Dumont expresses somewhat different views of hierarchy in the two editions of his book *Homo Hierarchicus*,[7] at the forefront of his work is an exploration of how Indian religion constructs social hierarchy around the contrast between pure and impure.[8] Catherine Bell, for her part, argues that ritual is not only a marker of difference, but the *creator* of difference; here, ritualized agents are produced through schemes of opposition and hierarchization.[9] The "history of the concept of ritual," she posits, "suggests that the term has been primarily used to define and mediate plurality and relationships between 'us and them.' "[10]

The notion that ritual abstinence is central to a religion's ability to "separate" and "distinguish" its practitioners has a scholarly history that extends back at least to Durkheim. In a few brief pages of *Elementary Forms of the Religious Life*, Durkheim underscores a theme important for consideration here: that although the ritual abstinences and interdictions of a

[4] Emile Durkheim, *The Elementary Forms of the Religious Life: A Study in Religious Sociology*, trans. J. W. Swain (London: George Allen & Unwin; New York: Macmillan, n.d.), p. 147.

[5] Pierre Bourdieu, *Distinction: A Social Critique of the Judgement of Taste*, trans. Richard Nice (Cambridge: Harvard University Press, 1984; French original, 1979), p. 479.

[6] Pierre Bourdieu, *Language and Symbolic Power*, ed. J. B. Thompson; trans. G. Raymond and M. Adamson (Cambridge: Harvard University Press, 1991), p. 120. Chap. 4 of Bourdieu's book ("Rites of Institution") offers a critique and reconstruction of the topic from the perspective of ritual's *social* function.

[7] Louis Dumont, *Homo Hierarchicus: The Caste System and Its Implications* (1st ed.: Chicago: University of Chicago Press, 1970 [French original, 1966]; 2nd ed.: Chicago, University of Chicago Press, 1980), pp. 2–4, 239–58, 212–13 (1st ed.); and pp. 239–45 (2nd ed.). See discussion in Smith, *To Take Place*, pp. 54–56.

[8] Dumont, *Homo Hierarchicus*, 2nd ed., pp. 46–60, 74, 212–13; note p. 59: "The opposition of pure and impure appears to us the very principle of hierarchy"; and Smith, *To Take Place*, pp. 54–56.

[9] Bell, *Ritual Theory*, pp. 104, 106–7.

[10] Catherine Bell, *Ritual: Perspectives and Dimensions* (New York/Oxford: Oxford University Press, 1997), p. 262.

religion (the "negative cult," in Durkheim's term)[11] usually prepare the way for more "positive" observances, rituals of denial can also be freed from subordination to the "positive cult" and claimed as the very center of religious observance. Such was the case with ascetic practices in some religions, Durkheim notes. He writes as follows on the function of ascetics in a religious system:

> there is something excessive in the disdain they profess for all that ordinarily impassions men. But these exaggerations are necessary to sustain among the believers a sufficient disgust for an easy life and common pleasures. It is necessary that an elite put the end too high, if the crowd is not to put it too low. It is necessary that some exaggerate, if the average is to remain at a fitting level.[12]

In Bourdieu's reflection on this Durkheimian theme, these "negative" rites, including the physical suffering they entail, are the very means through which are produced devotees "who are out of the ordinary, in a word, distinguished."[13] Specialized producers of religious rites and discourse are necessary to a religion, Bourdieu argues, and a division of religious labor entails a division into classes through which members of the laity are effectively "***dispossessed*** of the instruments of symbolic production."[14]

These themes inspire Jonathan Z. Smith's *To Take Place: Toward Theory in Ritual.* Eschewing the older phenomenological thesis that ritual is "an expression of or a response to 'the Sacred,' " Smith rather emphasizes that it is ritual that conveys sacrality on a thing or a person; thus ritual is, "above all, an assertion of difference."[15] Smith here explores (among other subjects) how the ritual activities performed in the Jerusalem Temple "consisted of a series of hierarchical and hieratic transactions concerning pure/impure. This is, above all, a matter of difference." Yet the activities themselves, Smith argues, give no clues for decoding the "meaning of the causes of impurity": "they signify sheer difference." If ritual highlights not the "meaning" or "content" of an activity, but "sheer difference," then, Smith suggests, the place (here, the Jerusalem Temple) can be "replicated in a system of differences transferred to another realm or locale (for example, Mishnah)."[16] Smith's emphasis on the transferability of the hierarchical schema—independent of previous meaning or content—is highly suggestive for a consideration of the ways in which details of Hebrew ceremonial law could be stripped of their earlier content and symbolically ap-

[11] Durkheim, *Elementary Forms*, p. 299.

[12] Ibid., pp. 309–16, citation at 316.

[13] Bourdieu, *Language and Symbolic Power*, p. 123.

[14] Ibid., pp. 168–69.

[15] Smith, *To Take Place*, pp. 105, 109.

[16] Ibid., pp. 85–86. For the Bible itself's "transformation of sacrifice into language," see Julia Kristeva, "Reading the Bible," in idem, *New Maladies of the Soul*, trans. Ross Guberman (New York: Columbia University Press, 1995), p. 120.

propriated by Christian ascetics to mark hierarchy and difference among Christians of later antiquity.[17] The purity of Israelite ceremonial spaces could be transferred to purity of Christian bodies.

Smith's exploration of how the ritual activities of the Jerusalem Temple were replicated in the literary register of the Mishnah suggests one way in which ancient Jewish ritual action, as prescribed in the Bible, could become a "new text." To Smith's observation we may usefully add the reflections of historian J. G. A. Pocock on how texts change meaning when placed in a different historical context. Taking his cue from speech-act theory, Pocock posits that texts should be seen as "events," as "sophisticated verbal performances."[18] The differing contexts in which texts are appropriated, he argues, allow the latter to perform "polyvalently."[19] When the language matrix of the text changes, or when successive generations of readers transpose texts to new contexts, texts find a "new history."[20] Pocock continues with an observation pertinent to the present study:

> The most interesting acts of translation are anachronistic. They are performed by readers who live in times during which the matrices, idioms, and language games have been modified, so that texts that are still current and still acting as the matrices for action are no longer limited to the performance of the illocutions they performed at first publication, and perhaps are no longer capable of performing those illocutions. Because the printed word is rather durable, many texts outlive the modification of their original contexts, as well as outliving their authors. Some of them acquire the sort of authority that leads individuals living in a series of modified contexts to recur to them, and these become the subjects of what are called traditions of interpretation, which are histories of anachronistic—or, if you prefer, diachronic—translation.[21]

Such was the case with the Jews' use of the ritual passages in their Scriptures: once the Jerusalem Temple had been destroyed, such texts could have no practical application for ritual observance. Nonetheless, although

[17] This theme resonates with Frits Staal's argument that ritual acts and sounds do not contain inherent meaning, although meanings may be supplied them. See Frits Staal, "The Meaninglessness of Ritual," *Numen* 26 (1975): 2–22, and the discussion in Bell, *Ritual*, pp. 70–71.

[18] J. G. A. Pocock, "Texts as Events: Reflections on the History of Political Thought," in *The Politics of Discourse: The Literature and History of Seventeenth-Century England*, ed. Kevin Sharpe and Steven N. Zwicker (Berkeley/Los Angeles/London: University of California Press, 1987), pp. 21–22.

[19] Ibid., p. 28.

[20] Ibid., p. 29.

[21] Ibid., p. 31. Pocock's reference to texts as "printed" indicates that his historical specialization pertains to a far later period than that of the Roman Empire. The chronological distance does not, however, affect the usefulness of his point for the present discussion.

the physical performance of the prescribed rituals had become impossible, the texts themselves could be assumed into a new literary context where, successively interpreted, they conveyed different religious meaning for new generations.

Christian ascetic interpreters, I posit, approached these Biblical texts in a functionally similar (albeit materially different) way. Since Christians from early times not only had retained the Hebrew Scriptures as part of their sacred literature, but also had claimed them as their own exclusive possession, they, too, were faced with making meaning of passages that had for them no direct ritual applicability. By imparting new meaning to these texts, Christian ascetic interpreters, like the rabbis, could speak inspiringly to later generations of devotees.

Although scholars of religion note instances in which texts themselves are turned into ritual objects,[22] a different situation obtained in early ascetically inspired Christianity. Here, Biblical texts prescribing rituals designed to separate ancient Hebrews from "pollution" and to mark off a class of holy priests were transformed into prescriptions for Christian sexual renunciation. Although both early Hebrews and late ancient Christians viewed the ritual texts as directives for righteous living, the "distinction" and hierarchy that the correct performance of ritual created for Hebrews of the Biblical era is transposed by Christians to a realm in which renunciants are accorded higher status than married laypeople. How the "negative cult" of early Christian asceticism produced "distinction" and "hierarchy" through its appropriation of and appeal to ritual texts is the subject of this chapter.

II: Techniques for Asceticizing

Ritual Law

Early Christian exegetes, although affirming the superiority of an ascetic Christian ethic to the lowly material and physical concerns of ancient Israelites, found that their ritual law—at first consideration, unfertile ground—could nonetheless be retrieved for the ascetic cause through creative interpretive strategies. If (as an older generation of Biblical scholars argued) the Hebrew prophets themselves had allegedly effected an "ethicization" of ritual practice, why could it not

[22] See Catherine Bell's discussion of Lu Hsiu-ching in her essay, "Ritualization of Texts and Textualization of Ritual in the Codification of Taoist Liturgy," *History of Religions* 27 (1988): 366–67, and her discussion of the work of Kristofer M. Schipper on Taoist texts (with reference to a "holocaust of texts"), p. 379.

also be "asceticized"?[23] This was a task broached by late ancient Christian exegetes who preserved the legal texts as "Scripture" in the midst of a deconstruction necessitated by Christianity's abandonment of Hebrew ritual law in practice. Somewhat paradoxically, the "narrow gate" (Matt. 7:13–14; cf. Luke 13:23–24) of renunciation was enabled by a "broader"—indeed, a profligate—exegesis, whose status as "supplement" could provide abundant grist for a Derridean mill.[24]

So effortless do these ascetic interpretations appear that scholars of our own era must read closely to isolate the techniques that enable subtle (and not so subtle) reconstructions of meaning. As noted above, a Christian exegete of ascetic persuasion could easily change the audience to whom ritual directives were given: commandments originally enjoined on Israelite priests alone could now be readdressed to Christian laypeople. Time frames could be vastly expanded, so that the temporary periods of renunciation commended for the ancient Hebrews were enlarged to encompass an entire lifetime, while the circumstances dictating those brief abstinences could be allegorized (e.g., ancient Israelite preparation for war could be reconstrued as the daily, but lifelong, ascetic "battles" of Christians). Certain ritual practices, such as circumcision, already assigned figurative significations by writers of the first three Christian centuries, were deftly reconfigured by ascetic enthusiasts of the fourth and fifth centuries to pertain to sexual renunciation. Last, if other interpretive techniques

[23] For, e.g., Julius Wellhausen, the process occurred in stages: from earlier, spontaneous ritual acts, the Hebrews moved to a prophetic and monotheistic religion with an emphasis on God's ethical relationship to humanity, the climax of Hebrew religion; yet the postexilic period witnessed the development of a hardened legalism and a nonspontaneous ritual worship. Nonetheless, ritual practice and morality intersected in various "ascetic exercises" that were gradually extended from the priestly class to the laity. See Julius Wellhausen, *Prolegomena to the History of Israel*, trans. J. Sutherland Black and Allan Menzies (Edinburgh: Adam & Charles Black, 1885 [German original, 1878]), esp. pp. 423–25. For Hegel, ancient Judaism's evaluation that the ceremonial law was as important as the moral law is a sign of the "servile consciousness" of the religion: see Hegel's *Philosophy of Religion*, trans. E. B. Speirs and J. Burdon Sanderson from the 2nd German edition (London: Routledge & Kegan Paul, 1962 [1895]; [German original, 1832]), II:211, 212.

[24] Jacques Derrida, *Of Grammatology*, trans. Gayatri Chakravorty Spivak (Baltimore/London: Johns Hopkins University Press, 1976), pp. 200, 226, 280–81, 295; and helpful discussion in Jonathan Culler, *On Deconstruction: Theory and Criticism after Structuralism* (Ithaca, N.Y.: Cornell University Press, 1982), esp. pp. 102–6, 164. Derrida's notion of "grafting" as a model for proliferation in texts is useful here: a central discussion can be found in *Dissemination* (Chicago: University of Chicago Press, 1982), p. 202; the term is lucidly explained in Culler, *On Deconstruction*, pp. 134–56. On the "insufficiency" of texts, the "lack" that calls forth exegesis, see Michael Fishbane, *Biblical Interpretation in Ancient Israel* (Oxford: Clarendon, 1985), pp. 271, 282.

failed, ascetic writers could either reassign the level of authority a particular text carried, or change, in effect, its status: thus what originally stood as "commandment" could with little effort be translated into "testimony."[25] In these ways, not only was the New Testament interpreted in an ascetic direction that highlighted its calls for stringent renunciation; through intertextual exegetical techniques, the ascetic import of Hebrew Scripture could be heightened as well.[26]

The appropriation of ancient Hebrew ritual language by Christian ascetics, however, carried a risk, for Christians had manifestly abandoned the observance of ritual law, even while claiming the Old Testament as "their" book—a claim that prompted the mockery of Faustus the Manichean, who could to good effect argue that Christians' renunciation of ritual law proved that the Old Testament might better be abandoned *in toto*.[27] Christians' unwillingness to ascribe any religious significance to the literal observance of Hebrew ritual taboos was, to be sure, noted long before the era of Mary Douglas and Jonathan Z. Smith: from the early centuries, interpretations were devised that would make meaning of the seemingly meaningless.

Typological interpretation early served this function, and persisted into the later patristic era. Still at the time of John Chrysostom, the Jerusalem Temple, sacrifices, and circumcision could be labeled "types" and "shadows" that were fulfilled in the new Christian order. (*We* have a spiritual, not a material, Temple; baptism, not circumcision; a spiritual Lamb, not a dumb beast, Chrysostom proclaims.)[28] Or, alternatively, allegory could rescue the day. Although some thought that Origen teetered dangerously close to denigrating the Old Testament in his seeming mockery of the levitical laws, "spiritual" meanings could be found in them via allegorical exegesis.[29]

[25] For a comparison to ancient Hebrew techniques, see Fishbane, *Biblical Interpretation*, p. 415: in aggadic exegesis, traditions are decontextualized and then reworked, relocated in a new literary setting. Whereas (according to Fishbane) the most important strategy of aggadic reformulation envisaged "the future in the light of the past," thereby emphasizing continuity between past and present (p. 412), Christian ascetic exegetes tended to emphasize the *discontinuity* between past and present, while nonetheless proclaiming the Old Testament as "theirs."

[26] For a discussion of rabbinic intertextual strategies, see Daniel Boyarin, *Intertextuality and the Reading of Midrash* (Bloomington/Indianapolis: Indiana University Press, 1990); for a discussion of Latin literary intertextuality, see Martin Irvine, *The Making of Textual Culture: 'Grammatica' and Literary Theory, 350–1100* (Cambridge: Cambridge University Press, 1994), esp. pp. 81–83.

[27] Faustus in Augustine, *Contra Faustum* 4.1; 6.1; 10.1 (CSEL 25, 268, 284–85, 310).

[28] John Chrysostom, *Hom. 3 Tit.* 4 (2:1ff.) (PG 62, 681); *Hom. 11 II Cor.* 2 (5:18) (PG 61, 476).

[29] E.g., Origen comments on the laws of Lev. 5 regarding corpse pollution: Why is

Moreover, some early Christian authors devised a "Wellhausian" type of interpretation that pointed to the spiritual "progress" present within the Old Testament itself and elevated the prophets' message above an allegedly earlier ritual observance, a developmental trajectory that could easily be extended to the ascetic agenda of Christianity. Thus according to Chrysostom, when the prophets instructed their hearers to "make themselves clean," they did not mean "bathe."[30] Likewise, according to a female orator in Methodius' *Symposium*, the Old Testament itself revealed a moral development that gradually ruled out incestuous marriages, polygamy, and adultery, preparing the way not just for marital continence (as verses in Ben Sirach and the Wisdom of Solomon suggest), but for virginity, heralded for the first time by Jesus.[31] The Old Testament itself, some posited, progressed toward the more explicitly "moral" and "spiritual" message of the Christian Dispensation. The *literal* fulfillment of Old Testament ritual was, in any event, now impossible: the Jerusalem Temple's destruction by divine ordination shows, for John Chrysostom, that Christ brought an end to the actual practice of the ritual law.[32]

The skill of patristic interpreters in deriving an ascetic message from seemingly insignificant details of Hebrew law is nothing short of ingenious. Thus the acacia wood that Hebrew men contributed for the building of the Temple (Exod. 35:24) contains an asceticizing message: since it is "wood not subject to rot," it portends for Origen virginity.[33] The bands of linen with which the priest is girded (Lev. 6:10; 16:4) signify that excessive lust can be restrained by a girdle of purity—-"pure," because linen is not a "mixed" fabric.[34] The vows of the Nazirites, by which they "separated themselves unto the Lord" (Num. 6:2), are now taken to mean the offering of virginity.[35] As for deciphering the laws of *kashrut*, Clement of Alexandria offers the inventive explanation that believers are instructed not to eat the meat of the hare or the hyena because of their deviant excre-

touching a corpse impure? What if it's the body of a prophet? of a patriarch? of Abraham himself?! (*Hom. 3 Lev.* 3.1 [GCS 29, 303]).

[30] John Chrysostom, *Hom. 6 II Tim.* 4 (2:26) (PG 62, 634).

[31] Methodius, *Symposium* 1.2–4 (GCS 27, 9–13). According to Methodius, Lev. 18:19, 20:17, and Gen. 17:24 (Abraham's circumcision) ruled out marriage with a sister. Polygamy was attacked by the prophets (Jer. 5:8; Prov. 5:8). Ben Sirach 23:1–6 and Wisdom of Solomon 4:1–2 claim that the "lust of the flesh" should be eradicated and that "virtue is a better memorial than children."

[32] John Chrysostom, *Hom. 7 II Cor.* 3 (PG 61, 446).

[33] Origen, *Hom. 13 Ex.* 6 (GCS 29, 278).

[34] Origen, *Hom. 4 Lev.* 6 (GCS 29, 324). Cf. Origen, *Hom. 9 Lev.* 2: if we imitate Christ's refusal to engage in marriage and procreation, we too will be clothed in bands of sacred linen.

[35] Methodius, *Symposium* 5.1–8 (GCS 27, 53–63).

mental and sexual practices that signify pederasty and adultery, practices condemned by Moses as well as by Christians.[36] Any detail of ceremonial law, it appears, could portend ascetic renunciation.

III: Asceticizing the Language of Temple and Sacrifice

The language of Temple and of sacrifice was readily appropriated for the ascetic campaign. Thus Christians could consider themselves "temples" of the Holy Spirit (I Cor. 3:16–17; 6:19–20) or "living sacrifices" (Rom. 12:1): ritual language is adept, Mary Douglas reminds us, in the production of "condensed symbols."[37] Of most interest for our purposes, however, is the way in which these identifications are displaced from their early ascription to *all* Christians[38] and arrogated to the celibate alone, especially to virgins and widows. Biblical imagery pertaining to holiness, sacrifices, temples, altars, and holy vessels is thus increasingly swept into the purview of ascetic discourse. Language of the ancient Hebrew cult could be used to underscore the superiority of ascetics to nonascetics within the Church.

Thus Jerome charges that Christians, such as his opponent Jovinian, who cite I Corinthians 6:19 (bodies as "temples of the Holy Spirit") to signal the equality of all baptized Christians are misguided, for surely even Jovinian knows that temples contain inner and outer courtyards, vestibules, kitchens and pantries, as well as the Holy of Holies—and so it is in the ranks of the Church.[39] The (possibly) Pelagian letter *On Virginity* (*To Claudia*) attempts an ameliorating solution to the question of whether *all* Christians are "holy and pure sacrifices," or only virgins. The author

[36] Clement of Alexandria, *Paedagogus* 2.10.83 (GCS 12, 208). Clement (*Paedagogus* 2.10.84) doubts the story that hyenas change sex: nature does not change. For an anthropological discussion of food taboos, see Mary Douglas, "Deciphering a Meal," in *Myth, Symbol, and Culture*, ed. Clifford Geertz (New York: W. W. Norton, 1971), pp. 61–81.

[37] Mary Douglas, *Natural Symbols* (New York: Vintage, 1973), p. 26.

[38] Applicable to all Christians: Tertullian, *De pudicitia* 16.1–2 (CCL 2, 1312); *De cultu feminarum* 2.1.1 (CCL 1, 352); Augustine, *Serm.* 278.9.9–10.10 (PL 38, 1272–73); Athanasius, Untitled (*Fragments on the Moral Life*) 6 (CSCO 150 = Scriptores Coptici 19, 124; ET, Brakke, p. 316); John Chrysostom, *Hom. 13 II Cor.* 3 (7:1) (PG 61, 494); *Hom. 9 I Cor.* 3 (3:16f.) (PG 61, 79); *De virginitate* 25 (SC 125, 174); *Hom. 29 Rom.* 1–2 (15:16) (PG 60, 655); Cyril of Jerusalem, *Or. Cat.* 4.23 (PG 33, 485). Cyprian, *De habitu virginum* 2 (CSEL 3.1, 188), although ostensibly writing to and about virgins, claims that after baptism, we are God's "temple"—thus ostensibly "opening up" the possibility to all baptized Christians.

[39] Jerome, *Adversus Iovinianum* 2.29 (PL 23, 340). For Methodius, virgins are "the Holy of Holies" (*Symposium* 5.8 [GCS 27, 62–63]).

acknowledges that all Christians receive "equal gifts of grace" and the "same blessings of the sacraments," but beyond this "common grace," virgins receive a "special grace" that qualifies them to be the "living sacrifices" of Romans 12:1; they will receive higher rewards, better rooms in the Father's divine mansions (John 14:2), than ordinary Christians.[40]

Other patristic writers, however, evince no qualms in appropriating the language of the cult for virgins alone. Carolyn Osiek has shown how the symbolic ascription of *widows* as "altars" gradually gave way to that of *virgins* as "altars."[41] I suggest that the phenomenon Osiek notes is part of a larger process by which lay Christians were progressively "desanctified" in favor of those espousing the ascetic ideals—and the more rigorously ascetic, the higher the status. Thus even within the ranks of celibates, virgins could be ranked above widows and those who took vows of continence within marriage.

Virgins are now described by ascetically inclined authors as "altars," from which no relative should try to drag them. Ambrose warms to this theme, citing the story in I Kings 13 of the withering of King Jeroboam's hand when he attempted (in Ambrose's construal of the passage) to "violate" the gifts of the altar.[42] The virgin's body as a "sacred vessel" is another favorite phrase of authors such as Basil of Caesarea and Jerome.[43] This "sacred vessel" stands in danger of pollution through a sexual "fall" that renders her liable to a charge of "adultery" against her Spouse, Christ.[44] For Jerome, the "vessels of the Lord's Temple," that is, virgins like Eustochium, are not to be exposed to public gaze. If Uzzah was struck down by God for touching the sacred ark of the covenant (II Sam. 6:6–7), how much more should virgins take care that no "unchaste eyes" defile their purity.[45]

Likewise, Paul's claim that Christian believers are "temples of God" is arrogated primarily to virgins by ascetic writers of the early Christian centuries. For the authors of the *Acts of Paul* and the *Acts of Thomas*, virgins who "keep their flesh pure" and "renounce filthy intercourse" can be called "temples of God."[46] Likewise, Basil of Ancyra, Eusebius of Emesa, Pseudo-Basil, and Gerontius are among the Christian writers who remark on virgins as "temples" and "sanctuaries."[47] Of such virginal "tem-

[40] (Anonymous), *ep. de virginitate* (= *Ad Claudiam*) 1–2 (CSEL 1, 225–26).

[41] Carolyn Osiek, "The Widow as Altar: The Rise and Fall of a Symbol," *The Second Century* 3 (1983): 159–69.

[42] Ambrose, *De virginibus* 2.4.27; 2.5.38 (PL 16, 226, 229); *De virginitate* 26 (PL 16, 286).

[43] Basil of Caesarea, *ep.* 199.18 (Loeb III:106); Jerome, *ep.* 22.23 (CSEL 54, 175).

[44] Basil of Caesarea, *ep.* 199.18 (Loeb III:106).

[45] Jerome, *ep.* 22.23 (CSEL 54, 175).

[46] *Acta Pauli et Theclae* 6 (Lipsius/Bonnet I:239–40); *Acta Thomae* 1.12 (Lipsius/Bonnet II:116–17).

[47] Basil of Ancyra, *De virginitate* 27 (Vaillant, pp. 20–21); Eusebius of Emesa, *De virginitate* 25, 27 (Buytaert I:192, 194);

ples," Mary provides the supreme example; in her, God prepared a "sanctuary" in order to bring something of the life of heaven to earth.[48] Parents are reminded by Eusebius of Emesa of their duty to help their virgin daughters fulfill their promises to Christ by honoring them as "temples of God."[49] In the context of the household asceticism popular in Asia Minor, fathers are expressly enjoined to serve as "priests" watching over the precious "sanctuary" entrusted to them, namely, their virgin daughters.[50] Eusebius of Emesa and John Chrysostom go so far as to call the matron Domnina a "priest" as she leads her sexually endangered virgin daughters to their martyrs' death.[51]

"Temples," however, are in constant danger of despoilation. For Basil of Ancyra, the virgin's body as a "temple" is equated with a nuptial chamber for her Spouse, Christ, and she is warned against "adultery."[52] Eusebius of Emesa's reference to the virgin as "temple" stands as a warning to any potential seducer or rapist: he should recall that sexual passion lasts only a moment, but that, in the words of Paul (I Cor. 3:17), "he who destroys a temple of God, God will destroy him."[53] The dangers of "falling" from one's virginal status can thus be described as "desolating the temple of Christ": so John Chrysostom, writing to his "fallen" friend Theodore.[54] In recounting the martyrdom of Domnina and her two daughters, Eusebius of Emesa puts on the mother's lips an exhortation to her daughters (who fear rape by their persecutors) that as martyred virgins, they will retain their status as "temples," not become *mulieres*, women who have experienced sexual intercourse.[55] Here we see, in Jonathan Z. Smith's phrase, "the language of vulnerability to degradation" that attends the hierarchical ranking of pure over impure.[56]

Likewise, it is now virgins who are the "living sacrifices" of Romans 12:1,[57] "sacrifices" that, in the eyes of their ascetic advocates, far outrank

---

(Gerontius), *Vita Melaniae Iunioris* 19 (SC 90, 182; ostensibly here spoken by Melania herself to her nuns); Ps.-Basil, *De virginitate* 2.41 (Amand de Mendietta/Moons, p. 43).

[48] John Chrysostom, *Hom. in servatoris nostri Jesu Christi diem natalem* 6 (PG 49, 360), citing Lev. 26:12; II Cor. 6:16; I Cor. 3:16.

[49] Eusebius of Emesa, *Hom. 6 de martyribus* 24 (Buytaert I:191).

[50] So Ps.-Basil, *De virginitate* 2.19–20; cf. 5.63 (here, of a son) (Amand de Mendietta/Moons, pp. 32, 37). For "household asceticism" in Asia Minor, see Susanna Elm, *"Virgins of God": The Making of Asceticism in Late Antiquity* (Oxford: Clarendon, 1994), pt. I.

[51] Eusebius of Emesa, *Hom. 6 de martyribus* 29 (Buytaert I:171); cf. John Chrysostom, *De SS. Bernice et Prosdoce* 6 (PG 50, 639).

[52] Basil of Ancyra, *De virginitate* 27 (Vaillant, pp. 20–21).

[53] Eusebius of Emesa, *Hom. 7 de virginitate* 27 (Buytaert I:194).

[54] John Chrysostom, *Ad Theodorum lapsum* 1.1 (PG 47, 277).

[55] Eusebius of Emesa, *Hom. 6 de martyribus* 18 (Buytaert I:162). The names of the mother and the daughters are sometimes confused in this and other sources pertaining to the story.

[56] Smith, *To Take Place*, p. 56.

[57] (Anonymous), *ep. de virginitate* (= *Ad Claudiam)* 1 (CSEL 1, 225); Athanasius,

those of the Old Testament. The virgin's sacrifice is superior in that it is an offering of chastity, not of blood; she is a "living" sacrifice, unlike the "dead and unclean" sacrifices of the Jews.[58] In fact, according to John Chrysostom, the stories of Abraham's almost-sacrifice of Isaac and Jephthah's sacrifice of his daughter teach God's disapprobation of the sacrificial cult.[59] Chrysostom argues that Christ put an end to the "impious and abominable" sacrifices of wicked Israelites who "sacrificed their sons and daughters to demons" (Ps. 106:37), the "sacrifice" of martyrdom serving as a worthy replacement.[60] Jerome, writing to Demetrias on her vow of virginity, claims that he consecrates to "eternal chastity" her "living sacrifice acceptable to God" (Rom. 12:1),[61] a verse to which Eusebius of Emesa and John Chrysostom also appeal in their exhortations to virgins.[62] Writers such as Athanasius likewise appropriate the language of the Hebrew cult, but stress the superiority of Christianity: the sacrifice of the virgin is a "whole" offering, not a "divided" one.[63] Moreover, for Athanasius, the virgin's "wholeness" contrasts with the "dividedness" of the matron, a "dividedness" that Athanasius attributes to her distraction by the "worldly things" of I Corinthians 7:34.[64] Hierarchy has been effectively signaled.

IV: Asceticizing Purity and Pollution

A related theme, but one which ascetic writers elaborated in a different direction, pertains to purity and pollution. Whereas in the linguistic appropriation of "the temple," "sacrifices," and "altars" I noted a gradual narrowing of the referent to the celibate alone, in the discussion of purity and pollution, the exegetical "move" of ascetically minded church fathers is to transfer Old Testament

Praecepta ad virgines (CSCO 150 = Scriptores Coptici 19, 99); Gregory of Nyssa, *De virginitate* 23.7 (SC 119, 554, 556). Earlier, Origen interpreted Rom. 12:1 to counsel the moral purity of Christians: the sacrifice of the heifer means the mortification of pride; the sacrifice of a ram denotes the suppression of anger, and so forth: see Origen, *Comm. Rom.* 9.1 (12:1) (PG 14, 1203–4).

[58] John Chrysostom, *Hom. 20 Rom.* 1 (12:1ff.) (PG 60, 596).

[59] John Chrysostom, *Hom. 14 de statuis* 3 (PG 49, 147); *Hom. 3 II Cor.* 6 (PG 61, 415); cf. Ambrose, *De virginitate* 3.10 (PL 16, 282); Eusebius of Emesa, *Hom. 7 de virginitate* 25 (Buytaert I:192); *Hom. 6 de martyribus* 29 (Buytaert I:171–72); Ps.-Basil, *De virginitate* 5.61–63 (Amand de Mendietta/Moons, pp. 53–55).

[60] John Chrysostom, *De SS. Bernice et Prosdoce* 5 (PG 50, 637).

[61] Jerome, *ep.* 130.2 (CSEL 56, 176–77).

[62] Eusebius of Emesa, *Hom. 7 de virginibus* 4 (Buytaert I:178); Gregory of Nyssa, *De virginitate* 23.7 (SC 119, 556). Gregory, in addition to citing Rom. 12:1–2, quotes Exod. 19:15, 22, and urges the virgins to be both pure priests and pure sacrifices (SC 119, 558, 560).

[63] Athanasius, *ep. 1 ad virgines* (CSCO 150 = Scriptores Coptici 19, 81; ET, Brakke, p. 280).

[64] Athanasius, *ep. 2 ad virgines* (Lebon, pp. 172–73; ET, Brakke, pp. 293–94); cf. *Vita prima graeca Pachomii* 1: Isaac as a "whole burnt offering" (SubsHag 19, 1).

regulations concerning purity and pollution not just to Christian celibates, but, as far as possible, to Christian laypeople as a whole. Particularly did their discussions focus on the issue of sexual relations within marriage. The decisive text picked to advance the Fathers' case was I Corinthians 7:5, Paul's advice that Christian married couples might separate sexually for prayer, but then should return to their sexual union so that Satan would not tempt them.

In general, Israel's call to holiness, especially as detailed in the book of Leviticus,[65] lay ready-to-hand for a transformed asceticizing interpretation. Since God is holy, all aspects of Israelite life (dietary, priestly, sexual, medical, and so forth) must be conformed to God's will for purity. The scope of holiness and pollution, cleanness and uncleanness, however, was sharply restricted by Christian ascetic interpreters to the human realm alone[66] and within this narrower compass, to the arena of sexuality in particular. Although Christian writers could sometimes appropriate a literal interpretation of ancient Hebrew purity laws (such as the prohibition of sexual intercourse during a wife's menstruation),[67] they more customarily align the Old Law's general call for "holiness" with the New Law's "counsels of perfection" (cf. Matt. 5:48) or its exhortation to live "without blemish" (Phil. 2:14–15), and interpret the resulting chain of verses to enjoin a life of abstinence, preferably of virginity.[68] Leviticus 11:44–45 (and parallel verses), "Be holy, for I am holy," is thus regularly cited by patristic authors to counsel sexual abstinence.[69] By such means, pollution-avoidance language could be borrowed from Hebrew Scripture for counsels quite foreign to its spirit: Christian widows, for example, are exhorted to remain celibate so that they can rise from their beds "clean" rather than

[65] As Fishbane notes (*Biblical Interpretation*, pp. 121–23), provisions in holiness codes diverge between assuming that Israel *is* corporately holy and must guard against defilement; or that Israel is not (yet) holy and must strive to become so. For purity regulations in ancient Greek and Roman religion, see Eugen Fehrle, *Die kultische Keuschheit im Altertum* (Giessen: Alfred Töpelmann, 1910).

[66] Augustine, *Contra Faustum* 6.7 (CSEL 25, 294–95); cf. Clement of Alexandria's explanation of "clean" and "unclean" animals as exemplary of human virtues and vices (*Paedagogus* 2.10.83–88). Likewise, John Chrysostom rejects the notion that any animal is "impure" by nature, for God created them all; it is only convention that separates pure from impure animals (*Hom. 24 Gen.* 5 [PG 53, 213]).

[67] E.g., Pelagius' interpretation of what "sanctification" means in I Cor. 7:14, according to Augustine in *De peccatorum meritis* 3.12.21 (CSEL 60, 148–49); Augustine ponders whether this is the correct interpretation of Paul's words. Ezek. 18:6 appears to be the Old Testament text in question. Pelagius does not offer this interpretation in his *Commentary on I Corinthians* 7:14.

[68] As by (Anonymous), *De possibilitate non peccandi* 4 (PLS 1, 1461–62).

[69] Tertullian, *De exhortatione castitatis* 10.4 (CCL 2, 1030); *De monogamia* 3.7 (CCL 2, 1232); Ps.-Clement, *ep. 1 de virginitate* 7 (Funk, pp. 12–13).

"unclean."[70] And with this sharper distinction between the pure and the impure, a new ascetic hierarchy was in the making.

Some Christian writers, however, evince discomfort at linking marital intercourse with pollution so as to distance themselves from Tatian, who allegedly interpreted Paul's words in I Corinthians 7:5 via Jesus' warning that no one can serve two masters (Matt. 6:24): sex and prayer are here deemed incompatible.[71] Thus other explanations that did *not* invoke the theme of pollution were sought by Catholic writers to explain I Corinthians 7:5. As will be detailed in chapter 10, various answers were posited: marital "busyness" provided one explanation;[72] marital "intemperance," another.[73] These answers were distinguished by their varying appeal to merely practical problems ("busyness") or to a more serious moral flaw ("intemperance"). When Chrysostom addresses congregations of married Christians in his homilies, for example, he assures them that sexual intercourse does not defile the married;[74] Paul in I Corinthians 7:5 refers only to "prayer with unusual earnestness," not "ordinary prayer," when he suggests the benefit of sexual separation.[75] Yet in an exhortation to virginity, Chrysostom raises the troubling question of how "Paul" in Hebrews 13:4 can claim that marriage is "honorable and the marriage bed free from stain," if he also suggests separation for prayer in I Corinthians 7:5.[76] Here, Chrysostom posits that the devil has an easier time diverting a man at prayer if the man has been "dissipated" through relations with a woman.[77]

Lastly, other church fathers skirted the theoretical issue of the polluting or nonpolluting quality of marital intercourse by simply lending the practical advice that Christian couples need not "wash" after sex: their one

[70] (Anonymous), *Ad viduitate servanda* 4 (PL 67, 1097); cf. Augustine's interpretation of Heb. 13:4 (on keeping the marriage bed "undefiled"): defilement signals "lust" and "excess," not the act of intercourse itself (*De nuptiis et concupiscentia* 1.24.27 [CSEL 42, 239]).

[71] Tatian, cited in Clement of Alexandria, *Stromata* 3.12.81 (GCS 52 [15], 232); Clement claims he quotes from Tatian's treatise, *On Perfection According to the Savior.*

[72] Ambrose, *Exhortatio virginitatis* 4.23 (PL 16, 358); cf. *Exp. Luc.* 8.37 (CCL 14, 310–11).

[73] Augustine, *De bono coniugali* 19.25, commenting on I Cor. 7:5 (CSEL 41, 219–20).

[74] John Chrysostom, *Hom. 51 Matt.* 5 (PG 58, 516); cf. *Hom. 3 Tit.* 4 (2:1) (PG 62, 681).

[75] John Chrysostom, *Hom. 19 I Cor.* 2 (PG 61, 153): otherwise, how could we fulfill the injunction of I Thess. 5:17 to "pray always"? Cf. *Hom. 51 Matt.* 5 (PG 58, 516).

[76] John Chrysostom, *De virginitate* 30.1 (SC 125, 188, 190). Chrysostom appeals to Old Testament examples of restraint as a "shaming device" for Christians: Exod. 19:15 and (a verse I have not found used by another patristic writer in this context) Joel 2:15–16, that in the "sanctification of the congregation," the bride and groom are to *leave* their chambers.

[77] John Chrysostom, *De virginitate* 31 (SC 125, 192).

baptism renders them clean.[78] By arguments such as these, some patristic authors retreated from the insinuation—skirting "heresy"—that even marital intercourse was polluting. Yet major church fathers, including Origen and Ambrose, suggest the polluting quality of marital relations, as will be explicated in the discussion of I Corinthians 7:5 in chapter 10.

For Jerome and for the (probably) Pelagian author of *De castitate*, pollution themes also stand in the forefront of consideration—although Jerome later, in the aftermath of the Jovinian controversy, attempts to soften his earlier remarks on this topic.[79] For Jerome, sex and prayer are simply incompatible[80]: "in view of the purity of the body of Christ," he declares, "all sexual intercourse is unclean."[81] Thus, according to Jerome, "Peter's" recommendation that men give honor to their wives as "the weaker sex" (I Pet. 3:7) means that they should abstain from marital intercourse.[82] Jerome also chastises couples who take the Eucharist at home after they have engaged in sexual relations—whereas they would not, Jerome claims, dare to "go to the martyrs" or "enter the churches"; "what is unlawful in church cannot be lawful at home," he intones.[83]

Pollution issues also stand at the center of the Pelagian treatise *De castitate*. Here, "chastity" means, tout court, that a Christian may not engage in any sexual relation.[84] The bodily "integrity" (i.e., virginal intactness) that marks our likeness to God is spoiled by "corruption," a term the anonymous author frequently uses for sexual intercourse.[85] The right to pray, the author argues, is categorically denied to the "incontinent" (i.e., to sexually active married couples), and, if this, "how much more" should the Eucharist be denied to them. Baptism cleanses us from "pollution," from our past "uncleanness" (*immunditia*), but once baptized, we are to maintain our newfound state of purity. Here, the author urges his readers to recall the blessed 144,000 men of Revelation 14:4 who have not "stained" themselves by sexual relations with women, which he explicitly

[78] Clement of Alexandria, *Stromata* 3.12.82 (GCS 15, 234); cf. *Constitutiones apostolorum* 6.29.4 (SC 329, 388): on the other hand, if a man has committed adultery or engaged in harlotry, all the rivers and oceans will not be able to cleanse him.

[79] Jerome, *ep.* 49 (48) (CSEL 54, 350–87, *passim*).

[80] Jerome, *ep.* 49 (48).15 (CSEL 54, 376) citing *Adversus Iovinianum* 1.7 (PL 23, 230).

[81] Jerome, *Adversus Iovinianum* 1.20 (PL 23, 249): "quod ad munditias corporis Christi, omnis coitus immunda sit."

[82] Jerome, *Adversus Iovinianum* 1.7 (PL 23, 230–31); *ep.* 49 (48).15 (CSEL 54, 376).

[83] Jerome, *ep.* 49 (48).15 (CSEL 54, 377).

[84] (Anonymous), *De castitate* 2 (PLS 1, 1466); cf. 3.1: "chastity" applies only to virgins, widows, and the married who do not engage in sexual relations (PLS 1, 1466).

[85] (Anonymous), *De castitate* 3.5 (PLS 1, 1467–68).

interprets as "sex with *wives*."[86] The theme of the polluting effects of sexual intercourse troubled the patristic discussion of the appropriate states for the offering of prayer and the reception of the Eucharist.

To argue their case that the polluting effects of sexual activity might render a Christian ineligible for prayer or Eucharistic communion, ascetically minded church fathers borrowed language of pollution-avoidance from the Old Testament. Two interpretive techniques surface prominently in their exegeses: first, Biblical verses enjoining temporary abstinences on the Hebrews are expanded to include longer, even lifelong, abstinences for Christians; and second, purity regulations originally prescribed only for Hebrew priests are now addressed to a wider audience, the married Christian laity. Whereas the language of "temple," "sacrifice," and "altar" was progressively *restricted* in its application from all Christians to celibates alone, here we note a *widening* of the audience. The effects in both cases, however, are the same: both promote an ascetic hierarchy of celibate over married and force sexual abstinence on the married as far as it seemed feasible to Christian leaders.

Moreover, the passage of Christian decades saw a progressively rigorous interpretation of purity regulations that counseled not just temporary abstinence or marital continence, but perpetual celibacy or virginity whenever possible. Thus Tertullian, writing in a period when ascetic propaganda had not yet voiced its most stringent demands, links the sentiment of the Holiness Code—"Be holy, for I am holy"—with I Corinthians 7:5 that recommends a temporary separation for couples so that they may engage in prayer. Tertullian approves this equation of marital "holiness" with sexual separation: prayers then have greater efficiency.[87] Jerome, however, heightens the ascetic message of I Corinthians 7:5 by reminding Christians that they must "pray always" (as Paul enjoins in I Thess. 5:17), thus allowing *no* time for sexual intercourse. Moreover, according to Jerome, if Paul thinks that mere "prayers" are hindered by the uncleanness of intercourse, how much more would he forbid couples who had recently indulged in sexual activity to receive the Eucharist.[88] To enforce this exegesis, Jerome cites Old Testament passages referring to brief and temporary periods of abstinence to press his own argument that since all sexual activity is polluting, no Christian who wishes to pray and to receive the

[86] (Anonymous), *De castitate* 10.4 (PLS 1, 1480–82).

[87] Tertullian, *De exhortatione castitatis* 10 (CCL 2, 1029–30), citing Lev. 11:45 (or 19:2 or 20:7 and 26).

[88] Jerome, *Adversus Iovinianum* 1.7 (PL 23, 230); earlier, he used the same argument in *ep.* 22.22. Cf. Jerome's interpretation of Eccles. 3:5: the time to "refrain from embracing" is the Christian present, so that Christians can give themselves to prayer, as Paul suggests in I Cor. 7:5 (*Comm. Eccles.* 3:5 [CCL 72, 275]).

Eucharist should engage—ideally, ever—in sexual relations. Jerome thus quotes I Samuel 21:4 (that holy bread would not be permitted to David's men if they had "polluted" themselves with women), and links this verse with other passages that he claims enjoin not just temporary abstinence, but permanent virginity. Thus he appeals to Deuteronomy 20:7 (that a Hebrew man who has just married should not go to war), now construed to mean that a man cannot be "Christ's soldier" if he engages in sexual relations.[89] And Jeremiah, who was (temporarily) forbidden by God to take a wife, now stands as a model of permanent virginity, whom Jerome holds up as exemplar to Eustochium.[90] Here, time frames and circumstances have been enlarged and generalized to provide Scriptural ballast for ascetic exhortation.

Pelagian authors, too, found the purity regulations of Hebrew Scripture a ready source for the sexual disciplining of married Christians. Pelagius himself links the command given by Moses that the Israelites should abstain from "women" for three days before the Law was to be given on Sinai (Exod. 19:15) with Paul's exhortation to the Thessalonians that they "abstain from *porneia*" (I Thess. 4:3), and cites the verses to support the demand that married Christian couples refrain from sexual relation if they wish to receive "the holy body of Christ": marriage relations are here rhetorically linked to pollution and to "fornication." Likewise, the "uncleanness" (*akatharsia*) against which Paul here warns the Thessalonians is interpreted by Pelagius as the "incontinence" which prevents the reception of Christ's body.[91] In his interpretation of I Corinthians 7:5 (refraining from marital relations for brief periods of prayer), Pelagius rehearses Moses' warning in Exodus 19 and further strengthens his ascetic exhortation by an appeal to I Samuel 21:4, in which the priest Ahimelech refuses to give "holy bread" to David's men unless they have "kept themselves from women"[92]—by now, a well-attested catena of verses. Thus, commandments that originally pertained to temporary abstinence have been expanded to warn Christians against indulgence in customary marital intercourse, which will (so ascetic writers warn) preclude their ability to receive the sacrament.

Pelagius' interpretation of such Scriptural verses pertaining to purity and pollution, however, is tightened by the yet more rigorous exegesis of the author of the anonymous Pelagian treatise, *De castitate.* Here, the argument does not recommend occasional marital restraint that makes room for prayer, but constitutes an appeal for virginity. According to this

[89] Jerome, *Adversus Iovinianum* 1.20 (PL 23, 249).

[90] Jerome, *ep.* 22.21 (CSEL 54, 172).

[91] Pelagius, *In I Thess.* 4:3; 4:7 (PLS 1, 1326, 1327).

[92] Pelagius, *In I Cor.* 7:5 (PLS 1, 1200).

Pelagian author, sexual intercourse itself entails "corruption" and "pollution," and is to be avoided entirely by any serious Christian.[93] The state of "cleanness" required for an Israelite to eat of the Lord's peace offerings (Lev. 7:19–20) is interpreted as the "absence of sexual relation" necessary for the Christian to receive the Eucharist. Following Jerome's logic, the author argues that if Paul in I Corinthians 7 claims that a couple cannot even pray when involved in sexual relation, how much more would he forbid the possibility of communicating?[94] And the author reinforces his argument from "uncleanness" with an appeal to two other New Testament passages. First, he explains why the man in John 15:15 can be called "a friend of God": namely, because he remained chaste and in appropriate condition to give and receive the Eucharist.[95] In addition, this Pelagian author puts an edge on the Parable of the Great Banquet in Luke 14:15–24: the banquet is first interpreted to mean "the Lord's Supper," that is, the Eucharist; next, the recently married man's declination of the invitation to partake of that Supper is noted—need we ask why, the Pelagian author archly queries?[96] Thus the ancient Hebrew desire to protect the "togetherness" of newly established couples (as, for example, in Deut. 20:7) is recast as an ascetic warning against the defilement of sexual relation.

If restraint of a temporary nature attending some few Old Testament passages could be extended by Christian ascetic writers to encompass a lifetime of abstinence, the enforcement of purity laws on Hebrew priests could be extended to all Christians, lay as well as clerics, monks, or nuns.[97] This move was cleverly facilitated by some ascetic writers through their repetition of such verses as Ephesians 6:9, that "God is no respecter of persons," now interpreted to mean that God does not wish for priests *alone* to enjoy the highest rewards for the fulfillment of divine law, but generously extends the requirements of priestly purity codes to *all* Christian believers so that they too may share in the divine blessing.[98]

[93] (Anonymous), *De castitate* 3.5; 2.1; 10.4 (PLS 1, 1467–68, 1465, 1482). The author pointedly remarks that it is only virgins, not the chaste married, who are called blessed in Rev. 14:4 (*De castitate* 10.4 [PLS 1, 1482]). Louis Dumont in *Homo Hierachicus* (p. 53, 1st and 2nd eds.) notes that in Hinduism, marriage is the only *rite de passage* that does *not* incur impurity—a sharp contrast with the views of the author of *De castitate*.

[94] (Anonymous), *De castitate* 10.4 (PLS 1, 1481). That some fourth-century Christians believed that they should not receive the Eucharist from a married priest (according to canon 4 of the Council of Gangra) shows how strong the fears of pollution might run in some quarters.

[95] (Anonymous), *De castitate* 17 (PLS 1, 1504–5).

[96] (Anonymous), *De castitate* 8.3 (PLS 1, 1477).

[97] On "changing the audience" as a technique of ascetic exegesis, see above, pp. 136–38.

[98] Tertullian, *De exhortatione castitatis* 7.4 (CCL 2, 1025); (Anonymous), *De castitate* 13.2 (PLS 1, 1492). Some Pelagian au-

Tertullian, for example, in his attack on remarriage appeals to an (alleged) Old Testament law that allows priests to marry only once.[99] His claim enables his argument that "even" the Old Testament stands against plural marriage. Tertullian next extends the alleged regulation prohibiting second marriage to Hebrew priests to every Christian, lay as well as clerical. He argues his case through an appeal to Revelation 1:6, "We are all priests"—and hence *all* Christians must be limited to one marriage,[100] in preparation for possible priestly service. Two centuries later, Jerome echoes the sentiment: laymen are bound by the same rules that prohibit priests from marrying a second time (an allusion to I Tim. 3:2?), and since all Christian men must stand ready for election to the priesthood, all must refrain from second marriage.[101]

Whereas Pelagius himself merely prohibited second marriage for priests and deacons,[102] the Pelagian author of *De castitate* insists that priests must be totally continent, thus imitating the chastity that is the condition of God and the angels.[103] Since this author has already insisted that the Old Testament "pollution" passages (e.g., Exod. 19:10–15; I Sam. 21:4) are relevant to all Christians,[104] they of necessity hold for priests. Any Christian who argues that marriage is still a favored state, as it was in ancient Israel, should commit himself to the entire (and to this author, disgusting) ritual law of the Hebrews, including animal sacrifice and circumcision:[105] marriage is here degradingly aligned with ritual practices that no Christian would presumably uphold.

In one instance, however, the widening of the audience of purity laws receives a different treatment: in the case of monks, regulations originally pertaining to marital sexuality needed to be recast, and other verses found, that would address the specific sexual problems encountered in an all-

thors cite Matt. 19:10–11 (only those to whom it is "given" can accept Jesus' teaching on eunuchs), but hastily assure the readers that the message is "given" to *all* Christians—although not to heathen or Jews; see (Anonymous), *De castitate* 8.2 (PLS 1, 1476–77).

[99] Tertullian says that he refers to a law in Leviticus, but no passage corresponds to his claim; Lev. 21:13–15 refers only to the chief priest's not taking as wife a woman who had been previously married. Probably he has in mind I Tim. 3:2.

[100] Tertullian, *De exhortatione castitatis* 7.1 (CCL 2, 1024); cf. Tertullian, *Ad uxorem* 1.7.4 (CCL 1, 381), in which he appeals to the Pastoral Epistles for Scriptural reinforcement against priests marrying more than once.

[101] Jerome, *ep.* 123.5 (CSEL 56, 79).

[102] Pelagius, *In I Tim.* 3:2, 3:12 (PLS 1, 1350, 1351); *In Tit.* 1:6 (PLS 1,1369).

[103] (Anonymous), *De castitate* 3.3 (PLS 1, 1466).

[104] (Anonymous), *De castitate* 5.2–3 (PLS 1, 1473).

[105] (Anonymous), *De castitate* 15.4 (PLS 1, 1498). For a fascinating discussion of the early Christians' attribution of "carnality" to the Israelites, see Daniel Boyarin, *Carnal Israel: Reading Sex in Talmudic Cul-*

male, supposedly celibate community. Here, John Cassian provides some enlightening exegeses.

In the rarified atmosphere of a male monastic community, Scriptural warnings against pollution acquired a distinctive resonance: masturbation[106] and nocturnal emissions[107] are here the almost-sole focus of purity discussions. Injunctions pertaining to male emissions could, of course, be adapted unproblematically from Hebrew law (e.g., Deut. 23:10–12) to fit the monastic regime: thus the Hebrew male who must remain outside the camp for a day following an emission is easily transmogrified into the monk who is deprived of worshiping with his ascetic confreres.[108] But more ingenious adaptations of Scripture are also evident in John Cassian's exhortations. Thus Cassian claims that only the monk who has reached the highest level of purity will be free from polluting emissions; indeed, he will (in an inventive interpretation of Hos. 2:18) "sleep in security."[109] In yet another creative gesture, Cassian transforms Paul's words to married Thessalonian men—that each possess his vessel ("his wife") in honor (I Thess. 4:4)—to apply to the purity of monks: monks who so possess their vessels (here, their genitals) are those who are not stained by the uncleanness of nocturnal emissions.[110] The flexibility of the word *skeuos* (= *vas*) doubtless enabled the verse's usefulness in a male monastic setting.

John Cassian likewise borrows Old Testament passages on ritual uncleanness to argue his special line, that a nocturnal emission prohibits a monk from receiving the Eucharist the next day. Cassian appeals to the "peace offerings" of Leviticus 7:20–21 that were prohibited to anyone in a state of uncleanness; specifying the offerings as "consecrated food" provides him with a convenient entrée to his topic of the Eucharist.[111] These verses are next interpreted in light of Paul's warning in I Corinthians 11:27–29 against "unworthy" eating and drinking of the Lord's body

---

ture (Berkeley: University of California Press, 1993), pp. 1–2.

[106] John Cassian, *Conlationes* 5.11 (SC 42, 200). Referring to Onan in Gen. 38, Cassian remarks that it was to avoid this kind of "impurity" that Paul wrote in I Cor. 7:9, "It is better to marry than to burn."

[107] Numerous passages in Cassian concern this topic; see, among others, *Institutiones* 2.13; 3.5; 6.7.2; 7.10; 7.11; 7.20; *Conlationes* 10.10; 12.2; 12.7–9; 12.16; 21.36; 4.15; 7.2; and all of book 22. For a comprehensive discussion, see David Brakke, "The Problematization of Nocturnal Emissions in Early Christian Syria, Egypt, and Gaul," *Journal of Early Christian Studies* 3 (1995): 419–60.

[108] John Cassian, *Conlationes* 12.2 (SC 54, 122). Cassian also cites Lev. 7:20 and Num. 19:22 for Scriptural support.

[109] John Cassian, *Conlationes* 12.7 (SC 54, 132).

[110] John Cassian, *Institutiones* 6.15.1–2; 6.20 (SC 109, 280, 284). On *skeuos/vas* = penis, see J. N. Adams, *The Latin Sexual Vocabulary* (Baltimore: Johns Hopkins University Press, 1982), pp. 41–43.

[111] John Cassian, *Conlationes* 12.2 (SC 54, 122); cf. *Institutiones* 6.8.

and blood, and with reference to Deuteronomy 23:10–11, the sole passage here cited which explicitly refers to the polluting effect of nocturnal emissions.[112] Cassian's exegesis of Scriptural purity regulations provides an illuminating illustration of the work that intertextual interpretation performed for the ascetic cause.

V: Interpretive Strategies for the Creation of Ascetic Meaning

These examples indicate how verses pertaining to the ritual law in Hebrew Scriptures could be appropriated and reinterpreted to apply to ascetically inclined Christians. Such appropriations required a skillful exegesis that employed transformations of audience, time frame, and circumstances, and that restricted the meanings of holiness, purity, and pollution almost exclusively to matters sexual. In addition, these ascetic writers did not eschew reversing their symbolic codes, if such reversals promoted an ascetic rhetoric.

The freedom with which these ascetic interpreters reverse their arguments is indeed a prime indication of the ideological nature of their rhetoric: where it suits their purposes, they can hold up exemplary Hebrew laypeople as models to Christian priests, and interpret the Old Testament itself as issuing a call for virginity. Thus Ambrose reverses the usual exegetical strategy of transferring injunctions incumbent on Hebrew priests to Christian laypeople; his argument—a nice instance of a "shaming" technique—proceeds from exemplary Hebrew laypeople, to less-than-ascetically-rigorous Christian priests. Ambrose's "proof" of the sexual renunciation undertaken by the Israelites is supplied by a now-familiar text, Moses' command that the people should stay pure from women for a few days before God was to descend on Sinai to give the Law (Exod. 19:10)—or, what Ambrose incorrectly (but conveniently for his purposes) refers to as a sacrifice, thus enabling an alignment of Moses' command with an injunction concerning the Christian Eucharist. If even "the people" were asked to abstain by Moses, how much more should Christian priests not "spot themselves" with marital intercourse? Ambrose registers shock that in some places—but only in out-of-the-way places, he assures his readers—Christian priests are fathering children and imagining that they do so with impunity.[113] Such men deserve the shame with which they are

[112] John Cassian, *Conlationes* 22.5 (SC 64, 120). Cassian, however, here moves toward considering "intention" in assigning culpability or innocence.

[113] Ambrose, *De officiis ministrorum* 1.50.248 (PL 16, 105). Another example of Exod. 19:15ff. used as a "shaming device" for Christian virgins can be found in John Chrysostom, *De virginitate* 30.1.

branded when their moral and spiritual standards are compared to the allegedly loftier ones of Hebrew laypeople.

Although Jerome's interpretive strategy customarily rests on an appeal to the "difference in times" that separates the Old Testament era from the Christian ascetic Dispensation (e.g., that priestly marriage in the Old Testament signals that era's vast inferiority to the "different times" inhabited by ascetic Christians),[114] he also locates a few passages in Hebrew Scripture that support his call for Christian virginity. Thus he cites the law in Leviticus 21:7 (that the head priest is required to marry an "undefiled woman") to argue that even among the ancient Hebrews, virginity could be valued[115]—rather overlooking the fact that the "undefiled woman" in question (explicitly identified by Jerome, but not by the text, as a virgin), was to be married. Moreover, since it is only a virgin sister at whose death a priest is allowed to "defile" himself by contact with a corpse, according to Leviticus 21:3, Jerome imagines that he has located yet another instance of the honoring of virginity in Hebrew Scripture.[116] Creating such links between Old Testament teaching and the demands of Christian asceticism was useful to Jerome in his attempted refutation of charges that he was a covert "Manichean" who denigrated God's good creation,[117] however ill this interpretive strategy accorded with his usual emphasis on "the difference in times." Strategies could be modified when a different argument seemed better suited to advance the ascetic agenda.

V: Circumcision

Interpreted literally, circumcision had, in Christian imagination, little to recommend it. As a sign of Jewish separateness, circumcision (in John Chrysostom's view) was imposed by God so as to rein in the Jews' "disordered appetites" and "blind instincts." Although this sign of "distinction" kept the Jewish bloodline pure from Abraham to Christ, Chrysostom concedes, it no longer has any useful

[114] E.g., Jerome, *Adversus Iovinianum* 1.34 (PL 23, 268–70).

[115] Jerome, *Adversus Iovinianum* 1.20 (PL 23, 249); contrast with *ep.* 52.10, where Jerome cites the passage to demonstrate the "lowliness" of the Old Law that required priests to marry. For rabbinic interpreters, the woman's defilement did not necessarily signal her lack of virginity but perhaps her relationship to someone who was disqualified from priestly status for various reasons (I thank my colleague Kalman Bland for this point).

[116] Jerome, *Adversus Iovinianum* 1.20 (PL 23, 249). Jerome may draw his inspiration from Tertullian, who argues that it is because all Christians are priests (Rev. 1:6) that Jesus tells the young man not to bury his father (Matt. 8:21–22; Luke 9:59–60), since priests must avoid the contamination of corpses, even those of their parents (Lev. 21:11) (*De monogamia* 7.8–9 [CCL 2, 1238–39]).

[117] See especially Jovinian's accusations, as reported in Jerome, *Adversus Iovinianum* 1.3.

function, for the "cutting of the flesh does not contribute to the freedom of the soul." This mark of "evil proclivities" can thus be safely discarded in the Christian era.[118] For Chrysostom, circumcision is a sign of the Jews' "carnality" that leads them (in Chrysostom's rhetorical representation) to chant, "Long life for the flesh!"[119] Actual circumcision is not to be practiced by Christians; John Cassian can interpret a monk's wish to be circumcised as the devil's delusion.[120]

A spiritualized understanding of circumcision, on the other hand, could easily be swept into Christian ascetic interpretation. Here, Christian exegetes had already been aided by Paul's allegorized readings of circumcision—"spiritual circumcision"—in such passages as Romans 2:29 and Philippians 3:3. Further, as is well known, Christian writers of the first few Christian centuries provided a typological analysis of circumcision that cast it as the forerunner of Christian baptism.[121] In the writings of Cyprian (mid-third century), the discussion of circumcision in relation to baptism begins to shift from issues of "pollution" to a speculation concerning the infant's possible sin.[122] From approximately the same period, in Origen's discussion of Jeremiah 4:4 ("circumcise yourselves to the Lord, remove the foreskin of your hearts"), circumcision is related to the "stain" that spots us from the time of our birth—but the "stain" is said to concern "evil thoughts,"[123] presumably, for Origen, a category pertaining to the will, not to "human nature." Here again, the language of pollution and the language of moral offense are linked. For all patristic authors, a spiritualizing exegesis would have to be provided for the circumcision texts if they were to be of use.[124]

Indeed, given the mockery of circumcision by Manichean opponents of Catholicism, some saving strategy was necessary. A good example of a recuperative technique is furnished by Augustine, who in his anti-Manichean treatises attempts to weave as tight a link between the Testaments

[118] John Chrysostom, *Hom. 39 Gen.* 4 (PG 53, 366–67).

[119] John Chrysostom, *Hom. 13 Heb.* 2 (PG 63, 103–4).

[120] John Cassian, *Conlationes* 2.8 (SC 42, 119).

[121] E.g., Justin Martyr, *Dialogus cum Tryphone* 19; 114; Augustine, *De baptismo* 4.24.32; *Contra Faustum* 19.9.

[122] Cyprian, *ep.* 58 (= 64) *Ad Fidum* 4–5 (CSEL 3.2, 719–21). Fidus advises an eight-day wait before baptism, comparable to circumcision, on the grounds that earlier, the infant is too close to the pollution of birth. Cyprian and his council rule against Fidus' position; are not infants "pure," as Titus 1:15 suggests ("To the pure, all things are pure")?

[123] Origen, *Hom. 5 in Jer.* 14–15 (SC 232, 316, 318), citing Job 14:4–5; cf. Origen, *Hom. 8 Lev.* 3, in which Job 3:3, Jer. 20:14–16, and Ps. 51:5 are also cited to signal our "impurity" from birth.

[124] Yet even a "spiritualizing" interpretation can mean something "physical": thus Cassian interprets Paul's words on "spiritual circumcision" as a warning to monks to avoid nocturnal emissions (*Conlationes* 21.26 [SC 64, 112]).

as possible. Augustine's Manichean opponent Faustus bluntly refers to circumcision as among the Jewish practices (like animal sacrifice) that Christianity calls us to abandon.[125] In a failed attempt at humor, Faustus jokes that the Jews and their God perhaps need the mark of circumcision to locate one another: the Jews might lose their moorings, wander blindly, unrecognized by their deity, if this physical sign were not impressed upon them![126] Faustus also mockingly queries Augustine as to why Catholics should not be circumcised, for they supposedly believe the testimony of Matthew 5:17 that Jesus came not to destroy the Law, but to fulfill it—and the commandment for circumcision was surely enjoined by the Law.[127]

Augustine is hard-pressed to respond. He first reminds Faustus of Paul's words, that Abraham's circumcision was "a seal of righteousness" (Rom. 4:11). Faustus should also reflect on Titus 1:15, "to the pure all is pure"—a sentiment foreign to Manichean teaching, which represents its deity as entangled in the reproductive process with those very organs that Faustus here mocks and reviles.[128] These points registered, Augustine argues that circumcision should be understood as one of the "symbolic" precepts that prefigured the teaching of Christianity;[129] just what it prefigured, he construes variously as "the removal of our fleshly nature,"[130] as "the circumcision of the heart,"[131] or as a sign of the original sin that needs "removing" from infants.[132]

Exegetes whose primary goal was to further the ascetic cause, however, could find other symbolic meanings for Biblical references to circumcision. Paul's words on circumcision and uncircumcision in I Corinthians 7, in the midst of his discussion of marriage and celibacy, stimulated patristic interpreters to elide the terms, sometimes adding Paul's dichotomy of slavery and freedom to the mix. Circumcision and uncircumcision now become interpretive metaphors for marriage and abstinence—but which was which? The equation could be run in more than one direction. Does

[125] Faustus in Augustine, *Contra Faustum* 25.1 (CSEL 25, 725–26).

[126] Ibid.

[127] Faustus in Augustine, *Contra Faustum* 19.6 (CSEL 25, 502); cf. 18.1–3 (CSEL 25, 490–92).

[128] Faustus in Augustine, *Contra Faustum* 6.3; 6.6 (CSEL 25, 287, 292); cf. 25.2 (CSEL 25, 727–28).

[129] Faustus in Augustine, *Contra Faustum* 6.2 (CSEL 25, 285–86).

[130] Faustus in Augustine, *Contra Faustum* 19.9 (CSEL 25, 507); cf. 25.2 (CSEL 25, 727–28).

[131] Faustus in Augustine, *Contra Faustum* 6.3 (CSEL 25, 286).

[132] In his anti-Pelagian writings, Augustine appeals to the ancient circumcision laws as a "proof" of original sin: the child would not deserve to be cut off from his people (Gen. 17:14) if he were not sinful. See Augustine, *De nuptiis et concupiscentia* 2.9.24; *Opus imperfectum* 1.50; 2.74; 2.119; 2.125; 2.151; 2.204; *De civitate Dei* 16.27. Moreover, the fact that a circumcised father begets an uncircumcised son is used by Augustine to argue that original sin is transmitted from even baptized parents to their children; see, for example, *ep.* 6*.7.

uncircumcision link to marriage as a code for uncleanness, or does circumcision link to marriage as a code for Jewishness? Either way, whether as uncleanness or as Jewishness, marriage is construed as the negative pole. Should the exegete assign a spiritual or a literal interpretation to the practice? The Logos in its overflowing creativity might suggest a variety of interpretations for this and other terms, thus (in Jon Whitman's words) standing as a "paradoxical counterpart" to the Fathers' commitment to a single "text" of Scripture.[133]

Origen's commentary on I Corinthians 7:18–20 (to be discussed further in chapter 10) set the pattern for later interpretations. Linking Paul's teaching on marriage and celibacy, circumcision and uncircumcision, and slavery and freedom, Origen posits that circumcision means being free of a wife, while uncircumcision refers to the married: thus the Jewish evaluation of the higher worth of circumcision is replicated in the new ascetic scale of values that places celibacy over marriage. Using this trope, Origen argues that those who come to the faith circumcised, that is, unmarried, should not seek to remove the marks of their circumcision by adding a wife; yet those who were called in uncircumcision, that is, marriage, should not cast aside their wives. A Christian can live a righteous life in uncircumcision, that is, in marriage, just as the circumcised, that is, the unmarried, can live righteously. Circumcision and uncircumcision, celibacy and marriage, are "indifferent" matters (*adiaphora*), Origen claims; salvation is rather won by keeping the commandments of God.[134] Here, Origen's discussion of marriage allows it an honored place alongside celibacy and contains no hint that marital intercourse is "polluting," as some of the passages cited earlier might suggest.[135]

Jerome borrows Origen's code that uncircumcision stands for the married, while the circumcised, by contrast, are those who have "cut off the foreskin of marriage" by adopting celibacy.[136] In one of his more complicated elaborations of this metaphor, Jerome notes that Adam, who was created physically uncircumcised, was given the "coat of marriage" (i.e., the "coat of skins" of Gen. 3:2) when he was expelled from Paradise. But, Jerome continues, if present-day Christians are "called in uncircumci-

[133] See Jon Whitman, *Allegory: The Dynamics of an Ancient and Medieval Technique* (Cambridge, Mass.: Harvard University Press, 1987), p. 62. Irvine, *The Making of Textual Culture*, p. 270, writes of the "semiotic anxiety" that the Word's "dispersal in multiple signs and interpretations" created for Augustine (citing *Confessions* 13.24 and 12.28–30) (see pp. 265–71 for full discussion of the point).

[134] Origen, *Comm. I Cor.* 7:18–20 (Jenkins [1908], pp. 506–7).

[135] See above, pp. 215–24.

[136] Jerome, *Adversus Iovinianum* 1.12; 1.20 (PL 23, 239–40, 249); Jerome, *ep.* 49 (= 48).6 (CSEL 54, 358), quoting from *Adversus Iovinianum* 1.11.

sion," that is, if they wear the "skins" of matrimony, they should not seek the "nakedness of virginity" by divorce. Remaining married, they should regulate their sexual practice so that they drink only from their own "wells," not from the dissolute cisterns of harlots who cannot hold the pure waters of chastity (Jer. 2:13; Prov. 5:15).[137] Circumcision, here coded as virginity, is in any event not a state that uncircumcised (i.e., married) Christians can regain by divorce.

Ambrose also deems physical circumcision to be unnecessary since Christ replaced it with his own bloody sacrifice: "who would use a needle in a battle while armed with stronger weapons," he asks? "Spiritual circumcision," however, is approved, and is linked with the teaching of Matthew 19:12 on "becoming a eunuch for the Kingdom of Heaven." It is rather the inner man, Ambrose concludes, who must be "circumcised of desire."[138] In this reading, circumcision is spiritualized and is understood as a trope for celibacy.

At other times, however, circumcision is read literally and is associated with the Old Law of Judaism that has now been superseded: here, those who wish to mark the "difference in times" between the two Dispensations can find useful ammunition. Manichean exegetes, for example, read circumcision literally as a way to discredit the Old Testament. Thus Augustine's Manichean opponents in their polemics customarily linked circumcision with the carnal delight that ancient Israelite men allegedly took in their wives and concubines. Yet not just Manicheans equated physical circumcision with marriage as a sign of Jewishness. Jerome in *Against Jovinian* can sneer that if Christians wish to follow Abraham in his marrying three wives, they should also follow him in circumcision: no halfway imitation should be allowed![139] Likewise in the presumably Pelagian treatise, *De castitate*, the equation of circumcision, Jewishness, and marriage is likewise manifest. It was only in the Old Dispensation that God wished for such observances—not now.[140] Those present-day Christians who argue illogically that marriage still has God's blessing, yet have abandoned other Hebrew practices, are urged to copy Abraham: let them offer animal sacrifice and get circumcised, as well as marry.[141] Ascetic authors' association of circumcision, Jewishness, animal sacrifice, and marriage provide an instructive illustration of how such a linkage serves to encode entire differing worldviews,[142] how these varied texts "implode" on the

[137] Jerome, *ep.* 128.3 (CSEL 56, 158).

[138] Ambrose, *ep.* 69 (= 72). 12; 26 (CSEL 82.2, 184, 191–92).

[139] Jerome, *Adversus Iovinianum* 1.19 (PL 23, 248).

[140] (Anonymous), *De castitate* 12.5 (PLS 1, 1491).

[141] (Anonymous), *De castitate* 15.4 (PLS 1, 1497) (perhaps borrowing from Jerome?).

[142] Cf. Bell, *Ritual Theory*, p. 104.

issue of ascetic renunciation. Thus circumcision is given a positive—and ascetic—valence if interpreted metaphorically (with help, for example, from Jer. 4:4), while a literal understanding of circumcision is associated with Jewish "carnality," with the rites of the Old Law that have been superseded in the new spiritual dispensation of Christianity.

VI: Status Readjustment of Ritual Texts

In addition to the ways discussed above in which Christian exegetes of an ascetic cast adapted the language of ancient Hebrew ritual for their own purposes, there remains one other method of rescuing the texts of ritual law: the reassignment of its "ontological status." This strategy does its work by retaining the text, but devaluing its authority for present-day Christians. This interpretive move was greatly assisted by the popularity of typological exegesis in the first few centuries of Christianity. Here, Old Testament legal injunctions could be taken as literal for the ancient Hebrews, who were in fact enjoined by God to practice the rituals listed in Leviticus. Such literal understandings, however, were not "the thing itself," which was made manifest only with the coming of Jesus: the ontological status of Old Testament ritual injunctions has here been shifted.[143]

A few examples of ascetic authors' "status readjustment" of particular texts will here suffice. Augustine, for example, is prone to change the level of authority, the "status," of Hebrew ritual law in accordance with the "difference of times": details that were designated "commandments" or "precepts" for the ancient Israelites are now reassigned to the nonlegal category of "testimonies" that point forward to Christianity, a move obviously dependent on earlier typological exegesis. Among the items that Augustine relegates to this category are keeping the Feast of Tabernacles, eschewing garments made of wool and linen mixed, and not plowing with an ox and an ass together.[144] Likewise, Augustine relegates God's injunction to "reproduce and multiply" from the category of commandment to that of remedy.[145] Through such readjustment of a text's authoritative

[143] It is worth noting that this typological technique differs from Origen's allegorizing, in which details of Old Testament law are taken "really" to have signified something "other" than the literal meaning of the text all along, even for spiritually minded Israelites. For an interesting discussion of the differences between typology and allegory, see Dawson, *Allegorical Readers*, p. 15.

[144] Augustine, *Contra Faustum* 6.9 (CSEL 25, 300–301).

[145] Augustine, *De bono viduitatis* 8.11 (CSEL 41, 317).

"status," the words could be saved as holy writ, yet incorporated into a new scheme of values that drastically changed their import.[146]

Augustine, however, unlike his colleagues of more rigorous ascetic persuasion, refrains from wedging too sharp a "difference of times" between the Old and the New Dispensations. Not only does he strive to preserve the holiness of Old Testament law as much as possible; he also wishes to discourage overly utopian estimations of the freedoms allowed in the Christian present. It is only in the Heavenly City to come that we will need no legal restraints upon us: here and now, the flesh still "lusts against the spirit" (Gal. 5:17).[147] Explicating the story of the Flood in Genesis 6, Augustine reminds his audience that men and women entered Noah's ark separately and remained so while in it; only when they left the ark did the sexes walk together. According to Augustine, the story suggests that while we are still in the ecclesiastical "ark" that floats on the waters of the world, we must heed rules that restrain sexual mingling; only in the new age of the resurrection, not in the Christian present, will these regulations be suspended.[148] Here, Christians are brought back to the realm of "the Law," whose supersession lies not in the Christian present, but only in the otherworldly future. Augustine's interpretation stands as a warning to Christians against displaying unwarranted pride at their imagined superiority to the rule-ridden Israelites.

Augustine's line of argumentation in this instance, however, was not the one advanced by his more ascetically inclined colleagues. For them, the proposition that certain deeds approved in olden times were unsuitable for the present—the axiology that undergirds typological interpretation for the church fathers—is far from suggesting a neutral attitude toward ancient Israelite practice. The ancient Israelites are not just to be construed as "different," but as morally inferior. "Difference" conveys a judgment of better and worse.

If from the time of Durkheim, ritual has been seen as a marker of "difference"—and in recent studies, as the creator of "difference"[149]—then the "asceticizing of ritual" might well be expected to carry its own hierarchical scheme of differentiation. The means by which a ritualized agent was produced through schemes of opposition and hierarchization (to use Cather-

[146] E.g., Augustine might have liked the maxim of Roland Barthes: "A text's unity lies not in its origin but in its destination" (*Image, Music, Text*, trans. Stephen Heath [New York: Hill and Wang, 1977], p. 148). For a discussion of ways in which the "alterity" of past literature was overcome by Roman writers, see Irvine, *The Making of Textual Culture*, p. 86.

[147] Augustine, *De spiritu et littera* 59 (33); *De natura et gratia* 61 (53); 64 (54); *De nuptiis et concupiscentia* 1.5.4. As Augustine puts it in his controversy with the Donatists, in the New Covenant are old men (*De baptismo* 1.15.24).

[148] Augustine, *Contra Faustum* 12.21 (CSEL 25, 349–50).

[149] Bell, *Ritual Theory*, p. 104.

ine Bell's language)[150] were easily transferred to the ascetic subject. As Jerome wrote to Eustochium upon the occasion of her ascetic renunciation, "Learn from me a holy arrogance: know that you are better than all of them."[151] Or in Athanasius' pithy phrase, "Where there is free will, there is inferiority."[152] Such language does not promote "the priesthood of all believers," but rather an ascetic caste who could appeal to ancient Hebrew priests and ritual for textual ballast in the creation of its own distinctive—and distinguishing—ethic.

[150] Ibid., pp. 106–7.

[151] Jerome, *ep.* 22.16 (CSEL 54, 163).

[152] Athanasius, *ep. 1 ad virgines* (CSCO 150 = Scriptores Coptici 19, 84; ET, Brakke, p. 281).

CHAPTER NINE

The Exegesis of Divorce

I: Introduction

The Fathers' interpretations of the Biblical divorce texts reveal with particular clarity the problems that beset ascetically minded Christian authors confronted with a Scriptural corpus that, on the surface, provided dubious support for their programs of renunciation. Yet Scriptural passages could, with imaginative assistance, be harnessed to carry a more strict ascetic agenda. The "supplementariness" of Biblical texts appears to have encouraged manifold exegeses of divorce: in this case, bodies, not interpretations, were restrained.

I wish to explore several questions in this chapter. First, I ask how the Fathers "managed" the diversity of texts pertaining to divorce: the texts of Roman law in relation to Scripture; of the Old Testament in relation to the New; of the Mosaic law in relation to other parts of the Old Testament (how does Deut. 24:1–4 square with Gen. 2:21–24?); of Jesus in relation to Paul; of some sayings of Jesus in relation to other sayings (how can the injunction to "leave one's wife" in Luke 18:29 be aligned with the antidivorce sayings?); of Paul in relation to "Paul" (how to square I Cor. 7 with the later New Testament literature that the Fathers attributed to Paul?). I do not here attempt to cover all the Fathers' discussions of the divorce texts—more will be found in chapter 10 below[1]—but I will rather focus on the interpretive problems that were occasioned by the uneasy relationship of various Biblical texts.

It was perhaps a simple task to set Roman law against Christian teaching, but did a patristic interpreter wish to set one portion of the Bible over against another? The battle to "save" Hebrew Scripture for the Church had been fierce, and in Augustine's era, Manichean exegetes such as Faustus—a skilled deconstructionist—still threatened Catholic affirmation of the Old Testament with their mockery of the patriarchs' sexual

[1] Especially important is Origen's discussion of divorce in the fragments of his *Commentary on I Corinthians* and Jerome's appropriation of that discussion, both of which are detailed in chap. 10.

exploits and the peculiarities of Mosaic ritual law.[2] How could ascetically minded church fathers extract a unified message from the diverse Scriptural texts so as to avoid bringing charges of heresy upon themselves, while effectively countering the scathing critiques of Scripture's detractors? The Old Testament texts pertaining to divorce tested the Fathers' hermeneutical ingenuity.

A second conceptual problem lay in the Bible's appeal to the metaphor of "one flesh" or "one body" in its marital rhetoric. This phrase was borrowed from Genesis 2:24 by Jesus (or, alternatively, by the editor of Matthew), developed by Paul in I Corinthians 6 for his attack on Christians' frequenting of prostitutes, and allegorized by the author of Ephesians. By late Christian antiquity, however, appeals to "one flesh" were deemed embarrassingly carnal in their emphasis, for even Roman law by that era held that consent, not sexual intercourse, stood as the defining feature of marriage. (Consider the definition attributed to the jurist Ulpian: "nuptias enim non concubitus sed consensus facit.")[3] And within the Christian

[2] For examples, see especially Augustine, *Contra Faustum*, books 19 and 22.

[3] "Not sleeping together, but consent, makes marriage": attributed to Ulpian in *Digest* 35.1.15 and 50.17.30. The anonymous author (Pseudo-Chrysostom) of the *Opus Imperfectum in Matthaeum*, commenting on Matt. 19:9, repeats this standard legal definition: "Matrimonium enim non facit coitus, sed voluntas," therefore concluding that marriage is not dissolved by "the separation of the body" but by "the separation of the will" (PG 56, 802). Earlier twentieth-century legal historians often understood phrases such as Ulpian's as interpolations that echo the sentiments of the church fathers, or as attempts to distinguish marriage from concubinage. See especially Hans Julius Wolff, "Doctrinal Trends in Postclassical Roman Marriage Law," *Zeitschrift der Savigny-Stiftung für Rechtsgeschichte*, Romanistische Abteilung, 67 (1950): 296–99. Wolff concludes that the notion of "consent" may have been stressed in postclassical Roman law not to overrule the importance of sexual union, but to emphasize that marriage could be concluded informally, without documentation (pp. 291–94). Contemporary legal scholars, such as Charles Donahue, do not think that the phrase is an interpolation but place it in its context, given in *Digest* 35.1.15 (when is a woman considered a "wife," for purposes of receiving a legacy?) (private correspondence of August 7, 1986).

For discussions of Roman marriage law and especially of "consent," see Riccardo Orestano, *La struttura giuridica del matrimonio romano dal diritto classico al diritto giustinianeo* (Milano: Antonio Giuffrè, 1951), vol. I; idem, "Alcune considerazioni sui rapporti fra matrimonio cristiano e matrimonio romano nell' età postclassica," in *Scritti di diritto romano in honore di Contardo Ferrini*, ed. Gian Gualberto Archi (Milano: Ulrico Hoepli, 1946), pp. 345–82; Emilio Albertario, *Studi di diritto romano* (Milano: Antonio Giuffrè, 1933) vol. I, esp. chaps. 10–12; Percy Ellwood Corbett, *The Roman Law of Marriage* (Oxford: Clarendon, 1930): Jean Gaudemet, *Sociétés et mariage* (Strasbourg: Cerdic-Publications, 1980) (Gaudemet's collected essays on the topic); idem, "Tendances nouvelles de la legislation familiale au IVe siècle," in *Transformations et conflits au IVe ap. J.-C.* Antiquitas I, 29 (Bonn: Rudolf Habelt Verlag, 1978), pp. 187–207; (Kunkel), "Matrimonium," *Realencyclopädie der classischen Altertumswissenschaft* 14.2 (1930): 2259–86; (Albertario), "Matrimonio," *Enciclopedia Italiana* 22 (1934): 580–81; Josef

camp, the belief enthusiastically endorsed by Augustine, that Joseph and Mary had pledged themselves in a genuine, indeed an ideal, marriage although they never engaged in sexual intercourse, provided further support for a more "spiritualized" understanding of marriage. But, on this understanding, if sex does not "make" marriage, how can sex (i.e., adultery) "break" it, as the common reading of Matthew 19:9 and 5:32 suggests? The dilemma posed by these questions underlies the sometimes incoherent approaches of the Fathers to the issue of divorce.

II: Roman Law and Christian Law

The issue of divorce was one on which the views of Christian leaders ran headlong against the freedoms granted by imperial law. If marriage was based on consent and was increasingly categorized as a species of contract in Roman jurisprudence, why did early Christian writers believe that the marital contract could not be dissolved, even if the two parties consented?[4] To what texts could they appeal to frame a notion of marriage that rested on volitional (i.e., nonphysical) factors, yet that would, in contrast to Roman law, pro-

---

Huber, *Der Ehekonsens im Römischen Recht, Studien zu seinem Begriffsgehalt in der Klassik und zur Frage seines Wandels in der Nachklassik*, Analecta Gregoriana 204 (Roma: Università Gregoriana Editrice, 1977); Wolff, "Doctrinal Trends," pp. 261–319; Alan Watson, *The Law of Persons in the Later Roman Republic* (Oxford: Clarendon, 1967), esp. chaps. 1–7; A. Esmein, *Le Mariage en droit canonique*, 3rd ed. (Paris: Librairie du Recueil Sirey, 1929); Giuseppe d'Ercole, "Il consenso degli sposi e la perpetuità del matrimonio nel diritto romano e nei Padri della Chiesa," *Studia et documenta historiae et iuris* 5 (1939): 18–75. Newer studies in English include Susan Treggiari, *Roman Marriage: Iusti Coniuges from the Time of Cicero to the Time of Ulpian* (Oxford: Clarendon, 1992); Suzanne Dixon, *The Roman Family* (Baltimore/London: Johns Hopkins University Press, 1992), esp. chaps. 2 and 3; Antti Arjava, *Women and Law in Late Antiquity* (Oxford: Clarendon, 1996), pp. 29–41, 158–60; and the collection of essays in *Marriage, Divorce and Children in Ancient Rome*, ed. Beryl Rawson (Oxford: Clarendon, 1991). For a summary of notions of "consent" in Roman and Christian marriage law, see Elizabeth A. Clark, " 'Adam's Only Companion': Augustine and the Early Christian Debate on Marriage," *Recherches Augustiniennes* 21 (1986), esp. 158–62. Exploring what a young woman's "consent" might (or might not) mean in Roman patriarchal society is Susan Treggiari, "Consent to Roman Marriage: Some Aspects of Law and Reality," *Echos du monde classique/Classical Views*, n.s. 1 (1982): 34–44.

[4] See discussions of the contractual nature of Roman marriage, especially as pertaining to betrothal and dowry, in Jane F. Gardner, *Women in Roman Law and Society* (Bloomington/Indianapolis: Indiana University Press, 1991), pp. 45–57; Treggiari, *Roman Marriage*, chaps. 3–4, esp. pp. 146–47; on how dowry came to be seen as a form of "contract," see Corbett, *Roman Law*, pp. 94–95 and chap. 6. Wolff ("Doctrinal Trends," p. 299) points out that in fifth- and sixth-century contract law, notions of "consent" became especially prominent and influenced marriage law.

vide a strong barricade against the permissibility of divorce? The most detailed patristic exposition of divorce was developed by Augustine, who explained that marriage as a *sacramentum* implied that *nothing* could break the marital pact: for Christians there could *be* no divorce as Roman law understood it.

Roman law provided an easy foil—conceptually, if not in practice—for the church fathers in their exegesis of divorce. Although Constantine (whether or not motivated by Christian concern) had attempted to limit the grounds on which a husband or a wife could initiate divorce,[5] his divorce legislation was undone by Julian at midcentury. In any event, no emperor of the fourth century, Constantine included, touched the right to divorce by mutual consent.[6] The difference between the freedom for divorce permitted under Roman law and the Christian rejection of such "laxity" is rhetorically expressed by Jerome in describing (and attempting to excuse) the divorce of his friend Fabiola: "The laws of Caesar are different . . . from the laws of Christ; Papinianus commands one thing, our own Paul another."[7] For a Christian to take refuge in the greater freedom for divorce allowed by civil law, Ambrose argues, renders the sin of divorce and remarriage even greater, and he posits the perhaps ethically dubious position that a hidden adultery would be preferable to an open one that

[5] Constantine's divorce legislation is found in *Codex Theodosianus* 3.16.1: a woman may initiate divorce only if her husband is guilty of homicide, sorcery, or destroying tombs; the husband may initiate divorce if he charges a wife's adultery, sorcery, or procuring. See discussion in Judith Evans-Grubbs, "Constantine and Imperial Legislation on the Family," in *The Theodosian Code: Studies in the Imperial Law of Late Antiquity*, ed. Jill Harries and Ian Wood (London: Duckworth, 1993), esp. pp. 125–29. Evans-Grubbs disputes older views which held that Christian ideals directly inspired all of Constantine's legislation on marriage and divorce (such as can be found in Michel Humbert's *Le Remariage à Rome: Etude d'histoire juridique et sociale* [Milano: Dott. A. Guiffrè Editore, 1972], pp. 360–71). For a discussion of divorce and the Roman family, see Keith R. Bradley, *Discovering the Roman Family: Studies in Roman Social History* (New York/Oxford: Oxford University Press, 1991), chap. 6.

[6] The first evidence that divorce by mutual consent was prohibited by imperial legislation comes from 542 (Justinian) and this legislation was repealed by his successor (*Novella* 117.10, overturned by Justin, *Novella* 140 of 566). See Evans-Grubbs, "Constantine," p. 128; Julian's decree repealing Constantine's limitations on divorce is no longer extant but is known from Ambrosiaster, *Liber quaestionum Veteris et Novum Testamenti* 115.12 (CSEL 50, 322); also see Henri Crouzel, *L'Eglise primitive face au divorce*, Théologie Historique 13 (Paris: Beauchesne, 1971), p. 128. Now see Evans-Grubbs' *Law and Family in Late Antiquity: Constantine's Legislation on Marriage* (Oxford: Oxford University Press, 1995).

[7] Jerome, *ep.* 77.3 (CSEL 56, 39). Papinianus was a celebrated early-third-century jurist. Gregory of Nazianzus declines to adjudicate a case in which a father was trying to force his daughter to divorce her husband, and appeals to the notion that "our" (i.e., Christian) law differs from Roman law on the issue of divorce: *ep.* 144 (PG 37, 248).

appealed to Roman law's permission of divorce.[8] Although occasionally a church father might attempt to rescue the less rigorous provisions of Roman divorce law (Tertullian, for example, argues that divorce legislation was a late addition even to Roman law),[9] the usual patristic view set Christian teaching firmly against the Roman tolerance of divorce.

Another feature of Roman divorce law criticized by many Fathers—Ambrosiaster excepted[10]—was that it prescribed different standards for men and for women, greater sexual freedom being allowed to men. Thus, for example, Basil of Caesarea expresses unease that men may leave their wives if the latter are unchaste, but that "custom" encourages women to remain with adulterous husbands. This is not the Biblical view, Basil concedes, but he appears unwilling to express stronger disapproval of societal mores. After all, Basil reasons, if Paul encourages women to remain with unbelieving husbands (I Cor. 7:13), why should they not stay with fornicating ones?[11] The Fathers usually argued that in theory Christianity upheld a higher standard that rendered men and women equal in regard to sexual conduct. But, as is evident, they raised the new "single standard" of sexual behavior in the direction of greater rigor, that is, men were to be bound by the restraints placed on women, rather than allowing women to "descend" to the freer sexual mores tolerated in males.[12]

III: Old Testament and New Testament on Divorce

If the texts of Roman civil law were, largely, something to be argued against, the texts of Scripture presented a far more difficult case: they could not be dismissed so easily without provoking cries of "heresy." First, was there not a problem with prohibiting divorce when God himself was seen as a (metaphorical) "divorcer"? Had he not, Origen asks, put away his former wife, the Synagogue, for her "fornications"? And had God not found a second wife, the Church, for his Son, who had left his heavenly Father, as well as his Mother (i.e.,

[8] Ambrose, *De Abrahamo* 1.7.59 (CSEL 32.1, 541), echoed by Chromatius of Aquileia, *Tract. in Matt.* 10.1 (PL 20, 347).

[9] Tertullian, *De monogamia* 9.8 (CCL 2, 1242).

[10] Ambrosiaster, *Comm. I Cor.* 7:11 (CSEL 81.2, 74–75): "the man is not bound by the law as the woman is, for 'the man is the head of the woman' " [I Cor. 11:3]). See discussion in Crouzel, *L'Eglise*, p. 269. For further discussion of Ambrosiaster's "misogyny," see the illuminating article by David Hunter, "The Paradise of Patriarchy: Ambrosiaster on Woman as (Not) God's Image," *Journal of Theological Studies*, n.s. 43 (1992): 447–69.

[11] Basil of Caesarea, *ep.* 188.9 (Loeb III:34–38).

[12] For example, Jerome, *ep.* 77.3; Augustine, *De serm. Domini in monte* 1.16.49; *Serm.* 9.3.3; *De coniugiis adulterinis* 2.7.8.

the "Jerusalem above" of Gal. 4:26) to be joined to his new wife, as Ephesians 5:31–32 proclaims? Did not Isaiah 50:1—"Thus says the Lord, 'Where is your mother's bill of divorce with which I put her away?' "—clearly indicate that God had "divorced" the Jews for their "unseemly" behavior in clamoring for Jesus' execution? The Jews, God's "first wife," had joined herself to the devil.[13] Origen finds a useful example in the story of Hosea, which he sees as an allegory of God's relationship with Israel. Hosea cast off his harlotrous wife but afterward, at God's command, took her back (Hos. 1:2; 2:2; 2:19), just as God could cast off the "hardened" Israelites (cf. Rom. 11:25–26) but later take *them* back.[14] God's "divorce" of the Israelites, his "first wife," is thus not seen as permanent, but as temporary and remedial—a characteristic Origenist understanding of divine chastisement. God's "divorce" of the Israelites, however, cannot be taken as a sanction for human divorce. Here, metaphors fail to sustain the rigor of Christian marital ethics.

Likewise, ascetically inclined patristic writers such as Basil of Caesarea could cast Jesus in the role of a divorcing husband to threaten consecrated virgins, "brides of Christ," who either had sexually strayed or appeared to be on the verge of doing so; they were the adulteresses whom Paul chastised in Romans 7:3. Yet here, too, correction was in order, for Christ had betrothed the virgin to himself "forever" (cf. Hos. 2:19). Although (in a nice example of gender-bending exegesis) the fallen virgin has taken "the members of Christ" and made them "members of a harlot" (I Cor. 6:15), she still may repent. She yet may imitate the Prodigal Son of Luke 15, return home, and hear her father's (i.e., God's) warm welcome, "This my daughter was dead and has come to life."[15] Virgins who had not fallen, however, were also to be warned that Christ their Bridegroom would write them a bill of divorce if he perceived even one act of unfaithfulness on his spouse's part.[16] As Basil of Ancyra assures his readers, Christ does not wish to divorce his virgin. Any man who attempts to corrupt Christ's "bride" should be told, "Leave her alone!" But if she deserts her Spouse for another man, she will fall into "fire and death."[17] Here, although Christ threatens "divorce," he does not wish to make use of his prerogative. Such metaphoric ascriptions of "divorce" to God and to Christ, however, seem to have played little part in discussions regarding the prohibition or allowance of divorce for Christians. A man's freedom to divorce as granted in Old Testament law is here metaphorically reassigned to Christ's relation

[13] Origen, *Comm. Matt.* 14.17 (GCS 40, 325–26).

[14] Origen, *Comm. Matt.* 14.20 (GCS 40, 333).

[15] Basil of Caesarea, *ep.* 46 (Loeb I:292, 294, 296, 306, 308, 310).

[16] (Anonymous), *ep.de virginitate* (= *Ad Claudiam*) 12 (CSEL 1, 241).

[17] Basil of Ancyra, *De virginitate* 42 (Vaillant, p. 45).

with the consecrated virgin; this freedom, however, does not extend to husbands in the "real world."

As for human divorce, the church fathers wrestled with the divergences between Old Testament law and Jesus' teaching, as they understood them. Moses' allowance of divorce was problematic to Christians both in itself (Deut. 24 suggests that the only restriction on divorce was the provision requiring the husband to deliver a written notice), and in that it was unilateral (only the husband could take the initiative). Origen's answer to this dilemma was blunt: the law of divorce in Deuteronomy 24 is "not from the Lord," but represents Moses' merely human opinion.[18] Here, the question of whose "voice" is more authoritative comes into play—and Jesus decisively wins. The Fathers frequently note the difference between the Law and the Gospel on the issue of divorce—whether more discreetly, as by Gregory Nazianzen,[19] or more stridently, as by Tertullian, who brashly claims that the New Law regarding divorce "abrogates" the Old.[20] Few church fathers write as bluntly to this point as Ambrose: any Christian who appeals to the freer divorce legislation of Deuteronomy 24 "speaks like a Jew," not acknowledging the great divide between Moses' concession and God's will.[21]

Yet even when the Fathers avoided such anti-Jewish insinuations, Jesus' treatment of Deuteronomy 24 in Matthew 19 enabled an interpretation that "saved" the text while simultaneously discarding it: if Moses' provision for divorce was occasioned by the Israelites' "hardness of heart," this condition should no longer obtain for Christians whose hearts have experienced the softening power of the Holy Spirit. The phrase "hardness of heart" stimulated the imaginations of patristic exegetes, especially those associated with the so-called Antioch school, to offer an explanation for the Mosaic allowance of divorce. According to these interpreters, Moses feared that irate husbands would murder their wives if they were forced to keep hateful ones, and hence he allowed the lesser evil of divorce rather than risk the greater sin of homicide.[22] The concession that Moses here

[18] Origen, *Comm. I Cor.* 7:8–12 (Jenkins [1908], p. 505); cf. *Comm. Matt.* 14.18 (GCS 40, 327–28).

[19] Gregory of Nazianzus, *Or.* 37.8 (PG 36, 292).

[20] Tertullian, *De monogamia* 14.4 (CCL 2, 1249).

[21] Ambrose, *Exp. Luc.* 8.7 (CCL 14, 300). For a summary of Jewish positions on divorce in the early Christian era, see Geza Vermes, "Bible and Midrash: Early Old Testament Exegesis," in *The Cambridge History of the Bible*, vol. I, *From the Beginnings to Jerome*, ed. P. R. Ackroyd and C. F. Evans (Cambridge: Cambridge University Press, 1970), pp. 206–7.

[22] John Chrysostom, *De virginitate* 41.1 (SC 125, 236); *Mulier alligata* 2 (PG 51, 219); *Hom. 17 Matt.* 4 (PG 57, 259–60); Theodore of Mopsuestia, *Comm. Mal.* 2:14–16 (PG 66, 616–17); Theodoret of Cyrrhus, *Interp. Mal.* 2:14–16 (PG 81, 1973, 1976); (Anonymous), *Opus imperfectum in Matt.* 19:8 (PG 56, 801); Jerome, *In Math.* 3 (19:8) (CCL 77, 166).

grants (but did not genuinely approve, according to John Chrysostom)[23] could be compared to the concession that Paul made for marriage (perpetual virginity was thus not to be forced on Christians)[24] and for the remarriage of widows who suffered "weakness of flesh."[25] Yet commentators eager to emphasize the unity of the two Testaments, such as John Chrysostom, press the meaning of Deuteronomy 24:2–4 (that a man may not remarry a wife he has dismissed if she married another in the interim). To Chrysostom, these verses signal that Moses' legislation was drawing closer to that of Christ, and the "closely read" detail he singles out to exemplify that unity focuses on the "stain" that the remarrying wife has acquired.[26]

Jesus' further claim in Matthew 19 that "from the beginning it was not so" (i.e., that there was no provision for divorce at the time of creation), and his citation of Genesis 2:24 ("two in one flesh"), offered further openings for the disparagement of the teaching of Deuteronomy 24: the "Moses" of Genesis 2 who promoted marital union could be pitted against the "Moses" of Deuteronomy who facilitated divorce.[27] According to John Chrysostom, God's intention at creation, superior to any later and merely human concession, should control the interpretation of all other Old Testament divorce legislation.[28] Ambrose calls the original decree of God in Genesis 2 a "law of nature,"[29] higher than the laws of mere mortals such as the all-too-human Moses of Deuteronomy 24. Jesus' more stringent teaching on divorce could thus be aligned with that of "Moses" in Genesis 2, trumping that of Deuteronomy 24. "Bone of bone and flesh of flesh" could stand as a graphic antidivorce teaching: "one rib, one wife," Jerome intoned, plagiarizing Tertullian.[30] Besides, if God had willed for there to be divorce, he would have formed more than one woman when he made the first man, John Chrysostom ingeniously reasons.[31]

[23] John Chrysostom, *Mulier alligata* 2 (PG 51, 219–20).

[24] Irenaeus, *Adversus haereses* 4.15.2 (PG 7, 1013–14).

[25] Tertullian, *De monogamia* 14.2 (CCL 2, 1249).

[26] John Chrysostom, *Mulier alligata* 2 (PG 51, 220).

[27] Augustine, *Contra Adimantum* 3 (CSEL 25, 118–22). The grave difficulties the various divorce texts caused for early Jewish exegesis is noted by Vermes, "Bible and Midrash," pp. 205–7. Vermes comments that the law of divorce is "perhaps the example *par excellence* of the necessity for halakhic midrash" (p. 205).

[28] John Chrysostom, *Mulier alligata* 2 (PG 51, 220).

[29] Ambrose, *De Abrahamo* 1.2.8 (CSEL 32.1, 508); cf. Jerome, *Adversus Iovinianum* 1.18.

[30] Jerome, *epp.* 79.10 (CSEL 55, 99); 123.11 (CSEL 56, 84); cf. *Adversus Iovinianum* 1.14; alluding to Tertullian, *De monogamia* 4; *Ad uxorem* 1.2. For Jerome's borrowing of such phrases from Tertullian in his ascetic writings, see Claudio Micaeli, "L'influsso di Tertulliano su Girolamo: le opere sul matrimonio e le seconde nozze," *Augustinianum* 19 (1979): 415–29, esp. p. 424.

[31] John Chrysostom, *Hom. 62 Matt.* 1 (PG 58, 597); *Mulier alligata* 2 (PG 51, 220).

A second exegetical move to bring Moses' divorce teaching into greater conformity with that of Jesus is provided by Augustine, customarily more anxious than Jerome to stress the harmony between the two Testaments. Thus Augustine seeks to ameliorate the divorce law of Deuteronomy 24 and align it with Jesus' teaching. He locates the point that enables retrieval of the Mosaic legislation in an imaginative speculation concerning Moses' motivation and intention in promulgating this law. According to Augustine, Deuteronomy 24 required the husband to provide a certificate of divorce in the hope that during the intervening period in which the document was being drawn up, his rash anger would subside and he would decide against divorce. In Augustine's construction, the scribes responsible for composing the divorce certificate would prudently advise the irate husband on the advantages of *not* separating. When Jesus repeated the Deuteronomic verses pertaining to the bill of divorce, Augustine argues, he wished to show his Jewish audience Moses' real intent, namely, that wives should not be divorced at all.[32] If nothing else, imagining that his divorced wife could freely marry another man would serve as a dissuasion for the husband: if "rational" argument fails, sexual jealousy piques him to retain exclusive possession of his spouse.[33]

Yet Augustine was not always so conciliatory toward the Old Testament divorce texts. He also could retreat to the standard explanation offered by the Latin Fathers, namely, that a great "difference in times" separated the standards appropriate for the ancient Israelites from those suitable for present-day Christians: behavior permissible to them is not to "us."[34] Like a skillful pedagogue, God tailored his ethical demands to fit the progressive maturity of the human race. As the author of the anonymous treatise *De castitate* more pointedly framed the "difference in times" argument, the Old Testament, while offering examples of God's mighty works and predicting future wonders, has been entirely superseded as a rule for life.[35] This principle also enabled Jerome's claim that New Testament passages that seemingly uphold Old Testament marital mores (e.g., the Pastorals' recommendation of second marriage for young widows) could be explained away: in sanctioning remarriage, "Paul" was "becoming a Jew for the Jews."[36] Too strong a rejection of the Old Testament, however, left a

[32] Augustine, *Contra Faustum* 19.26; 19.29 (CSEL 25, 527–29, 532–33).

[33] Augustine, *De serm. Domini in monte* 1.14.39 (CCL 35, 43).

[34] By Augustine, the "difference in times" argument is used in such passages as *Serm.* 260; *De bono coniugali* 13.15; 15.17; by Jerome, in *Adversus Iovinianum* 1.18; *ep.* 123.13; *Adversus Helvidium* 22; *Comm. in Mal.* 2:14–16; by Ambrose, in *Exp. Luc.* 8.7. A notable and developed instance is found in Methodius, *Symposium* 1.2.16–18. For a discussion of the "difference in times" argument, see above, pp. 145–52.

[35] (Anonymous), *De castitate* 12.4 (PLS 1, 1491).

[36] Jerome, *Adversus Iovinianum* 1.15 (PL 23, 245), alluding to I Cor. 9:20.

Christian open to charges of "Manicheanism," as Jerome learned to his distress.[37] The Fathers thus learned to walk a narrow tightrope in explaining Old Testament passages that pertained to divorce.

The diverse Gospel texts on divorce contained yet another source of difficulty: they seemed to contradict each other. Matthew 5:32 and 19:9 in their received form contain the so-called exception clause (that *porneia* is the one ground on which a man may divorce his wife),[38] a clause not found in either Mark 10 or Luke 16.[39] How could the Gospels differ on such an important point? Moreover, Mark 10:11–12 explicitly refers to a wife's divorcing her husband, a female initiative not countenanced by the other Gospels.[40] Despite such differences, all these passages constrain the grounds for divorce. But if such is the case, how then are they to be squared with Jesus' teaching in Luke 14:26 (that a man should "hate" his wife) and in Luke 18:29b (that a wife is one of the items a man may abandon in order to receive a manifold reward and eternal life in the age to come)? These difficulties were duly noted by the Fathers, even while they rhetorically proclaim that there *are* no discrepancies: do the Manicheans imagine that Gospel contradicts Gospel, that Matthew 19 (*porneia* of

[37] Jerome, *Adversus Iovinianum*, 1.3 (PL 23, 223); *ep.* 49(48).2 (CSEL 54, 352).

[38] *Porneia* is here often understood as adultery (*moicheia*), but an argument for interpreting it as premarital unchastity (and aligning the saying with Old Testament regulations governing the marriages of priests) is made by Abel Isaksson, *Marriage and Ministry in the New Temple. A Study with Special Reference to Mt. 19:3–12 and I Cor. 11:3–16*, Acta Seminarii Neotestamentici Upsaliensis 24 (Lund: C. W. K. Gleerup; Copenhagen: Ejnar Munksgaard, 1965), pp. 132–39. For other interpretations of *porneia* (including "prostitution"), see Joseph Bonsirven, " 'Nisi fornicationis causa': Comment résoudre cette 'crux interpretum'?", *Recherches de science religieuse* 35 (1948): 451–64. Opting for "concubinage" is Alberto Vaccari, who gives a succinct catalog of possible interpretations (and what stands against each) in "La clausola sul divorzio in Matteo 5,32; 19,9," *Rivista biblica* 3 (1955): 97–119.

[39] See discussion in Henri Crouzel, "Le Texte patristique de Matthieu V.32 et XIX.9," in idem, *Mariage et divorce, celibat et caractère sacerdotaux dans l'église ancienne: Etudes diverses*, Etudes d'Histoire du Culte et des Institutions Chrétiennes II (Torino: Bottega d'Erasmo, 1982), pp. 111–13: the present form of Matt. 19:9 is not attested by any ecclesiastical writer before Nicea. Crouzel argues that the change apparently occurred in the first half of the fourth century, as the present wording appears in citations by church fathers later in the fourth century; also see essays 8 and 12 in the same volume. In essay 8 ("Le Remariage après séparation pour adultère selon les Pères latins"), Crouzel argues that Matt. 5:32a is the original form of the saying (p. 147). Some commentators hold that the Matthean clauses should *not* be taken as "exceptions" but as "inclusions": on this interpretation, the meaning becomes "not even for adultery." See Vaccari, "La clausola," pp. 99–100, for discussion.

[40] The fact that the editor of Mark includes the provision for female-initiated divorce (permitted in Roman but not in Jewish law) is standardly taken by authors of New Testament textbooks to signal the "Gentile" audience of the Gospel of Mark.

the wife as the only grounds for divorce) should be taken to stand against Luke 18 (an eternal reward for "leaving" a wife), Augustine asks in perhaps feigned indignation?[41]

Could such passages be construed to agree with each other? One inventive interpretation, noted above,[42] posited that the disciples in Matthew 19 were not expressing "Jewish" shock at Jesus' pronouncement ("In that case, it would be better for a man not to marry at all!"), but signaling their immediate agreement with his position. The sentence should thus be read as a simple declarative statement, not as an exclamation of disbelief: "If such is the case of a man with his wife, it is *not* expedient to marry" (Matt. 19:10).[43] In this rendition of events, constructed entirely by a change of "tone," Jesus' ascetic message could be taken as finding a ready reception because at least some Jews (i.e., Jesus' disciples) understood it as compatible with their own sexual mores: a man could not be called to "leave" his wife for the sake of the Kingdom if he never had one.

A second option, found in the works of Cyril of Alexandria, conflates Paul's provision for a Christian married to a nonbeliever to separate (I Cor. 7:15) with Jesus' allowance of divorce for a wife's sexual straying (Matt. 19:9). Cyril then interprets other Gospel passages on the renunciation of family via these two allegedly permissible grounds for divorce. Thus, when Luke 18:29 enjoins the "leaving" of wife and family, Cyril declares that such a separation is allowable on the grounds of a wife's nonbelief or *porneia*. Yet Cyril assures his readers that such a separation is blessed: those who leave father will find their Father in heaven; leaving brothers, they will have the fraternity of Christ; leaving wife, they will enjoy the *sophia* of God above; and leaving mother, they will find the "Jerusalem above who is free and our mother" (Gal. 4:26).[44] The divorce texts are here construed as supporting ascetic renunciation by their alignment with the Gospel's antifamilial rhetoric. Similarly, divorce in order to pursue ascetic ends is also countenanced in a story reported by John Cassian: Theonas, a married man who wished to become a monk, argues that if Moses allows divorce for "hardness of heart" (Matt. 19:8), so Christ should allow it for the sake of chastity, and cites Luke 18:29 (the leaving of wife and family) as a justifying Scripture.[45]

The general patristic strategy, however, was to restrain possible implications of the injunction of Luke 18 to "leave one's wife." The injunction

[41] Augustine, *Contra Adimantum* 3 (CSEL 25, 119).

[42] See above, p. 142, for this text as an example of "changing tone."

[43] Jerome, *Adversus Iovinianum* 1.12 (PL 23, 238–39); Ambrose, *De virginitate* 6.29 (PL 16, 287).

[44] Cyril of Alexandria, *Comm. Luc.* 18:29 (PG 72, 860–61).

[45] John Cassian, *Conlationes* 21.9 (SC 64, 83). Cassian hastens to add that the story should not be taken to recommend

was not to be taken as Jesus' recommendation of divorce. Various intertexts were found that would smooth over any seeming discrepancies. Thus in Augustine's consideration of the Lucan passage, he notes that the only justification for a man's "leaving" is found in Paul's words in I Corinthians 7:12–15, concerning a Christian's separation from a nonbeliever. Augustine conflates the two passages and interprets them to mean that a Christian husband, if married to a nonbelieving wife and faced with the choice of either "leaving" her or "leaving" Christ, must choose separation from the woman.[46] Nowhere in his exegesis of Luke 18, however, does Augustine hint that he grasps the eschatological dimension of the saying or that its import must be considered in relation to Jesus' teaching on divorce as noted in Matthew 5 and 19. And in his *Commentary on the Sermon on the Mount*, Augustine argues that the sexual separation of spouses by mutual consent cannot be considered "divorce": the husband still has the wife "according to the spirit, but not according to the flesh," just as Paul counseled men in I Corinthians 7:29 to have their wives "as if not."[47] "Leaving," in other words, could be construed in ways that did not betoken divorce.

Jerome, less concerned than Augustine to uphold the indelibility of marriage, argues that the injunction to "leave all" (including wives) in Luke 18 serves as the explanation for why the Apostle Peter no longer had a wife after he became a Christian,[48] namely, he had left her. Nonetheless, it is interesting to note that even Jerome and Ambrose, who do not hesitate to counsel young people to defy their parents for the sake of ascetic living, are considerably more chary when dealing with the separation of married couples "for the sake of religion."[49]

The problem of the Gospels' divorce texts is compounded when Paul's writings are factored in, for in I Corinthians 7, Paul assumes (against the wording of Matthew and Luke) that a wife has the right to initiate divorce from her husband, as indeed she did in Roman law of Paul's time. Moreover, Paul in I Corinthians 7 is silent concerning the "exception" clause of Matthew 19:9 ("except for *porneia*"), mentioning divorce only in the

---

divorce (21.10).

[46] Augustine, *ep.* 157.31–32 (CSEL 44, 479–80).

[47] Augustine, *De serm. Domini in monte* 2.14.39 (CCL 35, 43).

[48] Jerome, *Adversus Iovinianum* 1.26 (PL 23, 256–57). It is interesting that Jerome's translation of I Cor. 9:5 opts for the reading "wife as a sister," thus implying that Peter no longer had sexual relations with his spouse. The evidence that Peter had once had a wife comes from Mark 1:30, which refers to Peter's mother-in-law.

[49] For examples of children being urged to leave their parents for the sake of religion (with frequent reference to Jesus' behavior), see Ambrose, *Exp. Luc.* 6.36; cf. 6.38; 7.33–34; 7.136; 7.146; 7.201; *Exhortatio virginitatis* 5.32; *De virginibus* 1.12.63–64.

context of an "unbelieving spouse" who does not wish to remain with his or her Christian partner (I Cor. 7:12–13). How could these discrepancies between the Gospels and Paul be accounted for? How could the texts be read to provide a near-seamless teaching whose import would be rigorous?

Ambrose, Jerome, John Chrysostom, and Augustine all wish to bring the texts from the Gospels into conformity with I Corinthians 7.[50] Jerome, for his part, claims that it is *because* Jesus forbade divorce in the Gospels that Paul writes in I Corinthians 7:1 that "it is good for a man not to touch a woman."[51] In this rendition, Paul sounds suspiciously like the disciples of Matthew 19, who conclude that if there can be no divorce except for fornication, marriage is "not expedient." Jerome's peculiar (and predictable) twist is to argue that whether with or without a provision for divorce, marriage is *never* "expedient."[52]

In his *Commentary on Matthew*, Jerome provides an intertextual reading of the divorce texts that supports his ascetic agenda. First, he appeals to Genesis 1–2 to explain and constrain the divorce teaching of Matthew 19: divorce was not part of God's original intention for women and men. He also appropriates Paul's distinction between human advice (*concilium*) and the command (*imperium*) of God, a move that allows him to assign Deuteronomy 24's permission for divorce to the lower realm of human "advice"—advice that can be safely discarded in light of the higher divine command. Yet Jerome is not content to leave these passages without lending them a distinctly ascetic coloration. Although he does not recommend that humans take "separation" upon themselves, he is quite willing for *God* to "separate" couples who, by mutual consent, live apart so as better to render religious service: having wives "as if not" (I Cor. 7:29) is highly applauded. Moreover, although Jesus had allegedly claimed that "not all" could receive his teaching on becoming a eunuch for the Kingdom of Heaven (Matt. 19:11–12), Jerome adds that the gift of continence is readily given to all who seek it, for "to all who seek is given" (Matt. 7:8 = Luke 11:10). Thus permission for human divorce has been superseded,

[50] A more extensive discussion of I Cor. 7:12–16 is found in chap. 10 below.

[51] Jerome, *Adversus Iovinianum* 1.7 (PL 23, 230).

[52] Jerome also interprets I Cor. 7:21 (whether a slave should use an opportunity to secure his freedom) in a way that sidesteps the issue of divorce. Since Jerome (and other authors) interpret the issues of circumcision/uncircumcision, slavery/freedom, eating meat/eating vegetables in I Corinthians all as relating to issues of marriage and sexuality, to read the verse on slavery as allowing the slave to "use the opportunity to secure freedom" might play into the hands of those would argue that married couples were encouraged to divorce. Jerome reads Paul's words as "use it rather" (*magis utere*), interpreting the phrase to mean "stay married"—but even within marriage, the wife may become a "sister" (i.e., sexual relation abandoned), thus providing "freedom." See *Adversus Iovinianum* 1.11 (PL 23, 236–37).

in effect, by the advocacy of "divine divorce" that enables chaste living—assisted by the power of human free will to master fate, *fortuna*, and sexual desire.[53]

Ambrose's treatment of the divorce texts differs from Jerome's in his grave concern for the problem of "pagan"-Christian marriage.[54] Here, it is tempting to speculate that Ambrose's divergent emphasis relates to his role as bishop of a societally important congregation in an imperial center, in contrast to Jerome's position as a reclusive scholarly monk in a backwater town in Palestine. Ambrose's most extensive discussion of the issue is found in his *Commentary on Luke*, in particular, his interpretation of Luke 16:18, "every one who divorces his wife and takes another commits adultery." Some people, Ambrose begins, mistakenly assume that because Matthew 19:6 appeals to God's joining of man and woman, that *all* marriage is from God. But this cannot be a correct inference, since Paul in I Corinthians 7:15 clearly believes that divorce between a Christian and an "unbeliever" is possible: thus a union between a Christian and a "pagan" is not marriage sanctioned by divine authority. The same conclusion can be reached, Ambrose posits, through an examination of Exodus 34:16 (an injunction to the Israelites against marrying "inhabitants of the land" who will encourage God's children to "play the harlot" after foreign deities). Only marriage between two Christians is true marriage sanctioned by God, according to Ambrose.

The consequences for Ambrose's understanding of divorce are clear: for a Christian to seek a divorce from a Christian spouse would imply that God was not the author of that union. Indeed, Ambrose freely concedes that the Mosaic divorce legislation was *not* written by God, for it stands against the sentiments of Genesis 2.[55] Since in Ephesians 5:27, the relation of Christ and the Church is figured in terms of human marriage, Christians should take heart that neither "philosophy" (a code for "paganism"?) nor "heretics" can separate the Lord and his Bride—and neither, by implication, should anything separate a Christian couple. Ambrose pointedly concludes his comments against divorce with the injunction, "What God has united, the Jew does not separate."[56] Interestingly, Ambrose nowhere here alludes to the Matthean "exception" clause. Rather, his whole discussion of divorce is framed by the context of Paul's advice on marriages between Christians and "unbelievers."

[53] Jerome, *In Math.* 3 (19:1ff.) (CCL 77, 166–68).

[54] For a commentary on Ambrose's views on marriage and divorce, see William Joseph Dooley, *Marriage According to St. Ambrose*, The Catholic University of America Press Studies in Christian Antiquity 11 (Washington, D.C.: Catholic University of America Press, 1948).

[55] Ambrose, *Exp. Luc.* 8.2; 8.4; 8.7–8 (CCL 14, 299, 300, 301).

[56] Ambrose, *Exp. Luc.* 8.9 (CCL 14, 301). For I Cor. 7:10–11 used as ballast against "the Jews," see Cyprian, *Ad Quiri-*

John Chrysostom discusses these passages in his attempt to explain that Paul's differentiation of his own voice from that of "the Lord's" in I Corinthians 7 does not signal any disagreement between the two: Paul could not endure speaking anything displeasing to Christ, Chrysostom argues. Although Paul knows Jesus' directives concerning the divorce of "believers," Jesus' silence concerning "unbelievers" leaves an opening for Paul's instruction in I Corinthians 7:12–13. Had not Jesus instructed the disciples that he would not reveal his complete teaching during his earthly life, but would leave some aspects for future disclosure (John 16:12)? Thus Paul, inspired by Christ, gives a recommendation for unbelievers in the I Corinthians passage. According to Chrysostom, when Paul distinguishes his own words from Christ's in I Corinthians 7:12, he points to a difference only in the time of delivery, not to a differing content.[57] Moreover, Chrysostom notes, when Paul finds a Christian man attached to a Gentile wife, he does not dissolve the marriage (I Cor. 7:12–13); Paul, like Jesus, knows that marriage makes the couple "two in one flesh" (Gen. 2:24; Matt. 19:5).[58] Unlike some other patristic writers, Chrysostom apparently believes that "mixed marriages" carry at least some degree of divine blessing.

Although Augustine comments in several places on the Biblical divorce texts,[59] his most extensive discussion—indeed, the most extensive discourse in all of patristic literature—is found in his treatise *On Adulterous Marriages.* Several themes Augustine develops in this treatise are already present in earlier works, such as *On Eighty-Three Diverse Questions.* In the latter treatise, Augustine aligns Jesus' teaching in the Matthean *porneia* clause with Paul's words on marriage between a "believer" and an "unbeliever," giving precedence to the "divine" speech of Jesus over the merely human opinion expressed by Paul that allowed for divorce in a situation of "mixed marriage." Augustine's central theoretical move in this short response is to interpret Paul's discussion of "paganism" as a code for "fornication,"[60] thus smoothing over the perceived difference between Jesus' teaching and Paul's: the "unbelief" of which Paul speaks is to be identified with the "fornication" that Jesus cites as the sole ground for a man's divorce. In another early work, his *Commentary on the Sermon on the Mount,*

---

num 3.90 (CSEL 3.1, 175).

[57] John Chrysostom, *De virginitate* 12.1; 12.2; 12.3 (SC 125, 128, 130).

[58] John Chrysostom, *Hom. 33 I Cor.* 5 (PG 61, 282).

[59] Augustine, *ep.* 157.31–32 (CSEL 44, 478–80); *Tract. in Ioan.* 9.2 (CCL 36, 91); *De diversis quaestionibus octoginta tribus* 83 (CCL 44A, 248–49).

[60] Augustine, *De diversis quaestionibus octoginta tribus* 83 (CCL 44A, 248). Cf. Gregory of Nazianzus, *Or.* 37.17 (PG 36, 301), where, conversely, the "adultery" of Matt. 19:9 is seen as "whoring concerning the Godhead." Real eunuchs should thus cut away "Arian impiety" and "Sabellian views" (*Or.* 37.17; 37.22 [PG 36, 301, 308]).

Augustine advances the same line: the Matthean *porneia* clause can be equated with "every sinful corruption," including "idolatry" (i.e., "paganism");[61] the "unbelief" mentioned by Paul is here subsumed into the rubric of the Matthean *porneia*. *Porneia* is, Augustine claims, "a generic and all-embracing" category[62]—a claim no doubt assisted by the frequent association in Old Testament texts of Israel's apostasy with "fornication."[63]

Augustine develops these themes, especially the puzzling discrepancies between the Gospels and Paul, in *On Adulterous Marriages*. In this treatise, Augustine responds to the interpretation of the divorce texts proposed by a certain Christian (presumably a cleric) named Pollentius.[64] Pollentius' general line of argument pressed for a wider interpretation of the grounds for divorce. Pollentius also sanctioned remarriage after divorce from an adulterous spouse, claiming that the latter could be understood as "dead," so that Paul's allowance of the remarriage of widows in I Corinthians 7:39 could apply to the case of divorce as well:[65] spousal adultery, just as spousal death, permits a second marriage.

Against Pollentius, Augustine argues that Paul's grudging acknowledgment of separation of Christian couples in I Corinthians 7:10–11 applies *only* to the situation in which one spouse committed adultery: there could be no other lawful grounds for separation. But if Paul here presumes the Matthean "exception clause," why does he not outrightly declare himself? Augustine replies, Paul did not need to add this point to his discussion "because it was so well known";[66] the "exception clause" is implicitly "in" the Pauline text.

Augustine's second move that aligns the Matthean texts with Paul's teaching is his now-familiar claim that the "unbelief" of which Paul speaks in I Corinthians 7:12–13 is actually "fornication in spirit," so that the *porneia* clause of Matthew 19 is present in these Pauline verses by covert allusion.[67] Moreover, Augustine also borrows an argument from the presumed equality of husband and wife in I Corinthians 7:4 to claim that even after a separation because of one partner's adultery, neither party can marry again without committing adultery. One spouse, in effect, cannot

[61] Augustine, *De serm. Domini in monte* 1.16.43 (CCL 35, 48); see discussion in Crouzel, *L'Eglise*, pp. 318–20.

[62] Augustine, *De serm. Domini in monte* 1.16.44–45 (CCL 35, 51, 52); cf. Cyprian, *De lapsis* 6: mixed marriage is a prostitution of a member of Christ.

[63] For example, Hos. 1–2; Ezek. 16; 23; Jer. 2:20–25; 3:1–3.

[64] For Pollentius' status and arguments about it, see Crouzel, *L'Eglise*, p. 337n. 52.

[65] Augustine, *De coniugiis adulterinis* 1.1.1; 1.7.7; 1.13.14; 2.2.2 (CSEL 41, 347–48, 353–54, 361–62, 383–84).

[66] Augustine, *De coniugiis adulterinis* 1.3.3; 1.7.7; 1.5.5 (CSEL 41, 350, 353–54, 351–52).

[67] Augustine, *De coniugiis adulterinis* 1.18.20 (CSEL 41, 367–68).

be deemed innocent while the other is pronounced guilty, for what applies to one, applies to both (I Cor. 7:4), since they both have "the same nature."[68] Such an interpretation, of course, functions as a strong dissuasion to divorce. The small differences in wording of the texts, Augustine claims, do not mean that their authors disagree. In any event, Paul really hopes, as I Corinthians 7:14–16 suggests, that the couple will stay together so that the "unbeliever" may eventually become a Christian.[69] In fact, the couple ought to stay together even in the case of adultery: just as Jesus forgave the adulterous woman of John 8, so a husband should forgive and take back an adulterous wife. Since the husband presumably has some sins to his account, Augustine counsels, he should not "cast stones" at a repentant wife.[70]

So strong is Augustine's aversion to remarriage that he not only prohibits it to the divorced, but also severely restricts the right of remarriage for widows to "the incontinent," the only ones to whom he thinks "Paul" conceded this right in I Timothy 5:14–15.[71] Elsewhere, Augustine bolsters his antidivorce stance through an interpretation of I Corinthians 7:27 ("Are you bound to a wife? Do not seek to be free. Are you free from a wife? Do not seek marriage") by claiming that the first part of the verse, taken as an antidivorce statute, is a "precept" and hence is completely binding, while the second clause, taken as an encouragement to celibate living, stands as a "counsel" for those of superior spirituality. Thus divorce is strictly forbidden, while the celibate life is encouraged.[72] In ways such

[68] Augustine, *De coniugiis adulterinis* 1.8.8 (CSEL 41, 355).

[69] Augustine, *De coniugiis adulterinis* 1.10.11; 1.13.14 (CSEL 41, 358–59, 362).

[70] Augustine, *De coniugiis adulterinis* 2.6.5; 2.7.6 (CSEL 41, 387–88). In the latter passage, Augustine adds the intriguing note that some were removing the John 8 story from Scripture on the grounds that women would infer from it that they could sin with impunity. Augustine's emphasis that the erring party should be taken back rather than divorced (and hence the "innocent" party allowed to remarry) appears to run counter to the evidence provided by the church fathers of the first few centuries. For the evidence and its assessment, see Pierre Nautin, "Divorce et remariage dans la tradition de l'église latine," *Recherches de science religieuse* 62 (1974): 9–46; Nautin argues against Henri Crouzel, who asserts in a variety of works that the Church never in early centuries allowed divorce with a provision for remarriage. See Crouzel, *Mariage et divorce*, esp. chaps. 3, 5, 8; and his *L'Eglise primitive face au divorce du premier au cinquième siècle*. One problem with the so-called Catholic position is that "divorce" or "repudiation" would not mean for Jesus or Paul what they meant in both Jewish and Roman law, that is, the freedom to remarry. For a blunt admission of this peculiarity, see Jacques Dupont, *Mariage et divorce dans L'Evangile: Matthieu 19, 3–12 et parallèles* (Bourges: Abbaye de Saint-André/Desclée de Brouwer, 1959), pp. 75–77, 221.

[71] Augustine, *De coniugiis adulterinis* 2.10.10; 2.14.14; 2.12.12 (CSEL 41, 393, 398–99, 395–96).

[72] Augustine, *De sancta virginitate* 15.15 (CSEL 41, 247–48).

as these, the exegeses of ascetically minded church fathers produce new meaning that tightens the moral demands on Christians and constrains their sexual and marital freedom.

IV: "Two in One Flesh"

Interpretive difficulties also beset the Gospels' seemingly more "carnal" understanding of marriage and divorce, as embodied in the phrase describing marriage as "two in one flesh" (Matt. 19:5), since by later antiquity, theologians and jurists had increasingly come to understand marriage more in terms of volition and intentionality than of bodily acts. Although this text was taken by various patristic commentators in simple fashion to denote the unacceptability of divorce for Christians,[73] it implied that marriage was to be understood in terms of a physical relationship. Hence, some ameliorating interpretation of the "two in one flesh" text was essential for Christian exegetes of ascetic inclination, who preferred that those Christians so unfortunate as to find themselves already married would agree to a purely "spiritual," that is, nonsexual, relationship.

Although the limitation of divorce in Matthew 19 to just one ground—*porneia*—could be seen as a restriction that worked to protect the wife,[74] its flaw, from a late ancient Christian standpoint, was that it linked divorce (and hence the "essence" of marriage) to a sexual act. Indeed, the "two in one flesh" text assured that arguments about marriage and divorce would be framed in ways that rested heavily on proper and improper sexual conduct, as is evident in the writings of such diverse authors as Basil of Ancyra,[75] Theodore of Mopsuestia,[76] and Zeno of Verona.[77] Yet in the works of Ambrose, Jerome, and Augustine, we begin to see some changes

[73] E.g., Origen, *Comm. I Cor.* 7:18–20 (Jenkins [1908], pp. 506–7); John Chrysostom, *Hom. 33 I Cor.* 5 (PG 61, 282); *Hom. 62 Matt.* 1 (PG 58, 597); Lactantius, *Divinae institutiones* 6.23 (CSEL 19, 567).

[74] See Bernadette Brooten for discussion on the debate over divorce in early Judaism and early Christianity: "Early Christian Women and Their Cultural Context: Issues of Method in Historical Reconstruction," in *Feminist Perspectives on Biblical Scholarship*, ed. Adela Yarbro Collins (Chico, Calif.: Scholars, 1985), pp. 73–74; idem, "Jewish Women's History in the Roman Period: A Task for Christian Theology," *Harvard Theological Review* 79 (1986): 23; idem, "Könnten Frauen im alten Judentum die Scheidung betreiben? Überlegungen zu Mk 10, 11–12 und I Kor 7, 10–11," *Evangelische Theologie* 42 (1982): 65–80; idem, "Zur Debatte über das Scheidungsrecht der jüdischen Frau," *Evangelische Theologie* 43 (1983): 466–78.

[75] Basil of Ancyra, *De vera virginitatis integritate* 41–42 (PG 30, 752).

[76] Theodore of Mopsuestia, *Comm. in Matt.* 5:31–32 (Reuss, p. 107).

[77] Zeno of Verona, *Lib. 1, Tract. 4* (PL 11, 297–99).

that imply less "sexual" conceptions of marriage, conceptions that in turn have repercussions for understandings of divorce.[78]

The simplest move by these Latin church fathers was merely to amend the phrase "one flesh" (or "one body") (Gen. 2:24; Matt. 19:5; Eph. 5:31) by the addition of the words "and one spirit." Thus Ambrose: the man and the woman in Paradise had not only "one flesh" but also "one spirit." So harmonious was their relation that Eve never experienced "ill will" until she encountered the serpent; in her innocence, she did not suspect his deceptive ploy.[79] According to Ambrose, the loving spouse, like the first couple, turns "conjugal love into nature, so that one flesh *and one spirit*" prevail.[80] By contrast, a fornicating wife does more than sever the "one flesh"; she also breaks the "one spirit" with her husband.[81] "One flesh," Ambrose concludes, entails "one marriage."[82]

Jerome, describing to Eustochium how Jesus will be her Bridegroom, cites the analogy in Ephesians 5:31–32 of bride and groom to Church and Christ, and bluntly "corrects" the author's "two in one flesh" citation. Jerome pointedly draws his reader's attention to the correction: "*rather*, 'two in one spirit.' "[83] Likewise, in his *Commentary on Matthew*, Jerome adds to Matthew 19:5 that marriage makes a couple not just "one in flesh," but also "one in spirit."[84] Yet preferable to becoming "one spirit" with a human sexual partner, according to Jerome, is to become "one spirit" through union with Christ. Here Jerome contrasts the Pauline distinction in I Corinthians 6:15–20 between the bodily union of a man with a prostitute, and a spiritual union with the Lord; the fact that Paul does not here consider that a man could become "one in spirit" with a human spouse serves as grist for Jerome's ascetic-interpretation mill.[85]

In any event, Jerome's reading of the story of Adam and Eve in Paradise renders the "one flesh" passage dubiously appropriable, for the prediction of the "one flesh" in Genesis 2, he notes, points ahead to a time after the couple have sinned and been expelled from Eden. To Jerome's mind, Adam and Eve were intended by God to remain as virgins, and if they had so remained, they never would have been "one flesh." The best that Jerome can do with the "one flesh" passage is to interpret it via a "close

[78] Even earlier, Origen had signaled that human creation in the "image of God" (Gen. 1:26–27) did not pertain to the "two in one flesh" teaching of Gen. 2:24 (*Comm. in Matt.* 14.16 [GCS 40, 321–22]).

[79] Ambrose, *De officiis ministrorum* 1.32.169 (PL 16, 78).

[80] Ambrose, *Exp. Ps.* 118.15.17 (CSEL 62, 339).

[81] Ambrose, *De interpellatione Iob et David* 3 (4).11.30 (CSEL 32.2, 266).

[82] Ambrose, *De viduis* 15.89 (PL 16, 276). Ambrose also adds "one spirit" to "one flesh" in *ep.* 42.3 (PL 16, 1124) and *Hexaemeron* 5.7.19 (CSEL 32.1, 154–55).

[83] Jerome, *ep.* 22.1 (CSEL 54, 145).

[84] Jerome, *In Math.* 3 (19:5) (CCL 77, 166).

[85] Jerome, *Adversus Iovinianum* 1.11

reading" of Ephesians 5:32 (the union of Christ and the Church): that Christ loves the Church in a holy and chaste manner, "without spot," suggests that husbands might love their wives more Christianly if they exhibited similar "spotlessness," that is, if they renounced sex within marriage.[86] Once again, by a clever exegetical route, the "one flesh" text has been changed into a "no flesh" injunction.

Augustine's exegeses of the "two in one flesh" passage spiritualize it in still other directions. For example, Augustine can appropriate it for Christological discussion: the "two"—the human and divine aspects of Jesus—become one in Mary's womb,[87] uniting the "bride" of the flesh and the "groom" of the Word of God.[88] Alternatively, the "two in one flesh" text is understood ecclesiologically as Christ's marriage to the Church,[89] an interpretation enabled by Ephesians 5:22–33, in which the "marriage" of Christ to the Church is held up as a model for human spouses. To be sure, Augustine did not abandon all physical associations of the "two in one flesh" passage. Early in his career, he found it a useful verse with which to assail Manicheans who censured marriage,[90] and later, to defend himself against the Pelagian charge that his theory of original sin entailed a denigration of marriage;[91] in these cases, he wished to champion the "fleshly" union of marriage. Nonetheless, even when defending himself against Pelagians, Augustine retreats from too "sexual" a construal of the verse which, he warns Julian of Eclanum, might suggest that Christ and the Church as described in Ephesians 5 were joined in carnal passion.[92]

The direction of Augustine's spiritualizing interpretation of Genesis 2:24 had consequences not just for his theory of marriage, but also for his understanding of divorce (or more precisely, "no divorce"). Most intriguingly, Augustine quotes Genesis 2:24 ("two in one flesh") to illuminate his understanding of the third "good" of marriage, the *sacramentum*.[93]

(PL 23, 236–37).

[86] Jerome, *Adversus Iovinianum* 1.16 (PL 23, 245–246); *ep.* 22.19 (CSEL 54, 168–69).

[87] Augustine, *Enn. in Ps.* 44.3 (CCL 38, 495).

[88] Augustine, *Tract. in ep. Ioan. ad Parthos* 1.2 (PL 35, 1979).

[89] Augustine, *Serm. Dennis* 12.2 (PL 46, 853).

[90] Augustine, *Contra Adimantum* 3 (CSEL 25, 119); *Contra Secundinum* 21 (CSEL 25, 939).

[91] Augustine, *Contra duas epistolas Pelagianorum* 1.5.9 (CSEL 60, 429–30); *De nuptiis et concupiscentia* 2.3.9 (CSEL 42, 261).

[92] Augustine, *Opus imperfectum contra Iulianum* 2.59 (CSEL 85.1, 206–7).

[93] The three "goods" of marriage, according to Augustine, are offspring, fidelity, and the "sacramental bond." See discussion in Nicolas Ladomérszky, *Saint Augustin, docteur de mariage chrétien. Etude dogmatique sur les biens du mariage* (Roma: Officium Libri Catholici, 1942), chap. 5. For other discussions on the "goods," see Bernard Alves Pereira, *La Doctrine du mariage selon Saint Augustine* (Paris: Gabriel Beauschesne, 1930), pp.

Although we might have expected "two in one flesh" to appear as a proof-text for Augustine's second "good" of marriage, *fides* or sexual fidelity, he does not cite it for that purpose. Rather, Augustine reserves the "two in one flesh" text to argue that the *sacramentum*, which he discusses in relation to Ephesians 5:32,[94] renders divorce impermissible.[95] "Two in one flesh" here suggests the permanence of marriage, not its sexual dimension.

Placing the "essence" of marriage in this spiritualized (albeit vaguely defined) "bond" had great implications for Augustine's views on divorce. Nothing "physical" can break a marriage, Augustine claims, so divorce is not justified even in cases of a wife's sterility[96] or chronic disease.[97] Nor does adultery break the pact between them.[98] (Here, Augustine argues against the view of some earlier church fathers that a Christian husband was obliged to separate from a fornicating spouse[99]: for Augustine, Jesus does not require this separation, and his forgiveness of the adulteress in John 8 stands as a model for spousal pardon.)[100] Likewise, although Paul tolerated the separation from an unbelieving spouse who would lead the Christian into impiety and sins, such separation, according to Au-

40–54; Emile Schmitt, *Le Mariage Chrétien dans l'oeuvre de Saint Augustin. Une théologie baptismale de la vie conjugale* (Paris: Etudes Augustiniennes, 1983), *passim*, esp. pt. 4, chap. 1. For a discussion of Augustine's notion of the family, see Brent D. Shaw, "The Family in Late Antiquity: The Experience of Augustine," *Past & Present* 115 (1987): 3–51 (although Shaw tends to read as "social reality" what I consider to be rhetorically ideological passages in Augustine's writings).

[94] Augustine, *De nuptiis et concupiscentia* 1.21.23 (CSEL 42, 236). Not only does Augustine use the "two in one flesh" text to illustrate the third "good" of marriage; he can also write of fornication (a violation of the second "good") in a way that emphasizes the volitional/intentional aspects. Thus in discussing the "except for *porneia*" clause in Matt. 19, Augustine notes that the woman's infidelity is a sign of her bad intention; she shows she did not wish to be a wife (*Tract. in Ioan.* 9.2 [CCL 36, 91]).

[95] Augustine's discussion of the three "goods" of marriage and the implication that it is the third "good," the *sacramentum*, that stands against the permissibility of divorce, can be found in his treatise *De bono coniugali* 7; 15.

[96] Augustine, *De bono coniugali* 3.3; 7.7 (CSEL 41, 190, 196–97); *De Gen. ad litteram* 9.7 (CSEL 28.1, 275–76); *De nuptiis et concupiscentia* 1.10.11 (CSEL 42, 223). Humbert (*Le Remariage*, p. 150) notes that facility of divorce *needed* to be an aspect of Augustus' earlier pro-marital and pro-reproductive legislation, if childless couples were to be encouraged to divorce and remarry with the hope of producing offspring.

[97] Augustine, *De conjugiis adulterinis* 2.13.13 (CSEL 41, 397–98).

[98] Augustine, *De nuptiis et concupiscentia* 1.10.11; 1.17.19 (CSEL 42, 222–23, 231); *De coniugiis adulterinis* 2.4.4 (CSEL 41, 385).

[99] See discussion in Crouzel, *L'Eglise*, pp. 318, 364. In *Retractiones* 1.18 (19).5–6, Augustine modifies this view: an adulterous wife can be sent away but then forgiven and brought back.

[100] Augustine, *De serm. Domini in monte* 1.16.43 (CCL 35, 48–49); cf. *De coniugiis adulterinis* 2.5.6, where the example is offered of David's taking back Michal (see I Sam. 25:44; II Sam. 3:14–15).

gustine, is not recommended;[101] it is more "Christian" for the believer to remain with the unbelieving partner.[102] Even if a man physically separates from his wife, the pact between them is not broken[103] and thus there can be no second marriage: they are still married, albeit physically separated.[104] If even "pagan" marriages share to a certain degree in the *sacramentum* (these couples are also to some extent "two in one flesh"),[105] how much more does Christian marriage? Indeed, Augustine compares the indelibility of marriage, lodged in the *sacramentum*, to the indelibility of baptism.[106]

For Augustine, even a couple's mutual vow of continence does not break the marriage pact—to the contrary, it enhances it—for the union then becomes more like that of Joseph and Mary.[107] Although Joseph and Mary never experienced sexual relations, and Mary's offspring (the first "good" of marriage) was miraculously conceived, they still had the *sacramentum* that linked them until Joseph's death.[108] As early as his treatise *Against Faustus the Manichean*, Augustine had argued that Joseph and Mary enjoyed a true marriage, because "intercourse of the mind is more intimate than that of the body": a couple can be husband and wife without the latter.[109] Thus the rigor with which Augustine imbues his argument against divorce rests on a spiritualized understanding of marriage that extends far beyond the "carnal" concession of Matthew 19, that divorce was not permitted to a man "except for *porneia*."

[101] Augustine, *De fide et operibus* 16.28 (CSEL 41, 72–73); cf. *De coniugiis adulterinis* 1.17.19–18.19 (CSEL 41, 366–67).

[102] Augustine, *De coniugiis adulterinis* 1.13.14 (CSEL 41, 361–62). Augustine comments that Paul was talking about a marriage in which both had been "unbelievers" but one had converted to Christianity, whereas now the situation is different: a Christian should marry only another Christian (*De coniugiis adulterinis* 1.21.25 [CSEL 41, 372–73]).

[103] Augustine, *De coniugiis adulterinis* 1.12.13 (CSEL 41, 361): she does not cease to be a "wife."

[104] Augustine, *De coniugiis adulterinis* 2.10.10 (CSEL 41, 393–94); cf. *De bono coniugali* 7.6 (CSEL 41, 195–96).

[105] Augustine, *Contra Iulianum* 5.12.46 (PL 44, 810); Adam and Eve had the *sacramentum* (*De nuptiis et concupiscentia* 1.21.23 [CSEL 42, 236]), as did the ancient Israelites (*De bono coniugali* 18.21 [CSEL 41, 214–15]).

[106] Augustine, *De coniugiis adulterinis* 2.5 (CSEL 41, 386). The analogy with baptism is stressed by R. Kuiters, "Saint Augustin et l'indissolubilité du mariage," *Augustiniana* 9 (1959): 10–11. Kuiters notes that Augustine avoids the language of "contract" in discussing marriage, preferring either *pactum* or *foedus* (pp. 7–8). Also see Schmitt, *Le Mariage chrétien*, pp. 260–65.

[107] Augustine, *De nuptiis et concupiscentia* 1.11.12 (CSEL 42, 224–25). Joseph and Mary are also models for Ambrose, who declares that they can be referred to as "spouses" (Matt. 1:24) because "non enim defloratio virginitatis facit conjugium, sed pactio conjugalis" (*De institutione virginis* 6.41 [PL 16, 331]).

[108] Augustine, *De nuptiis et concupiscentia* 1.11.13 (CSEL 42, 225).

[109] Augustine, *Contra Faustum* 23.8 (CSEL 25, 713); cf. *De consensu Evangelistarum* 2.1.3 (CSEL 43, 83); *De nuptiis et concupiscentia* 1.11.12 (CSEL 42, 224).

Not for a moment, though, did Ambrose, Jerome, and Augustine concede that they were adopting positions different from those attributed to Jesus and Paul: they would strongly resist the charge that they had altered the meaning of Biblical texts. Yet neither would these church fathers admit that they had constrained the sexual and marital practices of Christians further than had Scripture; for them, the Bible was understood to enable a rigorous ascetic renunciation. The teachings ascribed to Jesus, Paul, and Moses could, with exegetical labor, be brought into harmonious coexistence. And herein lies the beauty of commentary, which in Foucault's words, "allows us to say something other than the text itself, but on condition that it is the text itself which is said, and in a sense completed."[110] His claim finds an apt illustration in the church fathers' "exegesis of divorce."

[110] Michel Foucault, "The Order of Discourse," in *Untying the Text: A Post-Structuralist Reader*, ed. Robert Young; trans. Ian McLeod (Boston/London/Henley: Routledge and Kegan Paul, 1981), p. 58.

Reading Paul

CHAPTER TEN

I Corinthians 7 in Early Christian Exegesis

I: Introduction

How did patristic authors "read" I Corinthians 7 in a later Christian setting that pressured the Bible to ratify an escalating ascetic theory and practice? This famous chapter, containing Paul's most detailed teaching on marriage and sexual abstinence, proved sufficiently elastic to enable exegetes to express their varied ascetic preferences while expounding a text that they considered immutable and eternally valid. To be sure, almost all patristic writers rate sexual abstinence (if properly motivated) as "higher" on the scale of Christian values than marriage; nonetheless, they diverge considerably from each other in the weight they lend to this preference.

Given the Fathers' endorsement of Scripture's irrefragable authority, Biblical texts like I Corinthians 7 could not actually be "rewritten," but could be imbued with new (and diverse) meanings via commentary. Their expositions illustrate well Roland Barthes' claim concerning commentary that "[w]hat has been said cannot be unsaid, except by adding to it."[1] Patristic commentary on I Corinthians 7 stands as supplement, a "new text" that clarifies the chapter's ambiguities and compensates for its perceived (but unacknowledged) deficiencies.[2] The function of such commen-

[1] Roland Barthes, "The Rustle of Language," in idem, *The Rustle of Language*, trans. Richard Howard (New York: Hill and Wang, 1986; French original, 1984), p. 76. Also see Michel Foucault on the function of commentary in "The Order of Discourse," in *Untying the Text: A Post-Structuralist Reader*, ed. Robert Young, trans. Ian McLeod (Boston/London/Henley: Routledge and Kegan Paul, 1981), p. 58: commentary "allows us to say something other than the text itself, but on condition that it is this text itself which is said, and in a sense completed."

[2] On commentary as a new text: Roland Barthes, "Theory of the Text," trans. Ian McLeod, in *Untying the Text*, ed. Young, p. 44; Martin Irvine, *The Making of Textual Culture: 'Grammatica' and Literary Theory, 350–1100*, Cambridge Studies in Medieval Literature 19 (Cambridge: Cambridge University Press, 1994), p. 247. On the functions of supplementarity: Jacques Derrida, *Of Grammatology*, trans. Gayatri Chak-

tary is not, however, primarily literary: the Fathers wished their expositions to have extraliterary effects, namely, effects in the lives of Christians. In this case, when the newly supplemented text—the commentary—was deemed authoritative by the interpretive community of ascetic enthusiasts, it could enlist moral commitment and promote renunciation.[3] As Elisabeth Schüssler Fiorenza has succinctly expressed the point, "The evaluative criterion for rhetoric is not aesthetics, but praxis."[4]

Although the text of I Corinthians 7 with which these Fathers worked was relatively "set," several features of this important chapter encouraged diverse interpretations.[5] For example, Paul in various verses had addressed differing audiences (the married, virgins, widows) and had tailored his exhortations to suit their particular circumstances.[6] The diversity of Paul's audiences encouraged similarly varied ascetic stances among later interpreters who themselves addressed quite different readers and hearers. Were these interpreters seeking to persuade still-virginal adolescents to commit themselves to lives of permanent abstinence? To dissuade widows from second marriages? To console the married that the heavenly halls could also be theirs? To remind alleged heretics that the God who inspired Paul had *also* proclaimed "reproduce and multiply" (Gen. 1:28)? To warn monks for whom solitary sexual pleasures, not marriage, might be the immediate temptation? In each case, Paul's message could be adjusted to suit. Indeed, one and the same church father might emphasize different aspects of Paul's teaching in I Corinthians 7 to divergent audiences, for

---

ravorty Spivak (Baltimore/London: Johns Hopkins University Press, 1976; French original, 1967), pp. 200, 280.

[3] Brian Stock, *Listening for the Text: On the Uses of the Past* (Baltimore/London: Johns Hopkins University Press, 1990), p. 109, using the example of how the seemingly negative pronouncements on marriage in the Gospels receive the force of moral imperatives through the commentary in which they become entwined: a particularly apt example for the discussion that follows of I Cor. 7.

[4] Elisabeth Schüssler Fiorenza, "Rhetorical Situation and Historical Reconstruction in I Corinthians," *New Testament Studies* 33 (1987): 387. Cf. to Gerald Bruns' comments on Midrash: "Midrash is not method but form of life" ("The Hermeneutics of Midrash," in *The Book and the Text: The Bible and Literary Theory*, ed. Regina Schwartz [Oxford/Cambridge: Basil Blackwell, 1990], p. 200). Peter Rabinowitz argues that one of the most enduring legacies of New Criticism is for readers to assume that "ethical effects" are solely extraliterary (*Before Reading: Narrative Conventions and the Politics of Interpretation* [Ithaca, N.Y./London: Cornell University Press, 1987], p. 16).

[5] See chap. 5 above for an elaboration of these and other exegetical strategies.

[6] Particularly attentive to the question of the differing ages of Paul's varied audience is Norbert Baumert, *Ehelosigkeit und Ehe in Herrn: Eine Neuinterpretation von I Kor 7*, Forschung zur Bibel 47 (Würzburg: Echter Verlag, 1984), esp. pp. 18–19, 343–45. Baumert's approach in general is refreshing when compared to that of many (often Protestant) interpreters who try to "save" the chapter for a defense of Christian marriage; for Baumert, the theme of the chapter is not "marriage or celibacy?", but rather "cel-

words designed to chastise overly ascetic Marcionites were ineffective in rousing self-indulgent married Catholics to sexual restraint.

Thus the various verses of I Corinthians 7 were expounded in relation to particular interpretive communities and contexts.[7] To name this community "early Christian" cuts too broad a swathe: considerable differentiation was necessary if the Fathers wished to speak meaningfully to the Church's various constituents. I would expand Brian Stock's argument that the text is "what the community takes it to be,"[8] since diverse audiences within the larger *ecclēsia* often required that more than a single message be derived from the same passage. No one context permitted a "saturation" of the text;[9] rather, skillful exegesis allowed the commentator to promote his own interpretations among divergent audiences.[10] As we will see, the exhortations of patristic writers to *their* contemporaries intersected in unexpected ways with the varied advice Paul had addressed to specific Christian constituencies at Corinth.

Moreover, Paul provided a second encouragement to multiple interpretation by distinguishing within I Corinthians 7 differing levels of authoritative voice, sometimes stating his own preferences, while at others claiming to serve as spokesman for "the Lord's command." Since in the last verse of chapter 7, Paul alleges that he has "the Spirit of God," were interpreters to assume that the entire chapter was inspired by divine authority?

---

ibacy within marriage or outside of marriage?" (pp. 18, 340–42).

[7] See, for example, Stanley Fish, "Is There a Text in This Class?", in idem, *Is There a Text in This Class? The Authority of Interpretive Communities* (Cambridge/London: Harvard University Press, 1980), pp. 303–21; Brian Stock, *Listening for the Text*, pp. 100, 146, 151; idem, "Medieval Literacy, Linguistic Theory, and Social Organization," *New Literary History* 16 (1984): 18; John Mowitt, *Text: The Genealogy of an Antidisciplinary Object* (Durham, N.C.: Duke University Press, 1992), pp. 94–95, 99; Irvine, *The Making of Textual Culture*, pp. 15, 266. Fish readdresses the notion of "interpretive communities" in his essay "Change," in idem, *Doing What Comes Naturally: Change, Rhetoric, and the Practice of Theory in Literary and Legal Studies* (Durham, N.C.: Duke University Press, 1989), pp. 141–60.

[8] Stock, *Listening for the Text*, p. 146.

[9] Jacques Derrida, "Living On: Border Lines," in *Deconstruction and Criticism*, ed. Harold Bloom et al. (New York: Seabury/Continuum, 1979), p. 76; cf. Lee Patterson, *Negotiating the Past: The Historical Understanding of Medieval Literature* (Madison: University of Wisconsin Press, 1987), p. 151; Michel Foucault, *The Archaeology of Knowledge*, trans. A. M. Sheridan Smith (New York: Pantheon, 1972; French original, 1969), on how texts are "stabilized" by authors and audiences, p. 103. For a clear explication of Foucault's point, see Homi K. Bhabha, "The Commitment to Theory," in idem, *The Location of Culture* (London/New York: Routledge, 1994), p. 22: "Despite the schemata of use and application that constitute a field of stabilization for the statement, any change in the statement's conditions of use and reinvestment, any alteration in its field of experience or verification, or indeed any difference in the problems to be solved, can lead to the emergence of a new statement: the difference of the same."

[10] Foucault, "The Order of Discourse," p. 61.

Or did Paul speak "only as a human," holding no higher authorization for his views? Knowledgeable readers might also contrast Paul's teachings in chapter 7 with less ascetically rigorous Biblical injunctions in order to secure Scriptural props for their own ascetic preferences, just as Jesus had advanced his own superior teaching over the more "carnal" view of Moses on the question of divorce (Matt. 19:3–9). Far from proclaiming the "death of the author,"[11] the Fathers believed that I Corinthians 7 bespoke a plurality of authors, very much "alive"—but when and where did the author "Paul" speak in the same voice as the author "God"?

Still another complication: who was "Paul"? Since all patristic writers (unlike most modern Biblical scholars) believed that Paul had composed Ephesians, Colossians, and the Pastoral Epistles as well as I Corinthians and the other letters now considered genuinely Pauline, some interpretive work was required to explain how he could have expressed himself so discrepantly in various passages pertaining to marriage, procreation, and sexual renunciation. Although some patristic writers might freely criticize the teachings of the Old Testament in relation to the New, they shied from registering disagreement among the New Testament books themselves.

One attempted solution to this interpretive dilemma was, having differentiated "Paul's" various audiences by their degree of ascetic commitment, to argue that Paul met his readers at their own level. Thus I Corinthians 7:2–6 could be taken as a concession to sexually active married couples who might otherwise commit incest or fornicate with prostitutes (dangers detailed in I Cor. 5 and 6), whereas Ephesians 5 was directed to the spiritually perfect who conformed their relations to the model provided by Christ's (sexless) marriage to the Church. Likewise, I Timothy 5:14, counseling the remarriage of young widows, could be read as "Paul's" even greater concession to the morally weak who needed the remedy of a second marriage to stay them from a lapse into harlotry. Patristic commentators (unlike some of our contemporaries) did not hesitate to assign "authorial intention" in an effort to force a consistent and unitary voice—Paul's—among seemingly divergent texts.

There remains the question of interpreting Paul's "tone." Just as the reply of Jesus' disciples in Matthew 19:10 to his antidivorce teaching ("If such is the case of a man with his wife, it is not expedient to marry") could be construed as the shocked disbelief of carnally minded Jews or, conversely, as the ready agreement of experienced ascetic practitioners, so the assignment of "tone" could lend quite different nuances to Paul's

[11] The famous phrase of Roland Barthes, "The Death of the Author," in Barthes, *Image, Music, Text*, trans. Stephen Heath (New York: Hill and Wang, 1977; French original of this essay, 1968), pp. 142–48. Cf. Michel Foucault, "What Is an Author?", in *Textual Strategies: Perspectives in Post-Structuralist Criticism*, ed. Josué V.

words. Were they to be taken as stern warnings designed to pressure the young toward virginal commitment through an enumeration of the "woes of marriage"? Or as the remedies of a compassionate physician who cheerfully adjusted his prescriptions to match his patients' levels of medicinal tolerance?

The passage of time between Paul's composition of I Corinthians in *circa* 56–57 C.E. and the church fathers' exposition of his letter several centuries later contributed a further interpretive problem. Unlike modern commentators who stress the eschatological context of the epistle,[12] the patristic writers here considered, with the notable exception of Tertullian,[13] no longer anticipated the imminent and cataclysmic end of the world. Not imagining that Paul's words on sexual restraint might be undergirded by the expectation that "the day of the Lord will come like a thief in the night" (I Thess. 5:2), most patristic commentators sought other, noneschatologically dependent explanations for Paul's counsel of ascetic renunciation.

A final note: all the church fathers here cited deemed celibacy higher than marriage. On this general point there was little disagreement. Attempts by writers such as Jovinian to "equalize" marriage with celibacy prompted fierce rejoinders: "distinction" is built into the fabric of ascetic theory and practice. Yet there was also a need to counter Marcionite and Manichean denigration of reproduction. Although the church fathers had the parameters of their argument loosely set, within these limits there was nonetheless ample room for creative interpretation. Within that pale, generous assessments of marriage based on I Corinthians 7 could be proffered by writers such as John Chrysostom, preaching to urban congregations of the married at Antioch and Constantinople. At the other, still acceptable, end of the orthodox spectrum (yet dangerously broaching its borders) were the diatribes of the ascetically rigorous Jerome and the anonymous, allegedly Pelagian, author of the treatise *De castitate*, also inspired by I Corinthians 7.[14] Although the voices of laypeople, less ascetically inclined and not theologically educated, are largely absent from the historical record, we may perhaps hear their queries and protests in the

---

Harari (Ithaca, N.Y.: Cornell University Press, 1979), pp. 141–60.

[12] As revealed in verses such as "in view of the impending distress" (or "present distress") (v. 26); "the appointed time has grown very short" (v. 29); and "the form of this world is passing away" (v. 31). For modern commentators on I Cor. 7, see n. 17 below.

[13] Perhaps spurred later in his writing career by his conversion to the strongly eschatological Montanist movement?

[14] It is interesting to note that although the Pelagians were declared "heretics" for their views on original sin, its transfer (or nontransfer), and its effects (or noneffects), the extreme criticism of marriage in such treatises as *De castitate* appears not to have occasioned accusations of heresy. Jerome, however, suffered the ignominy of being labeled a "Manichean."

positions attributed to anonymous interlocutors ("Some say . . . ," or "You may reply" . . .),[15] or in reports that "some" argued that the more stringent demands of I Corinthians 7 were intended only for a priestly or monastic class, and were inapplicable to Christians-in-general.[16]

In this chapter I detail the major interpretive options attending the patristic exegesis of I Corinthians 7. In almost all cases, the positions I note are based on the Fathers' citation of the particular verse or verses in question. This chapter aims not to provide a complete catalog of any patristic author's ascetic teaching, but to illustrate how various verses of I Corinthians 7 could be summoned to support divergent agendas. It also illustrates how the exegetical strategies outlined in the first part of this book were deployed to enable different readings of this key Biblical chapter. (Citations to chapter and verse in my discussion refer to I Corinthians 7.)

II: Interpreting I Corinthians 7

> Now concerning the matters about which you wrote. It is well for a man not to touch a woman.
>
> *I Cor. 7:1 RSV*

Immediately we encounter an interpretive problem: who "speaks" I Corinthians 7:1b? Many modern exegetes argue that Paul here repeats a thesis posited by Corinthian Christians of an ascetic persuasion who counted themselves as "wise" and "strong." The force of Paul's repetition, these scholars claim, lies in his theoretical agreement with the ascetic Corinthians, promptly modified by his concession in 7:2 that such a goal was too difficult for most fallible Christians to pursue.[17]

[15] E.g., (Anonymous), *De castitate* 10.12 (PLS 1, 1487): how could the world continue if everyone adopted sexual renunciation? Also uttered, it appears, by Jerome's opponent Jovinian (Jerome, *Adversus Iovinianum* 1.36). Augustine cites this objection in *De bono coniugali* 10.10. Also frequent is the appeal to Gen. 1:28 ("Reproduce and multiply") by "laxer" Christians: see Pelagius, *Comm. I Cor.* 7:1–3; (Anonymous), *De castitate* 11.1; 14.4; Jerome, *Adversus Iovinianum* 1.3; 1.16, refuting an alleged objection of Jovinian, reported in Jerome, *Adversus Iovinianum* 1.5.

[16] Examples: according to Tertullian in his Montanist phase, the "psychics" (i.e., Catholic Christians) claim that the injunction against a second marriage holds only for priests, not for laypeople (*De monogamia* 12). According to John Chrysostom, "some allege" that I Cor. 7:1 ("It is good for a man not to touch a woman") applies only to priests, not to laypeople (*Hom. 19 I Cor.* 1).

[17] See, for example, the comments of John C. Hurd Jr., *The Origins of I Corinthians* (New York: Seabury, 1965), p. 67; W. E. Phipps, "Is Paul's Attitude towards Sexual Relations Contained in I Cor. 7:1?", *New Testament Studies* 28 (1982): 125–30; Gordon D. Fee, *The First Epistle to the Corinthians* (Grand Rapids: Eerdmans, 1987),

This modern interpretation was approximated by only a few of the church fathers. Ambrosiaster, the name assigned to an anonymous Latin writer of the later fourth century who is generally supportive of marriage (but not of gender equality),[18] ingeniously attributes the sentiment to the "pseudo-apostles," perhaps the "superlative" apostles who plagued Paul in Corinth (II Cor. 11–12), or to the wicked teachers of I Timothy 4:2–3. According to Ambrosiaster, these "pseudo-apostles" perversely and hypocritically condemn marriage so that they themselves may appear superior to other Christians. In Ambrosiaster's view, although Paul repeats "It is good not to marry," readers should not imagine that he intended this exhortation to be taken at face value; the concessions Paul makes in the following verses should be understood as his justified *critique* of the arrogantly self-righteous Corinthian "pseudo-apostles."[19] Those who pridefully boast that "it is well not to touch a woman" receive their proper chastisement from the Apostle.

Christian writers more sympathetic to ascetic exhortation but also supportive of marriage, on the other hand, such as Origen and John Chrysostom, read this verse somewhat differently: those who practice the sentiment of verse 1 are to be praised, not chastised. Origen thus takes the verse as Paul's congratulations to more "perfect" Christians who are able to sustain a high degree of abstinence. Noting that Paul urges the Corinthian Christians to practice "holiness" (*hagneia*, which for Origen usually entails sexual abstinence), Origen observes that Paul nonetheless conde-

---

pp. 270–71. Commentators eager to present Paul as no detractor of marriage often emphasize that Paul's anxiety about marriage stems from its "busyness" and/or from the imminence of the eschaton. In light of the end-times, all human relations are relativized. For a good presentation of the latter view, see Vincent L. Wimbush, *Paul, The Worldly Ascetic: Response to the World and Self-Understanding according to I Corinthians 7* (Macon, Ga.: Mercer University Press, 1987). According to Judith Gundry-Volf, Paul wishes to assure women that they can exercise pneumatic inspiration even *within* family structures; there is no need to leave ("Celibate Pneumatics and Social Power: On the Motivations for Sexual Asceticism at Corinth," *Union Seminary Quarterly Review* 48 [1994]: 105–26). Taking a rather sharper approach to I Cor. 7, Margaret M. Mitchell notes that the chapter's discussion is contained "under the overarching category of *porneia*" (*Paul and the Rhetoric of Reconciliation: An Exegetical Investigation of the Language and Composition of I Corinthians* [Tübingen: J. C. B. Mohr (Paul Siebeck), 1991], p. 235). Emphasizing Paul's concern with issues of purity and pollution in this chapter is Dale B. Martin, *The Corinthian Body* (New Haven, Conn./London: Yale University Press, 1995), pp. 205–17. Will Deming emphasizes that 7:1b may represent a Cynic position, corrected by Paul's words in 7:5 (*Paul on Marriage and Celibacy: The Hellenistic Background of I Corinthians 7* [Cambridge: Cambridge University Press, 1995], p. 115).

[18] See David Hunter, "The Paradise of Patriarchy: Ambrosiaster on Woman as (Not) God's Image," *Journal of Theological Studies*, n.s. 43 (1992): 447–69.

[19] Ambrosiaster, *Comm. I Cor.* 7:1 (CSEL 81.2, 70).

scends to the "weakness" of those unable to achieve this level of sexual restraint.[20] John Chrysostom agrees that abstinence is "better" but that Paul's concession to the married is necessary.[21] Nonetheless, the very fact that the Corinthians themselves had in verse 1 raised the issue of sexual renunciation indicates that they had "made progress" in the faith[22]— "progress," perhaps, from the incest and frequenting of prostitutes that Paul had earlier criticized in the Corinthian community.[23] Having taken the lead in raising the issue of abstinence with Paul, the speakers of verse 1 are to be applauded, not blamed. For Origen and Chrysostom, verse 1 is read as commendation for the ascetically rigorous, yet marriage is conceded for those of "weaker" moral fiber.

Other writers, less friendly toward marriage, adopt a more stringent tone. Thus the anonymous author of the Pelagian treatise *On Chastity* sharpens and narrows the import of the verse: it is not "women-in-general" whom Paul thinks are "good not to touch," for Paul does not sink to the moral depths of warning Christians against prostitutes or other illicit sexual relations. Rather, it is sex *within* marriage of which Paul speaks: it is good for the married couple "not to touch" each other.[24]

A further question: to whom was the exhortation in I Corinthians 7:1 directed? Although some Christians alleged that it applied only to priests,[25] patristic commentators generally argued that Paul recommended universal abstinence.[26] Yet other, more specialized audiences could also be imagined. For Cyprian, in the mid-third century, compiling a catena of Biblical passages that refute "Jewish" teaching and evince Christianity's superiority to Judaism, the verse serves as a weapon demonstrating the superiority of Christian abstinence to "Jewish" carnality:[27] the "difference in times" is here pointedly noted. Moreover, 7:1 reminded those committed to monastic abstinence to reject all impurity, a rejection symbolized by the belt that girds up the monks' loins.[28] This verse also provides Athanasius with ascetic ammunition for a particular interpretive community: warning virgins against the dangers of syneisaktism (in which abstinent men and women shared living quarters), Athanasius claims that if it is

[20] Origen, *Comm. I Cor.* 7:1–4 (Jenkins [1908], p. 500).

[21] John Chrysostom, *Hom. 19 I Cor.* 1–2 (PG 61, 151–52).

[22] John Chrysostom, *De virginitate* 12.6; 13.1–2 (SC 125, 132, 134).

[23] See I Cor. 5:1–2; 6:16–20—the subjects of John Chrysostom's *Homilies* 15, 16, and 18 on I Corinthians.

[24] (Anonymous), *De castitate* 10.1–2 (PLS 1, 1478–79).

[25] John Chrysostom, *Hom. 19 I Cor.* 1 (PG 61, 151).

[26] John Chrysostom, *Hom. 19 I Cor.* 1 (PG 61, 151); Jerome, *Adversus Iovinianum* 1.7 (PL 23, 228); (Anonymous), *De castitate* 9.1 (PLS 1, 1477–78).

[27] Cyprian, *Ad Quirinum* 3.32 (CSEL 3.1, 145).

[28] Evagrius Ponticus, *Praktikos, prologus* (SC 171, 488).

"good" in general not to touch a woman, "how much better" it is not to touch a "bride of Christ," that is, a consecrated virgin.[29]

We can identify two strategies in the commentaries of more ascetically inclined writers that boost the already-renunciatory import of 7:1. One tactic, devised by the anonymous author of the Pelagian treatise *On Chastity*, is to claim that 7:1, "it is good not to touch," overrules later verses that concede marriage. Thus the author appeals to this verse in discussing 7:38, which he alleges, "ignorant people" read as "he who marries does well, he who marries not does better."[30] The author flatly denies that Paul could have written "he who marries does well," because such a reading manifestly contradicts 7:1, Paul's true opinion.[31] All concessions Paul makes to marriage in chapter 7 must bow before the lofty standard of abstinence proposed in verse 1. In this explanation, we have an outright denial of Pauline authorship to verse 38, an unusual position for a Christian writer of this period to adopt.

A second strategy for raising the ascetic import of 7:1 appeals to an argument from "comparison," and borrows from the Old Stoic claim that the opposite of a virtue is always a vice, that there are no intermediate steps on the scale of virtue.[32] Ascetically rigorous writers press this argument with enthusiasm: if a good can be compared only to its opposite, then the good of "not touching" proves the "touching" of sexual relation to be an evil. This contention, found especially in the Latin Christian tradition, probably originates with Tertullian[33] and is adopted by the ascetic enthusiasts Jerome and the author of *On Chastity*—but is "corrected" by Augustine, more favorable to marriage.

Tertullian employs the argument from comparison in both his Catholic and his Montanist stages.[34] Although he claims in his treatise *To His Wife*

[29] Athanasius, *ep. 2 ad virgines* (Lebon, p. 182; ET, Brakke, p. 299).

[30] According to the critical apparatus pertaining to this verse, no early readings omit the phrase "his virgin." The earliest manuscript omitting the phrase (as the author of *De castitate* claims "the ignorant" read the verse) comes from the eighth or ninth century. I thank text critic Bart Ehrman for assistance on this point.

[31] (Anonymous), *De castitate* 10.14 (PLS 1, 1488). A similar denial of Pauline authorship (here, of I Tim. 4:1–3) is attributed by Augustine to Faustus the Manichean: Paul could not have written that dedicating virgins to Christ was a "doctrine of the devil," and cites the Apocryphal Acts and Matt. 19:12 to buttress his point. In general, Manicheans were quick to deny apostolic authorship to New Testament verses that stood against their teaching (e.g., the genealogies of the "fleshly" Jesus).

[32] See, for example, Zeno, frag. 188, 224, 225, *Stoicorum veterum fragmenta*, ed. Johannes von Arnim (Leipzig: B. G. Teubner, 1921), I:46–47, 54; Chrysippus, frag. 527, 529, 536 (*Stoicorum veterum fragmenta* III:141, 142, 143).

[33] Tertullian, *De monogamia* 3.2 (CCL 2, 1231).

[34] Johannes Quasten dates Tertullian's *Ad uxorem* to his Catholic period, in the opening years of the third century; the *De exhortatione castitatis* to a few years later, on his way to Montanism: and the *De monogamia* to the years of his full-blown Monta-

that he does not prohibit marriage or split the "one flesh" (Matt. 19:5–6), Tertullian nonetheless notes that if Paul grants the licitness of marriage only because of "necessity" (stemming from the sexual temptation into which Christians might otherwise fall), this is not much of a recommendation: what "necessity" grants, she also "depreciates." What kind of a good can it be that is commanded only in comparison with an evil?, Tertullian inquires. He then jumps ahead to 7:9 ("it is better to marry than to burn"): how much better to do neither, he exclaims![35] Employing the same argument in other treatises, Tertullian rhetorically inquires, it is "better to lack one eye than two," but who would claim that even lacking one were a good?[36]

Jerome in *Against Jovinian* directly appropriates Tertullian's argument, as he frequently does when commenting on moral topics.[37] According to Jerome, from I Corinthians 7:1 we must conclude, "if something is not good, it is bad." The evils of "touching" are then skillfully elaborated by an appeal to the dangers of "loose" or "foolish" women as described in Proverbs 6, 7, and 9. Such women who "touch" are said to "hunt for the precious life" [of young men], to cause heedless youths to lose their reason (Prov. 6:26–27).[38] "Touching" has here taken on decidedly sinister overtones via an intertextual analysis. Note that Jerome's intertexts do not describe "touching" in the context of marriage, but of illicit sexual relations deemed dangerous to men—intertexts in which women are cast in the role of the predators. Marriage is here subtly denigrated by its association with verses that warn young men against "dangerous" forms of sexual activity.

The anonymous author of the Pelagian treatise *On Chastity* shifts the discussion of 7:1 back to the realm of marital intercourse, but nonetheless appropriates Tertullian's (and now Jerome's) claim that "touching" is necessarily "bad," because the latter is the only opposite of "good." And if it is "good" for a man "not to touch" his wife, how much better it would be for him not to know her at all—presumably, to have remained unmarried! No man placed next to a fire can escape the heat, the author

---

nist commitment. See Quasten, *Patrology*, vol. II, *The Ante-Nicene Literature after Irenaeus* (Utrecht/Antwerp: Spectrum Publishers, 1953), pp. 302, 305–6. It could be argued that the dating of Tertullian's treatises as "late" on the basis of their increased rigor is a dubious methodological procedure.

[35] Tertullian, *Ad uxorem* 1.3.2–4 (CCL 1, 375–76).

[36] Tertullian, *De exhortatione castitatis* 3.7–10 (CCL 2, 1019–20); cf. *De monogamia* 3.2–6 (CCL 2, 1231–32).

[37] See, for example, Fr. Schultzen, "Die Benutzung der Schriften Tertullians *de monogamia* und *de ieiunio* bei Hieronymus *adv. Iovinianum*," *Neue Jahrbücher für deutsche Theologie* 3.1 (1894): 487–502; Claudio Micaeli, "L'influsso di Tertulliano su Girolamo: le opere sul matrimonio e le secondo nozze," *Augustinianum* 19 (1979): 415–29.

[38] Jerome, *Adversus Iovinianum* 1.7 (PL 23, 229).

of *On Chastity* ominously intones.[39] The argument as developed from Tertullian to Jerome to the author of *On Chastity* thus tends in an increasingly antimarital direction.

Augustine's treatise *On the Good of Marriage*, composed probably in 401,[40] responds to the alleged slanders that overly zealous ascetic interpreters (namely, Jerome) had leveled against marriage. Augustine seeks a mean between Jerome's excessive enthusiasm for asceticism and Jovinian's overly exuberant praise of marriage. Among the points that Augustine singles out for attack is the argument from comparison made by Tertullian and Jerome, albeit without naming them. For Augustine, more appreciative of the blessings of marriage, a "good" can be rightfully compared only with another "good," as Paul intends in his comparison of marriage and virginity. If marriage were a "good" only in contrast to fornication, both would be deemed evils . . . and then (in an argument moving from lesser to greater evils) fornication would be a "good" only in comparison with adultery, adultery only in comparison with incest . . . and below this, we sink to matters "unspeakable." Rather, it is only because *both* marriage and virginity are "goods" that Paul can compare them at all. The Virgin Mary, the widow Anna (Luke 2:36–38), and the chaste matron Susanna all participate in "good" states, although Augustine acknowledges continence as a higher "good" than marriage.[41] Here, Augustine turns the argument from comparison in a direction more favorable to marriage.

In general, patristic authors agree that the "not touching" of 7:1 depicts the ideal, but that only some Christians, the ascetic elite, can sustain this level of purity.[42] Jesus' concession in regard to becoming eunuchs for the sake of the Kingdom of Heaven ("not all can receive it") was sometimes quoted in conjunction with I Corinthians 7:1.[43] Methodius, writing in the early fourth century to praise Christian virginity, reads the opening verses of I Corinthians 7 in such a way that verses 2–4 constitute an "afterthought" on Paul's part. According to Methodius, Paul had expressed his

[39] (Anonymous), *De castitate* 10.2 (PLS 1, 1479). In alluding to Prov. 6:27–28 ("Can a man carry fire in his bosom and his clothes not be burned?"), the anonymous author appears to be following Jerome's discussion in *Adversus Iovinianum* 1.7. A similar argument from "fire/heat" is used by John Chrysostom, *De virginitate* 34.4.

[40] See Peter Brown, *Augustine of Hippo: A Biography* (Berkeley/Los Angeles: University of California Press, 1969), "Chronological Table C."

[41] Augustine, *De bono coniugali* 8.8 (CSEL 41, 199).

[42] For example, Augustine, *De nuptiis et concupiscentia* 1.16.18 (CSEL 42, 230–31); John Chrysostom, *Hom. 19 I Cor.* 1 (PG 61, 151).

[43] So Augustine, *De nuptiis et concupiscentia* 1.16.18 (CSEL 42, 230–31). It is interesting to note that Didymus ("the Blind") of Alexandria uses the same argument—that a good can be compared only to a good—to counter the Manichean claim that marriage is an evil while virginity is a good; see his *Contra Manichaeos* 8–9 (PG 39, 1096–97).

true belief in verse 1; only "afterward" did it come to his attention that many Christians were too weak to practice total sexual abstinence. Hence Paul lowered his expectations and permitted married sexual relations as a concession.[44] The verse also prompts Augustine's comment that God had not required lifelong virginity from Christians so that the voluntary commitment to sexual renunciation would be seen to surpass any mere "command."[45] Already, with verse 1, patristic writers can signal the "distinction" of Christians on the basis of ascetic renunciation. These more ascetically minded interpreters do not press Paul's message in order to champion the "concord" or "unity" of the Christian community, as Margaret Mitchell argues was Paul's intent in I Corinthians,[46] but rather in order to signal the superiority, the "distinction," of Christians who embrace ascetic living.

> But because of the temptation to immorality, each man should have his own wife and each woman her own husband. The husband should give to his wife her conjugal rights, and likewise the wife to her husband. For the wife does not rule over her own body, but the husband does; likewise the husband does not rule over his own body, but the wife does.
>
> *I Cor. 7:2–4 RSV*

Patristic commentators more favorable to marriage might now take heart: Paul thought that marriage was, after all, "allowable," an important point in the Christian arsenal of anti-Manichean polemic.[47] But for whom were Paul's words meant? The imagined audience might lend a more or a less positive "tone" to Paul's concession. Even Origen, more favorably disposed to marriage than some other patristic writers, thought that these verses were directed only to "infants," to the spiritually immature Corinthians who could not compare to the more ascetically advanced Christians at Ephesus.[48] Others stressed that these verses stood as no encouragement to the presently unattached to

[44] Methodius, *Symposium* 3.11 (GCS 27, 39).

[45] Augustine, *Serm.* 161.11.11 (PL 38, 884).

[46] See Mitchell, *Paul and the Rhetoric of Reconciliation*, pp. 121–25, 235–37. Mitchell sees Paul as promoting *concordia* throughout I Corinthians.

[47] An especially prominent theme in Ambrosiaster, *Comm. I Cor.* 7:2 (CSEL 81.2, 71).

[48] Origen, *Hom. 7 Ezech.* 10 (SC 352, 270, 272).

marry.[49] Jerome restricted the audience even further: Paul referred only to a man who had acquired a wife *before* he became a believer—the implication being that once he had converted, an unmarried man should have resisted taking a wife.[50]

For those writers most favorable to marriage, however, 7:2–4 was not read "negatively." Thus for Clement of Alexandria, Paul's words did not pertain to those chaste married couples who engaged in sexual relations for the sake of procreation alone, for such activity needs no "concession."[51] Clement here directly equates "giving conjugal rights" with "producing children."[52] Likewise, Augustine cites these verses to claim that although his contemporaries are overcome by lust and need this concession of marriage, the Hebrew worthies of yore, despite their polygamy, outshone them in that they engaged in sexual intercourse only to populate the earth, not from sexual desire.[53] Yet today, Augustine continues, when even Christians are overwhelmed by lust, the sexual outlet of faithful marriage can still be counted as one of its "goods."[54] Moreover, in his later writings, in which he was concerned to stress the effects and transfer of original sin, Augustine also argues that it is not the sexual act itself that is blameworthy, but the "lust" associated with it.[55] And Augustine's opponent Pelagius, despite his more critical assessment of marriage, agrees that Paul resembles a kind physician who willingly concedes something less than his optimal wish in order to forestall more harmful deeds: marriage here is a "remedy."[56] Thus 7:2–4 could be cited to signal the "good" of marriage.

Although patristic writers repeat Paul's reason for his concession to human weakness—"to avoid fornication"[57]—nuanced exegesis could pro-

[49] Tertullian, *De monogamia* 3.1–2 (CCL 2, 1230–31); Pelagius, *Comm. I Cor.* 7:1–3 (PLS 1, 1198–99).

[50] So Jerome, *Adversus Iovinianum* 1.7 (PL 23, 230); cf. Tertullian, *De monogamia* 11.

[51] Clement of Alexandria, *Stromata* 3.15.96.1–2 (GCS 52 [15], 240).

[52] Clement of Alexandria, *Stromata* 3.18.107.5 (GCS 52 [15], 246).

[53] Augustine, *De bono coniugali* 13.15; 16.18; 17.19; 19.22; 20.24 (CSEL 41, 207–8, 211–12, 212–13, 218); *De doctrina Christiana* 3.18.27 (CCL 32, 93–94); *Contra Faustum* 22.31; 22.49–50 (CSEL 25, 625, 642–44). Augustine is here clearly in a "pre-Pelagian" mode of argumentation; later he will claim that *all* humans from the time of Adam and Eve's sin have experienced "lust."

[54] Augustine, *De bono coniugali* 4.4 (CSEL 41, 191–93); *De gratia Christi* 2.34.39 (CSEL 42, 197–98).

[55] Augustine, *De nuptiis et concupiscentia* 1.1.1; 1.5.6 (CSEL 42, 211–12, 216–17); *Contra Iulianum* 3.14.28 (PL 44, 716–17).

[56] Pelagius, *Comm. I Cor.* 7:1–3 (PLS 1, 1198); cf. *Comm. I Tim.* 4:2 (PLS 1, 1342).

[57] Origen, *Comm. I Cor.* 7:1–4 (Jenkins [1908], pp. 500–501). For Origen, the "strong man" does not need this remedy for *porneia* because of his own weakness (but presumably because of his wife's). See also John Chrysostom, *Hom. 19 I Cor.* 1; *De virginitate* 15.2; *Propter fornicationes* 5; *Quales ducendae* 5; Methodius, *Symposium* 3.11, for other examples.

vide a more or a less positive assessment of its significance. So strongly does John Chrysostom argue that the concession is for the quelling of passion that he even discounts procreation as a reason: reproduction does not come about through a "natural act" but only as a gift from God.[58] With the Christian Dispensation, Chrysostom argues, resurrection is at the door; Christians no longer need to replace the human race or to leave memorials of ourselves in the form of children. The calming of passion is thus for Chrysostom the only present reason for married couples to engage in sexual relations.[59] In fact, Chrysostom argues (rather like the rabbis), it is the sexual relations of the couple that *keep* them chaste,[60] that protect them from illicit sex: "reading like a Jew" here prompts a warmer assessment of marital relations.

Other writers put a darker edge on Paul's concession. Tertullian in commenting on these verses resorts to an argument based on "levels of authority": Paul's indulgence for even a first marriage comes from a (mere) human being, whereas the Holy Spirit enjoins continence (presumably in 7:40?).[61] According to Tertullian, the Holy Spirit "takes back" the indulgence that Paul allowed earlier: the Christian present is not the "time" for the "embraces" of Ecclesiastes 3:5.[62] Tertullian notes further that it is only due to the "insidiousness of temptations" that Paul granted the indulgence of marriage in the first place.[63] The authority of human advice cannot compare with that of divine recommendation.

Tertullian also locates a second clear message in 7:2–4: if marriage is permitted to forestall fornication, then extramarital relations are not forgivable. Christians should not imagine that the fornicating man of I Corinthians 6:15–19 was forgiven. He had the choice of "marrying rather than burning" (7:9), and, having chosen not to marry but to frequent prostitutes, he and those like him must now look ahead to being "burned" in the punishing flames. Ordinary Catholics ("psychics," in Tertullian's Montanist parlance) who claim that fornication, adultery, and incest are

[58] John Chrysostom, *De virginitate* 19.1 (SC 125, 156, 158). In other treatises, Chrysostom also remarks that fecundity is not the result of human effort, but comes from God; see his discussion of Sarah's barrenness in his *Hom. 38 Gen.* 2.

[59] John Chrysostom, *Propter fornicationes* 3 (PG 51, 213).

[60] John Chrysostom, *De virginitate* 25 (SC 125, 174). See Daniel Boyarin, *Carnal Israel: Reading Sex in Talmudic Culture* (Berkeley/Los Angeles/Oxford: University of California Press, 1993), pp. 141–42; for sexual relations as a "prophylaxis" *against* desire in Paul, see Martin, *The Corinthian Body*, pp. 214–17; and more fully in idem, "Paul without Passion: On Paul's Rejection of Desire in Sex and Marriage," in *Constructing Early Christian Families: Family as Social Reality and Metaphor*, ed. Halvor Moxnes (London/New York: Routledge, 1997), pp. 201–15.

[61] Tertullian, *De exhortatione castitatis* 4.2–6 (CCL 2, 1021–22).

[62] Tertullian, *De monogamia* 3.6–8 (CCL 2, 1232).

[63] Tertullian, *Ad uxorem* 1.3.2 (CCL 1, 375).

forgivable do not recognize that Paul gave his "concession" not for these deeds, but for marriage alone.[64]

Jerome too scorns Paul's "concession": a Christian husband should rather be able to know his wife as a sister. Paul, he avers, is "too ashamed" even to name the deed that the married couple perform, and permits it only because of the "temptation of Satan" (7:5), a point that Jerome scores in an attempt to shame married, sexually active, Christians into abstinence. Unlike Tertullian, however, Jerome believes that the fornicating man of I Corinthians 6 *was* forgiven, because of Paul's words (taken as applying to the same case) in II Corinthians 2:5–10.[65]

Pelagius as well casts a dim light on Paul's "concession." In his *Commentary on I Corinthians*, it is "the incontinent" who protest against Paul's teaching on virginity and on marriage as a *remedium*. These "lovers of [sexual] indulgence" (*amatores luxuriae*) object that God's first blessing on humans was to "reproduce and multiply" (Gen. 1:28), pitting these words against Paul's recommendation for continence. Unlike John Chrysostom, however, Pelagius thinks that the production of children is the *only* reason for marrying: *libido*, sexual desire, should not count as a valid "excuse." Once children are conceived, there is no further reason for a couple to engage in sexual relations. Indeed, Pelagius remarks, chastity's superiority is shown in that it endures, whereas "incontinence" is limited in its use and depends on people's ages, their state of health, location, and so forth. Hence chastity is the preferable option.[66]

The author of the Pelagian treatise *On Chastity*, although borrowing from Pelagius, disagrees with his view that having children is the only reason for marital sex: rather, this author argues that Paul grants the concession of marriage in 7:2–4 so that the morally weak may escape fornication. Like Pelagius, however, he characterizes Paul as a good physician, but gives the metaphor a negative twist: only people who are "sick" need such a concession. If a Christian is "healthy," why yearn for the medicine appropriate for others? The body needs care, to be sure, but not "superfluous cures." If a man marries when he does not need to, he lays himself open to "needless slanders" about his moral condition. Next, a "close reading" of Galatians 5:22–23 bolsters the author's argument: since Paul here does not include marriage among the "fruits of the Spirit," although he explicitly praises *continentia* and *castitas*, the Pelagian commentator concludes that Paul must think marriage is incompatible with

[64] Tertullian, *De pudicitia* 16 (CCL 2, 1312–15).

[65] Jerome, *Adversus Iovinianum* 1.7; 1.8 (PL 23, 230, 231).

[66] Pelagius, *Comm. I Cor.* 7:1–3 (PLS 1, 1198). The Pelagian author of the letter *Honorificentiae tuae* (2.1 [PLS 1, 1690]) also claims that it is "the incontinent" to whom Paul here speaks.

such "fruits."[67] The author of *De castitate* also appropriates Pelagius' argument that whereas chastity can last "forever," sexual intercourse is limited by time of life, state of health, and so on—including one's endurance for performing the sexual act itself: not even for an entire hour, the author scoffs![68]

Another opportunity for exegetical disagreement was afforded by 7:4, the mutual "rule" of the spouses over each other's bodies. Did Paul's words point to a praiseworthy spousal equality, or to a mutual "bondage" which should dissuade Christians, especially the young, from marriage at all? Origen, of the earlier Fathers, is most concerned to read 7:3–4 "positively," as demonstrating the *homoiotēs* and *isotēs*, the likeness and equality, of the couple.[69] Chrysostom, too, notes the symmetry Paul establishes between husband and wife in these verses, and recommends that a husband recite them to a prostitute who tries to lure him, just as a wife might fend off unwanted advances from other men by their repetition. Yet Chrysostom hedges the verses about to forestall what he considers "misinterpretation": the equality of honor they bespeak applies only to the couple's sexual relation. In other areas, the husband is dominant, as Genesis 3:16 and Ephesians 5:25 and 33 teach. Yet I Corinthians 7:2–4 reminds Chrysostom of one other area of married life in which the couple mutually "share": their money.[70]

Likewise, in his short treatise on I Corinthians 7:1–2 ("On Account of Fornication . . . "), Chrysostom also parallels vigilance for one's own (and one's spouse's) body with that for his or her property: we should behave like the Watchful Servant of the Gospels, who can return the master's deposit (Matt. 24:43–51; Luke 12:35–46). In modesty and chastity, the husband has nothing more than the wife and is liable to the same punishment as she if he transgresses "the law of marriage." Just as a father will punish the husband for the misuse of his daughter's dowry, so God will punish the husband who offends against marital chastity.[71] The spouse's body constitutes a "trust" that is not to be squandered.

These discussions of the alleged "equality" of the marital partners, however, do not aim to signal their "equal rights," but rather their "equal restrictions." Thus, for Augustine, the "equality" these verses portend

[67] (Anonymous), *De castitate* 10.3; 10.15 (PLS 1, 1479–80, 1488–89). Perhaps the author hopes to refute I Cor. 7:7 (implying that marriage is a "gift" as well as virginity) with this other passage from Paul's writings? For the author of *De castitate*, marriage is decidedly *not* a "gift" (see 10.5).

[68] (Anonymous), *De castitate* 3.6 (PLS 1, 1468).

[69] Origen, *Comm. I Cor.* 7:3 (Jenkins [1908], p. 501).

[70] John Chrysostom, *Hom. 19 I Cor.* 1 (PG 61, 152). Chrysostom frequently reminds men of the problems occasioned by wives richer than they.

[71] John Chrysostom, *Propter fornicationes* 4 (PG 51, 214–15).

prohibits the couple from divorcing: neither may cast off the other.[72] Jerome likewise quotes 7:3–4 to forbid divorce, but adds an antimarital addendum via an intertext from the Gospels: it was because of Jesus' prohibition of divorce that Paul begins his letter to the Corinthians with the words, "It is good for a man not to touch a woman." Since a man will never be able to divorce after he marries, he is here warned by Paul against contracting a marriage in the first place.[73]

A second restriction that 7:2–4 suggests to patristic authors lies in the duty to provide sex for the partner: there can be no unilateral withdrawal into abstinence—a withdrawal that appears to have been more attractive to wives than to husbands, judging from the numerous texts that deal with this issue. Thus 7:3–4 means for Augustine and for the author of the *Letter to Celantia* that both husband and wife must agree to the relinquishing of sexual relations.[74] And Basil of Caesarea cites 7:4 to indicate that a married man may not remove himself to a monastery if his wife is unwilling for their sexual relation to be broken.[75] Marriage "dooms" a spouse to a life of "sex on demand."

That this "equality of restriction" could easily be turned in an even more antimarital direction by ascetically inclined Christian writers is evidenced by their frequent citation of 7:3–4 to characterize marriage as "bondage," a "bondage," as Jerome intimated above, that should dissuade the young from entering the marital relation in the first place. Ambrose rehearses this theme: although the "chain of love" is a "good," it is nonetheless a chain that inhibits one's freedom of will. Marriage, quite simply, binds a woman into servitude.[76] Since in marriage, Ambrose claims on the basis of 7:3–4, a Christian does not have "power over your own body," and since (adding a striking intertext) in marriage your garments cannot always be "white" (Eccles. 9:8), marriage renders a Christian less fit for religious duties.[77] It is no accident that these themes occur especially in Ambrose's exhortations to virgins that aim to dissuade them from marriage. Widows, too, are encouraged by Ambrose to recollect the bondage of marriage, and he cites 7:4 to jog their memories.[78]

[72] Augustine, *De coniugiis adulterinis* 1.8.8 (CSEL 41, 355).

[73] Jerome, *Adversus Iovinianum* 1.7 (PL 23, 230).

[74] Augustine, *ep.* 127.9 (CSEL 44, 28–29); (Anonymous), *Ad Celantiam* 28 (CSEL 29, 455–57).

[75] Basil of Caesarea, *Regulae fusius tractatae* 12 (PG 31, 948). Interestingly, Basil provides an "out" for this regulation: if the wife resists, the departing husband may cite to her Luke 14:26 ("If anyone comes to me and does not hate his own father and mother and wife and children and brothers and sisters, yes, and even his own life, he cannot be my disciple").

[76] Ambrose, *Exhortatio virginitatis* 4.21 (PL 16, 357–58).

[77] Ambrose, *Exhortatio virginitatis* 10.62 (PL 16, 370).

[78] Ambrose, *De viduis* 11.69 (PL 16, 268).

For Augustine, 7:3–4 should serve as dissuasion from marriage because the couple will come to understand that neither of them can live in continence unless both agree to it, that the wife must always "pay the debt" if her husband desires, whether she wishes to or not.[79] Pelagius tries to resolve the problem of potential marital conflict surrounding this issue by suggesting that the partner who desires to live in continence should so behave that the "incontinent" spouse is won over, provoked to a life of abstinence: *luxuria* should pass over to continence, not vice versa, he exhorts.[80] Pelagius does not, however, lend practical advice on what the partner aspiring to continence should do if this plan of spousal behavior modification does not achieve its desired effect.

Of all the Fathers here surveyed, John Chrysostom most frequently cites 7:3–4 to dissuade from marriage—even though he frequently affirms the goodness of marriage for those who need this "concession." Thus Chrysostom often sounds the theme of the "slavery" of marriage to young women from whom he hopes to press a virginal commitment.[81] Even the reason Paul advances for marriage in 7:2 (namely, forestalling fornication) is an attempt to shame his hearers to continence;[82] Paul writes so to turn his audience away from marriage. According to Chrysostom, Paul employs the same technique as the prophet Samuel (I Sam. 8:10–18) who predicted the negative effects of monarchy in order to dissuade the Israelites from its institution. Similarly in I Corinthians 7 Paul warns against the problems of marriage in order to lead Christians to continence.[83]

In his debates with the Manicheans, Augustine makes ingenious use of 7:3–4 to rationalize the nonascetic behavior of Old Testament figures (and of nonascetic Christians of the present) whom he nonetheless wishes to defend. While Manicheans point out stories of patriarchal "misbehavior" to justify rejecting the Old Testament, Augustine cleverly—and conversely—rescues the patriarchs for sanctity by arguing that Abraham's and Jacob's seemingly dubious sexual behavior was justified on the grounds that they themselves did not will their extramarital relationships, but were obediently following the wishes of their barren spouses. They are not to be judged guilty: marriage, as Paul claims in 7:3–4, entails that a husband's body is not "his own."[84] In particular, Augustine argues, Abraham's relation with Hagar was not prompted by sexual desire, a claim "proved" by his subsequent allowing of Sarah to treat Hagar harshly (Gen.

[79] Augustine, *ep.* 127.9 (CSEL 44, 28–29); *ep.* 262.2 (CSEL 57, 622–23).

[80] Pelagius, *Comm. I Cor.* 7:4 (PLS 1, 1199).

[81] John Chrysostom, *Hom. 19 I Cor.* 1 (PG 61, 152); *De virginitate* 28.1; 41.3 (SC 125, 182, 238).

[82] John Chrysostom, *Hom. 19 I Cor.* 1 (PG 61, 151).

[83] John Chrysostom, *De virginitate* 27.3; 29.2 (SC 125, 180, 186, 188).

[84] Augustine, *Contra Faustum* 22.31; 22.49 (CSEL 25, 624–25, 642–43); *De civitate Dei* 16.38 (CCL 48, 544).

16:6).[85] Here, Augustine gestures toward "asceticizing the Old Testament," recuperating the Old Dispensation for the New.

Jerome uses 7:3–4 in yet another way, as exegetical ballast ostensibly to defend Paula's daughter-in-law Laeta for not yet committing herself to continence. He writes that she is still under the Old Law of "reproduce and multiply" (Gen. 1:28); for her it is still "the time to embrace" (Eccles. 3:5)—and as a wife, she does not "have power over her own body" (7:4). Yet if Laeta defers giving herself to continence at this moment, at least she has "paid" in her daughter, whom she dedicates to virginity.[86] Through recitation of these verses, Jerome manages simultaneously to excuse Laeta and to shame her toward a life of continence.

> Do not refuse one another except perhaps by agreement for a season, that you may devote yourselves to prayer; but then come together again, lest Satan tempt you through lack of self-control.
>
> *I Cor. 7:5 RSV*

I Corinthians 7:5 was a verse that demanded explication: why would Paul have counseled sexual separation for prayer if marriage is "honorable" (Heb. 13:4)?[87] For those who argued that the New Testament supported rather than condemned marriage, the import of this verse might prove unsettling. That the "heretic" Tatian cited I Corinthians 7:5 to argue that sexual intercourse "destroyed" prayer[88] suggested troubling exegetical possibilities.

Those Fathers who wished to affirm marriage more (rather than less) enthusiastically insisted that the verse described the chaste, not the "incontinent" or the "wanton," among the married: so Clement of Alexandria and Cyril of Jerusalem.[89] On this interpretation, no negative implica-

[85] Augustine, *De civitate Dei* 16.25 (CCL 48, 529).

[86] Jerome, *ep.* 107.13 (CSEL 55, 304–5); cf. *ep.* 107.5 (CSEL 55, 296).

[87] John Chrysostom, *De virginitate* 30.1 (SC 125, 188, 190). Recently John C. Poirier and Joseph Frankovic have argued that Paul's advocacy of separation for prayer forms part of his view of the continuing validity of the Jewish law, that he is concerned with ritual purity issues, and that he understands his own celibacy as a prophetic charism, not necessarily applicable to other Christians ("Celibacy and Charism in I Cor. 7:5–7," *Harvard Theological Review* 89 [1996]: 1–18).

[88] Tatian, cited in Clement of Alexandria, *Stromata* 3.12.81.1–2 (GCS 52 [15], 232); Tatian apparently here cited Matt. 6:24 ("no one can serve two masters . . ."). Cf. Irenaeus, *Adversus haereses* 1.28.1: Tatian says that marriage is "corruption and fornication."

[89] Clement of Alexandria, *Stromata* 3.15.96.1–2 (GCS 52 [15], 240); Cyril of Jerusalem, *Or. Cat.* 4.25 (PG 33, 488).

tion attends the need for "separation." Thus for Chrysostom, 7:5 teaches that sexual desire is "natural" and that Paul permits lawful intercourse.[90] According to Augustine, this verse suggests that it is "incontinence," not the sexual act itself, that impedes prayer.[91] By such claims, the more negative implications of 7:5 might be mitigated.

Several Fathers posit that Paul had counseled couples to separate in order to pray not because of any sullying associations of sexual relation, but only because of the "busyness" of married life, the cares of the world (7:32–34). Here was a reason that did not seem to damn marriage, since Paul's recommendation for temporary abstinence was (so these Fathers alleged) motivated purely by practical considerations. Thus for Ambrosiaster, the worldly cares of the married suggest that they should set aside extra time from their sexual relation for prayer, even though this author acknowledges that they engage in "daily meditations."[92] According to Ambrose the married cannot freely give themselves to things divine when they must seek "to please a wife" (7:33); they are sold into servitude, deprived of the "freedom" enjoyed by virgins.[93] Athanasius, commenting on 7:5, contrasts the virgin, who can be a "whole burnt offering," with the busy distraction of the married.[94] Most of the Fathers' comments on the "busyness" of the married state, however, occur in their discussions of I Corinthians 7:32–35 on the cares and anxieties of the married; to this latter passage I will presently turn.

Other patristic writers, less enthusiastic toward marriage, read 7:5 more darkly. In Jerome's view, this verse should be interpreted in tandem with I Thessalonians 5:17 that instructs Christians to "pray without ceasing," an impossible task, he argues, while engaged in sexual intercourse.[95] Jerome and Augustine both locate another verse that they allege supports 7:5: I Peter 3:7. Here, "Peter" enjoins husbands to "bestow honor on the woman as the weaker sex . . . in order that your prayers may not be hindered," a verse Jerome interprets as meaning that a husband will refrain from marital relation if he wishes to "bestow honor" on his wife.[96] Intertextual readings thus strengthen the ascetic message of 7:5. Origen as well

[90] John Chrysostom, *Hom. 5 Tit.* 2 (2:11–14) (PG 62, 689).

[91] Augustine, *De bono coniugali* 10.11; 20.23 (CSEL 41, 202, 217–18). Augustine carried this view into his anti-Pelagian polemic; see, for example, *De nuptiis et concupiscentia* 1.14.16 (CSEL 42, 228–29); for his citation of I Cor. 7:5, *Opus imperfectum* 1.68.4–5 (CSEL 85.1, 74–75).

[92] Ambrosiaster, *Comm. I Cor.* 7:5 (CSEL 81.2, 71).

[93] Ambrose, *Exhortatio virginitatis* 4.23 (PL 16, 358). In *Exp. Luc.* 8.37 Ambrose appears to accept both "the cares of the world" and "the heaviness of intemperance" as reasons why a "respite" is necessary (CCL 14, 311).

[94] Athanasius, *ep. 1 ad virgines* (CSCO 150 = Scriptores Coptici 19, 81; ET, Brakke, p. 280).

[95] Jerome, *ep.* 22.22 (CSEL 54, 174).

[96] Augustine, *Contra Iulianum* 5.9.40 (PL 44, 807); Jerome, *Adversus Iovinianum* 1.7 (PL 23, 230).

hints that there may be tensions surrounding the separation for prayer. Thus he insists that the couple should agree on the separation so as to both prevent discord and forestall a lapse into the "incontinence" of too frequent sexual intercourse.[97]

Nonetheless, several of the Fathers sense that some shameful taint must adhere to the sexual act if Paul deems prayer and sex incompatible.[98] Ambrosiaster and John Chrysostom attempt to mitigate the force of this implication by suggesting that it is only especially "ardent" prayer, not ordinary devotions, that requires this restriction.[99] Origen, in contrast, advises that the bedroom is not the proper place for prayer[100]—without openly explaining why this is the case. Yet the passages he cites in his *Commentary on I Corinthians* 7:5 intimate the theme of impurity: Old Testament laws that require a man to abstain from his wife during the time of her menstrual "impurity" (Lev. 15:19–24; Ezek. 18:6). Christians, too, Origen argues, must be "completely pure" at the time of their prayers and fasts.[101]

In commenting on I Corinthians 7:5, Origen also identifies Old Testament verses suggesting that "even" the Israelites refrained from sexual activity before they were in the presence of the holy. The chain of verses he develops was later appropriated by Jerome and by the anonymous author of *On Chastity.* The first such passage concerns the separation of the Israelite men from their wives for three days before they approached God on Mount Sinai (Exod. 19:15); the second details the fitness of David's men to take the "holy bread" if (and only if) they had kept apart from women (I Sam. 21:4–6). Such passages prove to Origen that sexual separation for the sake of purity was a principle known to the Israelites, and should also govern Christian behavior.[102] If even Old Testament characters exhibited ascetic restraint, "how much more" can Christians be expected to live in chastity.

The theme of impurity is broached in other patristic discussions of 7:5 as well. Ambrose notes that Paul's injunction to sexual separation in 7:5 follows his words in 7:4, that spouses do not have control over their own bodies. If a married person does not have such control, he or she cannot always have "white" garments, cannot always be "clean" (Eccles. 9:8)[103]:

[97] Origen, *Comm. Matt.* 14.1–2 (GCS 40, 272–73); *De oratione* 2.2 (GCS Origenes 3, 300).

[98] See, for example, John Chrysostom, *Hom. 5 I Thess.* 3 (on 4:8) (PG 62, 426): if Paul was not ashamed to write I Cor. 7:5, Chrysostom will not be ashamed to counsel parents to marry their sons while the latter are young, before they fall into sexual dissoluteness.

[99] Ambrosiaster, *Comm. I Cor.* 7:5 (CSEL 81.2, 71); John Chrysostom, *Hom. 19 I Cor.* 2 (PG 61, 153).

[100] Origen, *De oratione* 31.4 (GCS Origenes 3, 397–98).

[101] Origen, *Comm. I Cor.* 7:5 (Jenkins [1908], p. 502).

[102] Ibid.

[103] Ambrose, *Exhortatio virginitatis* 10.62 (PL 16, 370).

marriage, it appears, renders a person impure against his or her will. Tertullian, in commenting on 7:5, also quotes "holiness" language from the Old Testament—"Be holy, as God is holy" (Lev. 11:44–45)—to recommend that sexual abstinence may be necessary for prayer.[104] And although Augustine in discussing marriage does not customarily employ the discourse of impurity, in his writings from the later 390s onward he repeatedly suggests that there is some "sinfulness" attached to the lust of sexual intercourse that portends the incompatibility of sex and prayer.[105] Yet citing 7:6, Augustine claims that God makes allowance for this sin because he so much blesses procreation—the *only* sin for which such allowance is made, Augustine pointedly remarks.[106]

Paul's words on sexual abstinence for the sake of prayer were expanded by the Fathers to include another type of religious devotion for which such abstinence was deemed necessary, partaking of the Eucharist. Once again, Origen's interpretation of I Corinthians 7:5 proved decisive for later writers. Perhaps I Samuel 21:4–6 (only David's "pure" men were allowed to take the showbread) here stimulated Origen's imagination concerning the "holy bread." If Paul urges Christians to keep pure from sexual contact in order to pray, Origen argues, how much more should they be pure if they wish to receive the bread of the Eucharist? Origen cites I Corinthians 11:27–29 (Paul's warning to Corinthian Christians not to eat or drink the Lord's Supper to their "judgment," but "worthily") in his discussion of I Corinthians 7:5 to threaten the dangers that await Christians who "take the bread" when they are in a sexually impure state.[107] Here, an intertext from the same epistle provides the requisite warning.

Most of the major Latin commentators on I Corinthians 7 appear to follow Origen in extending the separation for prayer to separation for the reception of the Eucharist. According to Ambrosiaster, perhaps the earliest of these writers, the married couple of I Corinthians 7:5 part so that they may "more worthily" receive the body of the Lord.[108] Jerome in *Against Jovinian* sharpens the provision: the couple "cannot" receive Christ's body if they have recently engaged in sexual relations.[109] He repeats Origen's two Old Testament examples of sexual restraint (Exod. 19:15; I Sam. 21:4–6) in his general discussion of sexual purity, conclud-

[104] Tertullian, *De exhortatione castitatis* 10.3–4 (CL 2, 1030).

[105] Examples in Augustine: *Contra Faustum* 30.5; *De bono viduitatis* 4.5; *Opus imperfectum* 1.4.29; *De nuptiis et concupiscentia* 1.14.16; 1.15.17; *Enchiridion* 21.78; *ep.* 6*.7; *De gratia Christi* 2.38.43.

[106] Augustine, *Contra Faustum* 30.5 (CSEL 25, 753–54).

[107] Origen, *Comm. I Cor.* 7:5 (Jenkins [1908], p. 502). Origen also cites I Cor. 7:5 in *Hom. 23 Num.* 3: the clergy should stay celibate if they are to offer the "bread."

[108] Ambrosiaster, *Comm. I Cor.* 7:5 (2) (CSEL 81.2, 72).

[109] Jerome, *Adversus Iovinianum* 1.7 (PL 23, 230).

ing, "in view of the purity of the body of Christ, all sexual intercourse is unclean."[110] Pelagius, for his part, relates these two Old Testament examples plus I Peter 3:7 to I Corinthians 7:5 in order to argue that only the continent may receive the holy bread.[111] Again we note the chain of asceticizing exegesis that runs from Origen to Jerome and Pelagius.

The anonymous author of *On Chastity* develops his own interesting exegesis of I Corinthians 7:5. He writes that as long as the married couple does not refrain from sex, their "instincts" always "defraud" them of the good of prayer and communion: this is the "defrauding" (RSV: "refusing") of which Paul speaks. If Paul here forbids even prayer to the "incontinent," it is certainly "not expedient" for such a person to take the Eucharist, prayer being "lesser" than communion.[112] For Scriptural parallels, however, the author turns to the Old Testament dietary laws. Leviticus 7:19–20 (the penalty on the "unclean" who eat the flesh of the sacrifices) is cited as an Old Testament "type" for the Christian injunction not to partake of the Eucharist while "unclean." If the Old Testament deprives "the incontinent" of sacrificial meat, the New Testament does not even let them pray! Although baptism cleanses a person from all impurity, the author of *De castitate* writes, the purpose of the "cleansing" is so that he may henceforth persevere in his newfound purity: falling into "incontinence" (for this author, including marital sex) renders a person defiled (*pollutus*) once more.[113] I Corinthians 7:5 manifestly carried graver implications for both the liturgical and the marital lives of Christians than at first glance might have been expected.

Patristic writers more affirming of marriage than the author of *De castitate* appealed to another aspect of 7:5: Paul's counsel that the couple "come together again." According to John Chrysostom, these words show that Paul permitted "lawful desire," that the sex drive was implanted in our natures for the sake of procreation.[114] "Coming together again" allows the couple to avoid the evils of fornication and incontinence, argue Clement of Alexandria and Methodius.[115] According to Athanasius, Paul did not mean for the couple to "abandon" the relation altogether, as Athanasius' ascetic opponent Hieracas apparently taught.[116] For Chrysostom,

[110] Jerome, *Adversus Iovinianum* 1.20 (PL 23, 249): "videlicet quod ad munditias corporis Christi, omnis coitus immunda sit."

[111] Pelagius, *Comm. I Cor.* 7:5 (PLS 1, 1200).

[112] (Anonymous), *De castitate* 10.4 (PLS 1, 1480–81); a good example of how *a fortiori* arguments can be employed in the debate.

[113] (Anonymous), *De castitate* 10.4 (PLS 1, 1481–82).

[114] John Chrysostom, *Hom. 23 II Cor.* 6 (PG 61, 563): unlike the desire for money, which is "unnatural," and the injunctions against it are thus harsher.

[115] Clement of Alexandria, *Stromata* 3.12.82.1 (GCS 52 [15], 233); Methodius, *Symposium* 3.11 (GCS 27, 39).

[116] Athanasius, *ep. 1 ad virgines* (CSCO

the verse forbids a unilateral withdrawal of one spouse from the sexual relation in order to pray[117]: he unleashes harsh words at women who cloak with a show of piety their sinful adoption of continence without their husbands' agreement.[118]

Others interpreted the verse to press their own views of sexual restraint. For Clement of Alexandria, 7:5 suggests that these respites for prayer teach a kind of continence that will endure even when the couple returns to sexual relation: thus the verse counsels more rigorous abstinence after they "come together again." (Clement, unlike the author of *On Chastity*, imagines that "continence" can obtain in a sexual relationship.)[119] Ambrose agrees: "temperance" in marriage is that for which Paul aims in 7:2–6.[120] Jerome allows that the couple, having separated for prayer, may give themselves once again "to the work of children"—but adds that after they do so, they might well return to continence.[121] Even more pointed is the interpretation advanced elsewhere by Jerome and by the anonymous *Letter to Celantia*: Paul intends for the couple to try out chastity "for a season" so that they will confidently be able to give their commitment to *perpetual* chastity. Here, "no return" to sexual relations is the preferable interpretation of 7:5.[122]

> I say this by way of concession, not of command. I wish that all were as I myself am. But each has his own special gift from God, one of one kind and one of another.
>
> *I Cor. 7:6–7 RSV*

That Paul here made a "concession," explicitly contrasted with a "command," gave patristic commentators so inclined the occasion to stress once more that marital sexual relations were permitted in order to exclude fornication.[123] Yet the negative overtones of "concession" could not be entirely erased. According to Pelagius, these words of indulgence were directed to "children" in the faith: that Paul gave "no command" on the issue indicates that he was leaving

150 = Scriptores Coptici 19, 86; ET, Brakke, pp. 282–83).

[117] John Chrysostom, *Hom. 19 I Cor.* 1 (PG 61, 153).

[118] John Chrysostom, *Hom. 86 Matt.* 4 (PG 58, 768).

[119] Clement of Alexandria, *Stromata* 3.12.79.1 (GCS 52 [15], 231).

[120] Ambrose, *ep.* 63.32 (PL 16, 1249).

[121] Jerome, *Comm. Eccles.* 3:5 (CCL 72, 275).

[122] Jerome, *Adversus Iovinianum* 1.12 (PL 23, 238); (Anonymous), *Ad Celantiam* 29 (CSEL 29, 456–57).

[123] Ambrosiaster, *Comm. I Cor.* 7:6 (CSEL 81.2, 72).

room for Christians to strive for "perfection."[124] Here, as elsewhere throughout the chapter, commentators could distinguish between "counsels" (exhortations for the strong) and "commands" (the lower level of righteousness required of all Christians).[125] Merely appropriating the "concession," however, leaves no room for praise: so John Chrysostom.[126] Such "concessions," Origen explains, were granted only because of the weakness of Paul's audience.[127] Yet, Augustine argues, the "concession" should not be understood as marriage itself, as "some" were taking it, for matrimony is no sin.[128] In any event, the "concession" is not taken to refer to Paul's allowance for a period of abstinence, as some modern commentators read the verse.[129]

For the Fathers, Paul's preference for virginity is underscored in his urging readers to "imitate himself,"[130] interpreted by ascetic commentators as a recommendation to live "in perpetual chastity."[131] Yet how to square Paul's words in 7:6–7 with such passages as I Timothy 5:14 that advise the remarriage of young widows? According to Chrysostom, the latter verse reveals a spirit of "condescension" with which God often indulges weak humans, not Paul's highest hope for Christians.[132] That 7:6–7 reinforced Paul's preference for virginity was widely accepted.

The same level of agreement did not attend the interpretation of the "gift" in 7:7: here, a striking divergence of opinion surfaced. According to Origen in his *Commentary on I Corinthians*, *both* marriage and celibacy are "gifts," a view that Jerome (somewhat surprisingly) adopts.[133] For Origen, the "gift" of marriage is harmony, *symphōnia*, that leads "not to confusion but to peace," a phrase he borrows from Paul's discussion of speaking in tongues in I Corinthians 14:33. Gentiles, however, do not in Origen's view partake of the "gift" of marriage unless they convert to Christianity. Moreover, Origen claims that understanding marriage as a

[124] Pelagius, *Comm. I Cor.* 7:6–7 (PLS 1, 1200); cf. John Chrysostom, *De virginitate* 2.2 (SC 125, 100).

[125] Methodius, *Symposium* 3.12 (GCS 27, 40).

[126] John Chrysostom, *De virginitate* 34.7 (SC 125, 204, 206).

[127] Origen, *Comm. I Cor.* 7:5–6 (Jenkins [1908], p. 502).

[128] Augustine, *ep.* 6*.7.11–12 (CSEL 88, 37).

[129] See, for example, Ben Witherington III, *Conflict and Community in Corinth: A Social-Rhetorical Commentary on 1 and 2 Corinthians* (Grand Rapids: Eerdmans; Carlisle, U.K.: Paternoster, 1995), p. 175; Deming, *Paul*, p. 115.

[130] John Chrysostom, *De non iterando coniugio* 3 (PG 48, 613); Ambrose, *Exhortatio virginitatis* 4.22 (PL 16, 358). A stimulating treatment of this theme is Elizabeth A. Castelli's *Imitating Paul: A Discourse of Power* (Louisville: Westminster/John Knox, 1991). Castelli appropriately notes that the call to "imitation" urges "sameness" while simultaneously reinforcing Paul's authoritative status (p. 103).

[131] (Anonymous), *Ad Celantiam* 29 (CSEL 29, 457).

[132] John Chrysostom, *Hom. 18 Hebr.* 1 (PG 63, 135).

[133] Origen, *Comm. I Cor.* 7:7 (Jenkins

"gift" condemns the Marcionite deprecation of marriage and reproduction: the same God who gave "holiness" (*hagneia*, that is, virginity) also gave marriage.[134] Likewise in his *Commentary on Matthew*, Origen quotes I Corinthians 7:6 to argue that both marriage and celibacy are "gifts," with "concord" as the special "gift" of marriage. Here, Origen cites Jesus' teaching in Matthew 19:6 (the couple is "not two but one") to reinforce his point. How does domestic concord prevail, Origen inquires? And answers: when the husband rules and the wife obeys.[135]

Origen's and Jerome's view that marriage is a "gift" may well have aroused the anonymous author of the treatise *On Chastity* to a rebuttal. If the bond of marriage were a "gift," then even pagans would enjoy a gift of God—a possibility that this author manifestly discounts. Here we see Origen's logic turned against itself: although Origen wishes to deny the "gift" to pagans, if the concord of the marriage bond is a sign of the "gift," then surely *some* pagans appear to enjoy it. Thus, for the author of *De castitate*, marriage cannot be called a "gift."[136]

Yet another question: was virginity to be considered a "gift"? Augustine, although abundant in his praise of marriage, answers "yes."[137] Claiming virginity as a "gift" shuts the mouths of those who, in their zeal to praise virginity, condemn marriage:[138] according to Augustine, persons who have not received the "gift" and who marry are thus not blameworthy. Understanding virginity as a "gift" preserves the importance of God's grace for Augustine, but simultaneously signals a more generous toleration for marriage.

Pelagian interpreters, on the other hand, stressed that the alleged "gift" of continence in 7:7 did not diminish the role of free will, so central to their theological position. Commenting on 7:7, Pelagius simply notes, "the gift, which we accept by our own free will."[139] The author of the treatise *On Chastity* waxes more expansive: virginity is not conferred as a "gift of God," but is preserved by free will. Otherwise, how could Christians expect a reward for their commitment to abstinence, for that which is a "gift" cannot be rewarded. If marriage and virginity were distributed as "gifts," how could Paul encourage all humans to "be as I am"? Unless free will were operative, Paul's words would ring hollow. The anonymous

[1908], p. 503); Jerome, *Adversus Iovinianum* 1.8 (PL 23, 232).

[134] Origen, *Comm. I Cor.* 7:7 (Jenkins [1908], p. 503).

[135] Origen, *Comm. Matt.* 14–16 (GCS 40, 323–24), citing Eph. 5:25, 33.

[136] (Anonymous), *De castitate* 10.5 (PLS 1, 1482).

[137] E.g., Augustine, *De continentia* 1.1; *Contra Iulianum* 5.16.66; *De nuptiis et concupiscentia* 1.3.3; *De gestis Pelagianorum* 13.29; *De gratia et libero arbitrio* 4.8; *ep.* 188.6.

[138] Augustine, *ep.* 157.37 (CSEL 44, 483–84).

[139] Pelagius, *Comm. I Cor.* 7:7 (PLS 1, 1200).

author ends his discussion of the "gift" (or, rather, the "nongift") of virginity with an ominous citation from Ben Sirach 15:17: "Before a man are life and death, and whichever he chooses will be given to him";[140] since virginity is clearly to be allied with "life," "death" must be the characteristic of the married state. Elsewhere in the treatise, the author of *De castitate* reinforces the same point: *all* humans have the choice to be "eunuchs for the Kingdom of Heaven," for to deny this choice would mean that God was a "respecter of persons" (Eph. 6:9) who wished some not to receive the reward. Since virginity is something humans possess "by nature," all they are asked is to preserve it by their own choice.[141]

It was not only alleged Pelagians, however, who pressed the theme that the "gift" of continence required an act of free will. John Chrysostom, too, faults interpretations of 7:7 that downplay human effort: although Paul calls continence a "gift," humans have to exert zeal as well.[142] Despite Paul's attributing his "gift" of virginity to God, Chrysostom argues, he most surely had struggled for it. Paul means to teach his audience that the ability to do God's will lies with them. Paul should not be faulted for arrogance when he exhorts the Corinthians to "do even as I do": he merely gives an example close at hand to show that the keeping of virginity is possible for them as well.[143]

> To the unmarried and the widows I say that it is well for them to remain single as I do.
>
> *I Cor. 7:8 RSV*

What level of authority does Paul here claim, asked patristic commentators? According to Ambrose, Paul does not here make a "law" but gives "advice." Just as doves—symbols of chastity—have no "laws" made for them, neither do those who live in virginity.[144] Cyril of Alexandria also expresses a caution: by writing "I say," Paul differentiates his voice from Christ's, since he knows that not everyone can dominate the flesh sufficiently to live as a virgin or a widow. In the verses that follow, Paul will make a concession for those who cannot.[145] Theodore of Mopsuestia apparently expressed the same caution: Jesus said

[140] (Anonymous), *De castitate* 10.5; 13.8 (PLS 1, 1482, 1494). Is marriage here to be equated with "death"?

[141] (Anonymous), *De castitate* 13.2; 3.6 (PLS 1, 1492, 1468).

[142] John Chrysostom, *Hom. 19 I Cor.* 2 (PG 61, 153).

[143] John Chrysostom, *De virginitate* 36.1; 36.3 (SC 125, 212, 216).

[144] Ambrose, *Hexaemeron* 5.8.19.62–63 (CSEL 32.1, 187–88): if, however, the chaste life of doves is too difficult for young widows, Paul advises them to marry (a shaming device?).

[145] Cyril of Alexandria, *Comm. I Cor.* 7:8 (PG 74, 872–73).

(in reference to "becoming a eunuch for the Kingdom of Heaven") that "not all could receive" his teaching, but only those "to whom it was given" (Matt. 19:12). Likewise here, for Theodore: it is only those receiving divine grace who can live as Paul did.[146]

The fact that this is Paul's first mention in chapter 7 of "widows" leads some commentators, such as John Chrysostom, to posit that he was directing his words—"remain single as I do"—especially to them.[147] Origen also thinks that Paul here speaks to widows: in their first marriages, the women did not yet have the opportunity to practice the "holiness" (*hagneia*) of continence, but now that their husbands are dead, they do.[148] Augustine attacks certain rigorous Christians who, claiming to be "pure," condemn the remarriage of widows; against them, Paul's concession in verses 8–9 can be cited.[149] In fact, so strongly do some commentators identify Paul with the widows that they claim him as a widower. Thus, remarking on these verses, Methodius writes that it is better for a once-married man to stay single after being widowed, "as he [Paul] did." Paul here becomes an example to those whose spouses have died, that they too may practice a more rigorous regime.[150] (Recall that Clement of Alexandria also furnished Paul with a wife.)[151] Jerome is perhaps familiar with diverging traditions regarding Paul's marital status; but for Jerome, 7:7–8 (as well as 9:5) stands against any interpretation that Paul had married. Don't listen to those who claim that Paul had a wife, Jerome warns Eustochium![152]

> But if they cannot exercise self-control, they should marry. For it is better to marry than to be aflame with passion [= burn].
>
> *I Cor. 7:9 RSV*

Paul speaks, but with what authority? Commentators might question the authority of Paul's words by contrasting them with other Biblical passages that carried no negative implications for marriage. Thus Paul's teaching should be differentiated from Christ's, Cyril of Alexandria stresses, since no divine command for abstinence is reported in the Bible.[153] For Tertullian, on the other hand, the

[146] Theodore of Mopsuestia, *Frag. in I Cor.* 7:8 (Staab, p. 182).

[147] John Chrysostom, *De virginitate* 37.4 (SC 125, 222).

[148] Origen, *Comm. I Cor.* 7:8 (Jenkins [1908], p. 504).

[149] Augustine, *De agone Christiano* 31.33 (CSEL 41, 136).

[150] Methodius, *Symposium* 3.12 (GCS 271, 41).

[151] Clement of Alexandria, *Stromata* 3.6.53.1 (GCS 52 [15], 220).

[152] Jerome, *ep.* 22.20 (CSEL 54, 170).

[153] Cyril of Alexandria, *Comm. I Cor.* 7:8ff. (PG 74, 872, 873).

concession for marriage that Paul here gives is overly generous, and should be deemed the opinion simply "of a man" that contrasts unfavorably with the more ascetically rigorous precepts of the Holy Spirit.[154] Paul permits this indulgence because of the "temptation" into which the Corinthians may fall,[155] according to Tertullian (presumably in his Montanist phase). Yet the Paraclete may abrogate permission for second marriage, which Paul tolerates—just as Christ abrogated Moses' permission for divorce.[156] Thus an interpreter's estimation of the authority of Paul's voice could carry rigorous or less rigorous implications.

Other Fathers favored a more flexible approach than Tertullian. John Chrysostom, like Cyril of Alexandria, argues that Paul's words indicate that the command for continence is not absolute; Chrysostom reminds his hearers/readers that Jesus declared that only some "could receive" his teaching on "becoming a eunuch for the sake of the Kingdom of Heaven."[157] Clement of Alexandria's commentary also aims in a less rigorous direction: the Apostle's advice here can be compared to that in 7:3, in which he concedes that the spouses should give each other their "due," not depriving each other in the work of reproduction. Clement's opponents—"Gnostics" of some stripe—counter with Luke 14:26, on hating one's father, mother, wife, and children in order to be a disciple of Jesus. Their interpretation is wrong, Clement argues, for the God of I Corinthians also commanded, "Honor your father and your mother" (Exod. 20:12).[158] Paul's advice in 7:9 is thus not to be understood as antifamilial or antireproductive. Clement also insists that Paul's concession concerns only *second* marriage, so eager is this author to praise the virtues of a single marriage. If a single marriage is undertaken with rational purpose, controlled will, and for the sake of reproduction,[159] it *needs* no concession.

A second question eliciting various answers asked what Paul meant by "burning" (*purousthai* [7:9]). The majority of patristic commentators (as well as the translators of the Revised Standard Version) interpret the "burning" as that of sexual desire, variously called "the fires of love,"[160] "the heat of the flesh,"[161] or "concupiscence."[162] Thus Origen in his *Com-*

[154] Tertullian, *De exhortatione castitatis* 3.6; 4.5 (CCL 2, 1019, 1021).

[155] Tertullian, *Ad uxorem* 1.3.2 (CCL 1, 375); cf. *De exhortatione castitatis* 4; *De monogamia* 14.

[156] Tertullian, *De monogamia* 14.2–3 (CCL 2, 1249).

[157] John Chrysostom, *Hom. 23 II Cor.* 6 (PG 61, 562).

[158] Clement of Alexandria, *Stromata* 3.15.97.1–3 (GCS 52 [15], 240).

[159] Clement of Alexandria, *Stromata* 3.1.4.3 (GSC 52 [15], 197); cf. *Stromata* 3.7.58; 3.11.71; 3.12.79. For a discussion of what Clement means by a "single marriage," see Yves Tissot, "Henogamie et remariage chez Clement d'Alexandrie," *Rivista di storia e letteratura religiosa* 11 (1975): 167–97.

[160] Ambrose, *Exp. Luc.* 4.63 (CCL 14, 128).

[161] Ambrosiaster, *Comm. I Cor.* 7:9 (2) (CSEL 81.2, 74).

[162] Especially Augustine; see, for exam-

mentary on I Corinthians so interprets the "burning": it is "the lust of the flesh" against which I John 2:16 and Galatians 5:16 warn, a burning that masters the soul of the sinner and is not quenched by reason. Origen, as well as other patristic commentators, reads the passage in connection with verse 8 ("to the unmarried and the widows . . . ") and thus believes that the verse does not pertain to first marriage, which is hereby removed from guilt-by-association. Although the Apostle does not declare second marriage to be impermissible, it is not a "good," for it is not in accordance with "temperance" (*sōphrosunē*), nor is it "according to nature" (*kata physin*). Of a second wife, Origen asserts, it is not possible to say, "Bone of my bones and flesh of my flesh" (Gen. 2:23), and as proof, he notes that only the first wives of the patriarchs were privileged to lie in the tomb of their husbands (Gen. 25:10; 49:31).[163] Later in his *Commentary*, Origen cites verse 7:9 as an example of Paul's "becoming weak for the weak" (9:22)—"weak" because he concedes the sexual relation on account of *porneiai* (7:2).[164] According to Methodius, Paul adds the provision of verse 9 for those whose "animal passion" is strong: Paul does not deem second marriage after the death of a spouse "good," but he concedes that it is better than "burning."[165]

Others, reading the verse to lend advice on second marriage after the death of a spouse, were slightly more lenient. Augustine emphasizes that the concession of verse 9 is meant only for those who cannot control themselves,[166] yet second marriage for widows should not be despised by those who deem themselves more "pure": remarriage is meant to prevent or forestall the "burning" of passion.[167] Jerome takes the verse similarly, when he writes that his friend Fabiola should be excused for marrying a second time (and this after divorce, not after widowhood); the marriage may have been necessary so that she would keep from "burning."[168] Since Jerome is scarcely a proponent of first marriage, let alone second, his words must be understood as an attempted justification of the dubious behavior of his devoted friend and patron; in other letters, Jerome argues it would be better for widows not even to *know* that Paul had conceded remarriage as an allowable option for them.[169] John Chrysostom, commenting on 7:9,

ple, *De sancta virginitate* 34.34; *De civitate Dei* 14; *De agone Christiano* 31.33; also Jerome, *Adversus Iovinianum* 1.9; *epp.* 49 (48).17; 77.3; 79.10.

[163] Origen, *Comm. I Cor.* 7:8–12 (Jenkins [1908], pp. 503–4).

[164] Origen, *Comm. I Cor.* 9:22 (Jenkins [1908], pp. 513–14).

[165] Methodius, *Symposium* 3.12 (GCS 27, 41).

[166] Augustine, *De bono coniugali* 10.10 (CSEL 41, 314): and is certainly better than the "burning" that leads a person to commit adultery (Augustine, *De coniugiis adulterinis* 2.12.12 [CSEL 41, 397]).

[167] Augustine, *De agone Christiano* 31.33 (CSEL 41, 136).

[168] Jerome, *ep.* 77.3 (CSEL 55, 39).

[169] Jerome, *ep.* 79.10 (CSEL 55, 99).

likewise appears to understand marriage as a deterrent for lust: since the "tyranny of concupiscence" brings great pain, one can withdraw from the struggle (by marriage) rather than be "subverted," that is, fall into fornication.[170] Yet the far superior state, Augustine adds, would be for the virgin not to burn even though she was not married, just as Daniel and his companions were preserved from the flames in the fiery furnace.[171]

A second group of interpreters, however, takes the "burning" of verse 9 to apply not to sexual desire, but to punishment,[172] a view that acquired force from a passive construal of the verb: "to be burned." Addressing verse 9, Tertullian rhetorically inquires, "What sort of good is it that is understood to be better [only] than a penalty?" Of course it is better to lose one eye than both, but neither option is good![173] Tertullian ponders the alternative interpretations of the verse: does Paul mean the fires of concupiscence or the fires of penalty? Since Paul granted marriage, he surely cannot believe that fornication is forgiven—and it is with fornication that Tertullian associates the "fire of concupiscence." Thus Paul must mean the "fire of penalty," specifically, the hellfire that awaits fornicators.[174] Tertullian reinforces this interpretation by appealing to the example of Dido, who he claims preferred "to burn rather than to marry."[175] The pun was deemed so witty that Jerome could not resist borrowing it (without attribution), even though his own interpretation of "burning" almost always pertains to the "fires of lust."[176]

Pelagius, for his part, does not even consider a more metaphoric interpretation of "burning" in his *Commentary on I Corinthians.* Most likely his understanding of the "burning" as punishment is derived from Tertullian, the source of so much moral teaching in the Latin patristic tradition. Thus according to Pelagius, when Paul writes that it is "better to marry than to burn," he alludes to the fiery punishment that will be meted out to fornicators. Pelagius finds his example in Genesis 38:24, the penalty that would have awaited Judah's daughter-in-law Tamar for her alleged

[170] John Chrysostom, *Hom. 19 I Cor.* 2 (PG 61, 153–54).

[171] Augustine, *De sancta virginitate* 56.57 (CSEL 41, 301).

[172] A modern argument for this position is made by Michael L. Barré, "To Marry or to Burn: *Purousthai* in I Cor. 7:9," *Catholic Biblical Quarterly* 36 (1974): 193–202; such a reading helps "rescue" Paul's views of marriage.

[173] Tertullian, *De monogamia* 3.4–5 (CCL 2, 1231–32).

[174] Tertullian, *De pudicitia* 16.15–16 (CCL 2, 1313–14).

[175] Tertullian, *De exhortatione castitatis* 13.3 (CCL 2, 1034); *De monogamia* 17.2 (CCL 2, 1252).

[176] Jerome, *Adversus Iovinianum* 1.43 (PL 23, 286). I have found just one example in Jerome that perhaps supports the option of "fire as penalty" and that cites I Cor. 7:9. In *ep.* 22.29 (CSEL 54, 187), Jerome writes that if a servant girl pretends to have a monastic vocation so as to escape her servitude, she should have read to her "better to marry than to burn" (assuming that the "burning" will be the penalty for her prevarication).

harlotries, had not Judah's responsibility for her pregnancy been revealed in a timely fashion.[177] "Burning as penalty" is also the only interpretive option considered for this verse by the anonymous author of *On Chastity.* Citing 7:9, the author briefly remarks, something is suspicious about a "good" that is reckoned as "better" than a serious punishment![178] Did these Pelagian authors believe that the "burning" Paul here faults could not have meant that which attends a desire they deemed "natural"? Or, alternatively, did they think that Christians should have overcome sexual desire and hence do not need to marry in order to avoid "burning"?[179] Their motivations are undecidable.

An *a fortiori* argument ("how much more!") could be used by several patristic writers to explicate I Corinthians 7:9, just as they used it to interpret verses 1–2 of the chapter. Of the early Fathers, Tertullian is the most vociferous: how can marriage be considered a "good" when it is commended only by comparison with an evil ("burning"), as Paul suggests in 7:9? How much better neither to marry nor to burn! Why should Christians not choose what is "profitable" (celibacy), rather than what is merely "not harmful" (marriage)?[180] Contrasting the good with an evil makes of it a "lesser evil,"[181] and prompts the question, what kind of a good is compared only to a penalty?[182] Jerome, too, argues that if marriage were truly a "good," Paul would not have compared it to a fire.[183] As noted above, for the author of *On Chastity,* something is suspicious about a "good" which is counted as "better" only in relation to a serious punishment.[184]

John Cassian provides yet another interpretive option for I Corinthians 7:9 that appears to be unique to him. In his Fifth *Conference,* Cassian teaches that there are three kinds of fornication: that of actual intercourse; that of lusting after a woman in one's heart (Matt. 5:28); and that of the "uncleanness" that can come about quite apart from "touching a woman." This latter is the "uncleanness" ascribed to Onan in Genesis 38. According to Cassian, it is this uncleanness—interpreted as masturbation—that prompts Paul to write that "it is better to marry than to burn."[185] Here

[177] Pelagius, *Comm. I Cor.* 7:9 (PLS 1, 1200).

[178] (Anonymous), *De castitate* 10.6 (PLS 1, 1483).

[179] The first complete discussion of various Pelagian authors' teaching on sexual desire will be provided in a Ph.D. dissertation by Michael Rackett, "Sexuality and Sinlessness: The Diversity of Pelagian Theologies of Marriage and Virginity," Duke University, 1999. On Pelagius' own views, which do not represent those of other Pelagian writers, see Carlo Tibiletti, "Teologia Pelagiana su celibato matrimonio," *Augustinianum* 27 (1987): 487–507.

[180] Tertullian, *Ad uxorem* 1.3.3–6 (CCL 1, 375–76).

[181] Tertullian, *De exhortatione castitatis* 3.7–9 (CCL 2, 1019–20).

[182] Tertullian, *De monogamia* 3.4 (CCL 2, 1231).

[183] Jerome, *Adversus Iovinianum* 1.9 (PL 23, 233).

[184] (Anonymous), *De castitate* 10.6 (PLS 1, 1483).

[185] Cassian, *Conlationes* 5.11 (SC 42, 200).

we have an excellent example of how a Biblical verse, when transported to a different venue in which its original referents were inapplicable (here, an all-male monastery), could be adapted to fit the new situation.

Still other writers use the verse to express their views of the broader nature of morality. Thus Ambrosiaster, writing from an ethical tradition that emphasizes the virtue of struggle, claims on the basis of 7:9 that the "perfect" person feels desire, but resists it.[186] His tradition differs from that of Basilides, who, on the basis of the same verse, concludes the opposite: that if a Christian must concentrate on endurance, he or she has already "lost hope."[187] These more general interpretations, however, go beyond the more narrow scope of most patristic exegesis of I Corinthians 7:9.

> To the married I give charge, not I but the Lord, that the wife should not separate from her husband (but if she does, let her remain single or else be reconciled to her husband)—and that the husband should not divorce his wife.
>
> *I Cor. 7:10–11 RSV*

Chapter 9 above, "The Exegesis of Divorce," discusses in some detail various church fathers' interpretations of various Biblical texts pertaining to divorce. Here, I wish to note the comments patristic writers make on I Corinthians 7:10–11 in particular.

Some authors explicitly puzzle over the seeming diversity of Biblical teaching on the topic of divorce. Few, however, take the line Tertullian did in his polemic against the Marcionites' separation of the Testaments: citing I Corinthians 7:10–11, Tertullian argues that since both Christ and the Old Testament allow divorce, we can infer that one and the same God inspires both Testaments.[188] Since Tertullian assuredly did not favor divorce, it seems prudent to understand his argument here as specifically tailored to his anti-Marcionite polemic. Cyprian, in contrast, cites Paul's aversion to divorce to demonstrate the manifest superiority of Christian to ancient, "laxer," Hebrew teaching.[189]

More often, some resolution of Biblical texts was attempted. Origen, for example, prefaces his remarks on 7:10–11 by noting that although Moses sometimes served as "an organ of the word of God," he also issued

[186] Ambrosiaster, *Comm. I Cor.* 7:9 (2) (CSEL 81.2, 74).

[187] Basilides (or followers), cited in Clement of Alexandria, *Stromata* 3.1.2.1 (GCS 52 [15], 195–96).

[188] Tertullian, *Adversus Marcionem* 5.7.7 (CCL 1, 683).

[189] Cyprian, *Ad Quirinum* 3.90 (CSEL

commands—such as the teaching on divorce—on his own authority, an authority that was overridden by Jesus' pronouncement against divorce in Matthew 19. Origen further notes that Paul distinguishes his own "voice" from that of the Lord when he writes of divorce in I Corinthians 7:10,[190] and claims that the Lord speaks directly to the believing husband and wife in 7:10–11, but not to unbelievers, for unbelievers are unworthy of receiving divine law from God himself. Paul, as a lesser authority than Christ, utters verses 12–13 that permit divorce to unbelievers, to couples in "mixed marriages."[191]

Augustine follows a similar strategy in interpreting 7:10–13. Like Origen, Augustine argues that Jesus' teaching against divorce concerns marriages in which both partners were Christians; Paul, on the other hand, directs his remarks to couples in which one spouse is "pagan." There is, then, no discrepancy between Jesus' and Paul's teaching. In considering verses 10–11, Augustine stresses that if one party should leave, the other must remain unmarried.[192] Moreover, verses 10–11, Augustine posits, apply only to a situation in which the man committed adultery, for this would be the only legitimate reason for his wife to separate from him. Paul certainly would not have written that she is to remain unmarried, if it were not lawful for her to abandon her husband in the first place![193] Augustine here strives to bring I Corinthians 7, which appears to permit separation on the grounds of religious difference, into conformity with Jesus' words in Matthew 19:9 that allowed divorce only on the grounds of the wife's "unchastity" (*porneia*). I Corinthians 7, however, does not list *porneia* as a grounds for divorce, but assumes the freer right to divorce for both women and men under Roman law, as I explicate in chapter 9.

Jerome also notes the discrepancy in Biblical divorce laws in his *Commentary on Matthew*, in which he provides an explanation that became standard with many authors: Paul knew that Moses allowed for divorce because he feared that hatred and murder would result if the couple were forced to stay together. Appealing to I Corinthians 7:10–13, Jerome proclaims that Paul's concession for divorce is a *concilium* of man, not an *imperium* of God.[194] Once again, the assignment of "voice" rescues the texts from apparent discrepancy.

John Chrysostom is likewise anxious that no one, on the basis of 7:10–13, should imagine that Paul's teaching differed from Jesus': Paul would not have put himself at odds with the Lord's pronouncements. Since

3.1, 175).

[190] Origen, *Hom. 16 Num.* 4 (GCS 30, 142).

[191] Origen, *Comm. I Cor.* 7:10–11 (Jenkins [1908], pp. 504–5).

[192] Augustine, *De diversis quaestionibus octoginta tribus* 83 (CCL 44A, 248–49).

[193] Augustine, *De coniugiis adulternis* 3.3 (CSEL 41, 350).

[194] Jerome, *In Math.* 3 (19:8) (CCL 77, 166–67).

Jesus already in the Gospels had pronounced a law against divorce (Matt. 5:32; 19:9), Paul's words in I Corinthians 7:10 merely repeat the "Lord's command" against divorce for Christian couples, in Chrysostom's estimation. Yet since Jesus had said nothing about unbelievers, Paul in verses 12–13 lends some counsel. Even here, however, readers should acknowledge that his words were inspired by Christ. Chrysostom cites 7:40 ("For I think that I also have the Spirit of God") to argue that all verses of the chapter are divinely inspired: Paul's words do not necessarily carry a lesser authority.[195]

Chrysostom also reflects on what the "separation" mentioned in verse 10 might mean. In his *Homily 19 on I Corinthians*, he urges the wife to stay with the husband, although not cohabit with him. Does this mean that they might continue living under the same roof, although without sexual relation? Or that she should not legally divorce, even though she physically separates from her husband? (Chrysostom's explicitly stated prohibition against her remarriage indicates his recognition that she has the right under Roman law to initiate a divorce.)[196] Elsewhere, Chrysostom links the requirement to stay single after separation (v. 11) with the couple's abstention from sexual relations for prayer in verse 5. Nonetheless, in commenting on verse 11, Chrysostom warns *against* the couple's reconciliation. If the couple "stays apart," they will have to master their passion, which is difficult enough; but if they reconcile, the woman will experience the woes of marriage. Returning to her "overbearing lord," she must flatter him and submit to his abuse, physical and psychological.[197] Chrysostom posits that a possible reason prompting the "separation" in verse 10 might have been one party's decision for continence without the other's agreement.[198] In still another discussion, Chrysostom argues against "unilateral withdrawal" from the marital relation, citing 7:10 along with 7:5: the devil can invest sin with a show of piety in the case of a woman who abdicates from sexual relations without her husband's agreement, and whom she thus drives into adultery.[199] Here, the "separation" Paul mentions is interpreted by Chrysostom as sexual separation *within* a marriage, not as divorce.

Other writers invest the interpretation of these verses with their own particular concerns. Thus Ambrosiaster, supportive of marriage, interweaves his interpretation of I Corinthians 7:10–13 on "not leaving" with

[195] John Chrysostom, *De virginitate* 12.1–4 (SC 125, 128, 130).

[196] John Chrysostom, *Hom. 19 I Cor.* 2 (PG 61, 154).

[197] John Chrysostom, *De virginitate* 40.2 (SC 125, 234).

[198] John Chrysostom, *Hom. 19 I Cor.* 2 (PG 61, 154).

[199] John Chrysostom, *Hom. 86 Matt.* 4 (PG 58, 768). Augustine worried that the separation might come about because one party withdraws from the sexual relation without the consent of the other: *De coniugiis adulterinis* 1.1.

citations from I Timothy (bishops can be married [3:2–5], young widows should marry [5:14]); through an intertextual exegesis Ambrosiaster provides encouragement for "staying together." Holiness obtains in marriage, he claims, not just in singleness.[200] Jerome, for his part, employs verse 11 to argue the case for the equality of men and women under Christian law, even though civil law does not so ordain.[201] In general, early Christian writers cite these verses to encourage the cementing of the marriage, not its dissolution. Origen thus quotes 7:29 ("If you are bound, do not seek to be loosed") to reinforce the advice of 7:10 not to separate.[202] And Clement of Alexandria, eager to rescue marriage from the deprecatory evaluation of some "Gnostics," cites verses 10–11 to prove that the New Testament favors marriage.[203]

> To the rest I say, not the Lord, that if any brother has a wife who is an unbeliever, and she consents to live with him, he should not divorce her. If any woman has a husband who is an unbeliever, and he consents to live with her, she should not divorce him. For the unbelieving husband is consecrated through his wife, and the unbelieving wife is consecrated through her husband. Otherwise, your children would be unclean, but as it is they are holy. But if the unbelieving partner desires to separate, let it be so; in such a case the brother or sister is not bound. For God has called us to peace. Wife, how do you know whether you will save your husband? Husband, how do you know whether you will save your wife?
>
> *I Cor. 7:12–16 RSV*

These verses posed similar problems for patristic commentators as did the previous ones: how to square them with the tolerance for divorce in the Old Testament, on the one hand, and with Jesus' near-total prohibition of it, on the other?

[200] Ambrosiaster, *Quaestiones Veteris et Novi Testamenti* 127.34 (CSEL 50, 414).

[201] Jerome, *ep.* 77.3 (CSEL 55, 39).

[202] Origen, *Comm. I Cor.* 7:10 (Jenkins [1908], p. 505).

[203] Clement of Alexandria, *Stromata*

As a first step, Tertullian, followed by Pelagius, argues that verses 12–14 are directed to Christians *already* married to unbelievers: Paul does not intend to promote such marriages among those currently unattached, for he does not wish for "holy flesh" to be defiled with "Gentile flesh." Tertullian ominously alludes to such intermarriage with "strange flesh" as reminiscent of the unions in which the men of Sodom and Gomorrah engaged, according to Jude 7. For Tertullian, believers who marry Gentiles are guilty of "fornication": the "members of Christ" have been joined with those of an adulteress (I Cor. 6:15).[204] Thus for Tertullian, 7:12–14 contains a strong message against intermarriage.

Moreover, the Fathers register discomfort about the seeming permission for divorce implied in these verses. Origen's handling of the passage, as we have seen, attempts a possible resolution: although "the Lord" earlier commanded the Christian couple of verses 10–11 to stay together, Paul now speaks to those in a "mixed marriage" in verses 12–16. Just as Moses' divorce teaching (Deut. 24:1–3) was corrected by a higher authority, Jesus, so Paul, too, takes second place to Jesus. Although Paul's teaching is still "holy," Origen assures his readers, it is nonetheless much inferior to the law of the Lord.[205]

Paul's words on divorce raise thorny problems for Ambrose as well. Commenting on Luke 16:18 ("anyone who divorces his wife and takes another, commits adultery"), Ambrose resolves his textual dilemma by distinguishing between "marriages which are made by God" (presumably those between two Christians), which *are* bound by Jesus' antidivorce teaching in Matthew 19:6, and the marriages of which Paul speaks in 7:12–13, which are not "from God," because God did not give permission for Christians to be united to Gentiles. "The Law forbids it," Ambrose intones, citing Exodus 34:16, which warns Israelite males against marriages with women of "the nations." Objectors should not cite Proverbs 19:14 (that God prepares a prudent wife for a man) to counter the seeming permission for divorce in I Corinthians 7:12–13, for the "harmony" of the former marital relation is not found in the Christian-"pagan" marriage here under discussion: in this instance, the argument of the "backtalkers" fails. According to Ambrose, Paul in I Corinthians 7 "verifies" that divorce arose because of human weakness and was contrary to God's intention.[206]

3.18.108.1–2 (GCS 52 [15], 246).

[204] Tertullian, *Ad uxorem* 2.2–3.1 (CCL 1, 384–87). Pelagius merely notes briefly the main point: the verses are directed toward those Christians *already* married to nonbelievers, and are not meant as encouragement for the unattached to do so: *Comm. I Cor.* 7:13f. (PLS 1, 1201).

[205] Origen, *Comm. I Cor.* 7:12–13 (Jenkins [1908], p. 505).

[206] Ambrose, *Exp. Luc.* 8.2–3; 8.8 (CCL 14, 299, 300–301).

Augustine too puzzles over these verses in relation to other Biblical texts pertaining to divorce. Struggling to understand why the Lord does not here forbid divorce in the case of "pagan" marriages since he had previously declared fornication to be the only grounds for divorce (Matt. 19:9), Augustine reasons that the "paganism" of these verses is to be equated with the "fornication" of the Gospels: the texts are not, after all, discrepant. Moreover, since Paul scrupulously claims his own voice for verse 12, no one should mistakenly propose that the Lord here is "commanding" divorce. Jesus' words against divorce in the Gospels are directed to Christians in marriages with fellow Christians, not to those in marriages with Gentiles. But Paul was not contradicting Jesus, Augustine hastens to add, attempting to bring harmony to these varying texts.[207]

Augustine also cites 7:12ff. to resolve the dilemma posed by the words ascribed to Jesus in Luke 18:29–30 on "leaving" one's house, wife, and children for the sake of the Kingdom of God, a verse that appeared to conflict with Jesus' teaching that a wife can be divorced for no other reason than fornication (Matt. 19:6). Most certainly (Augustine exclaims) she cannot be "sold," as could the "house" of Luke 18:29! I Corinthians 7:12 suggests to Augustine the answer to his interpretive dilemma: the "leaving" of Luke 18 must pertain *only* to a case of mixed marriage. As in I Corinthians 7:12, if the unbeliever refuses to stay with the Christian spouse, the latter is "free," not "enslaved." A Christian, however, should never renounce the faith to accommodate an unbelieving spouse[208]—a view that Augustine shares with his sometime-opponent Pelagius.[209]

Augustine likewise pits I Corinthians 7:12 against Luke 18:29–30 ("leaving one's wife") in his treatise against the Manichean Adimantus. Arguing for the goodness of marriage against its deprecation by Manicheans, Augustine claims on the basis of I Corinthians 7:12 that it is *not* always necessary for a man to leave his wife for the sake of Jesus: sometimes he can "stay," as Paul here advises.[210] Augustine's enthusiasm for the "good" of marriage here allows the more "pro-marriage" verses to constrain others that seem less well-disposed to the institution. Augustine notes elsewhere, however, that the unbelieving party should be baptized: Paul did not intend that he or she would remain an unbeliever forever.[211]

Basil of Caesarea's reflection on the New Testament divorce texts affords a revealing glimpse into how little headway Christian teaching had

[207] Augustine, *De diversis quaestionibus octoginta tribus* 83 (CCL 44A, 248–49).

[208] Augustine, *ep.* 157.31 (CSEL 44, 478–79).

[209] Pelagius, *Comm. I Cor.* 7:15 (PLS 1, 1201).

[210] Augustine, *Contra Adimantum* 3 (CSEL 25, 118–20).

[211] Augustine, *De peccatorum meritis* 2.26.42 (CSEL 60, 114).

made in changing customary sexual values and practice. Basil first wonders why "unchastity" as a grounds for divorce (Matt. 19:6) seems to apply only to women, not to men. Despite Paul's words in I Corinthians 6:16 against men's fornication with prostitutes, Basil admits that even in his day it still is customary for wives to take back fornicating husbands. Basil, like Augustine, finds his solution in comparing fornication to unbelief. If Paul writes (7:13) that the husband's unbelief is no reason for a Christian wife to separate from him—and Basil gratuitously adds, nor is her being beaten—neither should a wife leave a fornicating husband.[212] Basil here neatly justifies customary expectations regarding marital straying by an appeal to the Pauline text.

John Chrysostom in commenting on 7:12–16 also urges the Christian spouse to stay with the unbeliever. Just as Paul argues that a slave can be "free" while remaining enslaved (7:21–23), so the Christian man is not injured by staying with an unbelieving wife.[213] Although Christ did not raise the issue of marriage with unbelievers in his own divorce teaching, Chrysostom concedes, we are not to think that Paul's advice is at odds with Jesus' commands, for Paul is "inspired."[214] Stay married to an unbeliever, Chrysostom counsels,[215] for even in a "mixed" marriage the "two become one flesh" (Gen. 2:24).[216] Thus a wide variety of patristic commentators seek to reconcile Jesus' teaching on divorce with Paul's, often focusing on the difference in situations—the marriage of two Christians, or a "mixed marriage"—to justify the seemingly different advice given.

One disputed point attending these verses pertained to the meaning of "consecration" (or "sanctification") of the unbelieving spouse by the Christian one (7:14). Some interpretations could be summarily ruled out, according to Ambrose: for example, "sanctification" does not result from the act of sexual intercourse.[217] Was the verse intended to prohibit sexual relations during a wife's menstruation, Augustine muses, referring to Ezekiel 18:6?[218] For Clement of Alexandria, eager always to defend the sanctity of marriage against his "Gnostic" opponents, 7:14 proves that marriage is sanctioned by the New Testament,[219] but fornication is not.[220]

[212] Basil of Caesarea, *ep.* 188.9 (Loeb III:34, 36).

[213] John Chrysostom, *Hom. 19 I Cor.* 3 (PG 61, 155).

[214] John Chrysostom, *De virginitate* 12.2–3 (SC 125, 128, 130).

[215] John Chrysostom, *Hom. 26 Gen.* 2 (PG 53, 231–32).

[216] John Chrysostom, *Hom. 33 I Cor.* 5 (PG 61, 282).

[217] Ambrose, *De Cain et Abel* 1.10.46 (PL 14, 357).

[218] Augustine, *De peccatorum meritis* 3.12.21 (CSEL 60, 148–49). Most intriguing, Augustine notes that he has been reading Pelagius' exposition on I Corinthians. In his remarks on I Cor. 7:14, however, Pelagius does not comment on the point.

[219] Clement of Alexandria, *Stromata* 3.18.108.1–2 (GCS 52 [15], 246).

[220] Clement of Alexandria, *Stromata*

John Chrysostom likewise stresses that men are "sanctified" by wives, not by harlots.[221] The "uncleanness" of 7:14 comes not from the sexual act itself, Chrysostom insists, but from the "idolatry" of the unbelieving spouse, from the unclean mind.[222] Since even married Christians living in "the world" are saints, the faith that makes them holy also sanctifies the unbelieving spouse of a "mixed marriage."[223] Unlike Ambrose, Origen more daringly compares the "mixing" of the faith of the believing with the unbelieving partner to the sexual "mixing" of the man and woman, like the mixing of water and wine, that renders them "one flesh" (Gen. 2:24). Origen, like other patristic commentators, hopes that with time, the couple's conversation and relationship will enable the Christian spouse to "conquer" the unbelieving partner.[224]

A last debated point concerning these verses queried how the Christian spouse might "save" the non-Christian partner (7:16). The troubling aspect of this verse for several Fathers lay in the claim that the wife might "save" the husband: how could this be, if women were not allowed to teach, according to "Paul" in I Timothy 2:12? One answer posited that although women could not teach in public, they could instruct impious husbands at home: so Theodore of Mopsuestia and John Chrysostom.[225] Chrysostom explains that women were ordered not to teach in I Timothy because a woman was responsible for the first sin; she and her descendants, as punishment, have been subjected to men (Gen. 3:16). But, conversely, if men become the sinful sex, they may then need women's saving influence, as Paul writes in 7:16.[226] Women have even "spared nations," Chrysostom intones, citing I Corinthians 7:16 and Paul's female addressees in Romans 16 to illustrate women's capacity for heroic action.[227] It is not, of course, by performing routine marital or household duties that a wife "saves" her husband, Chrysostom quickly adds, but by her "practice of philosophy."[228]

An instructive example of how asceticism could "raise the stakes" for the interpretation of Biblical verses is found in Palladius' use of 7:16. Praising the adolescent couple Melania the Younger and Pinian, Palladius cites 7:16 to show how a wife "saved" her husband. Here, however, the "sav-

3.12.84.2–4 (GCS 52 [15], 234–35).

221 John Chrysostom, *Hom. 63 Ioan.* 4 (PG 59, 353).

222 John Chrysostom, *Hom. 19 I Cor.* 3 (PG 61, 154–55).

223 John Chrysostom, *Hom. 10 Heb.* 4 (PG 63, 87–88).

224 Origen, *Comm. I Cor.* 7:14 (Jenkins [1908], pp. 505–6).

225 Theodore of Mopsuestia, *Ad I Tim.* 2:12 (Swete II:93–94); John Chrysostom, *Hom. 31 Rom.* 1 (PG 60, 669); cf. *Hom. 26 Gen.* 2 (PG 53, 231–32).

226 John Chrysostom, *Serm. 5 Gen.* 1 (PG 54, 600).

227 John Chrysostom, *Hom. 61 Ioan.* 4 (PG 59, 341).

228 John Chrysostom, *De virginitate* 47.1 (SC 125, 262, 264).

ing" is not effected by Pinian's conversion from "paganism" to Christianity, the topic of Paul's discussion in this verse, but by his "conversion" to a more rigorously ascetic form of Christianity. Melania has "saved" Pinian from a mediocre Christian commitment.[229]

> Only, let every one lead the life which the Lord has assigned to him, and in which God has called him. This is my rule in all the churches. Was any one at the time of his call already circumcised? Let him not seek to remove the marks of circumcision. Was any one at the time of his call uncircumcised? Let him not seek circumcision. For neither circumcision counts for anything nor uncircumcision, but keeping the commandments of God. Every one should remain in the state in which he was called. Were you a slave when called? Never mind. But if you can gain your freedom, avail yourself of the opportunity. For he who was called in the Lord as a slave is a freedman, of the Lord. Likewise he who was free when called is a slave of Christ. You were bought with a price; do not become slaves of men. So, brethren, in whatever state each was called, there let him remain with God.
>
> *I Cor. 7:17–24 RSV*

These verses, which modern scholars might deem a digression from Paul's main theme of marital status, were not so read by many ancient commentators. Here Origen's interpretation decisively influenced later authors, especially Jerome, who relied heavily on him for their own ascetic exegesis. Conversely, it is of interest that writers such as Augustine, standing largely outside the Origenist exegetical tradition, make no use at all of these verses in their discussions of marriage and celibacy, despite their manifest interest in themes of "slavery" and "freedom."

[229] Palladius, *Historia Lausiaca* 61 (Butler, p. 156; also in [Gerontius], *Vita Melaniae Iunioris* 4 [SC 90, 134]).

Origen, and Jerome after him, recognize that Paul might here be accused of digressing to unconnected topics unless "slavery/freedom" and "circumcision/uncircumcision" were understood metaphorically as amplifying the main discussion on marriage:[230] the text is here taken to "implode" on the major topic of interest. Origen briefly makes this connection in his *Commentary on Romans.* Expounding Romans 1:1 (Paul as a "slave"), Origen turns to I Corinthians 7 for textual ballast. The "slavery" of marriage is proved by Paul's words in I Corinthians 7:4 (that neither spouse has freedom over his or her own body). Origen senses that 7:21 (if slaves can gain their freedom, "use it") must be carefully interpreted so that no reader imagines that "using one's freedom," by analogy, means the "freedom to divorce." Rather, a couple can be "free" within marriage if by mutual agreement they practice continence, such as Paul recommends in I Corinthians 7:5. Moreover, the person who is a "slave" in marriage can nonetheless be "free" in the cultivation of virtues such as faith, patience, mercy, and justice. Such a person Paul calls a "freedman (*libertus*) of the Lord" in 7:22. Yet even "freer," Origen argues, is the man without a wife who comes to Christ in the "purity of continence"—although even he can still be called a "slave of Christ" (7:22). Complete "freedom" will come only when we see "face to face," not in the "mirror or riddle" (I Cor. 13:12) that constitutes our present life in the flesh.[231] Romans 1:1 has prompted Origen to reflect on the "slavery" or "freedom" that marriage involves.

Origen's fullest discussion of I Corinthians 7:17–24 is found in his *Commentary on I Corinthians.* Fortunately, the fragments of this section of the *Commentary* are quite fully preserved. Here, Origen greatly expands the discussion of circumcision/uncircumcision, calibrating his evaluative code with the Jewish expectation that circumcision is more highly valued than the "uncircumcision" of the Gentiles. "Uncircumcision," on the new interpretive grid, stands as a code for marriage, but what might "circumcision," by contrast, mean? Does the "wifelessness" of circumcision simply connote "celibacy," or could it be taken to mean that becoming "wifeless" through divorce was also a possibility? The latter option Origen seeks to rule out through a complex exegesis of I Corinthians 7:18–20.

The first exegetical move Origen here makes is designed to forestall any notion that the act of "circumcision" might graphically suggest the "cutting" off of marriage by divorce—for could not someone reason that

[230] See Origen, *Comm. Rom.* 1.3.1 (1:1) (Hammond Bammel, p. 46); *Comm. I Cor.* 7:21–24 (Jenkins [1908], p. 508); *De principiis* 4.3.3 (GCS 22, 328); Jerome, *Adversus Iovinianum* 1.11 (PL 23, 235).

[231] Origen, *Comm. Rom.* 1.3.1 (1:1) (Hammond Bammel, pp. 46–48).

if marriage is described as becoming "one flesh" (Gen. 2:24), "circumcision" as a higher state might be taken to mean a permissible "cutting" of the "one flesh" by divorce? No, Origen retorts: "one flesh" betokens the solidity of the relation, which should precisely *not* be broken by divorce. Just as Paul counseled Jewish male converts (as circumcised, i.e., "wifeless") not to become "uncircumcised" (7:18) (in the transposed code, to acquire a wife), so now he instructs the married (= the uncircumcised) not to become "wifeless" (= circumcised) by divorce. If a man is at present without a wife, then he should not marry, Origen argues, but if married, he should not imagine divorce to be a legitimate option.

Further, since Paul writes that "neither circumcision nor uncircumcision counts for anything" (7:19), the same holds for marriage and for singleness: they are *adiaphora*, "indifferent things."[232] Countering the Marcionites, Origen argues that Christians can live in marriage "without reproach." According to Origen, Paul means that salvation depends neither on marriage nor on celibacy, but on "keeping the commandments of God" (7:19). Just as Paul counsels the circumcised and the uncircumcised, the slave and the free, to remain in the state in which they were called (7:20), so with the married and the single: the married should not seek divorce, and if the single have the strength to preserve their celibacy, they should remain in their state of "purity."[233]

The analogy of marriage and celibacy with slavery and freedom is beset with fewer interpretive problems for Origen: in this case, there is no doubt how the terms are to be aligned. Indeed, the metaphor of marriage as "slavery" appears so frequently in the ascetic writings of the fourth and fifth centuries that we are prone to forget its original referent. That marriage is "slavery" and singleness is "freedom," Origen posits, is supported by the intertext of I Corinthians 7:4 (on spouses not having power over their own bodies). According to Origen, Paul's advice to slaves in I Corinthians 7:21 (that if they have an opportunity to gain their freedom, they may "use it rather") should be taken, on the transposed code, as a recommendation for continence *within* the marriage relationship, an interpretation bolstered by 7:5, Paul's advice that couples separate to devote themselves to prayer by mutual agreement. In this way, one can be "free" while still a "slave" in marriage. Yet even the man who is called while he is "free" (i.e., unmarried) is still a "slave" to the Word of God, even though not the "slave" of a wife.[234]

[232] *Adiaphora* was a term used by Stoic philosophers to suggest that there was a "neutral" realm of things that in themselves neither hurt nor harmed a person, but whose effect depended on their right use. The concept muted the absoluteness of the Old Stoics' teaching on virtue and vice, which admitted no intermediary categories.

[233] Origen, *Comm. I Cor.* 7:18–20 (Jenkins [1908], pp. 506–7).

[234] Origen, *Comm. I Cor.* 7:18–20, 21–24 (Jenkins [1908], pp. 506, 508).

Jerome's discussion of these verses in *Against Jovinian* follows Origen's codes closely. Christians should not read Paul's advice on "slavery" in I Corinthians 7 too literally, Jerome advises, for then Paul would seem to be digressing in an incoherent manner, even to contradict himself. On a "literal" reading, the text might deconstruct itself. Had Paul not told slaves to obey their masters (Eph. 6:5; Col. 3:22; I Tim. 6:1; Titus 2:9) and in 7:20 and 24, to "remain in their calling"—yet now does he instruct them *not* to be "slaves of men"? The confusion that might result from such a literal understanding of "slavery" suggests that we ought rather to read "slavery" as portending something else, namely, "marriage."

Likewise, Jerome argues, if anyone is "uncircumcised," that is, married, let him not seek to become "circumcised," that is, unmarried (by divorce), for "neither circumcision nor uncircumcision counts for anything, but keeping the commandments of God" (7:19). Otherwise, the sheer fact of physical virginity, such as that observed by the Vestal Virgins, would imply that such women could be saints—without either Christian faith or works. When Paul counsels "slaves" that if they have a chance for freedom to "use it," he does not advocate divorce, but abstinence within marriage. So, Jerome continues, even if a man is still a "slave" of a wife, he can be a "freedman" of the Lord. Yet the unmarried, too, are "slaves of Christ," becoming "one spirit with him" (I Cor. 6:17), a verse that Jerome pointedly contrasts with the "becoming one flesh" (Gen. 2:24) of a marriage involving sexual relation.[235] Since we have been "bought with Christ's blood" (7:23), we must reject "poisonous pleasures."[236] It is evident how closely Jerome has followed Origen in his exegesis of this passage, how readily he agrees that the passages on slavery "implode" into the discussion of marriage.

Jerome repeats these sentiments in his letters, where he has further opportunity to demonstrate his exegetical ingenuity. For example, in *Epistle* 128 to Gaudentius in which Jerome gives advice on how to raise a daughter (for consecrated virginity, Jerome hopes), he cites 7:21 and repeats his equation of circumcision with virginity and uncircumcision with marriage, but expands the verse's import by means of intertexts. Adam received the "coat" (of skins: Gen. 3:21) of marriage at the time he was expelled from Paradise, Jerome claims. Those called in "uncircumcision" that is, in marriage, wear these "skins of matrimony" and should not seek the "nakedness" (Gen. 2:25) of virginity by divorce. Rather, let this man "possess his vessel (i.e., his wife) in sanctification and honor," as I Thessa-

[235] See, for example, Jerome, *ep*. 55.2; *Comm. Eph*. 3 (5:22–23).

[236] Jerome, *Adversus Iovinianum* 1.11 (PL 23, 35–37); cf. his explications in *epp*. 49 (48).6; 145.

lonians 4:4 commands. Married people should be further instructed to drink only from their own "wells," not from the dissolute cisterns of harlots that do not hold the waters of chastity (Jer. 2:13; Prov. 5:15): sexual fidelity within marriage is here absolutely commanded. Passing to the parallel of slavery and freedom, Jerome notes that for Paul, the married are "slaves" (7:21–22), and Jerome himself names their "master": "the flesh."[237] This ingenious example of intertextual exegesis pressures 7:17–24 in a highly ascetic direction.

I Corinthians 7:23 (not being "servants of men," since Christians are "bought with a price") could be given a decisively ascetic twist as well. Eusebius of Emesa, reciting the story of Bernice, Prosdoce, and Domnina (in which a mother urges her virgin daughters to martyrdom rather than expose them to sexual attack), frames a speech for the mother's lips. Prodding her daughters to remain virginal "temples" rather than to sink to the level of *mulieres* (here, women who have experienced sexual intercourse), the mother reminds them that they are consecrated vessels more precious than gold, not "servants of men" (*ancillae hominum*), for they have been "bought with a price" (7:23).[238] Here, Paul's counsel on "being free in the Lord" translates directly into "remaining free from sexual relation."

John Chrysostom can also put 7:23 ("do not become slaves of men") to novel use for a particular ascetic interpretive community. Writing against ascetic men who cohabit with women in syneisaktic relations, he spells out the servile behavior required of them in this domestic arrangement. Chrysostom cites 7:23 to pointed effect: if Paul commands that Christians should not become "slaves of men," how much more should male ascetics not become "slaves of women!"[239] Here, Chrysostom's intended audience lends an unexpected nuance to Paul's words.

> Now concerning the unmarried, I have no command of the Lord, but I give my opinion as one who by the Lord's mercy is trustworthy. I think that in view of the impending distress it is well for a person to remain as he is. Are you bound to a wife? Do not seek to be free. Are you free from a wife? Do not seek marriage. But if you marry, you do not sin, and if a girl mar-

[237] Jerome, *ep.* 128.3 (CSEL 56, 158).

[238] Eusebius of Emesa, *Hom.* 6.18 (Buytaert I:162–63).

[239] John Chrysostom, *Adversos eos qui apud se habent subintroductas virgines* 10 (PG 47, 509).

ries she does not sin. Yet those who
marry will have worldly troubles, and
I would spare you that.

I Cor. 7:25–28 RSV

I Corinthians 7:25–28 occasioned only minor points of disagreement among patristic exegetes. Paul's words in verse 25, that he had "no command of the Lord" for the unmarried, could nonetheless be read with varied nuance. To Jerome's opponent, Jovinian, Paul's admission suggests that since the Apostle has "no command," the virginal and the married states remain equal in value.[240] For most church fathers, however, the verse gave opportunity to stress that a commitment to virginity was higher than any mere "command"; as a "counsel," it prompted rigorous Christians to choose freely that which was above "the law." Sometimes Jesus' injunction to "become a eunuch for the sake of the Kingdom of Heaven," but concurrent admission that "not all could receive" this teaching (Matt. 19:12), was conjoined to verse 25. Arguments of this type are found in the writings of Ambrose, Jerome, Pelagius, anonymous Pelagian authors, Irenaeus, Methodius, Basil of Ancyra, Origen, and John Chrysostom.[241] Basil of Ancyra, for example, explains the verse thus: since God in Genesis 1:28 had already commanded reproduction, he could not make virginity a "law." Indeed, Basil notes, the choice of virginity was given to the world only at the time of Jesus, when swords were beaten into plowshares (Isa. 2:4; Mic. 4:3); Basil's intertexts here suggest that sexual activity signals a time of "war," while virginity is to be associated with "peace." Yet even in the Beatitudes, Basil notes, Jesus did not include a blessing on virginity so that the decision for abstinence would be attributed to free will, above any command and above "nature," which is governed by law.[242]

Yet various authors could press verse 25 ("Now concerning the unmarried, I have no command of the Lord, but I give my opinion as one who by the Lord's mercy is trustworthy") in an ascetic direction by the nuance they give it, the intertexts with which they read it, and the level of authority that they here concede to Paul. Thus Ambrose asks in regard to Paul's

[240] Jovinian in Jerome, *Adversus Iovinianum* 1.12 (PL 23, 237).

[241] Ambrose, *ep.* 63.35; *De virginibus* 1.5.23; Jerome, *Adversus Iovinianum* 1.12; *ep.* 22.20; Pelagius, *Comm. I Cor.* 7:25; *Ad Demetriadem* 9; (Anonymous), *De virginitate* 4.3; (Anonymous), *ep. de virginitate* (= *Ad Claudiam*) 4; Methodius, *Symposium* 3.13; Basil of Ancyra, *De virginitate* 55; Irenaeus, *Adversus haereses* 4.15.2; Origen, *Hom. 16 Num.* 4; *Comm. I Cor.* 7:25; John Chrysostom, *Hom. 19 I Cor.* 5; *De virginitate* 2.2; 47.4; *Hom. 78 Matt.* 1.

[242] Basil of Ancyra, *De virginitate* 55 (Vaillant, pp. 63, 65). Basil does not comment on the *Acts of Paul and Thecla* 5–6, which *does* include blessings on virginity among the macarisms.

admission that he had "no command," if *Paul* didn't, who else is likely to have had one? Ambrose puzzles: Paul certainly showed by his own example his preference for celibacy.[243] Moreover, verse 40, in which Paul claims for himself the "Spirit of God," could be summoned to argue that at verse 25 Paul had offered a divine, not a human, judgment: so the anonymous author of *De castitate*.[244] Pelagius likewise cites 7:25 to Demetrias, adding that although Paul denies his words are a "command," he also wrote to a skeptical audience in II Corinthians 13:3, "Do you desire proof that Christ is speaking in me?"[245] Here, an intertext from Paul's own writings bolsters his claim to divine authority.

Origen, for his part, interweaves his discussion of 7:25 with an appeal to Luke 17:10 (even when Jesus' followers have done all that they were commanded, they still must confess, "we are unworthy servants; we have only done what is our duty"): if Christians adopt Paul's recommendation of celibacy by their own free will, they need no longer confess that they are "unworthy." Christians have good reason to accept Paul's recommendation of celibacy, Origen argues, for in verse 25, Paul assures us that he is "trustworthy."[246] Pelagian authors could also appeal to verse 25 to emphasize a favorite theme: that we must fulfill all that is commanded before we can expect to receive any profit from doing what lies "above" the command.[247]

Since most patristic writers did not expect the imminent end of the world, there is little or no eschatological expectation fueling their interpretation of verse 26 concerning the "impending (or present) distress." Rather, the "distress" is read as signaling the "woes of marriage": virginity, it is argued, improves one's life here and now, not just in heaven.[248] So great are the stresses of the present world, the "perversity of things," that a married man, weighed down with cares and misfortunes, sins inadvertently, according to John Chrysostom.[249] Jerome thinks the "present distress" is good reason for choosing virginity,[250] but sharpens its meaning: the "distress" is to be identified with "swelling wombs and wailing infants."[251] Elsewhere, he puts an edge on the "distress" of verse 26 by read-

[243] Ambrose, *De virginibus* 1.5.23 (PL 16, 206).

[244] (Anonymous), *De castitate* 10.7 (PLS 1, 1483).

[245] Pelagius, *Ad Demetriadem* 9 (PL 30, 26).

[246] Origen, *Comm. I Cor.* 7:25 (Jenkins [1908], p. 509); cf. Origen's comments on I Cor. 9:16 (Jenkins [1908], p. 512).

[247] (Anonymous), *ep. de virginitate* (= *Ad Claudiam*) 4 (CSEL 1, 229); cf. (Anonymous), *De castitate* 10.8 (PLS 1, 1484), citing James 2:10 to argue that a person cannot be saved if he or she transgresses even one commandment.

[248] Ambrosiaster, *Comm. I Cor.* 7:26–27 (CSEL 81.2, 82).

[249] John Chrysostom, *De virginitate* 43 (SC 125, 250).

[250] Jerome, *Adversus Iovinianum* 1.5 (PL 23, 228).

[251] Jerome, *Adversus Iovinianum* 1.12 (PL 23, 239).

ing it via the intertext of Matthew 24:19, "Woe to those who are with child . . . "[252] The reproductive aspect of marriage here becomes the strongest signifier of "distress."

Augustine assumes a characteristically moderating view when discussing 7:26. Over against (presumably) Jovinian, Augustine argues that 7:26 implies that it is not only for the here-and-now that virgins are better off than married women, as if Paul believed that they will be equal in the world to come! Yet Augustine also deaccentuates the appeal to the practical problems of marriage as an interpretation of the "present distress," since, he argues, Paul's teaching is entirely directed to eternal life, not to the trivialities of the present era.[253] Pelagius has it both ways: by Paul's proclaiming that it is a "good" for the unmarried to stay as they are (v. 26), readers should understand a double benefit of virginity: present freedom from worldly cares and a heavenly reward for their virginity later.[254] For none of the writers here cited, however, does the "distress" of 7:26 signal the imminent arrival of the eschaton.

Verse 27 ("Are you bound to a wife? Do not seek to be free. Are you free from a wife? Do not seek marriage") buttressed the Fathers' understanding that although Paul preferred celibacy, he also opposed divorce as a means of gaining "freedom"; as we have seen, the Fathers tend rather to strengthen the relatively mild Pauline dissuasion of divorce. Tertullian, citing 7:27, reminds Christians that it is divine—not human—action which breaks marriages. If God wishes a marriage to cease, he will remove one spouse by death;[255] it does not devolve on the husband or wife to initiate a separation. Even the anonymous author of *De castitate*, who scorns marriage, emphasizes that both parts of 7:27 are to be taken seriously: a wife is not to be "loosed" if a man is married, but if he is not, neither should he seek a spouse.[256] Origen and Jerome, both of whom interpret marriage as "slavery," stress that those who are "bound" (i.e., married) must remain in servitude:[257] no divorce is countenanced.

I Corinthians 7:27 also prompts Augustine to note the difference between precepts and counsels: "if bound, do not seek to be free" is a precept, an absolute command against divorce, whereas "if free, do not seek to be bound" is a counsel, which Christians may reject or choose as they please.[258] Athanasius deploys 7:27 against virgins who wish to live in "spir-

[252] Jerome, *Adversus Helvidium* 21 (PL 23, 215); also cited in *Adversus Iovinianum* 1.12 (PL 23, 239).

[253] Augustine, *De sancta virginitate* 21.21; 13.13; 19.19 (CSEL 41, 255–56, 245–46, 252).

[254] Pelagius, *Comm. I Cor.* 7:26 (PLS 1, 1202).

[255] Tertullian, *Ad uxorem* 1.7.1–2 (CCL 1, 381).

[256] (Anonymous), *De castitate* 10.10 (PLS 1, 1486).

[257] Origen, *Comm. I Cor.* 7:27 (Jenkins [1908], p. 509); Jerome, *ep.* 145 (CSEL 56, 306).

[258] Augustine, *De sancta virginitate*

itual marriage" with men: "Are you free? Do not seek a wife," he recites (albeit with some gender-bending) to dissuade the women from such relationships.[259] For the most part, these verses were thought to point up the "difference in times" between the two Testaments: in the Old Dispensation, God had said, "It is not good to be alone" (Gen. 2:18); now, God counsels, "It is well to remain as is."[260]

Yet the unmarried do not sin if they marry (v. 28)[261]—if, and only if, the Fathers qualify, they have not made a prior commitment to virginity or celibacy, in which case they commit egregious sin.[262] Origen's comment on the verse is brief but pointed: Paul writes not that it is "good" to marry, but that it is "not a sin"; "note the difference."[263] According to Origen, "good" is rather reserved for "not touching" (7:1) and for remaining single "as I do" (7:7).

Discussion also attended verse 7:28b, the "worldly troubles" that Paul would spare the Corinthians by advising them against marriage.[264] Augustine rues that he did not hear this verse during his allegedly unruly adolescence, for doing so might have steered him toward the path of celibacy.[265] Yet Augustine takes care to assure his readers that it is the "burdensomeness" of marriage that Paul here signals, not any "evil"—although, to be sure, one cannot have marriage without these cares, the "tribulation of the flesh."[266]

For Origen, the virgin is free of these "worldly" troubles, predicted for women in Genesis 3:16. Human marriage, "becoming two in one flesh" (Gen. 2:24), Origen notes, commences in the dark. He cites for reinforcement—somewhat inappropriately, considering his moderating views on marriage—Romans 13:13, "Let us conduct ourselves becomingly as in the day, not in reveling and drunkenness, not in debauchery and licentiousness, not in quarreling and jealousy." Being joined to the Lord, like the marriage of Christ and the Church in Ephesians 5, by contrast, begins in the light, illumined by the lamps of the Wise Virgins of Matthew 25.

15.15 (CSEL 41, 247–48).

[259] Athanasius, *ep. 2 ad virgines* (Lebon, p. 185; ET, Brakke, p. 300).

[260] (Anonymous), *Admonitio Augiensis* (PLS 1, 1702).

[261] Augustine, *De nuptiis et concupiscentia* 1.16.18 (CSEL 42, 230–31): John Chrysostom, *Hom. 7 II Tim.* 4 (PG 62, 641).

[262] John Chrysostom, *Hom. 19 I Cor.* 6 (PG 61, 159); *Mulier alligata* 4 (PG 51, 223); *De virginitate* 39.1 (SC 125, 228).

[263] Origen, *Comm. I Cor.* 7:28a (Jenkins [1908], p. 510).

[264] Deming (*Paul*, pp. 173–77) argues that Paul here relies on positions formulated in the debate between Cynics and Stoics concerning the circumstances that might suggest refraining from marriage as a better course.

[265] Augustine, *Confessiones* 2.2.3 (CCL 27, 19).

[266] Augustine, *De sancta virginitate* 16.16 (CSEL 41, 249); *De bono coniugali* 13.15 (CSEL 41, 207).

In such a marriage to the Lord, Origen claims, we are joined "one in spirit" (I Cor. 6:17).[267]

What, moreover, was Paul "sparing" his listeners at the conclusion of 7:28? Augustine denies that the verse should be read so that what we are "spared" is hellfire.[268] For Methodius, Paul "spares" his audience any compulsion to adopt virginity; he leaves the matter entirely to their free will.[269] Most authors, however, resort to an enumeration of the "woes of marriage" as that which Paul would "spare them," often starting with wives (or husbands) and children.[270] Although Chrysostom declares that Christians are fully capable of enumerating such "woes" for themselves, he nonetheless provides them with ample assistance, mentioning the anguish of childbirth, the care of children, upsets of all kinds, sicknesses, premature deaths, misunderstandings, disputes, responsibility for the errors of others[271]—for starters!

> I mean, brethren, the appointed time has grown very short; from now on, let those who have wives live as though they had none, and those who mourn as though they were not mourning, and those who rejoice as though they were not rejoicing, and those who buy as though they had no goods, and those who deal with the world as though they had no dealings with it. For the form of this world is passing away.
>
> *I Cor. 7:29–31 RSV*

Most church fathers lacked Paul's apocalyptic vision of the world's imminent end and hence interpreted 7:29 ("the time is short") apart from the eschatological framework that most modern scholars think informed Paul's discussion in I Corinthians 7. The clearest exception is Tertullian. For Tertullian, that time has been "wound up" means that "the end of the ages" is upon us (I Cor. 10:11) and Chris-

[267] Origen, *Comm. I Cor.* 7:28b (Jenkins [1908], p. 510).

[268] Augustine, *De sancta virginitate* 20.20 (CSEL 41, 253).

[269] Methodius, *Symposium* 3.13 (GCS 27, 42–43).

[270] Although children are sent by God, wives and children still are "troubles," according to Paulinus of Nola, *ep.* 25.7. Labor pains and children also stand at the head of Ambrosiaster's list in his *Comm. I Cor.* 7:28. For Theodore of Mopsuestia, it is the cares of wife and household (*Frag. in I Cor.* 7:28–29 [Staab, p. 183]).

[271] John Chrysostom, *Mulier alligata* 4 (PG 51, 223).

tians should prepare themselves by cutting away worldly attachments.[272] The phrase particularly suggests to Tertullian that the laxer provisions of the Old Dispensation are to be abolished, replaced by the more stringent demands of the New. No more should Genesis 1:28 ("reproduce and multiply") hold sway; no more will the sour grapes [of second marriage] that the fathers chewed set the children's teeth on edge (Jer. 31:29–30; Ezek. 18:1–4). Rather, the harvest time has come and the planter will cut down the tree he formerly sowed.[273] In addition, Tertullian instructs the Marcionites that it was due to this "shortness of time" that Paul encouraged continence, not because (as the Marcionites believed) a God other than the Creator now reigns.[274] Thus Tertullian follows Paul in not forbidding marriage, but in urging celibacy because "the time is short."[275]

Ambrosiaster, although lacking any sense of apocalyptic denouement in his discussion of these verses, nonetheless proclaims that "daily the world grows old," that only "a short time" remains for it. Because "the end is near," we should turn from the cares of marriage to "divine deeds." Although Ambrosiaster here counsels his readers to "look ahead to the day of judgment,"[276] that day does not appear imminent. Likewise Origen, commenting on 7:29, links the verse to Matthew 6:10 ("Thy Kingdom come") and explains that the temporal kingdom is passing away so that the eternal one may come,[277] yet he does not seem to imagine divine intervention of a dramatic nature.

A more common explanation offered by the Fathers for the "shortness of time" linked Paul's admonition to the brevity of an individual's life. That "the time is short" means that death overtakes us all even if we were to live nine hundred years, as did the people of old: so Jerome.[278] Pelagius and the Pelagian author of the treatise *On Chastity* expand on this theme. For Pelagius, "the time is short" indicates not just the brevity of our lives, but that the part of a lifetime we might devote to sexual intercourse and reproduction is very short indeed, restricted by age, health, situation, and so forth; why not rather choose chastity, which is "eternal"? Pelagius here cites Ecclesiastes 3:5 on the "difference of times"—"a time to embrace and a time to cease from embracing"—as part of his exhortation

[272] Tertullian, *De cultu feminarum* 2.9.6–8 (CCL 1, 363–64).

[273] Tertullian, *De pudicitia* 16.19 (CCL 2, 1314); *De monogamia* 7.4 (CCL 2, 1238 [Tertullian ingeniously explains that second marriage is now to be considered as "levirate marriage," since all Christians are brothers]); *Adversus Marcionem* 1.29.4 (CCL 1, 473).

[274] Tertullian, *Adversus Marcionem* 5.7.8 (CCL 1, 683).

[275] Tertullian, *Ad uxorem* 1.3.2 (CCL 1, 375).

[276] Ambrosiaster, *Comm. I Cor.* 7:29 (2; 3) (CSEL 81.2, 84, 85).

[277] Origen, *Hom. 11 Ex.* 7 (GCS 29, 261).

[278] Jerome, *Adversus Iovinianum* 1.13 (PL 23, 240).

to abstinence.[279] The author of *De castitate* adds yet more: verse 29 should be read in conjunction with Psalm 90:10, that the years of our life, at best, are "threescore and ten." Since the "fruitfulness" of marriage ceases even at middle age, why forfeit the glory of eternal virginity for such a transient pleasure?[280]

Other patristic writers stress that since "the time is short," we should not postpone our vows of continence; in 7:29, Paul means to challenge his audience to lives of virginity.[281] Chrysostom argues that Christians should not wish to resemble the prosperous man who through bad luck is plunged into poverty and has no time to adapt to his new circumstances before he dies; applying the moral of this tale to sexual life, Chrysostom suggests that since "the time is short," Christians are advised to turn their minds now to the adoption of abstinence. Since resurrection "stands at the door," Christians should best reflect on heavenly things.[282] According to Jerome, "the time is short" should not be taken as Paul's encouragement for marriage, but as his discouragement.[283]

Paul's injunction to husbands "to have wives as though they had none" (7:29) was one of his most frequently cited sexual teachings by the Fathers: armed with this text, they might both advocate "sexless" marriage and rule out divorce as the proper means for married couples to attain "holiness." Yet no church father was as blatant as the author of the *Acts of Paul and Thecla*, who added "having wives as if not" to the Beatitudes, thus giving Jesus' blessing on the pure who abstained from sex.[284]

The context in which various Fathers cite 7:29 could lend it varying tones. Arguing against Marcionites who separate the two Testaments, Tertullian claims that the same God who pronounced Genesis 1:28 ("reproduce and multiply") now can declare, "as if not";[285] in a different context, however, Tertullian suggests that 7:29 casts further suspicion on the absolute goodness of marriage, which Paul only "permits."[286] Divergent audiences thus require differing exegeses. For Jerome, the "as if not" marks a contrast to the Old Testament encouragement of reproduction[287] and to

[279] Pelagius, *Comm. I Cor.* 7:29; 7:30 (PLS 1, 1203).

[280] (Anonymous), *De castitate* 10.1 (PLS 1, 1486–87).

[281] Paulinus of Nola, *ep.* 25.7 (CSEL 29, 227–28); Methodius, *Symposium* 3.13 (GCS 27, 43).

[282] John Chrysostom, *De virginitate* 72; 73.1 (SC 125, 348, 350); in 73.2 (SC 125, 352), Chrysostom cites Rom. 13:11 ("the night is far spent, the day draws near") but does not interpret the words in an apocalyptic mode.

[283] Jerome, *ep.* 123.5–6 (CSEL 56, 78–80).

[284] *Acta Pauli et Theclae* 5 (Lipsius/Bonnet I:238).

[285] Tertullian, *Adversus Marcionem* 1.29.4 (CCL 1, 473).

[286] Tertullian, *De monogamia* 3.2–3 (CCL 2, 1231).

[287] Jerome, *Comm. Eccles.* 3:5 (CCL 72, 275); cf. *Adversus Helvidium* 20: *now* we praise virginity instead.

the polygamy and serial marriages of the Old Testament patriarchs.[288] An anonymous Pelagian author also stresses that 7:29 signals the "difference in times": under the Old Dispensation, married men without sons were believed to be cursed, but now the greatest blessing falls on those who "have wives as if not."[289] Likewise for Augustine: citing 7:29, he remarks that earlier, the production of children was favored, but now is the time to "cease from embracing" (Eccles. 3:5).[290] Augustine stresses that 7:29 refers to those men who have wives "but are not subject to carnal concupiscence" since they no longer engage in "carnal generation," but in "spiritual regeneration."[291] Earlier, arguing against Manicheans, Augustine had cited 7:29 to prove that Catholics were good ascetics: Manicheans have no monopoly on asceticism, as Paul's words, "as if not," prove.[292] The theme "as if not" as a warning against concupiscence is also noted by Eusebius of Emesa, who adds that fasting makes possible the continent marriages that 7:29 encourages,[293] and by Origen, who associates 7:29 with the "mortification of the genital instincts" symbolized by John the Baptist's "girding up his loins" (Matt. 3:4).[294]

In general, 7:29 was taken to recommend that remaining single was better for those currently unattached, and remaining "continent," for the currently married.[295] To the Pelagian author of the treatise *On Chastity*, the verse signals that married people can live chastely like widows and virgins, that they can be "dead" to matters sexual: sexual activity has here been eradicated, not just tempered.[296]

Chrysostom, for his part, is careful when discussing 7:29 to stress that he is not "forbidding marriage"; he is not one of the evil teachers of I Timothy 4:2. Far from it: this verse rather indicates that married people as well as celibates can enter the Kingdom of Heaven.[297] Chrysostom argues that the married man who resides in the city has the same moral duties as do solitaries; he can live, if he tries, "as if not."[298] Chrysostom also emphasizes that the other provisions of 7:29 (e.g., "buying as though they had no goods") teach that a married man can manage with few possessions or servants, even if his wife is unwilling to do so—but the neces-

[288] Jerome, *Adversus Iovinianum* 1.24 (PL 23, 254–55).

[289] (Anonymous), *Admonitio Augiensis* (PLS 1, 702).

[290] Augustine, *De coniugiis adulterinis* 2.12.12 (CSEL 41, 395–96).

[291] Augustine, *De nuptiis et concupiscentia* 1.13.14–15 (CSEL 42, 227).

[292] Augustine, *Contra Faustum* 5.9 (CSEL 25, 281–82); cf. *De moribus ecclesiae Catholicae* 35.77.

[293] Eusebius of Emesa, *Hom.* 7.9 (Buytaert I:181).

[294] Origen, *Peri pascha* 36–37 (Guerard/Nautin, pp. 224, 226).

[295] Jerome, *ep.* 52.16 (CSEL 54, 439); Pelagius, *Comm. I Cor.* 7:29 (PLS 1, 1203).

[296] (Anonymous), *De castitate* 3.1 (PLS 1, 1466).

[297] John Chrysostom, *Hom. 7 Matt.* 8 (PG 57, 81–82); *Hom. 10 I Tim.* 1 (3:1–4) (PG 62, 549).

[298] John Chrysostom, *Hom. 7 Heb.* 4 (PG 63, 67–68).

sity of marital agreement for sexual separation (7:5) remains firm. Thus, for Chrysostom, sex is the one item of the domestic relationship for which the married man cannot make a unilateral renunciation "as if not."[299]

That 7:29 could also be read as an antidivorce text is demonstrated by the interpretations of several Fathers. Jerome cites the verse in conjunction with Matthew 19's prohibition of divorce, but suggests that godly couples might "separate" for serving God, as 7:5 advocates; this is "having wives as if not."[300] Pseudo-Basil also stresses that verse 29 does not recommend breaking up a marriage, but rather "choking out incontinence and sowing chastity."[301] Against Hieracas, who claimed that 7:29 commanded "no marriage," Athanasius counterargues that the verse should be read in conjunction with the intertext of 7:5 (on separating for prayer and then coming together again): Christians should understand that Paul gives such concessions so that marriages will *not* self-destruct.[302]

Verse 31 ("the form of the world is passing away") received less comment: the Fathers did not expect an imminent end of the world, and hence did not interpret this verse in an eschatological framework. Augustine remarks that Paul here shows he heeds I John 2:15–16 on not "loving the world," characterized by "the lust of the flesh and the lust of the eyes and the pride of life"; hence, as Paul exhorts, we should "use the world as if we have no dealings with it" (7:31).[303] The world's "aging" is suggested by Ambrosiaster as a proper way to read verse 31.[304] To John Chrysostom, 7:31 suggests, on the one hand, that Christians living in cities can retain their virtue, using the world "as if not," since "the form of the world is passing away"; and, on the other, 7:31 marks the "difference of times" between the world's beginning (when procreation was the means by which to perpetuate the memory of oneself) and the Christian present (when reproduction is unnecessary).[305] The verse could be put to other uses as well. Thus verses 29 and 31 buttress Basil of Caesarea's ruling that a man may not marry the sister of his dead wife: "don't make me laugh" by quoting "Increase and multiply" (Gen. 1:28), he sarcastically remarks.[306] For Evagrius Ponticus, that "the form of the world is passing away" strikes an Origenist note: with its passing, so dissolves the human body.[307]

[299] John Chrysostom, *De virginitate* 75.1 (SC 125, 358).

[300] Jerome, *In Math.* 3 (CCL 77, 166).

[301] Ps.-Basil, *De virginitate* 9.18 (Amand de Mendietta/Moons, p. 65). There is an implied intertext with the Parable of the Sower (Mark 4) here.

[302] Athanasius, *ep. 1 ad virgines* (CSCO 150 = Scriptores Coptici 19, 86; ET, Brakke, p. 283).

[303] Augustine, *Contra Iulianum* 5.16.60 (PL 44, 817).

[304] Ambrosiaster, *Comm. I Cor.* 7:31 (CSEL 81.2, 85).

[305] John Chrysostom, *Hom. 43 Gen.* 1 (PG 54, 396); *Hom. 44 Gen.* 6 (PG 54, 412).

[306] Basil of Caesarea, *ep.* 160 (Loeb II:408).

[307] Evagrius Ponticus, *Kephalaia Gnos-*

I want you to be free from anxieties. The unmarried man is anxious about the affairs of the Lord, how to please the Lord; but the married man is anxious about worldly affairs, how to please his wife, and his interests are divided. And the unmarried woman or girl is anxious about the affairs of the Lord, how to be holy in body and spirit; but the married woman is anxious about worldly affairs, how to please her husband. I say this for your own benefit, not to lay any restraint upon you, but to promote good order and to secure your undivided devotion to the Lord.

I Cor. 7:32–35 RSV

Again, the issue of Paul's authority comes to the fore. Paul writes to the Corinthians (7:35) that he wishes "not to lay them under restraint," but "to promote good order and to secure your undivided devotion to the Lord." Thus, according to various Fathers, Paul had not given the Corinthians (or later Christians) a "command," but had rather set an example by his own ascetic commitment.[308] Leaving the matter up to free choice, he had not made it one of compulsion, had not "forced" anyone "against nature."[309] But did not 7:32–35 seem to cast doubt on either the utility or the goodness of marriage, Tertullian queried?[310]

Paul's differentiation in 7:34 between the "unmarried woman and the virgin (*parthenos*)," on the one hand, and the "married woman," on the other, spurred several patristic authors to ponder the difference. Ambrosiaster concludes that the difference is not one of "nature" but of "act." While the word "woman" (*mulier*) encompasses females of varying marital statuses, Ambrosiaster notes, "virgin" designates one differentiated from the general category of femaleness.[311] Those Fathers who wished to put a

tica 1.26 (PO 28, 28–29).

[308] Ambrose, *De virginibus* 1.5.23 (PL 16, 206); Jerome, *Adversus Helvidium* 21 (PL 23, 215); Basil of Ancyra, *De virginitate* 56 (Vaillant, p. 67).

[309] John Chrysostom, *De virginitate* 76.1 (SC 125, 364); Jerome, *Adversus Helvidium* 21 (PL 23, 215).

[310] Tertullian, *Ad uxorem* 1.3.6 (CCL 1, 376); *De monogamia* 3.3 (CCL 2, 1231).

[311] Ambrosiaster, *Comm. I Cor.* 7:34 (CSEL 81.2, 86). Ambrosiaster perhaps borrows from Tertullian's discussion in *De virginibus velandis* 4–5, in which Tertullian notes that "woman" is a general category, with "virgin" a special distinction within it.

more positive face on Paul's evaluation of marriage, such as John Chrysostom, could argue that his distinction between "woman" and "virgin" does not equate with marriage or with continence, but pertains to the practical question of the amount of leisure for spiritual concerns that the virgin and the matron respectively experience. The problem for the married person is not sexual cohabitation, Chrysostom insists, but the impediment to rigorous living that domestic life poses.[312] Other writers, however, give 7:34 a more ascetic nuance. Thus Jerome comments that this passage extols "the happy state in which even the distinction of sex is lost," for "virgins" are not here called "women." It is "virgins," not "women," who Paul claims are "holy in body and spirit"—and don't cavil at Paul, God's "vessel of election," Jerome warns his readers.[313]

Several Fathers attempt "functional" explanations of the distinction between married and unmarried based on the two points mentioned by Paul: the virgin's freedom for the Lord contrasted with the matron's busy attendance upon her husband and worldly things; and the unmarried woman's holiness "in body and spirit" (7:34), a designation not accorded to the married woman. The first point appeared to signal a practical differentiation; the second, however, could be taken, more ominously, to imply that married women lack "holiness."

The first distinction between "virgins" and "married women" —that based on the cares and anxieties of marriage (7:32–34)—was easily linked to the "worldly troubles" (or "troubles of the flesh") that Paul had mentioned in 7:28. Thus according to Paulinus of Nola, although Paul is not an opponent of marriage, he wishes Christians to be free from the "troubles" of attending to spouse, children, and other domestic matters.[314] Several intertexts could be located to illumine these "troubles." For example, the "burdens" here mentioned could be reinforced by an appeal to the "inexpedience" of marriage mentioned by Jesus' disciples in Matthew 19:10.[315] In addition, the Parable of the Wise and Foolish Virgins (Matt. 25:1–13) suggested that the "foolish" ones were those who had not stripped themselves of the "cares" appropriate to married women.[316] Readers were also reminded of the worldly involvement that prompted the newly married man of Luke 14:16–24 to decline his invitation to the banquet.[317] For Pelagius, the intertext of the Parable of the Sower (Matt.

The argument later becomes important in the discussion of whether calling Mary the mother of Jesus a "woman" (Gal. 4:4) implies anything about her virginity.

[312] John Chrysostom, *Hom. 19 I Cor.* 6 (PG 61, 160); cf. *De virginitate* 77 (SC 125, 366, 368).

[313] Jerome, *Adversus Helvidium* 20 (PL 23, 213–14).

[314] Paulinus of Nola, *ep.* 25.7 (CSEL 29, 228–29).

[315] Ambrose, *De virginitate* 29–31 (PL 16, 287).

[316] John Chrysostom, *Hom. 78 Matt.* 2 (PG 58, 713).

[317] Ambrose, *Exp. Luc.* 7.196 (CCL 14,

13:3–9, 18–23) might be used to explicate I Corinthians 7:32–34: the "thorns" of domestic life choke the "good seeds."[318]

Yet what was the exact nature of these "anxieties" and "troubles" of married life? Although the phrase that (only) the unmarried are "holy in body and spirit" (v. 34) suggests that a purity issue might be involved, many Fathers appear to avoid this interpretive route.[319] On the one hand, they center on the "cares" that the married woman faces: she is bound by a multitude of duties and engagements that inhibit her leisure for spiritual matters.[320] Focusing on the "divided" nature of the matron's interests, Athanasius declares her to be a "divided" offering, in contrast to the "whole" burnt offering represented by the virgin.[321] Augustine claims, with regret, that if he had heard of these cares of marriage in his adolescence, he might have been impelled toward a virginal commitment.[322] Likewise, the pseudo-Basilian treatise *On Virginity* recommends to parents that they read these verses (among others) to their children to encourage more rigorous living.[323] And according to Evagrius Ponticus, 7:32–34 sums up the reasons why the prophet Jeremiah was told by God not to take a wife (Jer. 16:2): too many cares and anxieties.[324]

The practical problem of the married woman, however, could be focused by the patristic authors more precisely on her husband: *he* is the one who causes her cares and anxieties, since she is in servitude to him, as Genesis 3:16 states. It is this "curse" that the virgin escapes in rejecting marriage, according to Basil of Ancyra and Jerome.[325] For Basil of Caesarea, the fleshly attachments to family that marriage entails would be better replaced by "citizenship in heaven" (Phil. 3:20).[326] Whereas matrons spend time and money trying to "please" husbands with their clothing, ornaments, and makeup, virgins need not indulge in cosmetic interest, various church fathers claim.[327] Indeed, the attention patristic writers give to the issue of makeup is striking. Commenting on 7:34, Eusebius of

283); Pelagius, *Comm. I Cor.* 7:33 (PLS 1, 1204).

318 Pelagius, *Comm. I Cor.* 7:33 (PLS 1, 1204).

319 Explicitly ruled out in John Chrysostom, *Hom. 14 I Tim.* 2 (I Tim. 5:8) (PG 62, 573); *De virginitate* 77 (SC 125, 366).

320 Basil of Ancyra, *De virginitate* 23 (Vaillant, pp. 13, 15); John Chrysostom, *Hom. 19 I Cor.* 6 (PG 61, 159–60).

321 Athanasius, *ep. 2 ad virgines* (Lebon, p. 173; ET, Brakke, pp. 293–94).

322 Augustine, *Confessiones* 2.2.3 (CCL 27, 19).

323 Ps.-Basil, *De virginitate* 4.58 (Amand de Mendietta/Moons, p. 49).

324 Evagrius Ponticus, *Rerum monachalium rationis* 1 (PG 40, 1252–53).

325 Basil of Ancyra, *De virginitate* 23 (Vaillant, p. 15); Jerome, *Adversus Helvidium* 20 (PL 23, 214).

326 Basil of Caesarea, *Regulae fusius tractatae* 5.1–2 (PG 31, 920–21).

327 E.g., Tertullian, *De cultu feminarum* 2.4.1 (CCL 1, 357); Cyprian, *De habitu virginum* 5 (CSEL 3.1, 191); Ambrose, *De virginibus* 1.6.29–30 (PL 16, 207–8); John Chrysostom, *Hom. 36 I Cor.* 5 (PG 61, 313).

Emesa asks, do women forget that they will in the course of nature grow older and eventually die? Why then do they cover themselves with artificial cosmetics?[328] Tertullian reminds matrons that if they "pleased" their husbands well enough to receive their bids of marriage, they should not fear that their husbands' affection will turn to hate if they abstain from adorning themselves.[329] Chrysostom remarks that although Paul did not elaborate on how matrons attempt to "please" their husbands, the physical sufferings they endure and the abuse of their bodies through cosmetics come readily to mind.[330]

Some patristic authors believe that Paul here claims that the married woman cannot please God and a husband equally. To please a spouse before pleasing God, the author of the treatise *On Chastity* thus warns, is to put indulgence (*luxuria*) before God.[331] Gregory of Nyssa, in a surprisingly rare citation of I Corinthians 7 in his treatise *On Virginity*, comments that Christians cannot "please" in two marriages, so they should choose the better, the marriage to Christ.[332] According to Jerome, those women who "seek to please husbands" are in the same lowly category of Christians who on the basis of I Timothy 4:4 ("every creature created by God is good") attempt to justify their indulgence in eating meat.[333]

Modifications of these arguments are found in the writings of patristic authors more disposed to marriage, yet they offer differing reasons for Paul's warning against domestic "anxieties." Augustine, for example, objects to those (Jerome?) who overstress the worldly cares of marriage as an inducement to celibacy. Such "foolish" exegetes should be reminded that Paul's goal is eternal life, not mere relief from domestic distractions.[334]

Clement of Alexandria, for his part, adopts a line of argument more fully supportive of marriage. For Clement, there is no reason to distinguish between "caring for the things of the Lord" and "caring for a husband." Cannot the wife and the husband "care for the things of the Lord" together? Can she not care for the things of her husband "in the Lord" and also "care for the things of the Lord" more directly? In one role she acts as a wife, in the other, as a "virgin."[335] In a clever exegetical move, Clement expands the categories of 7:32–34 from two (wife, unmarried woman) to three (chaste wife, unchaste wife, unmarried woman). Thus he can argue that the chaste (*sōphrōn*) wife divides her life between God

[328] Eusebius of Emesa, *Hom.* 6.15 (Buytaert I:160).

[329] Tertullian, *De cultu feminarum* 2.4.1 (CCL 1, 357).

[330] John Chrysostom, *De virginitate* 75.4 (SC 125, 362).

[331] (Anonymous), *De castitate* 10.13 (PLS 1, 1487).

[332] Gregory of Nyssa, *De virginitate* 20.3 (SC 119, 496).

[333] Jerome, *ep.* 79.7 (CSEL 55, 96).

[334] Augustine, *De sancta virginitate* 13.13; 22.22 (CSEL 41, 245–46, 257).

[335] Clement of Alexandria, *Stromata* 3.12.88.2–3 (GCS 52 [15], 236–37).

and her husband, while the "unchaste wife" gives herself wholly to marriage (and, he implies, the unmarried woman devotes herself wholly to God).[336] Nonetheless, Clement warns, these verses do not mean that Paul wishes us to "hate" our families.[337] A similar theme emerges in Athanasius' comments on 7:32–34, in which he subtly "corrects" Paul: it is "worthy wives" who seek to please their husbands (7:34); it is they that keep the marriage bed "holy" (Heb. 13:4).[338] By such exegetical means were the more negative implications of 7:32–35 overcome.

Implicit in some readings of 7:32–35 is the Fathers' concern that these verses could be construed to deny that marriage was God's creation, and to contradict the advice pertaining to wives in the Pastoral Epistles. Thus Chrysostom ponders why "Paul" writes in I Timothy 3:1–4 that bishops should be once-married and manage their households well, when in I Corinthians 7:33 he observes that married people "care about the things of the world." Is it only those men who are free of a wife who are also free of such "care"? No, Chrysostom replies, because Paul in 7:29 has already stated that men can have their wives "as if not." Marriage is indeed compatible with the goal of reaching the Kingdom of Heaven, although Chrysostom admits that it is obtained with more difficulty by the married.[339] Chrysostom also cites these verses to argue against men and women living together in "spiritual marriage." Since Paul in 7:32–34 mentions only two categories, the married and the virgins, those living in syneisaktic relationships cannot be classified in either. They are rather involved in "adulteries," faithless in their "marriage" to Christ.[340]

A second theme of 7:34 required some interpretive skill on the part of patristic commentators: Paul writes that the unmarried woman strives to be "holy in body and spirit," but omits any mention of such "holiness" for married women. What is the significance of this omission? The verse was unpolemically cited by some Fathers simply to remind virgins that they are to keep "holy in body and spirit"[341]—especially if they wish to enter the company of the "wise virgins" of Matthew 25.[342] Rebecca is singled out as a young woman of ancient times who exemplified this dou-

[336] Clement of Alexandria, *Paedagogus* 2.10.109 (GCS 12, 223). Augustine's solution is to argue that the faithful wife *also* thinks to please the Lord as well as her husband—albeit somewhat less: *De bono coniugali* 11.13 (CSEL 41, 205).

[337] Clement of Alexandria, *Stromata* 3.15.97.1–3 (GCS 52 [15], 240–41).

[338] Athanasius, *ep. 1 ad virgines* (CSCO 150 = Scriptores Coptici 19, 90; ET, Brakke, p. 285).

[339] John Chrysostom, *Hom. 10 I Tim.* 1 (I Tim. 3:1–4) (PG 62, 549).

[340] John Chrysostom, *Adversus eos qui apud se habent virgines* 6 (PG 47, 504).

[341] E.g., Pelagius, *Ad Demetriadem* 10; (Anonymous), *ep. de virginitate* (= *Ad Claudiam*) 9; Ps.-Clement, *ep. 1 de virginitate* 5; Origen, *Hom. 11 Ex.* 7; Athanasius, *ep. 1 ad virgines* (34); *ep. 2 ad virgines* (4); *De virginitate* 2; Gregory of Nyssa, *De instituto Christiano* (Jaeger VIII.1:49).

[342] Pelagius, *Ad Demetriadem* 10 (PL 30, 27).

ble holiness.[343] Yet the explication of "holiness" could be given a sharper edge, and this in two quite different directions.

For a rigorously ascetic exegete such as Jerome, 7:34 warned virgins that bodily intactness is not enough: purity in spirit as well as in body is necessary, for many who appear to be virgins do not possess both qualifications.[344] Reflecting on Titus 2:6–7 and I Timothy 4:12, Jerome suggests that Christians should aim for both *incorruptio* (Jerome's translation of Titus' *aphthoria*) and *castitas* (his translation of Timothy's *hagneia*): *incorruptio* applies to the body and *castitas* to the mind. Thus Christians should be "holy [both] in body and spirit" (I Cor. 7:34).[345] Here, the Pastoral Epistles are pressed to promote ideals of abstinence, not of domestic life.

Ambrosiaster's explication of 7:34 reveals one ambiguity that attends its interpretation. For Ambrosiaster, it is the soul that either sanctifies or pollutes the body, so that having a "clean" body does not benefit a person if the soul is "polluted."[346] Ambrosiaster's comment could be read either as a warning to virgins (they may have "polluted" souls in their intact bodies)—or as an implicit argument that married people as well as virgins can be "holy," since it is the soul that lends sanctification to the body. In this reading, there is no suggestion that virginal "intactness" might count as a superior state in itself.

As Ambrosiaster's reflection suggests, 7:34 could be "rescued" for a pro-marriage argument, and was so by Augustine. In his treatise *On the Good of Marriage*, Augustine instructs his audience that they are not to read 7:34 as implying that the chaste Christian wife is not "holy in body," since *all* the faithful are "temples of the Holy Spirit" (I Cor. 6:19), although Augustine concedes that virgins have a claim to greater sanctity.[347] Likewise in his treatise *On the Good of Widowhood*, Augustine argues that Paul does not intend to exclude chaste married women from being called "holy in body" as well as "in spirit," and he summons up various intertexts to buttress his point. It is noteworthy that most of Augustine's intertexts (Col. 3:18; Titus 2:5; I Peter 3:1; Eph. 5:22) concern the subjection of women to their husbands; wifely subjection thus appears to stand, in Augustine's mind, as an essential aspect of "holiness" for married women. To these passages Augustine adds I Peter 3:5–6, in which the author claims the "holy women" of old served their husbands, with Sarah singled out for special mention. And since Paul himself considers the bodies of

[343] Origen, *Hom. 10 Gen.* 4 (GCS 29, 98); John Chrysostom, *Quales ducendae* 7 (PG 51, 236–37).

[344] Jerome, *ep.* 22.38 (CSEL 54, 203–5); cf. *Adversus Helvidium* 20 (PL 23, 213–14).

[345] Jerome, *Comm. Tit.* 2:6–7 (PL 26, 618).

[346] Ambrosiaster, *Comm. I Cor.* 7:34 (2) (CSEL 81.2, 87).

[347] Augustine, *De bono coniugali* 11.13 (CSEL 41, 204–5).

Christians to be "temples of the Holy Spirit" (I Cor. 6:19), Augustine urges no one to "sever the bodies of married Christians from the members of Christ."[348] Likewise, when in 7:35 Paul advises that the unmarried state contributes to "good order," he does not (according to Augustine) imply that the married state is dishonorable, for that would condemn even first marriage, which, he avers, neither Montanists, Novatianists, nor even Tertullian dared to do. "Promoting good order" here merely signals the higher degree of virtue attending virginity.[349] Augustine, once again, strives harder to rescue marriage for "holiness" than do several other patristic authors.

Augustine's defensive position regarding the "holiness" of the married woman signals that far more negative readings of 7:32–35 might be, and had been, given. The same fears that surrounded the interpretation of 7:5—that sexual relations "polluted" prayer—might here worry the interpretation of the matron's "holiness." As Jerome had noted, if only virgins, not married women, were called "holy in body and spirit,"[350] some degree of impurity must attend the married state. Nonetheless, even as rabid a critic of marriage as Jerome backed away from allegations of "impurity," retreating instead to the "practical" argument from marriage's "inexpedience." This "retreat" from the more damaging interpretation of 7:32–34 is well illustrated in Jerome's semi-comic description of the life of a married woman in his treatise *Against Helvidius.* The "practical" recommendation for ascetic living could scarcely be urged more convincingly than in his mocking elaboration of the "anxieties" of I Corinthians 7:32–34:

> Do you imagine that there is no difference between the woman who is free night and day for prayer, free for fasts, and the one who at her husband's approach makes up her face, prances about, fakes her flatteries? The virgin behaves so as to appear more ugly; she will wrong her appearance so as to obscure her handsomeness. But the married woman paints herself before the mirror; abusing herself, she tries by artifice to acquire a greater beauty than she was granted by birth. Next come the clamoring children, the noise of the household, the little ones waiting for her attention and her chatter; there is the adding up of costs, the preparation for future expenses. On the one side the cooks, armed for their task, rip into the meat; on the other, there is the murmuring throng of weavers. Meanwhile it is announced that the husband has arrived with his friends. Like a swallow the wife flits about to inspect the house. Is everything in place? Is the floor swept clean? Are the

[348] Augustine, *De bono viduitatis* 6.8 (CSEL 41, 312–13). Augustine again here adds the unmarried woman has a "greater holiness of body and spirit."

[349] Augustine, *De bono viduitatis* 5.7 (CSEL 41, 310–11).

[350] Jerome, *Adversus Helvidium* 20 (PL 213–14).

cups adorned (with flowers)? Is the meal ready? Tell me, I ask you, where amidst all this can there be any thought of God? Can these be happy homes? Where is there any fear of God amidst the beating of drums, the noise of pipes, the tinkling of lyres, the clash of cymbals? The hanger-on glories in his humiliation. The public victims of men's lusts are brought in, the scantiness of their attire the target of shameless eyes. The miserable wife must either rejoice in this—and die; or take offense—and her husband is pricked to a quarrel. *There* are dissensions, the seeds of divorce. Or if you find some home where such things don't happen—that would be a "rare bird"! Yet even here, there is the care of the house, the raising of children, the wants of a husband, the correction of the slaves: these things call us away from the thought of God. . . . For so long as the debt of marital intercourse is paid, perseverance in prayer is neglected.[351]

If any one thinks that he is not behaving properly toward his betrothed, if his passions are strong, and it has to be, let him do as he wishes; let them marry—it is no sin. But whoever is firmly established in his heart, being under no necessity but having his desire under control, and has determined this in his heart, to keep her as his betrothed, he will do well. So that he who marries his betrothed does well; and he who refrains from marriage will do better.

I Cor. 7:36–38 RSV

This passage of I Corinthians 7 is plagued with interpretive difficulties, since its different translations lend quite different meanings[352]or, more precisely, translators must guess Paul's meaning *before* they decide how to translate the several incompatible elements of these verses. What, for example, does *hyperakmos* mean? Does it refer to the young man, "full of vitality"? Or to the young woman? And if to the latter, is she "past her prime" or "in the flower of her youth"? And to whom does *gameitosan* refer, since Paul has not at this point presented readers with a potential bridegroom for the young woman?

Translators—who here surely are interpreters—must determine whether they think the verses concern a young man and his fiancée (should he

[351] Jerome, *Adversus Helvidium* 20 (PL 23, 214).

[352] For a discussion of the issue, see Elizabeth A. Clark, "John Chrysostom and the Subintroductae," *Church History* 46 (1977): 171–85; reprinted in idem, *Ascetic*

proceed forward with the marriage or "keep her as his virgin"?): this situation is imagined by the translators of the Revised Standard Version. Or do the verses concern a father and his virgin daughter (should he give her in marriage or "keep her as a virgin"?): this translation is favored by the King James Version. Or does the passage describe the situation of a male celibate and his female ascetic companion (should they agree to a marriage involving sexual relations or stay in their "spiritual marriage"?): this solution is adopted by the translators of the New English Bible and has found favor with several twentieth-century commentators.[353] As far as I am aware, Ephraem the Syrian was the only church father who thought the latter reading plausible[354]—although John Chrysostom, not advancing this interpretation, nonetheless expresses bewilderment at the wording of the text, for Paul here "seems to be talking about marriage, but all that he says relates to virginity."[355] Since most church fathers (including Chrysostom) were opposed to the practice of syneisaktism, or "spiritual marriage," and could not imagine that Paul could recommend this option, they read verses 36–38 to refer to a father and his daughter. (Interpreting the man and woman as a young couple, however, as do the translators of the RSV, are Ambrosiaster and perhaps Methodius.)[356] It is unfortunate that no fragments remain from this section of Origen's *Commentary on I Corinthians*, for they might have provided a clue whether Jerome's (and maybe Methodius') reading of verse 37 (that "keep his virgin" should be interpreted as "keep his flesh [pure]") derives from Origen's explication of this verse.[357]

Since patristic writers generally did not interpret I Corinthians 7 in the framework of Paul's eschatological expectation, they understood verses 36–38 to contain Paul's timeless advice for Christians: virginity is preferable to marriage, but marriage is acceptable for those pressed by (sexual) "necessity" (v. 37): so Clement of Alexandria,[358] Pelagius,[359] Basil of An-

---

Piety and Women's Faith: Essays on Late Ancient Christianity (Lewiston/Queenston: Edwin Mellen, 1986), pp. 265–90.

[353] Starting with Hans Achelis, *Virgines Subintroductae, Ein Beitrag zum VII Kapitel des I. Korintherbriefs* (Leipzig: J. C. Hinrichs, 1902); Hurd, *The Origin of I Corinthians*, esp. pp. 179–180; Jean Héring, *The First Epistle of Saint Paul to the Corinthians*, trans. from the 2nd French ed. by A. W. Heathcote and P. J. Allcock (London: Epworth, 1962), p. 64.

[354] For Ephraem's view, see Arthus Vööbus, *Celibacy, A Requirement for Admission to Baptism in the Early Syrian Church* (Stockholm: Estonian Theological Society in Exile, 1951), pp. 23–25.

[355] John Chrysostom, *Hom. 19 I Cor.* 6 (PG 61, 160).

[356] Ambrosiaster, *Comm. I Cor.* 7:36–38 (CSEL 81.2, 89–90); Methodius, *Symposium* 3.14 (GCS 27, 44–45).

[357] Jerome, *Adversus Iovinianum* 1.13 (PL 23, 242); Methodius, *Symposium* 3.14 (GCS 27, 44).

[358] Clement of Alexandria, *Stromata* 3.12.79.1–2 (GCS 52 [15], 231).

[359] Pelagius, *Comm. I Cor.* 7:36–38 (PLS 1, 1204–5).

cyra,[360] Augustine,[361] John Chrysostom,[362] and Ambrose.[363] What we might consider the historical context of these verses did not interest patristic authors so much as Paul's timeless assessment that virginity is "better" than marriage.

Nonetheless, some of the Fathers were eager to hedge this preference with assurances that Paul was not speaking against marriage; they often cite 7:36, "it is no sin."[364] Marriage is at least better than "uncomeliness" or "secret corruption."[365] Thus Ambrose, commenting on verse 38, explains that the one who "does well" by marrying does so "on account of a snare" (i.e., sexual temptation), whereas the one who "does better" by not marrying, does so "for profit"; the former is "for a remedy," the latter, "for a reward."[366] Eusebius of Emesa reads verses 36–38 in conjunction with the implied intertext of I Corinthians 15:41 (that heavenly bodies differ from one another in brightness): virginity shines "brighter." Yet Eusebius reminds readers that marriage is the "root" of virginity, presumably in producing children who may remain virgins; nonetheless, the life of "sanctification" is the "life of the angels" who neither marry nor give in marriage (Matt. 22:30 and parallels).[367] And such is the sentiment of other patristic writers.[368] Clement of Alexandria, predictably, offers a more ameliorating comment on the verse: 7:36–38 shows that marriage as well as celibacy is a form of service to God, and hence is good in its own right.[369]

Demurrers might be voiced by the more ascetically rigorous. For John Cassian, verse 38 ("he who gives his virgin does well") indicates that Paul is "becoming all things to all men" (I Cor. 9:22)[370]: does Cassian here approve Paul's gracious condescension to weaker humans, or, disdain his declining moral standards? The author of the Pelagian treatise *On Chastity* goes further: only "the ignorant" imagine that Paul wrote "he who mar-

[360] Basil of Ancyra, *De virginitate* 57 (Vaillant, p. 67). Basil interprets the father's guardianship of his virgin daughter as conforming to the second category of eunuchs Jesus mentions in Matt. 19: "eunuchs made by men," that is, according to Basil, through education and watchfulness.

[361] Augustine, *De doctrina Christiana* 3.17.25 (CCL 32, 93). Augustine, writing on types of Biblical interpretation, notes that if one takes this verse "literally," then one must read Ben Sirach 7:27 ("marry your daughter") figuratively.

[362] John Chrysostom, *De virginitate* 78.1 (SC 125, 368, 370).

[363] Ambrose, *De virginibus* 1.6.24 (PL 16, 206).

[364] For example, Ambrose, *De virginibus* 1.6.24; Eusebius of Emesa, *Hom.* 6.6; Athanasius, *De virginitate* (10); Augustine, *Contra Faustum* 32.17; *De bono viduitatis* 5.7.

[365] Methodius, *Symposium* 3.14 (GCS 27, 44).

[366] Ambrose, *Exhortatio virginitatis* 7.46 (PL 16, 365).

[367] Eusebius of Emesa, *Hom.* 6.6 (Buytaert I:155).

[368] Pelagius, *Comm. I Cor.* 7:36–38; Ps.-Basil, *De virginitate* 1.2–4; Athanasius, *ep. 1 ad virgines* (19); Augustine, *Contra Faustum* 30.6; *De bono viduitatis* 5.7; John Chrysostom, *De virginitate* 78.6.

[369] Clement of Alexandria, *Stromata* 3.12.79.5 (GCS 52 [15], 231).

[370] John Cassian, *Conlationes* 17.20 (SC 54, 268–69).

ries does well," for this claim runs counter to the whole thrust of his teaching in chapter 7, from verse 1 ("it is good not to touch a woman") forward.[371] Here, a more rigorous asceticism is promoted through an outright denial of apostolic authorship, an unusual position among Christian authors of this era.

A second unusual allusion to 7:36–38 is found in John Cassian's *Conferences*, in which Cassian recounts the story of Theonas and his wife. Theonas wishes to abandon his marriage so that he can devote himself to rigorous asceticism in the desert; the wife wishes them to remain in their marital and sexual relationship. In the dialogue that Cassian claims to report, she alludes to 7:37, that she is in "the flower of her age" and hence needs the sexual outlet.[372] Her alleged argument is novel not just in its tilting of verses 36–38 in a "pro-sexual" direction; it further attributes the desire to the woman, not to the man, a perfectly legitimate interpretation, given the ungendered ending of the Greek word *hyperakmos*.[373]

A last point of interest is the interpretive fodder that verse 37 ("under no necessity") provided. There is ample attestation in Greek literature that *anagkē* could mean "physical necessity";[374] among Christian writers, Methodius likewise understands this "necessity" as the "passion that calls forth a man's 'loins' to sexual intercourse."[375] Yet the verse prompted other authors to cite it in the debate concerning the relation between human free will and God's grace. For Athanasius, these verses illustrate that the virtue of virginity lies in free will.[376] With the eruption of the Pelagian controversy, however, the verse is pressed into more overtly polemical service. According to Augustine, the Pelagians quote 7:36–38 as ballast for their emphasis on free will. Augustine mocks this interpretation: the Pau-

[371] (Anonymous), *De castitate* 10.14 (PLS 1, 1488).

[372] John Cassian, *Conlationes* 21.9 (SC 64, 82). Theonas counters with such verses as Matt. 5:29–30 (that it is better to lose a "member" [here, his wife] and enter the Kingdom of Heaven maimed than to be condemned completely); Luke 18:29 (that everyone who leaves a wife for Jesus' sake will inherit eternal life); and Luke 14:26 (that a man who does not "hate" his wife cannot be Jesus' disciple). He accuses her of not being a "helper" (Gen. 2:18) but a deceiver. Theonas then fled to a monastery. Cassian argues (19.10) that no one should interpret the story as encouraging divorce; remember Heb. 13:4 ("marriage is honorable in everything, and the marriage bed undefiled").

[373] It reflects on the assumptions of modern translators that if they assign the *hyperakmos* of v. 36 to the man, they assume that he is "brimming with sexual desire," but if they assign the word to the woman, they translate that she is "past her peak" (as in the King James Version). Yet given the ancient understanding that women, too, were "brimming with sexual desire," as well as the linguistic neutrality of the term, there is no particular reason to disallow that the sexual desire characterizes *her*.

[374] See Liddell-Scott, *Greek-English Lexicon*, s.v. *anagkē*.

[375] Methodius, *Symposium* 3.14 (GCS 27, 44).

[376] Athanasius, *ep. 1 ad virgines* (CSCO 150 = Scriptores Coptici 19, 86; ET, Brakke, p. 283).

line passage concerns marriage, and it surely reveals no great virtue to be "willing" to marry![377] Yet late in his career, when he was under scrutiny by Gallic monks who suspected that his emphasis on God's predestinating activity abolished human freedom, Augustine adopts a mediating position that acknowledges the need for both grace (chastity is a "gift" [7:7]) and free will in the ascetic refusal of the married life. In this context, Augustine cites 7:36–37 as upholding freedom of the will, but balances it with Matthew 19:10, Jesus' concession that only "some" can receive his teaching on "becoming eunuchs for the Kingdom of Heaven."[378] Audience—and polemical context—again influences interpretation.

> A wife is bound to her husband as long as he lives. If the husband dies ["sleeps"], she is free to be married to whom she wishes, only in the Lord. But in my judgment she is happier if she remains as she is. And I think that I have the Spirit of God.
>
> *I Cor. 7:39–40 RSV*

With these verses, the Fathers find opportunity to speak against the remarriage of widows. Although Jerome's opponent Jovinian cited 7:39 to argue that God intended marriage and reproduction to continue throughout the world's history,[379] most patristic writers quote the verse to express a range of judgments against second marriage, from mild caution to disallowance. That Paul here claimed he has "the Spirit of God" (v. 40) lends authority to his teaching: so Ambrose, John Chrysostom, and Jerome.[380] Chrysostom informs his audience that in following the advice Paul here gives, they follow Christ.[381]

Even those who did not rule out second marriage reminded their hearers and readers of the "marital hierarchy" that Christianity taught: widows were more blessed than the married, but less blessed than virgins.[382] Paul had already declared that the absolutely good state was to be free, not

[377] Augustine, *De perfectione iustitiae hominis* 19.40–41 (CSEL 42, 42–43).

[378] Augustine, *De gratia et libero arbitrio* 4.7; 2.4 (PL 44, 886, 883–84).

[379] Jovinian, in Jerome, *Adversus Iovinianum* 1.5 (PL 23, 227); Jovinian counters Jerome's argument that it was only at the early stages of the world that God encouraged reproduction.

[380] Ambrose, *Exhortatio virginitatis* 7.46 (PL 16, 365); John Chrysostom, *Mulier alligata* 4 (PG 51, 223); *De non iterando coniugio* 1 (PG 48, 611); Jerome, *Adversus Iovinianum* 1.14 (PL 23, 243–44).

[381] John Chrysostom, *Mulier alligata* 1 (PG 51, 217).

[382] Pelagius, *Comm. I Cor.* 7:40 (PLS 1, 1205).

"bound" (v. 39), Jerome argues, and thus "Paul's" recommendation in I Timothy 5:14–15 for the remarriage of young widows cannot be taken to stand against his advice in 7:39.[383] According to Basil of Ancyra, if a woman has become "free in the Lord" by her husband's death, Paul advises her not to be swept into a new union by "fleshly voluptuousness"; if she opts for remarriage, it should be "with reflection."[384]

John Chrysostom also elaborates on the "boundness" (v. 39) of marriage. Just as fugitive slaves still bear their chains when they leave their master's house, so the woman, in place of "chains," has the law which forbids her to engage in a new marriage while her husband is alive. On this point, she is situated less advantageously than a slave, who at least can hope to change masters without death intervening. But once the "chain" of marriage is broken by the first husband's death, the widow is permitted to marry again—although Chrysostom mounts several arguments to dissuade her from doing so.[385] First, he notes Paul's euphemistic choice of word in verse 39: the husband "sleeps." Since the departed loved one is not "dead" but "sleeping," why does the widow not prudently wait for the moment when he "wakes up"?[386] Second, Chrysostom focuses on Paul's words in verse 40, that the widow will be "happier" if she does not remarry. There are many advantages to not remarrying, Chrysostom reports, even though Paul has not here enumerated them.[387] (Chrysostom himself provides lengthy lists in more than one of his treatises.)[388] Chrysostom also ingeniously reads the Pastoral Epistles as standing *against* remarriage of widows. He recounts how "happy" the widow can be in performing the deeds of charity recommended to widows in I Timothy 5:10 (and conveniently overlooks the recommendation for the remarriage of younger widows in the verses that follow).[389] Yet the "happiness" of the widow is not limited to this world, Chrysostom counsels: she will also be "happier" in the next, since she will receive a greater reward than if she had remarried.[390]

[383] Jerome, *ep.* 123.5 (CSEL 56, 76). In #4, Jerome explains that "Paul" prefers the young widows of I Tim. 5 to marry again rather than become prostitutes; he allows second marriages for the "incontinent" simply to rescue them from Satan.

[384] Basil of Ancyra, *De virginitate* 38 (Vaillant, p. 39).

[385] John Chrysostom, *Mulier alligata* 1 (PG 51, 218, 219).

[386] John Chrysostom, *Mulier alligata* 1 (PG 51, 219); cf. *Ad viduam iuniorem* 3 (the husband is sojourning [*apodēmia*] to heaven) (PG 48, 602). Chrysostom gives a long instruction against divorce, and an exegesis of the divorce texts, in *Mulier alligata* 2–3.

[387] John Chrysostom, *Mulier alligata* 4 (PG 51, 223).

[388] John Chrysostom, *De non iterando coniugio* 5–6 (PG 48, 617–19); cf. *Mulier alligata* 4 (PG 51, 223).

[389] John Chrysostom, *Hom. 7 II Tim.* 4 (II Tim. 3:1–7) (PG 62, 641–42).

[390] John Chrysostom, *Mulier alligata* 4 (PG 51, 223).

Although Ambrose, Clement of Alexandria, and Augustine all quote 7:39–40 in writing against remarriage,[391] it is Tertullian and Jerome who are the most vociferous, citing Paul's words in ways that tighten their import. For Tertullian, the fact that verse 40 (that Paul speaks with the authority of the Holy Spirit) stands at the end of the chapter gives an opportunity to argue that the Apostle here is "recalling" (i.e., "taking back") the "indulgence" for marriage he gave in the opening verses.[392] In another variation, Tertullian complains that Catholic Christians ("psychics") have misunderstood Paul when they appeal to 7:39 as permission for second marriage. Paul rather means that only if a person converts to Christianity *after* the spouse's death is he or she permitted to marry again, this time "in the Lord," that is, to another Christian. The verse does not, Tertullian argues, apply to women who were already Christians when their first husbands died. The Paraclete may now abrogate Paul's concession for second marriage, just as Christ abrogated the Mosaic concession for divorce.[393]

Jerome is scarcely less vociferous on this topic than Tertullian—and *his* views cannot be "blamed" on Montanism. Concluding his discussion of I Corinthians 7 in *Against Jovinian*, Jerome comes to the final issue of remarriage in verses 39–40, which he reads in conjunction with several intertexts that constrain Paul's words in an even more ascetic direction. A second marriage is certainly preferable to harlotry, Jerome muses; it is better for a widow to "prostitute herself to one man than to many." The one rib of Adam from which Eve was formed (Gen. 2:21–22) indicates that God intended single marriage. Moreover, the lowly state of second marriage is shown by "Paul's" prohibition of it for the clergy or for "real" widows (I Tim. 3:12; 5:9). For a woman to have had two husbands disbars her from the order of enrolled widows, and thus deprives her of the charity bread of the Church—and if she is so deprived, how much more is she deprived of "the bread of heaven" (John 6:32–35), that is, the Eucharist, through which Christians are condemned if they eat unworthily (I Cor. 11:27).[394] According to Jerome, Paul's words in 7:39–40 are

[391] Ambrose, *ep.* 63.39 (PL 16, 1251); *Exhortatio virginitatis* 7.46 (PL 16, 365); Clement of Alexandria, *Stromata* 3.12.80.1 (GCS 52 [15], 232). It is of interest that Augustine's treatise *On the Good of Widowhood* is mostly devoted to the goodness of first marriage, not to an explication of the benefits of widowhood, as we might expect. Augustine sets himself against Montanists, Novatianists, and Tertullian, all of whom attack second marriage, which Paul "soberly declared to be entirely lawful" (4.6 [CSEL 41, 309–10]).

[392] Tertullian, *De monogamia* 3.6 (CCL 2, 1232).

[393] Tertullian, *De monogamia* 11.1–9; 14.3 (CCL 2, 1244–45, 1249). In #12, Tertullian argues against Catholics who claim that Paul allowed second marriage for everyone except priests.

[394] Jerome, *Adversus Iovinianum* 1.14 (PL 23, 244). "One rib, one wife" is borrowed from Tertullian, *De monogamia* 4.2 (CCL 2, 1233). Cf. John Chrysostom, *Mu-*

in any event a "concession"; Christians should not believe that he advocated remarriage.[395]

Some Fathers also note that 7:39–40 stands against marriage between Christians and "pagans." For Tertullian, "the law of the patriarchs" against Gentile marriage conforms to 7:39,[396] and Cyprian cites 7:39—that intermarriage is precluded—in his catena of verses by which he intends to demonstrate the superiority of the Christian religion.[397]

One last interesting deployment of these verses is found in the argument offered by Augustine's correspondent Pollentius. Pollentius makes a case (rejected by Augustine) that a man should be permitted to remarry after divorcing an adulterous spouse, and bases his case, by analogy, on 7:39: if a woman may remarry after her husband is dead, can we not also consider the adulterous spouse as "dead" and allow remarriage for the nonadulterous partner?[398] Augustine counterargues that the "death of the soul" that constitutes adultery is not the same as the death of the body, of which Paul in these verses speaks.[399] Remarriage after a divorce from an adulterous spouse is not, for Augustine, compatible with Christian virtue.

III: Conclusion

How could I Corinthians 7, arguably the most ascetically directive chapter of the New Testament,[400] be read so as either to heighten or to diminish its ascetic import? Let me summarize the ways in which the verses of I Corinthians 7 were used to buttress patristic authors' own evaluations of marriage and sexual abstinence.

Although all of the patristic writers here surveyed encourage some level of sexual renunciation, the particular nuance each adopts frequently pertains to the audience to (or against) whom they write. Thus when Clement of Alexandria and Augustine criticize Christians whose rigorous asceticism seemingly implies a denigration of God's good creation, they champion marriage as best they can on the basis of Paul's verses: the "chaste married," for example, are here said *not* to be among those to whom Paul

---

lier alligata 2 (PG 51, 220): if God had wanted divorce, he would have created two women at the beginning so that Adam could have rejected one.

395 Jerome, *Adversus Iovinianum* 1.15 (PL 23, 245); likewise, John Chrysostom, *De non iterando coniugio* 3 (PG 48, 613), citing 7:6 ("concession not command") (presumably about sexual relations in a first marriage).

396 Tertullian, *De corona* 13.4–5 (CCL 2, 1061).

397 Cyprian, *Ad Quirinum* 3.62 (CSEL 3.1, 166).

398 Pollentius in Augustine, *De coniugiis adulterinis* 2.2.2 (CSEL 41, 383–84).

399 Augustine, *De coniugiis adulterinis* 2.4.4–5 (CSEL 41, 384–86).

400 A position strangely discounted by Will Deming, who argues that Paul should be placed "before and outside of" the history of Christian asceticism, "not within it as one of its founding fathers" (*Paul*, p. 212).

concedes marriage in the opening verses of the chapter, for such Christians need no "concession" for their praiseworthy marital relation. Yet against other Christians who appear too lax in their exertion of sexual control, authors such as Tertullian and the anonymous Pelagian author of the treatise *On Chastity* read I Corinthians 7 as sounding a highly astringent note: married sex is deemed scarcely higher than fornication. Roland Barthes' claim that a "text's unity lies not in its origin but in its destination"[401] here illumines the importance of audience for the interpretation of these commentaries.

Nuance could also be supplied by assigning various authoritative voices to different sections of the chapter. When Paul states that he is offering his own advice, should readers assign no special authority to his "merely human" opinion? Or does the Holy Spirit throughout inspire his teaching of a divinely ordained renunciation?

Other features of I Corinthians 7 also played into the exegetical hands of more rigorously ascetic commentators: thus Paul's excursus on slavery lent itself to exhortations regarding the "slavery" of marriage, while his recommendation that couples not separate is read as a divinely given command against divorce. Those commentators more sympathetic to marriage stress that it is only the "busyness" and "cares" of marriage that prompt Paul's mild dissuasions, while exegetes keen to press a more exacting ascetic line hint that there might be some "impurity" attending marital relations. These more ascetically minded exegetes also note that Paul's only justification for marriage (namely, to prevent fornication) scarcely constitutes a recommendation.

Although traditional Biblical critics assume that I Corinthians 7 is a single, unitary text, the readings presented in this chapter might better be characterized by the words of the demoniac in Mark 5:9: "My name is Legion: for we are many."[402] Readers—who in this case are patristic writers—have not so much "decoded" or "deciphered" Paul's text, but have "overcoded" it for their own ends.[403] Such multiple codings have been enabled by a variety of interpretive practices: by ingenious rhetoric, by intertextual interpretation, by "imploding" Biblical passages upon one another, by assignment of voice, by gender-bending. These divergent readings, however, exist not merely as multiple literary effects: they provide exegetical solutions to real-life problems that faced patristic commenta-

[401] Barthes, "The Death of the Author," in idem, *Image*, p. 148 (French original of this essay, 1968).

[402] Roland Barthes, "From Work to Text," in idem, *Image*, p. 160 (French original of this essay, 1971).

[403] Roland Barthes, "On Reading," in idem, *The Rustle of Language*, p. 42 (French original of this essay, 1976).

tors.[404] The "ends" pursued by these exegetes should thus be viewed not so much as personal interpretive resolutions to textual problems, but as informed by the religious, ecclesiastical, and moral (not to speak of social and material) circumstances of the interpreters. Their literary effects thus stand in history "as part of the ensemble of social practices."[405] Here historical work and literary work are effectively married.

[404] Michael Fishbane, *Biblical Interpretation in Ancient Israel* (Oxford: Clarendon, 1985), p. 271 (writing of the Hebrew Bible).

[405] Etienne Balibar and Pierre Macherey, "On Literature as an Ideological Form," trans. Ian McLeod, John Whitehead, and Ann Wordsworth, in *Untying the Text*, ed. Young, p. 83.

CHAPTER ELEVEN

From Paul to the Pastorals

I: Introduction

My survey of the patristic exegesis of I Corinthians 7 suggests that despite the widespread praise for ascetic renunciation, the Fathers' interpretations varied in accord with their own purposes and the contexts within which they reflected on particular verses. Nonetheless, for ascetically inclined exegetes, all New Testament passages pertaining to marriage and sexuality must be conformed to the lofty standard of I Corinthians 7. In some cases, this task proved easy; in others, more difficult.

Paul's teaching on sexual issues elsewhere than in I Corinthians 7 posed few difficulties for the Fathers; such verses were to be read in accord with the directives of this famous chapter. Other Pauline passages, however, that did not manifestly speak to issues of sexuality needed more interpretive work to render them useful for exegetes promoting ascetic renunciation. The Pastoral Epistles and other late New Testament books, however, proved most recalcitrant of all; that the Fathers believed that Paul himself had composed these books rendered their hermeneutical task both necessary and difficult. To square the assumption of marital preference contained in these books with the teaching of I Corinthians 7 that favored celibacy required intensive exegetical labor and considerable intellectual ingenuity. This chapter illustrates the progressive degrees of interpretive dexterity required for ascetically inclined writers to "read renunciation" from various verses of the Pauline, deutero-Pauline, and other later New Testament literature. I begin by examining verses in Paul's letters that speak directly to sexual issues.

II: Passages Concerning Sexual Behavior

Some passages, insofar as they directly concern issues of sexual behavior, lay ready for ascetically inclined exegetes to arrogate for their own purposes. Three such passages will here illustrate how easily some Pauline texts could be appropriated by various patristic writers with a minimum of exegetical labor.

> For this reason God gave them up to dishonorable passions. Their women exchanged natural relations for unnatural, and the men likewise gave up natural relations with women and were consumed with passion for one another, men committing shameless acts with men and receiving in their own persons the due penalty for their error.
>
> *Rom. 1:26–27 RSV*

Patristic interpretations of Romans 1:26–27 do not surprise. To some exegetes, the passage is said to reveal the evil consequences of "pagan" belief and practice, namely, "unnatural relations."[1] To other commentators, the verses imply, by way of contrast, the "goodness" of (hetero)sexual relations within marriage. Augustine thus argues that these verses support his view that the "pardon" for returning to marital relations after separation for prayer that Paul concedes in I Corinthians 7:6 concerns only "incontinent" sexual intercourse; the peccadillo of marital intemperance, however, is far removed from the "unnatural" acts against which Paul here, in Romans 1:26–27, rails.[2] Augustine's Pelagian opponent Julian of Eclanum reads the passage even more exuberantly: in these verses, Paul proclaims men's sexual relations with women—and sexual desire itself—to be both laudable and "natural."[3]

John Chrysostom, also supportive of marriage, sees in Romans 1:26–27 a description of the devil's attempt to sunder the "two in one flesh" (Gen. 2:24) of heterosexual coupling. The "unnatural" relations to which Paul here alludes are even more transgressive than the fornication with prostitutes described in I Corinthians 6; the latter unions, Chrysostom

[1] Origen, *Comm. Rom.* 1.22(19) (Hammond Bammel, pp. 93–96); Origen insists that changing "the image of God" should not be taken to imply that God has a body. Also see Athanasius, *Vita Antonii* 69 and *Contra gentes* 1.26; Pelagius, *Comm. Rom.* 1:27, cf. his comment on 1:24: "impurity" is described as "the filthy rites of idols"; Ambrosiaster, *Comm. Rom.* 1:26. For a discussion of female homoeroticism and Rom. 1, see Bernadette J. Brooten, *Love Between Women: Early Christian Responses to Female Homoeroticism* (Chicago/London: University of Chicago Press, 1996), chaps. 9 and 10; for discussion of the Fathers' attitudes, pp. 314–57.

[2] Augustine, *De bono coniugali* 10.11 (CSEL 41, 202–3).

[3] Julian of Eclanum in Augustine, *De nuptiis et concupiscentia* 2.19.34 (CSEL 42, 287); *Contra Iulianum* 3.20.40 (PL 44, 724–25); *Opus imperfectum* 5.17; 5.46 (PL 45, 1450, 1482).

concedes, are at least "in accord with nature." Men who engage in "unnatural" relations injure *both* sexes by disdaining the behavior proper to each.[4] Thus Augustine and Chrysostom read Romans 1:26–27 in accordance with Paul's teaching on sexual relations in I Corinthians, a move requiring little exegetical labor.

Pelagius, on the other hand, does not contrast sexual relations "in accord with nature" with those that are "contrary to nature," but rather understands Romans 1:26–27 to exemplify the evil that results when unbridled *libido* does not observe a "mean"; for Pelagius, same-sex relations illustrate "excessive" rather than "unnatural" sexuality.[5] Paul's condemnation of same-sex relations here serves as a foil for the Fathers to express their tolerance of a tempered sexual relation within marriage. A far sharper critique of marriage would, however, be prompted by other passages.

I Thessalonians 4:3–7 likewise provides an opportunity for the Fathers to contrast appropriate and inappropriate sexual relations:

> For this is the will of God, your sanctification: that you abstain from immorality; that each one of you know how to take a wife for himself [= hold his vessel] in holiness and honor, not in the passion of lust like heathen who do not know God; that no man transgress, and wrong his brother in this matter, because the Lord is an avenger in all these things, as we solemnly forewarned you. For God has not called us for uncleanness, but in holiness.
>
> *I Thess. 4:3–7 RSV*

Writers keen to praise—or least to justify—marriage here found another set of useful verses. Thus when Tertullian writes against Marcionites who (he alleges) destroy "the God of marriage," he explains that in I Thessalonians 4:3–7, Paul instructs Christians to abstain from fornication, not from marriage. The "lust" which Paul here mentions does not pertain to Christian marital relations, but only to "extravagant, unnatural, and enormous sins." The law of nature, Tertullian argues, accommodates our "vessel" (here, probably to be equated with "body," or more specifically,

[4] John Chrysostom, *Hom. 4 Rom.* 1–3 (1:26–27) (PG 60, 417–20).

[5] Pelagius, *Comm. Rom.* 1:27 (PLS 1, 1119). For a discussion of the ancient understanding of same-sex relations as "excess," see Dale B. Martin, "Heterosexism and the Interpretation of Romans 1:18–32," *Biblical Interpretation* 3 (1995):

with "penis")[6] through the honorable estate of matrimony.[7] Thus Tertullian does not interpret Paul's rebuke of the lustful as an indictment of Christian couples, but as a testimony to the divine ordination of marriage and as a censure of "Gentile" immorality.

Theodore of Mopsuestia provides a second "pro-marriage" reading of I Thessalonians 4:3–7, but, unlike Tertullian, understands the passage as a chastisement of those Thessalonian Christian husbands who pursued women other than their own spouses. Here, the "vessels" that the men are to "hold in holiness and honor" are their wives; they are not to soil themselves with adultery. Since concupiscence ("lust") is not a "crime" but merely a "motion of nature," Theodore denies that Paul's words apply to faithful Christian marriage. Rather, he argues, "lust" obtains when a man has sexual relations with a woman other than his wife. According to Theodore, Paul warns in these verses against "defrauding" one's brother of his "possession" (i.e., his wife), a sin whose guilt is exacerbated when the defrauded party is a "brother in the faith."[8] Faithful Christian marriage is here carefully removed from Paul's critique of "lust," as it also was by Tertullian when writing against the Marcionites.

John Chrysostom reads I Thessalonians 4:3–7 as an attack on both fornication and adultery. In an argument typical of Chrysostom's concern for social and economic relations, he stresses that *any* extramarital sex (whether with prostitutes, slave girls, or the empress herself) is adultery; the class of the woman is not the issue at hand. Rather, for a married man, any sexual relation other than with his wife is adultery, to be punished by God—the injured party—if not by the Roman state.[9] When Paul writes that a Christian man should "do no wrong to his brother" (v. 6), he implies that the sexual appropriation of a woman other than one's wife is "taking more than what belongs to us": fornication and adultery are here aligned with covetousness. Chrysostom also appears to understand the *skeuos* ("vessel") as either the penis, or more generally, the body. We "possess our vessel" when we keep it in a state of purity. According to Chrysostom, the "vessel" becomes "impure," however, when "it" refuses to do as we wish, but impels us into sin.[10]

341–43, 346.

[6] For discussions of ancient and modern understandings of *skeuos*, see John W. Bailey, "The First and Second Epistles to the Thessalonians," in *The Interpreter's Bible* (New York/Nashville: Abingdon, 1955), XI:294–95; Ernest Best, *A Commentary on the First and Second Epistles to the Thessalonians* (London: Adam & Charles Black, 1972), pp. 161–64.

[7] Tertullian, *Adversus Marcionem* 5.15.3 (CCL 1, 709).

[8] Theodore of Mopsuestia, *Comm. I Thess.* 4:3–4 (Swete II:22–23).

[9] John Chrysostom, *Hom. 5 I Thess.* 1–2 (4:5–8) (PG 62, 424–25); cf. *Propter fornicationes* 4 (4:8) (PG 51, 213–24).

[10] John Chrysostom, *Hom. 5 I Thess.* 1–2 (4:4–6) (PG 62, 424).

While Augustine praises marriage, he (unlike Theodore of Mopsuestia) does not understand "concupiscence" as a natural bodily desire, but as the result of sin that infects all humans, not merely fornicators and adulterers: Christians are not exempt from "the passion of lust" (4:5). Thus Augustine faults his Pelagian opponent Julian of Eclanum for differentiating the sexual instincts of the body (which Julian deems so praiseworthy that he even introduces them into Paradise) from "lust," a word that Julian reserves for sexual relations characterized by "fornication and excess."[11] Julian's distinction is meant to rescue the sexual acts of married Christians from any implied taint. For Augustine, to the contrary, "lust" attends *all* sexual acts.

Taking the "vessel" in this passage to mean "wife,"[12] Augustine further argues that by using their "vessels" for procreation alone, both Adam and the patriarchs can be exonerated of any suspicion of sexual excess. Does not Hebrews 11:4–6 report that they were "pleasing to God"?[13] In the present, however, Christians have to fear this "disease" of lustful desire.[14] Any sexual intercourse beyond what is necessary to produce children offends against not only Christian morality, but even the ancient Roman marriage tables that stipulated children to be the purpose of marriage:[15] "pagan" law of the distant past is here enlisted to support Augustine's sexual ethic. Augustine notes that the Latin manuscripts of I Thessalonians 4:5 contain two different readings ("*in morbo desiderii vel concupiscentiae*"; "*in passione concupiscentiae*"); whichever reading one adopts, Augustine claims, the "diseased condition" obtains even in "the lawful and honorable sexual union of husband and wife." "*Passio*," Augustine informs his readers, in the usage of the church is not a neutral term, but one of censure.[16]

For writers of a more ascetically rigorous bent, I Thessalonians 4:3–7 takes on darker associations. Pelagius, although not as antimarital as the anonymous Pelagian author of *De castitate*, nonetheless wrests unflattering sentiments concerning the married from these verses. Appealing to the story in Exodus 19:15 (the prohibition to Israelite men against approaching a woman for three days before God's appearance on Mount Sinai), Pelagius instructs the Christian "incontinent" that they cannot

[11] Augustine, *Contra Iulianum* 4.10.56; 5.9.39 (PL 44, 765, 807).

[12] Augustine, *Contra Iulianum* 5.9.35 (PL 44, 805); *De nuptiis et concupiscentia* 1.8.9 (CSEL 42, 220).

[13] Augustine, *De nuptiis et concupiscentia* 1.8.9; 2.8.19 (CSEL 42, 221, 271); *De bono coniugali* 12.14 (CSEL 41, 206–7).

[14] Augustine, *Contra Iulianum* 4.10.56; 5.9.39 (PL 44, 765, 807).

[15] Augustine, *Serm.* 278.9.9 (PL 38, 1272).

[16] Augustine, *De nuptiis et concupiscentia* 2.33.55 (CSEL 42, 312–13). The editors of CSEL 42 (following most manuscripts) have omitted the *nisi*—which renders pointless Augustine's argument.

"lay hands on the holy body of Christ" (i.e., receive communion) if they have so approached any woman, for "uncleanness" renders one unfit to receive the Eucharist. The "Gentiles" whom Paul here accuses of acting "in passion" are ignorant that God is a "lover of chastity."[17] Pelagius warns that the Lord will "avenge" (I Thess. 4:6) those who vow continence to God and do not keep their promises.[18] When Paul exhorts the Thessalonians to take their "vessels" (here, "wives") in "sanctification and honor," he condescends to them in the same way that he did to the "weak Corinthians."[19] Marital relations have here suffered a subtle demotion—but they were to receive a more severe devaluation by Jerome.

Beginning with a concession, Jerome cites I Thessalonians 4:3–7 to instruct those who are already married when they were "called" to Christianity (I Cor. 7:20) not to desert their marriages for abstinence, but rather to drink only of their own "wells" (i.e., "wives"), not those of prostitutes.[20] Jerome nonetheless extracts a more rigorous ascetic implication from the passage through a complex intertextual exegesis.[21] By reading "hold your vessel in sanctification and honor" (I Thess. 4:4) in tandem with Ephesians 5:21–33, Jerome concludes that husbands should love their wives in the same (sexless) chastity as Christ in Ephesians 5 is said to love the Church. Since the "image of God" does not involve marriage, Jerome declares, our re-creation in that image (Col. 3:10) implies that difference of sex will be erased, as Paul signifies by his phrase "no male and female" (Gal. 3:28). "Putting off the old man" and "putting on the new man" (Col. 3:9–10) mean for Jerome that sexual difference is overcome in the new creation.[22] Through intertextual exegesis, I Thessalonians 4:3–7 has been recast to advocate the virginal life, seen by Jerome as the true "sanctification." The values of I Corinthians 7, aided by a subtle "close reading" of Ephesians 5, "improve" Paul's teaching in I Thessalonians 4:3–7.

A third Pauline passage that receives considerable attention from ascetically inclined exegetes is I Corinthians 6:15–20:

> Do you not know that your bodies are members of Christ? Shall I therefore take the members of Christ and make them members of a prostitute? Never! Do you not know that he who joins

[17] Pelagius, *Comm. I Thess.* 4:3; 4:7; 4:5 (PLS 1, 1326, 1327).

[18] Pelagius, *Comm. I Thess.* 4:6 (PLS 1, 1326).

[19] Pelagius, *Comm. I Thess.* 4:4 (PLS 1, 1326); cf. I Cor. 7:1–3.

[20] Jerome, *ep.* 128.3 (CSEL 56, 158), alluding to Jer. 2:13 and Prov. 5:15.

[21] For an elaboration of "intertextual exegesis," see above, pp. 122–28.

[22] Jerome, *Adversus Iovinianum* 1.16 (PL 23, 246).

> himself to a prostitute becomes one
> body with her? For, as it is written,
> "The two shall become one" (Gen.
> 2:24). But he who is united to the
> Lord becomes one spirit with him.
> Shun immorality. Every other sin
> which a man commits is outside the
> body; but the immoral man sins
> against his own body. Do you not
> know that your body is a temple of the
> Holy Spirit within you, which you
> have from God? You are not your
> own; you were bought with a price. So
> glorify God in your body.
>
> *I Cor. 6:15–20 RSV*

According to the church fathers, these verses, in their "plainest" interpretation, constituted a strong critique of fornication and adultery.[23] That Christians were "temples of the Holy Spirit" (6:19) demanded a special purity of them, a purity that required modesty in female attire and opposed the use of cosmetics.[24] For some writers, a Christian's joining his members with a prostitute betokened idolatry;[25] to others, the verses stood as a warning against intermarriage with "Gentiles."[26] Particular classes of Christians could also be corrected by recitation of these verses: wives who opted for a unilateral withdrawal from marital relations;[27] a widower who had taken a concubine after his wife's death;[28] potential martyrs (here reminded that they are "joined to the Lord" to whom they witness);[29] those living in syneisaktic relationships;[30] fallen virgins, both female and male.[31]

[23] Tertullian, *Adversus Marcionem* 5.7.4–5 (CCL 1, 682–83); *De pudicitia* 16.8–10 (CCL 2, 1312–13); Ps.-Cyprian (Novatian), *De bono pudicitia* 6 (CSEL 3.3, 17–18); Lactantius, *Divinae institutiones* 6.23 (CSEL 19, 566–67); Origen, *Hom. 5 Jesu Nave* 6 (SC 71, 172); Eusebius of Emesa, *Hom.* 7.26 (Buytaert I:193); Athanasius, *Frag.* 6 (CSCO 150 = Scriptores Coptici 19, 124; ET, Brakke, p. 316); Nilus of Ancyra, *De monastica exercitatione* 12 (PG 79, 733); John Chrysostom, *Hom. 4 Rom.* 3 (1:26–27) (PG 60, 419); *De virginitate* 25 (SC 125, 174); *Hom. 63 Ioan.* 4 (PG 59, 353–54); *Hom. 18 I Cor.* 1 (PG 61, 145–46).

[24] Tertullian, *De cultu feminarum* 2.1.1 (CCL 1, 352); Ambrose, *Hexaemeron* 6.9.8.47 (CSEL 32.1, 238).

[25] Augustine, *De fide et operibus* 12.18 (CSEL 41, 58).

[26] Tertullian, *Ad uxorem* 2.3.1–4 (CCL 1, 387–88); Cyprian, *Ad Quirinum* 3.62 (CSEL 3.1, 166).

[27] (Anonymous), *Ad Celantiam* 30 (CSEL 29, 458).

[28] Augustine, *ep.* 259.3 (CSEL 57, 613), citing I Cor. 6:15.

[29] Origen, *Exhortatio ad martyrium* 10 (GCS Origenes 2, 10).

[30] Athanasius, *ep. 2 ad virgines* (Lebon, p. 185; ET, Brakke, p. 300).

[31] Female: Basil of Caesarea, *ep. 46* (Loeb I:296); male: John Chrysostom, *Ad*

Manicheans' negative assessments of the body could likewise be reproached through the citing of I Corinthians 6:15–20.[32]

Exegetes also tightened the interpretation of these verses by elaborating their import in a more emphatically ascetic direction. For example, Origen suggests that since Christians are "temples of the Holy Spirit" (6:19), they should disdain sexual union for the sake of pleasure.[33] According to Clement of Alexandria, the "fornication" against which 6:18 warns is to be identified with "second marriage."[34] Several authors agree that maintaining a pure "temple" is particularly important for virgins: so the authors of the *Acts of Thomas* and the *Acts of Paul*, Athanasius, and Gerontius, author of the *Life of Melania the Younger*.[35] Although commentators more favorable to marriage cite these verses to stress its goodness, especially its salutary provision of an alternative to fornication,[36] several features of I Corinthians 6:15–20 encouraged a still more rigorous assessment.

First, commentators note that "two becoming one [flesh]," a phrase which in Genesis 2:24 and Matthew 19:6 signals a blessing on marriage, here describes relations with a prostitute. Although Paul's Corinthian audience may have been shocked that he applied this honored text applauding marriage to prostitution, in the hands of an ascetically rigorous critic such as Jerome, the negative connotations of unions with prostitutes could spill over "backwards," so to speak, to remind readers that the sexual act in marriage did not necessarily differ from that performed with a prostitute.[37] If "two in one flesh" portends something evil when applied to prostitutes, why should it suggest anything different for the married? *All* sexual intercourse, according to Jerome, is suspect.

Theodorum lapsum 1.1 (PG 47, 277) (the Christ-bearing temple [Theodore] has been thrown down).

[32] Augustine, *Contra Faustum* 20.15 (CSEL 25, 555–56); *De moribus ecclesiae Catholicae* 35.78 (PL 32, 1343).

[33] Origen, *Comm. I Cor.* 6:19 (Jenkins [1908], p. 372).

[34] Clement of Alexandria, *Stromata* 3.12.88–89 (GCS 52 [15], 236–37).

[35] *Acta Thomae* 12 (Lipsius/Bonnet II:116–17); *Acta Pauli et Theclae* 5 (Lipsius/Bonnet I:238); Athanasius, *ep. 2 ad virgines* (Lebon, p. 172; ET, Brakke, p. 293); (Gerontius), *Vita Melaniae Iunioris* 29 (SC 90, 182, 184) (the teaching is attributed to Melania herself).

[36] Augustine, *De moribus ecclesiae Catholicae* 35.78 (PL 32, 1343); *De bono coniugali* 11.13 (CSEL 41, 204–5); *De bono viduitate* 3.4 (CSEL 41, 308); John Chrysostom, *De virginitate* 25 (SC 125, 174).

[37] Jerome, *Adversus Iovinianum* 2.24 (PL 23, 334), *ep.* 55.2 (CSEL 54, 489); cf. *Adversus Iovinianum* 1.20 and 1.7, where passages pertaining to marriage and fornication are elided. The source of this sentiment is probably Tertullian, who in *De exhortatione castitatis* 9.3 (CCL 2, 1028) claims that the sexual act is the same in marriage as in fornication. See James L. Kugel, *In Potiphar's House: The Interpretive Life of Biblical Texts* (San Francisco: HarperSanFrancisco, 1990), pp. 132, 173, 261, on "back-referring" in rabbinic exegesis of the Hebrew Bible.

The most common pressure to interpret I Corinthians 6:15–20 in an ascetic direction, however, comes from Paul's wording in verses 16–17: a man becomes "one body" with a prostitute,[38] "but (*de*) he who is united to the Lord becomes one spirit with him." While marriage, as well as fornication and adultery, involved a "union of body," the higher Christian life, by contrast, advised a "union of spirit." The (sexless) union "with the Lord" here praised might be enlarged to encompass a sexless marital union as well: how much better to be "one in spirit" than "one in flesh."[39]

It is not only the most vociferous critics of marriage, such as Jerome,[40] who press this interpretation. Although the anonymous author of *To Celantia* criticizes his addressee for adopting sexual abstinence without her husband's consent, his preference nonetheless is for a mutually chosen sexless union in which the couple can be "one in spirit."[41] Thus Genesis 2:24 ("two in one flesh") and I Corinthians 6:17 ("one in spirit") are read over against each other as demonstrating "the difference in times" that obtains between the Old Dispensation and the New.[42] Likewise, Origen, commenting on the different statuses of Christians addressed by Paul in I Corinthians 7, cites 6:16–17, distinguishing the "one flesh" that pertains to marriage from the "one spirit" that attends a higher holiness.[43] For the author of the letter *To Claudia*, it is *virgins* who are "one in spirit with the Lord,"[44] as it is for Athanasius, Basil of Ancyra, and Gregory of Nyssa.[45]

Augustine, however, resists such exclusive co-optation of I Corinthians 6:15–20 for the sexually abstinent. Defending marriage as a "good," Augustine argues that verse 19 (our bodies as "temples of the Holy Spirit") corrects any "misimpression" that readers might derive from I Corinthians 7:34, namely, that married women might not be "holy in body," since the latter phrase is there explicitly used only of *unmarried* women. Yet

[38] For a helpful discussion, see Bruce N. Fisk, "*Porneuein* as Bodily Violation: The Unique Nature of Sexual Sin in I Corinthians 6:18," *New Testament Studies* 42 (1996): 540–58.

[39] For Daniel Boyarin, these verses signal Paul's attempt to displace sexuality entirely in favor of "an allegorical becoming-one-spirit with Christ" (*A Radical Jew: Paul and the Politics of Identity* [Berkeley/Los Angeles/London: University of California Press, 1994], pp. 171–72).

[40] Jerome, *epp.* 71.3 (CSEL 55, 4); 22.1 (CSEL 54, 145); *Adversus Iovinianum* 1.11; cf. 1.16 (PL 23, 236, 246).

[41] (Anonymous), *Ad Celantiam* 30 (CSEL 29, 457–58).

[42] (Anonymous), *Admonitio Augiensis* (PLS 1, 1702). For a discussion of the "difference in times," see above, pp. 145–52.

[43] Origen, *Comm. I Cor.* 7:28b (Jenkins [1908], p. 510).

[44] (Anonymous), *ep. de virginitate* (= *Ad Claudiam*) 1–2 (CSEL 1, 225–26).

[45] Athanasius, *ep. 1 ad virgines* (CSCO 150 = Scriptores Coptici 19, 74; ET, Brakke, p. 275); *ep. 2 ad virgines* (Lebon, p. 185; ET, Brakke, p. 300); Basil of Ancyra, *De virginitate* 49 (Vaillant, p. 55); Gregory of Nyssa, *De virginitate* 15.1 (SC 119, 446).

married women, too, Augustine claims, are "holy in body" as well as "holy in spirit," since *all* Christians are "temples of the Holy Spirit" (6:19).[46] The married as well as the unmarried may join their "members" with Christ; this is not, in Augustine's view, a privilege reserved for virgins and widows alone.[47]

Romans 1:26–27, I Thessalonians 4:3–7, and I Corinthians 6:15–20, insofar as they pertain directly to sexual issues, required little exegetical labor on the part of patristic interpreters—although even in these cases, greater or lesser degrees of ascetic renunciation could be "read" from them.

III: "Flesh" and "Spirit"; "No Male and Female"

I next turn to some Pauline passages that do not explicitly concern sexual issues, but which were easily adapted by patristic commentators to speak to them. Two such groups of passages are those in which Paul opposes "flesh" to "spirit" (Rom. 7:13–24; 8:4–9; Gal. 5:16–26; 6:8), and his phrase, "no male and female" (Gal.3:28). Both sets could be pressed with minimal exegetical effort to provide reinforcement for the ascetic agenda. In the first case, the Fathers take care to avoid "heretical" readings that denigrate "the flesh," even as they extol ascetic values.

In the patristic discussion of Paul's teachings on "flesh" and "spirit" (or variously, "Spirit"), several questions arose. What did Paul mean by the words "flesh" and "lust"? With what voice did he speak: was he the "wretched man" who was "sold under sin," or the one who could "thank God" for his redemption (Rom. 7:24–25)? And to whom did he speak? To married Christians? To "heretics"? To ascetics? Both "voice" and "audience" were major factors governing the interpretation of these verses.

All patristic writers were concerned to exclude the overly ascetic interpretations of "flesh" by Encratites and Manicheans that seemingly denigrated the created order. Thus Jerome attacks the Encratite interpretation of Galatians 6:8 ("sow to his own flesh/sow to the Spirit"), which, he claims, posits "sowing in the flesh" to mean the marital union whose end was "reaping corruption from the flesh." Jerome faults the Encratites' failure to "read closely": Paul does not here write "sow in the flesh," but "sow in *his* flesh." No man cohabiting with his wife is "sowing in *his* flesh"; thus the verse cannot apply to marital relations, as the Encratites assume.

[46] Augustine, *De bono coniugali* 11.13 (CSEL 41, 204–5).

[47] Augustine, *De bono viduitatis* 3.4; 6.8 (CSEL 41, 308, 312).

Not only are the Encratites bad readers, they also carp at God's good creation, a more serious fault. Rather, those who "sow in the flesh and reap corruption from it," Jerome argues, are those who pursue sexual pleasure. Christians who eat, drink, and sleep "in the name of the Lord" and "with reason," by contrast, are *not* "sowing in the flesh" but "in the spirit." Genesis 1:28 ("reproduce and multiply"), read in tandem with Galatians 6:8, counsels us to a "rational" reproductive act which can be called "sowing in the spirit."[48] Rarely is Jerome so irenic regarding sexual relations; it is worth noting that his desire to rebut extreme ("heretical") ascetic interpretations here prompts his moderating tone.

More frequently, Manichean interpretations of the "flesh/spirit" passages come under attack. Pelagius argues against Manicheans in his exegesis of Romans 7 and 8, and hence he has little reason to read these chapters as an ascetic directive. Commenting on Romans 8, Pelagius notes that by *caro* Paul does not mean the "flesh" itself, but the "carnal sense" (*sensus carnalis*); otherwise, Christians might imagine that the flesh were evil, as Manicheans claim.[49] When explicating Galatians 5:19–21 (the "works of the flesh"), Pelagius argues that these "works" are more appropriately referred to vices prompted by the soul or the mind. If Christians attribute them to the flesh *per se*, they might, like Manicheans, deem the flesh an evil nature.[50]

Augustine also fears Manichean interpretations of Paul's flesh/spirit passages, not least when he himself is facing the accusations of "Manicheanism" that were leveled against him by his Pelagian opponent, Julian of Eclanum. Thus he repeatedly notes that "flesh" and "spirit" should not be understood as two "natures," as in Manichean teaching.[51] Augustine appeals to Ephesians 5:28–29, that no man "hates his own flesh," as is evidenced by husbands' love for their wives "as their own bodies"; through these verses, he posits, Manichean denigration of the flesh stands corrected. To be sure, Augustine adds, Paul acknowledges that Christians have fleshly desires, but his concession does not mean that they should act upon them. According to Augustine, humans are not free from the opposition between flesh and spirit while they remain in "this body of death" (Rom. 7:24); this they achieve only in the afterlife.[52] Here, Augustine not only faults Manicheans as poor readers,[53] but also cautions

[48] Jerome, *Comm. Gal.* 3 (6:8) (PL 26, 459–60).

[49] Pelagius, *Comm. Rom.* 8:7 (PLS 1, 1146).

[50] Pelagius, *Comm. Gal.* 5:19–21 (PLS 1, 1285).

[51] Augustine, *Serm.* 152.4 (PL 38, 821); *Opus imperfectum* 3.178 (CSEL 85.1, 479); 6.6 (PL 45, 1510); 6.14 (PL 45, 1531); *De continentia* 7.18 (CSEL 41, 161).

[52] Augustine, *Opus imperfectum* 6.14 (PL 45, 1531), commenting on Gal. 5:16–17; cf. *Opus imperfectum* 4.77 (PL 45, 1385).

[53] Augustine, *De continentia* 9.22 (CSEL 41, 168).

that the Pauline verses should not be taken by Christians as declaring a (Manichean) "war against the body."[54] "Heretics' " deeply ascetic interpretations of the Pauline "flesh/spirit" verses thus provide a "brake" on the exegesis of patristic writers concerned to uphold the goodness of God's creation.

A few church fathers astutely note that words such as "flesh" and "lust" carry different meanings even within Scripture itself. Thus John Cassian, commenting on the "desires of the flesh" in Galatians 5:17, observes that "flesh" sometimes means "the whole man," as in "the Word was made flesh" (John 1:14), while at other times, it means "carnal will and desires," as in Galatians 5:17.[55] Likewise, Pelagius and Chrysostom both note that "flesh" does not always mean "the body." According to Chrysostom, "flesh" in Galatians 5:17 rather means "the depraved will"; Paul charges the sins he here enumerates against the "slothful soul," not against the body.[56] Augustine's opponent Julian of Eclanum also attempts to shift the interpretation of "lusts of the flesh" (Gal. 5:17) away from the domain of the sexual: thus the sin of the Sodomites can (with assistance from Ezek. 16:49) be interpreted as excessive eating and drinking rather than as sexual deviance.[57] Augustine, too, argues that by "the works of the flesh" Paul means not only "sensual pleasures" (fornication and impurity standing as examples), but also "faults of the mind," such as devotion to idols, sorcery, and enmity.[58] And in *The City of God*, Augustine argues that "lust" is a general word for all kinds of desires, the desire for revenge, money, and domination, as well as for sex.[59] The Fathers' wish to avoid overly negative—and thus "heretical"—interpretations of "flesh" appears evident.

Some patristic interpretations of the Pauline passages depicting "the war of flesh against spirit" exempt faithful Christians from these battles: it is more convenient that others suffer from this warfare. Thus the anonymous (Pelagian?) author of the letter *To Celantia* assumes that Christians are oblivious to the struggles of flesh against spirit noted in Galatians 5. Having "crucified the flesh with its passions and desires" (Gal. 5:24), Christians should separate from "unbelievers," who stand as the proper targets of Paul's correction.[60] For this author, Christians are not the audience whom Paul here chastises.

[54] Augustine, *De doctrina Christiana* 1.24.25 (CCL 32, 19–20).

[55] John Cassian, *Conlationes* 4.10–11 (SC 42, 174, 175).

[56] Pelagius, *Comm. Rom.* 8:7 (PLS 1, 1146); John Chrysostom, *Hom. 5 Gal.* 5 (5:17) (PG 61, 671).

[57] Julian of Eclanum, in Augustine, *Contra Iulianum* 3.20.41 (PL 44, 722–23).

[58] Augustine, *De civitate Dei* 14.2 (CCL 48, 415–16).

[59] Augustine, *De civitate Dei* 14.15–16 (CCL 48, 438).

[60] (Anonymous), *Ad Celantiam* 9 (CSEL 29, 442–43).

Another popular interpretation assumed that Jews were the discredited group who "lusted against the spirit," a view enabled by the assumption that Paul referred to his old "Jewish" sinful self in Romans 7. Thus Augustine confesses that earlier in his exegetical career he had assumed that Romans 7:18 ("I know that no good dwells in me, that is, in my flesh") was spoken by Paul as a sinful Jew, not as a Christian.[61] This position, Augustine later complains, his Pelagian opponent Julian of Eclanum still holds. By ascribing such statements to a "Jewish," not a "Christian," Paul, Julian and his supporters smugly (and mistakenly) believe that they as Christians live entirely "according to the Spirit."[62] Augustine in his mature years posits rather that Christians are not delivered from the tussle of "flesh against spirit" in the here-and-now. Romans 7:15 ("I do not understand my own actions. For I do not what I want, but I do the very thing I hate") signals that the warfare of "flesh" against "spirit" still applies to the present life of the faithful.[63] Similarly, for Tertullian in his Montanist phase, only Catholic Christians ("psychics") suffer from "flesh that lusts against the Spirit" (Gal. 5:17); piously "spiritual" Christians have overcome such lust, as proved by their prohibition of second marriage.[64] By such interpretations, "lusting against the Spirit" could be assigned to "others," not to one's own group.

Moreover, those Fathers eager to defend the (relative) goodness of marriage read Paul's injunctions on "flesh and spirit" in a way that accords with this goal. Thus John Chrysostom, preaching on Romans 7 to urban, largely married Christians, argues that when the body became mortal after the first sin, it needed concupiscence, anger, pain, and other passions. These qualities are not reprehensible in themselves, but only when they become "unbridled." If concupiscence is limited in its operation to "the laws of marriage," then it is not sinful; only when it passes beyond marriage and leads to adultery is it blameworthy. Thus it is not desire itself that Paul faults, but the "exorbitant" uses of desire.[65]

Augustine, for his part, chastened by Pelagian allegations of his covert "Manicheanism," belatedly concedes that there *could* have been a legitimate sexual desire in the Garden of Eden, different from the evil concupis-

[61] Augustine, *Contra Iulianum* 3.26.61 (PL 44, 733); *Contra duas epistolas Pelagianorum* 1.10.21–22 (CSEL 60, 442–43). Cf. Augustine's earlier work on Romans, *Expositio ad Romanos* 37 (44)–38 (46) (CSEL 84, 19–20).

[62] Augustine, *Contra Iulianum* 3.26.61 (PL 44, 733); Julian in Augustine, *Opus imperfectum* 1.67.2–4 (CSEL 85.1, 66–67).

[63] Augustine, *Opus imperfectum* 1.67.1–4 (CSEL 85.1, 69–71).

[64] Tertullian, *De monogamia* 1.2–3 (CCL 2, 1229).

[65] John Chrysostom, *Hom. 13 Rom.* 1 (7:14) (PG 60, 507–8). Chrysostom's appeal to "unbridled desire" is reminiscent of Pelagius' comment on Rom. 1:27: "Effrenata libido modum servare non novit" (PLS 1, 1119).

cence which, Paul says, "wars against the law of the mind" (Rom. 7:23). Augustine also here cites Galatians 5:17 to make the same point: the sexual appetite that Adam and Eve in Paradise might conceivably have felt had they not sinned would not have been such that the "desires of the flesh" opposed those of the spirit.[66]

Despite these caveats aimed to rescue the goodness of Christian marriage, it is nonetheless clear that most patristic authors find the Pauline passages on flesh and spirit more useful to reinforce their views on sexual restraint. Sometimes the frame of reference for discussing "the lust of the flesh" is fornication, the first such "work of the flesh" listed by Paul in Galatians 5:19–21. Jerome thus notes that other deeds a man performs "outside his body," but fornication is sinning "in his body," joining his members to those of a prostitute and defiling his body, his "temple of the Holy Spirit" (I Cor. 6:18–19).[67] The unmarried, too, can feel their "members" war against their minds (Rom. 7:23); if they do, as did his friend Fabiola, they may marry so as to prevent the "burning" of I Corinthians 7:9, Jerome concedes.[68] Augustine, for his part, interprets his own adolescent sexual behavior, now the subject of much regret, as a manifestation of succumbing to "the lusts of the flesh" (Gal. 5:17).[69]

Moreover, in a move that was to have momentous implications for later Christianity, Augustine shifts the explication of Paul's phrases "the flesh lusting against the spirit" and "the war of the members" to the arena of *marriage*: it is not merely men's frequenting of prostitutes and other illicit acts that here qualify for inclusion. Paul speaks not only of sexual desire outside of marriage.[70]

In his anti-Pelagian treatise *On Marriage and Concupiscence*, Augustine cites Paul's phrases—"the law of sin," "the war of the members," "the flesh"—over and again,[71] and in his other anti-Pelagian writings, sexual desire *within* marriage is his target.[72] He argues that married couples know "that no good dwells in [their] flesh" (Rom. 7:18) when they act on their sexual desires beyond the minimum necessary for procreation; in this case,

[66] Augustine, *ep.* 6*.5; 6*.8 (CSEL 88, 34, 38).

[67] Jerome, *Comm. Gal.* 3 (5:19–21) (PL 26, 443).

[68] Jerome, *ep.* 77.3 (CSEL 55, 39), on Fabiola's remarriage.

[69] Augustine, *Confessiones* 8.5.11 (CCL 27, 120).

[70] Augustine on desire and lust in general, citing these Pauline passages: *De nuptiis et concupiscentia* 1.1.1; 1.21–22.24; 1.28–29.31; 1.30.33; 1.31.35; *Contra Iulianum* 3.13.26; 3.13.27; 3.20.41; 3.21.50; 3.26.61; 4.1.2; 4.4.34; 4.14.72; 5.7.24; 5.15.58; 6.23.73; *Opus imperfectum* 1.68; 1.72; 2.180; 4.77; 6.14; 6.17; 6.37; *Serm.* 151.3.3; *ep.* 6*.5; *De civitate Dei* 14.2; 15.20; 19.4.

[71] For example, Augustine, *De nuptiis et concupiscentia* 1.1.1; 1.21–22.24; 1.28–29.31; 1.30.33; 1.31.35.

[72] For example, Augustine, *Contra Iulianum* 4.2.6; *Opus imperfectum* 1.68; *De gratia Christi* 2.34.39; *ep.* 6*.7; *De civitate Dei* 14.18.

they experience a "war" between the "law of the members" and the "law of the mind" (Rom. 7:23).[73] Not only have Paul's words on "flesh and spirit" here been given a decisively sexual turn; they have been given this within the context of marriage. Of course, Augustine is not alone in making such an exegetical move. Earlier, Origen interprets the story of the newly married man who refused the invitation to the dinner (Luke 14:18–20) with the help of the "flesh/spirit" passages in Paul's writings; described as a "friend of pleasure rather than a lover of God," the new husband exemplifies those who are "in the flesh" and thus "cannot please God" (Rom. 8:8).[74]

Virgins, however, can be declared exempt from the battle of flesh versus spirit. According to the pseudo-Clementine letters on virginity, true virgins do not have "the mind of the flesh" (Rom. 8:6–7), defined via a catalog of sixty-three sins that leads off with fornication, uncleanness, and wantonness.[75] For Jerome, it is the married, not the virginal, who "serve [the] two masters" (Matt. 6:24) of the flesh as well as the spirit (Gal. 5:17); virgins are exempt from the double loyalty.[76] Other authors, however, assume that even those committed to ascetic living might also hear the "flesh/spirit" passages to good effect. Thus Athanasius and Eusebius of Emesa recite Galatians 5:16–24 to communities of virgins.[77] And parents who wish their children to commit themselves to lives of virginity should frequently rehearse the Pauline verses on "flesh and spirit" to them, according to Pseudo-Basil.[78]

More specialized ascetic audiences could also be envisioned as the recipients of Paul's advice on the sinful flesh. Basil of Ancyra thus warns virgins against contact with "eunuchs of the church," since such a eunuch "remains a man by nature." If even touching another virgin's body while sleeping in the same bed can arouse "the law of sin in [her] members" (Rom. 7:23), relations with eunuchs are even more dangerous.[79] Widows also can be disciplined through these verses: Jerome cites Romans 8:8 ("they that are in the flesh cannot please God") to warn them against excessive attention to their attire and wearing makeup.[80] Still other passages suggest that patristic authors may have been addressing the problem

[73] Augustine, *Contra Iulianum* 4.2.6 (PL 44, 739); *Opus imperfectum* 1.68.3–5 (CSEL 85.1, 74–75), citing Rom. 7:18; *De gratia Christi* 2.34.39 (CSEL 42, 197–98).

[74] Origen, *Frag.* 84 *Hom. Luc.* (SC 87, 542).

[75] Ps.-Clement, *ep. 1 de virginitate* 8 (Funk, pp. 13–15).

[76] Jerome, *ep.* 49 (48).20 (CSEL 54, 385).

[77] Athanasius, *Frag.* 2 (CSCO 150 = Scriptores Coptici 19, 121; ET, Brakke, p. 314); Eusebius of Emesa, *Hom.* 7.13 (Buytaert I:184).

[78] Ps.-Basil, *De virginitate* 4.58 (Amand de Mendietta/Moons, p. 51), citing Rom. 8:8 and Gal. 6:8.

[79] Basil of Ancyra, *De virginitate* 62 (Vaillant, p. 81).

[80] Jerome, *ep.* 38.3 (CSEL 54, 291).

of syneisaktic relationships. Galatians 5:13–16 can, according to the pseudo-Titus epistle, be recited to male and female virgins who stray after human partners,[81] and Basil of Ancyra's citation of Romans 7:23 to warn virgins against "eunuchs of the church" may point in the same direction.[82] Yet another category of ascetics addressed by these verses were those who after long periods of abstinence "grow wanton" and marry; Jerome reserves his special venom for such, and cites the Pauline verses from Romans and Galatians on "flesh and spirit" against them.[83]

Last, John Cassian quotes the Pauline verses in an all-male monastic environment. He argues first that the passages should not be taken as referring primarily to sinners. Romans 7:18–20 suggests that the subjects are Christians who "defile themselves" against their own good intent; sinners, by contrast, willingly defile themselves.[84] It is those on their way to perfection (presumably monks) who cry out "Wretched man that I am!" (Rom. 7:24); it is the "saints" who confess, "For I do not do the good I want, but the evil I do not want is what I do" (Rom. 7:19).[85] From what particular evil these monks are not exempt becomes clear in the course of Cassian's extended discussion: nocturnal emissions.[86] Thus Paul's teaching on flesh and spirit could be adapted to provide edification in a variety of sexual contexts.

Another set of verses that proved relatively easy to "asceticize" was Galatians 3:27–28: "For as many of you as were baptized into Christ have put on Christ. There is neither Jew nor Greek, there is neither slave nor free, there is neither male nor female; for you are all one in Christ Jesus" (RSV). Scholars of our day claim these verses as part of an early Christian baptismal formula, but debate the extent to which—if at all—Paul meant to counsel transformation of gender relations in the here-and-now.[87] Some church fathers, stimulated by Origen's exegesis, took that the passage to signal the original sexless condition of humans formed after "the image of God."[88] Others, such as John Chrysostom, employed the verses as a

[81] Ps.-Titus, ep., (de Bruyne, pp. 51–52).

[82] Basil of Ancyra, *De virginitate* 62 (Vaillant, p. 81).

[83] Jerome, *Adversus Iovinianum* 1.37–38 (PL 23, 273–76), citing Rom. 7:14, 24, 25; 8:5–9; Gal. 3:3–4; 5:16–17, 24–25; 6:7–8.

[84] John Cassian, *Conlationes* 23.1 (SC 64, 137–38).

[85] John Cassian, *Conlationes* 23.10; 23.13 (SC 64, 152–53, 157).

[86] John Cassian, *Conlationes* 12.1–2 (SC 54, 121–22); 22.14 (SC 64, 133) (the problem of nocturnal emissions).

[87] For a discussion of the scholarship, see Dennis R. MacDonald, *There Is No Male and Female: The Fate of a Dominical Saying in Paul and Gnosticism*, Harvard Dissertations in Religion 20 (Philadelphia: Fortress, 1987). An especially important analysis can be found in Wayne A. Meeks, "The Image of the Androgyne: Some Uses of a Symbol in Earliest Christianity," *History of Religions* 13 (1974): 165–208.

[88] Gregory of Nyssa, *De opificio hominis* 16.7; 16.9 (PG 44, 180, 181). Antony, *ep.* 7 (PG 40, 1019); Evagrius Ponticus, *De diversis malignis cogitationibus* 3 (PG 79,

"shaming device" for his contemporaries, pointing back to the apostolic age when men and women could mingle, oblivious to sexual temptation, "no male and female."[89]

Galatians 3:27–28 was early pressed in an asceticizing direction. According to Clement of Alexandria, the Docetist Julius Cassianus cited a saying from the *Gospel according to the Egyptians* that contained the line: "When Salome asked when she would know the answer to her questions, the Lord said, 'When you trample on the robe of shame, and when the two shall be one, and the male with the female, and there is neither male nor female.' " Apparently Julius Cassianus quoted the verse to promote sexual abstinence: the Lord blessed eunuchs, he reminds his readers. Clement rejects this interpretation, arguing rather that it is the Christian's resisting of wrath, desire, and evil habits that promotes "no male and female."[90] In another, less polemical, context, Clement interprets "no male and female" to mean that "all who abandon the desires of the flesh are equal and spiritual."[91]

Although some patristic commentators take Galatians 3:27–28 to pertain only to the postresurrection life when there will be "no marrying and giving in marriage" (Matt. 22:30),[92] others claim that the verses apply in the present to the sexually abstinent. Thus Gregory of Nyssa cites Galatians 3:27–28 to virgins: instead of entering two marriages (one to Christ and one to a human spouse), forbidden by Paul in I Corinthians 7:32–33, Christians should follow the advice of Solomon in Proverbs 4:6–8 and "marry wisdom." Both male and female virgins, Gregory argues, can participate in this sapiential marriage.[93]

Jerome also cites Galatians 3:27–28 to encourage chastity. In his *Apology against Rufinus*, Jerome defends himself against Rufinus' charges that he is an Origenist. Among the points he must counter is his earlier explication of Ephesians 5:21–33 in his *Ephesians Commentary.* There, Jerome had written that wives would be turned into men and souls into bodies, so that there would be no difference of sex, "no male and female." Yet Jerome now, in the midst of the Origenist controversy, claims that he had not meant to take away the difference of sex, but had merely advocated the

1204). These references suggest an Origenist background; it is unfortunate that Origen's *Commentary on Galatians* is not extant.

[89] John Chrysostom, *Hom. 3 Acta* 1 (1:16) (PG 60, 34); *Hom. 73 Matt.* 3 (PG 58, 677).

[90] Clement of Alexandria, *Stromata* 3.13.91–93 (GCS 52 [15], 238–39).

[91] Clement of Alexandria, *Paedagogus* 1.6.31 (GCS 12, 108).

[92] Theodore of Mopsuestia, *Comm. Gal.* 3:28 (Swete I:57).

[93] Gregory of Nyssa, *De virginitate* 20.4 (SC 119, 498, 500, 502). Gregory's exegesis appears to borrow from Origen's allegorical reading of the patriarchs' plural marriages; see the discussion in chap. 6 and Origen, *Hom. 11 Gen.* 1 (GCS 29, 101–2).

erasure of lust and sexual intercourse: this is Paul's intent in urging men to have their wives "as if not" (I Cor. 7:29), and Jesus', in pronouncing that in the resurrection there will be "no marrying and giving in marriage" (Matt. 22:30). Jerome bolsters his defense by citing Galatians 3:27–28: when chastity abounds among men and women, then gradually dawns "no male and female," a condition "like the angels" (Matt. 22:30). The message of Galatians 3:27–28, according to Jerome, is thoroughly ascetic.[94]

Most interesting, Jerome can cite Galatians 3:27–28 to advocate sexless marriage. In the 390s, Jerome corresponded with a Spanish couple, Lucinius and Theodora, who had taken a vow of continence.[95] Late in the decade, after Lucinius' death, Jerome wrote to console the widow. He tells Theodora that because of their continence she can be called Lucinius' "sister"; theirs was a marriage in which there was "no male and female." If they achieved this lofty state of purity even while living in the body, what greater holiness they will gain when they "put on incorruption" (I Cor. 15:53) and become "like the angels," who "neither marry nor give in marriage" (Matt. 22:30). Jerome nonetheless adds a caveat to rebuff any accusation of Origenism. Difference of sex will obtain in the afterlife, he concedes; "Paul will still be Paul, Mary will still be Mary."[96] "No male and female" must now be understood metaphorically in order to ward off charges of Origenism.

Thus the "flesh/spirit" passages in Romans and Galatians, in addition to the "no male and female" of Galatians 3:28, could be pressed in an ascetic direction by church fathers who deployed Paul's text to advance a more rigorous agenda. Still, explication of these verses demanded only limited exegetical labor from ascetically inclined exegetes.

IV: Food, the Resurrection Body, and Sex

I turn next to two sets of Pauline verses that required more ingenious elaboration if they were to be taken to advocate sexual renunciation: Paul's teachings on food practices and on the resurrection body.

In various passages (Rom. 14; I Cor. 3, 6, 8, and 10), Paul addresses the issue of "food offered to idols." Here, Paul counsels that although in theory no food impairs holiness, Christians should avoid offending their

[94] Jerome, *Apologia contra Rufinum* 1.29 (CCL 79, 28–29). The passage in question comes from Jerome's *Ephesians Commentary* 3 (PL 26, 567–68); Rufinus attacks Jerome's interpretation in *Apologia contra Hieronymum* 1.24–25 (CCL 20, 58–60).

[95] Jerome, *ep.* 71, esp. #3 (CSEL 55, 4).

[96] Jerome, *ep.* 75.2 (CSEL 55, 31).

"weaker" brothers and sisters in the faith who fear that eating meat offered in pagan sacrifices—a customary source of meat in antiquity—will "pollute" them. At Corinth, "the Strong" mocked this fear, claiming that "an idol has no real existence" (I Cor. 8:4) and that "all things are lawful for me" (I Cor. 6:12). Paul cautions them that the duty of "the Strong" is to edify "the Weak," not to flaunt their own sense of freedom.[97]

Such passages were readily, and unsurprisingly, incorporated into the numerous patristic discussions of fasting. What does surprise, however, is the ease and frequency with which they could be swept into the discourse of sexual renunciation. Such discussions provide an excellent example of exegesis by "textual implosion,"[98] in which seemingly irrelevant verses are marshaled to provide support for the promotion of sexual abstinence. Patristic authors enlist the Pauline passages pertaining to food in two ways for their exhortations to sexual renunciation: either they lift general principles from Paul's discussion that they then transfer from the arena of food to that of sexuality; or, conversely, they appeal directly to particular words ("meat," "milk," and "vegetables/herbs") which, when taken metaphorically, describe the different sexual statuses of Christians.

In his reflections on the eating of meat offered to idols, Paul frequently appeals to such general principles as that the Strong must care for the Weak, that Christians are responsible for "our brother's salvation," that they should not put "stumbling blocks" in the paths of their fellow Christians (Rom. 14:13; 15, 21; I Cor. 8:9; 10:24). Transferring these principles to the realm of sex, the Fathers cite Paul's words to warn against the "scandal" of celibate men and women living together, behavior that injures other Christians and causes them "to stumble." Thus the author of the pseudo-Clementine letters on virginity instructs the male reader that if on his missionary journeys he should happen upon a place with only one Christian woman available to provide hospitality, he should speedily depart. Otherwise, people will gossip, and his behavior will be seen as a "stumbling block." Lifting verses from Paul's discussion of the proper use of food, the pseudo-Clementine author urges, "If your brother is being injured by what you eat, you are no longer walking in love" (Rom. 14:15). He also cites I Corinthians 10:32–33 on "not giving offense"; Christians should rather try to "please men" so that "they may be saved."[99]

[97] For an analysis of these terms, see Gerd Theissen, "The Strong and the Weak in Corinth: A Sociological Analysis of a Theological Quarrel," in idem, *The Social Setting of Pauline Christianity: Essays on Corinth*, ed. and trans. John H. Schütz (Philadelphia: Fortress, 1982; German original of this essay, 1975), pp. 121–43; Dale B. Martin, *The Corinthian Body* (New Haven, Conn./London: Yale University Press, 1995), pp. 179–89.

[98] For a discussion of "textual implosion," see above, pp. 132–34.

[99] Ps.-Clement, *ep. 2 de virginitate* 5 (Funk, pp. 35–37).

Cyprian likewise cites I Corinthians 8:13 ("Therefore, if food is a cause of my brother's falling, I will never eat meat, lest I cause my brother to fall") to warn against the dangers of virgins living with celibate men. Separate them while they are still innocent, he urges, so that they not scandalize their brothers and sisters in the faith.[100] Both Eusebius of Emesa and John Chrysostom quote I Corinthians 10:32–33 ("give no offense . . . please all men in everything . . . ," words originally written to counsel Christians on food regulation) to warn against syneisaktic relationships that scandalize fellow Christians for whose salvation, Paul would claim, the suspected parties are responsible.[101]

A second and related principle to which Paul appeals in his discussion of food purity centers on the difference between what is "lawful" and what is "expedient." Christians have "rights" that they may choose not to use if by their non-use they better upbuild others in the faith; such is the case with meat that may have been offered to "idols." Passages such as I Corinthians 6:12–13; 8:13; 10:23–25, and Romans 14:20 are cited to press home this point. Thus Jerome, Ambrose, and Tertullian all rehearse I Corinthians 6:12 (" 'all things are lawful for me,' but not all things are helpful"—the first phrase apparently uttered by "the Strong" at Corinth to justify their freer food practices) to counsel against second marriage. According to Ambrose, God does not prohibit second marriage for widows, but nonetheless the practice is "not expedient."[102] For Jerome, when Paul allowed second marriages "to the incontinent," he was "becoming a Jew to the Jews" (I Cor. 9:20). Although "all things [here, second marriages] are lawful," not all "are expedient"; hence Christians are warned against remarriage.[103] Moreover, the Fathers can quote Paul's words on "inexpedience" against him, so to speak: Paul's concession to second marriage in I Corinthians 7:39–40 is "corrected" by the higher principle of renouncing this "right," since it is "not expedient." Here, Paul "talks back" to himself, restricting his concession by a more rigorous injunction. Tertullian agrees (in his pre-Montanist period) that although second mar-

[100] Cyprian, *ep.* 4(= 61).2 (CSEL 3.2, 474).

[101] Eusebius of Emesa, *Hom.* 7.20 (Buytaert I:188–89); John Chrysostom, *Adversus eos qui apud se habent subintroductas virgines* 4 (PG 47, 500). Basil of Ancrya, worrying that virgins may "fall," recites to them I Cor. 8:11–13 (originally counseling against table fellowship with "idolators" in their temples), urging them not to scandalize the brother "for whom Christ died" (*De virginitate* 43 [Vaillant, p. 47]).

[102] Ambrose, *De viduis* 11.68 (PL 16, 268). It is interesting that Ambrosiaster, generally a partisan of marriage and not given to "ascetic" readings, explains the meaning of "not all is expedient" by an appeal to Matt. 19:10; Ambrosiaster attributes the phrase "if this is the way of a man with his wife, it is not expedient to marry" to the Apostle Peter and links "inexpedience" to *first* marriage (*Comm. I Cor.* 10:22–23 [CSEL 81.2, 116]).

[103] Jerome, *Adversus Iovinianum* 1.15 (PL 23, 245); cf. *ep.* 49(48).8, 18 (CSEL 54, 363, 383).

riage is "lawful," it is not "expedient" (I Cor. 10:23); Paul's merely "permitting" this practice suggests that some doubt lingers about its goodness.[104] But even this concession of second marriage seems better to Tertullian than intermarriage with Gentiles, which to his mind is *neither* "lawful" *nor* "expedient."[105]

Ambrose also cites I Corinthians 6:12 ("not all is expedient") to a high-born correspondent who sought Ambrose's sanction for allowing his son to marry his daughter's daughter. Even of lawful acts, Ambrose rejoins, some are "not expedient."[106] Augustine appeals to the same theme of not using "rights" (I Cor. 6:12–13; 8:13; 10:23–25; Rom. 14:20) against Pollentius, who argues that a Christian man should be allowed to remarry after divorcing his wife: some "rights," Augustine counters, should not be used.[107] Clement of Alexandria adopts a simple solution to the use of "rights." Since "self-control" is among the "lawful things" (I Cor. 6:12; 10:23), why do not Christians simply embrace it as their way of life?[108] Thus the general principle embedded in Paul's discussion of food practices—"lawful but not expedient"—could be extracted from its original setting and redeployed in a new exegetical arena, that pertaining to sexual renunciation.

The Fathers counseling sexual renunciation could appeal even more directly to Paul's "meat-eaters," "milk-drinkers," and "vegetable-eaters" (Rom. 14:2; I Cor. 3:1–3). In the Latin tradition, Tertullian appears to be the first to use this argument. Citing I Corinthians 3:1–3 (Paul's condescension to the Corinthian "infants" who need "milk," not "solid food"), Tertullian judges Paul's words relevant to the topic of second marriage. Tertullian excuses Paul's leniency in allowing Christian widows to remarry (I Cor. 7:39); he was offering "milk" to a fledgling and inexperienced church. But Tertullian restricts those to whom Paul's words apply: not to a Christian widow who was married to a Christian, but to one who converted after her marriage and is now allowed to take a partner in the faith after her "pagan" husband's death.[109] Ambrose, for his part, cites Romans 14:2 ("he who is weak, let him eat vegetables/herbs") as describing the state of marriage: the "vegetable-eater" is the "weak" man who takes a wife. Virginity is rather for the "strong," presumably for Paul's "meat-eaters."[110]

Origen, on the Greek side of the tradition, claims that admonitions such as Paul gives in Romans 13:9 against adultery, as well as his concessions to

[104] Tertullian, *De exhortatione castitatis* 8.1 (CCL 2, 1026).

[105] Tertullian, *Ad uxorem* 2.8.9 (CCL 1, 394).

[106] Ambrose, *ep.* 60.6 (PL 16, 1236).

[107] Augustine, *De coniugiis adulterinis* 1.14.15 (CSEL 41, 363–64).

[108] Clement of Alexandria, *Stromata* 3.5.40 (GCS 42 [15], 214).

[109] Tertullian, *De monogamia* 11.6–11 (CSEL 2, 1245–46).

[110] Ambrose, *De virginibus* 1.6.24 (PL

marriage in I Corinthians 7, are like "milk" for children, a beverage Origen here disdains. Mature Christians who partake of "solid food, not milk" (Heb. 5:12) need not be admonished to cease visiting prostitutes. An example of "solid food," according to Origen, is Paul's teaching in Ephesians. Here the subject is not fornication or idolatry, but Christ's spiritual marriage to the Church. Origen also characterizes those who understand Scripture only in a moral sense as "milk-drinkers," positioned below "the perfect" who receive the "solid food" of Scripture's mystical meaning.[111]

Following Origen, Jerome also reads I Corinthians 3:1–3 (on "solid food" in comparison to "milk") as providing useful ascetic directives. Arguing against marriage, he claims that mature Christians who "eat meat" are those who are able to keep chaste (i.e., remain sexually abstinent), while the "infants" who need "milk" are those who marry. The "milk-drinkers," he complains, are in an "animal" state and cannot receive the things of God's Spirit.[112] Texts pertaining to food here "implode" into a discussion of marriage and abstinence.

A second set of verses—I Corinthians 15:41–54, on the resurrection body—seemingly distant from discussions of sexuality and renunciation, was also, with some assistance, swept into the ascetic discussion. A first useful point for ascetic exegetes could be found in verse 41, the differing brightness of the sun, moon, and stars, "for star differs from star in glory." Although some authors cite this verse in a general sense to promote sexual restraint among Christians,[113] others interpret the verse according to the specific code of the hundredfold, sixtyfold, and thirtyfold harvests of the Parable of the Sower that signify (in Jerome's rendition) virginity, widowhood, and marriage.[114] Thus Augustine enumerates the differing "glory" of the stars as "chaste marriage," widowhood, and virginity.[115] He acknowledges that although the married may receive eternal life, they will not enjoy the highest glory that befits the brightest "star."[116] Athanasius extends the comparison to other Biblical verses. Not only does I Corinthians 15:41 speak to the greater glory of virgins than the married, so does Matthew 13:18–23 (the Sower's three harvests), Luke 19:17–19 (those

---

16, 206); *ep.* 63.39 (PL 16, 1251).

[111] Origen, *Hom. 7 Ezek.* 10 (SC 352, 270, 272). John Chrysostom probably follows Origen in declaring that Paul's advice (and concessions) to the Corinthian Christians should be considered "milk, not solid food" (*De virginitate* 49.3 [SC 125, 278]).

[112] Jerome, *Adversus Iovinianum* 1.37 (PL 23, 275).

[113] So Pelagius, *Ad Demetriadem* 17 (PL 30, 33); cf. (Pelagius?), *De divina legis* 7 (PL 30, 116).

[114] Jerome, *Adversus Iovinianum* 1.3 (PL 23, 223); *ep.* 49 (48).3 (CSEL 54, 354).

[115] Augustine, *Serm.* 132.3.3 (PL 38, 736); cf. *De bono viduitatis* 6.9 (CSEL 41, 313).

[116] Augustine, *De sancta virginitate* 14.14 (CSEL 41, 247).

who rule over ten cities [the virgins] compared to those who rule over five [the married]); and John 14:2 ("my Father's house has many mansions").[117] Methodius argues that virgins, as "martyrs," are the brightest "lights" of I Corinthians 15:41. He pairs with this text Song of Songs 6:8–9: there are sixty queens, eighty concubines, and maidens without number, but only "one dove," "my perfect one," namely, the virgin.[118] Verses that could be taken to imply ranking of various sorts are all collapsed into the hierarchy of ascetic renunciation. Yet to claim that the virgin's "lights" are brighter should not be taken as a denigration of marriage, Eusebius of Emesa warns.[119]

That "the physical comes first and the spiritual afterwards" (I Cor. 15:46), another phrase from Paul's discussion of the resurrection body, suggests to Tertullian a comparison based on an ascetic distinction between Adam and Christ. Writing against second marriage, Tertullian notes that Adam was at least a monogamist (although not "perfect," as he was in his virginal, pre-Fall condition in Eden). Yet the "last man" (v. 45), Christ, representing "the spiritual," comes after "the physical"—and, Tertullian pointedly notes, Jesus did not marry at all.[120] This "second man" (v. 47), the "man of heaven" who is characterized by virginity,[121] should serve as the model for Christians. Likewise, according to Cyprian, it is virgins who bear the "image" of this "man of heaven" (v. 49).[122]

I Corinthians 15:52–53 provided another useful pair of verses for ascetically minded writers, for they claim that "corruption must put on incorruption" (RSV: the "perishable" puts on "imperishability"). "Corruption" and "incorruption" could with little effort be decontextualized and be made to stand as judgments on sexual relation. For Augustine, "incorruption" is found only when carnal concupiscence is banished, a removal that obtains only in the afterlife.[123] Clement of Alexandria, more optimistic about sinlessness in the present order, thinks that "corruption" can be changed to "incorruption" in the here-and-now, when intense desire, "educated to self-control," results in chastity.[124] Further along the ascetically rigorous spectrum is Pseudo-Basil, who includes the verse "corruption shall not inherit incorruption" among those that parents should re-

[117] Athanasius, *ep. 1 ad virgines* (CSCO 150 = Scriptores Coptici 19, 82; ET, Brakke, p. 280).

[118] Methodius, *Symposium* 7.3 (GCS 27, 73–75).

[119] Eusebius of Emesa, *Hom.* 6.6 (Buytaert I:155).

[120] Tertullian, *De monogamia* 5.5–6 (CCL 2, 1235).

[121] (Augustine?), *Serm.* 74.5 (PL 39, 1889).

[122] Cyprian, *De habitu virginum* 23 (CSEL 3.1, 204).

[123] Augustine, *De nuptiis et concupiscentia* 1.25.28 (CSEL 42, 240–41); *Serm.* 151.2; 128.8.10 (PL 38, 815, 718).

[124] Clement of Alexandria, *Paedagogus* 2.10.100.2 (GCS 12, 217).

cite to their children when urging them toward virginal commitment.[125] For Jerome, "corruption" attaches to all sexual intercourse, whereas "incorruption" is characteristic of chastity; the rewards of chastity, he claims, cannot belong to marriage.[126]

Thus, with some ingenuity, Paul's discussions of pure and impure food and the resurrection of the body could be marshaled for the promotion of celibate living.

V: Post-Pauline Literature

When we move to New Testament literature that is identified by modern scholarship as post-Pauline, the difficulties of finding a message of ascetic renunciation multiply. Not least of the problems was occasioned by the Fathers' belief that Paul himself had written Ephesians, Colossians, the Pastoral Epistles (I and II Timothy and Titus), and (usually) Hebrews. Should not I Timothy agree with I Corinthians 7, Jerome asks, since they "are the work of one author?"[127] While the Fathers labored to create a seamless harmony among these texts, they nonetheless could not avoid noting their many discrepancies. Why would Paul write in I Corinthians 7:5 that married couples should separate for prayer, if the marriage bed is "undefiled" (Heb. 13:4)?[128] Why does I Timothy 2:12 forbid women to teach, when Paul in I Corinthians 7:16 says that they may "save" their husbands?[129] If women themselves are "saved by childbearing"(as I Tim. 2:15 claims), what should we imagine as the fate of virgins and childless widows?[130] Why should pastors urge widows to remarry (I Tim. 5:14), when Paul writes that the "time is short" and that married men should live with their wives "as if not" (I Cor. 7:29)?[131] Did not Paul know the example of Anna (Luke 2:36–37), who preserved her widowhood for many decades without remarrying?[132] Why enjoin widows to remarry, when Paul writes in I Corinthians 7:32–34 that the mar-

[125] Ps.-Basil, *De virginitate* 4.58 (Amand de Mendietta/Moons, pp. 49, 51).

[126] Jerome, *Adversus Iovinianum* 1.37 (PL 23, 275): "corruptio ad omnem coitum pertinet."

[127] Jerome, *ep.* 123.5 (CSEL 56, 76). It is of interest that Jerome denied to Paul the authorship of Hebrews on the grounds of that book's differences in style and language from "true" Pauline works, but did not make similar comments on the Pastorals: see Jerome, *De viris illustribus* 5; cf. 25.

[128] John Chrysostom, *De virginitate* 30.1 (SC 125, 188, 190): cf. *Hom. 51 Matt.* 5 (PG 58, 516).

[129] John Chrysostom, *Serm. 5 Gen.* 1 (PG 54, 599–600).

[130] John Chrysostom, *Hom. 9 I Tim.* 1 (2:11–12) (PG 62, 545).

[131] Jerome, *ep.* 52.16 (CSEL 54, 439).

[132] Ambrose, *De viduis* 2.12 (PL 16, 251); cf. Ambrosiaster, *Comm. I Tim.* 5:3 (CSEL 81.3, 278).

ried have "many cares"?[133] Why should a bishop be "the husband of one wife" (I Tim. 3:2), if Paul states that the married "care about the things of the world" (I Cor. 7:33)?[134] The later New Testament books were fraught with problems for exegetes pressing ascetic readings of Scripture.

Although the more uxorious sentiments of these later Scriptural books were useful to mainstream exegetes in warding off excessively ascetic interpretations such as those proffered by Hieracas[135] and the Manicheans,[136] this post-Pauline literature is also cited by the enthusiastic champions of marriage, such as Jerome's opponent Jovinian. It is Jovinian who quotes I Timothy 5:14 (the remarriage of widows), Hebrews 13:4 (the marriage bed as "undefiled"), I Timothy 2:15 (women are "saved by childbearing"), and I Timothy 3:2 (clergy should be married) to argue for the "equality" of marriage and virginity.[137] According to the author of *On Chastity*, I Timothy 4:1–5 (the predicted advent of evil teachers who will forbid marriage) was Jovinian's favorite text.[138] And John Chrysostom reports that Christians of a less rigorous stamp than himself were urging his friend, the "fallen Theodore," to marry by citing Hebrews 13:4 to him.[139] Such citations of these Scriptural verses needed to be countered by more ascetically inclined writers—but in a way that would not incur charges of "heresy."

Against such "anti-ascetic" uses of later New Testament literature, the Fathers developed numerous textual strategies. Translations from the Greek New Testament into Latin, as we saw above,[140] could press texts in an ascetic direction (e.g., Jerome translates the Pastorals' frequent recommendation of *sōphrosunē* as *castitas*).[141] Second, although "virgins" do not figure in these texts, they can be "introduced"—a kind of "textual syneisaktism"—often in an *a fortiori* argument. Thus the restraint on women's behavior dictated in I Timothy 2:8–15 prompts comments of the sort, "if this is enjoined for married women, how much more should virgins. . . ."[142] Several patristic authors attempt to answer the puzzling ques-

[133] Theodore of Mopsuestia, *Comm. I Tim.* 5:14 (Swete II:165).

[134] John Chrysostom, *Hom. 10 I Tim.* 1 (3:1–4) (PG 62, 548–49).

[135] So Athanasius, *ep. 1 ad virgines* (CSCO 150 = Scriptores Coptici 19, 86; ET, Brakke, p. 283), citing I Tim. 5:4 on young women marrying and bearing children.

[136] Especially Augustine, *Contra Faustum* 5.9; 14.11; 15.10; 20.16 (CSEL 25, 282, 411, 437, 556); *Contra Felicem* 1.7 (CSEL 25, 808–9), citing Col. 3:18 and I Tim. 4:4. Jerome cites Heb. 13:4 to prove that he is not a Manichean: *Adversus Iovinianum* 1.3 (PL 23, 223).

[137] Jovinian in Jerome, *Adversus Iovinianum* 1.5; 1.27; 1.34 (PL 23, 227, 259–60, 268).

[138] (Anonymous), *De castitate* 16 (PLS 1, 1498).

[139] John Chrysostom, *Ad Theodorum lapsum* 2.3 (PG 47, 312).

[140] See above, pp. 113–18.

[141] Jerome, *Adversus Iovinianum* 1.27 (PL 23, 260); *Comm. Tit.* 2:3 (PL 26, 615).

[142] Ambrose, *Exhortatio virginitatis*

tion of why virgins do not appear in these texts, as the exegetes obviously thought they should. According to the author of the Pelagian treatise *On Virginity*, "Paul" did not give any command for virgins in I Timothy 2 because he thought it unnecessary; in fact, he deemed it an insult, for virgins would not attempt to do what was forbidden to married women.[143] Another solution is offered by John Chrysostom: when "Paul" says to "honor widows" (I Tim. 5:3) but omits any mention of virgins, perhaps his silence indicates that there were not any consecrated virgins yet, or (alternatively) that they had already fallen from their high estate.[144] Conversely, Chrysostom posits that although "Paul" chastises widows who had "fallen," "straying after Satan" (I Tim. 5:15), he has nothing for which to rebuke virgins and hence is silent concerning them.[145]

Even if virgins were not "in" the text, other authors could remind their readers that the reproduction so abundantly praised in these New Testament passages was that which produced "virgins for Christ."[146] Moreover, when "Paul" wrote that the marriage bed was "undefiled" (Heb. 13:4), his message, according to Athanasius, was directed to virgins as a warning not to become "puffed up" at their superior status.[147] Here, a "hidden audience" of virgins is subtly "introduced" and their superior condition noted. The conflicting explanations for why no consecrated virgins are mentioned in these texts, and the Fathers' attempt to "read them in," is another indication of the Fathers' puzzlement regarding the discrepancies between I Corinthians 7 and other New Testament literature that they believed had been composed by Paul.

A third exegetical strategy that promoted an asceticizing interpretation of the New Testament involved deploying the Paul of I Corinthians 7 to "answer back" the "Paul" of the Pastoral Epistles and other late New Testament books, much as Jesus as rabbi countered the temptations of Satan with Biblical citations (Matt. 4:1–11; Luke 4:1–13).[148] Thus when Jovinian cites the "pro-marriage" verses in I Timothy 2:14, 5:14, and Hebrews 13:4, Jerome responds with I Corinthians 7:29, that men may have their wives "as if not."[149] If I Timothy 2:8–15 (the subjection of

13.86 (PL 16, 377); Cyprian, *De habitu virginum* 8 (CSEL 3.1, 193–94); Basil of Caesarea, *ep.* 199.18 (Loeb III:106, 108); Pelagius, *Comm. I Tim.* 5:12 (PLS 1, 1355).

[143] (Anonymous), *ep. de virginitate* (= *Ad Claudiam*) 12 (CSEL 1, 242–43).

[144] John Chrysostom, *Hom. 13 I Tim.* 2 (5:3) (PG 62, 566).

[145] John Chrysostom, *Hom. 15 I Tim.* 1 (5:11–15) (PG 62, 579).

[146] Jerome, *ep.* 66.3 (CSEL 54, 650); Eusebius of Emesa, *Hom.* 6.17 (Buytaert I:162), commenting on I Tim. 2:15.

[147] Athanasius, *De virginitate* 10 (Lebon, pp. 213–14; ET, Brakke, p. 306); Cyril of Jerusalem, *Catecheses* 4.25 (PG 33, 488); John Chrysostom, *De virginitate* 8.2 (SC 125, 116).

[148] On "talking back" as an exegetical strategy, see above, pp. 128–32.

[149] Jerome, *Adversus Iovinianum* 1.5 (PL 23, 227).

women and their "salvation" in childbearing) is adduced, Pauline replies can be found in I Corinthians 7:37–38 (that singleness is preferable to marriage) and I Corinthians 15:41 (that some heavenly bodies are "brighter" than others).[150] Against "Paul's" chastisement of women's speech and deceitful ways (I Tim. 2:11–14), readers are reminded (by John Chrysostom) that Paul thought women might "save" their husbands (I Cor. 7:16)—in fact, might "save" men *not* their husbands, as Priscilla's instruction of Apollos (Acts 18:24–26) testifies.[151] Indeed, married women might even "save" their children—as Domnina did her virgin daughters—rather than be "saved" by them, as I Timothy 2:15 assumes.[152]

Likewise, a celibate clergy could be promoted by having Paul "talk back." To the injunction in I Timothy 3:2 that bishops should be "once-married," Jerome retorts that if marriage were a necessary qualification for the bishopric, Paul would never have exclaimed, "Would all men be like me!" (I Cor. 7:7): never-married bishops are clearly preferable.[153] Citing Paul's directive that married men might have their wives "as if not" (I Cor. 7:29) made allowance for married clergy—who are hereby enjoined to renounce sexual relations while in office.[154]

Widows, too, could be counseled through "talking back." The Pastor's injunction that younger widows should remarry (I Tim. 5:14) was countered with the claim that Paul gave this advice only for widows who, lacking self-control, should "marry rather than burn" (I Cor. 7:9).[155] If the widows of I Timothy 5 consider Paul's warning against the many cares of marriage (I Cor. 7:32–34), however, they will refrain from remarrying.[156] That the widow will be "happier" if she remains in her single state (I Cor. 7:40) is read as Paul's recommendation for the "real widows" of I Timothy 5:5.[157] Moreover, that Paul in Romans 7:6 claims Christians are "dead to the law," suggests (to Tertullian) that the remarriage of widows (I Tim. 5:14), sanctioned by the "law" of the Old Dispensation, is not an option for those who live in the newness of Christ's spirit.[158] Thus Pauline texts could be deployed as "back-talk" in a variety of situations to override the domestic assumptions of these later New Testament books.

[150] Eusebius of Emesa, *Hom.* 6.17 (Buytaert I:162).

[151] John Chrysostom, *De virginitate* 46.1; 47.1–2 (SC 125, 262, 264); cf. *Serm. 5 Gen.* 1 (PG 54, 599–600).

[152] John Chrysostom, *De SS. Bernice et Prosdoce* 6 (PG 50, 639).

[153] Jerome, *Adversus Iovinianum* 1.34 (PL 23, 270).

[154] John Chrysostom, *Hom. 10 I Tim.* 1 (3:1–4) (PG 54, 549). Cf. Chrysostom's explanation at the beginning of these homilies: the man came from "secular life" already married and was advanced to the office of bishop (PG 62, 503–4).

[155] Ambrose, *De viduis* 2.12 (PL 16, 251); cf. John Chrysostom, *De non iterando coniugio* 3 (SC 138, 174).

[156] Theodore of Mopsuestia, *Comm. I Tim.* 5:14 (Swete II:165).

[157] John Chrysostom, *Ad viduam iuniorem* 2 (SC 138, 122, 124); (Anonymous), *De viduitate servanda* 1 (PL 67, 1094).

[158] Tertullian, *De monogamia* 13.2–3

Three topics surface with regularity in the Fathers' commentary on these passages: the audience addressed in the Household Codes and related literature; the requirement of "monogamy" for the clergy; and the regulations concerning widows in I Timothy 5. Let me address these in turn.

Ascetically minded Fathers could gain some argumentative leverage by hypothesizing that the intended audience for the sexual directives of this later literature was an inferior grade of Christian.[159] The audience for whom such writings were composed, they assumed, consisted not of the celibates of I Corinthians 7:29, but rather of "the Weak" to whom Paul allows the indulgence of marriage and sexual intercourse in 7:5–6 and in Colossians 3:18.[160] Jerome thus characterizes the "honorableness" of marriage (Heb. 13:4) as "the safe track of a lower path," even when the wife is motivated solely by a desire to bring forth "virgins for Christ."[161] Marriage may be considered "honorable" (Heb. 13:4), Gregory of Nazianzus reasons, but only for the temperate who engage in sexual intercourse simply for the sake of producing children.[162] According to Athanasius, although in heaven the patriarchs will greet the "honorable" married of Hebrews 13:4, it will nonetheless be virgins who will lead the way to the altar (Ps. 43:4) and offer the sacrifice (Ps. 116:17–18).[163] The assumptions of late New Testament literature regarding the normativity of marriage are here skillfully challenged by more ascetically inclined church fathers.

As for the "bearing of children" (I Tim. 2:15) that affords women salvation (despite their unhappy descent from the treacherous Eve and their ensuing subjection), various exegetical treatments rescued the verse for readers of more rigorous propensities. As John Chrysostom pointedly put the question, if women are "saved by childbearing," what is the fate of virgins and childless widows?[164] One solution, proffered by Jerome, concludes that the woman's "salvation" might result from her bearing children "for virginity"; her virginal offspring then compensate for what she herself has lost.[165] Moreover, commenting on I Timothy 2:15, Pelagius is quick to remind his readers that much more is needed for salvation than "just faith"[166]—certainly not, we may assume, the mere physical fact of becoming a mother, as Jovinian's female disciples allegedly claimed.[167] In

(CCL 2, 1248–49).

[159] On "changing the audience" as a strategy of ascetic exegesis, see above, pp. 136–38.

[160] Augustine, *Contra Faustum* 5.9 (CSEL 25, 281–82).

[161] Jerome, *ep.* 66.3 (CSEL 54, 650).

[162] Gregory of Nazianzus, *Or.* 37.9 (PG 36, 293).

[163] Athanasius, *ep. 1 ad virgines* (CSCO 150 = Scriptores Coptici 19, 82–83; ET, Brakke, pp. 280–81).

[164] John Chrysostom, *Hom. 9 I Tim.* 1 (2:11–15) (PG 62, 545).

[165] Jerome, *Adversus Iovinianum* 1.27 (PL 23, 260); cf. *ep.* 66.3 (CSEL 54, 650).

[166] Pelagius, *Comm. I Tim.* 2:15 (PLS 1, 1349–50).

[167] Jerome, *Adversus Iovinianum* 2.37 (PL 23, 351).

any event, Chrysostom argues, it is not merely bearing children that is laudable, but educating them in virtue: "will," not "nature," is the operative category.[168]

Still another intervention—by Origen—applied I Timothy 2:15 to the divine childbearing of the Virgin Mary: "salvation" is here effected through Mary's bearing of Christ.[169] Origen also allegorizes I Timothy 2:15 to denote the soul who conceives the words of Christ and "bears children"; sharing her bed with the Word of God, this fecund soul brings forth virtues such as chastity and justice. Such, Origen claims, is the proper interpretation of Psalm 128:3, that "your children will be like olive shoots around your table."[170]

Gregory of Nyssa, probably influenced by Origen's allegory, also spiritualizes the meaning of I Timothy 2:15 in his advice to virgins. The verse, he explains, counsels them to cultivate a spiritual union that bears "life" and "incorruptibility." Psalm 113:9, which describes the joy of the barren woman who conceives, is similarly applicable to the virgin; she is a "mother" who bears immortal children through the spirit.[171] In ways such as these, the physicality of childbearing could effectively be erased from the text, while the words of I Timothy 2:15 remained enshrined as Holy Scripture. In these cases, allegorical interpretation rescues Biblical texts from their excessive carnality.

Yet another post-Pauline passage that was read as promoting ascetic values is Ephesians 5:21–33 (the analogy of marital relations to those of Christ with the Church). Verses could be ingeniously extracted from the resolutely marital context of this Household Code to encourage more rigorous sexual renunciation, not female subservience.[172] For example, 5:27 (that the Church should be presented to the Bridegroom "without spot or wrinkle") provided a phrase that could be variously deployed to discourage second marriage (so Origen),[173] to encourage virginity (so Pelagius and Gregory of Nyssa),[174] and to urge female ascetics living with celi-

[168] John Chrysostom, *De Anna* 1.3–4 (PG 54, 636–38). Recall that Chrysostom does not believe that children are conceived simply "by nature," in any event; see above, p. 272.

[169] Origen, *Frag. 20 Hom. Luc.* (Luke 1:43) (SC 87, 478).

[170] Origen, *Hom. 20 Num.* 2 (GCS 30, 188–89).

[171] Gregory of Nyssa, *De virginitate* 13.3 (SC 119, 430).

[172] On the many uses of these passages to enforce domestic arrangements and wifely submission, see, for example, Tertullian, *Ad uxorem* 2.8; Augustine, *Tract. in Ioan.* 2.14.3; *Contra duas epistolas Pelagianorum* 1.5.9; *ep.* 262.7; Ambrose, *De viduis* 15.89, *Comm. Luc.* 8.9; (Anonymous), *Ad Celantiam* 26; Pelagius, *Comm. Eph.* 5:22–33; Basil of Caesarea, *Hexaemeron* 7.5; John Chrysostom, *Propter fornicationes* 4; *Hom. 20 Eph.*; *Hom. 14 Gen.* 4; *Serm. 2 Gen.* 2.

[173] Origen, *Hom. 17 Luc.* 10 (SC 87, 262).

[174] (Anonymous), *ep. de virginitate* (= *Ad Claudiam*) 11 (CSEL 1, 241); Gregory of Nyssa, *De virginitate* 1 (SC 119, 256).

bate men to abandon their syneisaktic relationships (so John Chrysostom).[175] Jerome, commending Eustochium on her virginal commitment, instructs her that the "one" the man and the woman are here said to become (5:31) is not the "one flesh" of Genesis 2:24 but the "one spirit" of I Corinthians 6:17. The virgin can look forward to this spiritual union with Christ.[176] Even Augustine, a defender of Christian marriage, cites the Ephesians 5 verses to refer not to the sexual union, but to the third "good" of marriage, the sacramental bond.[177] That this "bond" obtains despite failure to produce children (the first "good") or to preserve the second "good" of fidelity supported Augustine's argument that Joseph and Mary were truly married, despite their lifelong lack of sexual relation.[178] Thus, although Ephesians 5 is most often quoted to reinforce the sanctity of Christian marriage, the "bond" could be interpreted in a less sexual direction.

Augustine affords an instructive instance of how Christian exegetes could heighten or lessen the ascetic import of Ephesians 5:21–35. Pondering the principles of Scriptural exegesis in *On Christian Doctrine*, Augustine notes that some Christians devoted to the "higher" spiritual life read as figurative passages that provide useful moral instruction for those at less advanced levels. As an example, Augustine reports that some who have "become eunuchs for the sake of the Kingdom of Heaven" (Matt. 19:12) interpret Biblical passages on "loving and governing a wife"—such as Ephesians 5:21–35—as figurative, an exegetical ploy that Augustine, sympathetic to marriage, deems artificial.[179]

We in fact have examples of such figurative interpretations of passages that if "literally" read, seem to endorse marriage. The anonymous (and highly ascetic) author of the treatise *On Chastity* claims that Christians *should* read some Biblical passages figuratively. For support, he argues that the Genesis stories concerning Abraham's wife Sarah and concubine Hagar are taken by Paul himself as an allegory of the two covenants, the "present Jerusalem" and the "Jerusalem above" (Gal. 4:22–26). An analogous approach should govern the interpretation of Genesis 2:24 (man and

[175] John Chrysostom, *Quod regulares feminae viris cohabitare non debeant* 6 (PG 47, 526).

[176] Jerome, *ep*. 22.1 (CSEL 54, 145).

[177] Augustine, *De nuptiis et concupiscentia* 1.10.11; 1.21.23 (CSEL 42, 222–23, 236).

[178] For Augustine's understanding of the "bond" as holding for those couples who have no children or who do not engage in sexual relations, see *De bono coniugali* 3.3 (CSEL 41, 190). As early as *Against Faustus* (23.8), ca. 398, Augustine was arguing that there can be husband and wife without sexual intercourse (CSEL 25, 713). Also see Augustine, *De consensu Evangelistarum* 2.1.2–3 (CSEL 43, 82–83); *Serm.* 51.13.21 (PL 38, 344–45), and discussion in Elizabeth A. Clark, " 'Adam's Only Companion': Augustine and the Early Christian Debate on Marriage," *Recherches Augustiniennes* 21 (1986): 139–62.

[179] Augustine, *De doctrina Christiana* 3.17.25 (CCL 32, 92–93).

woman becoming "one flesh"); Ephesians 5:31–32 (the union of Christ and the Church) explains its "true" meaning, according to the author of *De castitate*.[180] The physical marriages of "real" men and women in the world are here subtly devalued by more figurative readings.

Jerome—typically—also proffers more rigorously ascetic readings of Ephesians 5:21–35. If Christ loves the Church chastely, "without spot or wrinkle," so should husbands love their wives *in chastity*, which for Jerome (unlike for some other church fathers), means "no sex." He reinforces this interpretation by an appeal to I Thessalonians 4:4–7, that Christians should possess their "vessels" in "sanctification and honor, not in the passion of lust like the Gentiles who know not God. . . . For God has not called us for uncleanness, but in holiness." Citing Colossians 3, Jerome proceeds to argue that "putting on the new man" and "being renewed in the image" of Christ mean that now there is "no male and female" (Gal. 3:28); we are rather born again in Christ, *a virgin*. By this complex intertextual exegesis, Jerome has skillfully recouped Ephesians 5 for the promotion of virginity, which "replenishes" Paradise, unlike marriage, which "reproduces" (Gen. 1:28) only to have its "crop" cut down by death.[181]

A few years earlier in his *Ephesians Commentary*, Jerome sets a more "spiritual" interpretation of Ephesians 5 over against the lowly concessions that Paul made to the married in I Corinthians 7:3–5. Borrowing Origen's gender code, Jerome interprets "bodies" (coded female) as the Church and "souls" (coded male) as Christ; these two may be made "one spirit" (I Cor. 6:17). Jerome suggests that there is both a "simple" interpretation of loving and nourishing a wife and a "higher," "tropological" one. According to the "higher" exegesis, wives will be transformed into men and bodies into spirits, so that there will be no difference of sex in the resurrection; "like angels" (Matt. 22:30), there will be "no male and female" (Gal. 3:28). The message, according to Jerome, is that we should now begin to be "what is promised for us in heaven."[182] Thus in his *Ephesians Commentary* as well as in his debate with Jovinian, Jerome interprets Ephesians 5 so that it promotes sexual renunciation in the present.[183] That this interpretation of Ephesians 5 could be the centerpiece of Rufinus' attack on Jerome's covert "Origenism" is another story, told elsewhere.[184]

[180] (Anonymous), *De castitate* 15.2 (PLS 1, 1496–97).

[181] Jerome, *Adversus Iovinianum* 1.16 (PL 23, 246).

[182] Jerome, *Comm. Eph.* 3 (5:22–23; 5:29) (PL 26, 564, 567–68).

[183] John Oppel, omitting this part of Jerome's exegesis from his discussion of the passage, contrives to make Jerome a supporter of marriage ("Saint Jerome and the History of Sex," *Viator* 24 [1993]: 1–22, esp. pp. 20–21).

[184] Rufinus, *Apologia* 1.24–25 (CCL 20, 58–60); see discussion in Elizabeth A. Clark, "The Place of Jerome's *Commentary on Ephesians* in the Origenist Controversy:

A second issue of the later New Testament literature—clerical marriage—also attracted the attention of patristic exegetes. I Timothy 3:2, 3:12, and Titus 1:6 were the contested verses. Surprisingly, several church fathers think that the injunction for clergy to be married not more than once is too rigid. What if (they posit) a man married and was widowed before he was baptized; if he then remarries, is he to be excluded from the clergy? Jerome, Origen, and Theodore of Mopsuestia[185] think not; opposed to any relaxing of ecclesiastical rigor, however, is Ambrose.[186] Origen argues that if a man lost his second wife while he was still young and lived until his declining years in chastity, he should not be debarred from the priesthood. Is not such a man more chaste than he who married only once, but engaged in an a sexual relation with his wife until old age? Why should the latter man be eligible for elevation to the clergy when the former is not?[187] Jerome and Theodore of Mopsuestia modify Origen's argument so that the man lives with his *second* wife until old age (but "continently," Jerome adds): why should such a man be excluded from the clergy?[188] Nonetheless, most writers (including these same writers elsewhere) urge a more "ascetic" approach to these verses.

First, some explanation was needed why "Paul" would permit clergy to be married even once. Jerome attempts to provide a reason: in the early days of the faith, Gentiles were flocking to the Church and lighter regulations were needed so as not to drive them away, as is evidenced by the decisions made by the Jerusalem Council (Acts 15).[189] Elsewhere, and conversely, Jerome claims that "Paul" permitted clerical marriage because the new converts to the faith were coming from Judaism, which allowed polygamy; decisively ruling out the latter, "Paul" commanded that a priest have *only* one wife.[190] It appears from these examples that Jerome believed Jewish as well as Gentile converts to the early Church were morally weak and in need of special consideration—or at the least, they provided convenient foils for his rhetoric. Jerome offers hypothetical reasons why, even in his own day, married priests are sometimes chosen in preference to virginal ones: perhaps the latter lack other virtues; perhaps lay Christians

---

The Apokatastasis and Ascetic Ideals," *Vigiliae Christianae* 41 (1987): 154–71.

185 Jerome, *ep.* 69.2–4 (CSEL 54, 680–86) (all sins are washed away in baptism); *Comm. Tit.* 1:6 (PL 26, 598); Origen, *Comm. Matt.* 14.22 (GCS 38, 336–39); Theodore of Mopsuestia, *Comm. I Tim.* 3:2 (Swete II:100–101).

186 Ambrose, *ep.* 63.62–64 (PL 16, 1257–58); cf. *De officiis ministrorum* 1.247 (PL 16, 103).

187 Origen, *Comm. Matt.* 14.22 (GCS 38, 337–38).

188 Jerome, *Comm. Tit.* 1:6 (PL 26, 598); Theodore of Mopsuestia, *Comm. I Tim.* 3:2 (Swete II:103–4).

189 Jerome, *Adversus Iovinianum* 1.34 (PL 23, 268).

190 Jerome, *ep.* 69.5 (CSEL 54, 686–87).

want priests who are more like themselves; perhaps bishops give clerical positions to their own relatives rather than to the best candidates.[191] Why "Paul" and the later Church tolerated married priests is here answered.

John Chrysostom and Theodore of Mopsuestia likewise appeal to the notion that "Paul" gave these lighter regulations since the first converts came from Judaism and had been accustomed to polygamy (and to extramarital relations, Theodore adds). On this point, these Fathers appear to assume that the sexual mores depicted in the patriarchal narratives still obtained in the "real world" of first-century C.E. Judaism. Chrysostom further reasons that "Paul" did not place any more demanding requirements upon bishops because there were presumably very few who espoused the "angelic life" (of total sexual abstinence), yet sufficient clergy were needed to furnish each city with a bishop.[192] Elsewhere, Chrysostom comments that "Paul" wrote Titus 1:6 to stop the mouths of the heretics who condemn marriage; if bishops are allowed to marry, marriage must be considered a "good."[193]

Yet why would Paul have allowed even one marriage for the clergy if in I Corinthians 7:33 he had written that the married care about "the things of the world"? One answer rests on the assumption that even if a cleric *were* married, he would not engage in sexual relations with his wife. Thus John Chrysostom appeals to the notion that even married men, priests included, can have their wives "as if not" (I Cor. 7:29).[194] Chrysostom further assumes that "Paul" must have been referring to men who, raised to priestly office from "secular life," were already married.[195]

For Jerome, "Paul" means that a bishop could be "the husband of one wife"—in the past. When in office, the bishop certainly will not beget children or he will be condemned as an adulterer (presumably, faithless in his "marriage" to Christ or to the Church). According to Jerome, Paul did not believe that it was *necessary* for a man to be married in order to be a bishop, or he never would have exclaimed, "Would all men be like me!" (I Cor. 7:7). If Christian laypeople cannot pray without abstaining from sexual relations (I Cor. 7:5), how much more must a priest be sexually pure, he who must always be ready to "offer sacrifices" and pray?[196] Pelagius, commenting on I Timothy 3:12 (that deacons should be

[191] Jerome, *Adversus Iovinianum* 1.34 (PL 23, 269).

[192] John Chrysostom, *Hom. 10 I Tim.* 1 (3:1–4) (PG 62, 547); Theodore of Mopsuestia, *Comm. I Tim.* 3:2 (Swete II:102–3).

[193] John Chrysostom, *Hom. 2 Tit.* 1 (1:6) (PG 62, 671).

[194] John Chrysostom, *Hom. 10 I Tim.* 1 (3:1–4) (PG 62, 549).

[195] John Chrysostom, *Hom. I Tim.* argumentum (PG 62, 503–4).

[196] Jerome, *Adversus Iovinianum* 1.34–35 (PL 23, 268–70). Ambrose as well expresses shock that in some places (but only in "out-of-the-way places") priests were begetting children: *De officiis ministrorum* 1.248 (PL 16, 105).

married only once), argues that if a man is not already married when he assumes the diaconate, he should not take this verse as an injunction to wed.[197] As Athanasius remarks, appealing to Paul's evaluative code in I Corinthians 7, married deacons may be "good," but virginity is certainly the "better" state.[198] Thus any hint that clergy might be required to be married is dispelled.

The spectrum of opinion on married clergy ranged from Jovinian and Clement of Alexandria, who cite I Timothy 3:2 to argue that "Paul" deemed marriage "good" for clergy as well as for laity,[199] to Jerome, who doubts the goodness of *first* marriage for priests,[200] and Tertullian, for whom second marriage for any Christian, clerical *or* lay, should be ruled out.[201] According to Jerome, "Paul's" statement in I Timothy 3:2 that bishops should be *sōphrona* means that they are to be "chaste" (i.e., "not engaging in sexual relations").[202] "Preachers of continence"—Jerome's definition of a priest in *Epistle* 52—should not urge others, whether virgins or widows, to marry. Has not the priest read I Corinthians 7:29, that the "time is short" and that those who have wives "should live as though they have not"?[203]

Tertullian drives the argument in a different direction to claim that there should be no second marriage for either laypeople or priests. Readers should infer that "Paul" deemed second marriage detrimental to the faith of all Christians since he prohibited it to the clergy.[204] Since members of the clergy come from the ranks of laypeople, *all* Christians must keep to the bounds of "monogamy" so that all are ready to serve: "we are all priests" (Rev. 1:6), Tertullian intones. Since God is "no respecter of persons" (Eph. 6:9), what is required of the clergy applies to everyone.[205] Others, such as Pelagius and Jerome, note that although second marriage is forbidden to clerics, it is allowable for laypeople, although Jerome adds that "Paul" in writing Titus 1:6 does not "exhort" laypeople to second marriages, but merely relaxes the harder rule laid upon priests.[206]

[197] Pelagius, *Comm. I Tim.* 3:12 (PLS 1, 1351).

[198] Athanasius, *ep. 1 ad virgines* (CSCO 150 = Scriptores Coptici 19, 81; ET, Brakke, p. 279).

[199] Jovinian, in Jerome, *Adversus Iovinianum* 1.34 (PL 23, 268); Clement of Alexandria, *Stromata* 3.12.90; 3.18.108 (GCS 52 [15], 237, 246). Ambrosiaster, commenting on I Tim. 3:12, says God blesses marriage with one spouse but not with two (*Comm. I Tim.* 3:12 [CSEL 81.3, 268]).

[200] Jerome, *Adversus Iovinianum* 1.34–35 (PL 23, 268–70); *ep.* 52.16 (CSEL 54, 439).

[201] Tertullian, *De monogamia* 12.4–5 (CCL 2, 1247–48); *Ad uxorem* 1.7.4 (CCL 1, 381); *De exhortatione castitatis* 7.2–3 (CCL 2, 1024–25).

[202] Jerome, *Adversus Iovinianum* 1.35 (PL 23, 270).

[203] Jerome, *ep.* 52.16 (CSEL 54, 439).

[204] Tertullian, *Ad uxorem* 1.7.4 (CCL 1, 381).

[205] Tertullian, *De monogamia* 12.1–2 (CCL 2, 1247); *De exhortatione castitatis* 7.2–4 (CCL 2, 1024–25).

[206] Pelagius, *Comm. Tit.* 1:6 (PLS 1,

A third passage in the Pastorals that received extensive attention from ascetically inclined patristic writers was the discourse on widows in I Timothy 5, a chapter integral to the "pro-marriage" stance of the Household Codes. Recent scholars note the Pastor's attempt to limit the number of widows supported by the Church by tightening qualifications for entry to the group. Moreover, by urging young widows to remarry, the Pastor disqualifies them for future support as enrolled widows.[207] Various verses of I Timothy 5 were cited by those early Christian writers most concerned to defend marriage: Jovinian in his battle with Jerome, and Theophilus of Alexandria, when warning against the allegedly heretical asceticism of Origenists.[208] The vast majority of Fathers, however, find ways to tame the import of I Timothy 5 for the service of ascetic values. They adopt two chief interpretive strategies for doing so: by letting the Paul of I Corinthians 7 and other Pauline texts "talk back" to the "Paul" of I Timothy 5, and by devising deconstructive readings of the chapter so that its advocacy of remarriage for widows comes unraveled.

Ambrose's treatise *On Widows* illustrates the tensions the Fathers sensed between the Pastorals' and I Corinthians 7's evaluation of marriage. Why would "Paul" in I Timothy 5 have urged younger widows to remarry, Ambrose puzzles? Surely he understood from the example of the elderly widow Anna in Luke (2:36–37) that the preservation of widowhood until old age was possible.[209] Already in I Corinthians 7 Paul had called Christians to a higher "grace" through his counsel of virginity and post-marital continence.[210] Had he not there instructed his readers that marriage is a "bondage" in which one's body belongs to the spouse (I Cor. 7:3–4)? Remarriage after a spouse's death is not forbidden, Ambrose concedes, but even acts that are "lawful" are not always "expedient" (I Cor. 6:12).[211] Had not Paul clearly stated that marriage (and the remarriage of widows) was only for those who could not control themselves (I Cor. 7:9)?[212] *Despite* I Timothy 5, widows should not think of remarrying, Ambrose concludes.[213]

Other writers as well favor the advice of I Corinthians 7 over that of I Timothy 5, often appealing to arguments from "the hierarchy of voice."[214]

1370); Jerome, *Comm. Tit.* 1 (1:6) (PL 26, 599).

[207] Jouette Bassler, "The Widows' Tale: A Fresh Look at I Tim. 5:3–16," *Journal of Biblical Literature* 103 (1984): 23–41.

[208] Jovinian in Jerome, *Adversus Iovinianum* 1.5 (PL 23, 227); Theophilus of Alexandria, *ep. paschalis* (404) (= Jerome, *ep.* 100). 12 (CSEL 55, 225–26).

[209] Ambrose, *De viduis* 2.12 (PL 16, 251).

[210] Ambrose, *De viduis* 12.72; 14.82 (PL 16, 269, 273).

[211] Ambrose, *De viduis* 11.68–69 (PL 16, 267–68).

[212] Ambrose, *De viduis* 2.12 (PL 16, 251).

[213] Ambrose, *De viduis* 11.59 (PL 16, 265).

[214] On the "hierarchy of voice," see above, pp. 141–45.

Jerome compares I Timothy 5's provision for the second marriage of widows to Paul's justification for the marriage of virgins in I Corinthians 7, namely, so that they will not fall into fornication—but what is "excusable," he hastily adds, is not necessarily "desirable."[215] In I Corinthians 7:39–40, Paul had declared that the widow was better off not being "bound" in a marriage—and I Timothy 5 must agree, Jerome argues, for both books are "the work of one author." Since Paul in I Corinthians 7:29 had already proclaimed that "the time is short," he certainly would not recommend marriage in I Timothy 5. "Paul's" words in I Timothy 5 on remarriage show rather that he sometimes acquiesced on issues in ways that did not represent his true wishes.[216] The teaching of I Corinthians 7 takes precedence over the "voice" of the Pastor.

Augustine, although more favorable to marriage than Jerome, nonetheless also balks at the prescription for the remarriage of widows in I Timothy 5:14. "Paul" here meant to allow remarriage only for the "incontinent," Augustine argues, just as he had allowed virgins and widows who "burned" to marry in I Corinthians 7:8–9. Surely "Paul" in I Timothy 5 was not trying to impose the rule of remarriage on those who had already chosen continence.[217]

John Chrysostom likewise believed that Paul's authoritative voice was best heard in I Corinthians 7:7, that all should be (continent) as he was. Some widows, Chrysostom speculates, must have "compelled" Paul against his will to impose the rule of I Timothy 5:14 on them, a rule that should be understood as a "concession" not as a "command" (I Cor. 7:6). For those widows who otherwise would live as "harlots," Chrysostom concedes, remarriage is allowable,[218] but Paul's advice in I Corinthians 7:40—that a widow will be "happier" remaining in her single state—should be preferred.[219] Since widows are "married to Christ," they should not think of uniting themselves to anyone else, Chrysostom concludes.[220] And to such arguments, Theodore of Mopsuestia adds that if a woman recalls the many "cares" of marriage (I Cor. 7:32–34), she will be dissuaded from second marriage.[221] In all these cases, the Paul of I Corinthians "talks back" to refute the encouragement to remarriage given by the

[215] Jerome, *Adversus Iovinianum* 1.14 (PL 23, 243–44).

[216] Jerome, *ep.* 123.5–6 (CSEL 56, 76–80).

[217] Augustine, *De bono viduitatis* 8.11 (CSEL 41, 316–17); cf. *De coniugiis adulterinis* 2.12.12 (CSEL 41, 395–97) and *ep.* 3*.2 (CSEL 88, 22–23).

[218] John Chrysostom, *De non iterando coniugio* 3 (SC 138, 172, 174).

[219] John Chrysostom, *Ad viduam iuniorem* 2 (SC 138, 124)—a verse also cited by the Pelagian(?) author of *De viduitate servanda* 1 (PL 67, 1094).

[220] John Chrysostom, *Ad viduam iuniorem* 2 (SC 138, 124); *Hom. 15 I Tim.* 1 (5:11–15) (PG 62, 579).

[221] Theodore of Mopsuestia, *Comm. I Tim.* 5:14 (Swete II:165).

"Paul" of I Timothy 5; the "voice" of I Corinthians 7 commands greater authority than that of I Timothy 5.

Moreover, the text of I Timothy 5 could, when "deconstructively" read, press a more ascetic message. First, the *neōteras* ("young women") of I Timothy 5:14 could be understood as females contemplating marriage for the first time, *not* as widows; on this reading, the verse does not counsel the remarriage of widows, but merely recommends first marriage.[222] Thus Clement of Alexandria, a champion of first marriage but a critic of remarriage, which he equates with "fornication," cites I Timothy 5:14 in his praise of "young women" marrying.[223] Athanasius also cited I Timothy 5:14 against the heretically ascetic Hieracas to defend (first) marriage, although he concedes that virginity is surely the better choice.[224] Augustine likewise argues that the verse refers to first marriage; marriage is not sinful, as "Paul's" allowance of it to "young women" (*iuniores*) of I Timothy 5:14 shows, although continence is nonetheless preferable, as is proved by Matthew 19:12 ("eunuchs for the Kingdom of Heaven") and I Corinthians 7:1 ("it is well not to touch a woman").[225] Thus the ambivalence of the referent of "*neōteras*"—whether "young women" in general or more specifically, "young widows"—provided one convenient loophole by which ascetically inclined church fathers could reject the recommendation for the remarriage of widows.

A second aspect of the text of I Timothy 5 that could be pressed to provide a more ascetic reading lay in the implied contrast between the "real" widows of verse 5 (who, remaining single, have set their hopes on God and spend their days and nights in prayer) and the "wanton" widows of verses 11–14 (who violate their pledge to Christ, are idle gadabouts, gossips, and busybodies; to forestall such behavior, they should marry and have children). It was an easy exegetical task to argue that "Paul" meant for women to endorse the former rather than the latter vidual mode of life. Thus two sections of I Timothy 5—verses 5–10 (the "real" widows) and verses 11–15 (the "wanton" widows)—could be set over against each other to encourage ascetic renunciation. According to Tertullian, since "Paul" praises the first set of widows who married only once, readers can infer that he believes second marriage is detrimental to the faith.[226] Even Ambrosiaster, supportive of marriage, argues that the "true widows" of verse 5, like Anna, are "worthier" of God in that they have rejected second

[222] On "ascetic translation," see above, pp. 113–18.

[223] Clement of Alexandria, *Stromata* 3.12.89 (GCS 52 [15], 237).

[224] Athanasius, *ep. 1 ad virgines* (CSCO 150 = Scriptores Coptici 19, 86; ET, Brakke, p. 283) citing I Cor. 7:38–40 over against I Tim. 5:14.

[225] Augustine, *De nuptiis et concupiscentia* 1.16.18 (CSEL 42, 231).

[226] Tertullian, *Ad uxorem* 1.7.4 (CCL 1, 381).

marriage.[227] Jerome elaborates: it is only for those widows who have "outraged Christ" by "fornicating" against him (i.e., those who have "strayed after Satan," according to v. 15) that "Paul" urges a second marriage. As for their bearing children (v. 14), "Paul" wrote these words so that the women "would not be prompted by fear to kill the children they had conceived in adultery." For women of this type, Jerome concedes, remarriage is preferable to becoming a prostitute or to taking several lovers—yet far better, of course, would be to imitate the "ideal" widow of verses 5–10.[228]

The Pelagian(?) author of *De viduitate servanda* reminds his widowed addressee that the "real" widows whom she should emulate are described in I Timothy 5:4–6. By remaining celibate, she shows that she has abandoned her former delight "in the lust of the flesh." She now can "lie alone in bed and rise up clean," not in the "uncleanness of the flesh" as she did in marriage.[229] The "real" widows of verses 3–6 (and Anna of Luke 2) are also contrasted by the Pelagian(?) author of *On the Christian Life* with two other sets: with widows still preoccupied with home and children, and with those given to "feasts and sensual delights" (the widows criticized in vv. 13–15). The "dearly beloved sister" to whom this treatise is directed is expected to place herself amid the first group, the "real" widows.[230] And Pelagius himself offers a "correction" of I Timothy 5:14. "Paul" here addresses only those women who have not made a commitment to Christian widowhood; if they marry and have children *after* they have taken their vow, they stand condemned.[231]

John Chrysostom, for his part, divides the widows of I Timothy 5 into three groups. The "real" widows of 5:5 who, "all alone," have no children to whom they must attend, are closer to God than those in the second category who bring up children (5:10).[232] The third type, the widows of 5:11–15, however, should be deemed "fallen." Espoused to Christ, they violated their faith. Nonetheless, their marriages provided a "safeguard" so that they would not slip into an even worse condition of life. To them should be contrasted virgins who had *not* fallen, whose lack of sin precludes any allusion to them here, Chrysostom ingeniously argues.[233] Addressing verse 5 ("Honor widows who are real widows"), Chrysostom remarks, if we are to honor "real widows," what about virgins?[234] Here, it

[227] Ambrosiaster, *Comm. I Tim.* 5:3f. (CSEL 81.3, 278).

[228] Jerome, *ep.* 123.3–4 (CSEL 56, 74–75).

[229] (Anonymous), *De viduitate servanda* (PL 67, 1094).

[230] (Anonymous), *De vita Christiana* 15 (PL 40, 1045).

[231] Pelagius, *Comm. I Tim.* 5:14 (PLS 1, 1355); cf. 5:12.

[232] John Chrysostom, *Hom. 6 I Thess.* 4 (4:13f.) (PG 62, 434).

[233] John Chrysostom, *Hom. 15 I Tim.* 1 (5:11–15) (PG 62, 579).

[234] John Chrysostom, *Hom. 13 I Tim.* 2 (5:5) (PG 62, 566).

is not only the "real widows" of verse 5 who are contrasted with the "wanton" ones of verses 11–15, but widowhood itself is seen as inferior to Christian virginity—an option not offered by the author of the Pastorals, but pressed by later writers of an ascetic inclination.[235]

Still another aspect of I Timothy 5 prompted a more ascetically rigorous reading of that chapter. Verse 6, "she who is self-indulgent is dead" (or as the Fathers phrased it, "she who gives herself to pleasure is dead"), could be removed from its context as a warning to the "real widows" of verse 5 and repositioned to describe the "wanton" young widows of verses 11–15. Stirred by their unruly sexual desires ("giving themselves to pleasure"), they contract second marriages—which, in the logic of the Fathers' creative repositioning of this verse, implies that these widows are "dead." Thus Augustine, writing to the widow Proba (who had not opted for remarriage), assures her that she is among the "real widows" of verse 5; she is not one of those who "living in pleasure, is dead."[236] John Chrysostom, inveighing against second marriage, which he holds "defiles" the bed of the dead husband, cites the verse "she who lives in pleasure is dead" to advance his argument. According to Chrysostom, "Paul" counsels remarriage only for widows who have not been able to live in seemly fashion, such as those in verses 11–15 who have "strayed after Satan." Against such widows, Chrysostom claims, "Paul" sets the "good widows" of verse 10 who are attested by their righteous deeds and many virtues.[237] "Paul's" warning in verse 6 is thus understood as directed to the morally weak, not to the "real widows" of verse 5.

Yet for many Fathers, it is not merely "wanton" widows (5:11–12) who are chastised. All remarriage is here recast as only one step up from prostitution,[238] as "fornication,"[239] or more politely, as "weakness of the flesh"[240] or "incontinence."[241] Chrysostom is sure that Paul wanted all Christians to be continent, "as he himself was" (I Cor. 7:7), not to remarry;[242] the

235 "Virgins" are introduced into the text by Pelagius (*Comm. I Tim.* 5:12), Basil of Caesarea (*ep.* 199.18), and Theodore of Mopsuestia (*Comm. I Tim.* 5:14).

236 Augustine, *ep.* 130.3.7 (CSEL 44, 47–48).

237 John Chrysostom, *Hom. 7 II Tim.* 4 (3:1–7) (PG 62, 641).

238 Jerome, *Adversus Iovinianum* 1.14 (PL 23, 244); *epp.* 54.15 (CSEL 54, 482); 79.10 (CSEL 55, 99–100, comparing the "harlotry" to that of Israel and Jerusalem in Ezek. 16:25; 28:3); 123.4 (CSEL 56, 75).

239 John Chrysostom, *De non iterando coniugio* 3 (PG 138, 176, 178); Tertullian, *De exhortatione castitatis* 9.1 (CCL 2, 1027) (second marriage as a *species stupri*); Clement of Alexandria, *Stromata* 3.12.89 (GCS 52 [15], 237).

240 Tertullian, *De monogamia* 14.4 (CCL 2, 1249); cf. *Ad uxorem* 1.64.1 (CCL 1, 377).

241 Ambrose, *De viduis* 13.75; 15.88 (PL 16, 270–72, 275); Augustine, *De bono viduitatis* 8.11 (CSEL 41, 315–16); *De coniugiis adulterinis* 2.12.12 (CSEL 41, 396–97); John Chrysostom, *Hom. 15 I Tim.* 1 (5:11–15) (PG 62, 579–80).

242 John Chrysostom, *Hom. 18 Heb.* 1 (PG 63, 135).

Paul of I Corinthians 7 once again provides a foil against the "Paul" of the Pastorals. Ambrose attempts to shame widows who remarry by unfavorably comparing their "wantonness" with the chastity of doves, mere dumb animals.[243] Appealing to an economic calculus, Jerome asks the widow contemplating remarriage why she should put "an uncertain thing before a certain feeling of shame?"[244] Such negative assessment of a widow's desire for remarriage cast I Timothy 5:14 in a dim light.

Two church fathers, Jerome and John Chrysostom, note that the Pastor's recommendation of remarriage for young widows (I Tim. 5:14) comes unraveled within the chapter itself. They provide a deconstructive reading that reveals the inconsistency of the chapter. Both Jerome and Chrysostom recognize that the advice that young widows remarry (v. 14) effectively removes their eligibility for church support in future years; to the once-married only is this privilege reserved, according to verse 9.[245] If the young widows follow the Pastor's advice in 5:14 and remarry, they can never find a place among the ranks of "real widows" in 5:9 who are supported by the Church. Hence, Chrysostom concludes, "Paul" did not mean that he wished *all* young widows to remarry, but only those "more fragile" ones who might lapse into dubious behavior.[246] Jerome elaborates this point via an ingenious intertextual exegesis: according to 5:9, if a widow has had more than one husband, she is deprived of "the bread of charity" (i.e., the Church's support of the "real widows")—and if this, "how much more" will she be deprived of "the bread of heaven" (John 6:33, 41), the body of Christ in the Eucharist that Christians are warned not to eat unworthily (I Cor. 11:27–29) lest they commit an "outrage" and bring condemnation on themselves.[247] Dark insinuations are here made regarding the reception of the Eucharist by the twice-married.

Chrysostom and Jerome thus effectively demonstrate that the advice to widows offered in I Timothy 5 is self-contradictory. Although they do not speculate on the Pastor's motivations as a modern Biblical commentator might (e.g., that the Pastor was attempting to decrease the number of widows the Church must support by tightening the eligibility requirements and urging the widows' families to provide for them), they nonetheless teach that widows cannot remarry if they later wish to be "real widows" who receive the support provided for the once-married. According to the author of the *Life of Olympias*, his young widowed heroine understood well that since "the law is laid down for the unruly" (I Tim.

[243] Ambrose, *Hexaemeron* 5.8.19.63 (CSEL 32.1, 187–88).

[244] Jerome, *ep.* 54.15 (CSEL 54, 482).

[245] Jerome, *ep.* 123.5 (CSEL 56, 78).

[246] John Chrysostom, *Vidua eligatur* 4 (PG 51, 324–25).

[247] Jerome, *Adversus Iovinianum* 1.14 (PL 23, 244).

1:9), the "law" of remarriage in I Timothy 5:14 is inapplicable to well-disciplined widows such as herself.[248]

Thus ascetically inclined Fathers read the later New Testament books in ways that mitigated their domestic emphases and encouraged a more rigorous renunciation, that brought these passages into conformity with I Corinthians 7 and Paul's stated preference for celibacy. While verses from Paul's letters that echoed the themes of I Corinthians 7 were easy for the Fathers to appropriate for their ascetic agenda, the Pastoral Epistles and other late New Testament books required more ingenious exegetical assistance to align them with the mores of I Corinthians 7. By differentiating authorial voice and intended audience, by using the Paul of I Corinthians 7 to "talk back" to the "Paul" of the Pastoral Epistles, by understanding Pauline texts such as those concerning food purity and the resurrection body to "implode" into issues of sexuality and marriage, by "differentiating the times" of the gloriously ascetic Christian present from the "infant" days of the Church when new Jewish and Gentile converts required coddling, the Fathers found a harmonious and united message of renunciation in the New Testament. Thus both Old and New Dispensations could be understood to promote a thoroughly ascetized Christianity.

[248] (Anonymous), *Vita Olympiadis* 3 (SC 13bis, 410).

Afterword

In his essay, "Reading as Poaching," the French theorist and historian Michel de Certeau imaginatively posits a contrast between writers and readers:

> Far from being writers—founders of their own place, heirs of the peasants of earlier ages now working on the soil of language, diggers of wells and builders of houses—readers are travellers; they move across lands belonging to someone else, like nomads poaching their way across fields they did not write, despoiling the wealth of Egypt to enjoy it themselves.[1]

In this book, I hope to have shown how the church fathers were *both* readers who "poached" *and* writers who "founded their own place." Deeply embedded in a culture of Christian texts whose authors had "despoiled the wealth of Egypt" in their appropriation of the Jewish Scriptures as well as the treasures of classical learning, the Fathers created a new, highly asceticized version of Christianity that was to shape religious and moral values for centuries to come.

Traditional patristics scholarship excelled in its attention to philological and theological detail, yet from a contemporary, more theoretically invested, standpoint might be deemed insufficiently attentive to the mechanics of textual construction[2] (including issues of power embedded in the process) and to the productive role of readers, who sometimes become writers[3]—in de Certeau's words, who "poach" as well as "found their own place"

Much recent literary (and other) theory, I have argued, is relevant to the study of patristic commentary. By expanding the meaning of a text,

[1] Michel de Certeau, "Reading as Poaching," in *The Practice of Everyday Life*, trans. Steven Rendall (Berkeley/Los Angeles/London: University of California Press, 1984), p. 174. That de Certeau's language *itself* is highly resonant with that of the Fathers (e.g., "spoiling the Egyptians" is the metaphor they commonly use to describe their appropriation of classical texts) reveals his own imbrication in a Christian culture.

[2] See, for example, Valentine Cunningham, "Renoving That Bible: The Absolute Text of (Post) Modernism," in *The Theory of Reading*, ed. Frank Gloversmith (Sussex: Harvester; Totowa, N.J.: Barnes and Noble, 1984), p. 2; see also Shoshana Felman, "Turning the Screw of Interpretation," *Yale French Studies* 55–56 (1977): 119.

[3] Daniel Boyarin, *Intertextuality and the Reading of Midrash* (Bloomington/Indianapolis: Indiana University Press, 1990), p. 17; cf. Harold Bloom, *Kabbalah and Criticism* (New York: Seabury, 1975), p. 125.

commentary creates in effect a "new text,"[4] thus illustrating the "supplementary" quality of writing to which Jacques Derrida has called attention.[5] Yet, as Foucault has counterargued, the text itself remains: commentators thus "say something other than the text itself, but on condition that it is this text itself which is said, and in a sense completed."[6] Patristic commentators, to be sure, assume that they are merely drawing out the meaning implicit in the texts they discuss, not creating a new or "foreign" message. Yet their comments illustrate how it is the present readers, not the original authors, who provide meaning.[7] As I have suggested throughout, intertextual explorations that attend to how words have "always already been used and carry within themselves the traces of preceding usage"[8] reveal the decontextualization and relocation of Biblical texts in commentary-writing, and show how "new texts" are constructed from old.[9]

Some contemporary literary critics imagine that such theoretical insights are applicable only to the poetry and prose written since the late nineteenth century.[10] At best, they single out Augustine as the one patristic writer recuperable for contemporary literary criticism.[11] I would argue otherwise: Derridean supplementarity, Bakhtinian dialogism or Kristevan intertextuality, and ideology critique are theoretical tools highly illuminating of the works of patristic authors.[12]

[4] Roland Barthes, "Theory of the Text," in *Untying the Text: A Post-Structuralist Reader*, ed. Robert Young (Boston/London/Henley: Routledge and Kegan Paul, 1981), p. 44; cf. Robert Scholes, *Protocols of Reading* (New Haven, Conn./London: Yale University Press, 1989), p. 8.

[5] Jacques Derrida, *Of Grammatology*, trans. Gayatri Chakravorty Spivak (Baltimore/London: Johns Hopkins University Press, 1976), pp. 200, 226, 280–81, 295.

[6] Michel Foucault, "The Order of Discourse," in *Untying the Text*, ed. Young, p. 58.

[7] Roland Barthes, "The Death of the Author," in idem, *Image, Music, Text*, trans. Stephen Heath (New York: Hill and Wang, 1977), p. 148.

[8] Tzvetan Todorov, *Mikhail Bakhtin: The Dialogical Principle*, trans. Wlad Godzich, Theory and History of Literature 13 (Minneapolis: University of Minnesota Press, 1984; French original, 1981), p. 63.

[9] Michael Fishbane, *Biblical Interpretation in Ancient Israel* (Oxford: Clarendon, 1985), p. 415; cf. the explanation of deconstruction's project exposed in these themes in Jonathan Culler, *On Deconstruction: Theory and Criticism after Structuralism* (Ithaca, N.Y.: Cornell University Press, 1982), p. 128.

[10] E.g., Roland A. Champagne, "The Writer Within the Intertext," in *Intertextuality. New Perspectives in Criticism*, ed. Jeanine P. Plottel and Hanna Charney (New York: Literary Forum 2, 1978), p. 131.

[11] E.g., Geoffrey Galt Harpham, *The Ascetic Imperative in Culture and Criticism* (Chicago/London: University of Chicago Press, 1987), esp. pp. 122–34 (Augustine emerges as a postmodern reader).

[12] Martin Irvine, *The Making of Textual Culture: 'Grammatica' and Literary Theory 350–1100* (Cambridge: Cambridge University Press, 1994), is one of the relatively few works that uses these tools to illuminate the literary traditions of late antiquity and the early Middle Ages.

I would propose, however, that a strictly literary approach to texts should be expanded to include a more material analysis, an analysis that raises issues of social power and cultural interests—a sociology of interpretation, if you will. In the case of the ascetic readers and writers who have here served as my subjects, religious and cultural need required that Scripture be placed in relation to a contemporary Christian ascetic practice.[13] It is here, in the investigation of the social location of texts, that the issues of power, of the creation of "difference" that I have stressed, come to the fore.

When in early Christianity the ascetic body came to occupy a central discursive position, "strong readings"[14] of the Bible, readings that found in Scripture what the exegete needed, provided ballast for the changing cultural project. In Harold Bloom's elegant phrase, "Interpretation is revisionism, and the strongest readers so revise as to make every text belated, and themselves as readers into children of the dawn, earlier and fresher than any completed text ever could hope to do."[15]

[13] Ibid., pp. 110, 189–243.

[14] Harold Bloom, *Kabbalah and Criticism* (New York: Seabury, 1975), p. 125; cf. his *A Map of Misreading* (New York: Oxford University Press, 1975).

[15] Bloom, *Kabbalah*, p. 126.

Bibliography

Primary Sources

All primary sources in standard series (as listed on the abbreviations page at the beginning of this volume) are identified in the footnotes and are not given here. Primary sources not in the above series are as follows:

Acta Pauli et Theclae. In *Acta Apostolorum Apocrypha*. Vol. I:235–72. Ed. R. A. Lipsius and M. Bonnet. Leipzig: Hermann Mendelssohn, 1891. Reprinted 1959, Hildesheim: Georg Olms Verlagsbuchhandlung.

Acta Thomae. In *Acta Apostolorum Apocrypha*. Vol. II.2:99–291. Ed. R. A. Lipsius and M. Bonnet. Leipzig: Hermann Mendelssohn, 1903. Reprinted 1959, Hildesheim: Georg Olms Verlagsbuchhandlung.

Athanasius. (*De virginitate*). "Athanasiana Syriaca I: Un *logos peri parthenias* attribué à saint Athanase d'Alexandrie." Ed. and trans. Joseph Lebon. *Le Muséon* 40 (1927): 205–48.

———. (*Ep. 2 ad virgines*). "Athanasiana Syriaca II: Une lettre attribué à saint Athanase d'Alexandrie." Ed. and trans. Joseph Lebon. *Le Muséon* 41 (1928): 169–216.

Basil of Ancyra. *De virginitate*. Ed. and trans. A. Vaillant. Textes publiés par l'Institut d'Etudes Slaves 3. Paris: Institut d'Etudes Slaves, 1943.

Basil of Caesarea. *Epistulae*. *Letters*. 4 vols. Trans. Roy J. Deferrari. Loeb Classical Library. London: William Heinemann/New York: G. P. Putnam's Sons, 1926.

Clement of Alexandria. *Fragmenta*. "Fragments de Clément d' Alexandrie conservés en arabe." Ed. H. Fleisch. *Mélanges de l'Université Saint Joseph* (Beyrouthe) 27 (1947–48): 64–71.

Codex Theodosianus. *Theodosiani libri xvi cum constitutionibus sirmondianis*. Ed. T. Mommsen. Berlin: Weidmann, 1905.

Corpus Iuris Civilis. Vol. I, *Institutiones*. Ed. Paulus Krueger. *Digesta*. Ed. Theodorus Mommsen. Berlin: Weidmann, 1893. Vol. II, *Codex Iustinianus*. Ed. Paulus Krueger. Berlin: Weidmann, 1892. Vol. III, *Novellae*. Ed. Rudolphus Schoell. Berlin: Weidmann, 1895.

Epistula (Ps.-) Titi. "Epistula Titi, discipuli Pauli, De dispositione sanctimonii." Ed. Donatien de Bruyne. *Revue Bénédictine* 37 (1925): 47–72.

Epistulae Barnabae. In *Patres Apostolici*. I:38–97. Ed. F. X. Funk. Tübingen: Heinrich Laupp, 1901.

Eusebius of Emesa. *Eusèbe d'Emése. Discours conservés en latin*. 2 vols. Ed. E. M. Buytaert. Spicilegium Sacrum Lovaniense Etudes et Documents 26–27. Louvain: Spicilegium Sacrum Lovaniense, 1953–57.

Evagrius Ponticus. *Opera. Euagrius Ponticus.* Ed. W. Frankenberg. Abhandlungen der königlichen Gesellschaft der Wissenschaften zu Göttingen, philologisch-historische Klasse, n.f. 13, 2. Berlin: Weidmann, 1912.

Gregory of Nyssa. *Gregorii Nysseni Opera, auxilio aliorum virorum doctorum edenda.* Ed. Werner Jaeger et al. Leiden: Brill, 1960–.

Horsiesius. (*Testamentum Horsiesii*). "Liber patris nostri Orsiesii quam moriens pro testamento fratribus tradidit." In *Pachomiana Latina.* Ed. Amand Boon, 109–47. Bibliothèque de la Revue d'Histoire Ecclésiastique 7. Louvain: Bureaux de la Revue, 1932.

Origen. *Commentarius in I. Epistolam ad Corinthios, fragmenta.* "Documents: Origen on I Corinthians." Ed. Claude Jenkins. *Journal of Theological Studies* 9 (1908): 231–47, 353–72, 500–514; 10 (1909): 29–51.

———. (*Commentarius in Epistolam ad Romanos*). *Der Römerbrief Kommentar des Origenes: Kritische Ausgabe der Übersetzung Rufins, Buch 1–3.* Ed. Caroline Hammond Bammel. Vetus Latina: Aus der Geschichte der Lateinischen Bibel 16. Freiburg im Breisgau: Verlag Herder, 1990.

———. *Peri Pascha. Sur la Pâque.* Ed. O. Guérard and P. Nautin. Christianisme Antique 2. Paris: Beauchesne, 1979.

Palladius. *Historia Lausiaca. The Lausiac History of Palladius.* 2 vols. Ed. Cuthbert Butler. Texts and Studies VI, 1–2. Cambridge: Cambridge University Press, 1898, 1904.

Pseudo-Basil. (*Peri parthenias*). "Une Curieuse Homélie grecque inédite sur la virginité addressée aux pères de famille." Ed. and trans. David Amand de Mendietta and Matthieu Ch. Moons. *Revue Bénédictine* 63 (1953): 18–69.

Pseudo-Clement. *Epistulae de virginitate.* In *Patres Apostolici.* II:1–49. Ed. F. X. Funk. Tübingen: H. Laupp, 1913.

Stoicorum Veterum Fragmenta. 3 vols. Ed. Johannes von Arnim. Leipzig: B. G. Teubner, 1905.

Theodore of Mopsuestia. *Commentarius in Epistolas Pauli. Theodori Episcopi Mopsuesteni in Epistolas B. Pauli Commentarii: The Latin Version with the Greek Fragments.* 2 vols. Ed. H. B. Swete. Cambridge: Cambridge University Press, 1880, 1882.

———. *Commentarius in I. Epistolam ad Corinthios. Pauluskommentare aus der griechischen Kirche.* Ed. Karl Staab, 172–96. Neutestamentliche Abhandlungen 15. Münster: Aschendorff, 1933.

———. *Commentarius in Mattheum. Matthäus-Kommentare aus der griechischen Kirche.* Ed. Joseph Reuss, 96–150. Texte und Untersuchungen 61. Berlin: Akademie-Verlag, 1957.

Selected Secondary Sources

Achelis, Hans. *Virgines Subintroductae: Ein Beitrag zum VII Kapitel des I. Korinthianerbriefs.* Leipzig: J. C. Hinrichs, 1902.

Ackroyd, P. R., and C. F. Evans, eds. *The Cambridge History of the Bible.* Vol. I, *From the Beginnings to Jerome.* Cambridge: Cambridge University Press, 1970.

Adams, J. N. *The Latin Sexual Vocabulary.* Baltimore: Johns Hopkins University Press, 1982.

Albertario, Emilio. "Matrimonio." In *Enciclopedia Italiana.* Vol. 22:580–82. Roma: Instituto della Enciclopedia Italiana, 1934.

———. *Studi di diritto romano.* Milano: Antonio Giuffré, 1933.

Alexander, Philip S. "Quid Athenis et Hierosolymis? Rabbinic Midrash and Hermeneutics in the Graeco-Roman World." In *A Tribute to Geza Vermes: Essays on Jewish and Christian Literature and History.* Ed. Philip R. Davies and Richard T. White, 101–24. JSOT Supplement Series 100. Sheffield: JSOT, 1990.

Arjava, Antti. *Women and Law in Late Antiquity.* Oxford: Clarendon, 1996.

Arns, Evaristo. *La Technique du livre d'après Saint Jerôme.* Paris: E. de Boccard, 1953.

Aubineau, Michel. "Les Ecrits de Saint Athanase sur la virginité." *Revue d'ascetique et de mystique* 31 (1955): 140–73.

Auerbach, Eric. *Literary Language and Its Public in Late Latin Antiquity and in the Middle Ages.* Trans. Ralph Mannheim. Bollingen Series 74. New York: Pantheon/Random House, 1965. German original, 1958.

———. *Scenes from the Drama of European Literature.* Theory and History of Literature 9. Minneapolis: University of Minnesota Press, 1984. Original English edition, 1959.

Baer, Richard A., Jr. *Philo's Use of the Categories Male and Female.* Arbeiten zur Literatur und Geschichte des Hellenistischen Judentums 3. Leiden: Brill, 1970.

Bagnall, Roger S. *Egypt in Late Antiquity.* Princeton, N.J.: Princeton University Press, 1993.

Bailey, John W. "The First and Second Epistles to the Thessalonians." In *The Interpreter's Bible.* XI:245–339. New York/Nashville: Abingdon, 1955.

Bakhtin, Mikhail M. *The Dialogic Imagination: Four Essays.* Ed. Michael Holquist; trans. Caryl Emerson and Michael Holquist. Austin: University of Texas Press, 1981.

Balibar, Etienne, and Pierre Macherey. "On Literature as an Ideological Form." Trans. Ian McLeod, John Whitehead, and Ann Wordsworth. In *Untying the Text.* Ed. Robert Young, q.v., 79–99.

Barns, John W. B. "Greek and Coptic Papyri from the Covers of the Nag Hammadi Codices: A Preliminary Report." In *Essays on the Nag Hammadi Texts: In Honour of Pahor Labib.* Ed. Martin Krause, 9–18. Leiden: Brill, 1975.

Barr, James. *Old and New Interpretation: A Study of the Testaments.* London: SCM, 1966.

Barré, L. "To Marry or to Burn: *Purousthai* in I Cor. 7:9." *Catholic Biblical Quarterly* 36 (1974): 193–202.

Barrett, C. K. "The Bible in the New Testament Period." In *The Church's Use of the Bible, Past and Present.* Ed. D. E. Nineham, q.v., 1–24.

Barthélemy, Dominique. "Est-ce Hoshaya Rabba qui censura le 'Commentaire Allégorique?' " In idem, *Etudes d'histoire du texte de l'Ancien Testament,* 140–73. Orbis Biblicus et Orientalis 21. Fribourg: Editions Universitaires; Göttingen: Vandenhoeck & Ruprecht, 1978.

Barthes, Roland. "The Death of the Author." In idem, *Image, Music, Text,* q.v., 142–48. French original of this essay, 1968.

Barthes, Roland. "From Work to Text." In idem, *Image, Music, Text,* q.v., 154–64. French original of this essay, 1971.

———. *Image, Music, Text.* Trans. Stephen Heath. New York: Hill and Wang, 1977.

———. "On Reading." In idem, *The Rustle of Language,* q.v., 33–43. French original of this essay, 1971.

———. "The Rustle of Language." In idem, *The Rustle of Language,* q.v., 76–79.

———. *The Rustle of Language.* Trans. Richard Howard. New York: Hill and Wang, 1986. French original, 1984.

———. "Theory of the Text." Trans. Ian McLeod. In *Untying the Text.* Ed. Robert Young, q.v., 31–47.

Bassler, Jouette. "The Widows' Tale: A Fresh Look at I Tim. 5:3–16." *Journal of Biblical Literature* 103 (1984): 23–41.

Bauer, Walter. "Matt. 19, 12 und die alten Christen." In *Aufsätze und Kleine Schriften.* Ed. Georg Strecker, 253–62. Tübingen: J. C. B. Mohr, 1967. Original edition, 1914.

———. *Orthodoxy and Heresy in Earliest Christianity.* Ed. Robert A. Kraft and Gerhard Krodel; trans. The Philadelphia Seminar on Christian Origins, from the second German edition. Philadelphia: Fortress, 1971.

Baumert, Norbert. *Ehelosigkeit und Ehe in Herrn: Ein Neuinterpretation von I Kor 7.* Forschung zur Bibel 47. Würzburg: Echter Verlag, 1984.

Baumgarten, Joseph M. "The Qumran-Essene Restraints on Marriage." In *Archaeology and History in the Dead Sea Scrolls. Journal for the Study of Pseudepigrapha.* Ed. Lawrence H. Schiffman, 13–24. Suppl. 2, JSOT/ASOR Monograph 2. Sheffield: Sheffield Academic Press, 1990.

Beard, Mary. "Writing and Religion: Ancient Literacy and the Function of the Written Word in Roman Religion." In *Literacy in the Roman World.* Ed. Mary Beard et al., q.v., 35–58.

———, et al., eds. *Literacy in the Roman World.* Journal of Roman Archaeology Supplementary Series 3. Ann Arbor: University of Michigan Press, 1991.

Bell, Catherine. *Ritual: Perspectives and Dimensions.* New York/Oxford: Oxford University Press, 1997.

———. *Ritual Theory, Ritual Practice.* New York/Oxford: Oxford University Press, 1992.

———. "Ritualization of Texts and Textualization of Ritual in the Codification of Taoist Liturgy." *History of Religions* 27 (1988): 366–92.

Best, Ernest. *A Commentary on the First and Second Epistles to the Thessalonians.* London: Adam & Charles Black, 1972.

Bhabha, Homi K. "The Commitment to Theory." In idem, *The Location of Culture,* 19–39. New York/London: Routledge, 1994.

Biale, David. *Eros and the Jews: From Biblical Israel to Contemporary America.* Berkeley/Los Angeles/London: University of California Press, 1997. Original edition, New York: Basic, 1992.

Bianchi, Ugo. "La Traditione de l'enkrateia: Motivations ontologiques et protologiques." In Ugo Bianchi, ed., *La tradizione dell' enkrateia: Motivazione ontologiche e protologiche,* q.v., 293–315.

———, ed. *La tradizione dell' enkrateia: Motivazione ontologiche e protologiche.* Roma: Edizioni dell' Ateneo, 1985.

Biarne, Jacques. "La Bible dans la vie monastique." In *Le Monde latin antique et la Bible.* Ed. Jacques Fontaine and Charles Pietri, q.v., 409–29.

Biller, Peter, and Anne Hudson, eds. *Heresy and Literacy, 1000–1530.* Cambridge: Cambridge University Press, 1994.

Binns, John. *Ascetics and Ambassadors of Christ: The Monasteries of Palestine 314–631.* Oxford: Clarendon, 1994.

Blond, Georges. "L' 'Héresie' encratite vers la fin du quatrième siècle." *Recherches de science religieuse* 31 (1944): 157–210.

Bloom, Harold. *Kabbalah and Criticism.* New York: Seabury, 1975.

———. *A Map of Misreading.* New York: Oxford University Press, 1975.

Bloomfield, Morton W. "Allegory as Interpretation." *New Literary History* 3 (1971–72): 301–17.

Blowers, Paul M. "Origen, the Rabbis, and the Bible: Toward a Picture of Judaism and Christianity in Third-Century Caesarea." In *Origen of Alexandria: His World and His Legacy.* Ed. Charles Kannengiesser and William L. Petersen, q.v., 96–116.

Boissevain, Jeremy. *Friends of Friends: Networks, Manipulators and Coalitions.* New York: St. Martin's; London: Macmillan, 1974.

Bonsirven, Joseph. " 'Nisi fornicationis causa': comment résoudre cette 'crux interpretum'?" *Recherches de science religieuse* 35 (1948): 442–64.

Bostock, Gerald. "Allegory and the Interpretation of the Bible in Origen." *Journal of Literature and Theology* 1 (1987): 39–53.

Bourdieu, Pierre. *Distinction: A Social Critique of the Judgement of Taste.* Trans. Richard Nice. Cambridge: Harvard University Press, 1984. French original, 1979.

———. *Language and Symbolic Power.* Ed. J. B. Thompson; trans. G. Raymond and M. Adamson. Cambridge: Harvard University Press, 1991.

Bowman, Alan K. "Literacy in the Roman Empire: Mass and Mode." In *Literacy in the Roman World.* Ed. Mary Beard et al., q.v., 119–31.

———, and Greg Woolf, eds. *Literacy and Power in the Ancient World.* Cambridge: Cambridge University Press, 1994.

Boyarin, Daniel. *Carnal Israel: Reading Sex in Talmudic Culture.* The New Historicism 25. Berkeley/Los Angeles: University of California Press, 1993.

———. *Intertextuality and the Reading of Midrash.* Bloomington/Indianapolis: Indiana University Press, 1990.

———. *A Radical Jew: Paul and the Politics of Identity.* Berkeley/Los Angeles/London: University of California Press, 1994.

———. "The Song of Songs: Lock or Key? Intertextuality, Allegory and Midrash." In *The Book and the Text: The Bible and Literary Theory.* Ed. Regina Schwartz, q.v., 214–30.

Boyarin, Jonathan, ed. *The Ethnography of Reading.* Berkeley/Los Angeles/Oxford: University of California Press, 1993.

Boyd, Clarence Eugene. *Public Libraries and Literary Culture in Ancient Rome.* Chicago: University of Chicago Press, 1915.

Bradley, Keith R. *Discovering the Roman Family: Studies in Roman Social History.* New York/Oxford: Oxford University Press, 1991.

Brakke, David. *Athanasius and the Politics of Asceticism.* Oxford: Clarendon, 1995.

———. "The Problematization of Nocturnal Emissions in Early Christian Syria, Egypt, and Gaul." *Journal of Early Christian Studies* 3 (1995): 419–60.

Brooks, Roger. "Straw Dogs and Scholarly Ecumenism: The Appropriate Jewish Background for the Study of Origen." In *Origen of Alexandria: His World and His Legacy.* Ed. Charles Kannengiesser and William L. Petersen, q.v., 63–95.

Brooten, Bernadette. "Early Christian Women and Their Cultural Context: Issues of Method in Historical Reconstruction." In *Feminist Perspectives on Biblical Scholarship.* Ed. Adela Yarbro Collins, 65–71. Chico, Calif.: Scholars, 1985.

———. "Jewish Women's History in the Roman Period: A Task for Christian Theology." *Harvard Theological Review* 79 (1986): 22–30.

———. "Könnten Frauen im alten Judentum die Scheidung betrieben? Überlegungen zu Mk 10, 11–12 und I Kor 7, 10–11." *Evangelische Theologie* 42 (1982): 65–80.

———. *Love Between Women: Early Christian Responses to Female Homoeroticism.* Chicago/London: University of Chicago Press, 1996.

———. "Zur Debatte über das Scheidungsrecht der jüdischen Frau." *Evangelische Theologie* 43 (1983): 466–78.

Brower, Gary R. *Ambivalent Bodies: Making Christian Eunuchs.* Unpublished Ph.D. dissertation, Duke University, 1996.

Brown, Dennis. *Vir Trilinguis: A Study in the Biblical Exegesis of Saint Jerome.* Kampen: Kok Pharos, 1992.

Brown, Peter. *Augustine of Hippo: A Biography.* Berkeley/Los Angeles: University of California Press, 1969.

———. *The Body and Society: Men, Women, and Sexual Renunciation in Early Christianity.* New York: Columbia University Press, 1988.

———. "The Diffusion of Manichaeism in the Roman Empire." *Journal of Roman Studies* 59 (1969): 92–103.

———. *Power and Persuasion in Late Antiquity: Towards a Christian Empire.* Madison: University of Wisconsin Press, 1992.

———. "The Rise and Function of the Holy Man in Late Antiquity." *Journal of Roman Studies* 61 (1971): 80–101.

———. "The Rise and Function of the Holy Man in Late Antiquity, 1971–1997." *Journal of Early Christian Studies* 6 (1998): 353–76.

———. "The Saint as Exemplar in Late Antiquity." In *Saints and Virtues.* Ed. John Stratton Hawley, 3–14. Comparative Studies in Religion and Society 2. Berkeley/Los Angeles/London: University of California Press, 1987.

Bruns, Gerald. "The Hermeneutics of Midrash." In *The Book and the Text: The Bible and Literary Theory.* Ed. Regina Schwartz, q.v., 189–213.

———. *Inventions: Writing, Textuality, and Understanding in Literary History.* New Haven, Conn./London: Yale University Press, 1982.

———. "The Problem of Figuration in Antiquity." In *Hermeneutics: Questions and Prospects.* Ed. Gary Shapiro and Alan Sica, q.v., 147–64.

Bultmann, Rudolph. "Ursprung und Sinn der Typologie als hermeneutischer Methode." *Theologische Literaturzeitung* 75 (1950): 205–12.

Burghardt, Walter. "On Early Christian Exegesis." *Theological Studies* 11 (1950): 78–116.

Burrus, Virginia. "Ascesis, Authority, and Text: The Acts of the Council of Saragossa." *Semeia* 58 (1992): 95–108.

———. *The Making of a Heretic: Gender, Authority, and the Priscillianist Controversy.* The Transformation of the Classical Heritage 24. Berkeley/Los Angeles/London: University of California Press, 1995.

Burton-Christie, Douglas. *The Word in the Desert: Scripture and the Quest for Holiness in Early Christian Monasticism.* New York/Oxford: Oxford University Press, 1993.

Cameron, Averil. *Christianity and the Rhetoric of Empire: The Development of Christian Discourse.* Berkeley/Los Angeles/Oxford: University of California Press, 1991.

Campenhausen, Hans von. *Die Asketische Heimatlosigkeit im Altkirchlichen und Frühmittelalterlichen Mönchtum.* Tübingen: J. C. B. Mohr (Paul Siebeck), 1930.

Castelli, Elizabeth A. *Imitating Paul: A Discourse of Power.* Louisville: Westminster/John Knox, 1991.

Certeau, Michel de. *The Practice of Everyday Life.* Trans. Steven Rendall. Berkeley/Los Angeles/London: University of California Press, 1984.

Chadwick, Henry. "The Bible and the Greek Fathers." In *The Church's Use of the Bible.* Ed. D. E. Nineham, q.v., 25–39.

———. "The Domestication of Gnosis." In *The Rediscovery of Gnosticism.* Ed. Bentley Layton, 3–16. Leiden: Brill, 1980.

Champagne, Roland A. "The Writer within the Intertext." In *Intertextuality. New Perspectives in Criticism.* Ed. Jeanine Plottel and Hanna Charney, q.v., 129–37.

Charity, A. C. *Events and Their Afterlife: The Dialectics of Christian Typology in the Bible and Dante.* Cambridge: Cambridge University Press, 1966.

Childs, Brevard S. "The Sensus Literalis of Scripture: An Ancient and Modern Problem." In *Beiträge zur alttestamentlichen Theologie: Festschrift für Walther Zimmerli zum 70. Geburtstag.* Ed. Herbert Donner, Robert Hanhart, and Rudolf Smend, 80–93. Göttingen: Vandenhoeck & Ruprecht, 1977.

Chitty, Derwas J. *The Desert a City: An Introduction to the Study of Egyptian and Palestinian Monasticism under the Christian Empire.* Crestwood, N.Y.: St. Vladimir's Seminary Press, 1966.

Clanchy, M. T. *From Memory to Written Record: England, 1066–1307.* Cambridge, Mass.: Harvard University Press, 1979.

Clark, Elizabeth A. " 'Adam's Only Companion': Augustine and the Early Christian Debate on Marriage." *Recherches Augustiniennes* 21 (1986): 139–62.

———. *Ascetic Piety and Women's Faith: Essays on Late Ancient Christianity.* Lewiston/Queenston: Edwin Mellen, 1986.

———. "Devil's Gateway and Bride of Christ: Women in the Early Christian World." In idem, *Ascetic Piety and Women's Faith: Essays on Late Ancient Christianity,* q.v., 23–60.

———. "Friendship Between the Sexes: Classical Theory and Christian Practice." In idem, *Jerome, Chrysostom, and Friends: Essays and Translations,* q.v., 35–106.

———. *Jerome, Chrysostom, and Friends: Essays and Translations.* New York: Edwin Mellen, 1979.

Clark, Elizabeth A. "John Chrysostom and the Subintroductae." *Church History* 46 (1977): 171–85. Reprinted in idem, *Ascetic Piety and Women's Faith*, q.v., 265–90.

———. "New Perspectives on the Origenist Controversy: Human Embodiment and Ascetic Strategies." *Church History* 59 (1990): 145–62.

———. *The Origenist Controversy: The Cultural Construction of an Early Christian Debate.* Princeton, N.J.: Princeton University Press, 1992.

———. "The Place of Jerome's *Commentary on Ephesians* in the Origenist Controversy: The Apokatastasis and Ascetic Ideals." *Vigiliae Christianae* 41 (1987): 154–71.

———. "Sexual Politics in the Writings of John Chrysostom." *Anglican Theological Review* 59 (1977): 3–20.

———. "The Uses of the Song of Songs: Origen and the Later Latin Fathers." In idem, *Ascetic Piety and Women's Faith: Essays on Late Ancient Christianity*, q.v., 386–427.

———. "The Virginal *Politeia* and Plato's *Republic*: John Chrysostom on Women and Sexual Relation." In idem, *Jerome, Chrysostom, and Friends: Essays and Translations*, q.v., 1–34.

Cohen, Jeremy. *"Be Fertile and Increase, Fill the Earth and Master It": The Ancient and Medieval Career of a Biblical Text.* Ithaca, N.Y./London: Cornell University Press, 1989.

Cooper, Kate. *The Virgin and the Bride: Idealized Womanhood in Late Antiquity.* Cambridge/London: Harvard University Press, 1996.

Corbett, Percy Ellwood. *The Roman Law of Marriage.* Oxford: Clarendon, 1930.

Countryman, L. William. *The Rich Christian in the Church of the Early Empire: Contradictions and Accommodations.* Texts and Studies in Religion 7. New York/Toronto: Edwin Mellen, 1980.

Coyle, J. Kevin. "The Cologne Mani Codex and Mani's Christian Connections." *Eglise et Théologie* 10 (1979): 179–93.

Crouzel, Henri. "La Distinction de la 'typologie' et de l''allégorie.' " *Bulletin de littérature écclésiastique* 65 (1964): 161–74.

———. *L'Eglise primitive face au divorce.* Théologie Historique 13. Paris: Beauschesne, 1971.

———. *Mariage et divorce, celibat et caractère sacerdotaux dans l'église ancienne: Etudes diverses.* Etudes d'Histoire du Culte et des Institutions Chrétiennes II. Torino: Bottega d'Erasmo, 1982.

———. *Origen: The Life and Thought of the First Great Theologian.* Trans. A. S. Worrall. San Francisco: Harper & Row, 1989. French original, 1985.

———. "Le Remariage après séparation pour adultère selon les Pères latins." In idem, *Mariage et divorce, celibat et caractère sacerdotaux dans l'église ancienne: Etudes diverses*, q.v., 143–58.

———. "Le Texte patristique de Matthieu V.32 et XIX.9." In idem, *Mariage et divorce, celibat et caractère sacerdotaux dans l'église ancienne: Etudes diverses*, q.v., 98–119.

Culler, Jonathan. *On Deconstruction: Theory and Criticism after Structuralism.* Ithaca, N.Y.: Cornell University Press, 1982.

Cunningham, Valentine. "Renoving That Bible: The Absolute Text of (Post) Modernism."In *The Theory of Reading*. Ed. Frank Gloversmith, 1–51. Sussex: Harvester; Totowa, N.J.: Barnes and Noble, 1984.

Dagron, Gilbert. *Vie et miracles de Sainte Thècle: Texte grec, traduction et commentaire*. Subsidia Hagiographica 62. Bruxelles: Société des Bollandists, 1978.

Dan, Joseph. "Midrash and the Dawn of Kabbalah." In *Midrash and Literature*. Ed. Geoffrey H. Hartman and Sanford Budick, q.v., 127–39.

Daniélou, Jean. *Sacramentum Futuri: Etudes sur les origines de la typologie biblique*. Etudes de théologie historique. Paris: Beauschesne, 1950.

Daube, David. "Alexandrian Methods of Interpretation and the Rabbis." In *Essays in Greco-Roman and Related Talmudic Literature*. Ed. Henry A. Fischel, 165–82. New York: Ktav, 1977.

———. "Rabbinic Methods of Interpretation and Hellenistic Rhetoric." *Hebrew Union College Annual* 22 (1949): 239–64.

Dawson, David. *Allegorical Readers and Cultural Revision in Ancient Alexandria*. New Haven, Conn./London: Yale University Press, 1992.

Deal, William E. "Towards a Politics of Asceticism." In *Asceticism*. Ed. Vincent L. Wimbush and Richard Valantasis, q.v., 424–42.

D'Ercole, Giuseppe. "Il consenso degli sposi e la perpetuità del matrimonio nel diritto romano e nei Padri della Chiesa." *Studia et documenta historiae et juris* 5 (1939): 18–75.

Deferrari, Roy. "St. Augustine's Method of Composing and Delivering Sermons." *American Journal of Philology* 43 (1922): 97–123.

Deming, Will. *Paul on Marriage and Celibacy: The Hellenistic Background of I Corinthians 7*. Cambridge: Cambridge University Press, 1995.

Derrida, Jacques. *Dissemination*. Chicago: University of Chicago Press, 1982.

———. "Living On: Border Lines." In *Deconstruction and Criticism*. Ed. Harold Bloom et al., 75–176. New York: Seabury/Continuum, 1979.

———. *Of Grammatology*. Trans. Gayatri Chakravorty Spivak. Baltimore/London: Johns Hopkins University Press, 1976. French original, 1967.

Dixon, Suzanne. *The Roman Family*. Baltimore/London: Johns Hopkins University Press, 1992.

Dooley, William Joseph. *Marriage According to St. Ambrose*. The Catholic University of America Press Studies in Christian Antiquity 11. Washington, D.C.: Catholic University of America Press, 1948.

Douglas, Mary. "Deciphering a Meal." In *Myth, Symbol, and Culture*. Ed. Clifford Geertz, 61–81. New York: W.. Norton, 1971.

———. *Natural Symbols*. New York: Vintage, 1973.

———. *Purity and Danger: An Analysis of Concepts of Pollution and Taboo*. New York/Washington, D.C.: Praeger, 1966.

Drijvers, Han. "Facts and Problems in Early Syriac-Speaking Christianity." *The Second Century* 2 (1982): 157–75.

Dumont, Louis. *Homo Hierarchicus: The Caste System and Its Implications*. 1st ed. Chicago: University of Chicago Press, 1970. French original, 1966. 2nd ed.: Chicago: University of Chicago Press, 1980.

Dupont, Jacques. *Mariage et divorce dans L'evangile: Matthieu 19, 3–12 et parallèles*. Bourges: Abbaye de Saint-André/Desclée de Brouwer, 1959.

Durkheim, Emile. *The Elementary Forms of the Religious Life: A Study in Religious Sociology.* Trans. J. W. Swain. London: George Allen & Unwin; New York: Macmillan, n.d.

Duval, Yves-Marie. "La Problématique de la *Lettre au Vièrges* d'Athanase." *Le Muséon* 88 (1975): 405–33.

Easterling, P. E. "Books and Readers in the Greek World: The Hellenistic and Imperial Periods." In *The Cambridge History of Classical Literature.* Vol. I, *Greek Literature.* Ed. P. E. Easterling and B. M. W. Knox, 1–41. Cambridge: Cambridge University Press, 1985.

Edwards, Catharine. *The Politics of Immorality in Ancient Rome.* Cambridge: Cambridge University Press, 1993.

Ehrman, Bart D. *The Orthodox Corruption of Scripture: The Effect of Early Christological Controversies on the Text of the New Testament.* New York/Oxford: Oxford University Press, 1993.

Elm, Susanna. *"Virgins of God": The Making of Asceticism in Late Antiquity.* Oxford: Clarendon, 1994.

Emmett, Alanna. "An Early Fourth Century Female Monastic Community in Egypt?" In *Maistor: Classical, Byzantine and Renaissance Studies for Robert Browning.* Ed. Ann Moffat, 77–83. Byzantina Australiensia 5. Canberra: The Australian Association for Byzantine Studies, 1984.

Esmein, A. *Le Mariage en droit canonique.* 3rd ed. Paris: Librairie du Recueil Sirey, 1929.

Evans-Grubbs, Judith. "Constantine and Imperial Legislation on the Family." In *The Theodosian Code: Studies in the Imperial Law of Late Antiquity.* Ed. Jill Harries and Ian Wood, 120–42. London: Duckworth, 1993.

———. *Law and Family in Late Antiquity: Constantine's Legislation on Marriage.* Oxford: Oxford University Press, 1995.

Fee, Gordon D. *The First Epistle to the Corinthians.* Grand Rapids: Eerdmans, 1987.

Fehrle, Eugen. *Die kultische Keuschheit im Altertum.* Giessen: Alfred Töpelmann, 1910.

Felman, Shoshana. "Turning the Screw of Interpretation." *Yale French Studies* 55–56 (1977): 94–207.

Fineman, Joel. "The Structure of Allegorical Desire." In *Allegory and Representation.* Ed. Stephen Greenblatt, q.v., 26–60.

Finnegan, Ruth. *Literacy and Orality: Studies in the Technology of Communication.* Oxford/New York: Basil Blackwell, 1988.

Fiorenza, Elisabeth Schüssler. "Rhetorical Situation and Historical Reconstruction in I Corinthians." *New Testament Studies* 33 (1987): 386–403.

Fish, Stanley. "Change." In idem, *Doing What Comes Naturally: Change, Rhetoric, and the Practice of Theory in Literary and Legal Studies,* 141–60. Durham, N.C.: Duke University Press, 1989.

———. "Is There a Text in This Class?" In idem, *Is There a Text in This Class? The Authority of Interpretive Communities,* 303–21. Cambridge, Mass./London: Harvard University Press, 1980.

Fishbane, Michael. *Biblical Interpretation in Ancient Israel.* Oxford: Clarendon, 1985.

———, ed. *The Midrashic Imagination: Jewish Exegesis, Thought, and History.* Albany: State University of New York Press, 1993.

Fisk, Bruce N. "*Porneuein* as Bodily Violation: The Unique Nature of Sexual Sin in I Corinthians 6:18." *New Testament Studies* 42 (1996): 540–58.

Flusin, Bernard. *Miracle et histoire dans l'oeuvre de Cyrille de Scythopolis.* Paris: Etudes Augustiniennes, 1983.

Fontaine, Jacques, and Charles Pietri, eds. *Le Monde latin antique et la Bible.* Bible de Tous le Temps 2. Paris: Beauschesne, 1985.

Foucault, Michel. *The Archaeology of Knowledge.* Trans. A. M. Sheridan Smith. New York: Pantheon, 1972. French original, 1969.

———. *The Care of the Self.* Trans. Robert Hurley. New York: Pantheon, 1986. French original, 1984.

———. "The Order of Discourse." Trans. Ian McLeod. In *Untying the Text: A Post-Structuralist Reader.* Ed. Robert Young, q.v., 48–78.

———. "What Is an Author?" In *Textual Strategies: Perspectives in Post-Structuralist Criticism.* Ed. Josué V. Harari, 141–60. Ithaca, N.Y.: Cornell University Press, 1979.

Fraade, Steven D. "Ascetical Aspects of Ancient Judaism." In *Jewish Spirituality I.* Ed. Arthur Green, 253–88. New York: Crossroad, 1986.

Frei, Hans. "The 'Literal Reading' of Biblical Narrative in the Christian Tradition: Does It Stretch or Will It Break?" In *The Bible and the Narrative Tradition.* Ed. Frank McConnell, 36–77. New York/Oxford: Oxford University Press, 1986.

Froehlich, Karlfried. *Biblical Interpretation in the Early Church.* Philadelphia: Fortress, 1984.

Frow, John. "Intertextuality and Ontology." In *Intertextuality: Theories and Practices.* Ed. Michael Worton and Judith Still, 45–55. Manchester/New York: Manchester University Press, 1990.

Frye, Northrop. *The Great Code: The Bible and Literature.* New York/London: Harcourt Brace Jovanovich, 1981.

Gamble, Harry. *Books and Readers in the Early Church: A History of Early Christian Texts.* New Haven, Conn./London: Yale University Press, 1995.

Gardner, Jane F. *Women in Roman Law and Society.* Bloomington/Indianapolis: Indiana University Press, 1991.

Gasparro, Giulia Sfameni. *Enkrateia e antropologia: le motivazioni protologiche della continenze e della verginità nel cristianesimo dei primi secoli e nello gnosticismo.* Studia Ephemeridis "Augustinianum" 20. Roma: Institutum Patristicum "Augustinianum," 1984.

Gaudemet, Jean. *Sociétés et mariage.* Strasbourg: Cerdic-Publications, 1980.

———. "Tendences nouvelles de la legislation familiale au IVe siècle." In *Transformation et conflits au IVe ap. J.-C.* Fédération Internationale des Etudes Classiques, 187–207. Antiquitas I, 29. Bonn: Rudolph Habelt Verlag, 1978.

Gertner, M. "Midrashim in the New Testament." *Journal of Semitic Studies* 7 (1962): 267–92.

Goehring, James E. "Asceticism." In *Encyclopedia of Early Christianity.* I:127–30. Ed. Everett Ferguson. 2nd ed. New York/London: Garland, 1997.

———. "The Encroaching Desert: Literary Production and Ascetic Space in Early Egyptian Christianity." *Journal of Early Christian Studies* 1 (1993): 281–96.

Goehring, James E. "Monastic Diversity and Ideological Boundaries in Fourth-Century Christian Egypt." *Journal of Early Christian Studies* 5 (1997): 61–84.

———. "New Frontiers in Pachomian Studies." In *The Roots of Egyptian Christianity.* Ed. B. A. Pearson and J. E. Goehring, 236–57. Philadelphia: Fortress, 1986.

———. "The Origins of Monasticism." In *Eusebius, Christianity, and Judaism.* Ed. Harold W. Attridge and Gohei Hata, 235–55. Detroit: Wayne State University Press, 1992.

———. "Through a Glass Darkly: Diverse Images of the APOTAKTIKOI (AI) of Early Egyptian Monasticism." *Semeia* 58 (1992): 25–45.

———. "Withdrawing from the Desert: Pachomius and the Development of Village Monasticism." *Harvard Theological Review* 89 (1996): 267–85.

———. "The World Engaged: The Social and Economic World of Egyptian Monasticism." In *Gnosticism and the Early Christian World.* Ed. James E. Goehring et al., 134–44. Sonoma, Calif.: Polebridge, 1990.

Gögler, Rolf. *Zur Theologie des biblischen Wortes bei Origenes.* Dusseldorf: Patmos-Verlag, 1963.

Gold, Barbara K., ed. *Literary and Artistic Patronage in Ancient Rome.* Austin: University of Texas Press, 1982.

Goody, Jack. *The Interface Between the Written and the Oral.* Cambridge: Cambridge University Press, 1987.

———. *The Logic of Writing and the Organization of Society.* Cambridge: Cambridge University Press, 1986.

Gorce, Denys. *La Lectio divina des origines du cénobitisme à Saint Benoit et Casiodore. T. I: Saint Jérôme et la lecture sacrée dans le milieu ascétique romain.* Wépion-sur-Meuse: Monastère du Mont-Vierge; Paris: Librairie Auguste Picard, 1925.

Gougaud, L. "Les Critiques formulées contre les premiers moines d'Occident." *Revue Mabillon* 24 (1934): 145–63.

Gould, Graham. *The Desert Fathers on Monastic Community.* Oxford: Clarendon, 1993.

———. "The Influence of Origen on Fourth-Century Monasticism: Some Further Remarks." In *Origeniana Sexta: Origène et la Bible/Origen and the Bible.* Ed. Gilles Dorival, Alain Le Boulluec et al., 591–98. Actes du Colloquium Origenianum Sextum Chantilly, 30 août–3 septembre 1993. Leuven: University Press/Uitgeverij Peeters, 1995.

Grant, Robert M. *The Letter and the Spirit.* London: SPCK, 1957.

———. *A Short History of the Interpretation of the Bible.* Rev. ed. New York: Macmillan, 1963.

Greenblatt, Stephen J., ed. *Allegory and Representation.* Selected Papers from the English Institute, 1979–80. New Series 5. Baltimore/London: Johns Hopkins University Press, 1981.

Gregg, Robert C., and Dennis E. Groh. *Early Arianism: A View of Salvation.* Philadelphia: Fortress, 1981.

Gribomont, Jean. "Eustathe de Sébaste." In idem, *Saint Basile: Évangile et église. Mélanges.* I:95–106. Spiritualité orientale 36. Bégrolles-en-Mauges: Abbey de Bellefontaine, 1984.

———. "Le Monachisme au sein de l'église en Syrie et en Cappadoce." *Studia Monastica* 7 (1965): 7–24.

Griffith, Sidney H. "Asceticism in the Church of Syria: The Hermeneutics of Early Syrian Monasticism." In *Asceticism*. Ed. Vincent L. Wimbush and Richard Valantasis, q.v., 220–45.

———. "Singles in God's Service: Thoughts on the Ihidaye from the Works of Aphrat and Ephrem the Syrian." *The Harp* 4 (1991): 145–59.

Gruenwald, Ithamar. "Midrash and the 'Midrashic Condition': Preliminary Considerations." In *The Midrashic Imagination: Jewish Exegesis, Thought, and History.* Ed. Michael Fishbane, q.v., 6–22.

Guillaumont, Antoine. "Perspectives actuelles sur les origines du monachisme." In idem, *Aux Origines du monachisme chrétien*, 215–27. Spiritualité orientale 30. Bégrolles-en-Mauges, Abbaye de Bellefontaine, 1979.

Guillet, Jacques. "Les Exégèses d'Alexandrie et d'Antioche: Conflit ou malentendu?" *Recherches de science religieuse* 34 (1947): 257–302.

Gundry-Volf, Judith. "Celibate Pneumatics and Social Power: On the Motivations for Sexual Asceticism at Corinth." *Union Seminary Quarterly Review* 48 (1994): 105–26.

Hadot, Pierre. *Philosophy as a Way of Life: Spiritual Exercises from Socrates to Foucault.* Ed. A. I. Davidson; trans. M. Chase. Oxford: Blackwell, 1995. French 2nd ed., 1987.

Hagendahl, Harald. "Die Bedeutung der Stenographie für die spätlateinische christliche Literatur." *Jahrbuch für Antike und Christentum* 14 (1971): 24–38.

———. *Latin Fathers and the Classics. A Study on the Apologists, Jerome, and Other Christian Writers.* Studia Graeca et Latina Gothoburgensia 6. Göteborg: Elanders Boktr. Aktiebolag, 1958.

Haines-Eitzen, Kim. "Hearing and Reading: Literacy and Power in the Early Christian Church." Unpublished M.A. thesis, University of North Carolina–Chapel Hill, 1993.

Halivni, David Weiss. *Midrash, Mishnah, and Gemara: The Jewish Predilection for Justified Law.* Cambridge/London: Harvard University Press, 1986.

Halperin, David J. *The Faces of the Chariot: Early Jewish Responses to Ezekiel's Vision.* Texte und Studien zum Antiken Judentum 16. Tübingen: J. C. B. Mohr (Paul Siebeck), 1988.

Hamman, Adalbert G. "Les Origines du mônachisme chrétien au cours de deux premiers siècles." In *Homo Spiritalis: Festgabe für Luc Verheijen.* Ed. Cornelius Mayer and Karl Heinz Chelius, 311–26. Würzburg: Augustinus-Verlag, 1987.

Handelman, Susan A. "Freud's Midrash." In *Intertextuality.* Ed. Jeanine P. Plottel and Hanna Charney, q.v., 99–112.

———. "Jacques Derrida and the Heretic Hermeneutic." In *Displacement: Derrida and After.* Ed. Mark Krupnik, 98–129. Bloomington: Indiana University Press, 1983.

———. *The Slayers of Moses: The Emergence of Rabbinic Interpretation in Modern Literary Theory.* Albany: State University of New York Press, 1988.

Hanson, Ann Ellis. "Ancient Illiteracy." In *Literacy in the Roman World.* Ed. Mary Beard et al., q.v., 159–97.

Hanson, R. P. C. *Allegory and Event: A Study of the Sources and Significance of Origen's Interpretation of Scripture.* Richmond: John Knox; London: SCM, 1959.

———. "Biblical Exegesis in the Early Church." In *The Cambridge History of the Bible.* Vol. I, *From the Beginnings to Jerome.* Ed. P. R. Ackroyd and C. F. Evans, q.v., 412–53.

Harnack, Adolph von. *Bible Reading in the Early Church.* Trans. J. R. Wilkinson. Crown Theological Library 36. London: Williams & Norgate; New York: G. P. Putnam, 1912.

———. *Outlines of the History of Dogma.* Trans. E. K. Mitchell. Boston: Beacon, 1957. German original, 1889.

Harpham, Geoffrey Galt. *The Ascetic Imperative in Culture and Criticism.* Chicago/London: University of Chicago Press, 1987.

———. "Asceticism and the Compensations of Art." In *Asceticism.* Ed. Vincent L. Wimbush and Richard Valantasis, q.v., 357–68.

Harris, William V. *Ancient Literacy.* Cambridge, Mass./London: Harvard University Press, 1989.

Harrison, Verna E. F. "Allegory and Asceticism in Gregory of Nyssa." *Semeia* 57 (1992): 113–30.

Hartman, Geoffrey H., and Sanford Budick, eds. *Midrash and Literature.* New Haven, Conn./London: Yale University Press, 1986.

Hegel, G. W. F. *Philosophy of Religion.* Trans. E. B. Speirs and J. Burdon Sanderson from the 2nd German edition. London: Routledge & Kegan Paul, 1962 [1895]. German original, 1832.

Heinemann, Joseph. "Profile of a Midrash: The Art of Composition in Leviticus Rabba." *Journal of the American Academy of Religion* 39 (1971): 141–50.

Henrichs, Albert. "The Cologne Mani Codex Reconsidered." *Harvard Studies in Classical Philology* 83 (1979): 339–67.

Héring, Jean. *The First Epistle of Saint Paul to the Corinthians.* Trans. A. W. Heathcote and P. J. Allcock from the 2nd French edition. London: Epworth, 1962.

Herman, Jozsef. "Spoken and Written Latin in the Last Centuries of the Roman Empire: A Contribution to the Linguistic History of the Western Provinces." In *Latin and the Romance Languages in the Early Middle Ages.* Ed. Roger Wright, 29–43. University Park: Pennsylvania State University Press, 1996.

Hernadi, Paul, ed. *The Rhetoric of Interpretation and the Interpretation of Rhetoric.* Durham, N.C.: Duke University Press, 1989.

Hirschfeld, Yizhar. *The Judean Desert Monasteries in the Byzantine Period.* New Haven, Conn./London: Yale University Press, 1992.

———. "The Life of Chariton: In Light of Archaeological Research." In *Ascetic Behavior in Greco-Roman Antiquity.* Ed. Vincent Wimbush, q.v., 425–47.

Hirshman, Marc. *A Rivalry of Genius: Jewish and Christian Biblical Interpretation in Late Antiquity.* Trans. Batya Stein. Albany: State University of New York Press, 1996.

Holl, Karl. "Die Schriftstellerische Form des griechischen Heiligenlebens." *Neue Jahrbücher für das Klassische Altertums* 29 (1912): 406–27.

Holquist, Michael. "The Politics of Representation." In *Allegory and Representation.* Ed. Stephen J. Greenblatt, q.v., 163–83.

Hopkins, Keith. "Conquest by Book." In *Literacy in the Roman World*. Ed. Mary Beard et al., q.v., 133–58.

Horbury, William. "Jews and Christians on the Bible: Demarcation and Convergence (325–451)." In *Christliche Exegese zwischen Nicaea und Chalcedon*. Ed. J. van Oort and U. Wickert, 72–103. Kampen: Kok Pharos, 1992.

Horsfall, Nicholas. "Statistics or State of Mind?" In *Literacy in the Roman World*. Ed. Mary Beard et al., q.v., 59–76.

Huber, Josef. *Der Ehekonsens im Römischen Recht: Studien zu seinem Begriffsgehalt in der Klassik und zur Frage seines Wandels in der Nachklassik*. Analecta Gregoriana 204. Roma: Università Gregoriana Editrice, 1977.

Humbert, Michel. *Le Remariage à Rome: Etude d'histoire juridique et sociale*. Milano: Dott. A. Guiffrè Editore, 1972.

Hunter, David G. "The Paradise of Patriarchy: Ambrosiaster on Woman as (Not) God's Image." *Journal of Theological Studies*, n.s. 43 (1992): 447–69.

———. "Resistance to the Virginal Ideal in Late-Fourth-Century Rome: The Case of Jovinian." *Theological Studies* 48 (1987): 45–64.

Hurd, John C., Jr. *The Origins of I Corinthians*. New York: Seabury, 1965.

Irvine, Martin. *The Making of Textual Culture: 'Grammatica' and Literary Theory, 350–1100*. Cambridge: Cambridge University Press, 1994.

Isaksson, Abel. *Marriage and Ministry in the New Temple. A Study with Special Reference to Mt. 19:3–12 and I Cor. 11:3–16*. Acta Seminarii Neotestamentici Upsaliensis 24. Lund: C. W. K. Gleerup; Copenhagen: Ejnar Munksgaard, 1965.

Jameson, Fredric. "Metacommentary." In idem, *The Ideologies of Theory: Essays 1971–1986*. Vol. 1, *Situations of Theory*, 3–16. Theory and History of Literature 48. Minneapolis: University of Minnesota Press, 1988. Originally in *PMLA* 86, 1 (1971): 9–18.

———. *The Political Unconscious: Narrative as a Socially Symbolic Act*. Ithaca, N.Y.: Cornell University Press, 1981.

———. *The Prison-House of Language: A Critical Account of Structuralism and Russian Formalism*. Princeton, N.J.: Princeton University Press, 1972.

Jobling, David, Peggy L. Day, and Gerald T. Sheppard, eds. *The Bible and the Politics of Exegesis: Essays in Honor of Norman K. Gottwald on His Sixty-Fifth Birthday*. Cleveland: Pilgrim, 1991.

Jones, A. H. M. *The Later Roman Empire 284–602*. Oxford: Basil Blackwell, 1964.

Jorion, Paul. "Emic and Etic. Two Anthropological Ways of Spilling Ink." *Cambridge Anthropology* 8 (1983): 41–68.

Judge, E. A. "The Earliest Use of Monachos for 'Monk' (P. Coll. Youtie 77) and the Origins of Monasticism." *Jahrbuch für Antike und Christentum* 20 (1977): 72–89.

Junod, Eric. "La Virginité de l'apôtre Jean: Recherche sur les origines scriptuaires et patristique de cette tradition." In *Lectures anciennes de la Bible*, 113–36. Cahiers de Biblia Patristica 1. Strasbourg: Centre d'Analyse et de Documentation Patristiques, 1987.

Kaelber, Walter O. "Asceticism." In *The Encyclopedia of Religion*. I:441–45. Ed. Mircea Eliade. New York: Macmillan; London: Collier Macmillan, 1987.

Kannengiesser, Charles, and William L. Petersen, eds. *Origen of Alexandria: His World and His Legacy.* Christianity and Judaism in Antiquity 1. Notre Dame, Ind.: University of Notre Dame Press, 1988.

Kaster, Robert A. *Guardians of Language.* The Transformation of the Classical Heritage 11. Berkeley/Los Angeles/London: University of California Press, 1988.

Kelly, J. N. D. *Jerome: His Life, Writings, and Controversies.* New York: Harper & Row, 1975.

Kennedy, George A. *Classical Rhetoric and Its Christian and Secular Tradition from Ancient to Modern Times.* Chapel Hill: University of North Carolina Press, 1980.

———. *Greek Rhetoric Under Christian Emperors: A History of Rhetoric. Vol. 3.* Princeton, N.J.: Princeton University Press, 1983.

Kenney, E. J. "Books and Readers in the Roman World." In *The Cambridge History of Classical Literature.* Vol. II, *Latin Literature.* Ed. E. J. Kenney and W. V. Clausen, 3–32. Cambridge: Cambridge University Press, 1982.

Kenyon, Frederic G. *Books and Readers in Ancient Greece and Rome.* Oxford: Clarendon, 1932.

Kimelman, Reuven. "Rabbi Yohanan and Origen on the Song of Songs: A Third-Century Jewish-Christian Disputation." *Harvard Theological Review* 73 (1980): 567–95.

Koenen, Ludwig. "Manichäische Mission und Klöster in Ägypten." In *Das Römisch-Byzantische Agypten (Akten des internationalen Symposions 26–30 September 1978, Trier.* II:93–108. Mainz am Rhein: Verlag Philipp von Zabern, 1983.

Kort, Wesley A. *"Take, Read": Scripture, Textuality, and Cultural Practice.* University Park: Pennsylvania State University Press, 1996.

Koschorke, Klaus. *Die Polemik der Gnostiker gegen das kirchliche Christentum.* Leiden: Brill, 1978.

Kristeva, Julia. "Reading the Bible." In idem, *New Maladies of the Soul,* 115–26. Trans. Ross Guberman. New York: Columbia University Press, 1995.

———. "Word, Dialogue and Novel." In idem, *Desire in Language: A Semiotic Approach to Literature and Art.* Ed. Leon S. Roudiez; trans. Thomas Gora et al., 64–91. New York: Columbia University Press, 1980. French original in Julia Kristeva, *Sêmeiôtikê,* 143–73. Paris: Seuil, 1969.

Kugel, James L. *In Potiphar's House: The Interpretive Life of Biblical Texts.* San Francisco: HarperSanFrancisco, 1990.

———. "Two Introductions to Midrash." *Prooftexts* 3 (1983): 131–55.

Kuiters, R. "Saint Augustin et l'indissolubilité du mariage." *Augustiniana* 9 (1959): 5–11.

Kunkel, W. "Matrimonium." *Realencyclopädie der classischen Altertumswissenschaft* 14, 2 (1930): 2259–86.

Ladomérszky, Nicolas. *Saint Augustin, docteur de mariage chrétien. Etude dogmatique sur les biens du mariage.* Roma: Officium Libri Catholici, 1942.

Lampe, G. W. H. "The Reasonableness of Typology." In *Essays on Typology.* Ed. G. W. H. Lampe and K. J. Woollcombe, 9–38. London: SCM, 1957.

Lange, N. R. M., de. *Origen and the Jews: Studies in Jewish-Christian Relations in Third-Century Palestine.* Cambridge: Cambridge University Press, 1976.

Lauterbach, Jacob. "Midrash and Mishnah: A Study in the Early History of the Halakah." *Jewish Quarterly Review* 5 (1914–15): 503–27; 6 (1915–16): 23–95, 303–23.

Lawless, George. *Augustine of Hippo and His Monastic Rule.* Oxford: Clarendon, 1987.

Legrand, Lucien. *La Virginité dans la Bible.* Lectio Divina 39. Paris: Les Editions du Cerf, 1964.

LePelley, Claude. *Les Cités de l'Afrique romaine au Bas Empire*, t. I. Paris: Etudes Augustiniennes, 1979.

Lieberman, Saul. "Rabbinic Interpretation of Scripture." In idem, *Hellenism in Jewish Palestine: Studies in the Literary Transmission, Beliefs and Manners of Palestine in the I Century B.C.E.–IV Century C.E.*, 47–82. Texts and Studies of the Jewish Theological Seminary of America 18. New York: Jewish Theological Seminary of America, 1962.

Lieu, Samuel N. C. *Manichaeism in the Later Roman Empire and Medieval China: A Historical Survey.* Manchester: Manchester University Press, 1985.

———. "Precept and Practice in Manichaean Monasticism." *Journal of Theological Studies*, n.s. 32 (1981): 153–73.

———. "Some Themes in Later Roman Anti-Manichaean Polemics: I." *Bulletin of the John Rylands Library of Manchester* 68 (1986): 434–72.

Lim, Richard. *Public Disputation, Power, and Social Order in Late Antiquity.* The Transformation of the Classical Heritage 23. Berkeley/Los Angeles/London: University of California Press, 1995.

Lizzi, Rita. "Ascetismo e monachesimo nell' Italia tardoantica." *Codex Aquilarensis* 5 (1991): 55–76.

———. "Una socièta esortata all' ascetismo: misure legislative e motivazioni economiche nel IV-V secolo D.C." *Studi Storici* 30 (1989): 129–53.

Loewe, Raphael. "The 'Plain' Meaning of Scripture in Early Jewish Exegesis." *Papers of the Institute of Jewish Studies London I.* Jerusalem: Magnes, 1964.

Louth, Andrew. *Discerning the Mystery: An Essay on the Nature of Theology.* Oxford: Clarendon, 1983.

Lubac, Henri de. *Exégèse médiévale: Les quatre sens de l'Ecriture.* Théologie 41. Paris: Aubier, 1959.

———. " 'Sens spirituel'." *Recherches de science religieuse* 36 (1949): 542–76.

———. " 'Typologie' et 'allégorisme.' " *Recherches de science religieuse* 34 (1947): 180–226.

MacDonald, Dennis R. *The Legend and the Apostle: The Battle for Paul in Story and Canon.* Philadelphia: Westminster, 1983.

———. *There Is No Male and Female: The Fate of a Dominical Saying in Paul and Gnosticism.* Harvard Dissertations in Religion 20. Philadelphia: Fortress, 1987.

MacDonald, Margaret Y. "Women Holy in Body and Spirit: The Social Setting of I Corinthians 7." *New Testament Studies* 36 (1990): 161–81.

Madsen, Deborah L. *Rereading Allegory: A Narrative Approach to Genre.* New York: St. Martin's, 1994.

Malone, Edward. *The Monk and the Martyr: The Monk as the Successor of the Martyr.* Studies in Christian Antiquity 12. Washington, D.C.: Catholic University Press, 1950.

Margerie, Bertrand de. *Introduction à l'histoire de l'exégèse.* Vol. I, *Les Pères grecs et orientaux.* Paris: Les Editions du Cerf, 1980.

Markgraf, B. "Clemens von Alexandrien als asketischer Schriftsteller in seiner Stellung zu den natürlichen Lebensgütern." *Zeitschrift für Kirchengeschichte* 22 (1901): 487–515.

Markus, Robert. *The End of Ancient Christianity.* Cambridge: Cambridge University Press, 1990.

Martin, Dale B. *The Corinthian Body.* New Haven, Conn./London: Yale University Press, 1995.

———. "Heterosexism and the Interpretation of Romans 1:18–32." *Biblical Interpretation* 3 (1995): 332–55.

———. "Paul without Passion: On Paul's Rejection of Desire in Sex and Marriage." In *Constructing Early Christian Families: Family as Social Reality and Metaphor.* Ed. Halvor Moxnes, 201–15. London/New York: Routledge, 1997.

Martindale, Charles. *Redeeming the Text: Latin Poetry and the Hermeneutics of Reception.* Cambridge: Cambridge University Press, 1993.

McKitterick, Rosamund. "Women and Literacy in the Early Middle Ages." In idem, *Books, Scribes and Learning in the Frankish Kingdoms, 6th–9th Centuries,* 1–43. Aldershot, U.K.: Variorum, 1994.

McLynn, Neil B. *Ambrose of Milan: Church and Court in a Christian Capital.* The Transformation of the Classical Heritage 22. Berkeley/Los Angeles/London: University of California Press, 1994.

Meeks, Wayne A. "The Image of the Androgyne: Some Uses of a Symbol in Earliest Christianity." *History of Religions* 13 (1974): 165–208.

Meershoek, G. Q. A. *Le Latin biblique d'après Saint Jérôme: Aspects linguistiques de la rencontre entre la Bible et le monde classique.* Latinitas Christianorum Primeva 20. Nijmegen/Utrecht: Dekker & Van de Vegt, 1966.

Merkelbach, Reinhold. "Manichaica (1–3)." *Zeitschrift für Papyrologie und Epigraphik* 56 (1984): 45–53.

Micaeli, Claudio. "L'influsso di Tertulliano su Girolamo: le opere sul matrimonio e le seconde nozze." *Augustinianum* 19 (1979): 415–29.

Miller, Patricia Cox. "The Blazing Body: Ascetic Desire in Jerome's Letter to Eustochium." *Journal of Early Christian Studies* 1 (1993): 21–45.

Mitchell, Margaret M. *Paul and the Rhetoric of Reconciliation: An Exegetical Investigation of the Language and Composition of I Corinthians.* Tübingen: J. C. B. Mohr (Paul Siebeck), 1991.

Mitchell, W. J. T., ed. *The Politics of Interpretation.* Chicago/London: University of Chicago Press, 1983.

Mohrmann, Christine. "Mulier. A propos de II Reg. 1, 26." *Vigiliae Christianae* 2 (1948): 117–19.

———. "Saint Augustin écrivain." *Recherches Augustiniennes* 1 (1958): 43–66.

Morard, Françoise-E. "Monachos, moine: Histoire du terme grec jusqua' au 4e siècle." *Freiburger Zeitschrift für Philosophie und Theologie* 19 (1972): 332–411.

Mowitt, John. *Text: The Genealogy of an Antidisciplinary Object.* Durham, N.C.: Duke University Press, 1992.

Moxnes, Halvor, ed. *Constructing Early Christian Families: Family as Social Reality and Metaphor.* London/New York: Routledge, 1997.

Nautin, Pierre. "Divorce et remariage dans la tradition de l'église latine." *Recherches de science religieuse* 62 (1974): 9–46.

Neusner, Jacob. *Midrash as Literature: The Primacy of Documentary Discourse.* Lanham, Md./New York/London: University Press of America, 1987.

Nineham, D. E. *The Church's Use of the Bible, Past and Present.* London: SPCK, 1963.

North, Helen. *Sophrosyne: Self-Knowledge and Self-Restraint in Greek Literature.* Cornell Studies in Classical Philology 35. Ithaca, N.Y.: Cornell University Press, 1966.

Oberhelman, Steven M. *Rhetoric and Homiletics in Fourth-Century Christian Literature: Prose Rhythm, Oratorical Style, and Preaching in the Works of Ambrose, Jerome, and Augustine.* American Philological Association American Classical Studies 26. Atlanta: Scholars, 1991.

O'Keefe, John J. "Christianizing Malachi: Fifth-Century Insights from Cyril of Alexandria." *Vigiliae Christianae* 50 (1996): 136–58.

———. "Impassible Suffering? Divine Passion and Fifth-Century Christology." *Theological Studies* 58 (1997): 39–60.

Olson, David R., and Nancy Torrance, eds. *Literacy and Orality.* Cambridge: Cambridge University Press, 1991.

Ong, Walter J. *Orality and Literacy: The Technologizing of the Word.* London/New York: Routledge, 1982.

Oppel, John. "Saint Jerome and the History of Sex." *Viator* 24 (1993): 1–22.

Orestano, Riccardo. "Alcune considerazioni sui rapporti fra matrimonio cristiano e matrimonio romano nell' età postclassica." In *Scritti di diritto romano in honore di Contardo Ferrini.* Ed. Gian Gualberto Archi, 121–37, 345–82. Milano: Ulrico Hoepli, 1946.

———. *La struttura giuridica del matrimonio romano dal diritto classico al diritto giustinianeo.* Milano: Antonio Giuffrè, 1951.

Orlandi, Tito. "Giustificazioni dell' encratismo nel testi monastici copti del IV–V secolo." In *La tradizione dell' enkrateia: Motivazione ontologiche e protologiche.* Ed. Ugo Bianchi, q.v., 342–63.

Osiek, Carolyn. "The Widow as Altar: The Rise and Fall of a Symbol." *The Second Century* 3 (1983): 159–69.

Parker, Robert. *Miasma: Pollution and Purification in Early Greek Religion.* Oxford: Clarendon, 1983.

Patte, Daniel. *Early Jewish Hermeneutic in Palestine.* SBL Dissertation Series 22. Missoula, Mont.: Scholars, 1975.

Patterson, Lee. *Negotiating the Past: The Historical Understanding of Medieval Literature.* Madison: University of Wisconsin Press, 1975.

Pearson, Birger A. "Biblical Exegesis in Gnostic Literature." In idem, *Gnosticism, Judaism, and Egyptian Christianity,* q.v., 29–38.

———. *Gnosticism, Judaism, and Egyptian Christianity.* Minneapolis: Fortress, 1990.

———. "Jewish Elements in Gnosticism and the Development of Gnostic Self-Definition." In idem, *Gnosticism, Judaism, and Egyptian Christianity,* q.v., 124–35.

Pépin, Jean. *Mythe et allégorie. Les origines grecques et les contestations judéo-chrétiennes.* 2nd ed. Paris: Etudes Augustiniennes, 1976. 1st ed., 1958.

Pereira, Bernard Alves. *La Doctrine du mariage selon Saint Augustine.* Paris: Etudes Augustiniennes, 1983.

Petrucci, Armando. *Public Lettering: Script, Power, and Culture.* Trans. Linda Lappin. Chicago/London: University of Chicago Press, 1993. Original Italian edition, 1980.

Phipps, W. E. "Is Paul's Attitude towards Sexual Relations Contained in I Cor. 7:1?" *New Testament Studies* 28 (1982): 125–31.

Pizzolato, Luigi Franco. *La dottrina esegetica de sant' Ambrogio.* Studia Patristica Mediolanensia 9. Milano: Università Cattolica del Sacro Cuore, 1978.

Plottel, Jeanine P., and Hanna Charney, eds. *Intertextuality. New Perspectives in Criticism.* New York: Literary Forum 2, 1978.

Pocock, J. G. A. "Texts as Events: Reflections on the History of Political Thought." In *Politics of Discourse: The Literature and History of Seventeenth Century England.* Ed. Kevin Sharpe and Steven N. Zwicker, 21–34. Berkeley/Los Angeles/London: University of California Press, 1987.

Poirier, John C., and Joseph Francovic. "Celibacy and Charism in I Cor. 7:5–7." *Harvard Theological Review* 89 (1996): 1–18.

Preus, James Samuel. *From Shadow to Promise: Old Testament Interpretation from Augustine to the Young Luther.* Cambridge, Mass.: Harvard University Press, 1969.

Quasten, Johannes. *Patrology.* Vols. I–III. Utrecht/Antwerp: Spectrum, 1953–60.

Quispel, Gilles. "The Study of Encratism: A Historical Survey." In *La tradizione dell' enkrateia: Motivazione ontologiche e protologiche.* Ed. Ugo Bianchi, q.v., 35–81.

Rabinowitz, Peter. *Before Reading: Narrative Conventions and the Politics of Interpretation.* Ithaca, N.Y./London: Cornell University Press, 1987.

Rackett, Michael. "Sexuality and Sinlessness: The Diversity of Pelagian Theologies of Marriage and Virginity." Ph.D. dissertation, Duke University, forthcoming, 1999.

Rajan, Tilottama. "Intertextuality and the Subject of Reading/Writing." In *Influence and Intertextuality in Literary History.* Ed. Jay Clayton and Eric Rothstein, 61–74. Madison: University of Wisconsin Press, 1991.

Rawson, Beryl, ed. *Marriage, Divorce and Children in Ancient Rome.* Oxford: Clarendon, 1991.

Rebenich, Stefan. *Hieronymus und sein Kreis. Prosopographie und socialgeschichtliche Untersuchungen.* Historia 72. Stuttgart: Franz Steiner Verlag, 1992.

Reitzenstein, Richard. *Des Athanasius Werk über das Leben des Antonius.* Sitzungsberichte der Heidelberger Akademie des Wissenschaften, Philosophisch-Historische Klasse 5, 1914.

Reynolds, L. D., and N. G. Wilson. *Scribes and Scholars: A Guide to the Transmission of Greek and Latin Literature.* 3rd ed. Oxford: Clarendon, 1991. 1st ed., 1968.

Ricoeur, Paul. "Epilogue: The 'Sacred' Text and the Community." In *The Critical Study of Sacred Texts*. Ed. Wendy Doniger O'Flaherty, 271–76. Berkeley, Calif.: Graduate Theological Union, 1979.

Riffaterre, Michael. *Text Production*. Trans. Terese Lyons. New York: Columbia University Press, 1983. French original, 1979.

Roberts, Colin H. *Manuscript, Society and Belief in Early Christian Egypt*. London: Oxford University Press, 1979.

Robinson, James M. "The Pachomian Monastic Library at the Chester Beatty Library and the Bibliothèque Bodmer." *Occasional Papers* 15. Claremont, Calif.: Institute for Antiquity and Christianity, 1990.

Rosen, Stanley. *Hermeneutics as Politics*. New York/Oxford: Oxford University Press, 1987.

Rousseau, Philip. *Ascetics, Authority, and the Church in the Age of Jerome and Cassian*. Oxford: Oxford University Press, 1978.

———. *Basil of Caesarea*. Berkeley/Los Angeles/Oxford: University of California Press, 1994.

———. "The Structure and Spirit of the Ascetic Life." Unpublished typescript.

Rousselle, Aline. "Aspects sociaux du recrutement ecclésiastique au IVe siècle." *Mélanges d'archéologie et histoire de l'Ecole Française de Rome* 89 (1977): 333–70.

Rouwhorst, G. A. M. "Das Manichaeische Bemafest und das Passafest der Syrischen Christen." *Vigiliae Christianae* 35 (1981): 397–411.

Rubenson, Samuel. *The Letters of St. Antony: Origenist Theology, Monastic Tradition and the Making of a Saint*. Lund: Lund University Press, 1990.

Said, Edward. "The Problem of Textuality: Two Exemplary Positions." *Critical Inquiry* 4 (1978): 673–714.

———. "The Text, the World, and the Critic." In *Textual Strategies: Perspectives in Post-Structuralist Criticism*. Ed. Josué V. Harari, 161–88. Ithaca, N.Y.: Cornell University Press, 1979.

———. *The World, the Text, and the Critic*. London/Boston: Faber and Faber, 1983.

Säve-Söderbergh, Torgny. "Holy Scriptures or Apologetic Documentations? The 'Sitz im Leben' of the Nag Hammadi Library." In *Les Textes de Nag Hammadi*. Ed. Jacques-E. Ménard, 3–14. Leiden: Brill, 1975.

Saxer, Victor. *Bible et hagiographie. Textes et thèmes bibliques dans les Actes des martyrs authentiques des premiers siècles*. Berne: Peter Lang, 1986.

Schäublin, Christoph. *Untersuchungen zu Methode und Herkunft der Antiochenischen Exegese*. Theophaneia 23. Köln/Bonn: Peter Hanstein Verlag, 1974.

Schmitt, Emile. *Le Mariage chrétien dans l'oeuvre de Saint Augustin. Une théologie baptismale de la vie conjugale*. Paris: Etudes Augustiniennes, 1983.

Scholes, Robert. *Protocols of Reading*. New Haven, Conn./London: Yale University Press, 1989.

———. *Textual Power: Literary Theory and the Teaching of English*. New Haven, Conn./London: Yale University Press, 1985.

Scholten, Clemons. "Die Nag-Hammadi-Texte als Buchbesitz der Pachomianer." *Jahrbuch für Antike und Christentum* 31 (1988): 144–72.

Schultzen, Fr. "Die Benutzung der Schriften Tertullians *de monogamia* und *de ieiunio* bei Hieronymus *adv. Iovinianum.*" *Neue Jahrbücher für deutsche Theologie* 3, 1 (1894): 487–502.

Schwartz, Regina, ed. *The Book and the Text: The Bible and Literary Theory.* Cambridge/Oxford: Basil Blackwell, 1990.

Shapiro, Gary, and Alan Sica. *Hermeneutics: Questions and Prospects.* Amherst: University of Massachusetts Press, 1984.

Shapiro, Michael J. *The Politics of Representation: Writing Practices in Biography, Photography, and Political Analysis.* Madison: University of Wisconsin Press, 1988.

Shaw, Brent D. "The Family in Late Antiquity: The Experience of Augustine." *Past & Present* 115 (1987): 3–51.

Simon, Marcel. "L'Ascéticisme dans les sectes juives." In *La tradizione dell' enkrateia: Motivazione ontologiche e protologiche.* Ed. Ugo Bianchi, q.v., 393–426.

Smith, Jonathan Z. *To Take Place: Toward Theory in Ritual.* Chicago/London: University of Chicago Press, 1987.

Smith, Wilfred Cantwell. "Scripture as Form and Concept: Their Emergence for the Western World." In *Rethinking Scripture: Essays from a Comparative Perspective.* Ed. Miriam Levering, 29–57. Albany: State University of New York Press, 1989.

Staal, Frits. "The Meaninglessness of Ritual." *Numen* 26 (1975): 2–22.

Starn, Randolph. "Meaning-Levels in the Theme of Historical Decline." *History and Theory* 14 (1975): 1–31.

Starr, Raymond J. "The Circulation of Literary Texts in the Roman World." *Classical Quarterly* 37 (1987): 213–23.

Stead, G. Christopher. "Rhetorical Method in Athanasius." *Vigiliae Christianae* 30 (1976): 121–37.

Stern, David. "Midrash and Indeterminacy." *Critical Inquiry* 15 (1988): 132–61.

———. *Parables in Midrash: Narrative and Exegesis in Rabbinic Literature.* Cambridge/London: Harvard University Press, 1991.

Stock, Brian. *The Implications of Literacy: Written Language and Models of Interpretation in the Eleventh and Twelfth Centuries.* Princeton, N.J.: Princeton University Press, 1983.

———. *Listening for the Text: On the Uses of the Past.* Baltimore/London: Johns Hopkins University Press, 1990.

———. "Medieval Literacy, Linguistic Theory, and Social Organization." *New Literary History* 16 (1984): 13–30.

Strack, Hermann L. *Introduction to the Talmud and Midrash.* Philadelphia: Jewish Publication Society of America, 1931.

Stratton, Jonathan G. *The Problem of the Interaction of Literacy, Culture and the Social Structure, With Special Reference to the Late Roman and Early Medieval Periods.* Unpublished Ph.D. dissertation, University of Essex, 1978.

Street, Brian. *Literacy in Theory and Practice.* Cambridge Studies in Oral and Literate Culture 9. Cambridge: Cambridge University Press, 1984.

———. "Orality and Literacy as Ideological Constructions: Some Problems in Cross-Cultural Studies." *Culture & History* 2 (1987): 7–30.

Strousma, G. "Monachisme et Marranisme chez les Manichéens d'Egypte." *Numen* 29 (1982): 184–201.

Tanner, Kathryn. "Theology and the Plain Sense." In *Scriptural Authority and Narrative Tradition*. Ed. Garrett Green, 59–78. Philadelphia: Fortress, 1987.

Tardieu, Michel. "Les Manichéens en Egypte." *Bulletin de la Société français d'Egyptologie* 94 (1982): 5–19.

———. "Principes de l'exégèse manichéenne du Nouveau Testament." In idem, *Les Règles de l'interpretation*, 123–46. Paris: Cerf, 1987.

Taussig, Michael. *Shamanism, Colonialism, and the Wild Man: A Study in Terror and Healing*. Chicago/London: University of Chicago Press, 1987.

Theissen, Gerd. *Sociology of Early Palestinian Christianity*. Trans. John Bowden. Philadelphia: Fortress, 1978. German original, 1977.

———. "The Strong and the Weak in Corinth: A Sociological Analysis of a Theological Quarrel." In *The Social Setting of Pauline Christianity: Essays on Corinth*. Ed. and trans. John H. Schütz, 121–43. Philadelphia: Fortress, 1982. German original of this essay, 1975.

Thomas, Rosalind. *Literacy and Orality in Ancient Greece*. Cambridge: Cambridge University Press, 1992.

Thurman, Robert A. F. "Tibetan Buddhist Perspectives on Asceticism." In *Asceticism*. Ed. Vincent L. Wimbush and Richard Valantasis, q.v., 108–18.

Tibiletti, Carlo. "Motivazione dell' ascetismo in alcuni autori cristiani." *Atti della Accademia delle Scienze di Torino* 106 (1972): 489–537.

———. "Teologia Pelagiana su celibato/matrimonio." *Augustinianum* 27 (1987): 487–507.

Tilley, Maureen A. *The Bible in Christian North Africa: The Donatist World*. Minneapolis: Fortress, 1997.

Tissot, Yves. "Encratisme et Actes Apocryphes." In *Les Actes Apocryphes des Apôtres: Christianisme et monde païen*. Ed. François Bovon et al., 109–19. Publications de la Faculté de Théologie de l'Université de Genève 4. Geneva: Labor et Fides, 1981.

———. "Henogamie et remariage chez Clement d'Alexandrie." *Rivista di storia e letteratura religiosa* 11 (1975): 167–97.

Todorov, Tzvetan. *Mikhail Bakhtin, The Dialogical Principle*. Trans. Wlad Godzich. Theory and History of Literature 13. Minneapolis: University of Minnesota Press, 1984. French original, 1981.

Torjesen, Karen Jo. *Hermeneutical Procedure and Theological Method in Origen's Exegesis*. Berlin/New York: Walter DeGruyter, 1986.

Treggiari, Susan. "Consent to Roman Marriage: Some Aspects of Law and Reality." *Echos de monde classique/Classical Views*, n.s. 1 (1982): 34–44.

———. *Roman Marriage: Iusti Coniuges from the Time of Cicero to the Time of Ulpian*. Oxford: Clarendon, 1991.

Trigg, Joseph Wilson. *Origen: The Bible and Philosophy in the Third-Century Church*. Atlanta: John Knox, 1983.

Urbach, Ephraim E. *The Sages: Their Concepts and Beliefs*. Trans. Israel Abrahams. 2nd ed. Cambridge, Mass./London: Harvard University Press, 1979. Hebrew original, 1969.

Vaccari, Alberto. "La clausola sul divorzio in Matteo 5, 32; 19, 9." *Rivista biblica* 3 (1955): 97–119.

———. "La *theôria* nella scuola esegetica di Antiocha." *Biblica* 1 (1920): 3–36.

Valantasis, Richard. "Constructions of Power in Asceticism." *Journal of the American Academy of Religion* 63 (1995): 775–821.

Van Dam, Raymond. *Leadership and Community in Late Antique Gaul*. The Transformation of the Classical Heritage 8. Berkeley/Los Angeles/London: University of California Press, 1985.

Vaux, Roland de. *Archaeology and the Dead Sea Scrolls*. London: Oxford University Press, 1973.

Veilleux, Armand. "The Origins of Egyptian Monasticism." In *The Continuing Quest for God: Monastic Spirituality in Tradition and Transition*. Ed. William Skudlarek, 44–50. Collegeville, Minn.: Liturgical, 1982.

Vermes, Geza. "Bible and Midrash: Early Old Testament Exegesis." In *The Cambridge History of the Bible*. Vol. I, *From the Beginnings to Jerome*. Ed. P. R. Ackroyd and C. F. Evans, q.v., 199–231.

Vessey, Mark. "The Forging of Orthodoxy in Latin Christian Literature: A Case Study." *Journal of Early Christian Studies* 4 (1996): 495–513.

Vogüé, Adalbert de. *Histoire littéraire du mouvement monastique dans l'antiquité. Première partie: Le monachisme latin de la mort d'Antoine à la fin du séjour à Rome (356–385)*. Paris: Les Editions du Cerf, 1991.

Vööbus, Arthur. *Celibacy, A Requirement for Admission to Baptism in the Early Syrian Church*. Stockholm: Estonian Theological Society in Exile, 1951.

———. *History of Asceticism in the Syrian Orient: A Contribution to the History of Culture in the Near East*. Vol. I, *The Origin of Asceticism: Early Monasticism in Persia*. CSCO 184 = Subsidia 14. Louvain: CSCO, 1958.

Ward-Perkins, Bryan. *From Classical Antiquity to the Middle Ages: Urban Public Building in Northern and Central Italy A.D. 300–850*. Oxford: Oxford University Press, 1984.

Watson, Alan. *The Law of Persons in the Later Roman Republic*. Oxford: Clarendon, 1967.

Weiss, Johannes. *The Proclamation of Jesus on the Kingdom of God*. Ed. and trans. R. H. Hiers and D. L. Holland. Philadelphia: Fortress, 1971. German original, 1892.

Wellhausen, Julius. *Prolegomena to the History of Israel*. Trans. J. Sutherland Black and Allan Menzies. Edinburgh: Adam & Charles Black, 1885. German original, 1878.

White, Hugh E. Evelyn. *The Monasteries of the Wâdi 'N Natrûn*. Pt. II, *The History of the Monasteries of Nitria and of Scetis*. Ed. Walter Hauser. New York: Metropolitan Museum of Art, 1932.

Whitman, Jon. *Allegory: The Dynamics of an Ancient and Medieval Technique*. Cambridge, Mass.: Harvard University Press, 1987.

Wiles, Maurice. "Theodore of Mopsuestia as Representative of the Antiochene School." In *The Cambridge History of the Bible*. Vol. I, *From the Beginnings to Jerome*. Ed. P. R. Ackroyd and C. F. Evans, q.v., 489–510.

Wilken, Robert L. *The Christians as the Romans Saw Them*. New Haven, Conn./ London: Yale University Press, 1984.

———. *The Land Called Holy: Palestine in Christian History and Thought*. New Haven, Conn./London: Yale University Press, 1992.

———. "The Lives of the Saints and the Pursuit of Virtue." In idem, *Remembering the Christian Past*, 121–44. Grand Rapids: Eerdmans, 1995.

Williams, Michael A. *Rethinking "Gnosticism": An Argument for Dismantling a Dubious Category*. Princeton, N.J.: Princeton University Press, 1996.

Wilson, Robert McL. "Alimentary and Sexual Encratism in the Nag Hammadi Tractates." In *La tradizione dell' enkrateia: Motivazione ontologiche e protologiche*. Ed. Ugo Bianchi, q.v., 317–332.

Wimbush, Vincent L. *Paul, The Worldly Ascetic: Response to the World and Self-Understanding according to I Corinthians 7*. Macon, Ga.: Mercer University Press, 1987.

Wimbush, Vincent L., ed. *Ascetic Behavior in Greco-Roman Antiquity: A Sourcebook*. Minneapolis: Fortress, 1990.

———, and Richard Valantasis, eds. *Asceticism*. New York/Oxford: Oxford University Press, 1995.

Wisse, Frederik. "Gnosticism and Early Monasticism in Egypt." In *Gnosis: Festschrift für Hans Jonas*. Ed. Barbara Aland, 431–37. Göttingen: Vandenhoeck & Ruprecht, 1978.

Witherington, Ben, III. *Conflict and Community in Corinth: A Social-Rhetorical Commentary on 1 and 2 Corinthians*. Grand Rapids: Eerdmans; Carlisle: Paternoster, 1995.

Wolde, Ellen Van. "Trendy Intertextuality?" In *Intertextuality in Biblical Writings: Essays in Honour of Bas van Iersel*. Ed. Sipke Draisma, 43–49. Kampen: J. H. Kok, 1989.

Wolf, Peter. *Vom Schulwesen der Spätantike: Studien zu Libanius*. Baden-Baden: Verlag für Kunst und Wissenschaft, 1952.

Wolff, Hans Julius. "Doctrinal Trends in Postclassical Roman Marriage Law." *Zeitschrift der Savigny-Stiftung für Rechtsgeschichte* 67 (1950): 261–319.

Wolfson, Elliot R. "Beautiful Maiden without Eyes: *Peshat* and *Sod* in Zohairic Hermeneutics." In *The Midrashic Imagination: Jewish Exegesis, Thought, and History*. Ed. Michael Fishbane, q.v., 155–203.

Wright, Addison G. "The Literary Genre Midrash." *Catholic Biblical Quarterly* 28 (1966): 105–38, 417–57.

Wyschogrod, Edith. *Saints and Postmodernism: Revisioning Moral Philosophy*. Chicago/London: University of Chicago Press, 1990.

Young, Frances. "Allegory and the Ethics of Reading." In *The Open Text: New Directions for Biblical Studies?* Ed. Francis Watson, 103–20. London: SCM, 1993.

———. *Biblical Exegesis and the Formation of Christian Culture*. Cambridge: Cambridge University Press, 1997.

Young, Frances. "The Rhetorical Schools and Their Influence on Patristic Exegesis." In *The Making of Orthodoxy: Essays in Honour of Henry Chadwick*. Ed. Rowan Williams, 182–99. Cambridge: Cambridge University Press, 1989.

———. *Virtuoso Theology: The Bible and Interpretation*. Cleveland: Pilgrim, 1993. Published originally as *The Art of Performance: Towards a Theology of Holy Scripture*. London: Darton, Longman and Todd, 1990.

Young, Robert. "Post-Structuralism: An Introduction." In idem, *Untying the Text: A Post-Structuralist Reader*, q.v., 1–28.

———, ed. *Untying the Text: A Post-Structuralist Reader*. Boston/London/Henley: Routledge and Kegan Paul, 1981.

Youtie, Herbert C. "Bradeôs graphôn: Between Literacy and Illiteracy." *Greek, Roman and Byzantine Studies* 12 (1971): 239–61.

Zetzel, James E. G. *Latin Textual Criticism in Antiquity*. Salem, N.H.: Ayer, 1984.

Select Index of Biblical Passages

OLD TESTAMENT

Select General Index